Ordines Coronationis Franciae

The Middle Ages Series

Ruth Mazo Karras, General Editor

Edward Peters, Founding Editor

A complete list of books in the series is available from the publisher.

Ordines Coronationis Franciae

Texts and Ordines for the Coronation
of Frankish and French Kings
and Queens in the Middle Ages

VOLUME II

Edited by
RICHARD A. JACKSON

PENN

UNIVERSITY OF PENNSYLVANIA PRESS

Philadelphia

10 9 8 7 6 5 4 3 2 1

Published by the University of Pennsylvania Press
Philadelphia, Pennsylvania 19104-4011

Library of Congress Cataloging-In-Publication Data

Jackson, Richard A., 1937-
   Ordines coronationes Franciae : texts and ordines for the coronation of Frankish
and French kings and queens in the Middle Ages / edited by Richard A. Jackson.
         p.   cm.— (Middle Ages series)
   Includes bibliographical references and index
   ISBN 0-8122-3263-1 (v. 1, alk. paper).—ISBN 0-8122-3542-8 (v. 2, alk. paper)
1. France—Kings and rulers—Religious aspects—Sources. 2. Coronations—
France—History—Sources. 3. Rites and ceremonies—France—Sources.
4. Monarchy—France—History—Sources. 5. France—History—Medieval period,
987–1515—Historiography. I. Series.

DC33.15J3   1995
394'.4–dc20   94-48121
                                                                              CIP

For
Louise C. Jackson

CONTENTS

Volume II

PREFACE

Rarely, if ever, can a work of this magnitude be the work of a single individual, and I take pleasure in noting that I have been most fortunate in obtaining financial aid and in having the help of outstanding advisors and collaborators. In 1994–95 the National Endowment for the Arts provided me with an Editions Grant that enabled me to devote the entire year to this volume, as well as to travel to France and to the Vatican City for one final examination of several manuscripts. A grant from the University of Houston covered the cost of the photographs and the publication rights for the plates. As with Vol. I, Elizabeth A. R. Brown, Reinhard Elze, Edward M. Peters, and Hervé Pinoteau provided encouragement, help, and occasional readings from manuscripts or books that were not readily available to me. Abbé Raymond Etaix discovered a most important manuscript in Paris (Ordo XXIII, MS *F*), and he requested that Abbé Jean Goy communicate his discovery to me. Craig Taylor provided me with a careful transcription of Ordo XXA, MS *J*. Anne Walters Robertson gave me helpful advice concerning the liturgy at several points. Bernard Barbiche, the late T. Julian Brown, Patrick Demouy, and Sylvie Lefèvre also provided help with texts in Vol. II. Virginia Jackson proofread and corrected the English parts of my manuscript of Vol. II, just as she did for Vol. I. Special gratitude is due to four individuals. Hans-Erich Keller, whose knowledge of Middle French has few equals, examined my editions of the French texts in detail and made copious suggestions that not only improved my transcriptions of the texts in Vol. II, but that also enabled me to avoid a legion of ignorant mistakes. Claude Buridant gave me excellent advice concerning which variants to retain and which to discard in some of the Middle French texts, he minutely examined Ordo XXB in the attempt to determine the date of the translation, and he suggested many improvements to my edition of Ordo XXIIB-C, even going so far as to make his own transcription of Ordo XXIIB. Reinhard Elze carefully read the entire manuscript, suggested numerous improvements, and corrected my typing errors, whether in Latin, German, French, or English. Dr. Dennis Levi of the University of Houston's School of Optometry was particularly helpful over the years as he resolved my visual problems and provided me with carefully designed corrective lenses that enabled me to devote uncountable hours to the computer screen and microfilm reader. Once again, I appreciate the help given by the gentle staff of the University of Pennsylvania Press: Alison Anderson, Managing Editor; Carl Gross, Design and Production Manager; Jerome Singerman, Humanities Editor; and Patricia A. Steele, Copy Editor.

Finally, I wish to acknowledge the encouragement given to me by Robert L. Benson. He took great pleasure in Vol. I and intended to use it extensively; I regret that his death in early 1996 prevents me from giving him similar pleasure in Vol. II.

This volume is dedicated to my mother on her eightieth birthday. She is an exceptional woman who, when young, was prevented by the circumstances of life from getting the education she wanted, so she made up for the deficit by going to college and receiving an Associate in Arts degree when she was in her seventies. Her childhood and youth on farms in Kansas and Minnesota did not hinder her from instilling in all her children a love of learning and an appreciation of the best in Western Civilization's culture.

Five hundred years have lapsed between the last medieval French coronation ceremony, that of Louis XII on 27 May 1498, and the completion of this volume. I began to collect material for the edition in 1973, and although I did not work exclusively on the edition during the past twenty-five years, nearly all my research time since 1981 has been devoted to it alone. I have held some wonderful manuscripts in my hands, and the project has occasionally produced exciting findings, but frequently the work has been boring and often little short of sheer drudgery, and it has almost always been difficult. Therefore, it is with great relief that I conclude with a word that one finds at the end of so many texts in medieval manuscripts, and with deep feeling add the last three words of the last text in this volume to my own *Explicit*.

Calvert, Texas
August 1998

ABBREVIATIONS AND FREQUENTLY CITED WORKS

Note: For full references, see Works Cited, pp. 628–651.

Arch. nat.	Paris, Archives nationales
Baluze, *Capitularia*	Etienne Baluze, ed., *Capitularia regum Francorum.*
Bibl.	Biblioteca, Bibliotheek, Bibliothek, Bibliothèque
Bibl. Apos. Vat.	Biblioteca Apostolica Vaticana
Bibl. mun.	Bibliothèque municipale
Bibl. nat.	Bibliothèque nationale de France
Baluze	Collection Baluze
Dupuy	Collection Dupuy
fran., lat.	fonds français, fonds latin
nouv. acq. fran.	nouvelles acquisitions françaises
nouv. acq. lat.	nouvelles acquisitions latines
Bouman, *Sacring*	Cornelius A. Bouman, *Sacring and Crowning.*
CCSL	Corpus Christianorum Series Latina
Cod. lat.	Codex latinus
DACL	Fernand Cabrol and Henri Leclercq, *Dictionnaire d'archéologie chrétienne et de liturgie.*
Delisle, "Mémoire"	Léopold Delisle, "Mémoire sur d'anciens sacramentaires."
Dewick	E. S. Dewick, *The Coronation Book of Charles V of France.*
Duchesne, *Scriptores*	André Duchesne, ed., *Historiae Francorum scriptores.*
ed., edd.	edition, editions
Elze or Elze's Ordo	Reinhard Elze, ed., *Ordines coronationis imperialis.*
Godefroy	Théodore Godefroy and Denis Godefroy, eds., *Le cérémonial françois.*
Grat, *Saint-Bertin*	Félix Grat et al., eds., *Annales de Saint-Bertin.*
Jackson	Richard A. Jackson
"Manuscripts"	"Manuscripts, Texts and Enigmas."
Vivat rex	*Vivat rex: Une histoire des sacres et couronnements en France.*
Vive le roi	*Vive le Roi! A History of the French Coronation Ceremony.*
Leroquais	Victor Leroquais

Pontificaux	*Les pontificaux manuscrits des bibliothèques publiques de France.*
Sacramentaires	*Les sacramentaires et les missels manuscrits des bibliothèques publiques de France.*
Mansi	Giovan Domenico Mansi, ed., *Sacrorum conciliorum nova et amplissima collectio.*
Martène	Dom Edmond Martène, ed., *De antiquis ecclesiae ritibus.*
Martimort	Aimé-Georges Martimort, *La documentation liturgique de Dom Edmond Martène.*
MGH	Monumenta Germaniae Historica
Capitularia	Alfred Boretius and Victor Krause et al., eds., *Capitularia regum Francorum.* MGH Legum sectio 2,2.
Leges	Georg Heinrich Pertz, ed., *MGH Leges* (in folio).
MS, MSS	manuscript, manuscripts
Nelson, *Politics*	Janet L. Nelson, *Politics and Ritual in Early Medieval Europe.*
PL	Jacques Paul Migne, ed., *Patrologiae cursus completus latinae.*
n., nn.	note number, numbers
no., nos.	paragraph number, numbers
Recueil des historiens	*Recueil des historiens des Gaules et de la France,* ed. Dom Martin Bouquet et al.
Schramm	Percy Ernst Schramm
Frankreich	*Der König von Frankreich.*
Kaiser	*Kaiser, Könige und Päpste.*
"Ordines-Studien II"	"Ordines-Studien II: Die Krönung bei den Westfranken und den Franzosen."
"Westfranken"	"Die Krönung bei den Westfranken und Angelsachsen von 878 bis um 1000."
Sirmond	Jacques Sirmond
Opera varia	*Opera varia.*
Hincmari opera	ed., *Hincmari archiepiscopi Remensis opera.*
Karoli Calvi capitula	ed., *Karoli Calvi et successorum aliquot Franciae regum capitula.*
var., vars.	variant, variants
Vogel-Elze	Cyrille Vogel and Reinhard Elze, eds., *Le pontifical romano-germanique du dixième siècle.*
Warren, *Leofric*	F. E. Warren, ed., *The Leofric Missal as Used in the Cathedral of Exeter.*

INTRODUCTION TO VOLUME II

This is the second and last volume of all known medieval French coronation ordines and related texts. Every text in this volume dates after 1200, and every one, as explained in Vol. I: 3, is peculiarly French in that it provides not only for the king's anointing with chrism from the Holy Ampulla, but also for the dominant ceremonial roles played by the peers of France. This distinguishes these texts from the first nineteen ordines, which are all generically Frankish or even western European. The General Introduction to Vol. I contains a full discussion of the texts selected, the manuscript sources, features of earlier editions, the development of the ritual, the reliability of the ordines, and the presentation of the edition.

The ordines in this volume are very much based upon the traditions of the past. Every Latin formula in Ordo XXII A appears in one ordo or another in Vol. I, and every formula in Ordo XXIV is to be found in an earlier ordo. Ordo XXIII adds nineteen formulas from several older sources, some of which cannot be precisely identified. The only novel formulas in Ordo XXV (nos. 26 and 28) are drawn from the liturgy of Reims cathedral.

Four manuscripts in the cathedral of Reims were particularly important for the ordines in Vol. II, and they deserve a special note in this introduction. Two of them, both pontificals, survive to the present. Reims, Bibl. mun., MS 343 (= Ordo XIX, MS *A*) provided most of the text of Ordo XXI, and some readings in later ordines demonstrate that it was consulted several times thereafter. Reims, Bibl. mun., MS 342 (= Ordo XV, MS *G*) moved the coronation oath to a place very near the beginning of the ceremony, and it also continued to be consulted.

The other two manuscripts have been lost since the eighteenth century. Known as the *livre bleu* (= Ordo XXII A, lost manuscript *2*) and the *livre rouge* (= Ordo XXIII, lost manuscript *4*) from their respective bindings of dark blue and red velvet, they were kept in the cathedral treasury rather than in the cathedral library. The *livre bleu* was an authoritative copy of the Last Capetian Ordo (Ordo XXII A). It is the manuscript that is likely to have been the major source of Charles V's ordo (Ordo XXIII); it was probably the ordo used at Charles VII's coronation in 1429; it furnished some readings in the first half of Louis XI's ordo (Ordo XXIV) and nearly all the text in the second half of that ordo; and in 1484 some of its readings were adopted for the Ordo of Charles VIII (Ordo XXV). The *livre rouge* was an equally authoritative copy of a slightly modified version of

Charles V's ordo, the ordo that, the evidence suggests, was used at Charles VI's coronation in 1380. The *livre rouge* was not written in the fourteenth century, however; it postdates Louis XI's coronation in 1461. Perhaps composed in 1478, it provided nearly all the liturgy for the coronation in 1484, and it established a relatively fixed liturgy for ceremonies in the early-modern period, during which there was very little liturgical change. The *livre rouge* essentially concluded the development of a ritual that had had its origins with the anointings of Pepin in the 750s.[1]

General Principles of the Edition

The edition retains all significant variants from nearly all medieval manuscripts of each ordo, as well as from a few early-modern manuscripts and early printed editions that preserve the text of manuscripts now lost. In both French and Latin texts I make a distinction between *u* and *v*, but *i* and *j* are always presented as *i* in Latin, although I distinguish between *i* and *j* in French. Minor variants of the *ae* diphthong and of *c* and *t* (e.g., *iusticia* and *iustitia*) are not retained, although the orthography of the first manuscript in which a variant appears is always respected. For a full explanation of the general principles of the edition, see Vol. I: 41–48. The Principles of the Edition in the introductory apparatus of each ordo explain any deviations from the general principles.

A number scribes inserted a ✠, the sign of the Cross, in a benediction. Rather than multiply the notes by referring to each of these instances, they are indicated in the variants (e.g., ✠ *add.* D F). The ✠ is normally after *bene* and *Spiritus* in *benedictio* and *Spiritus sancti*, but this edition always shows its location in the base manuscript only.

Two-thirds of the texts in this volume are in French, and only one-third entirely in Latin. This differs markedly from Vol. I, in which only one text (Ordo XVII B) is in French. This raised problems of punctuation because the French rules for punctuation differ from those currently applied in the United States. I adopted a hybred solution: in the texts themselves I followed the French rules for punctuation in editing documents and texts, including the use of chevrons (the *guillemets* « and ») instead of quotation marks (" and "), and the spacing around punctuation marks, but I placed single quotation marks around quotations from the Bible, and in the introductory material and in the notes I adopted the practices customary in the United States.

---

[1] For details concerning these two, see my study, "The *livres bleu* and *rouge*, Two Coronation Manuscripts in the Cathedral of Reims," in ... *The Man of Many Devices, Who Wandered Full Many Ways ...: Festschrift in Honor of János M. Bak*, ed. Balázs Nagy and Marcell Sebők (Budapest: Central European University Press, 1999), 176–86.

Punctuating the French texts was difficult because the syntax of these texts is not modern French. To the extent possible, I observed the rules listed by Maurice Grevisse,[2] but they were often not appropriate. Although I did omit many of what I consider the excessive (or misplaced) commas of some earlier editors, I inserted other commas, or semicolons, where I thought they would be helpful to understanding the often convoluted syntax. Furthermore, where a comma was not strictly called for, I occasionally inserted one simply to indicate a passage of time.

I offer apologies to my colleagues who wanted to see spellings like *aprés* and *dés* (both prepositions), *roÿne* (two syllables pronounced *ro-ine*), or *beneïçon* (four syllables pronounced be-ne-i-çon) instead of *apres*, *des*, *royne*, and *beneïçon*. I consulted with authorities on such matters, and the current practice of the Ecole des Chartes is to discourage the use of accents in these words when editing historical texts in Middle French.

A Technical Note

When I began to edit these two volumes, I worked with the technical aids available at the time: photocopies, typewritten transcripts, and pen and paper. The microcomputer became available in the late 1970s, and I acquired my first one in 1978. Computer succeeded computer, and software came again and again to be replaced by better software. Most of the editing was done using various versions of Microsoft Word for DOS, a program that, for technical reasons, I continued to use to the very end of the editing process. The files were then translated into the format of Microsoft Word for Windows. Once that had been done, I temporarily widened the margins so that an entire line would be visible on the screen at 200 percent of its normal size. This enabled me to see errors, usually punctuation marks, that had continuously evaded my eye even when printed out.

The final format of both volumes was produced using Quark XPress for Windows, a program that possesses far more sophisticated formatting capabilities than Word for Windows. From Quark XPress the text was printed as camera-ready copy on a Hewlett-Packard LaserJet printer. That copy was printed one-third larger than the final printed page and was reduced to seventy-five percent of its size when published. This reduction produced an effective resolution that is close to the resolution of the text produced by most electronic typesetters. I worked closely with Carl Gross, Design and Production Manager of the University of

---

[2] Maurice Grevisse, *Le bon usage*, 11th ed. (Paris: Duculot, 1980), 1412–25 (nos. 2754–70).

Pennsylvania Press, in order to determine the font sizes and the precise measurements for the page layout for the camera-ready copy. I myself suggested using the font in which this edition is printed, ITC Century, because its italic font is easier to read than most italic fonts, an important consideration when so much of each of these volumes is set in an italic font. One month after the press had received the camera-ready copy of Vol. I, it had the bound volume on hand, which must have come close to setting a speed record for publishing an academic book.

The computer has been essential in preparing this edition, partly because it enabled me easily to correct so many of my own errors of transcription and typing. In each volume I occasionally noted mistakes made by earlier editors, but in doing so I did not intend to appear overly critical. On the contrary, I acknowledge that, before 1900, scholars did not even have typewriters, but had to work entirely with pen and paper. Given such technological limitations, earlier editors' accomplishments are nothing short of astounding, and we would know far less than we do about the past were it not for their Herculean labors.

TEXTS OF THE ORDINES

ORDO XX A

The Ordo of Reims

Date: ca. 1230
Other names: Ordo of Louis IX (Schreuer, Buchner)

Introduction

This text is not really an ordo, but a modus, because it gives only the instructions for carrying out the ceremony, omitting the liturgical texts. It was intended to be used in conjunction with a pontifical, to which it refers as an "ordinarius" (nos. 8 and 13). Nevertheless, it calls itself an ordo, and the custom of referring to it as such is now so well entrenched that it seems necessary to retain that appellation.[1]

Despite its brevity, this is an extremely important text, for it marks the transition from a coronation ritual that has much in common with other countries' rites to a ritual that is specifically French. This is an appropriate text to begin the second volume of this collection because it is the first text to make provisions for the Holy Ampulla, for the participation of the peers of France, for the oath requiring the king to expel heretics from the kingdom, and for investiture with ankle boots and spurs; it is also the first to disclose the nature of the king's offering in the course of the mass. This is the first truly French ordo in a series that continued until the end of the monarchy: almost all its specifications were repeated in practically every succeeding ordo.

The scholarship concerning this ordo has had an interesting history since Ulysse Chevalier first published the text, which became a focal point of a controversy during the early years of the twentieth century. Chevalier (ed. *a*, pp. xxxi–xxxv) proved that the manuscript's *terminus a quo* is 1271 and its *terminus ad quem* could be as early as 1274, so he

---

[1] The terminology can be confusing; see Vol. I: 7, n. 12, where I attempt to clarify it. The pontifical to which the ordo refers could have been Ordo XV (the Ratold Ordo), MS *G* (Reims, Bibl. mun., MS 342). This is suggested by the wording "ubi tria promittenda et iuranda" in no. 8, a wording easily derived from the rubric in manuscript *G*'s marginal addition (Ordo XV,5): "Hec triplicia se servaturum iura promittat," a phrase that appears nowhere else in the ordines. It is true that the sequence of the insignia in the Ordo of Reims (summarized in no. 13) differs from the sequence in the Ratold Ordo, but that does not prove that Reims 342 was not the pontifical in question, for the Ordo of Reims altered the sequence and simply refers (in no. 13) to the "orationes que suis in locis in ordinario continentur."

dated the manuscript to about 1274 — without asserting anything about the possible date of the ordo's composition. In 1909 Hans Schreuer recognized from the French translation (Ordo XX B) that most of the ordo had been incorporated into the Ordo of 1250 (Ordo XXI), which Schreuer dated to the coronation of Louis VIII in 1223. He then attempted to reconstruct the Latin text (he did not yet know ed. *a*) by extracting it from the Ordo of 1250, and he followed that with a partial edition of the French translation of the Ordo of Reims (Ordo XX B, ed. *g*), which he believed to have been written for the coronation of Louis IX in 1226. Despite his dispute with Schreuer over the date of Ordo XXII C, Maximilian Buchner agreed with Schreuer's attributions for the ordo and its French translation.[2] In the 1930s Percy Ernst Schramm thought that the text had been composed during the period 1260–74,[3] and in 1960 H. G. Richardson suggested that it was based upon a lost text older than 1215.[4] I have argued that the ordo was composed between 1226 and 1250 and have assigned an approximate date of 1230 to it.[5]

Parts of the Ordo of Reims were not incorporated into the Ordo of 1250. It has not previously been possible to know whether this was the case because the ordo, as we now have it, postdated the Ordo of 1250, or whether the compiler of 1250 omitted those parts that he did not deem appropriate to his compilation. I believe the latter, i.e., that the Ordo of Reims in MSS *A*, *B*, and *C* essentially reproduces a text that predated the Ordo of 1250. This view is staunchly supported by the variants that *B* and *C* have in common with Ordo XXI (see Principles of the Edition below): they show that the manuscript of the Ordo of Reims that was one of Ordo XXI's sources is largely preserved in *B* and *C*, which are independent of *A*.

Sometime after 1300, the greater part of the ordo was copied into the twelfth-century manuscript *D* of Lambert of Saint-Omer's *Liber Floridus*, and several manuscripts were copied from that.[6] Variants from most of them are given here, because, although they had no influence upon the development of the French ceremony, they do represent one way in which knowledge of the ceremony became public.

---

[2] Schreuer's and Buchner's studies are cited, in full in Vol. I: 4, n. 7. Schreuer's "edition" of Ordo XX A is in "Über altfranzösische Kröungsordnungen," 176–83.

[3] Schramm, "Ordines-Studien II," 24–26.

[4] Richardson, "Coronation in Medieval England," 114.

[5] Jackson, "Manuscripts," 53–55, where I evaluated Richardson's suggestion on p. 54, n. 81.

[6] The ordo was not yet in the manuscript when Leiden, Bibl. Univ., MS Voss. Lat. Fol. 31 was copied from *D*.

Manuscripts

A—Reims, Bibl. mun., MS 328, fols. 70v–73r. An ordinary of the cathedral of Reims. Late thirteenth century. A note by M. de la Salle on the manuscript's flyleaf reads: "Ancien Ordinaire de l'Eglise de Reims ecrit dans le 13ᵉ siecle. Cela paroit par les festes qui y sont marquees a leur rang entre lesquelles on ne voit pas celles du St. Sacrement ny de S. Louis mais bien celle de S. Francois." A note, also by M. de la Salle, on the inside of the cover of *B* says that the "feste la plus recente qu'on y trouve dans le propre des saints est celle de S. Louis." A manuscript that was obviously intended to be consulted regularly, *A* is not very carefully executed, despite its use of red and black ink and decorated initials. Its lines are often not straight, and the letters are quite uneven (the minims sometimes slope to the right, sometimes to the left—perhaps the manuscript was copied by a left-handed writer). Ulysse Chevalier (ed. *a*) mistakenly referred to manuscripts *A*, *B*, and *C* as nos. 326, 327, and 328. Description: Chevalier, *Sacramentaire*, xxxi–xxxv; Martimort, 178–79, no. 251. See Plate 15.

B—Reims, Bibl. mun., MS 329, fols. 3v–5v. Ca. 1300. An ordinary of the cathedral of Reims. More carefully executed than *A*, in red and black ink, with rather uneven letters, lines that sometimes slant, and decorated initials. Chevalier, *Sacramentaire*, xxxv–xxvii, dated the manuscript (referred to as no. 327), on the basis of a note on the flyleaf, to the end of the thirteenth century, but I believe that it could be a little later. Description: Chevalier, *Sacramentaire*, xxxv–xxxvii; Martimort, 178–79, no. 251.

C—Reims, Bibl. mun., MS 330, fols. 104v–106v. Fourteenth century, first quarter. An ordinary of the cathedral of Reims. The most carefully written of the three Reims ordinaries, in red and black ink, with even letters, neatly drawn lines, and decorated initials. Chevalier, *Sacramentaire*, xxxviii, argued that the manuscript (mistakenly referred to as no. 328) dates before 1313. Description: Chevalier, *Sacramentaire*, xxxvii–xli; Martimort, 178–79, no. 251.

D—Wolfenbüttel, Herzog August Bibl., MS Guelf 1 Gud. lat. 20, fols. 72v–73r. The ordo is no. 113, a fourteenth-century addition at the end of this manuscript of the *Liber Floridus* by Lambert de Saint-Omer, although parts of the ordo were omitted in this and in the other manuscripts of the *Liber Floridus*. The manuscript was copied in the diocese of Thérouanne, Tournai or Cambrai in the second half of the twelfth century. Description: Léopold Delisle, "Notice sur les manuscrits du *Liber Floridus* de Lambert, chanoine de Saint-Omer" (Paris: C. Klincksieck, 1906; reprinted from *Notices et extraits des manuscrits*, 38), 593–600, 743–44; Otto von Heinemann et al., *Die Handschriften der herzoglichen Bibliothek zu Wolfenbüttel: vierte Abt.: Die Gudischen Handschriften* (Wolfenbüttel: J. Zwissler, 1913), 77.

E—Chantilly, Musée Condé, MS 1596, fols. 73v–74r. Fifteenth century, second half (ca. 1470?). The *Liber Floridus*, copied from *D*. Description: Delisle, "Notice sur les manuscrits," 601–602.

F—The Hague, Koninklijke Bibl., MS 72 A 23, fol. 86r–v. Formerly MS 759, then MS Y.392. 1460. The *Liber Floridus*, copied from *D* at Lille or Ninove. Description: Delisle, "Notice sur les manuscrits," 602–604; Gerard I. Lieftinck, *Manuscrits datés conservés dans les Pays-Bas*, vol. 1: *Les manuscrits d'origine étrangère (816–C. 1550)*, (Amsterdam: North Holland Publishing Co., 1964), 32, no. 74a.

G—Genoa, Bibl. Durazzo-Giustiniani, MS A IX 9, fols. 70r–71r. Fifteenth century, last quarter. The *Liber Floridus*, copied from *D*. Description: Delisle, "Notice sur les manuscrits," 600–601; Dino Puncuh, *I manoscritti della raccolta Durazzo* (Genoa: Sagep, 1979), 162–64. Not collated.

H—Vatican City, Bibl. Apos. Vat., MS Reg. lat. 574, fols. 17r–19r. Fifteenth century. In the seventeenth century Paul Petau possessed this manuscript of Guillaume de Nangis's works; the ordo was inserted into the manuscript between an abbreviated version of Guillaume's chronicle and his *Gesta Ludovici regis*.[7] Description: none.

---

[7] I failed to see this manuscript when I first worked in the Vatican Library. E. A. R. Brown kindly provided me with her most careful transcription of it, which I verified against a photocopy and, when I returned to Rome, the manuscript itself. Prof. Brown also established the provenance of the manuscript. Manuscript *H* could be older than manuscripts *E*, *F*, and *G*. Because its date is not precisely determined, I assigned the sigla as I did in order to display closely related manuscripts with consecutive letters in the stemma.

The manuscript was mentioned in Godefroy, 1: 26, in a passage that is ambiguous and misleading: "L'ordre du sacre et couronnement des roys; recueilly du regne du roy Sainct Louys. Traduit en ce temps mesme du Latin en François : Et qui est au devant d'une vie manuscrite dudit Sainct Louys, faite par Guillaume de Nangis, lequel roy commença de regner, et fut sacré en l'an 1226. Ce manuscrit se trouve, tant en Latin qu'en François, és bibliotheques de Messieurs du Puy, et Petau." The passage implies 1) that there were both Latin and French copies of Guillaume de Nangis's *Gesta Ludovici regis*; 2) that the French translation of the Ordo of Reims was to be found in one manuscript of that work; and 3) that, presumably, the Latin text of the ordo was in the Latin copy of the *Gesta*. Only the present MS *H*, which Petau possessed, contained both the *Gesta* and the ordo, and they are both in Latin. There can be no doubt that the Godefroys copied their French translation of the ordo from a manuscript that belonged

I— Chantilly, Musée Condé, MS 1149 (côte XIX^D–17), fols. 1r–3r. Seventeenth century. Copied from *H*. Description: Henri, duc d'Aumale, *Chantilly*, 3: 296.

J—Oxford, Bodleian Library, MS Ashmolean 842, fols. 75r–76v. Seventeenth century, second half. A note by Elias Ashmole says, "Transcribed from an old vellum manuscript which the Duke of York delivered to Sir Edward Walker 23 Oct. 1660." Description: William Henry Black, *A Descriptive Catalogue of the Manuscripts Bequeathed unto the University of Oxford by Elias Ashmole*, Catalogi codicum manuscriptorum bibliothecae Bodleiana, pars 10 (Oxford: The University Press, 1845), 590–92. [8]

Editions

a—Cyr Ulysse Chevalier, *Sacramentaire et martyrologe de l'abbaye de Saint-Remy*, Bibliothèque liturgique 7 (Paris: Alphonse Picard, 1900), 222–26, from *A*, with some variants from *B* and *C*.

b—Schreuer, *Die rechtlichen Grundgedanken*, 174–78 (from *a*). Incomplete because Schreuer omitted everything after the beginning of the queen's ordo.

The Stemma

It is impossible to establish a complete stemma of the Reims ordinaries. Manuscripts *B* and *C* are descended from a common source (x^2), but *C* is not copied from *B*, and neither is copied from *A*. Although *H* has many of the readings of *C*, it was not copied from *C*, which implies that there was an additional lost manuscript (x^3) between x^2, on the one hand, and *C* and *H*, on the other. There is no reason to assume, however, that any of the three ordinaries was copied directly from the lost source indicated here. Not knowing how many manuscripts are represented by the lost manuscripts (x^1, x^2, and x^3), the stemma can be only approximately correct for manuscripts *A*, *B*, *C*, and *H*.

It is even more difficult to locate manuscript *J*'s place in the stemma. The manuscript contains many corrupt readings that show that the script of its source, lost manuscript x^4, was difficult for a seventeenth-century reader. Those readings apart, *J* shares a number of readings with *B*, *C*, and *H*, all descended from x^2, and it contains some readings that otherwise

---

to Pierre Dupuy (Ordo XX B, MS *E*), and that manuscript does not contain the *Gesta*. This corrects the remarks of Brown, *Franks, Burgundians, and Aquitanians*, 81, n. 313.

[8] Manuscript *J* was kindly and carefully transcribed for me by Craig Taylor, for whose help I am deeply grateful.

appear only in H, so J is not only descended from x^2, but also is more closely related to H than to any other surviving manuscript.

Another set of manuscripts is another matter, though. The manuscript tradition of the *Liber Floridus* has been thoroughly studied, and the accompanying stemma incorporates J. P. Gumbert's stemma of those *Liber Floridus* manuscripts that contain the Latin text of the ordo (the sigla are those of this edition, not of Gumbert's study).[9] A number of variants that D has in common with B and C suggest that D is descended from lost manuscript x^2.

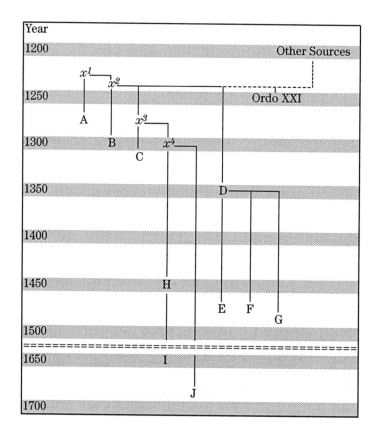

---

[9] J. P. Gumbert, "Recherches sur le stemma des copies du Liber Floridus," in *Liber Floridus Colloquium: Papers Read at the International Meeting Held in the University Library, Ghent on 3–5 December 1967*, ed. Albert Derolez (Ghent: E. Story-Scientia, 1973), 37–50.

Principles of the Edition

The orthography is that of base manuscript *A*; I added the paragraphing and modernized the punctuation. A few variants are given from Ordo XXI when they accord with *B* or *C* because the manuscript of Ordo XXI is older than manuscript *A*, and these readings show that the text of *B* or *C*, both of which are younger than *A*, is sometimes more correct than *A*. The scribe of *F* sometimes omitted the second of doubled letters (e.g., *ampula* instead of *ampulla*); these variants are seldom retained. Variants from *I* are normally given only when they are identical with *H*, its source; MS *I* illustrates some of the problems in unraveling the transmission of these texts because, although *I* is clearly copied from *H*, the scribe took the liberty of correcting a few of the errors in *H*, thus reverting to the correct readings in other manuscripts. MS *J* indiscriminately reads *archiepiscopus* or *archiespiscopus*; these variants are not retained. Unless the letter appears in a variant for other reasons, I did not retain variants of *c* for *t* (e.g., *eciam* for *etiam*) or of *y* for *i* (e.g., *dyaconibus* for *diaconibus*). I did not collate MS *G*.

ORDO XX A

The Latin Text

1. [fol. 70v] Ordo ad inungendum regem[a].

1. [a] Ordo ... regem *om.* B C D E F H I; Ordo ... regem] Coronatio regis Francie J.

2. Hic est[a] ordo ad inungendum[b] et coronandum regem[c].[10] Paratur primo[d] solium[e] in modum eschafeudi[f] aliquantulum eminens, contiguum[g] exterius choro ecclesie inter utrumque chorum, positum in medio, in quod[h] per gradus ascenditur, et in quo possint[i] pares regni, et eciam si necesse fuerit, alii cum rege consistere.

2. [a] Hic est] Incipit D E F. —[b] ungendum B J. —[c] *No.* CXIII *in marg.* D F; Hic est ... regem] De sacra regum Galliae unctione H I. —[d] autem J. —[e] Paratur primo solium] Primo quando rex debet inungi et coronari paratur solium in ecclesia Remensi cathedrali H I. —[f] eschefudi B, eschafudi C, eschaffendi D E F, escaufendi H, eschaufodi J. —[g] contiguum] et contiguum J. —[h] in quo J. — [i] possint *om.* H I.

3. Rex autem[a], die quo ad coronandum venerit[b], debet processionaliter recipi tam a canonicis quam ab ecclesiis ceteris[c] conventualibus.

---

[10] This sentence is treated as a title C, D, E, and F. Manuscript B leaves a blank space for the superfluous title. The variant reading of H and I is treated as a title; E. A. R. Brown has informed me that *H*'s variant title is in the seventeenth-century script of Paul Petau.

Sabbato[d] precedente diem dominicam in qua[e] rex est consecrandus et coronandus, post complectorium[f] completum[g], committitur ecclesie custodia custodibus a rege deputatis cum propriis custodibus ecclesie. Et debet rex in tepestive[h] noctis silencio venire in ecclesiam[i] orationem facturus, et ibidem, si voluerit, in oratione[j] aliquantulum vigilaturus.

3. [a] enim B C D E F.—[b] venerat J.—[c] ab ecclesiis ceteris] ceteris ecclesiis B C, a ceteris ecclesiis D E F H I, ab ceteris ecclesiis J.—[d] vero add. H I.—[e] in qua] qua B, in quo D E F J.—[f] completorium E H I J.—[g] expletum B C D E H I J.—[h] intempestive B E F, in tempestive C D H, in tempesto J.—[i] eccliam H.— [j] in oratione si voluerit H I.

4. Cum autem pulsatur ad matutinas, debent esse parati[a] custodes regis[b] introitum ecclesie observantes, qui, aliis aditibus ecclesie obseratis firmius et munitis, inter ceteros canonicos et clericos[c] ecclesie, et tunc et[d] postmodum eciam de die, si necesse fuerit, debent honorifice ac diligenter[e] intromittere.

4. [a] parari B.—[b] regii J.—[c] clericos et canonicos D E F.—[d] et om. H I J.— [e] diligenter ac honorifice H I.

5. Matutine more solito decantantur. Quibus expletis, pulsatur ad primam, et cantatur[a] prima, cum visum fuerit expedire. Post primam[b] cantatam, debet rex cum archiepiscopis et[c] episcopis, baronibus et aliis, quos intromittere voluerit, in ecclesiam[d] venire antequam fiat benedictio[e]; et debent esse sedes disposite[f] circa altare, ubi honorifice episcopi et archiepiscopi, episcopis regni paribus[g] sedentibus [seorsum[h]] ab oppositis altaris, non longe a rege, nec multis indecenter interpositis.

5. [a] canitur B—[b] autem add. H I.—[c] et om. D E H I.—[d] ecclesia B C D F.— [e] benedictio] aqua benedicta B C and Ordo XXI,8, aqua benedicto J.— [f] deposite H I J.—[g] ubi honorifice ... paribus] ubi honorifice archyepiscopis episcopis regni D E F, ubi archiepiscopi et episcopi sedere valeant episcopis regni paribus H I, ubi honorifice sedent episcopi et archiepiscopi episcopis paribus regni J.—[h] seorsum om. A, but add. B C D E F H I J and Ordo XXI,8.

6. Inter primam[a] et terciam debent venire monachi sancti[b] Remigii[c] processiona [fol. 71r] liter cum crucibus et cereis, cum sacrosancta ampulla, quam debet abbas reverentissime[d] deferre sub cortina serica IIII[or] [e] perticis a IIII[or] [f] monachis albis indutis sublevata. Et cum venerit[g] ad ecclesiam beati[h] Dyonisii, vel, si magis oportuerit[i] propter turbam comprimentem[j], usque ad maiorem ianuam ecclesie, debet archiepiscopus

ABCHIJ   DEF

cum ceteris archiepiscopis et[k] episcopis, nec[11] non
et canonicis, si fieri potest, occurrere, vel, si magis
oportuerit fieri[l] propter multitudinem turbe exterius
comprimentis, saltem cum aliquibus de episcopis et
baronibus, et eam de manu abbatis

cum pollicitacione de reddendo bona fide[m] suscipere, et sic ad altare
cum magna populi reverencia deferre, abbate et[n] aliquibus de monachis
pariter comitando[o], ceteris exspectantibus[p] donec omnia perfecta
fuerint et[q] sacrosancta ampulla referatur sive[r] in ecclesiam[s] beati Dyonisii sive in capella beati[t] Nicholai[u].[12]

6. [a] vero *add.* H. —[b] beati B C D E F J. —[c] Remigi F; Remensis *add.* H I. —
[d] reverendissime *corr. to* reverentissime *in a later hand* E. —[e] quatuor B C D
E F H I J. —[f] quatuor E H I; a IIII[or] et quatuor J. —[g] venerint B C J. —[h] sancti
H I. —[i] opportuerit C. —[j] comprimantem D E, *but the* a *expuncted and corr.
above line to* comprimentem E. —[k] et *om.* H I. —[l] si fieri ... fieri] si fieri non
potest B C H I, si fieri potest occurrere vel si fieri non potest J. —[m] sic *add.* D
E F I. —[n] cum J. —[o] comittando C. —[p] expectantibus B C E F H I J. —[q] tunc
add. J. —[r] sive *om.* H I. —[s] ecclesia J. —[t] sancti H I. —[u] Nycolai E.

7. Hiis ita gestis[a], archiepiscopus ad missam se preparat cum diaconibus et[b] subdiaconibus vestimentis insignioribus et pallio[c] induendus[d]. In hunc modum autem[e] indutus, venit processionaliter[f] more solito
ad altare. Cui venienti, debet ibi astans rex[g] assurgere reverenter.

7. [a] ita gestis] factis D E F. —[b] et *om.* H I. —[c] palleo C J, palliis H. —[d] indutis
J. —[e] autem *om.* D E F H I. —[f] processionaliter *om.* D E F. —[g] rex ibi astans
B C J.

8. Cum autem venerit archiepiscopus ad altare, debet vel[a] ipse vel
aliquis de omnibus episcopis pro universis ecclesiis[b] sibi subditis a rege[c]
petere, ut[d] promittat et iuramento firmet se observaturum[e] iura[13] episcoporum et ecclesiarum, sicut debet[f] regem in regno facere[g] custodire[h], et
cetera, quemadmodum in[i] ordinario continentur[j], ubi tria promittenda et
iuranda eidem[k] proponuntur, preter iuramentum Lateranensis[l] concilii[m],

---

[11] *A* erroneously begins a new sentence with *Nec.*

[12] The abbey church of Saint-Denis still stands some 150 meters southwest of the
cathedral church (but now houses a museum). The chapel of Saint-Nicholas was in the
Hôtel-Dieu, across the street from the west corner of the cathedral; this building has
disappeared. Cf. the description of Francis I's ceremony in Godefroy, 1: 247, and also
Ordo XXIV,19.

[13] *A* is not carefully written, and this looks like *irna*; in any case, it is not *iura.*

videlicet de hereticis de regno suo extirpandis[n]. Hiis[o] itaque[p] promissis a rege et iuramento super sacrosancta eewangelia[q] [14] firmatis[r], [fol. 71v] cantatur ab omnibus "Te Deum laudamus."

8. [a] vel *om.* H I. —[b] aliquis de omnibus ... ecclesiis] aliquis de episcopis pro omnibus et ecclesiis B C D E F, aliquis ex episcopis pro omnibus H I, alius de episcopis pro omnibus et pro ecclesiis J. —[c] hic add. D F, hic promittere *add.* E, *but* promittere *expuncted by scribe* E. —[d] et B. —[e] serviturum H. —[f] decet C D E F H. —[g] et *add.* B C J. —[h] custodiri H I. —[i] in *om.* J. —[j] continetur H. — [k] et iuranda eidem] eidem D F, ei E. —[l] Latheranensis D F. —[m] consilii E; iuramentum Lateranensis concilii] iuramentum nove constitutionis Lateranensis concilii J. —[n] exstirpendis D F, exstirpandis E H I. —[o] Hic B. —[p] ita J. — [q] ewangelia B, evangelia C. —[r] promissis a rege ... firmatis] a rege super sancta Dei ewangelia (evangelia E) promissis D E F; super ... firmatis] firmatis supra sacrosancta evangelia H I.

9. Postmodum iam antea preparatis et positis super altare[a] corona regia, gladio in vagina incluso, calcaribus aureis, sceptro deaurato et virga[b] ad mensuram unius cubiti vel amplius habente desuper manum eburneam[c]. Item, caligis sericis et iacinctinis intextis per totum liliis[d] aureis, et tunica eiusdem coloris

A B C H I J	D E F
et operis, in modum tunicalis quo induuntur subdiaconi ad missam[e]. Nec non et socco prorsus eiusdem coloris et operis[f], qui est factus fere in modum cape serice absque caparone[g],	necnon et socco prorsus, quo induuntur subdyaconi ad missam,

que omnia abbas sancti[h] Dyonisii in Francia de monasterio suo debet Remis asportare[i] et stans ad altare custodire[j].

9. [a] altari H I. —[b] virgam J. —[c] eburneum B. —[d] liis C. —[e] ad missam *om.* J. — [f] eiusdem ... operis] et operis eiusdem coleris C. —[g] caprone H I, caperone J. —[h] beati B C J. —[i] apportare D E F; de monasterio ... asportare] debet Remis afferre H, de monasterio suo ad Remum debet asportare J. —[j] altare ea custodire J.

10. Rex[a] ante altare[b] stans deponit vestes suas, preter tunicam suam[c] sericam et camisiam apertas profundius ante[d] et retro in pectore, videlicet[e] et inter scapulas aperturis tunice sibi invicem connexis ansulis argenteis. Tunc in primis ibi[f] a magno camerario Francie regi[g] dicte calige calciantur[h]. Et postmodum a duce Borgundie[i] calcaria eius pedibus

---

[14] Again, *A* is not clear; the third letter seems to be *w* and not *uu*, but the word is clearly written *evangelii* near the end of the ordo.

astringuntur et statim tolluntur[j]. Postmodum rex[k] [15] a solo archiepiscopo
gladio cum[l] vagina accingitur. Quo accincto, statim idem gladius[m] de
vagina ab archiepiscopo extrahitur, vagina[n] super altare[o] deposita[p], et
datur ei ab archiepiscopo in manibus[q], quem[r] debet rex afferre humiliter[s] ad altare, et statim resumere de manu archiepiscopi, et incontinenti
dare seneschallo[t] Francie[u] ad portandum ante se, et[v] in ecclesia usque ad
finem misse, et post missam[w] cum ad palacium vadit.

10. [a] autem *add.* H I. —[b] Rex autem ad altare J. —[c] suam *om.* B C D E F H
I J. —[d] autem J. —[e] in pectore videlicet] videlicet in pectore D E F. —[f] ibi *om.*
H I. —[g] regis J. —[h] regi ... calciantur] Regi calciantur calige *beginning a new
sentence* D F; Regi calige calciantur E, *which has no punctuation here*; quas
ei tradit abbas beati Dionisii *add.* J. —[i] Burgundie B C E H I J, Burgondie
D F. —[j] et statim tolluntur *om.* D E F; quo similiter ei tradit predictus abbas
add. J. —[k] autem *add.* H I. —[l] et J. —[m] statim idem gladius] idem gladius statim D E F. —[n] ab archiepiscopo extrahitur vagina *om.* B, *but add. in marg.
by scribe.* —[o] altari H. —[p] reposita B C, posita J; vagina super altare deposita
om. D E F. —[q] in manibus *om.* D E F. —[r] quam D E. —[s] afferre humiliter]
humiliter deferre H I. —[t] senescallo B C D E H I J, senescalo F. —[u] et *add.* D
E F. —[v] et *om.* D E F J. —[w] in ecclesia *add.* B.

11. Hiis itaque[a] gestis, crismate in altari[b] super patenam[c] consecratam preparato[d], debet archiepiscopus sacrosanctam ampullam super
altare[e] aperire, [fol. 72r] et inde cum[f] acu aurea aliquantulum de oleo
celitus misso[g] attrahere[h], et crismati[i] parato[j] diligencius immiscere ad
inungendum[k] regem, qui solito[l] inter universos reges terre hoc[m] glorioso[n] prefulget privilegio, ut oleo celitus misso[g] singulariter inungatur.
Tunc dissutis ansulis aperturarum[o] ante et retro, et genibus in terram
positis, primo archiepiscopus eum eodem loco oleo inungto[p] in summitate[q] capitis. Secundo in pectore. Tercio inter scapulas. Quarto in
scapulis. Quinto in compagibus brachiorum[r]. Et, dum inungitur,
cantatur[s] a circonstantibus[t] hec antiphona[u], "Inunxerunt regem
Salomonem."

11. [a] ita B C D E F H I J. —[b] altare J; in altari *om.* D E F. —[c] pathenam E. —
[d] prepararo J. —[e] altari H I; super altare *om.* E. —[f] cum *om.* J. —[g] emisso D E
F. —[h] atrahere B C. —[i] chrismari B, chrismate E. —[j] preparato D E F H. —
[k] ungendum B, in ungendum F. —[l] solus B C D E F H I J. —[m] hec B. —[n] reges
terre hoc glorioso] hoc reges terre D E F. —[o] aperturam B C. —[p] eum eodem
loco oleo inungto] cum eodem oleo inungat B, eum eodem oleo inungit C D F
H, eum eodem loco inungit E; primo ... inungto] primo eodem loco inungitur
J. —[q] summitatio J *with marginal note in the same hand* Sic l. summitate. —

_____

[15] *H* and *I* end the previous sentence with *postmodum* and begin a new one with
Rex.

^r braciorum C. —^s cantatur *om.* H I. —^t circumstantibus B J, circunstantibus E F H. —^u anthiphona D E F.

ABCHIJ   DEF

12. Post hec connectuntur ansule aperturarum propter inunctionem, et tunc a camerario Francie induitur tunica iacinctina^a, et desuper socco, ita quod dextram manum habet^b liberam in apertura socci, et super sinistram soccum elevatum, sicut elevatur casula sacerdoti^c. Deinde datur ei ab archiepiscopo sceptrum in manu dextra^d et virga^e in sinistra. Ad ultimum^f convocatis^g ex nomine paribus^h regni et circumstantibusⁱ,[16] archiepiscopus accipit de altari coronam regiam, et solus imponit^j eam capiti regis. Qua imposita, omnes pares regni^k tam clerici quam laici^l manum apponunt^m corone et eam undique sustentant.

12. ^a iacinctina tunica H I; quam ei tradit abbas beati Dionisii *add.* J. —^b dextram manum habet] dextram me habet H, dexteram manum habeat J. —^c sacerdotis J. —^d dextera B C H I J. —^e virgam C. —^f ultimam B. —^g cum vocatis B. —^h partibus B. —ⁱ circumstantibus] circunstantibus (circumstantibus I) videlicet archiepiscopo Remensi dux (duce I), Lingonensi dux (duce I), Laudunensi dux (duce I), Noviomensi comes (comite I), Belvacensi comes (comite I), Cathalanensi comes (comite I), episcopis; Normannie, Aquitanie, Burgundie, ducibus; Tolose, Britannie et Flandrie, comitibus H I. —^j preponit C. —^k regni *om.* B C H I J. —^l tam laici quam clerici C. —^m imponunt H I J.

13. Tunc archiepiscopus, cum paribus coronam sustentantibus, regem taliter insignitum deducit in solium sibi preparatum, sericis stratum et ornatum, ubi collocat eum in sede eminenti, unde ab omnibus possit videri. Quem in sede sua taliter residentem, mox archiepiscopus, mitra ob^a reverenciam deposita^b, osculatur. Et postea^c episcopi et laici pares qui eius coronam sustentant.[17] Porro in accinctione gladii^d, in unctione, in dacione sceptri et virge, [fol. 72v] in imposicione^e corone, et cum in solio collocatur, archiepiscopus dicit orationes que suis in locis in ordinario^f continentur. Rege itaque in solio suo taliter residente, et paribus regni cum eo coronam eius^g sustentantibus^h, ad altare revertitur.

---

[16] The scribe of *H* added *dux* and *comes* above the line for each of the episcopal peers in var. 12i, which probably shows that those words were not in his source. The scribe of *I* corrected the grammar to *duce* and *comite* respectively.

[17] *Sic l. mutus Sic. eum redundat* add. in marg. by scribe *J*.

13. [a] mitra ob] mitra B, mitre ob J. — [b] depositum B, enim J. — [c] post eum B C H I J. — [d] et *add.* J. — [e] inpositione B. — [f] ordonario J. — [g] eius *om.* H I. — [h] archiepiscopus *add.* B C H I J.

ABCDEFHIJ

14. Ordo ad inungendam reginam[a].

14. [a] Ordo ... reginam *om.* B C D E F H I J.

15. Verum si regina inungenda fuerit et coronanda[18] cum rege, paratur[a] similiter ei[b] solium a sinistra parte chori, solio regis[c] aliquantulum eminenciori a parte chori dextra[d]

ABCHIJ	DEF
collocata[e]. Et postquam rex in modum premissum in[f] solio suo[g] resederit, archiepiscopo ad altare regresso, regina,[19] sericis induta, ab ipso inungitur in[20] capite et in pectore tantum[h], non in unctione[i] regis celitus missa[j], sed oleo sanctificato simplici. Post inunctionem[k] datur ei ab archiepiscopo sceptrum modicum, alterius modi quam sceptrum regium, et virga consimilis[l] virge regie. Deinde imponitur ab archiepiscopo solo corona capiti ipsius. Quam impositam sustentant[m] undique barones, et sic[n] deducunt eam ad solium[o], ubi in sede parata collocatur, circumstantibus[p] eam baronibus et matronis nobilioribus.	collocata, sed non inungitur de oleo celitus emisso, sed oleo sanctificato simplici.

15. [a] patur J. — [b] ei similiter B C J; ei *om.* D E F. — [c] regio H I. — [d] dextera B D F H I J. — [e] collocato B C H, collocat J. — [f] in *om.* B. — [g] suo *om.* J. — [h] et in pectore tantum] tantum et in pectore B C H I J. — [i] inunctione B C, unctione H I. — [j] emissa H I. — [k] unctionem J. — [l] cum similis B. — [m] sustentent B. — [n] sic *om.* H I. — [o] suum *add.* J. — [p] circunstantibus C H.

16. Hiis expletis, missa tunc[a] demum a cantore et succentore, chorum servantibus, inchoatur et sollempniter decantatur[b]. Lecto tamen[c] Ewangelio[d], maior inter archiepiscopos et episcopos[e] assistentes librum Evangelii[f] accipit, et tam ad regem quam ad reginam ad

---

[18] *coronanda* followed by a half-line blank in *H;* the following line begins with *cum rege.*

[19] *A* incorrectly begins a new sentence with *Regina; B* and *C* do not, although a later hand has added what appears to be a punctuation mark (probably a comma) before *regina.*

[20] *A* incorrectly begins a new sentence with *In; B* and *C* do not.

ABCHIJ | DEF

deosculandum deportat. Deinde refert^g eum ad archiepiscopum qui missam celebrat^h.

16. ^{a}tunc *om.* J. —^{b} incipitur et sollenniter decantatur J. —^{c} autem B C H
I J. —^{d} evangelio C H I. —^{e} et episcopos *om.* H I. —^{f} ewangelium B, evangelii
C H I, ewangeli J. —^{g} defert H I. —^{h} celebrat *om.* J.

17. Dum autem cantatur^a offertorium, deducitur tam rex quam
regina sollempniter de solio^b, et offert uterque ad manum^c archiepiscopi
tam panem unum^d quam vinum in urceo argenteo et XIIIe aureos^f

[fol. 73r] postmodum^g.

17. ^{a} canatur J. —^{b} sollempniter de solio] de soliis suis D E F, sollenniter de
solio J. —^{c} ad manum] de manu H I. —^{d} vinum B. —^{e} undecim J. —^{f} Bisancios *add. above* aureos, *and* et regina similiter *add. in marg. in a later hand*
C. —^{g} postmodum *om.* J.

18. Quo facto^a, reducitur uterque^b ad solium suum
et sedem suam. Tunc^c celebratur missa ab archiepiscopo; antequam^d dicat "Pax vobis," facit benedictionem
super regem^e, reginam et populum. Et, accepto osculo
pacis ab archiepiscopo, is^f qui librum evangelii^g deosculandum ante detulerat, defert pacem regi et regine in
soliis suis residentibus. Et postea^h omnes archiepiscopi
et^i episcopi dant osculum pacis unus post alium regi in
suo solio^j residenti.

18. ^{a} postmodum *add.* J. —^{b} usque J. —^{c} et tunc J. —^{d} autem *add.* B C H I J. —
^{e} et *add.* H I J *and, in a later hand,* B. —^{f} his C. —^{g} ewangelium B, Ewangelii J; pacis ... evangelii] pacis is qui evangelii librum ad H. —^{h} postea] post
eum J. —^{i} et *om.* H. —^{j} solio suo H I.

ABCHIJ | DEF

19. Post percepcionem eucharistie factam ab archiepiscopo^a, iterum^b descendunt
rex et regina de soliis suis, et accedentes
humiliter ad altare, percipiunt^c corpus et
sanguinem Domini de manu archiepiscopi.
Et missa^d expleta, deponit archiepiscopus
coronas de capitibus eorum. Quibus exutis

19. post perceptionem
eucharistie ab archiepis-
copo factam.[21] Interim
descendunt rex et regina
de soliis suis, et accipiunt
corpus et sanguinem Domi-
ni de manu archyepiscopi,

---

[21] *D, E,* and *F* treat *post perceptionem ... factam* as the conclusion of the sentence
in no. 17.

regalibus insignibus, iterum imponit capitibus eorum modicas coronas. Et sic vadunt
ad palacium, nudo gladio precedente[e].

et sic vadunt ad palacium,
nudo gladio precedente.

19. [a] ab archyepiscopo factam D, ab archiepiscopo factam E F. —[b] Interim D
E F. —[c] et accedentes ... percipiunt] et accipiunt D E F. —[d] misse H . —
[e] gladio nudo precendente J.

ORDO XX B AND ORDO XX C

French Translations of the Ordo of Reims

Dates: ca. 1300–1320, 1512

Other names for Ordo XX B: French Translation of the Ordo of Louis IX
(Schreuer, Buchner)

Introduction

The Ordo of Reims (Ordo XX A) is important not only because it transformed a generic coronation ceremony into a specifically French one, but also because, in translation, it was the first ordo to make its way from the relatively private pages of liturgical books into the more public volumes of secular government. The original translation of the Ordo of Reims is presented here with its variants both on account of its official position at the heart of the French government and because the translation has been the subject of scholarly discussion on its own account.

The translation, made in the language of the Ile-de-France around 1300, was copied into each of the four earliest registers of the Chambre des comptes in Paris. These registers, which came to be known as the *Libri memoriales*, or *Mémoriaux*, were entitled, rather waggishly, ✠ (i.e., *Croix*, the symbol for the sign of the Cross), *Pater*, *Noster*, and *Qui es in celis*, the beginning words of the Lord's Prayer. It cannot have been fortuitous that a prescriptive coronation text should have found its way into these registers, for the most important royal financial institution would have borne a significant part of the expenses of the most costly of all royal ceremonies. The practical necessity of producing an informed royal officialdom had the side effect of making the ceremony known to a wider audience than it had ever had before — the ordines in pontificals and ordinaries would have been little known outside the churches or monasteries that possessed them.

Less than half a century after the French translation of the Ordo of Reims entered the Chambre des compte's registers, knowledge of its contents began to spread in another way. The translation was combined with the Ordo of Charles V (Ordo XXIII) and other coronation materials to form the collection that was Charles V's official coronation book. There were several copies of that book, including the lavishly illustrated one that Charles V himself added to the royal library.[1]

---

[1] For details concerning this manuscript, see the introduction to Ordo XXIII.

A compilation made from the early registers in the fifteenth century was also known as *Noster* (now called *Noster²* in order to distinguish from the original *Noster*). *Noster²* was itself copied in the fifteenth century (manuscript *F*). *Croix* was recopied in the sixteenth century because the original *Croix* had become nearly illegible. References to *Croix* in early-modern manuscripts or books almost always were to this sixteenth-century copy (sometimes known as *Nouveau Croix*), and references to *Noster* were likewise to the fifteenth-century *Noster²*. These fifteenth- and sixteenth-century copies hardly contributed to the dissemination of knowledge concerning the coronation, however, for the printing presses of France began to turn out printed descriptions of the ceremony, and the coronation ceremony became truly a matter of public knowledge.[2]

The original *Noster*, which dates from about 1320, is the only one of the Chambre des comptes's *Libri memoriales* that has survived to the present. The remaining three early registers, and apparently *Noster²* and *Nouveaux Croix*, were destroyed in the fire that consumed the financial institution's archives on 27 October 1737. *Noster* survives because it had disappeared from the archives of the Chambre des comptes, apparently before the middle of the sixteenth century. It had resurfaced only in 1728, when it was in the library of the abbey of Saint-Germain-des-Prés, where its presence at the time of the fire explains its survival. Almost immediately after the fire, an official attempt was made to recover the contents of the lost registers; the task had not been completed when the Revolution brought it to an end. Unfortunately, those who copied texts in the recovery attempt did not identify their sources.[3] It is clear, though, that the recovery attempts did not make use of *Noster*, the importance of which was not recognized in the eighteenth century; instead, later copies and even printed editions were consulted.

It does not seem likely that either *Noster* or *Croix* contained the original of the translation of the Ordo of Reims.[4] The copy in *Noster* has a

---

[2] From at least the early fifteenth century, the ceremony itself was a relatively private affair, though, visible only to a few; the evidence does not show whether the same was or was not true during the thirteenth and fourteenth centuries. See Richard A. Jackson, "Le pouvoir monarchique dans la cérémonie du sacre et couronnement des rois de France," in *Représentation, pouvoir et royauté à la fin du Moyen Age*, ed. Joël Blanchard (Paris: Picard, 1995), 237–51.

[3] This has made it difficult to establish stemmata both for this ordo and for Ordo XXII A.

[4] *Croix* was usually regarded as the most authoritative of the four registers. Joseph Petit et al., *Essai de restitution des plus anciens mémoriaux de la Chambre des comptes de Paris (Pater, Noster¹, Noster², Qui es in Cœlis, Croix, A¹)*, Université

number of archaic readings that suggest a date somewhat older than ca. 1320, although, interestingly enough, manuscript B, the younger copy in Charles V's coronation book, which appears to have descended from *Croix*, has a few readings that are even more archaic than some of those in *Noster*. The language of this translation is important because it is an early example of non-literary French.[5]

The second translation (manuscript Q) was made independently at the beginning of the sixteenth century. It has never been published, and it has some interesting peculiarities and is philologically fascinating because its language is that of northeastern France, not the Ile-de-France.[6] The text does not contain the complete ordo because it is a translation of Ordo XX A, manuscript F, the incomplete ordo added to some manuscripts of Lambert de Saint-Omer's *Liber floridus*.

I place these translations immediately after the Ordo of Reims, the text that they translate, even though this puts them out of chronological order: the Ordo of 1250 (Ordo XXI) and the Last Capetian Ordo (Ordo XXII A) were composed before the Ordo of Reims was first translated.

---

de Paris: Bibliothèque de la Faculté des Lettres 7 (Paris: Félix Alcan, 1899), vi–xix, discussed the dating, ownership, and contents of the four *Libri memoriales*. Petit stated that *Noster* (which Petit termed *Noster¹*) is older than *Croix* and *Qui es in celis* (and on p. 67 he noted that *Croix* and *Qui es* seem to have been composed after and from *Noster*). He provided evidence that *Croix* contained texts dating from 1223 to 1332 (or 1334); *Pater* from 1254 to 1330; *Noster* from 1226 to 1315; and *Qui es* from 1223 to 1330.

Petit concluded that it is not possible to determine whether *Pater* or *Noster* is the oldest of the four, and he cautiously stated that *Croix* and *Qui es in celis* were copied "en partie" from *Noster*. If I am correct in detecting older linguistic forms in the present translation in manuscripts descended from *Croix*, then it would appear that the translation in *Croix* was not copied from *Noster*, but either from a common lost source or from *Pater* (lost manuscript *2*). For coronation matters, the authority of *Croix* was enhanced when it was selected to receive a copy of the Last Capetian Ordo (Ordo XXII A, lost manuscript *4*).

[5] My colleague Claude Buridant, who specializes in translations from Latin into French, very kindly and carefully examined the text. He informed me that, on the basis of language alone, it is impossible to tell whether the translation was made in the late thirteenth or the early fourteenth century. I am most grateful to Professor Buridant for his help with this and other French texts. I particularly followed his advice in deciding which of the many variants to retain in this edition of the translation.

[6] Some of its words are unfamiliar to most modern readers, so I added a few lexicographical and philological notes as an aid to understanding the text.

Lost Manuscripts

There are two groups of lost manuscripts.[7] The first consists of early registers of the Chambre des comptes, the *Libri memoriales*, and contains five manuscripts.

1—Paris, Chambre des comptes, register (*mémorial*) ✠ (*Croix*), fols. 25 (the king's ordo) and 27–29v or 30r (the queen's ordo).[8] Ca. 1320–1330.

2—Paris, Chambre des comptes, register *Pater*, fols. 163 (the king's ordo) and 164 (the queen's ordo). Ca. 1320–1330.

3—Paris, Chambre des comptes, register *Qui es in celis*, fols. 27 (the king's ordo) and 29v (the queen's ordo). Ca. 1320–1330.

4—Paris, Chambre des comptes, register *Noster²*, fols. 250 (the king's ordo) and 252 (the queen's ordo), apparently from *Pater*. *Noster²* is a fifteenth-century compilation made from the early registers. After the original *Noster* disappeared definitively from the Chambre des comptes, *Noster²* came to be called *Noster* in its stead; the designation *Noster²* is a modern one devised to avert confusion with the original *Noster* (manuscript *A*).

5—Paris, Chambre des comptes, register *Nouveau Croix* (or *Saint-Just* or *Saint-Just²*), fols. 30ff. 1574. This was a copy of the register *Croix* (lost manuscript *1*), which the *greffier* of the Chambre des comptes ordered copied in 1574 because the original had become nearly illegible. It was called, apparently officially, *Saint-Just*, after having been known as the *Liber viridis sine asseribus, signatus* ✠, but it was sometimes called *Nouveau Croix*. When most early-modern manuscripts and books refer to *Croix*, they refer to this copy rather than to the original *Croix*. Modern scholars devised the name *Saint-Just²* in order to avert confusion with the original *Saint-Just*, an early register of the Chambre des comptes that contained no coronation text.

The second group consists of manuscripts that were formerly in the library of Charles V and Charles VI.

6—Lost manuscript from the library of Charles V and Charles VI. No. 228 in the inventory by Léopold Delisle, *Recherches sur la librairie de*

---

[7] I originally thought that there was a third category, which consisted of a single manuscript containing a translation of Guillaume de Nangis's *Gesta Ludovici regis*. There was no such manuscript, however; see Ordo XX A, n. 7.

[8] The final folio number of the text in these registers cannot be precisely determined, nor is it possible to know whether the text began on the recto or verso side of the folio.

Charles V, 2 vols. (Paris: H. Champion, 1907), 2: 40, this manuscript
also contained a copy of the Ordo of Charles V (Ordo XXIII, lost MS
3); it was deposited in the abbey of Saint-Denis in 1380. Description:
Richard A. Jackson, "Les manuscrits des *ordines* de couronnement
de la bibliothèque de Charles V, roi de France," *Le Moyen Age* (1976),
78–85.

7—Lost manuscript from the library of Charles V and Charles VI. No. 229
in Delisle, *Recherches*, this manuscript almost certainly contained a
copy of Charles V's ordo (Ordo XXIII, lost MS *1* or *2*). Description:
Jackson, "Les manuscrits des *ordines*," 74–75.

8—Lost manuscript from the library of Charles V and Charles VI. No. 231
in Delisle, *Recherches*, this manuscript also contained a copy of
Charles V's ordo (Ordo XXIII, lost MS *1* or *2*). Description: Jackson,
"Les manuscrits des *ordines*," 75–76.[9]

Manuscripts

ORDO XX B

A—Paris, Bibl. nat., MS lat. 12814 (= Chambre des comptes, mémorial
Noster), fols. 27r–30v. Ca. 1320. This is the only *Liber memorialis* to
survive to the present. Description: Petit, *Essai de restitution*, x–xiii,
xvi–xix, 67–85. See Plate 16.

B—London, British Library, MS Cotton, Tiberius B.viii, fols. 35r–41r (foliation in pencil). 1365. Description: see Ordo XXIII, MS *A*.

C—Paris, Bibl. nat., MS lat. 8886, fols. 58r–62v (foliation in pencil). Early
fifteenth century. Description: Leroquais, *Sacramentaires*, 2: 373–77,
no. 546, and *Pontificaux*, 2: 148–54, no. 140, which use the foliation
in ink and which are entirely superseded by Mathieu Lescuyer's very
detailed description in Jacqueline Sclafer and Marie-Pierre Lafitte
(eds.), *Catalogue général des manuscrits latins, n° 8823–8921*
(Paris: Bibliothèque nationale de France, 1997), 106–111. See Plates
17–18.

D—London, British Library, MS Additional 32097, fols. 148v–150v
(296v–299v in old foliation). Fifteenth century. As in *B* and *C*, the
ordo in this manuscript is followed by the coronation oaths (fol.
150r–v), lists of the Peers of France (fol. 150v), and the Ordo of
Charles V. Description: *Catalogue of Additions to the Manuscripts in*

---

[9] I now believe that no manuscript in the royal library contained both the translation of the Ordo of Reims and the Last Capetian Ordo, and that the only copy of the
Last Capetian Ordo in the library (Ordo XXII A, lost MS *3*) may have been a copy of the
cathedral of Reims's *livre bleu* (Ordo XXII A, lost MS *2*). See also Ordo XXIII, lost MSS
1–3.

the British Museum in the Years MDCCCLXXXII–MDCCCLXXXVII (London: British Museum, 1889), 73–75.

E—Paris, Bibl. nat., MS Dupuy 365, fols. 22r–28r. Fifteenth century, third quarter. Copied from *C*. Formerly in the possession of Pierre Dupuy.[10] Description: Dorez, *Catalogue de la collection Dupuy*, 1: 340. See Plates 19–20.

F—Paris, Bibl. nat., MS fran. 2833, fols. 184r–185v. Formerly MS lat. 8406. Fifteenth century. Copied from lost manuscript *4* (*Noster²*). Description: *Bibliothèque nationale: Catalogue des manuscrits français: Ancien fonds*, 1: 500–502.[11]

G—Paris, Bibl. nat., MS fran. 4596, fols. 124v–129v. Formerly MS fran. 9475. Sixteenth century. Copied from *F*. Description: *Bibliothèque nationale: Catalogue des manuscrits français: Ancien fonds*, 4: 32–35.

H—Paris, Bibl. nat., MS nouv. acq. fran. 7232, fols. 1r–4v, 5v–6v. Formerly MS Brienne 263. Seventeenth century, first half; initialed by Paul Petau and Pierre Dupuy on 15 January 1652 (unpaginated leaf 1r). Copied from lost manuscript *5* (*Nouveau Croix*). Description: Omont, *Catalogue général des nouvelles acquisitions françaises*, 3: 62, 83.

I— Paris, Bibl. de l'Institut de France, MS Godefroy 380, pp. 335–50. Mid-seventeenth century. Source not stated or determined. Not collated.

J— Paris, Bibl. de l'Institut de France, MS Godefroy 382, pp. 123–34. Mid-seventeenth century. Copied from *E*. Not collated.

K—Paris, Bibl. de l'Arsenal, MS 4227, fols. 2r–4r, 5r–6r. Seventeenth century, second half. Copied indirectly from *H*. Description Martin, *Catalogue des manuscrits de la Bibliothèque de l'Arsenal*, 4: 331.

L—Paris, Bibl. nat., MS fran. 16600, fols. 316r–321r. Seventeenth century.

---

[10] Dupuy's signature is on fol. 1r, followed by a note, "donné par M. de Lomenie." The reference is to Antoine de Loménie, seigneur of Ville-aux-Clercs, who was a *secrétaire d'Etat* under Henry IV and Louis XIII; see Léopold Delisle, *Le cabinet des manuscrits de la Bibliothèque impériale*, Histoire générale de Paris 10, 3 vols. (Paris: Imprimerie impériale/nationale), 1868–81, 1: 214–17. On fol. 59v a note that appears to be seventeenth century reads, "Ce Livre a esté escript en l'an 1378 du Regne du Roy Charles V," a date that is clearly incorrect. The miniatures in the manuscript were painted by an artist in the circle of Jean Colombe (verbal communication from François Avril), the same artist who executed the second set of miniatures in the *Très riches heures* of the duke of Berry; on Colombe, see Ulrich Thieme (ed.), *Allgemeines Lexikon der bildenden Künstler*, 7 (Leipzig: Verlag von E. A. Seemann, 1912), 244–45.

[11] Manuscript *F* is not *Noster²*, but was either copied from it or from a very similar manuscript (Petit, *Essai de restitution*, xiii). See also Charles Victor Langlois, *Registres perdus des archives de la Chambre des comptes de Paris* (Paris: Imprimerie nationale, 1916).

Copied from lost manuscript *4* (*Noster²*).[12] Description: Henri Omont, *Catalogue général des manuscrits français*, 3 vols. (Paris: Ernest Leroux, 1898–1900), vol. 2: Lucien Auvray, *Ancien Saint-Germain français*, (Paris: Ernest Leroux, 1898), 1: 487.

M—Paris, Bibl. de l'Assemblée nationale, MS 195, fols. 12r–16v. Formerly MS B.105ⁱ, tome 68. Late seventeenth or early eighteenth century. Copied from *K*.[13] Description: see Ordo XVII B, MS *G*.

N—Paris, Arch. nat., KK 1442, fols. 3r–8r, 9r–10v. Eighteenth century. Copied indirectly from *H*. Description: see Ordo XVII B, MS *I*.

O_1—Paris, Arch. nat., P 2288, pp. 706–12, 714–15. Eighteenth century (after 1737 because the manuscript contains an attempt to recover the lost contents of the early registers after the fire). Copied from a copy of lost manuscript *1* (*Croix*), beginning on fol. 25. Description: Petit, *Essai de restitution*, 5.

O_2—Paris, Arch. nat., P 2288, pp. 716–25. Eighteenth century (after 1737). Supposedly copied from lost manuscript *4* (*Noster²*), beginning on fols. 250 and 252, but actually from *F* or a copy of *F* (but not from *G*). Description: Description: Petit, *Essai de restitution*, 5.

P—Paris, Bibl. nat., MS nouv. acq. fran. 7938, fols. 117r–127r. Eighteenth century (before 1767). Copied from *F*. Description: Omont, *Catalogue général des nouvelles acquisitions françaises* 3: 169, 195.[14]

ORDO XX C

Q—The Hague, Koninklijke Bibl., MS 128 C 4, fols. 179r–181r. Formerly MS Y.407. 1512. Numbered 113, this French translation of Ordo XX A, MS *F* was made in Enghien (Hainault) for Philip of Cleves. Description: Delisle, "Notice sur les manuscrits," 604–605; Lieftinck, *Manuscrits datés conservés dans les Pays-Bas*, 1: 44, no. 104.

---

[12] Petit, *Essai de restitution*, 7, no. 23, stated that MS 16600 contains most of the documents from *Pater* and *Noster²*.

[13] After collating the manuscripts of Ordo XVII B, I knew that MS 195 (that ordo's MS *G*) was copied either from nouv. acq. fran. 7232 (MS *H*) or from Arsenal 4227 (MS *K*), but I could not determine which one. Variants in the present text prove that MS 195 was copied from Arsenal 4227. This also corrects Elizabeth A. R. Brown's statement that MS 195 was copied from nouv. acq. fran. 7232 (Brown, *Franks, Burgundians, and Aquitanians*, 102, n. 1).

[14] Petit, *Essai de restitution*, 6 (no. 10) and 7 (no. 18), asserted that Paris, Bibl. nat., MSS fran. 2755 and fran. 5317 are each independent and nearly complete copies of the original *Croix*, but neither manuscript contains Ordo XX B. Manuscript fran. 2755 was copied from several of the *Chambre de compte*'s early registers, and fran. 5317 contains (pp. 59–98) only extracts from *Croix*. Manuscript fran. 5317, pp. 1–3, does have the table of contents of *Croix*, but this does not list either Ordo XX B or the copy of Ordo XXII A (lost manuscript *4*) sewn at the end of the register.

Editions — Ordo XX B

a — Godefroy, 1: 26–29, with the lists of the peers on p. 30, from E.[15]

b — Philippe Labbe, *L'abrègé royal de l'alliance chronologique de l'histoire sacrée et profane* (Paris: Gaspar Meturas, 1651; reprinted 1664), 1: 619–24, from lost manuscript 5 (*Nouveau Croix*), fol. 30 (with a reference to lost manuscript 3 [*Qui es*], fol. 27).[16]

c — Varin, *Archives administratives de la ville de Reims*, 1, part 2: 528–30, from O_1.

d — Guillaume Marlot, *Histoire de la ville, cité et université de Reims*, 4 vols. (Reims: L. Jacquet, 1843–1846) 3: 786–90, from c.

e — G. Leroy, "Le livre du sacre des rois, ayant fait partie de la librairie de Charles V, au Louvre, actuellement conservé au British Museum, à Londres," *Bulletin historique et philologique du Comité des travaux historiques et scientifiques* (1896), 616–20, from B. Pp. 620–21 contain very brief incipits of nos. 20b–21b, the *petitio* and *promissio* (but not no. 22b, the oath of the kingdom), followed by nos. 23b–24b, the material on the Peers of France.

f — Dewick, *Coronation Book of Charles V*, cols. 5–12, from B. The list of the peers of France is in cols. 13–14.

g — Schreuer, "Über altfranzösische Krönungsordnungen," 183–92. Nos. 1–13 from f.[17]

The Stemma — Ordo XX B

Apart from A, there are three groups of manuscripts. Manuscripts B C D E form a group derived from a source in the royal library (lost manuscript 6). Manuscripts F G L O_2 P form a second group derived from

---

[15] The Godefroys took considerable liberties in modernizing the spelling both in the ordo and in the lists of peers. See also Ordo XX A, n. 7.

[16] On p. 624 Labbe wrote that he compared the text in *Croix* and *Qui es* with Godefroy's edition (edition a) and that he decided to publish it from the *Libri memoriales* because "j'ay trouvé que celuy cy portoit des marques plus evidentes de son antiquité, et qu'il avoit esté moins alteré par les copistes." Although he did not say which manuscript he used for his edition, the variants show that he copied *Nouveau Croix* (lost manuscript 5). Schreuer, "Über altfranzözische Krönungsordnungen," 162, n. 1, mistakenly cited this as an edition by Jacques Lelong.

[17] In addition, the text has sometimes been printed in collections of texts for the use of French university students, e.g., by Jean Imbert, Gérard Sautel, and Marguerite Boulet-Sautel, *Histoire des institutions et des faits sociaux (X^e–XIXe siècle)*, « Themis »: Textes et documents (Paris: Hachette, 1956), 77–79, from e (nos. 1–13 only), and (from Imbert et al.) by Marcel Reinhard (ed.), *Textes et documents d'histoire, Agrégation d'histoire, 1959* (Paris: Hachette, 1960), 138–41 (nos. 1–13 only).

Noster² (lost manuscript *4*). Manuscripts $H\,K\,M\,N\,O_1$ (and ed. *b*) form a third group derived from lost manuscript *1* (*Croix*).

In the $B\,C\,D\,E$ group, *E* was certainly copied from *C*. Manuscripts *B* and *D* share many readings, but *D*, which was copied in England, was not copied from *B*, even though *B* had been taken to England by the Duke of Bedford. Therefore, *B* and *D* were each copied from a lost manuscript, x^3. Manuscript *C* was not copied from x^3, but from a lost manuscript that was the source of x^3, doubtless lost manuscript *6*, here labeled x^2. The stemma of this group (the "royal group") is as follows:

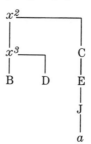

The stemma of the $F\,G\,L\,O_2\,P$ group is quite clear. Manuscript *F* was copied from lost manuscript *4* (*Noster²*), but *Noster²* appears to have been copied from *Pater* rather than from from *Noster* (see below). Manuscripts *G*, *P*, and O_2 were copied from *F*, but *L* was not copied from *F*. Because *L* does share many readings with *F*, it appears to be an independent copy of *Noster²*. Therefore, the stemma of this group is as follows:

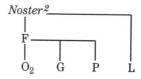

The stemma of the $H\,K\,M\,N\,O_1\,b$ group can also be established with a fair degree of certitude. Several scribal peculiarities in *H*, which was copied from *Nouveau Croix* (lost MS *5*), appear also in *K M N*, showing that these four manuscripts form their own subgroup and that *K*, *M*, and *N* are descended from *H*. Manuscript *M* is clearly copied from *K*, but *N* was copied from neither *K* nor *M*. A number of readings (not retained in the variants) show that *K* and *N* were not directly copied from *H*, but independently copied from a lost intermediate manuscript (x^5).[18] Manu-

---

[18] In this text the evidence for a lost manuscript between nouv. acq. fran. 7232 and Arsenal 4227 (MSS *H* and *K*) is clearer than it was in Ordo XVII B (MSS *E* and *F*). See also n. 13 above.

script H shares some readings with ed. b, and both appear to have been copied from *Nouveau Croix* rather than from *Croix* or *Qui es* (lost MSS *1* and *3*)—simply the fact that *Croix* had become nearly illegible in the sixteenth century makes this probable, and *Croix* appears to have been regarded as more authentic than *Qui es*. On the other hand, O_1 was not copied from H, K, M, or N. It does have a number of readings in common with b; it does not appear to have been copied from b, but rather to have descended from b's ultimate source. This was not *Nouveau Croix*, however, because O_1 retains many spellings of an older manuscript that must have contained readings from the original *Croix*. Because *Croix* had been destroyed by the time O_1 was copied, O_1 had to have been copied from a careful copy of *Croix*, here labeled x^4. In O_1 a few spellings typical of the period from 1450 to 1550—*ung*, for example—suggest that x^4 was copied then. Thus the stemma for this group is as follows:

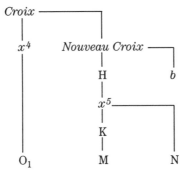

It might even be possible to combine the stemmata of the three groups. Manuscript O_1, only one step removed from *Croix*, has several readings in common with the royal group $B\ C\ D\ E$ (e.g., *ampole* instead of *ampoule*, *dedens* instead of *dedans*, *ceptre* instead of *sceptre*). These must surely show that x^2 in the royal group (lost manuscript *6*, *7*, or *8*) was a copy of *Croix* (a copy because x^2 also contained the coronation oaths, information on the peers of France, and the Ordo of Charles V). The differences between the presumed readings of *Croix* and the readings of *Noster* would seem to show that they were copied from their source independently. We do not have the readings of *Pater* or *Qui es* (excepting two readings in *Pater*—see below and nn. 32 and 37), so it is impossible to determine the relationship between all four of the early registers of the Chambre des comptes. Two readings in F and L suggest that the ordo in their source, *Noster^2*, was copied from neither *Croix* nor *Noster*, but from another manuscript. These readings are 1) the untranslated Latin title (no. *2b*, var. *e*), which is in none of the manuscripts or editions descended from *Croix* or *Noster*; and 2) the reading *ordonnance* in no. *8b*, var. *q*, where all manuscripts or editions (except *D*, which is not very trustworthy) descended from *Croix* and *Noster* read *ordinaire*. The parenthetical note in MS *H* (quoted in n. 32), which was copied when *Pater* was still in existence, states that *Pater* read *paulle* where the other manuscripts read *palle* (no. *7b*, var. *e*—the reading *pallé* in O_1 and *b* is a modern misreading of one possible Middle-French spelling). Because both *F* and *L* read *paule*, it appears that their source, the ordo in *Noster²*, was copied from *Pater*. This evidence is slender, however, and the stemma indicates that by means of a question mark between *Pater* and

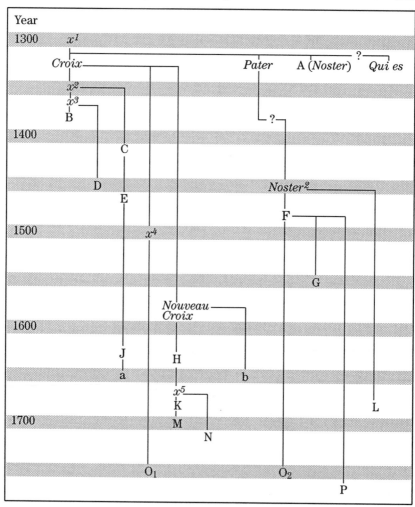

Noster[2]. Manuscript *Qui es* could have been copied either from the common source or from one of the other registers; only for the sake of simplicity is it here shown as possibly the former. The stemma shows all known and putative manuscripts (with a minimum of lost manuscripts). Spacial constraints disguise the probable dates of 1354–65 for x^2 and x^3 as well as for *B*, which is dated. Also, one must keep in mind that the dates of many of the manuscripts, particularly the lost ones, are approximate.

Principles of the Edition

The text of the official translation (Ordo XXB) is the previously unpublished text in MS *A*. The orthography of *A* is respected, but I have added apostrophes in contractions and otherwise followed the rules outlined in the General Principles of the Edition (Vol. I: 41–48). Except as noted, the sentences are those of *A*; other manuscripts often differ.[19] The paragraphing often differs from manuscript to manuscript, and it would be impossibly complex to attempt to indicate the peculiarities of each manuscript, so I have adopted for both translations the paragraphing of Ordo XXA. This results in identical paragraph numbers in Ordines XXA, XXB, and XXC. Nonetheless, where the paragraphing in *A* and *B* differs from that of Ordo XXA, I indicate it in a note.[20] Capitalization varies widely from manuscript to manuscript and even within a manuscript; therefore, both capitalization and punctuation have been modernized.

I retain the variants from *B*, *C*, and *D*, but only those variants from *E* that are identical with *C*. Variants from O_1 are retained because it was copied from a copy of lost manuscript *1* (*Croix*). Variants from *H* and from edition *b* (Labbe) are retained because they appear to be independent copies of lost manuscript *5* (*Nouveau Croix*). Similarly, variants from *F* and *L* are retained because they are independent copies of lost manuscript *4* (*Noster*[2]).

The scribe of *C* had four peculiarities. 1) His *n* sometimes looks like a *u*, and he wrote a double *n* like *un*, usually in *couroune* or *courouner* (and their other forms); those readings have been rendered *u* and *nn* respectively when they appear in a retained variant, and the same is true of *E*, which closely follows *C* in this respect. 2) He placed a line over an *i* before an *n*, which would normally indicate a succeeding *n*, but in these

---

[19] In many instances the scribe of *B* capitalized the *E* in *et* even where it is not possible to begin a new sentence; it did not seem worthwhile to retain these as variants.

[20] In *A* the paragraphs are indicated by a double period and a sign much like the modern English-language paragraph sign (..¶); in *B* they are indicated by relatively ornate capital letters.

cases it is simply a dot over the i to distinguish *in* from *m*. 3) He indiscriminately terminated a word with a normal curved s or one that looks like a cursive z; this orthography has not been retained unless the word is a variant for another reason. 4) It is sometimes impossible to determine whether he wrote *ct* or *tt* (e.g., *mectre* or *mettre*); I have rendered the readings of such words to the best of my ability.

The scribe of D wrote his s at the end of words either as a normal curved letter or like a cursive z, and his r sometimes looks like an i; these features have not been retained unless there is another reason for a variant. The scribe often appears to have copied words incorrectly from his source, and a number of his spellings show that his French was not that of the Ile-de-France. He sometimes wrote *nt* with a line over the letters (in *do$\overline{nt}$*, for example), suggesting that this is an abbreviation for *nnt* (i.e., *donnt*); this might be simply a scribal peculiarity, but instances of it been retained because in Ordo XX C (MS Q) the letter n is often doubled. The scribe's double initial f, as in *ffrance*, is doubtless a capital letter, but I have retained it as it appears in the manuscript.

The scribe of H usually wrote a final *nt* in such a way that it looks like n only; this has been rendered as *nt*. His l apostrophe sometimes looks like li, which is often the reading of the manuscripts copied from H; these have been transcribed so as to reflect the probable readings of H's source (e.g., *l'eglise* rather than the incorrect reading, *li eglise*).

The scribe of L sometimes wrote an initial i like a j (as in *jra*), and sometimes not; no attempt has been made to preserve this peculiarity. He wrote *doibt* for *doit*, as the scribes of K, M, and N occasionally did; this reading is not retained.

These manuscripts were written over the course of four hundred years in French, a language that had no standard spelling. To make matters worse, the scribes sometimes copied the spelling of their source, and sometimes they modernized the spelling, using the spelling current for their time and their part of France, but they were often quite inconsistent in their modernization. Therefore, there are an enormous number of variants, which made this text more difficult to present legibly than any other.[21] This necessitated several methods of eliminating many variants.

---

[21] This is illustrated by no. 2, the shortest paragraph in the text, as it appears in my computer files. Variants are placed within the diagonals / and \, and hidden (i.e., non-printing) notes to myself are surrounded by the angle brackets < and >. Obviously, retaining all variants would render the edition incomprehensible and practically useless.

Premierement. <B D (I think - D is abbr.) E K M N also> /Premerement C, Premieremen <sic - no t> O_1\ L'en <O_1 also> /l'on H K M N\ doit /doibt N\ apparellier /appareillier B, appareiller C E H K M N

In addition to those stated in the General Principles of the Edition (Vol. I: 42–48), these are:

1) All readings from *K*, *M*, and *N*, and from *G*, O_2, and *P* have been rigorously excluded because these manuscripts were copied directly or indirectly from surviving manuscripts.

2) Readings from *E* are retained only if they are identical with those of *C*, its source.[22] This departure from the edition's stated intention (Vol. I: 3) of providing all readings of nearly all medieval manuscripts was made particularly reluctantly because *E* is the source of MS *J* (and indirectly of ed. *a*).

3) Variants of *c* and *t* (e.g., *constitucion*, *constitution*), of *i* and *y* (e.g., *lui*, *luy*), and of terminal *s* or *z* (e.g., *assés*, *assez*) are more often than not simply scribal conventions. These are not retained for their own sake, although they might appear in a variant that is retained for another reason.

O_1 *a b*, appellier <sic - scribe did not cross the descender on the p> D, appereiller <sic for the e> E; Premeierement ... apparellier] L'en (L'on G O_2) <an independent correction, not a proof that O_2 is from G> doit (doibt L) appareiller (appareiillier G L, appareiller O_2 P <first proof that O_2 is not from G>) premierent <sic - rechecked F in Paris 1995> (premierement L O_2 P, premierement *om.* G <but not F O_2 - rechecked F G in Paris - clear proof that O_2 is not from G>) F G L O_2 P)\ I /un B C H K L M N O_1 *a*, ung D <D looks more like ungi, but that is his peculiar terminal g, which is elsewhere also> E F G O_2 P *b*\ eschaufau <H L M *b* also> /eschaufaut B E K, eschafaut C, eschauffaut D <I had esthauffaut, but decided on 11/29/94 that that t was actually a c - it looks like a halfway crossed t; his c often looks like this>, eschauffau F O_2, eschaffeau O_1, eschaffau N P, eschaffaut *a*\ un poi <H L also> /un pou B C, un peu D *a*, ung peu E, un poy O_1, ung poy F O_2 P *b*\ haut <H b also> /hault D F G O_2 P; un poi haut] un poisant K M N\ joignant <F H P *b* also> /joingnant C D E O_2\ au cuer <B D F L O_1 O_2 P *b* also> /cuer E H <but the first stroke of the first u is blotted in H, leading to the reading of K M N>, coeur K M N, Choeur *a*\ de l'yglise /l'eglise B C D E F G H K L M N O_1 O_2 P *a b*\ audehors <au dehors B C D E F G H K L N O_1 P *b* <but not O_2, but in O_2, many separate words appear written as one; one or two words in M> mis ou /au E K L *b*\ milieu /meilleu <sic - rechecked in Paris> F, milleu <sic> L O_2 P, mileu <sic> *b*\ entre l'un <B F H K L M N P *b* also> /l'ung O_1 O_2; entre l'un] de l'un C *a*, de l'ung E, <except for Godefroy's modernization, a proof that *a* was copied from E> l'une D <sic for the e - rechecked>\ et l'autre /l'aultre M\ cuer, <P also> /cueur E H, choeur K M <spelling varies in K M>, coeur N, Choeur *a*\ ou quel /Ou quel F P, auquel H K M N, ouquel L *a b* <one or two words in O_1>\ l'en /l'on N\ montera /monstera F O_2 P\ par degrez, <F H L M N *a b* also> /degres C D E K O_1 <actually degrés in O_1>\ et ou quel <F P also> /ouquel H L *a b*, où quel K M, ou quel N <one or two words in O_2>\ puissent /puissant <sic for the a> C E, puisse <not plural> *b*\ estre /être O_1\ ovecques /avecques B C D O_1, avecquez E, avec F G H K L M N O_2 P *a b*\ le roy /roi D <spelling varies in D>\ les pers <F O_2 P *b* also> /pairs H K M N\, peres L O_1\ dou /du B C D E F H K L M N O_1 O_2 P *a b*\ royaume /royalme <abbr., but spelled out roialme later> D, reaume <sic> E\ de France /ffrance D\ et autres <abbreviated H M N> /aultres C E, autrez D\ se <P also> /si E H *a*, sy K M N\ mestier <D E F H K L M N O_2 P a also> /mestiers B C *b*, metiers O_1\ est.

[22] Some noteworthy differences: *E* fairly consistently reads *autier, chef, chouses, cueur, ung* instead of *C*'s *autel, chief, choses, cuer, un*.

4) Variants of several words are not retained for their own sake, although they might appear in a variant that is retained for another reason. These variants are numerous, so they are listed separately in Appendix I along with the manuscripts in which they appear.

5) In a number of instances in *A* two words are written as one or vice versa, and the scribes of later manuscripts either separated or combined them, sometimes indiscriminately. Except for manuscript *B*, these variants are not normally retained.

6) Where the scribe of *A* employed roman numerals, other scribes often did not, but spelled the words out. Except for manuscript *B*, these variants are not retained when the sense of *A* is clear.

Anyone who finds that what remains is still daunting should keep in mind that most readers will need only the base text, or, perhaps, the readings from manuscript *B*, Charles V's personal coronation book.[23] Those who seek the probable readings of lost manuscripts *4* (*Noster²*) and *5* (*Nouveau Croix*) should concentrate on the variants from *F* and *L* and from *H* and *b* respectively. To approach the readings of the original *Croix* will require taking into account the readings of *C* and O_1, as well as *H* and *b*; very few will find it necessary to go to such lengths, however. Only specialists in the history of the French language will need all the variants.

In Ordo XX C the sentences are those of manuscript *Q*, but the punctuation has otherwise been modernized to the extent permitted by the sentence structure. Like the scribe of *D*, the scribe of *Q* sometimes doubled the letter *m* or *n* by adding a line above the word (e.g., *donnt* for *dont*); these have been retained. He wrote both *del eglize* and *de leglize* (among other words); this orthography is retained, except that the customary modern apostrophe is added where called for. The acute accent is also added if necessary—there are no accents at all in the manuscript of this translation. Because the paragraph numbers are the same as those in Ordo XX A, there are a few lacunae in the sequence of numbers, which, like Ordo XX B, begins with no. 2.

Each translation's identical paragraph numbers are distinguished by the addition of *b* or *c* (to accord with the translations' labels), and the numbers are always the same as those in Ordo XX A.

---

[23] All readings from *B* are retained, no matter how minor (except as noted in n. 19 above). Therefore, substituting *B*'s readings for *A*'s readings will produce the exact text of *B*. This is not possible with the other manuscripts because many minor variants have been suppressed and because a given manuscript will often have two or more spellings of the words listed in Appendix I.

Ideally, these two translations should have been presented in parallel columns like the translations of the Last Capetian Ordo (Ordo XXII B and Ordo XXII C), but the large number of variants in Ordo XX B rendered this impractical, so the two texts are presented seriatim.

ORDO XX B

The Official Translation

A B C D F H L O$_1$ b

2b. [fol. 27r] C'est[a] [24] l'ordenance[b] a enoindre et a[c] couronner[d] le roy[e].[25]

Premierement[f], l'en[g] doit apparellier[h] I eschaufau[i] un poi[j] haut[k] joingnant[l] au cuer de l'yglise[m] audehors[n], mis ou milieu[o] entre l'un[p] et l'autre cuer, ou quel[q] l'en montera[r] par degrez et ou quel puissent[s] estre ovecques[t] le roy les pers dou[u] royaume de France[v] et autres se[w] mestier[x] est.

2b. [a] C'est *om.* [b]. —[b] l'ordinance D, l'ordonnance H *b*, l'ordonace O$_1$. —[c] a *om.* C D E. —[d] coronner B. —[e] en ffrance *add.* D; C'est l'ordonance … le roy]

---

[24] No manuscript of this translation contains Ordo XX A,1.

A is preceded by a marginal note in a contemporary hand: "Melius hec ordinacio ponitur et scribitur in fine libri memorialis signato ✠ [*Croix*]." This refers to lost manuscript 4 of the Last Capetian Ordo (Ordo XXII A). Also in *A*, fol. 27r, there is a long note in the margin on the coronation rights and obligations of Reims, but it has nothing directly to do with this text, so I do not reproduce it here. It was published by C. Couderc, "Note sur le manuscrit latin 12814 de la Bibliothèque nationale," *Bibl. de l'Ecole des Chartes*, 49 (1888), 645–53. See Plate 16.

In *C*, fol. 58r, a high-quality miniature depicts the king enthroned on the elevated platform with the six lay peers seated on his right and the six ecclesiastical peers on his left (see Plate 17). There is a somewhat modified copy of it in *E*, fol. 22r (see Plate 19).

A marginal note in *O$_1$* refers to the location of the king's ordo in the Chambre des compte's registers: "Registre ✠, fol. xxv. / Registre Pater, fol. 163. / Noster, fol. 250 [i.e., *Noster²*]. / Qui es, fol. 27." Another hand added "Sacre et Couronnement des Rois et Reines" above the title.

The folios of *Noster²* are given in the upper left corner of *O$_2$*, p. 716 ("Registre noster / 250 et 252"), and *O$_2$*'s supposed source stated immediately below ("fol. 250"). Below that the folio numbers of the other *Libri memoriales* were added in another hand ("Registre Qui es in caelis fol. 27 et 29 / Registre Pater fol. 163 et 164 / Registre ✠ fol. 205" [sic—should be fol. 25]). Another hand added "Sacre et couronnement des roys et reines" in the upper right corner of the page, and the name "Brailly" (presumably the man who copied this part of the manuscript) appears just above that. In fact, *O$_2$* was copied from *F* rather than directly from lost manuscript 4 (*Noster²*).

L adds in the margin the reference to the page number in *Noster²* ("ii [c].l.").

[25] "Du livre ✠ ancien fol. xxv. et du nouveau fol. xxx" added after no. 1 in *H*.

Modus coronandi regem Francie F L. —[f] Premerement C, Premieremen O_1. —
[g] l'on H. —[h] appareillier B, appareiller C E H O_1 b, appellier D; Premeierement
... apparellier] L'en doit appareiller premierent (appareillier premierement L)
F L. —[i] un eschaufaut B. —[j] un pou B C, un peu D, ung poy F b, un poy O_1. —
[k] hault D F. —[l] joingnant C D E. —[m] l'eglise B C D E F H L O_1 b. —[n] au dehors
B. —[o] ou meilleu F, au milleu L, au mileu b. —[p] l'ung O_1; entre l'un] de l'un C,
l'une D. —[q] auquel H. —[r] monstera F. —[s] puissant C E, puisse b. —[t] avecques
B. —[u] du B C D E F H L O_1 b. —[v] royalme de ffrance D. —[w] si H. —[x] mestiers
B C b, metiers O_1.

3b. Au[a] jour que li roys vient a[b] estre couronnez[c], il doit estre receu a
procession[d] des chanoines[e] de la mere[f] eglise, et des persones[g] et[h] des
autres eglises conventuaus[i]. Le[26] samedi[j] devant le dymenche[k] que le
roy[l] doit estre consacrez[m] et couronnez[n], apres complie[o] chantee, doit
estre bailliee l'yglise a garder au gardes[p] qui seront a ce establiz[q] du roy[r],
ovecques[s] les propres gardes de l'eglise[t]. Et[u] [27] a[v] la nuit[w] assez tost[x], le
roy[y] doit venir a la dicte eglise[z] pour faire s'oroison[a] et veillier[b] illecques[c] en oroison[d] une piece[e] se il[f] vuest[g].

3b. [a] Processio *add. in marg.* B. —[b] a *om.* F L. —[c] coronnez B. —[d] processions F. —[e] des channoinez D, dechanoinnes F. —[f] mestre C. —[g] personnes B
C D E F H L O_1 b. —[h] et *om.* F H L O_1 b. —[i] conventuaux B C E H, conventu-
alx D. —[j] sabmedi C D E, samedy H O_1 b. —[k] dimenche B C D E F b,
dimanche H L, diemanche O_1. —[l] ly roys F, li roy L. —[m] sacrez D, consacré F
H L. —[n] coronnez B. —[o] compline F. —[p] bailliee (bailee H, baillié O_1) l'eglise
a garder aus (aux H O_1 b) gardes B H O_1 b, l'eglise baillee a garder aux gardes
C E, baillié l'eglise a garder aux gardez du roi D, baillee a garder l'esglise aux
gardes F, baillee a l'eglise aux gardes L; Custodes ecclesie *add. in marg.* B. —
[q] establiz a (ad C D E) ce B C D E. —[r] a ce establiz du roy] de par le roy F L. —
[s] avecques B. —[t] l'esglise F. —[u] Oracio regis *add. in marg.* B, *but partially
erased.* —[v] a *om.* F L. —[w] nuict H L O_1 b; vint L, *but corr. in another hand to*
nuict. —[x] toust F. —[y] li roys F, li roy L; assez tost le roy] le roy assez tost H. —
[z] a la dicte eglise] a l'eglise F H L. —[a] s'oroyson C D, oroison F, s'oraison H b,
l'oroison *corr. to* s'oroison L, l'oraison O_1. —[b] veillez F, veiller H L b. —
[c] illuecques B D, ileuquez C, illec F H O_1 b, illuec L. —[d] oroyson D, oraison H
O_1 b. —[e] pieche D. —[f] se il] Et s'il F, s'il H. —[g] veult B D O_1 b, vuelt C, vieult F,
veut H L.

4b. Quant l'en sonne aus matines[a], les gardes le roy doivent estre
apparelliez[b] pour garder l'entree de l'eglise et doivent mectre[c] enz[d] honorablement[e] et o diligence[f] entre les[g] autres les chanoines et les clers[h] de
l'eglise, et adonques et par apres[i] de[j] jour quant mestier en sera[k]. Et les

---

[26] B begins a new paragraph with *Le.*

[27] Beginning here, the marginal notes in *B*, which describe the contents of the
text, have usually been erased and are largely illegible.

autres entrees de l'eglise doivent estre bien et fermement[l] fermees et garniés.

4b. [a] a mattines D, aux matines F H L O_1 b; aus *om.* C. —[b] appareilliez B, appareillés C E O_1, appelliés D, appareillees F L, appareillez H b. —[c] mettre B. —[d] ens B F D b, eulx C E, eux H L O_1. —[e] honourablement C, honnourablement F. —[f] a diligence O_1. —[g] ces L. —[h] clercs F H L O_1 b. —[i] apprez C E. —[j] le H. —[k] mester en sera C, mestier est sera F L, métier sera H, mestier sera O_1 b. —[l] estre bien et fermement] bien et fermement estre B C D E.

5b. Les matines[a] doivent estre chantees sicomme[b] il est acoustumé[c]. Et icelles[d] matines[e] chantees, l'en sonne prime, et apres prime chantee, li roys[f] doit venir a l'eglise, et ovecques[g] lui[h] les arcevesques et[i] les evesques et les barons que il voudra[j] faire mectre enz[k], et si[l] doit venir ençois[m] que l'eaue[n] benoite[o] soit faite ; et doivent estre les sieges ordenez[p] environ l'autel, ou les arcevesques et les[q] evesques se[r] doivent soer[s] honorablement[t]. Et les evesques [fol. 27v] qui sont[u] pers du royaume[v] un poi audehors[w], a l'encontre[x] de l'autel[y] non pas loing[z] du roy, ne[a] ne doit pas avoir moult[b] de gens mis entre euls[c] desavenaument[d].

5b. [a] mattines D. —[b] si comme B. —[c] accoustumé D H L O_1 b. —[d] ycelles B. —[e] mattines O_1. —[f] le roys D, li roy L. —[g] avecques B. —[h] li O_1 b. —[i] et *om.* H. —[j] qu'il vouldra C E F, qu'il voudra H L, qu il voldra O_1 b. —[k] mettre ens B, mettre eux H. —[l] si *om.* B C D E. —[m] ainçois B C E F H L, ainchois D, ançois O_1 b. —[n] l'yaue B D, l'eyoue C E, l'eaüe *with the final e crossed out* L. —[o] l'eaue benoiste F, l'iaue benoiste H O_1 b. —[p] ordenés B, ordonnés D, ordonnez F H, ordennez O_1, ordonez b; li sieiges ordennés C. —[q] les *om.* B C D E F. —[r] se *om.* O_1. —[s] seoir B C D E F H L O_1 b. —[t] honourablement C, honnorablement F. —[u] seront C E. —[v] royalme D. —[w] un pou au dehors B C D, un poi au dehors H L, un poy au dehors O_1 b. —[x] alencontre F L, en l'encontre H O_1 b. —[y] del autel D. —[z] loin H b. —[a] et H. —[b] mout D, mont F L. —[c] eulz B, eulx C E, eux D H L; entre euls] entrens F. —[d] desavenamment B O_1 b, desavenement D H; desavenaument *om.* C E.

6b. Entre prime et tierce doivent venir les moines de Saint Remi a procession o les croiz[a] et[b] les cierges[c] et ovecques la sainte ampoule[d], la quele[e] li abbés[f] doit porter a tres grant reverence[g] souz[h] une courtine[i] de soie portee sur[j] IIII[k] perches de IIII moines vestuz[l] en[m] aubes ; et quant[28] il[n] vendront[o] a l'eglise Saint Denys[p], ou se il couvenoit mieulz[q] pour la presse[r] se elle[s] estoit[t] trop grant[u], jusques a la porte greigneur[v] de l'eglise, li[w] arcevesques doit aler encontre[x], et ovecques lui li autres[y] arcevesques et[z] les evesques et les chanoines, se ce se pouet faire[a], et[b] se ce ne peut estre fait[c] pour la grant[d] presse qui seroit dehors, alassent[e]

---

[28] Largely illegible erased marginal note in *B*.

ovecques[f] lui[g] aucuns des evesques et des barons. Adonques[29] li arcevesques doit prendre l'ampoule[h] de la main de l'abbé, et si[i] li[j] doit promectre[k] en bonne foy[l] que il[m] li[n] rendra, et[o] en tele maniere[p] li arcevesques doit[q] porter icelle ampoule[r] a l'autel o grant reverence[s] du pueple[t], et le doit acompeignier[u] li abbés avec aucuns[v] de ses moines, et les autres doivent attendre tant que tout soit parfait[w], et donques[x] la sainte ampoule[y] sera rapportee[z] ou en l'eglise[a] Saint Denys[b] ou en la chapelle[c] Saint Nicolas[d].[30]

6b. [a] o les croix D H L _b_, o les crois F, a les croix H. — [b] o _add._ C F L. — [c] ciorgez D. — [d] avecques la sainte ampolle B. — [e] la quelle C D E O$_1$, laquelle F H L _b_. — [f] abbé L. — [g] o tresgrant reverance F, a tres grand reverence H L. — [h] soubz C D E F, sous H L O$_1$ _b_. — [i] cortine C E. — [j] sus B. — [k] trois F L. — [l] vestus B. — [m] en _repeated at top of following folio_ B. — [n] ilz C D E F H. — [o] viendront H. — [p] Denis B; Saint Denys] de Reins C. — [q] couvenoit miex B, convenoit mieulx C F, convenoit mieux D H L O$_1$ _b_. — [r] parrpesse (_or something similar_) L, _but corr._ (_perhaps in another hand_) _to_ presse. — [s] elle _om._ B. — [t] etoit O$_1$. — [u] grande H, grand L. — [v] grigneur C E. — [w] Li B. — [x] aler alencontre C E, aller allencontre D, aller encontre H L O$_1$ _b_. — [y] avecques lui li autres B, avec lui les autres F L, avec (avecques O$_1$ _b_) li les autres H O$_1$ _b_. — [z] et _om._ C H O$_1$ _b_. — [a] se ce se puet (puet F) faire B C F L, se ce puet faire D _b_, si ce se pooit faire H, et se ce pooet faire O$_1$. — [b] ou L. — [c] et se ce ne puet estre fait (faite D, faict L) B C D L, et si ce ne peut estre fait H, et se ne se puet faire _b_; et se ... fait _om._ F. — [d] le grant D, la grande H, la grand L. — [e] allassent D H O$_1$ _b_. — [f] avecques B. — [g] li O$_1$. — [h] l'ampole B. — [i] si _om._ C E. — [j] lui F H. — [k] promettre B. — [l] bon foi D. — [m] qu'il F L. — [n] lui C E H, la _b_. — [o] et _om._ F L. — [p] manere L. — [q] doit li archevesque (arcevesques O$_1$, archevesques _b_) H O$_1$ _b_. — [r] ycelle ampole B. — [s] reverance F. — [t] peuble C, poeple D, peuple F H O$_1$ _b_. — [u] acompaignier B, acompaigner C D F, accompagner H, accompaigner L O$_1$, accompagnier _b_. — [v] li abbés avecq ascuns D, ly abbés ou aucun F, li abbé ou aucun L. — [w] parfoit D, parfaict L. — [x] et donques] et donquez D, et adoncques F, et dont H _b_, Et adonques L, et donc O$_1$. — [y] ampole B. — [z] raportee C D E F H O$_1$. — [a] de _add._ O$_1$. — [b] Remi C. — [c] chapele B, chappelle F L. — [d] Nicholas C D E.

7b. Ces[31] choses faites, l'arcevesque s'apparallera[a] a la messe vestuz[b] des[c] plus nobles vestemenz[d] et du palle[e] [32] ovecques[f] les dyacres et ovecques[f] les souzdyacres[g], et doit en ceste maniere vestuz[h] venir a l'autel a procession, sicomme[i] il est acoustumé[j], et li roys[k] se doit[l] lever o reverence[m] et ester[n] illecques[o].

---

[29] Illegible erased marginal note in _B_.

[30] See Ordo XX A, n. 12.

[31] Illegible erased marginal note in _B_.

[32] _au livre Pater y a, et doit Paulle_ add. in parentheses _H_. The "livre Pater" was lost MS _2_.

7b. [a] s'appareillera B C D E F, s'apareillera H, se pareillera L, se appareillera O_1 b. —[b] vestus B, vestu H L. —[c] de D H O_1. —[d] vestemens B C D E H L O$_1$ b; vestuz ... vestemenz] des plus nobles vestemens vestuz F. —[e] paule F L, pallé O_1 b. —[f] avecques B. —[g] subdyacres C E, soudiacres F b, sousdiacres H L, souz-diacres O_1; et ovecques les souzdyacres om. D. —[h] maniere vestu H, manerevestu L. —[i] si comme B. —[j] acustumé D, accoustumé H L b, accoutumé O_1. —[k] li roy L. —[l] soit D. —[m] o grant reverance F, o grand reverance L. —[n] oster b. —[o] illuecques B D, yleucques C E, illec H O_1 b.

8b. Et[33] quant l'arcevesque sera venuz[a] a l'autel, il, ou aucuns[b] des evesques pour touz et pour les eglises qui leur[c] sont souzmises[d], doivent demander au roy que il[e] promecte[f] et afferme[g] par son serement[h] a garder et affaire[i] garder les droitu [fol. 28r] res[j] des[k] evesques et des eglises, sicomme[l] il avient au roy affaire[m] en son royaume[n], et les autres choses, sicomme[o] elles sont contenues[p] en l'ordinaire[q], ou[r] III[s] choses li sont proposees a estre promises[t] et jurees, hors[u] le serement[v] de la novele[w] constitucion[x] du concile[y] du[z] Latran[a]. C'est assavoir[b] de mectre[c] hors de son royaume les[d] hereges[e]. Et[34] ces[f] choses promises du roy et fermees par son serement[g] sus les[h] saintes Evangiles[i], tuit ensemble[j] chantent[k] « Te Deum laudamus[l] ».

8b. [a] venus B, venu F H L, vestus b. —[b] a l'autel ou il ou aucuns C E, a l'autel il ou ascuns D, a l'autel il ou aucun F H O_1 b. —[c] lour D, leurs O_1. —[d] souzmises *corr. from* mises A, *apparently by the scribe*; soubmises C E L b, soubz mises D, sousmises F, soumises H O_1. —[e] qu'il H. —[f] promette B. —[g] aferme F, ferme L. —[h] serment C E H L, serrement O_1. —[i] a faire B C D E F H L O$_1$ b. — [j] droiturez C D, droictures F O_1 b. —[k] de F L. —[l] si comme B C F L O_1, se comme H, si come b. —[m] au roy a faire B C D E H O$_1$ b, a roy a faire F L. — [n] roialme D. —[o] si comme B F H L O$_1$ b, ainci comme C, si come b. —[p] tenues H. —[q] l'ordenance D L, l'ordonnance F. —[r] au F L. —[s] trois B. —[t] pronmises D. —[u] hors *om.* C E. —[v] sairement B D, serment C E H L, serrement O_1. — [w] nouvelle C D E H O$_1$ b, novele *om.* F L. —[x] nouvele constitution B. —[y] consile D, consire L. —[z] de B C D E F H L O$_1$ b. —[a] Lautran b. —[b] a sçavoir H L b. — [c] a savoir de mettre B. —[d] les *om.* A, *but add. above line in a contemporary hand, perhaps by the scribe.* —[e] ereges H b; les hereges *om.* D. —[f] ses B. — [g] serment C E H L, sairement D, serrement O_1. —[h] les *om.* F L. —[i] Ewangilles F, Evangilles O_1; Evangiles *corr. from* Evangeles L. —[j] tout ensamble D, tous ensemble F H. —[k] chantent *om.* B, le *add.* b. —[l] te dominum *add.* C E.

---

[33] Neither *A* nor *B* begin a paragraph here. In *A* and *H* this sentence is treated as a continuation of the previous one, although *B* and most other manuscripts do begin a new sentence here.

[34] *A* and *B* begin a new paragraph with *Et*; the text then continues as a single paragraph to the end of no. 11.

9b. Entre ce l'en doit avoir apparellié[a] [35] et mis sus[b] l'autel la couronne[c] le[d] [36] roy et s'espee[e] mise[f] dedenz[g] son fuerre[h],[37] ses esperons[i] d'or, son ceptre doré[j] et sa verge[k] a la mesure d'un coute[l] ou de plus, qui aura[m] audessus[n] une main d'yvoire. Item, les chauces[o] de soie[p] de couleur de[q] violete[r], broudees[s] ou tissues[t] de flour de lys[u] d'or, et la cote[v] de celle[w] couleur[x] et de celeuvre[y] meismes[z], faite en manere[a] de tunique[b] dont les souzdyacres[c] sont[d] vestuz[e] a la messe[f], et ovecques[g] ce le sercot[h], qui doit estre du[i] tout en tout de celle[j] meismes[k] couleur[l] et de celle[m] meismes[k] euvre[n], et si est fait a[o] bien pres en maniere[p] d'une[q] chappe[r] de soie sanz[s] chapperon[t]. Toutes les queles[u] choses devant dites[v], li abbés[w] de Saint Denys en France doit apporter[x] de son moustier[y] a Reins[z] et doit estre[a] a l'autel et garder les[b].

9b. [a] appareillié B D, appareillé C E F L O₁ b, apareillé H. —[b] sur corr. to sus L. —[c] coronne B. —[d] du C E. —[e] l'espee O₁ b. —[f] mise] et mise C E. —[g] dedens B D F L O₁, dedans C E H b. —[h] son furre C E, sa fuerrel D, son feurte F, son fuerrel H O₁, son feurre L, son fuerel b. —[i] esporons D. —[j] d'or B C D E. —[k] sa vierge C, la verge L. —[l] couste D F, coude H. —[m] ara B C E. —[n] au dessus B. —[o] chausses C E H b, chauses D. —[p] soye B. —[q] de om. b. —[r] violette D H L O₁ b. —[s] brodees C D E F H O₁ b. —[t] thissues C E, tieussues O₁ b; par tout add. F H L. —[u] flours de lys (liz O₁ b) B C H O₁ b, fflours de lis D, fleur de lis (lys L) F L. —[v] cotte D H O₁. —[w] cele B, ceste C E, cette O₁. —[x] color or colour D. —[y] celeuvre] celle oeuvre B H, celle euvre C F O₁, celle oevre L, cel oeuvre b; et de celeuvre om. D. —[z] meisme D, mesmes F L b, mesme H O₁. —[a] maniere B C E F H O₁ b, manniere D. —[b] tunicque C, tuniques b. —[c] soubsdiacrez C, soudiacres F b, sousdiacres H L O₁. —[d] donnt les sousdiacres sonnt D. —[e] vestus B. —[f] le messe D. —[g] avecques B. —[h] surcot F L. —[i] de F b. —[j] telle corr. to celle L. —[k] meisme C D, mesme F H L b; celles mesmes O₁. —[l] coulor or coulour D. —[m] de celui C E, d'icelle D, il celle H. —[n] oeuvre B H b, oevre L, euvres O₁; oeuvre] oeuvre d'une fachon D. —[o] de H b. —[p] a maniere D, en manere L. —[q] du corr. to d'une in a contemporary hand in A, perhaps by the scribe. —[r] chape L b. —[s] soye sens B. —[t] chapprin H, chaperon L b. —[u] les quelles B C E O₁, lesquellez D, lesquelles F H L b. —[v] dictes B. —[w] li abbé L. —[x] aporter B C D E H. —[y] monstier B F. —[z] Rains C D E, Rayms F, Rayns L, Reims O₁ b. —[a] ester L. —[b] les garder C E, les y garder b.

10b. Li roys[a] sera en estant[b] a l'autel[c] et despoillera[d] sa robe[e] fors sa cote[f] de soye et sa chemise, qui seront ouvertes bien aval devant et

---

[35] What remains of a partially effaced marginal note in *B* is not legible enough to make sense: "__ _ vestur_ non solet de s_pat_ ad altar."

[36] Corrected to *le* from *du* in O₁, and a signed marginal note reads, "approuvé cy endroit un mot rayé et un mot a l'interligne." The writer's mark is illegible, but see n. 45 below.

[37] *oudit livre Pater, y'a fuirre* add. in parentheses *H*.

derrieres[g], c'est assavoir[h] ou piz[i] et entre les espaules[j], et les ouvertures de la cote[f] seront a la foiz[k] recloses et rejointes[l] ovecques achaces[m] d'argent. Adonc tout premierement li granz chamberiers[n] de France[o] chaucera[p] illeques[q] au roy les devant[r] dites[s] chauces[t]. Les queles[u] li[v] abbés[w] de Saint Denys[x] li[y] baudra. Et apres li dus[z] di Bourgoingne[a] li[b] mectra[c] les esperons[d] es piez[e], que li abbés[f] de Saint Denys[g] li[y] baudra, [fol. 28v] et meintenant[h] li[y] seront ostez[i]. Apres li arcevesques tout seul[j] ceindra[k] au roy s'espee[l] ovecques[m] le feurre[n], la quele[o] espee ceinte[p], li arcevesques meismes[q] traira[r] hors[s] du feurre[t], et le fuerre[u] sera mis sus[v] l'autel, et li arcevesques mectra[w] au[x] roy l'espee[y] en sa main, et le roy[z] la doit offrir[a] humblement a l'autel, et meintenant[b] il la reprendra de la main[c] [38] l'arcevesque[d], et la baudra tantost[e] au seneschal[f] de France[g] a[h] porter devant lui en l'eglise jusques a la fin de la messe, et apres la messe quant il yra au pales[i].

10b. [a] Li roy L. —[b] en estant *om.* A, *but add. above line, perhaps by the scribe.* —[c] a l'autel en estant B C D. —[d] desplouillera C E, despouillera D H, despoueillera F, despoüillera L, depoüillera *b.* —[e] robbe H. —[f] cotte D H O$_1$. — [g] darrieres B, darriere C E, derriere L *b*; bien aval … derrieres] biel et devant et deriere D, bien avant et devant et derriere H. —[h] sçavoir H L *b.* —[i] a savoir ou pis B. —[j] espaulles F *b.* —[k] foy L. —[l] rejointez C, rejoinctes F L. — [m] achaces *later corr. to* ataiches A, *perhaps by the scribe*; atachez C, athatez D; ovecques achaches] avecques (avec H *b*) attaches B H O$_1$ *b*, a estaches F L. —[n] li grans chamberiers B C D, ly grans chambriers F, le grand chamberier H, le grands chamberier (*corr. from* les grands chamberiers) L, li grans chamberer O$_1$, li grans chamberers *b.* —[o] ffrance D. —[p] chaussera C E O$_1$, changera H. —[q] illuecques B D, illeucques C, illec H O$_1$ *b*, illeques *om.* F L. — [r] devantes O$_1$. —[s] dictes B, des *corr. to* dites L. —[t] chausses C H, chaussez D. —[u] Les quelles B, les quelles C E O$_1$, lesquellez D, Lesquelles F, lesquels H, lesquelles L *b.* —[v] li *om.* C, *but later add. above line, perhaps by the scribe.* — [w] abbé H L O$_1$. —[x] Denis B. —[y] lui F. —[z] dux B, ducs D L, duc F H O$_1$ *b.* —[a] de Borgoigne B, de Bourgoigne C E L O$_1$, de Burgoigne D, de Bourgongne F H, de Bourgogne *b.* —[b] luy F. —[c] mettra B. —[d] ses esperons C E, les esporons D, les esperons d'or O$_1$. —[e] es pies C D, es pieds H L *b.* —[f] li abbé H L O$_1$. —[g] de Saint Denys *om.* F L. —[h] maintenant B C D E F H L O$_1$ *b.* —[i] ostés C E O$_1$, estez D. —[j] suel D, seuls F; seul] seus L, *but* seus *crossed out and* sens *later corr. to* seus. —[k] seindra B D, saindra C E O$_1$ *b*, seindra *corr. to* ceindra L. —[l] l'espee H O$_1$ *b.* —[m] avecques B. —[n] fuerre B C D, fuerrel H O$_1$ *b.* —[o] la quelle B C D O$_1$, Laquelle F, laquelle H L *b.* —[p] sainte C E O$_1$ *b*, chaintee D. — [q] mesmes F O$_1$, mesme H L *b.* —[r] traira] traira maintenant F, trairra maintenant L. —[s] hors] hors l'espee C E. —[t] fuerre B C D, fuerrel H O$_1$ *b.* —

---

[38] The scribe of O$_1$ originally added *de*, but then he crossed it out and wrote *a*; a signed marginal note comments: "approuvé cy endroit un mot Rayé et un mot a l'interligne." The writer's mark is illegible, but see n. 45 below.

[u] ly feurre F L, le fuerrel H O_1 b, le feurrel b. —[v] seur B. —[w] mettra B. —[x] au /
au b. —[y] s'espee F b. —[z] la main et ly roys F, la main li roy L. —[a] osfrir B. —
[b] maintenant B C D E F H L O_1 b, mainttenant O_1. —[c] a *add*. C O_1 b, de *add*.
H. —[d] rependra de la l'archevesque D. —[e] tantot H O_1. —[f] senechal O_1. —
[g] ffrance D. —[h] pour F L. —[i] palais B C D E F H L O_1 b.

11b. Ces choses ainsi[a] faites et le cresme mis a l'autel sus une
patene[b] consacree, li[c] arcevesques doit appareller[d] a ouvrir[e] la sainte
ampoule[f] sus l'autel, et en[g] doit traire a une aguille[h] d'or aucun petit de
l'uyle envoiee des ciex[i], et mesler[j] o[k] grant diligence[39] ovecques[l] le
cresme qui est apparellié[m] a en oindre[n] le roy, li quel[o] roys resplendist
seulement[p], devant touz[q] les autres roys du monde, de ce[r] glorieus[s] privi-
leige[t] que il singulierement[u] soit enoint de l'uyle envoiee des ciex[v]. Adonc
l'en[w] li[x] defferme[y] les devant dites achaces[z] des ouvertures devant et
derriere[a]. Apres[b] il se doit mectre[c] a genouz[d] a terre, et doncques[e] il doit
estre enoint[f]. Premierement, audessus[g] du chief[h] de la devant dite ouyle[i].
La seconde foiz[j], ou piz[k]. La tierce, entre les espaules[l]. La quarte, aus[m]
espaules[n]. La quinte, en la jointure[o] des braz[p]. Et en dementieres[q][40] que
l'en le enoint[r], cil[s] qui sont[t] entour doivent chanter ceste antienne :
« Inunxerunt regem Salomonem[u] ».

11b. [a] ainci C. —[b] pateine F L. —[c] Li A B, *beginning a new sentence.* —
[d] appareillier B D, appareiller C F H L O_1 b. —[e] ovrir L, a ouvrir *om.* B C
D E. —[f] ampole B. —[g] en *om.* H O_1 b. —[h] o une aguille F, a une aiguille H O_1,
o une aiguille L, a un aguile b. —[i] de l'uyle envoyee des cieux B, de l'uille
envoié des cieulx C, de l'uille anvoyee des cieulx D, d'uille envoiee des cieulx
F, de l'huile envoyee des cieux H b, de oille envoyee des cieux L, de l'huile
envoyé des cieux O_1. —[j] meller B D F b. —[k] a: L; a *corr. by the scribe to* o
O_1. —[l] avecques B. —[m] appareillié B b, appareillé C E F H L O_1. —[n] enoindre
B, enoinndre D. —[o] Li quiex B, liquieur C, li quelx D, li quelz F, Liquel H b,
liquiex L, Li quels O_1. —[p] seulement (suelement D) resplendist (resplandit F
L) B C D F L O_1 b, resplendit seulement H. —[q] tous B, toutz D. —[r] cest F. —
[s] glorieux B C D E F H L O_1 b. —[t] privilege B C D H L O_1 b, privillege F. —
[u] singulerement C D. —[v] enoint de l'uyle envoyee des cieux B, enoint de l'uille
envoié des cieulx C, enoindt de l'uille anvoyee des chieux D, enoint de hulle
envoiee des cieux F, enoint de l'huile envoyee des cieux H, en oint de l'uille
envoyee des cieux L, enoint de l'uille envoyé des cieux O_1, enoint de l'huille
envoyee des cieux b. —[w] l'en *om.* B C E. —[x] lui F L. —[y] differme H; defferme
li l'en D. —[z] les devant dictes attaches B, les devant dictes athaches C, les
devantdictes attachez D, les devantdictes ataches F, les devans desdictes
attaches H, les devantdites attaches L, les devant des attaches O_1, les devant

---

[39] *o grand diligence* underlined *H*, and *Magna praeminentia rex Francorum oleo
coelitus misso inungitur* add. in marg. *H*.

[40] This word is abbreviated in *A* and could read *dementiers*, although I do not
think so.

desdites attaches *b*. —[a] darrieres C E. —[b] Et apres F L. —[c] mettre B. —
[d] a genoulz B, a genoulx C D E, a genous F L *b*, a genoux H. —[e] donques B,
donc C E O_1, adoncques F, adonques L *b*. —[f] enoindt D, enoinct H. —[g] au
dessus B. —[h] du chef H, dau chief L. —[i] oyle C D E, huille F H, oille L *b*, oylle
O_1; devant dicte huyle B. —[j] La seconde foiz] le seconde D. —[k] au pis C E, au
piz *b*. —[l] espaules O_1, *corr. by the scribe to* espaulles. —[m] aux C D H O_1 *b*, es
F L. —[n] espaulles O_1. —[o] joincture L. —[p] bras C D E H O_1 *b*, beas L. —[q] en
dementres C E F, en dementiers D, endementres L, en demantieres O_1, en
deventiers *b*. —[r] l'en le enoindt D, l'en l'ennoint F, l'on l'enoint H, l'en
l'enuoient L, l'en enoint O_1 *b*. —[s] cilz C E F. —[t] sonnt D. —[u] Ininxerunt regem
Salamonem D, Innunxerunt regem Salomonem H.

12b. Apres[a] [41] l'en li[b] doit reffermer[c] les achaces[d] des ouvertures
pour l'oncione[e]. Adoncques[f] le chamberiers[g] de France[h] li[b] doit vestir la
devant dite[i] cote[j] de l'euvre[k] et de la couleur devisees[l] ci dessus[m], et li
abbés[n] de Saint Denys la[o] doit baillier[p] a[42] icelui chamberier[q], et aussi[r] li
doit li chamberier[s] vestir pardessus[t] le devant dit[u] sercot[v], en tele [fol.
29r] maniere[w] que il[x] doit avoir la destre[y] main[z] delivré[a] devers l'ouverture du sercot[b], et sus la senestre main doit estre levé le sercot[c] aussi[d]
comme la chasuble[e] d'un[f] prestre ; et[g] apres li evesques[h] li met[i] le ceptre[j]
en la main destre[k] et la verge en la[l] senestre[m] ; et darrenierement[n]
appellez[o] les pers de France[p], qui s'estent[q] entour, li[r] arcevesques prent[s]
la couronne[t] royal et il seul[u] la met ou chief du roy[v], et icelle couronne[w]
mise, tuit[x] li per et clers et loyz[y] y doivent mectre[z] les mains[a] et soustenir
la deça et dela[b].

12b. [a] Apres] Et apres ce F L. —[b] lui F. —[c] refermer B H L O_1, refremer D. —
[d] ataches B F, attaches C E H L O_1 *b*, attachez D. —[e] l'onction B. —[f] Adonc B
H O_1 *b*, Adont C D, et adonc F L. —[g] li chamberiers B C O_1, ly chambrier F, li
chambriers H, li chamberer L, li chambrier *b*. —[h] li chamberiers de ffrance
D. —[i] devant dicte B. —[j] cotte D H. —[k] l'oeuvre D H, l'oevre L. —[l] devisee C
H, doviseez D, devisez O_1 *b*. —[m] si dessus C E, chi dessus D, pardessus F. —
[n] li abbé H L. —[o] lui F, li L. —[p] bailler C E F H L O_1 *b*. —[q] ycelui chamberier B,
y cellui chambrier C, y cellui chamberier D, icelui chambrier F, iceluy chambrier H *b*, iceluy chamberier L, icelluy chamberier O_1. —[r] ausy C, ainsy F L. —
[s] li doit li chamberiers B, le doit li chambrier C E H *b*, le doit li chamberier D,
doit ledit chambrier F, le doibt li chamberier L, li doit le chamberier O_1. —
[t] par dessus B. —[u] dit *om.* A, *but add. above line in another contemporary
hand.* —[v] surcot C D E F L, sarcot O_1. —[w] manere L. —[x] qu'il F L. —[y] dextre
C E L. —[z] doit ... main] doit avoit avoir la main destre *b*. —[a] delivré] a delivré
F L. —[b] sucot C, surcot F L; en tele maniere ... du sercot *om.* H. —[c] surcot C

[41] Neither *A* nor *B* begins a new paragraph here; the text continues as a single
paragraph to the end of no. 13.

[42] *Corr.* from *au* to *a* in O_1, and a signed marginal note reads, "approuvé cy endroit
un mot Rayé et un mot a l'interligne." The writer's mark is illegible, but see n. 45 below.

D E F L. —[d] ainsi F H, ainsin L. —[e] la chasule D, le chasuble H O_1. —[f] d'un] du L. —[g] En F L. —[h] evesques *corr. in another hand to* arcevesques A; arcevesques B C D E F L O_1, archevesque H *b*. —[i] lui mect F, luy met H. —[j] la ceptre C. —[k] dextre C E H L O_1. —[l] la *om.* B; la] lan main D. —[m] main *add.* L, *but crossed out.* —[n] darrainnement B, darranniement C, derrainement D, derrenierement F O_1, dernierement H *b*, derreniement L. —[o] appellés C E O_1, appeller H. —[p] les pers de ffrance D, les pers (peres L) du royaume F L; et *add.* B. —[q] qui estent H, qui s'entend L. —[r] Li B, lui F. —[s] prend H. —[t] coronne B. —[u] suel D. —[v] en chef du roy H, au choix dou roy *corr. to* au chef dou roy L. —[w] ycelle coronne B. —[x] tout D, tous F H. —[y] clers et laiz (lais C D) B C D, clerc et lay F L, clercs et laiz H O_1 *b*. —[z] ydoivent mettre B. —[a] la main F L. —[b] soustenir la de ça et de la B, soustenir deça et dela C E, soubstenir la de cha et dela D, soutenir la deça et dela H *b*.

13b. Lors doit li arcevesques, ovecques les pers[a] qui[b] sostienent[c] la couronne[d], mener le[e] roy ainssi[f] aourné[g] en la chaere[h] qui li[i] est apparelliee[j] et aournee[k] de draps de soye, et le doit[l] illecques[m] mectre[n] en son siege, qui doit estre si haut[o] que touz[p] le puissent veoir[q]; et doit li arcevesques pour reverence baisier[r] le[e] roy soiant en tele maniere[s] en son siege. Et apres li evesques[t] et li lay[u] pers qui soustiennent[v] la couronne[w]; et en ceignant[x] lui l'espee[y], sicomme[z] il est dessus dit[a], et[43] quant li arcevesques l'enoint[b], et quant il li[c] baille le ceptre et la verge et il li met[d] la couronne[e], et quant il s'asiet[f] en sa chaire[g], il dit[h] les oroisons[i] qui en leurs lieus[j] sont escriptes[k] en l'ordinaire[l]. En tele[m] maniere[n] assis le roy[o] en sa chaere[p], et les pers du royaume[q] ovecques[r] lui[s] qui soustiennent[t] la couronne[e], li[44] arcevesques retourne a l'autel.[45]

---

[43] All manuscripts begin a new sentence with *Et*, which makes the passage nearly incomprehensible, so I altered this to *et* in order to bring the passage in accord with the structure of the Latin text.

[44] *A* and all other manuscripts begin a new sentence with *Li* (or its variants — see Appendix I, pp. 618–20), making the passage difficult to understand, so I changed *Li* to *li* and added the following clause to what precedes, bringing the translation into accord with the Latin text.

[45] *H* (fol. 4v–5v) here adds, "Et au marge est escrit du Registre vieux seulement," and inserts a marginal note that is similar to the one in *A*, fol. 27 (referred to above, n. 24). Because *H* was copied from *Nouveau Croix* (lost MS *5*), this addition's "Registre vieux" refers to the original *Croix* (lost MS *1*). There are significant variants and additions between the versions in *A* and *H*, however. Manuscript *H* does refer (on fol. 5v) to the passage in the register *Noster* ("et similiter in alio libro memorialium signato, noster fol. 14 scribitur, nihil reperies in dicto folio"); this doubtless refers to *Noster²* (lost MS *4*) because the original *Noster* (MS *A*) was lost from the sixteenth to the eighteenth century.

O₁ adds: "Collationné par nous conseiller maitre a ce commis. Bizeau." The signature is followed by the same mark as in the previous marginal notes in this manuscript

13b. ᵃ avecques li pers B. — ᵇ la *add.* F L. — ᶜ soustiennent B C F O₁ *b*, soustienent D, soutiennent H, sostiennent L. — ᵈ coronne B. — ᵉ li H. — ᶠ ainsi B F H O₁, ainsin L. — ᵍ orné H, ainsi aourné *om.* C E. — ʰ chaiere B C D F L, chere H, chaire O₁. — ⁱ lui D F L. — ʲ appareilliee B H, appareillee C E F L O₁ *b*, appareillié D. — ᵏ ornee H. — ˡ doivent F L. — ᵐ illuecques B D, illeucquez C, illec F H O₁ *b*, illuec L. — ⁿ mettre B. — ᵒ hault C D E F. — ᵖ toutz D. — ۹ voir H L. — ʳ baiser H O₁. — ˢ en tele (telle C D E) maniere soiant (seiant C E) B C D E, seant en telle maniere (tel manere L) F L, seant en telle maniere H *b*, seant en telle maniere O₁. — ᵗ li evesque B D, l'arcevesque O₁, li archevesque *b*. — ᵘ lai B, lays C E H. — ᵛ soutiennent H O₁. — ʷ la coronne B, a coronne D. — ˣ seignant C E, chaignant D, saignant *b*. — ʸ li s'espee F L, li l'espee H, luy l'epee O₁. — ᶻ si comme B. — ᵃ dessus dit] dit dessus D F L, dit cy dessus H. — ᵇ l'ennoint *or* l'enuoint F, l'enuoint L, l'enuoint O₁. — ᶜ lui D F *b*. — ᵈ et lui mect F, et li met L. — ᵉ coronne B. — ᶠ s'assiet C E F *b*, assiet D, l'assiet F H, la siet L. — ᵍ chaiere B F L O₁, cheiere C E, chayere D, chaere *b*. — ʰ dist D. — ⁱ oraisons H O₁ *b*. — ʲ leur lieu B C, lour lieu D, leurs lieux F H L, leurs lieues O₁. — ᵏ escrites H L. — ˡ l'ordenance *corr. in another hand to* l'ordenire L. — ᵐ celle C D E. — ⁿ manere L. — ᵒ le roy assis F L. — ᵖ chaiere B F L O₁, chieire C, chayere D, chere H. — ۹ roialme D. — ʳ avecques B. — ˢ li O₁. — ᵗ soustienent D, soutiennent H, sostiennent L.

14b. [fol. 29v] C'est ᵃ ⁴⁶ comment ᵇ la royne doit estre ᶜ enointe et coronnee ᵈ. ⁴⁷

14b. ᵃ l'ordinance *add.* D. — ᵇ comme *b*. — ᶜ etre O₁. — ᵈ C'est comment ... coronnee] Modus inungendi seu coronandi reginam F L.

15b. Et ⁴⁸ se il avient ᵃ que la royne doie ᵇ estre enointe et coronnee avecques le roy, l'en li ᶜ appareille ᵈ un eschaufau ᵉ devers la senestre partie du cuer, et lors doit estre ᶠ mis l'eschaufau ᵍ le ʰ roy ⁱ devers la destre ʲ partie du cuer, un poi ᵏ plus haut ˡ que celui a ᵐ la royne. Et puis que

---

(nn. 36, 38, and 42 above). The signature is not fully legible; I here follow Varin (ed. *c*, p. 530) without being absolutely certain that the reading is correct. The king's ordo in *O₁* is followed by a blank folio page and then the queen's ordo.

⁴⁶ After leaving the bottom third of fol. 29r blank, a different scribe copied the remainder of the text in *A*. This explains the differences in spelling in the two parts of the text. The scribe of *O₁* added "Registre ✠ fol. xxvii." in the left margin (p. 713). A different hand added "Registre Pater fol. 164. Reg. Noster fol. 252 [i.e., *Noster²*]. Reg. Qui es fol. 29" in the top margin. Still another hand added "Sacre et couronnement des Rois et Reines" in the upper right corner of the page.

⁴⁷ This title is followed in *C* by a very detailed miniature (fol. 61r) depicting the queen receiving the scepter, while the king, seated at the left, looks on (see Plate 18). The similar miniature in *E*, fol. 25v, also after the title and also of very high quality, is based upon it (see Plate 20).

In *L* a later hand added "Couronement du Roy" above the title, an appropriate addition because much of what follows continues the ordo for the king's coronation.

⁴⁸ A page reference to *Noster²* added in marg. in *L*.

li roys[n] sera[o] assis en son eschaufau[e] en la maniere[p] devant dicte[q], et que li arcevesques sera retourné[r] a l'autel[s], il enoindra la royne, qui doit estre vestue[t] de soye, et sera enointe ou chief[u] tant seulement[v] et ou piz[w], non pas de l'oncion[x] le roy envoiee[y] des ciex[z], mes[a] d'uyle simple saintefiee[b]. Et apres[c] l'oncion[d] li arcevesques li[e] baille I[f] petit sceptre[g] d'autre maniere[h] que le sceptre[i] royal[j], et si li[e] baille une verge semblable[k] a la verge le roy[l]. Et[49] apres l'arcevesque tout seul[m] li[e] met sa[n] coronne en son chief[o]. La quele[p] coronne mise, doivent soustenir[q] li baron[r] deça et dela, et en tele[s] maniere il[t] la[u] doivent mener en son[v] eschaufau[w], ou elle doit estre[x] assise en son siege qui li[y] est apparellié[z], et li baron[a] et les plus nobles dames[b] doivent estre[c] environ.

15b. [a] Et s'il advient F, Et s'il avient H L. —[b] doyne F, doit H O_1 b. —[c] lui F — [d] apparellie D, apareille L; l'on luy doit appareiller H. —[e] eschaufaut B. — [f] coeur et lors doit être O_1. —[g] l'eschaufaut B. —[h] du B C D E. —[i] mis l'escha-ufau le roy] l'eschauffau. Le roy mis F L. —[j] dextre C E H L. —[k] un pou B C, ung pou D, ung poy F, un peu H, un poy O_1 b. —[l] hault C D E F. —[m] cellui a C, celuy de H, celluy de L. —[n] le roy H, li roy L. —[o] est H O_1 b. —[p] manere L. — [q] devantdit D, devant dite L O_1 b. —[r] retorné D. —[s] l'ostel F. —[t] vestuee D. — [u] en chief B C, au chief F H, au chef L. —[v] soulement D, seullement O_1. —[w] au pis L. —[x] nompas de l'onction B, non pas de l'unction C E, non pas del onction D. —[y] anvoyee D, envoié F, envoyé L. —[z] cieux B F H L O_1 b, cieulx C D E. —[a] mais B C D E F H L O_1 b. —[b] d'uyle simple saintifiee B, d'uyle simple saintefié C, d'oile simple saintefyé D, de celle simple saintifiee F, d'huille simple sanctifiee H, de celle simple saintefiee L, d'uille simple saintefiee O_1, d'huile simple sanctifiee b. —[c] Et apres] Apres b. —[d] l'onction B D F H L O_1, l'unction C E. —[e] lui F H. —[f] un B. —[g] ceptre B C D E F O_1 b, septre H. — [h] manere L. —[i] ceptre B C D F O_1 b, septre H. —[j] roial D. —[k] semblant B C E, samblant D. —[l] le roy] royal C E. —[m] suel D. —[n] la C E F H L. —[o] chef H L. — [p] la quelle C D O_1, Laquelle F, laquelle H L b. —[q] soutenir H. —[r] li barons H L. —[s] icelle b. —[t] ens F, ils H b, eux L. —[u] doivent soustenir ... maniere il la om. D. —[v] a son F L. —[w] eschaufaut B. —[x] doit estre om. C E. —[y] lui D F H. — [z] appareillié B, appareillé C E F H L O_1 b. —[a] li barons C. —[b] dames om. H O_1 b. —[c] ester L.

16b. Ces choses acomplies[a], l'en doit chanter la messe sollempnee-ment[b], et le chantre[c] et le souzchantre[d] doivent garder le[e] cuer; et l'Evangile[f] leue, li greigneur[g] des arcevesques et des[h] evesques doit predre[i] l'evangilier[j] et porter au roy et a la royne a besier[k], et apres le doit rapporter[l] a l'arcevesque qui chante la messe.

16b. [a] accomplies H L O_1 b. —[b] sollempnelment B, solempnelment D F, sollemnellement L; l'en doit ... sollempneement] on dit la messe chantee

---

[49] A and B begin a new paragraph with Et; the text continues as a single paragraph through le sacrement de la Messe in no. 18.

solennellement H, l'en doit la messe chanter solempnellement (solemnelle-ment *b*) O_1 *b*. —^{c}ly chantres F, li chantres L. —^{d}le soubxchantre C E, ly souschantre F, le souschantre D H O_1, li souchantres L, le sous-chantre *b*. — ^{e}ly F. —^{f}l'Ewangile C, l'Ewangille F, l'Evangille O_1. —^{g}le greigneur B H, le grigneur C E, le greignour D, ly grandres F L. —^{h}des *om.* H *b*. —^{i}prandre C E. —^{j}l'evangelier B C D E F H, l'euvangiler O_1, l'Evangile *b*. —^{k}a baisier B C D E O_1, pour baisier F L, a le baiser H, a le baisier *b*. —^{l}raporter B D H.

17b. Et^{50} quant l'en chante^a l'offrende^b, l'en^c doit sollempneement^d mener le roy et la royne de leurs^e eschaufauz^f affaire^g leurs^h offrendes^i, et offre^j l'un et l'autre^k a^l la main^m l'arcevesque I^n pain, et vin en^o I orciau^p d'argent, et XI deniers^q d'or.

17b. ^{a}quant l'en a chanté F L, quant l'on chant H, quant on chant *b*. —^{b}l'offe-rende B, l'offrande C D E F H L *b*. —^{c}on H. —^{d}sollempnelment B, solemp-nelment C D F, solennellement H, solempnellement L *b*, solempnellement O_1. —^{e}lours D, leur H. —^{f}eschaufaus B. —^{g}a faire B C D E F H L O_1 *b*. — ^{h}lours D, leur L. —^{i}offerendes B, offrandes C D E F H *b*. —^{j}offrer H. — ^{k}l'autre] li autre O_1. —^{l}en C E. —^{m}de *add.* H, a *add.* O_1 *b*. —^{n}I *om.* H. —^{o}et D F L. —^{p}orceau C D E F H, ceceau L. —^{q}deners C; un pain et vin en un orceau d'argent et XIII deniers B.

18b. Laquele^a chose faite, l'un et l'autre doit^b estre ramené en son^c eschaufau^d et a^e son siege. Apres [fol. 30r] c'en^f repaire^g li arcevesque^h a l'autel pour faire le sacrement de la Messe^i. Et^{51} ençois^j que il die^k « Pax vobis », il doit faire la beneyçon^l sur^m le roy et sus^n la royne et sus^m le peuple^o ; et apres^p cil qui l'evangelier^q a besié^r doit prendre la pes^s de^t l'arcevesque et la doit porter au roy^u et a la royne^v qui se sieent^w en leurs^x sieges. Et par apres^y touz^z les arcevesques et touz^a les evesques, l'un apres l'autre, doivent donner le besier^b de^c la pes^d au roy soiant^e en sa chiere^f.

18b. ^{a}La quele B, la quelle C, La quelle D F, Laquelle H, laquelle L O_1 *b*. — ^{b}doit *om.* D. —^{c}a son C E F L, ei son L. —^{d}eschaufaut B. —^{e}en C D E. — ^{f}s'en B C E, s'on D, ce F H L O_1 *b*. —^{g}retourne C E. —^{h}li arcevesques B. —^{i}a l'autel l'arcevesque pour faire le sacrement de la Messe F, a l'autel l'archevesque pour faire le sacrement de l'autel la Messe L. —^{j}ainçois B C E H L O_1 *b*, ainchois D, ainçoys F, *ançois corr. to* ainçois L. —^{k}qu'il die B C D E F L O_1 *b*, qu'il dit H. —^{l}beneicion C, beneichon D, beneiçon F L O_1 *b*, bene-diction H. —^{m}seur B. —^{n}seur B, sus *om.* D. —^{o}peuble C, pueple D L. — ^{p}appres C; ce *add.* F L. —^{q}cilz qui a baillié (baillé C E) l'Evangile B C E, chilz qui a baillié l'Evangile D, cil qui porta l'ewangelier (evangelier L) F L, cil qui

---

^{50}In *A, H, L,* and *O_1* this sentence is treated as a continuation of the previous one.
^{51}*A* and *B* begin a new paragraph with *Et*; the text continues as a single paragraph to the end of no. 19.

l'euvangelier O_1, cil qui l'evangilier *b*. —^{r} a baisier B C D E F L, a baisé H, a baisié O_1 *b*. —^{s} paiz B C E, paix D F H *b*, pays L. —^{t} Diu C, *corr. in a contemporary hand to* Deiu. —^{u} de sa bouche (boche C) *add.* B C D. —^{v} du livre *add.* B C D E. —^{w} sient D F L *b*. —^{x} lours D. —^{y} appres C. —^{z} tous B, toutz D, tuit L. —^{a} toutz D, tuit L; touz *om.* B C E F. —^{b} baisier B C D E F L, baiser H, besié *b*. —^{c} et H. —^{d} paiz B C E, paix D F H L. —^{e} seant B C D E F H L. — ^{f} chaiere B L O_1, cheiere C E, chayere D, chere H, chaire *b*; sa chiere] son siege F.

19b. Apres cen que^a li arcevesques aura pris^b le cors Nostreseigneur^c, le roy^d et la royne doivent descendre de leur^e eschaufauz^f et venir humblement^g a l'autel et prendre de la main^h l'arcevesque le cors et le sanc Nostreseigneur^i. Et la^j messe chantee, l'arcevesque oste leurs^k coronnes de leurs chies^l. Aus quiex^m ostees^n les enseignes royaus^o, il leur^p met^q en leurs^r chies^s autres petites^t coronnes. En^u tele^v maniere^w il^x s'en vont^y au pales^z, l'espee nue portee devant^a. ^{52}

19b. ^{a} Apres ce que B C D E, Par apres et (ce L) que F L, Et apres que H, Et apres ce que O_1 *b*. —^{b} prins C E F. —^{c} corps Nostreseigneur B C D E F L *b*, corps de Nostre Seigneur H, corps Notre Seigneur O_1. —^{d} ly roys F, li roy L. — ^{e} leurs B C E F H L O_1 *b*, lours D. —^{f} eschaufaus B. —^{g} himblement C. —^{h} de *add.* H, a *add.* O_1 *b*. —^{i} le corps et le sanc Nostre Seigneur B, le corps et le sanc Nostreseigneur C E, le corps et le le sang de Nostre Seigneur D, le corps et le sang Nostre Seigneur F H L *b*, le corps et le sant Notre Seigneur O_1. — ^{j} Et la] La *b*. —^{k} lours D, leur L. —^{l} leurs chiefs B F *b*, leurs chefs C E H, lours chiefs D, leur chief *or* chiefs L. —^{m} Au quelx C E, aux quelx D, Ausquelz F, ausquels H, auxquels L, aus quiex *or* ausquiex O_1, ausquiels *b*. —^{n} ostés D H O_1. —^{o} enseignes royaulx C E F, enseignes roiaulx D, enseignes royaux H L O_1, ensignes royaux *b*. —^{p} leurs C E, lour D. —^{q} mect F. —^{r} lours D. —^{s} chiefs B C D F *b*, chefs H L. —^{t} petittes O_1. —^{u} Et en F L. —^{v} celle H *b*. —^{w} manere L. —^{x} ils D H *b*, eulx F, eux L. —^{y} vant C E. —^{z} palais B C D E F H L O_1 *b*. — ^{a} devannt eux D, devant eulx F O_1, devant eux H L *b*.

---

^{52} *F* ends here. *H* (fols. 6v–7r) adds: "Tout ce qui dessus est pris dudit registre ✠ vieux et nouveau, et est de mot a mot inseré aux registres [fol. 7r] et memoriaux Pater, fol. viii^{xx}.iii. Noster, fol. ii^c.l., et qui es in coelis, fol. xxv." It is followed in *H* (fols. 7r–v) by extracts from old and new *Croix* (lost MSS *1* and *5*), then on fol. 7v by the Last Capetian Ordo from *Croix* (Ordo XXII A, lost MS *4*). The register *Noster* that this refers to is *Noster*^{2} (lost manuscript *4*).

L is signed "Croisady." Manuscript O_1 adds: "Collationné par Nous Conseiller Maitre a Ce Commis. Fremin." This text in O_1 is then followed on the next page (p. 716) by manuscript O_2 (fol. 716r). Manuscript O_2 adds: "Collationné Par Nous conseiller maistre a ce commis. Jean Demomae."

ABCDE

20b. Requisicio[53] episcoporum regni Francie[a] facienda regi in sua coronacione[b].

A vobis perdonari petimus, ut unicuique de nobis et ecclesiis nobis commissis canonicum privilegium ac debitam legem atque iusticiam conservetis et deffensionem[c] exhybeatis[d], sicut rex in suo regno debet unicuique episcopo et ecclesie sibi commisse[e].

20b. [a] ffrancie D. —[b] coronatione B. —[c] deffencionem C, defensionem D. — [d] exhibeatis B. —[e] ecclesiis sibi commissis B C D E.

21b. Responsio[a] regis ad episcopos.

Promitto vobis et perdono, quia unicuique de vobis et[b] ecclesiis vobis commissis canonicum privillegium[c] et debitam legem atque[d] iusticiam servabo et deffensionem[e] quantum potuero, adiuvante Domino, exibebo[f], sicut rex in suo regno unicuique episcopo et ecclesie sibi commissis[g] per rectum exibere[h] debet.

21b. [a] Requisicio C E. —[b] de add. B C D E. —[c] privilegium B C D E. —[d] ac B C D E. —[e] defensionem C E, deffencionem D. —[f] exhibebo B C D E. —[g] commisse B C D E. —[h] exhibere B C D E.

22b. [fol. 30v] *Hec tria populo christiano et mihi[a] subdito in Christi promitto[54] nomine.*

In primis, ut ecclesie Dei omnis populus christianus veram pacem nostro arbitrio in omni tempore servet[b].

Aliud, ut rapacitates et omnes iniquitates omnibus gradibus[c] interdicam.

Tercium, ut in omnibus iudiciis equitatem et misericordiam precipiam, ut mihi[a] et vobis indulgeat suam[d] [55] misericordiam clemens et misericors Deus.

22b. [a] michi B C D E. —[b] Et superioritatem, iura et nobilitates corone Francie (ffrancie D) inviolabiliter custodiam, et illa nec transportabo nec alienabo add. B C D E. —[c] gradibus om. D. —[d] suam] per suam B C D E.

---

[53] The oaths are written in another contemporary hand in *A*. These are in *A, B, C, D,* and *E* only.

[54] MS *A* could equally well read *Promicto* both here and at the beginning of no. 21b. In both instances *Promicto* is the reading of *C*.

[55] All manuscripts except *A* read *per suam*. The only previous ordo with the oath is Ordo XV (the Ratold Ordo), nos. 5 and 37, which likewise omit *per*, as do most manuscripts of the Last Capetian Ordo (Ordo XXII A,8).

B C E

23b. Ou[56] temps ancien ne avoit[a] que XII pers en France, VI clers et VI lays, dont ne se remuent les clers. Ce sont les clers dux.

    L'arcevesque de Reins[b].
    L'evesque de Laon.
    L'evesque de Lengres.
Ce sont les clers contes.
    L'evesque de Beauvais.
    L'evesque de Chaalons.
    L'evesque de Noyon.

   23b. [a] n'avoit C E. —[b] Rains C E.

24b. Ce sont les pers laiz.
    Le duc de Borgoigne[a].

    Le duc de Normendie[b].
    Le duc d'Aquitaine[c].
Ce sont les contes.
    Le conte de Tholose.
    Le conte de Flandres.
    Le conte de Champaigne[d].
    Le roy de France tient en sa main[e] la conté de Tholose et la conté de Champaigne.
    Le conte d'Alençon.
    Le duc de Bourbon.
    Le conte d'Estampes.
    Le conte d'Artoys.
    Le duc de Bretaigne[f].
    Le conte de Clermont.

D

23b. Ou temps anchien n'avoit que XII pers en ffrance, VI clers et VI lais, dont ne se remuent les clers.

    L'arcevesque de Rains.
    L'evesque de Laon.
    L'evesque de Longres.
Che sont les clers comtes.
    L'evesque de Biauvais.
    L'evesque de Chaalons.
    L'evesque de Noyen.

24b. Che sont lez pers lais ducs.[57]
    Le duc de Bourgoigne.
    Le comte d'Alençon.
    Le duc de Bourbon.
    Le comte d'Estampes.
Che sont lez pers ducs.
    Le duc de Normandie.
    Le duc d'Acquitaine.
Che sont lez comtes.
    Le comte de Tholoso.
    Le comte de fflandres.
    Le comte de Champaigne.
    Le roy de ffrance tient en sa mayn la comtee de Tholose et la comté de Champaigne.

    Le comte d'Artois.
    Le duc de Bretaigne.
    Le comte de Clermont.

---

[56] Edition *a*, having omitted the oaths (nos. 20–22), skips from no. 19a to nos. 23a and 24a, but the Godefroys modernized the spellings of the peers.

[57] In thus ordering the lay peers, the scribe of *D* makes utter nonsense of the subject.

BCDE

Le roy de Navarre[g] pour cause de sa conté d'Esvreux[h] et la terre qu'il tient ou royaume[i] de France[j].

Ces VII pairies sont[k] nouvelles et doivent seoir selonc leur[l] temps, c'est a savoir[m] selonc[n] ce qu'il sont fait per.

Ces pers anciens[o] sont mis si comme il[p] doivent seoir en jugement en la presence du roy, et doivent les pers laiz seoir a la destre[q] et les pers clers a la senestre du roy.[58]

24b. [a] Bourgoingne C. —[b] Normandie C E. —[c] d'Aquictaine C E. —[d] *written* Chāpāigne B, Champaigne C E. —[e] a sa main C. —[f] Bertaigne C E. —[g] Navare D. —[h] la conté d'Esvieux C E, sa comté d'Esvreux D. —[i] en royaume C. —[j] ffrance D. —[k] sont *om.* C E. —[l] selond leur C E, selonque lour D. — [m] *perhaps* asavoir B, assavoir C D E. —[n] selond C, selonque D. —[o] Ches pers anchiens D. —[p] ils D. —[q] dextre C.

ORDO XX C

The Unofficial Translation

Q

2c. [fol. 179r] S'ensieult l'ordre que pour oindre et couroner le roi.

Premierement, on apareille ung siege en maniere d'unne eschaffaux aulchunnement apparant hault, tenant par dehors au chuer [fol. 179v] del eglize, poset en la moienne entre les II chueres, dedens le quel on monte par degrés. Et la ou que puissent seoir avoec le roi les peres du roialme et oci des aultres se il est de besoing.

3c. Et sur le jour que le roi doit venire pour estre couronés, il doit estre processionalement rechupt, tant des chanonnes quant des aultres eglizes conventuales, le samedi precedant le dimance en quoi le roi doit estre consacrés et couronnés. Et complies accompliies, on doit commettre le garde del eglize aux gardiens deputés de par le roi, ensamble avoec les propres gardes del eglize. Et se doit le roi en silence environ la minuit venire en l'eglize pour faire oraison. Et la se il veult demorer et veillier en oraison quelque petis.

4c. Et quant on sonne a matinnes, les gardes du roi doivent estre prestres gardans la entree del eglize, les quelz les aultres entrees del eglize bien fremees et bien asseurés, entre tous les aultre cleres et chanonnes del eglize, et allors, et depuis oci de jours se il est de besoing, doivent honourablement et diligentement lesser entrer dedens.

5c. Et les matinnes comme il est de coustumme chanter. Et tous che acomplist, on doit sonner primes, et quant il samble estre heure, on doit

---

[58] *B, C, D*, and *E* next proceed to the Ordo of Charles V (Ordo XXIII).

chanter primes. Apres primes chantees, le roi doit, ensamble avoec les
archevesques et evesques et barons et aultres le quelz il voldra avoir
lessies dedens l'eglize, venire devant que se face la benediction. Et
doivent des kaneres[59] et aultres sieges estre disposés empres l'aultel, la
ou les archevesques, evesques et peres du roialme seantes en bas, aux
opposittes del aultel point loing du roi, ne pluseurs indecentement entre
mis.

6c. Entre prime et tierce doivent venire les moiesnes de Sainct
Remis processionalement a tout les croix et confanons[60] et torches
avoec la saincte sacree ampulle, la quele doit l'abbés reverentement
aporter soubz unne courtinne de soie enlevee de quattre moiesnes a tout
quattre perses vestis de blanc. Et quant il sera venus jusques al eglize de
Sainct Denis, ou se il est de besoing plus oultre pour la multitude des
gens [fol. 180r] pressantes. Jusques a la porte majour del eglize, doit
l'archevesque en promettant sa foi de la rendre telement rechepvoir. Et
telement le porter avoec grande reverence du peuple al aultel, l'abbés et
aulchuns de ces moisnes ensamble le siewant, tous les aultres attendans
jusques a tant que tout soit parfait et accomplis. Et la saincte sacree
ampulle soit reposee ou en l'eglize de Sainct Denis ou en la chapelle de
Sainct Nicolas.

7c. Et che fait, l'archevesque se doit preparer a la messe avoec ces
diacques et soudiacques vestis de nobles abis[61] et manteaux ou cappes
ou casure.[62] En ceste maniere vestis, il doit venire a usance accoustumee
al aultel. Au quel venant, se doit le roi la present soi lever reveramment.

8c. Et quant l'archevesque est venus jusques al autel, doit lui ou aulchuns des evesques, pour tous et pour touttes les eglizes subjectes a lui,
du roi cela demander que il prommette et que il le afferme par serment
soi devoir observer les drois des evesques et des eglizes, comme il apar-

---

[59] The word "kaneres" is a derivative of "chanoine," according to Hans-Erich
Keller, who referred me to Adolf Tobler and Erhard Lommatsch, *Altfranzösisches
Wörterbuch*, 10 vols. to date (Berlin: Weidmannsche Buchhandlung, and Wiesbaden:
Franz Steiner Verlag, 1925–1974), 2: 223, s.v., "chanieres," a reference that I did not find
very helpful. The context makes clear that the sense of the word is "canons' stalls" or
"canons' chairs," which is a mistranslation of the Latin.

[60] "confanons" = "gonfanons," which is not in the Latin text.

[61] The scribe originally wrote *cappe*, then crossed it out and replaced it with *abis*;
"abis" = "abisse" = "lin très-fin"; cf. Frédéric Godefroy, *Dictionnaire de l'ancienne
langue française et de tous ses dialectes du IXe au XVe siècle*, 10 vols. (Paris: Vieweg
[1–4], and Bouillon [5–10], 1880–1902; reprints Vadus, Liechtenstein: Scientific Periodicals Establishment, and New York: Kraus Reprint Corporation, 1962; and Geneva and
Paris: Slatkine, 1982), 1: 23.

[62] "casure" = "chasuble."

tient au roi de faire garder et observer en son roialme chretien en ceste forme et maniere que il sont contenus en l'ordinaire, la ou li sont proposee a tenire trois chozes et promettre, excepté le conseil lateransis ou du lateran, c'est a sçavoir de extirper et mettre a fin tous les hereticques du roialme. Et cela telement prommis du roi sur les sainctes Ewangiles de Dieu. On doit chanter tous ensemble « Te Deum laudamus ».

9c. Ou apres desia par avant la couronne regale et l'espee en la ghaine enclose preparés et mis sur l'autel, les esperons dorés, le sceptre dorés et la verge a la mesure d'ung cubitte ou plus aiant par desus unne mains de yvoire. Item, les cauches de soie et touttes jacinctes bordees et tissoittés par toute a fleur de lis dorees et la robe de ceste mesmes couleur et ung socco avoec de quoi on veste les subdiacques a la messe. Et touttes les dittes chozes doit l'abés de Sainct Denis en France aporter de son monastere a Rains et estant al autel les garder.

10c. Et le roi estant devant l'autel doit despoullier ces abillements, exceptés sa robe de soie et sa chemise ouvertes bien par fons devant et deriere, c'est a sçavoir en la poitrine [fol. 180v] et entre les espaules. Les ouvertures de la cottelle lachiés ensemble ou aultrement conjoinctes a anneles d'argent, allors la tous premier du grant chamberlain de Franche li doient cauchier[a] ces cauches. En apres du duc de Bourgongne li soient cauchiés les espourons au pies et nueles ou bloucquies.[63] Et cela fait, l'archevesque doit lui seul li cheindre l'espee ensemble avoec la ghaine ou foureau, le quel chaintes, l'archevesque doit tirer hors du foureau la ditte espee et le donner au roi en sa mains. La quele doit le roi humblement apporter al autel, et incontinent la reprendre de la mains del[b] archevesque, et incontinent la donner au senechale que pour porter devant lui dedens l'eglize jusques a fin de la messe, et apres messe quant il s'en vat au palaix.

10c. [a] cauchies Q. —[b] del *repeated* Q.

11c. Et tout che telement accomplist[a], le cresme aparilliet sur la patene consacree, doit l'archevesque ouvrire la saincte sacree ampulle sur l'autel et de icelle quelque petis prendre de ceste ole envoiiés du ciel a tout unne aguille d'or et le attraire dehors et le meler diligentement le plus que faire le puelt ensamble avoec le cresme preparés que pour oindre le roi, le quel li seul est previlegiiet de che previlege entre tous les rois du monde, que il est singulierement oingt del ole envoiet du ciel. Et allors les

---

[63] "nueler" = "nouler" = "boutonner" and "blocquier" = "blouquier" = "bouclier"; cf. Edmond Huguet, *Dictionnaire de la langue française du XVIe siècle*, 7 vols. (Paris: E. Champion, then Paris: Didier, 1925–73) 1: 453, and 1: 608. The phrase could be translated "buttoned or buckled."

anneles destachiés des ouvertures devant et deriere, et mis a terre en II genoulz, premierement l'archevesque le oingt du dit ole au couppries[64] de la test. Secondement, en la poitrine. Tiercement, entre deux espaules. Quartement, sur les espaules. Et quintement, en les jointures des bras. Et quant on l'oinct, on chante ceste anthiphonne : « Inunxerunt regem Salomonem ».

11c. ᵃ accoplist Q.

15c. Et se la roine est a oindre et couronner ensamble avoec le roi, on doit samblablement aprester ung siege de la partie senestre du chuer, aulchunnement plus hault[65] le siege du roi, estant colloquiet[66] a la partie dextre du chuer. Mais on ne la oingt point del ole envoiiet du ciel.

17c. Et [fol. 181r] quant on chante l'offertore, tant le roi, comme la roynne, soient menés jus de leur sieges, et doivent offrire ung cheschun de eulx pains et vin a la main del archevesque dedens unne kanne d'argent, et XIII piece d'or.

19c. Et apres la perception del eucharistie faitte de par l'archevesque. En ceste apendant[67] descendent le roi et la royne de leur sieges et prendent le corps et le sanc de Nostre Seigneur de la main del archevesque, et telement s'en vont il au palaix, l'espee nue devant eulx.

---

[64] "couppries" = Old French "copulees," normally masculine "couplez," meaning "sommet"; cf. Godefroy, *Dictionnaire*, 2: 235c. I owe this reference and interpretation to Hans-Erich Keller.

[65] "que" add., then crossed out by the scribe.

[66] "colloquiet" = "colloquer" = "placer"; cf. Godefroy, *Dictionnaire*, 9: 126.

[67] "apendant" = "pente," the throne or platform.

ORDO XXI

The Ordo of 1250

Date: 1240–1250

Other names: Ordo of Louis VIII (Godefroy, Schreuer, Buchner) or Compilation of 1223 (Schreuer, Buchner)

Introduction

The Ordo of 1250 is an anomaly in the history of the French rite because the manuscript that contains it (MS *A*) is far more important than the text itself. The text is a compilation that was perhaps hastily— and certainly poorly—put together from four sources slightly before 1250. The four sources are: 1) a Reims manuscript of the Ordo of 1200 (Ordo XIX, MS *A*); 2) a lost copy of the Ordo of Reims (Ordo XX *A*); 3) a Reims copy of the Ratold Ordo (Ordo XV, MS *G*); and 4) an unidentified manuscript that was the source of the coronation oaths (which in this ordo differ from those in any other French ordo) and perhaps of the litany.[1] The skeleton and the liturgy of the ordo are largely those of the Ordo of 1200, not greatly modified. Into the skeleton the compiler inserted large pieces of the Ordo of Reims, obviously as rubrics. A few borrowings from the other two texts and a litany suggestive of Châlons-sur-Marne round out the text.[2]

The text could not have been used to carry out a coronation ceremony. For example, it has the king make his promise to the bishops and swear his tripartite oath in nos. 10 and 12, then undergo a scrutinium in no. 20, and finally swear another oath in no. 48. In no. 37, the king is to be led to his throne before investiture with the insignia of kingship, and again in no. 46, after the crowning of the king. The king is anointed in nos. 26–27, but the prayer of consecration (no. 36), which in other ordines precedes the anointing, follows the anointing in this ordo. The

---

[1] I considered the possibility that the oaths were copied from Reims 342 with some carelessness and that they were also truncated in order to make room for the miniatures. Some of the wording here is close enough to some of the wording in Ordo XXII A,6–8, however, to demonstrate that there was indeed a lost manuscript source, parts of which apparently found their way into Ordo XXII A.

[2] The portions of the ordo that are copied from the Ordo of Reims (Ordo XX A) are copied either from that ordo's lost manuscript x^1 or lost manuscript x^2 (see the stemma on p. 296). For a few further details concerning the treatment of the sources, see Jackson, "Manuscripts," 56–58.

text also repeats the Ordo of 1200's peculiarity that concludes the queen's coronation with part of the marriage liturgy.

These faults do not mean that the text itself is without value, for it does preserve most of the Ordo of Reims's contents from a source that is older than any that otherwise survives. It has the distinction of being the first complete ordo to incorporate the thirteenth-century elements of French (as distinguished from European) kingship (see the introduction to Ordo XX A). It is also a source for the conceptions of kingship during the reign of St. Louis.[3]

That which makes the ordo truly important is the manuscript's series of miniatures that illustrate principal moments of the ceremony. It is the first of three surviving medieval French coronation manuscripts that accompany the written text with a program of pictures. Such a series of miniatures is rare in liturgical texts, and in manuscript *A* the illustrations work together and in parallel with the text to form a kind of mirror of princes.[4] Certain features of the manuscript prove that scribe and illuminator worked very closely together to produce the manuscript (see, for example, n. 17 below).

Even though the entire text of the ordo was copied by a single scribe who wrote a uniform and very legible gothic book script, the manuscript is more complex than it appears initially. Traces of eight or ten other hands appear in one way or another in the ordo. To the extent possible, this edition identifies them and attempts to date these hands (see the Principles of the Edition below).

Then, there are questions concerning the manuscript's provenance. Probably no one would doubt that it came from Reims and was illuminated in a Parisian workshop, were it not for some features of the ordo's litany (nos. 13–18). E. S. Dewick noted the presence of saints of Châlons-sur-Marne (Memmius, Donatianus, Domitianus, Alpinus, Ludomirus, and Elaphius) in the litany, and an absence of Reims saints (Sixtus, Sinicius, Rigobert, and Eutropia), although he failed to notice that it does address Nichasius and Remigius, two saints particularly venerated in the diocese of Reims. On the basis of the litany Victor Leroquais declared the manuscript to be a fragment of a pontifical of Châlons-sur-Marne.[5] Argument

---

[3] See Le Goff, "The Ordo of 1250."

[4] See Bonne, "The Manuscript of the Ordo of 1250." I give just brief descriptions of the miniatures with indications of their place on the page, excepting the historiated initials, all of which occupy a square at the left of the respective folios and about one-third the height of the text on the page; see Bonne's study for fuller descriptions and art-historical comments.

[5] Dewick, *Coronation Book of Charles V*, 89–90; Leroquais, *Pontificaux*, 2: 145–46.

from absence can be hazardous, though. For example, Reims MS 342 (Ordo XV, MS *G*), a known pontifical of Reims and one of the provable sources of the Ordo of 1250, contains an *Ordo ad visitandum infirmum*, in which the litany (fol. 91v–92v) is like the Ordo of 1250's litany in that the typical Reims saints, Nichasius, Sixtus, Sinicius, Rigobert, and Eutropia are not in it, although Remigius is.[6] It is not easy to explain the presence of the Châlons saints in the Ordo of 1250, but it is doubtful that that feature of the manuscript alone is proof that the manuscript came from Châlons.

Furthermore, whether or not the manuscript was copied at Châlons, Leroquais was most certainly wrong to call it a fragment of a pontifical. It is a fully independent manuscript in its own right, never having formed part of a larger work.

Manuscripts

A—Paris, Bibl. nat., MS lat. 1246, fols. 1r–41v. Formerly MS lat. 4464. (I use the foliation in red Arabic numerals at the top of the page, not the one in black Roman numerals or the black Arabic numerals at the bottom of the page.) Ca. 1250. Description: Branner, *Manuscript Painting in Paris*, 13–14, 69, 87–91, 211, 225; Martimort, 174, no. 243; 386, no. 776; Bonne, "The Manuscript of the Ordo of 1250," 58–71. See Plate 21.

B—Paris, Bibl. de l'Institut de France, MS Godefroy 380, pp. 179–227. Seventeenth century. Copied from *A*. Not collated.

C—Reims, Bibl. mun., MS 1489 (nouv. fonds), no. 3, pp. 1–28. Eighteenth century. Copied from edition *a*. Not collated.

Editions

a—Godefroy, 1: 13–25, from *A*.

b—Martène. Three editions:

   b₁—(Rouen, 1700–1702), 2: 198–209 (Ordo V), from *A*.

   b₂—(Antwerp, 1736–38), 2: 610–21 (Ordo VI).

   b₃—(Venice, 1763–65; reprints Venice, 1783, and Venice, 1788), 2: 219–23 (Ordo VI).

Principles of the Edition

The text and orthography are from manuscript *A*. The punctuation has been modernized to accord with the ordo's sources (Ordines XIX and XX *A*) as much as possible.

---

[6] On the other hand, in the other provable source of the Ordo of 1250, Reims 343 (= Ordo XIX, MS *A*), there is a litany that does contain these saints in the *Ordo qualiter dedicatio ęcclesię fieri debeat* (fols. 10v–12v).

There are two major sets of corrections to the manuscript, in addition to those made by the scribe himself. The earlier of the two appears to date from the later Middle Ages. The added passages in the second hand in notes 47 and 48 are long enough to identify the script as dating from the fifteenth century (probably the second half). Whenever possible, the writer of each set of corrections is identified as the Earlier or the Later hand.[7] In nos. 29–30 and 69 the Earlier hand added superscript feminine forms to the masculine forms (as in Ordo XIV,4 and 8, and in Ordo XIX,57), these are identified as *aliter* because they are variant readings rather than corrections or emendations.

At least one correction was made in still another hand, probably in the thirteenth century, and still another hand made at least one correction, probably in the fourteenth century.

Even with all these corrections, many errors remain in the text. I correct some of the worst of them, either by giving the correct reading in the text with the manuscript's reading in a variant or a note, or by supplying missing letters or words within square brackets, or by referring to *A*'s source. I did not seek to correct all errors, however, and the reader is cautioned to compare *A*'s readings with those of its surviving sources (Ordo XV, MS *G*, and Ordo XIX, MS *A*) or other ordines.

ORDO XXI

1. [fol. 1r] Incipit[8] ordo ad consecrandum et coronandum regem.

2. Paratur primo solium in medio chori. Exeunte autem rege de thalamo, dicitur hec oratio ab uno episcoporum.

Omnipotens sempiterne Deus, qui famulum tuum N. reg [fol. 1v] *ni fastigio dignatus es sublimare, tribue ei, quesumus, ut ita in huius seculi cursu cunctorum in commune salutem disponat, quod a tue veritatis tramite non recedat. Per.*

3. Postea ducitur processionaliter ad ecclesiam, cantando hoc resp.

Ecce mitto angelum meum, qui precedat te et custodiat semper; observa et audi vocem meam et inimicus ero inimicis tuis et affligentes te affligam. Et pre [fol. 2r] *cedet te angelus meus.*

---

[7] Identification of the two hands is based partially upon the colors of the ink: the ink of the Earlier hand is fairly black, whereas that of the Later hand tends to be brown.

[8] "Ici comance le corunement des rois de France" is written in gothic script on the verso of the second of the two flyleaves (facing fol. 1r) at the beginning of manuscript *A*. The hand is not that of a professional scribe. The decoration of the initial *I* on *Ici* suggests that this was written in the thirteenth century. The top half of fol. 1r is occupied by a miniature depicting both the king's reception at the church and the king in prayer at the altar.

4. Vers.

Israel, si me audieris, non erit in te deus recens neque adorabis deum alienum, ego enim Dominus. Et precedet.[9]

5. Ad hostium ecclesie subsistant archiepiscopus et episcopi. Et archiepiscopus hanc orationem dicat.

Dominus vobiscum.

Oremus.

Deus, qui scis humanum genus nulla sua virtute posse subsistere, concede propicius, ut famulus tuus N., quem populo tuo voluisti preferri, ita tuo fulciatur [fol. 2v] *adiutorio, quatinus quibus potuit preesse valeat et prodesse. Per.*

6. Introeuntes autem ecclesiam cantent hanc antiphonam.

Domine, salvum fac regem et exaudi nos in die qua invocaverimus te.[10]

Usque in introitum chori.

Psalmus. *Exaudiat te Dominus in die tribulationis; protegat te nomen Dei Iacob.*[11]

Gloria Patri.

Sicut erat.

7. Tunc metropolitanus dicat hanc orationem.

Dominus vobiscum.

Et cum spiritu tuo.

Oremus.

[fol. 3r] *Omnipotens sempiterne Deus, celestium terrestriumque moderator, qui famulum tuum N. ad regni fastigium dignatus es provehere, concede, quesumus, ut a cunctis adversitatibus liberatus, ecclesiastice pacis dono muniatur et ad eterne pacis gaudia te donante pervenire mereatur. Per dominum nostrum.*

8. Post primam cantatam, debet rex venire in ecclesia antequam fiat aqua benedicta, et debent esse sedes disposite circa altare, ubi honorifice sedeant archiepiscopi et episcopi, et regni pares se [fol. 3v] deant seorsum ab oppositis altaris. Inter primam et terciam debet abbas sancti Remigii Remensis processionaliter cum crucibus et cereis deferre

---

[9] *A gives the musical notation for the response and versicle: conventional square notation on five four-line staffs, followed by two five-line staffs.

[10] *A provides two four-line staffs for this antiphon, but the musical notation was never added. The absence of notation demonstrates that the musical annotator was someone other than any of the other participants in creating the manuscript, the production of which was carefully orchestrated, as Le Goff, "The Ordo of 1250," and Bonne, "The Manuscript of the Ordo of 1250," rightly contend.

[11] Ps. 19: 2.

reverentissime sacrosanctam ampullam sub cortina serica quatuor[a] perticis a quatuor monachis albis indutis sublevata. Cum autem venerit
archiepiscopus ad altare, debet vel ipse vel aliquis de episcopis pro
omnibus et ecclesiis sibi subditis a rege petere, ut promittat et iuramento
firmet se observaturum et iura episcoporum et ecclesiarum ita dicendo.

8. [a] perdicis *after* quatuor *crossed out by scribe* A.

9. [fol. 4r] *A*[12] *vobis perdonari petimus, ut nobis et ecclesiis nostris
canonicum privilegium ac debitam legem atque iusticiam conservetis
ac defendatis.*

10. Responsio regis.

Promitto vobis, quod vobis et ecclesiis vestris canonicum [fol. 4v]
*privilegium et debitam legem atque iusticiam servabo. Et defensionem
quantum potuero, adiuvante Domino, exhibebo, sicut rex in suo regno
unicuique episcopo et ecclesie sibi commisse per rectum exhibere
debet.*

11. Postea inquirant alte duo episcopi assensum populi, quo habito,
cantent "Te Deum." Et prosternat se usque in finem "Te Deum."[13] [fol. 5r]
Cantato "Te Deum laudamus," erigatur rex de solo ab episcopis et hec
promittens dicat.

12. *Hec tria populo christiano et michi subdito in Christi nomine
promitto. In primis, ut ecclesie Dei omnis populus christianus veram
pacem, nostro arbitrio, servet in omni tempore. Secundo, ut*[14] *omnes
rapacitates et iniquitates interdicam. Tercio, ut in omnibus iudiciis
equitatem et misericordiam precipiam.* Dicant omnes, *Amen.*

13. Postea prosternat se rex humiliter totus in cruce [fol. 5v] cum
episcopis et presbyteris hinc inde prostratis. Ceteris in choro breviter
psallentibus letaniam que sequitur.[15]

14. *Kyrieleyson.*
Christe eleyson.
Kyrieleyson.
Christe, audi nos.
Pater de celis Deus, miserere nobis.

---

[12] The top half of fol. 4r is occupied by a miniature depicting the arrival of the
Holy Ampulla.

[13] The bottom third of fol. 4v is occupied by a miniature depicting two bishops
seeking the people's assent, the king kneeling at the altar, and prelates chanting the Te
Deum.

[14] *ut* added in superscript, apparently by the scribe of *A*.

[15] The middle half of fol. 5v is occupied by a miniature depicting the king pros-
trated before the altar while the clergy chants the litany in responding choirs.

Fili redemptor mundi Deus, miserere nobis.
Spiritus sancte Deus, miserere.
[fol. 6r] *Sancta Trinitas, unus Deus, miserere nobis.*

Sancta Maria,	*ora pro nobis.*
Sancta Dei genitrix,	*ora pro nobis.*
Sancta virgo virginum,	*ora.*
Sancte Michael,	*ora.*
Sancte Gabriel,	*ora.*
Sancte Raphael,	*ora.*
Omnes sancti angeli et archangeli Dei,	*orate pro nobis.*
Omnes sancti beatorum spirituum ordines,	*orate.*
Sancte Iohannes Baptista,	*ora pro nobis.*
Omnes sancti patriarche et prophete,	*orate.*
Sancte Petre,	*ora.*
Sancte Paule,	*ora.*
Sancte Andrea,	*ora.*
Sancte Iacobe,	*ora.*
Sancte Iohannes,	*ora.*
Sancte Thoma,	*ora.*
Sancte Iacobe,	*ora.*
[fol. 6v] *Sancte Phylippe,*	*ora.*
Sancte Bartholomee,	*ora pro nobis.*
Sancte Mathee,	*ora.*
Sancte Symon,	*ora.*
Sancte Iuda,	*ora.*
Sancte Mathia,	*ora.*
Sancte Barnaba,	*ora.*
Sancte Marce,	*ora.*
Sancte Luca,	*ora.*
Sancte Marcialis,	*ora.*
Omnes sancti apostoli et evangeliste,	*orate.*
Omnes sancti discipuli domini,	*orate.*
Omnes sancti innocentes,	*orate.*
Sancte Stephane,	*ora.*
Sancte Line,	*ora.*
Sancte Clete,	*ora.*
Sancte Clemens,	*ora.*
Sancte Syxte,	*ora.*
Sancte Grisogone,	*ora.*
Sancte Corneli,	*ora.*

Sancte Cypriane,	*ora.*
Sancte Cosma,	*ora.*
Sancte Damiane,	*ora.*
Sancte Laurenti,	*ora.*
[fol. 7r] *Sancte Vincenti,*	*ora.*
Sancte Georgi,	*ora.*
Sancte Christophore,	*ora.*
Sancte Dyonisi cum sociis tuis,	*orate.*
Sancte Maurici cum sociis tuis,	*orate.*
Sancte Ypolite cum sociis tuis,	*orate.*
Sancte Nichasi cum sociis tuis,	*orate.*
Omnes sancti martyres,	*orate.*
Sancte Silvester,	*ora.*
Sancte Leo,	*ora.*
Sancte Gregori,	*ora.*
Sancte Martine,	*ora.*
Sancte Augustine,	*ora.*
Sancte Ambrosi,	*ora.*
Sancte Iheronime,	*ora pro nobis.*
Sancte Germane,	*ora.*
Sancte Vedaste,	*ora.*
Sancte Amande,	*ora.*
Sancte Memi,	*ora.*
Sancte Donatiane,	*ora pro nobis.*
Sancte Domiciane,	[fol. 7v] *ora pro nobis.*
Sancte Alpine,	*ora.*
Sancte Leudomire,	*ora pro nobis.*
Sancte Elaphi,	*ora.*
Sancte Nicholae,	*ora.*
Sancte Benedicte,	*ora.*
Sancte Remigi,	*ora.*
Sancte Eligi,	*ora.*
Sancte Hylari,	*ora.*
Sancte Egidi,	*ora.*
Sancte Leonarde,	*ora.*
Omnes sancti confessores,	*orate pro nobis.*
Omnes sancti monachi et heremite,	*orate.*
15. *Sancta Maria Magdalena*[a],	*ora.*
Sancta Maria Egyptiaca,	*ora.*
Sancta Felicitas,	*ora.*
Sancta Perpetua,	*ora.*

Sancta Petronilla,	*ora.*
Sancta Agnes,	*ora.*
Sancta Agatha,	*ora.*
Sancta Lucia,	*ora.*
Sancta Cecilia,	*ora.*
Sancta Anastasia,	*ora.*
[fol. 8r] *Sancta Katerina,*	*ora.*
Sancta Margareta,	*ora pro nobis.*
Sancta Iuliana,	*ora pro nobis.*
Sancta Barbara,	*ora.*
Sancta Brigida,	*ora.*
Sancta Eufemia,	*ora pro nobis.*
Sancta Fides,	*ora.*
Sancta Spes,	*ora.*
Sancta Caritas,	*ora.*
Omnes sancte virgines,	*orate.*
Omnes sancti et sancte,	*orate.*

15. ª Magdalene A.

16. *Propicius esto,*	*parce nobis Domine.*
Ab omni malo,	*libera nos Domine.*
Ab insidiis dyaboli,	*libera nos Domine.*
A dampnatione perpetua,	*libera.*
Ab ira et odio et omni mala voluntate,	*libera.*
A subitanea et eterna morte,	*libera.*
[fol. 8v] *Ab impetu inanis glorie,*	*libera.*
A spiritu fornicationis,	*libera.*
A cecitate cordis,	*libera nos Domine.*
A penis inferni,	*libera.*
In hora mortis,	*succurre nobis Domine.*
Per annunciationem tuam,	*libera.*
Per adventum tuum,	*libera.*
Per nativitatem tuam,	*libera.*
Per circumcisionem tuam,	*libera.*
Per apparitionem tuam,	*libera.*
Per baptismum tuum,	*libera.*
Per ieiunium tuum,	*libera.*
Per passionem et crucem tuam,	*libera.*
Per piissimam mortem tuam,	*libera.*
[fol. 9r] *Per gloriosam resurrectionem tuam,*	*libera.*

Per admirabilem ascensionem tuam,   *libera.*
Per adventum Spiritus sancti paracliti,   *libera.*
In die iudicii,   *libera nos Domine.*
17. *Peccatores, te rogamus, audi nos.*
Ut pacem nobis dones, te rogamus.
Ut remissionem peccatorum et emendationem vite nobis dones, te rogamus.
Ut ecclesiam tuam regere et defensare digneris, te rogamus.
Ut famulum tuum N. in regem eligere digneris, te rogamus.
Ut eum regere benedicere et sublimare digneris, te rogamus.
[fol. 9v] *Ut eum ad regni fastigium perducere digneris, te rogamus.*
Ut eum et omnes principes nostros in tua voluntate custodias, te rogmus.
Ut locum istum et omnes habitantes in eo conservare digneris, te rogamus.
Ut cunctum populum christianum precioso sanguine tuo redemptum conservare digneris, te rogamus.
Ut fructus terre dare et conservare digneris, te rogamus.
Ut oculos misericordie tue super nos reducere digneris, te rogamus.
Ut animas nostras et parentum nostrorum ab eterna dampnatione [fol. 10r] *eripias, te rogamus.*
Ut omnibus fidelibus defunctis requiem eternam donare digneris, te rogamus.
Ut nos exaudire digneris, te rogamus.
Fili Dei, te rogamus, audi nos.
18. *Agnus Dei, qui tollis peccata mundi, parce nobis Domine.*
Agnus Dei, qui tollis peccata mundi, exaudi nos Domine.
Agnus Dei, qui tollis peccata mundi, dona nobis pacem.
Kyrieleyson.
Christeleyson.
Kyrieleyson.

    19. *Pater noster.*
    Et ne nos in.
    Et veniat super [fol. 10v] *nos misericordia tua, Domine.*
    Salutare tuum secundum eloquium tuum.
    Esto nobis, Domine, turris fortitudinis.
    A facie inimici.
    Memor esto, Domine, congregationis tue.
    Quam possedisti.
    Domine, salvos fac reges.
    Et exaudi nos in die.

Salvos fac servos tuos et ancillas tuas.
Deus meus sperantes in te.
Fiat pax in virtute tua.
Et habundantia in turribus tuis.
Oremus pro benefactoribus nostris.
Miserere eis, Domine.
Ut pro fidelibus defunctis.
Requiem eternam.
Domine, exaudi ora [fol. 11r] *tionem meam.*
Et clamor meus ad te veniat.
Dominus vobiscum.
Et cum spiritu tuo.

20. Finita autem letania, erigant se. Sublatus vero princeps, interrogetur a domino metropolitano hoc modo.

Vis fidem sanctam a catholicis viris tibi traditam tenere et operibus iustis observare? Responsio regis. *Volo.*

Iterum metropolitanus. *Vis sanctis ecclesiis ecclesiarumque ministris tutor et defensor esse?* Responsio regis. *Volo.*

Iterum metropolitanus. *Vis regnum tuum a Deo* [fol. 11v] *concessum secundum iusticiam patrum tuorum regere et defendere?* Responsio regis. *Volo. Et in quantum divino fultus adiutorio ac solatio omnium suorum valuero, ita me per omnia fideliter acturum esse promitto.*

21. Si sanctas Dei ecclesias ac rectores ecclesiarum nec non et cunctum populum sibi subiectum iuste ac religiose regali providentia iuxta morem patrum suorum defendere ac regere velit, illo autem profitente in quantum divino fultus adiutorio ac solatio omnium suorum [fol. 12r] valuerit, ita se per omnia fideliter esse acturum, ipse episcopus affatur populum si tali principi ac rectori se subicere ipsiusque regnum firma fide stabilire atque iussionibus illius obtemptare velint iuxta apostolum, qui dicit, 'Omnis anima potestatibus sublimioribus subdita sit,'[16] regi quasi precellenti. Tunc ergo a circumstante clero et populo unanimiter dicatur, "Fiat, fiat. Amen." Postea vero, illo devote inclinato, dicatur ab uno episcopo hec oratio.

22. *Dominus vobiscum.*
Oremus.

[fol. 12v] *Benedic, Domine, hunc regem nostrum N., qui regna omnium moderaris a seculo et tali benedictione glorifica, ut davitice teneat sublimitatis sceptrum et glorificatus in eius protinus inveniatur merito. Da ei tuo inspiramine cum mansuetudine ita regere*

---

16 Rom. 13: 1.

populum, sicut Salomonem fecisti regnum obtinere pacificum; tibi semper cum timore sit subditus tibique militet cum quiete. Sit tuo clipeo protectus cum proceribus. Et ubique tua gracia victor existat. Ho [fol. 13r] *norifica eum pre cunctis regibus gentium, felix populis dominetur. Et feliciter eum nationes adornent. Vivat inter gentium catervas magnanimus; sit in iudiciis equitatis singularis. Locupletet eum tua predives dextra; frugiferam obtineat patriam, et eius liberis tribuas profutura. Presta ei prolixitatem vite per tempora, ut in diebus eius oriatur iusticia, a te robustum teneat regiminis solium. Et cum iocunditate et iusticia eterno glorietur in regno. Per.*

23. Dein [fol. 13v] de ab uno episcoporum dicatur hec oratio.

Deus inenarrabilis auctor mundi, conditor generis humani, gubernator imperii, confirmator regni, qui ex utero fidelis amici patriarche nostri Abrahe, preeligisti reges seculi profuturos, tu presentem regem hunc N. cum exercitu suo, per intercessionem beate Marie semper virginis et omnium sanctorum, ubere benedictione locupleta et in solium regni firma stabilitate connecte; visita eum sicut Moysen in rubro, Iesu [fol. 14r] *Nave*ᵃ *in prelio, Gedeon in agro, Samuelem in templo, et illa eum benedictione syderea ac sapiencie tue rore perfunde, quam beatus David in psalterio, Salomon filius eius te remunerante percepit e celo. Sis ei contra inimicorum acies lorica, in aversis galea, in prosperis paciencia, in protectione clipeus sempiternus; et presta, ut gentes illi teneant fidem, proceres sui habeant pacem, diligant caritatem, abstineant se a cupiditate, Loquantur iusticiam, custodiant* [fol. 14v] *veritatem; et ita populus iste sub eius imperio pululet coalitus benedictione eternitatis, ut semper maneant tripudiantes in pace victores. Quod ipse prestare.*

23. ᵃ Iesi [fol. 14r] mane A.

24. Postmodum positis super altare corona regia, gladio in vagina incluso, calcaribus aureis, sceptro deaurato et virga ad mensuram unius cubiti vel amplius habente desuper manum eburneam. Item, caligis sericis et iacintinis intextis per totum liliis aureis, et tunica eiusdem coloris et operis, in modum [fol. 15r] tunicalis quo induuntur subdiaconi ad missam. Nec non et socco prorsus eiusdem coloris et operis, qui est factus fere in modum cappe serice absque caparone. Que omnia abbas sancti Dyonisii in Francia de monasterio suo debet Remis aportare et stans ad altare custodire.

25. Rex autem [anteᵃ] altare stans deponit vestes suas, preter tunicam sericam bene profunde apertas ante in pectore et retro in dorso. Videlicet inter scapulas aperturis tunice sibi invicem connexis ansulis

argenteis. [fol. 15v] Tunc in primis ibi a magno camerario Francie regi dicte calige calciantur. Et postmodum a duce Borgondie calcaria eius pedibus astringuntur [17] et statim tolluntur. Postmodum rex a solo archiepiscopo gladio cum [fol. 16r] vagina accingitur. Quo accincto, statim idem gladius de vagina ab archiepiscopo extrahitur, vagina super altare reposita, et datur ei ab archiepiscopo in manibus, quem debet rex humiliter afferre ad altare. Et statim resumere de manu episcopi. Et incontinenti dare senescallo Francie ad portandum ante se, et in ecclesia usque ad finem misse, et post missam cum ad palacium vadit.

25. ᵃ ante *om.* A, *here add. from Ordo XX A,10.*

26. Hiis ita gestis, crismate in altari super patenam consecratam preparato, debet archiepiscopus sa [fol. 16v] crosanctam ampullam super altare aperire, et inde cum acu aurea aliquantulum de oleo celitus misso attrahere, et crismati parato diligentius inmiscere ad inungendum regem, qui solus inter universos reges terre hoc glorioso prefulget privilegio, ut oleo celitus misso singulariter inungatur. Tunc dissutis ansulis aperturarum ante et retro, et genibus in terram positis, primo archiepiscopus cum eodem oleo inungit regem in summitate capitis, secundo in pectore, [fol. 17r] tercio inter scapulas, quarto in scapulis, quinto in compagibus brachiorum, dicens. [18]

27. *Ungo te in regem de oleo sanctificato, in nomine Patris et Filii et Spiritus sancti.* Dicant omnes, *Amen.*

28. Et cantetur hec antiphona.

[fol. 17v] *Unxerunt Salomonem Sadoch sacerdos et Nathan propheta regem in Gyon, et accedentes leti dixerunt, 'Vivat rex in eternum.'* [19]

29. Dum cantatur hec antiphona, dicit basseᵃ archiepiscopus.

Christe perunge hunc regemᵇ in regimen.

29. ᵃ basso A. —ᵇ hanc [re]ginam *aliter* (*in the Earlier hand*) A.

30. Oratio.

Unde unxisti sacerdotes, reges, prophetas ac martyres, qui per fidem

---

[17] The sentence is here broken by a miniature, which shows that the copyist and the miniaturist worked together to produce the finished result. Therefore, for this manuscript, the text would appear to have been copied from an interim manuscript that was the result of collating the four sources of the text. The miniature, which occupies the middle half of fol. 15v, depicts the investitures of the buskins and the spurs (see Plate 21).

[18] The middle half of fol. 17r is occupied by a miniature that depicts the anointing of the king's head while the constable of France holds the upright sword.

[19] *A* adds the musical notation for the antiphon (conventional square notation on a five-line staff).

*vicerunt regna operati sunt iusticiam et adepti sunt promissiones, tua
sacratissima* [fol. 18r] *unxio super caput eius defluat, atque ad interiora descendat et cordis illius intima penetret, et promissionibus, quas
adepti sunt victoriosissimi reges, gracia tua dignus*[a] *efficiatur, quatinus et in presenti seculo feliciter regnet et ad eorum consorcium in
celesti regno perveniat. Per dominum nostrum Iesum Christum filium
tuum. Qui unctus est oleo leticie pre consor-tibus suis. Et virtute crucis potestates aerias debellavit, tarthara destruxit regnumque dyaboli
superavit et ad celos vic* [fol. 18v] *tor ascendit, in cuius manu victoria,
omnis gloria et potestas consistunt, et tecum vivit et regnat Deus in
unitate eiusdem Spiritus sancti Deus, per omnia secula seculorum.
Amen.*

30. [a] [di]gna *aliter* (*in the Earlier hand*) A.

31. Alia oratio.

*Deus, Dei filius, dominus noster Iesus Christus, qui a Patre oleo
exultationis unctus est pre participibus suis, ipse per presentem sacri
unguinis infusionem Spiritus paracliti super caput tuum infundat
benedictionem eandemque usque ad interiora cordis tui penetrare
faciat, quatinus hoc visibili* [fol. 19r] *et tractabili dono invisibilia
percipere, et temporali regno iustis moderaminibus executo, eternaliter cum eo regnare merearis. Per dominum nostrum Iesum Christum.*

32. Post hoc ungat ei manus, dicens.

Ungantur[20] *manus iste de oleo sanctificato, unde uncti fuerunt
reges et prophete et sicut unxit Samuel David in regem, ut sis benedictus et constitutus rex in regno isto super populum istum, quem dominus Deus tuus dedit tibi ad regen* [fol. 19v] *dum ac gubernandum.
Quod ipse prestare dignetur.*

33. Sequitur oratio.

Dominus vobiscum.

Et cum spiritu tuo.

Oremus.

*Prospice, omnipotens Deus, serenis obtutibus hunc gloriosum
regem N., et sicut benedixisti Abraham, Ysaac et Iacob, sic illum largis
benedictionibus spiritualis gracie cum omni plenitudine tue potencie
irrigare atque perfundere dignare; tribue ei de rore celi et de pinguedine terre habundantiam frumenti, vini et olei, et omnium frugum
opulentiam, ex*[a] *largita* [fol. 20r] *te divini muneris longa*[b] *per tempora,*

---

[20] In *Ungantur* the historiated initial *U*, which occupies the left half of the middle
third of fol. 19r, depicts the anointing of the king's hands.

*ut, illo regnante, sit sanitas corporum in patria, et pax inviolata sit in
regno, et dignitas gloriosa regalis palacii maximo splendore regie
potestatis oculis omnium fulgeat, luce clarescat atque splendore quasi
splendidissima fulgura maximo perfusa lumine videatur; tribue ei,
quesumus omnipotens Deus, ut sit fortissimus protector patrie et consolator ecclesiarum, atque cenobiorum sanctorum maxima cum
pietate regalis munificientie, atque* [fol. 20v] *ut sit fortissimus regum,
triumphator hostium, ad opprimendas rebelles et paganas nationes.
Sitque suis inimicis sat terribilis pre maxima fortitudine et regalis
potencie; obtimatibus quoque atque precelsis, proceribusque ac
fidelibus sui regni sit magnificus et amabilis et pius, ut ab omnibus
timeatur atque diligatur. Reges quoque de lumbis eius per successiones
temporum futurorum egrediantur, regnum*[c] *hoc regere totum, et post
gloriosa tempora atque felicia presentis vite* [fol. 21r] *et gaudia sempiterna, in perpetua beatitudine habere mereatur. Quod ipse prestare
dignetur.*

33. [a] et A. —[b] longua A. —[c] egrediantur. Regnum A.

34. Alia oratio.
Dominus vobiscum.
Et cum spiritu tuo.
Oremus.

*Deus, qui es iustorum gloria et misericordia peccatorum, qui misi-
sti filium tuum preciosissimo sanguine suo genus humanum redimere, qui conteris bella et propugnator es*[21] *in te sperantium, et sub
cuius arbitrio omnium regnorum continetur potestas, te humiliter
deprecamur, ut presentem famulum tuum N. in tua misericordia
confiden* [fol. 21v] *tem in presenti sede regali benedicas eique propicius adesse digneris, ut qui tua expetit protectione defendi, omnibus
sit hostibus fortior; fac eum, Domine, beatum esse et victorem de
inimicis suis, corona eum corona iusticie et pietatis, ut ex toto corde
et tota mente in te credens tibi deserviat, sanctam tuam ecclesiam
defendat et sublimet, populumque a te sibi commissum iuste regat;
nullus insidiantibus malis eum* [in[22]] *iniusticiam vertat; accende,
Domine, cor eius*[a] *ad amorem gracie tue per hoc unctionis* [fol. 22r]
*oleum, unde unxisti sacerdotes, reges et prophetas, quatinus iusticiam
diligens per tramitem similiter iusticie populum ducens*[b]*, post peracta a te disposita in regali excellentia annorum curricula, pervenire*

---

[21] Written *pro / pugnatores* as one word broken at the end of the line in *A*, but a
line was added to separate the two words, apparently by the Later hand.

[22] *in* added by the Earlier hand; *in iniusticiam* Ordo XIX,23.

ad eterna gaudia mereatur pervenire.[23] *Per dominum nostrum Iesum Christum filium tuum, qui tecum vivit et regnat in unitate spiritus sancti Deus. Per omnia secula seculorum. Amen.*

34. [a] tuis A. — [b] dicens A.

35. *Dominus vobiscum.*
Et cum spiritu tuo.
Sursum corda.
Habemus ad dominum.
Gracias agamus domino Deo nostro.
Dignum et iustum est.
36. [fol. 22v] Prefatio.
Vere[24] *dignum et iustum est, equum et salutare, nos tibi semper et ubique gracias agere.*

37. *Domine*[a] *sancte Pater omnipotens, eterne Deus, creator ac gubernator celi et terre, conditor et dispositor angelorum et hominum, rex regum et dominus dominorum, qui Abraham fidelem famulum tuum de hostibus triumphare fecisti, Moysi et Iosue populo tuo prelatis multiplicem*[b] *vic* [fol. 23r] *toriam tribuisti, humilem quoque puerum tuum David regni fastigio sublimasti, eumque de ore leonis et de manu bestie atque Golie sed et de gladio maligno Saul et omnium inimicorum liberasti, et Salomonem sapiencie pacisque ineffabili munere ditasti, respice propicius ad preces nostre humilitatis, et super hunc famulum tuum N., quem supplici devotione in regnum pariter eligimus, benedictionum tuarum dona multiplica, eumque dextera tue potencie semper ubique* [fol. 23v] *circumda, quatinus predicti Abrahe fidelitate firmatus, Moysi mansuetudine fretus, Iosue fortitudine munitus, David humilitate exaltatus, Salomonis sapiencia decoratus, tibi in omnibus complaceat et per tramitem iusticie in offenso*[c] *gressu semper incedat, et tocius regni ecclesiam deinceps cum plebibus sibi annexis ita enutriat ac doceat, muniat et instruet,*[25] *et contraque omnes visibiles et invisibiles hostes idem potencialiter regaliterque tue virtutis regnum admi* [fol. 24r] *nistret, ut regale solium videlicet Saxonum, Merciorum*[d], *Nordan, Chymbrorum sceptra non deserat, sed ad pristine fidei pacisque concordiam eorum animos, te opitulante, reformet, ut, utrorumque horum populorum debita subiectione fultus, condigno amore glorificatus, per longum vite spacium*

---

[23] *pervenire* is thus repeated, but the Later hand deleted its second occurrence by drawing a line around three sides of the word.

[24] In *Vere* the historiated initial *V* depicts a priest praying at the altar.

[25] Corrected to *instruat* by the Later hand.

paterne apicem glorie tua miseratione unatum[26] *stabilire et gubernare*
mereatur; tue quoque protectionis galea munitus et scuto insuperabili
iugiter protectus. Armisque celestibus circumdatus optabi- [fol. 24v]
lis victorie triumphum feliciter capiat terroremque sue potencie infi-
delibus inferat. Et pacem tibi militantibus letanter reportet, virtutibus
necnon quibus prefatos fideles tuos decorasti, multi[pli]ci[27] *honoris*
benedictione condecora et in regni regimine sublimiter colloca. Et oleo
gracie Spiritus sancti perunge.[28]

37. ^a salutare. Nos tibi semper et ubique gracias agere, domine A. —^b multitudinem A, *but* multiplicem *Ordo XIX,26.* —^c in officioso A, *but* in offenso
Ordo XIX,26; read inoffenso. —^d Mentiorum A, *but* Merciorum *Ordo XV,9.*

38. Post inunctionem omnium predictorum sic factam, connectuntur
ansule aperturarum propter inunctionem, et tunc a camerario Francie
induitur tunica iacinctina, et desuper soccus, [fol. 25r] ita quod dexteram
manum habet liberam in apertura socci. Et super sinistram soccum
elevatum, sicut elevatur casula sacerdotis. Demum datur ei ab archiepiscopo sceptrum in manu dextera et virga in sinistra. Ad ultimum convo-
catis ex nomine paribus regni et circumstantibus, archiepiscopus accipit
de altari coronam regiam, et solus imponit capiti regis. Qua imposita,
omnes pares tam clerici quam laici manum apponunt corone et eam
undique sustentant. Tunc archiepiscopus coronam sustinentibus re- [fol.
25v] gem taliter insi[g]nitum deducit in solium sibi preparatum, sericis
stratum et ornatum, ubi collocat eum in sede eminenti, unde ab omnibus
possit videri, quem in sede sua taliter residentem, mox archiepiscopus,
mitra ob reverentiam deposita, osculatur, et post eum episcopi et laici
pares qui eius coronam sustentant.

39. Postea ab episcopis ensem accipiat et cum ense totum sibi
regnum fideliter ad regendum secundum supradicta verba sciat esse
commendatum, dicente metropolitano.[29]

[fol. 26v] *Accipe*[30] *gladium per manus episcoporum licet indignas,*
vice tamen et auctoritate sanctorum apostolorum consecratas, tibi
regaliter impositum nostreque benedictionis officio, in defensionem
sancte Dei ecclesie divinitus ordinatum. Et esto memor de quo psalmista

---

[26] The letter *a* in *unatum* expuncted by the Later hand; *unatim* Ordo XV,9.

[27] *multici* corrected to *multiplici* by the Later hand.

[28] No. 36 was compiled from Ordo XIX,26 and Ordo XV,9.

[29] The whole of fol. 26r is devoted to a miniature that depicts the retying of the
king's tunic, the investiture of the mantle, the peers supporting the crown on the king's
head, and the standing king receiving the archbishop's kiss.

[30] The historiated initial *A* in *Accipe* depicts the bestowal of the sword.

prophetavit dicens, 'Accingere gladio tuo super femur tuum, potentis-
sime,' ut in hoc per eundem vim equitatis excerceas, molem iniqui-
tatis potenter destruas et sanctam Dei [fol. 27r] *ecclesiam eius[que]* [31]
fideles propugnes ac protegas, nec minus sub fide falsos quam chris-
tiani nominis hostes exec[r]eris [32] *ac destruas, viduas ac pupillos*
[clementer [33]*] adiuves ac defendas, desolata restaures, restaurata con-*
serves, ulciscaris iniusta, confirmes bene disposita, quatinus hec in
agendo virtutum triumpho gloriosus iusticieque cultor egregius cum
mundi salvatore, cuius tipum [34] *geris in nomine, sine fine merearis*
regnare. Qui cum Patre etc.

40. Accinctus autem en [fol. 27v] se, similiter ab illis armillas et pal-
lium accipiat et anulum, dicente metropolitano.

Accipe [35] *regie dignitatis anulum, et per hunc in te catholice fidei*
cognosce signaculum, quia ut hodie ordinaris caput et princeps populi,
ita perseverabilis auctor ac stabilitor christianitatis et christiane
fidei, ut felix in opere, locuplex [36] *in fide, cum rege regum glorieris. Per*
eundem cui est honor et gloria per infinita secula se [fol. 28r] *culorum.*
Amen.

41. Oratio post anulum.

Deus, cuius est omnis potestas et dignitas, da famulo tuo pro spiritu
sue dignitatis effectum, in qua, te remunerante, permaneat tibique
iugiter [37] *placere*[a] *contendat. Per.*

41. [a] placendus A.

42. Postea sceptrum et baculum accipiat, dicente sibi ordinatore.

Accipe [38] *virgam virtutis atque equitatis, qua intelligas mulcere pios*
et terrere reprobos, errantibus viam pandere, lapsis manum porrigere,

---

[31] *eius A*, corrected to *eiusque*, apparently by the Later hand; *eiusque* in Ordo XIX,28.

[32] *execeris A*, corrected to *execreris* by the Later hand; *execreris* in Ordo XIX,28.

[33] *clementer* is the reading of the Ordo XIX,28. In *A* there is a blank space between *pupillos* and *adiuves*, and the Later hand added the word *protegas* in the margin. The blank space provides evidence that there was an intermediate copy between Ordo XIX and *A* and that this copy was probably written in some sort of cursive and was difficult to read, for Ordo XIX, MS *A* is very legible.

[34] *cipum* in *A*, corrected to *tipum* in the Later hand; *typum* in Ordo XIX,28.

[35] The historiated initial *A* in *Accipe* depicts the bestowal of the ring.

[36] *locuplex* in *A* and Ordo XIX,29, MS *B* (var. 29b), but *locuples* in Ordo XIX,29, MS *A*.

[37] *permaneat semperque timeat tibique iugiter* in Ordo XV,17, the source here.

[38] The historiated initial *A* in *Accipe* depicts the bestowal of the short scepter (the *baculum*).

dis [fol. 28v] *perdas et superbos et releves humiles, ut aperiat tibi hostium Iesus Christus dominus noster, qui de ipso ait, 'Ego sum hostium; per me si quis introierit, salvabitur,' et ipse qui est clavis David et sceptrum domus Israel, 'qui aperit et nemo claudit, claudit et nemo aperit.' Sitque tibi auctor, qui educit 'vinctum de domo carceris, sedentem in tenebris et in umbra mortis.' Et in omnibus sequi merearis eum, de quo propheta David cecinit, 'Sedes tua Deus in seculum seculi, virga equitatis virga regni tui.'* [fol. 29r] *Et imitando ipsum 'diligas iusticiam, et odio habeas iniquitatem; quia propterea unxit te Deus, Deus tuus,' ad exemplum illius, quem ante secula unxerat 'oleo exultationis pre participibus suis,' Iesum Christum dominum nostrum, qui vivit et regnat per omnia secula seculorum. Amen.*

43. Tunc solus metropolitanus [re]verenter[39] coronam capiti regis imponat, dicens.

Accipe[40] *coronam regni, que licet ab indignis, nostris tamen manibus capiti* [fol. 29v] *tuo imponitur, et quia sanctitatis gloriam et honorem et opus fortitudinis expresse signare intelligas, et per hanc te participem ministerii nostri non ignores, ita ut, sicut nos in interioribus pastores rectoresque animarum intelligimur, tu quoque in exterioribus verus Dei cultor strenuusque*[a] *contra omnes adversitates ecclesie Dei defensor regnique tibi a Deo dati et per officium nostre benedictionis, in vice apostolorum omniumque sanctorum tuo regimini commissi, utilis executor regnatorque pro* [fol. 30r] *ficuus semper appareas*[b], *ut inter gloriosos athletas virtutum gemmis ornatus et premio sempiterne felicitatis coronatus cum redemptore ac salvatore Iesu Christo, cuius nomen vicemque gestare crederis, sine fine glorieris, qui vivit et imperat Deus cum Deo Patre in unitate Spiritus sancti. Per omnia secula seculorum. Amen.*

43. [a] strennusque A. — [b] apparens A.

44. Et ab eo statim dicatur benedictio super eum, que et tempore [synodi[a]] dicenda est super regem.

Benedicat tibi Dominus, custodiat et te[b] *et sicut voluit te super* [fol. 30v] *populum suum esse regem, ita in presenti seculo felicem et eterne felicitatis tribuat esse consortem. Amen.*

---

[39] *verenter* in *A*, corrected in very faint ink or pencil to *reverenter* by a hand that appears contemporary (according to François Avril in conversation), rather than either the Earlier or the Later hand.

[40] The historiated initial *A* in *Accipe* depicts the archbishop crowning the standing king.

44. ᵃsynodi *om.* A, *here add. from Ordo XIX,32.* —ᵇ custodiat et te] custodiatque te *Ordo XIX,32.*

45. *Clerum ac populum, quem sua voluit opitulatione in tua sanctione congregari, sua dispensatione et tua amministratione per diuturna tempora faciat feliciter gubernari. Amen.*

46. *Quatinus divinis monitis parentes, adversitatibus carentes, bonis omnibus exuberantes, tuo imperio fideli amore obsequentes, et in presenti seculo pacis tranquillitate fruantur et tecum eter-* [fol. 31r] *norum omnium consortio potyri mereantur. Amen.*

Quod ipse prestare.

47. Deinde coronatus honorifice per chorum ducatur de altari ab episcopis usque ad solium, cantante choro hoc resp.

Desiderium anime eius tribuisti ei. Et voluntate labiorum eius non fraudasti eum, Domine. Quoniam prevenisti eum in benedictionibus dulcedinis posuisti in capite eius coronam [fol. 31v] *de lapide precioso. Et voluntate labiorum.*⁴¹

48. Deinde dicat ei domnusᵃ metropolitanus.

*Sta et retine locum a modo, quem hucusque paterna successione tenuisti, hereditario iure tibi delegatum per auctoritatem Dei omnipotentis et presentem traditionem nostram, omnium scilicet episcoporum ceterorumque Dei servorum; et quanto clerum sacris altaribus propinquiorem prospicis*ᵇ*, tanto ei potiorem in locis congruis honorem impendere memineris, quatinus medi* [fol. 32r] *ator Dei et hominum te mediatorem cleri et plebis.*⁴²

Hoc in loco domnusᵃ metropolitanus sedere eum faciat super sedem dicendo.

In hoc regni solio te confirmet et in regno eterno secum regnare faciat Iesus Christus dominus noster, rex regum et dominus dominantium, qui cum Deo Patre et Spiritu sancto vivit et regnat Deus. Per omnia secula seculorum. Amen.

48. ᵃ donnus A. —ᵇ perspicis A.

49. Professio regis ante solium coram Deo, clero et populo.

Profiteor et promitto coram Deo et angelis tuis a modo et [fol. 32v] *deinceps legem et iusticiam pacemque sancte Dei ecclesie populoque michi subiecto, pro posse et nosse facere et conservare salvo condigno misericordie respectu, sicut in consilio fidelium nostrorum melius*

---

⁴¹ A adds the musical notation for this response (conventional square notation on a five-line staff). This is a response and versicle in Ordo XIX,35.

⁴² *constituat* added above the line in the Later hand.

*invenire poterimus, pontificibus quoque ecclesiarum Dei condignum
et canonicum honorem exhibere, atque ea, que ab imperatoribus et regibus ecclesiis sibi commissis collata et reddita sunt, inviolabiliter conservare abbatibus eciam comitibus et vassis dominicis nostris
congruum honorem secundum consilium fidelium nostro-* [fol. 33r]
rum prestare. Amen. Amen.

50. Tunc det illis oscula pacis; cunctus autem cetus clericorum tali
rectore gratulans, sonantibus campanis, alta voce concinat "Te Deum
laudamus." Cantante populo "Kyrieleyson." Tunc episcopus metropolitanus missam celebret plena processione. Sequitur ordo missarum, si in
feria evenerit, sed melius et honorabilius est in die dominica.

51. *Pax vobis.*

Oremus.[43]

Oratio.

*Deus, qui miro ordine universa disponis et ineffabiliter gubernas,
presta, quesumus, ut fa* [fol. 33v] *mulus tuus N. hec*[a] *in huius seculi
cursu implenda discernat*[b], *unde tibi imperpetuum*[c] *placere prevaleat.
Per dominum nostrum.*

51. [a] hoc A, *but* hęc *Ordo XIX,40.* — [b] discernas A. — [c] in perpetuum *Ordo
XIX,40.*

52. Secreta.

*Concede, quesumus omnipotens Deus, his salutaribus sacrificiis
placatus, ut famulus tuus ad peragendum regalis dignitatis officium
inveniatur semper ydoneus et celesti patrie reddatur acceptus. Per.*

53. Benedictio.

*Omnipotens Deus, qui te populi sui voluit esse rectorem, ipse te
celesti benedictione* [fol. 34r] *sanctificans eterni regni faciat esse consortem. Amen.*

*Concedatque tibi contra omnes christiane fidei hostes visibiles
atque invisibiles victoriam triumphalem, et pacis et quietis ecclestice
felicissimum te fieri longe lateque fundatorem. Amen.*

*Quatinus te gubernacula regni tenente, populus tibi subiectus
christiane religionis iura custodiens undique totus*[a] *pace tranquilla
perfruatur, et te in concilio regum beatorum collocato, eterna felicitate
ibidem tecum pariter gaudere mereatur.* [fol. 34v] *Amen.*

Quod ipse prestare dignetur.

Et pax eius sit semper vobiscum.

53. [a] tutus A *and Ordo XIX,42, MS A.*

---

[43] *Oremus* mistakenly rubricated in *A*.

54. Postcommunio.

Hec, Domine, salutaris sacrificii perceptio famuli tui N. pecca-
torum maculas[a] *diluat et ad regendum secundum tuam voluntatem*
populum ydoneum illum reddat, ut hoc salutari mysterio contra visi-
biles atque invisibiles hostes reddatur invictus, per quod mundus est
divina dispensatione redemptus. Per dominum.

54. [a] maculis A, *but* maculas *Ordo XIX,43.*

55. Alia missa.

Deus, cuius regnum est omnium seculorum, supplicatio- [fol. 35r]
nes nostras clementer exaudi, et christianissimi regis nostri protege
principatum, ut in tua virtute confidens et tibi placeat et super omnia
regna precellat. Per dominum.

56. Secreta.

Sacrificiis, Domine, placatus oblatis, pacem tuam nostris tempo-
ribus clementer indulge. Per.

57. Postcommunio.

Deus, qui diligentibus te facis[a] *cuncta prodesse, da cordi regis nos-*
tri inviolabilem caritatis affectum, ut desideria de tua inspiratione
concepta nulla possint temptatione mutari. Per dominum.

57. [a] facies *corr. to* facis *by scribe* A.

58. [fol. 35v] Verum si regina fuerit inungenda[44] et coronanda cum
rege, paratur ei similiter solium a sinistra parte chori, solio regis aliquantulum eminentior[i] ex parte chori dextera collocata. Et postquam rex in
modum premissum in solio suo resederit, archiepiscopo ad altare
regresso regina, sericis induta, ab episcopo dicente que inferius scripta
sunt post consecrationem regis. Inungitur in capite tantum et in pectore.
Nec inunctione regis celitus emissa, sed oleo sanctificato sim- [fol. 36r]
plici. Post inunctionem datur ei ab archiepiscopo sceptrum modicum,
alterius in omni quam sceptrum regium, et virga consimili[s] virge regie.
Deinde imponitur ab archiepiscopo solo corona capiti ipsius, quam
impositam sustentant undique barones, et sic deducunt eam ad solium,
ubi in sede parata collocatur, circumstantibus eam baronibus et matronis
nobilioribus.

59. Hiis expletis, missa cum demum a cantore et succentore, chorum
servantibus, inchoatur et sollempniter decantatur. Lecto autem ewan-
[fol. 36v] gelio, maior inter episcopos et archiepiscopos assistentes
librum ewangelii accipit, et tam ad regem quam ad reginam ad eum osculandum deportat. Deinde refert eum ad archiepiscopum qui missam

_____

[44] A second *fuerit* in *A* after *inungenda* was crossed out by the Later hand.

celebrat; dum autem cantatur offertorium, deducitur tam rex quam regina sollempniter de solio, et offert uterque ad manum archiepiscopi tam panem unum quam vinum in urceo argenteo et tresdecim aureos. Postmodum hoc facto deducitur uterque ad solium suum et sedem. Tunc celebratur missa ab archi [fol. 37r] episcopo; antequam autem dicat "Pax vobis," facit benedictionem super regem et populum; et accepto osculo pacis ab archiepiscopo, is qui librum ewangelii deosculandum ante detulerat, defert pacem regi et regine in soliis suis residentibus. Et postea omnes archiepiscopi et episcopi dant osculum pacis unus[45] post alium regi in suo solio residenti; post perceptionem eucharistie factam ab archiepiscopo, iterum descendunt rex et regina de soliis suis, et accedentes humiliter ad altare, percipiunt corpus et sanguinem Domini de [fol. 37v] manu archiepiscopi; et missa expleta, deponit archiepiscopus coronas de capitibus eorum; quibus exutis regalibus insi[g]nibus,[46] iterum imponit capitibus eorum modicas coronas, et sic vadunt ad palacium, nudo gladio precedente.

60. Incipit benedictio regine. Hec oratio dicatur in ingressu ecclesie.[47]

61. [fol. 38r] *Dominus vobiscum.*

Oremus.

Oratio.

Omnipotens sempiterne Deus, fons et origo tocius bonitatis, qui feminei sexus fragilitatem nequaquam reprobando adversaris, sed dignanter comprobando potius eligis, et qui infirma mundi eligendo forcia queque confundere decrevisti, quique eciam glorie virtutisque tue triumphum in manu Iudith femine olim Iudaice plebi de hoste sevissimo resignare voluisti, respice, quesumus, ad preces humilitatis nostre, et super hanc [fol. 38v] famulam tuam N., quam supplici devotione in reginam eligimus, benedictionum tuarum dona multiplica, eamque dextera tue potencie semper et ubique circumda, ut umbone muniminis tui undique secus firmiter protecta, visibilis seu invisibilis hostis nequicias triumphaliter expugnare valeat, et una cum

---

[45] *unum* in *A*, corrected to *unus* in the Later hand.

[46] *A*'s reading, *insinibus*, was later corrected in another hand in red ink to *insignibus*. The *g* is not like that in the Later hand. The manuscript contains no example of the Earlier hand's *g*, but I doubt that the correction was made in the Earlier hand for all corrections in that hand are in black ink.

[47] The bottom third of fol. 37v is occupied by a double miniature that depicts the substitution of a lighter crown for the king's coronation crown and the royal couple's communion. Below it, in the bottom margin, the Later hand added (perhaps from Ordo XV,47, MS *G*):

"*Adesto, Domine, supplicationibus nostris, et quod humilitatis nostre gerendum est misterio, tue virtutis impleatur effectu. Per dominum.*"

Sarra atque Rebecca, Lya et Rachel, beatis reverendisque feminis, fructu uteri sui fecundari seu gratulari mereatur ad decorem tocius regni statumque sancte [fol. 39r] *Dei ecclesie regendum nec non protegendum. Per Christum dominum nostrum, qui ex intemerato beate Marie virginis alvo nasci, visitare et renovare dignatus est mundum. Qui tecum vivit et gloriatur Deus in unitate Spiritus sancti, per immortalia secula seculorum. Amen.*

62. Item benedictio eiusdem ante altare.

Deus, qui solus habes immortalitatem lucemque habitas inaccessibilem, cuius providencia in sui dispositione non fallitur, qui fecisti ea que futura sunt et vocas ea que non sunt tamquam ea que [fol. 39v] *sunt, qui superbos equo moderamine de principatu deicis atque humiles dignanter in sublime provehis, inestimabilem misericordiam tuam supplices exoramus, ut sicut Hester reginam Israhelis causa salutis de captivitatis sue compede solutam ad regis Assueri thalamum regnique sui consortium transire fecisti, ita hanc famulam tuam N. humilitatis nostre benedictione christiane plebis gracia salutis ad dignam sublimemque regis nostri copulam regnique sui participium miseri* [fol. 40r] *corditer transire concedas, et ut in regalis federe coniugii semper manens pudica proximam virginitatis palmam continere queat, tibique Deo vivo et vero in omnibus et super omnia iugiter placere desideret, et te inspirante que tibi placita sunt toto corde perficiat. Per.*

63. In sacri olei unctionem.

Spiritus sancti gracia, humilitatis nostre officio.

64. Supra[48] est in rege ad corone impositione.

---

[48] The following text was later added in the left margin of *A*. The first four words, *Ungo te in reginam*, were written in black ink in a hand that I think is fourteenth century, but that is not the Earlier hand. The remainder was written in the Later hand in brown ink.

"*Ungo te in reginam de oleo sanctificato. In nomine Patris et Filii et Spiritu sancti. Prosit tibi hec unctio olei in honorem et confirmationem eternam.*

Postea datur sceptrum et virga et annulus."

The Later hand also added the following texts in brown ink in the right margin of *A*:

"Ante coronam datur sceptrum et virga et postea an[n]ulus.

Accipe annulum fidei signaculum sancte trinitatis, quo possis omnes hereticas pravitates devitare et barbaras gentes virtute tibi prestita ad agnitionem veritatis advocare.

Oratio.

Deus, cuius est omnis potestas et dignitas, da famule tue signo tue fidei prosperum sue dignitatis effectum, in qua tibi semper firma maneat tibique iugiter placere contendat. Per dominum."

Officio indignitatis nostre seu congregatoris in reginam benedictam. Accipe[49] *coronam regalis excellencie, que licet ab in* [fol. 40v] *dignis episcoporum tamen manibus capiti tuo imponitur, unde sicut exterius auro et gemmis redimita enites,*[50] *ita et interius auro sapientie virtutumque gemmis decorari contendas, quatinus post occasum huius seculi cum prudentibus virginibus sponso perenni*ᵃ *domino nostro Iesu Christo, digne et laudabiliter occurens, et regiam celestis aule merearis ingredi ianuam, auxiliante eodem domino nostro Iesu Christo, qui cum Deo Patre.*

64. ᵃ perhenni A.

65. Introitus ad missam.

Sicut oculi servorum.

Psalmus. *Ad te levavi o* [fol. 41r] *culos.* [51]

66. Epistola ad Ephesios.

Fratres. "Mulieres viris suis subdite sint, sicut Domino" etc.[52]

Resp. *Protector noster.*

Vers. *Domine Deus virtutum. Alleluia.*

Vers. *Domine refugium.*

67. Ewangelium secundum Mattheum.

In illo tempore. "Accesserunt ad Iesum Pharisei, temptantes et dicentes: Si licet homini dimittere uxorem" etc.[53]

68. Offertorium.

In te speravi, Domine.

69. Communio.

Domine memorabor.

70. Oratio.

Deus tuorum corona fidelium, qui quos ad regnum vocas, in misericordia et miseratione coronas, huic corone plenitudinem [fol. 41v] *tue benedictionis digneris infundere, ut per istam unctionem et nostram benedictionem sanctificetur et insigne regni habeatur. Quatinus eius impositione famulus tuus rex noster insi[g]nitus*ᵃ*, cetere plebi tue emineat, et memor desponsationis et honoris a te sibi collati, ita tibi*

---

[49] Ordo XIX,51, *A*'s source, reads "benedictam, accipe." Ordo XIV,13, MSS *D* and *E*, correctly read "benedicta, accipe." Ordo XVI,59 reads "benedicta, retine."

[50] *emicas* in *A*, but *enites* in *A*'s source, Ordo XIX,51.

[51] Ps. 122: 1.

[52] Eph. 5: 22 et seq. The opening word, *Fratres,* is not rubricated in *A*, so it looks like part of the quoted Biblical text.

[53] Mt. 19: 3 et seq. The opening words, *In illo tempore,* are not rubricated in *A*, so they look like part of the quotation.

devotus[b] *existat, ut in diebus suis iusticia et habundantia pacis oriatur, et ad ianuam paradysi de manu tua qui es rex regum coronam regni celestis percipere mereatur. Qui vivis et regnas.*[54]

70. [a] insinitus A, *but* insignitus *Ordo XIX,57;* [famu]la [tu]a [regi]na [nost]ra [insini]ta *aliter (in the Earlier hand)* A. —[b] [devo]ta *aliter (in the Earlier hand)* A.

---

[54] In *A,* "Ici finist le corunement des rois de France" is added at the bottom of fol. 41v. This is in the same hand as the title facing fol. 1r; it is different from any of the hands that made corrections to the text itself. Fol. 42r is completely filled with a double miniature depicting the replacement of both the king's and the queen's coronation crowns with lighter ones and the return to the archiepiscopal palace; this miniature appears to be slightly later than the other miniatures in the manuscript (see Bonne, "The Manuscript of the Ordo of 1250," 68–69). Fol. 42v is blank. Fol. 43r–v contains (in a sixteenth-century hand) a "Memoire de ce qui se doibt faire au coronement de la Royne de France quand elle n'est coronnée avec le Roy." It is essentially an index to certain prayers in the ceremony and is of no interest within the context of the present edition. Fol. 44r is blank.

Fol. 44v is most interesting. At the top of the page a fifteenth-century hand wrote, "L'an de grace mil quatre cens Soixante et ung le mercredi vint deux[me]. Jour de Juillet trespassa le Roy charles. Sept[me]." Below that in a fourteenth-century cursive documentary hand is the line "Anno domini millesimo CCC[mo] nonagesimo quarto et nono." Finally, there is a partially erased signiture that appeared to be the name "Charles" when examined under ultraviolet light. On the signature see Jackson, "Manuscripts," 56, n. 93.

Ordo XXII A

The Last Capetian Ordo

Date: 1250–1270

Other names: Ordo of Sens (Martène, Schreuer, Buchner)

Introduction

This present text (although not the Latin ordo) has been known since Jean du Tillet published a French translation of it in the sixteenth century (Ordo XXII C). Du Tillet and Théodore and Denis Godefroy dated it to 1179. Dom Edmond Martène published the Latin text in more or less its original form from manuscript *D*, which came from Sens, thereby furnishing the name formerly attached to it. Percy Ernst Schramm demonstrated that the text had nothing to do with Sens, and he assigned to it the new name retained here.[1] Schramm thought that the text had been composed around 1300–1320, but the date of manuscript *A* shows that the ordo must date from the latter part of the reign of St. Louis. It was, therefore, the third of the three ordines that appear to date from the reign of Louis IX (the other two are Ordines XX A and XXI).[2]

The Ordo of Reims introduced specifically French traits into the liturgy of the French coronation, but it was incomplete and could not have been used except in conjunction with a pontifical, and the succeeding Ordo of 1250 would have been quite useless as a guide to carrying out a ceremony. Therefore, the present text is the first complete ordo that is

---

[1] In *Franks, Burgundians, and Aquitanians*, E. A. R. Brown insisted on styling the ordo "the last direct Capetian ordo" because France's Valois and Bourbon kings were descended from Hugh Capet every bit as much as the direct Capetians. Strictly speaking, Brown is correct, of course, but I cannot agree with her terminology for at least three reasons. 1) Whether in English, French, or German, it is customary to speak of the kings from Hugh Capet to Charles IV as Capetian kings, and their successors as Valois or Bourbon kings. 2) The term "last Capetian ordo" is well entrenched in the literature, and there is no compelling reason to expand the terminology by creating a new (and awkward) name. 3) The present ordo is the last one that we know of that does not appear to have been devised for a specific coronation, but for the French rite in general — the succeeding ordines are all associated with particular kings; the only possible exception to this statement is the cathedral of Reims's *livre rouge*, and it is just a slightly modified version of the Ordo of Charles V (see the introduction to Ordo XXIII).

[2] For an additional argument for a date from the reign of Louis IX, see Jackson, "Manuscripts," 59.

both "French" and useable at a coronation.[3] It combines elements of earlier texts, particularly the Ratold Ordo (Ordo XV) and the Ordo of Reims, to form what was in some ways the most felicitous medieval French coronation ordo, even though its texts are not always in the correct order. Excepting only the French prayer (no. 70), every one of its formulas appears in an ordo in Vol. I. The ordo's compilers were men who knew what they were doing, and the success of their undertaking may be measured by the triumph of the ordo itself. It appears to have supplied the structure of the ceremony from the late thirteenth century (probably since the coronation of Philip III) to the coronation of John in 1350. Then, it was modified and expanded for the Ordo of Charles V in 1364; the latter appears to have been reused at the coronation of Charles VI in 1380. There is evidence that the Last Capetian Ordo was used again at the coronation of Charles VII in 1429. In 1461 the Ordo of Louis XI (Ordo XXIV) was compiled from the Last Capetian Ordo and the Ordo of Charles V. In 1484 some of the Last Capetian Ordo's essential features reappeared, via the cathedral of Reims's *livre rouge*, in the Ordo of Charles VIII (see the introduction to Ordo XXV), and they thereafter remained in the ceremony until the end of the Old Regime. Only the vastly altered circumstances of the Restoration monarchy made it necessary to depart markedly from the liturgy of this most successful of all French coronation ordines.[4]

Although manuscript *A* is the oldest surviving copy of the Last Capetian Ordo, it is a pontifical from Meaux and can hardly have been the first manuscript of the ordo, for it is unreasonable to assume that a manuscript from Meaux should have contained the original text of a rite that was to be observed at Reims. Manuscript *B*, now at the University of Illinois, is noteworthy for its historiated initials, but, unfortunately, is now missing two sections that contained larger miniatures. Each of the other medieval manuscripts has its own contribution to make to the construction of a stemma for this ordo, but, although one of them is very pretty (MS *C*), one is beautiful (MS *D*), and every one has some interesting features, none is otherwise unusually remarkable.

The lost manuscripts are interesting and particularly intriguing. They

---

[3] The ordo could be appropriately named the "first French ordo" because it is the first complete, usable ordo that incorporates the features typical of the later medieval and modern French ceremony, but I avoided assigning a new name to it for my reason 2 in n. 1 above.

[4] For details concerning the statements in this paragraph, see the introductions to Ordines XX A and XXI; Vol. I: 30–32; Jackson, "Manuscripts," 53–64; and Jackson, *Vive le roi*, 30–40 (= *Vivat rex*, 37–43).

include a manuscript (lost manuscript *1*) that appears to have contained nothing but the ordo; located in the library of the abbey of Saint-Remi in Reims, it would doubtless have given us useful information about the early history of the ordo if it had survived the fire of 1774. A manuscript known as the *livre bleu* (lost manuscript *2*), which was in the treasury of the cathedral church of Notre Dame in Reims, was the official version of the ordo and was cited or quoted several times from the sixteenth to the eighteenth centuries; it is likely to have been lost or even purposely destroyed during the Revolution.[5] Lost manuscript *3* first turns up in an inventory of the royal library made in 1373, but the manuscript was older because an inventory refers to it as "un livre ancien."[6] A copy from the royal library is likely to have been the stemma's lost manuscript x^5 because manuscript *B* was copied for a member of the royal family.[7]

The ordo was given a kind of official royal sanction in the Chambre des comptes's early register known as *Croix*.[8] Not originally part of *Croix*, which is a parchment manuscript, a paper copy of the Last Capetian Ordo (lost manuscript *4*) was sewn at the end of *Croix*. There it was able to assist royal officials as they prepared future coronations, particularly in matters relating to the costs of those coronations, and there it contributed to the composition of the British Library's manuscript Cotton Tiberius B.viii and its siblings.[9] *Croix* was destroyed by fire in 1737, as was a sixteenth-century copy of it, *Nouveaux Croix* (lost manuscript *5*).[10]

Manuscript G_1 has the distinction of having been written in the smallest script of any surviving coronation ordo, and the only way to read it is with the aid of a magnifying glass (see the full-size image, Plate 26). Manuscript G_1 is relatively late, though, and its diminutive script would not be sufficient to make it the really exciting manuscript that it is. Only

---

[5] I say "purposely destroyed" because in its attempt to eradicate vestiges of the "religion royale" the Convention did send a special commissioner to Reims to destroy the Holy Ampulla; it also broke open the royal tombs in Saint-Denis and cast away their human remains.

[6] In my study, "Les manuscrits des *ordines*," 73, n. 23, I argued that "ancien" probably meant 100 years or so; I now think that it could mean even less because so many new works were added to the royal library during the reign of Charles V.

[7] It is almost certain that x^5 was in the royal library; see n. 28 below.

[8] On these registers, see the introduction to Ordo XX B.

[9] Jackson, "Les manuscrits des *ordines*," 69–72, and Ordo XXIII, MS *A*.

[10] The eighteenth-century attempts to recover the contents of the lost *Libri memoriales* are discussed in the works cited in Ordo XX B, nn. 4, 11. See Brown, *Franks, Burgundians, and Aquitanians*, for many details concerning the copy of the ordo in *Croix*; Brown sought to recover its contents on the basis of MSS *J*, *N*, and *O*.

in collating all the manuscripts of this ordo and in comparing its different readings and variants did it become clear that G_1 was very closely related to MSS J and O, which we know to have descended from the ordo sewn at the end of *Croix*. Manuscripts J and O were copied from *Nouveau Croix*. Manuscript G_1 was copied before *Nouveau Croix* was copied, however, so G_1 was copied from *Croix* and is the only surviving manuscript copied from that ordo in an early register of the Chamber des comptes (see also the discussion of the stemma below. With G_1, therefore, we have the text (although not the manuscript) that the king's officials consulted when they prepared the coronations of their monarchs from the mid-fourteenth century on.[11]

None of the previous editions of the ordo is satisfactory. Edition a (Martène) contains many errors, including the omission of three liturgical formulas. Edition b (Gatticus) likewise contains errors, among them omitted words. Edition c (Brown) is reliable, but it is based upon three late manuscripts descended from lost manuscript *5*, itself a relatively late manuscript.[12]

Lost manuscripts

1—Reims, Bibl. de l'abbaye de Saint-Remi, MS 59, L. 8. 1285 or 1286. Destroyed by fire in the abbey in 1774. Description: Lelong, *Bibliothèque historique*, no. 25947.[13]

---

[11] The dates of the cathedral of Reims's *livre bleu* (lost manuscript *2*) and MS C, and the presumed date of *Croix*, suggest that the latter two manuscripts' source (MS x^6 in the stemma) may have been the *livre bleu*, or a copy of the *livre bleu*, but the evidence for this identification is very slender. The addition in no. 69, var. d suggests that *Croix*'s source was a manuscript from Saint-Denis. If it was, and if the ordo in *Croix* is descended from the *livre bleu*, then there was an intermediate manuscript between the *livre bleu* and the copy in *Croix*. Lost manuscripts *1* and *2* cannot be identified with any degree of certainty with any of the lost manuscripts in the stemma.

[12] On Martène's edition, see Vol. 1: 16–17; on Gatticus's edition, see n. 26 below. Brown did not attempt to edit all manuscripts of the ordo, but only those that preserved the text of lost manuscript *4*, and, without collating all manuscripts of the ordo, she could not know that MS G_1 is the only surviving manuscript copied directly from *Croix*.

[13] Jacques Lelong, *Bibliothèque historique de la France*, 2nd ed., 5 vols., ed. Fevret de Fontette and Barbeau de la Bruyère (Paris: Herissant, 1768–78), 2: 704, no. 25947:

"MS. Ordo ad consecrandum et coronandum regem Franciae, cum ritibus in eo observandis, et precibus recitari solitis: *in*-8.

Ce Manuscrit est dans la Bibliothèque de l'Abbaye de S. Remi de Reims, num. 59, L. 8. Il a environ 500 ans, et est conform à l'*Ordo VII. ex Mss. Pontif. Eccles. Senonensis*, que le Père Martenne a donné dans son Ouvrage *De ritibus antiq. Eccles. in-fol. tom. II. pag.* 622" (i.e., ed. a_2).

Synoptic Table of Ordo XXIIA*						
A E	I	B** D	H	F	C	G₁ J O
1–15	1–15	1–15	1–15	1–15	1–15	1–15
		16–20	16–20			
	21	21	21	21	21	21
22–52	22–52	22–52	22–52	22–52	22–52	22–52
					55	
53	53	53	53	53	53	53
					56	
					71–73	
					56	
54	54	54	54	54	54	54
55	55	55	55	55		55
						71–73
56–57	56–57	56–57	56–57	56–57		56–57
58		58	58	58	58	58
59–68	59–68	59–68	59–68	59–68	59–68	59–68
69	69	69	69	69		69
						70
71–73	71–73	71–73	71–73	71–73		
			74			
					56	
	75–79					

* The table provides a general survey only. In some instances a given manuscript will contain just part of a given number, and in other cases there are significant variations within a number.

** Manuscript *B* is now wanting nos. 1–11 and the first part of no. 12, as well as the last part of no. 19, nos. 21–22, and the first part of no. 23. Because it otherwise contains the same texts as *D*, and in order to restrict the table to seven columns, it is included here without indication of the missing sections. Excepting the addition of no. 74, *H* is identical to *B* and *D*.

The date of the manuscript thus works out to the second half of the thirteenth century. This accords with the precise date (1285 — the year of Philip III's coronation) given by M. de la Salle in Reims, Bibl. mun., MS 1485, no. 4, pp. 1, 3 (see n. 70 below and Ordo XXIII, n. 131).

2—Reims, Trésor de la cathèdrale, manuscript known as the *livre bleu*. Ca. 1330. See Jackson, "The *livres bleu* and *rouge*."

3—Lost manuscript from the royal library of Charles V and Charles VI. No. 227 in Léopold Delisle's inventory of manuscripts in the royal library. See Ordo XX B, n. 9, and Jackson, "Les manuscrits des *ordines*," 73–74.

4—Paris, Chambre des comptes, register (*mémorial*) ✠ (*Croix*), fols. 199ff.[14] Ca. 1350.[15] This copy was sewn at the end of the register,[16] so it had great official importance, but it disappeared in the fire in the Chambre des comptes in 1737. *J* and *O* are supposedly copies of it, but in fact they were copied from *Nouveau Croix* (lost manuscript *5*) instead. The only surviving manuscript copied directly from *Croix* is G_1.

5—Paris, Chambre des comptes, register *Nouveau Croix* (also called *Saint-Just* or *Saint-Just²*), fols. 213ff. (see n. 35 below). Description: see Ordo XX B, lost manuscript *5*.

Manuscripts

A—Paris, Bibl. nat., MS nouv. acq. lat. 1202, fols. 121r–143v. Ca. 1250–1270; this pontifical of Meaux is dated by its script, decorations, and, even more, by its miniatures.[17] Base text of this edition. Description: Leroquais, *Pontificaux*, 2: 235; Martimort, 147, no. 184; J. B. Molin, "Un pontifical de Meaux du XIIIᵉ siècle," *Bulletin de la Société d'histoire et d'art du diocèse de Meaux*, 6 (1955), 257–59. See Plate 22.

B—Urbana, University of Illinois Library, unnumbered MS entitled *Ordo ad consecrandum et coronandum regem et reginam Franciae*, fols. 1r–23v (the whole of the manuscript). Ca. 1330. This is one of only three illuminated French coronation manuscripts from the Middle Ages. In this case, the miniatures are small (about 3 cm by 3 cm) because they were painted within the framework of historiated initials. The text of this manuscript of 24 folios is incomplete—the

---

[14] We know the beginning folio number of the text in lost manuscripts *4* and *5*, but not the ending one.

[15] *Croix* was copied 1320–1330. Because the present ordo was later added to the manuscript, I have assigned an approximate date of 1350 to it.

[16] See Ordo XX B, n. 24, and Ordo XXII B, n. 3.

[17] I am grateful to François Avril for having confirmed my dating of this manuscript. There are several signatures on fols. 178r–180r. Molin, 258, stated that the oldest of them dates from 1281 or 1282, and he thought that the manuscript was copied for Jean III, bishop of Meaux from 1274 to 1288. Neither François Avril nor I believe that the miniatures could have been executed so late, however.

first six folios and the two folios that follow fol. 4v (in the present foliation) have been lost, so the text begins in no. 12, and all or parts of nos. 19–23 are missing.[18] Description: Anne D. Hedeman, "The Commemoration of Jeanne d'Evreux's Coronation in the *Ordo ad Consecrandum* at the University of Illinois," in *Essays in Medieval Studies: Proceedings of the Illinois Medieval Association* 7 (1990): 13–28. See Plate 23.

C—Vatican City, Bibl. Apos. Vat., MS Chigi C VI 182, fols. 72r–85v (new foliation stamped at bottom of page). Formerly Chisianus 468. Mid-fourteenth century. Pontifical of Cambrai or (less likely) Reims.[19] Description: Salmon, *Les manuscrits liturgiques*, 3: 23, no. 47. See Plate 24.

D—London, British Library, MS Egerton 931, fols. 183v–203r. This beautiful pontifical was probably copied for Guillaume de Melun, archbishop of Sens from 1346 to 1378. Description: *Catalogue of Additions to the Manuscripts in the British Museum in the Years MDCCCXLI–MDCCCXLV* (London: George Woodfall and Son, 1850), 1842: 104; Martimort, 203–204, no. 298, and 386–87, no. 777. See Plate 25.

E—Vatican City, Bibl. Apos. Vat., MS lat. 4733, fols. 61r–67r. Fifteenth century. Written in at least two hands, this manuscript is an incomplete copy of the Roman pontifical in the "Caeremoniale Jacobi Stefaneschi." Description: Marc Dykmans, *Le cérémonial papal de la fin du moyen âge à la Renaissance*, Bibliothèque de l'Institut historique belge de Rome 24 (Brussels and Rome: Institut historique belge de Rome, 1977), 1: 219; Salmon, *Les manuscrits liturgiques*, 3: 122, no. 413.

F—Paris, Bibl. nat., MS lat. 3968, fols. 208r–210r. Fifteenth century. The manuscript is a miscellaneous collection that consists of mostly legal commentaries. Description: none.

---

[18] Manuscript *B* was kindly brought to my attention by François Avril.

[19] A litany on fols. 166r–168v points to Cambrai more than to Reims. (I am grateful to Anne Walters Robertson for her opinion concerning this point.) There are nearly three dozen detailed, high-quality, historiated miniatures in the manuscript, all in the bottom margin. Most seem to be related to the text, but a few are not. My apparatus notes those that are on the leaves that contain the coronation ordo. The manuscript contains extensive musical notation (conventional square notes on a four-line staff), although none in the coronation ordo. In the mid-seventeenth century the manuscript was given to the cathedral chapter of Sens by "Iacobus Picolonineus [?] Arag[s]. de Castella" (note pasted on flyleaf, and fol. 1v). The manuscript was examined and described in detail for me by Reinhard Elze before I had the opportunity to go to the Vatican Library to examine it; I am most grateful to Professor Elze for his help.

G—Paris, Bibl. nat., MS fran. 14371, fols. 318r–324v. Ca. 1475.[20] The manuscript is a collection of various acts and is entitled "Protocolle de la chancellerie royale sous le règne de Charles VII."[21] It is composed of previously separate volumes, as is shown by the old foliation (fols. 1r–40r) on fols. 318r–357r. Description: Henri Omont, *Catalogue général des manuscrits français: Ancien supplément français*, 3 vols. (Paris: Ernest Leroux, 1895–96), 1: 183–84. See Plate 26.

> G_1—fols. 318r–324v. The complete ordo (nos. 1–78), except that it is wanting the litany.

> G_2—fol. 356r. The coronation oaths (nos. 6–8) only, copied in a contemporary hand different from that of the scribe who copied G_1.

H—London, British Library, MS Arundel 149, fols. 23r–30v. Late fifteenth century (after 1484).[22] Description: *Catalogue of Manuscripts in the British Museum*, New Series I, Part I: *The Arundel Manuscripts* (London: British Museum, 1834), 39.

I—Paris, Bibl. nat., MS lat. 12080, fols. 1r–10v (the entire manuscript). Formerly S. Germ. lat. 400. Ca. 1500. Description: Leroquais, *Pontificaux*, 2: 174–75, no. 150.[23]

J—Paris, Bibl. nat., MS nouv. acq. fran. 7232, fols. 7v–21v. Seventeenth century, first half. Copied from lost manuscript 5 (*Nouveau Croix*). The variants from this manuscript and from O are given because they contain the readings of lost manuscript 5, which had come to replace *Croix* after 1574. Description: see Ordo XX B, MS H.

K—Sens, Bibl. mun., MS 11, fols. 144r–155r. 1671. Copied from D. Description: Leroquais, *Pontificaux*, 2: 334–36, no. 201.

---

[20] The text of the complete coronation ordo (manuscript G_1) concludes on fol. 324v; then fifteen blank lines precede the title of the following text, "Christianissimi Francorum regis commandacio," which is on fol. 325r–v. On fol. 326r is a letter patent of Louis XI, dated 29 January 1472 in the same hand as the ordo. Two succeeding documents (fols. 326r–327r) are dated February and March 1472, so the manuscript was copied after March 1472. The manuscript otherwise appears to date from the third quarter of the century, so it was probably copied in 1472 or shortly thereafter.

[21] The fact that this particular ordo found its way into a collection of acts concerning Charles VII supports my contention that Charles VII was crowned in accordance with the Last Capetian Ordo; see Jackson, *Vive le roi*, 34–36 (= *Vivat rex*, 38–40).

[22] The *terminus a quo* is given by abstracts from the Ordo of Charles VIII, which immediately precede the Last Capetian Ordo, and which are written in the same hand. See the introduction to Ordo XXV.

[23] A printed note at the bottom of fol. 1r reads: "Ex Bibliotheca MSS. COISLINIANA, olim SEGUERIANA, quam Illust. HENRICUS DU CAMBOUT, DUX DE COISLIN, Par Franciae, Episcopus Metensis, etc. Monasterio S. Germani à Pratis legavit. An. M.DCC.XXXII."

L—Bibl. de l'Arsenal, MS 4227, fols. 6v–19r. Seventeenth century. Copied indirectly from *J*. Description: see Ordo XX B, MS *K*.

M—Paris, Bibl. de l'Assemblée nationale, MS 195, fols. 17r–27r. Eighteenth century. Copied from *L*. Description: see Ordo XVII B, MS *G*.

N—Paris, Arch. nat., KK 1442, fols. 11v–29r. Eighteenth century. Copied indirectly from *J*. Description: see Ordo XVII B, MS *I* (= Ordo XX B, MS *N*).

O—Paris, Arch. nat., P 2288, pp. 1290–1317. Eighteenth century (after 1737 because the manuscript contains an attempt to recover the lost contents of the early registers after the fire). Copied indirectly from lost manuscript *5* (*Nouveau Croix*), fol. 205 (fol. 199 is crossed out).[24] Description: see Ordo XX B, MS *O₁*.

Editions[25]

a—Martène. Three editions:

 a₁—(Rouen, 1700–1702), 3: 209–21 (Ordo VI), from *D*.

 a₂—(Antwerp, 1736–38), 2: 622–34 (Ordo VII).

 a₃—(Venice, 1763–65; reprints Venice, 1783, and Venice, 1788), 2: 223–27 (Ordo VII, but misprinted Ordo VIII).

b— Gatticus, *Acta selecta caeremonialia*, 1: 218–25, from *E* with variants from *C*.[26]

c— Brown, *Franks, Burgundians, and Aquitanians*, 102–16, from *J*, *N*, and *O*.

---

[24] Fol. 199 was the beginning folio of the text in the original *Croix*. In *Nouveau Croix* it was fol. 213, so *O*'s "fol. 205" must be either a scribal error or the beginning folio in *O*'s source (MS *x³* in the stemma).

[25] A Latin version of the ordo, based upon ed. *a₁* or *a₂* of Jean du Tillet's French translation (Ordo XXII C), was published by "Lotarius Philoponus," *Joan. Tilii actuarii in suprema Curia Parisiensi celeberrimi Commentariorum et disquisitionum de rebus Gallicis libri duo, nunc primùm Latinè redditi* (Frankfurt am Main: Apud Andream Wechelum, 1579), 104–11. From there it was published by Abraham Bzowski (=Bzovius) in his continuation of Caesar Baronius, *Annales ecclesiastici*, 14 (Cologne: Apud Antonii Boëtzeri haeredes, 1625), cols. 256–62. See Brown, *Franks, Burgundians, and Aquitanians*, 4–5.

From Bzovius the translation back into Latin was republished in the anonymous *Respublica, sive status regni Galliae diversorum autorum* (Leiden: ex officina Elzeviriana, 1626), 591–606.

[26] Gatticus modernized much of the spelling, as was customary in early-modern editions. Unlike Martène, he did not omit any formulas, but he had the irritating tendency to omit words, and many of his readings are wrong, partly because manuscript *E* is itself often ambiguous (it would be often impossible to read if one did not already know what the reading should be). By the time I had collated to the middle of the ordo

The Stemma

Despite the relatively large number of surviving manuscripts of this ordo (second only to Ordo XV), and even though no surviving medieval manuscript was copied from any other surviving manuscript, the stemma proved to be surprisingly easy to establish. Examination of the synoptic table (p. 371) and of places in the text where there are parallel columns shows that membership in the various groupings was largely determined, not by subtle differences like misspellings or use of wrong words or inversions of words (as in Ordo XV, for example), but by the addition of entire sections, whether parts of rubrics or formulas. Manuscripts A and E represent the earliest form of the ordo, and MSS B, D, H, I, and K a slightly revised version of it. Manuscripts C, F, G_1, J, L, M, N, and O belong to a second revised form that was probably produced in the first half of the fourteenth century.[27]

Because MS A can hardly have been the first manuscript of the ordo, it was copied from a lost original, MS x^1. The order of the texts in MS E is identical to that in MS A, but E was not copied from A, so E is an independent copy derived from x^1. All MSS except A and E add no. 21, so they are all descended from x^2, a lost manuscript descended from x^1. The conclusion of no. 14, no. 21, and the two long variant readings (in parallel columns) in no. 32 all show that MS x^3 is the common ancestor of MSS B, D, H, and I.

Manuscript I is, however, in some ways closer to the primitive forms of the A E group than it is to the B D H subgroup (cf. no. 1 and the conclusion of no. 9). Also, B, D, and H, but not I, add nos. 16–20 and 58, so B, D, and H share their descent from a common source. Therefore, I was copied from x^3, but B, D, and H are descended from x^4, a copy of x^3. Number 51, var. j and n. 74, and no. 58, var. a (where D omits the words "benedici sive coronari et" that are in B and H), show that B and H were copied from x^5, a copy of x^4.[28] Manuscript K was copied from D.

Working chronologically backward through the second group of manuscripts (containing the second revised form of the ordo), the late

---

I had counted some ninety erroneous readings in edition b, and I ceased to note them thereafter.

[27] Perhaps at one of the five coronations between 1315 and 1350: Louis X (3 August 1315), Philip V (9 January 1317), Charles IV (21 February 1322), Philip VI (29 May 1328), or John (26 September 1350).

[28] Because B appears to have been copied and illuminated for a member of the royal family, and because H was copied in England after the royal library had been taken to England by the Duke of Bedford (or by his executors or heirs after his death), it appears that B and H are descended from a lost manuscript in the royal library and that x^5 was lost MS 3.

MSS *J*, *L*, *M*, *N*, and *O* are clearly related. Manuscript *M* was copied from *L*. Manuscripts *L* and *N* share most variant readings, but there are enough common differences between them and *J* to prove that they were independently copied from a copy of *J*.[29] Therefore the relationship between *J*, *L*, *M*, and *N* is the same as Ordo XXB, MSS *H*, *K*, *M*, and *N*.

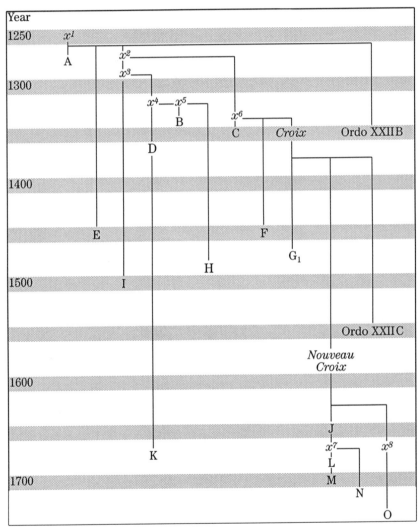

<hr>

[29] I carefully considered the possibility that *J* and *N* were copied from the same manuscript, but had to reject it because *N* shares some of *L*'s erroneus readings in places where the reading is correct in *J*. These readings are not retained in the variants.

The relationship between this ordo's MSS O (Arch. nat. P 2288) and J differs from the relationship between the two copies of Ordo XX B (MSS O_1 and O_2) in P 2288, however. Manuscript O was not copied from J, but from a copy of J's source — it had to have been a copy because J's source had been destroyed in the fire of 1737. Therefore, where their readings coincide, J and O provide independent evidence of the readings of that source, which, as in the case of Ordo XX B (MS H and ed. b), was *Nouveau Croix* (lost MS 5) rather than *Croix* (lost manuscript 4).[30]

Manuscript G_1 shares a number of the features of J and O, including the location of nos. 71–73 and the addition of no. 70, but it has to have been copied from *Croix* because it antedates *Nouveau Croix*. The text that it contains is, therefore, the closest that we can come to the text of the ordo that was sewn at the end of *Croix*.

Manuscripts C and F likewise belong to the second revision of the ordo, as is demonstrated by the title (no. 1) or the conclusion of no. 9, for example. Manuscript F, which otherwise shares most features of the manuscripts descended from *Croix*, is wanting no. 70, and nos. 71–73 are in the same location as in the $A B D E F H I$ group, showing that F was not copied from *Croix*, but from a manuscript more closely related to the original form of the ordo. Manuscript C is peculiar in many ways, and the ordering of its text seems to have been the work of the scribe who copied it. Still, C has enough readings in common with F and *Croix* (as represented by G_1) to show that the three manuscripts share a common source, here labled x^6.

As in other stemmata, a designation like x^x for a lost manuscript might stand for more than one manuscript or copies of it. We have no idea how many manuscripts have disappeared. The indicated dates of lost manuscripts on the stemma are somewhat arbitrary. In preparing the stemma, I assumed that the various revisions of the text were made at the time of coronations in Reims, so I placed the lost manuscripts at the approximate times of those ceremonies, if possible. These are Philip III in 1271 for x^2, Philip IV in 1285 for x^3, Louis X in 1315 for x^4, Philip V in 1317 for x^5, Charles IV in 1322 or Philip VI in 1328 for x^6 (I think the latter date is more likely for x^6).

Principles of the Edition

The text is from manuscript A. The scribe failed to write a number of rubrics in red ink; those instances are not noted, and the rubrication here is standardized. Despite the relatively large number of manuscripts of

---

[30] The stemma requires revision of some of Elizabeth A. R. Brown's arguments in *Franks, Burgundians, and Aquitanians.*

this ordo, none contains the original of any recension of the ordo or is authorative enough to retain its punctuation, so the punctuation has been standardized to accord with that of other ordines in this volume (usually with the punctuation of Ordo XXIII).

The letters c and t are often indistinguishable or not clear in C, E, F, and G_1. I have transcribed them to the best of my ability, but another reader might read them differently.

In many places in E the ink did not penetrate the parchment well, so the manuscript is often difficult to read. The script is a somewhat rounded, spidery, late Gothic book script that sometimes just suggests a line or curve, which contributes to its difficulty and doubtless to some of Gatticus's erroneous readings.[31] Thus, for example, the scribe did not always form the letter e well, with the result that it sometimes looks like c, and the word *eum* appears to read *cum* in several instances; in these instances I render E's readings as they appear to read rather than as they should read, doing so because, in fact, they might reflect the apparent reading of the scribe's source and provide evidence of the appearance of that source. The scribe of the ordo often wrote something that looks like the letter i at the end of a line in order to achieve something like right justification. Those instances are not noted. On the other hand, the manuscript contains many nonsensical readings, which are retained.[32]

The scribe of J usually wrote out *ae* or *oe* (e.g., *terrae, coeli*), either as two separate letters or as a diphthong (æ or œ), an orthography that is hardly to be found in late-medieval French manuscripts; these are rendered simply as *e*.[33] The other modernizations in J are retained, however.

The scribe of O sometimes wrote a single word as two (e.g., *supra dicta*) or two words as one (e.g., *inmanu*); these instances are not noted. The manuscript has little punctuation or indication of sentences or paragraphs.

Variants of c and t and of i and y are not retained, although the spelling of the base manuscript or a variant is respected (but only from the first manuscript if the variant applies to more than one manuscript).

---

[31] The script is similar to the Italian Bolognese Gothic book script illustrated by Michelle P. Brown, *A Guide to Western Historical Scripts from Antiquity to 1600* (Toronto and Buffalo: University of Toronto Press, 1990), 124–25, no. 48.

[32] Either E was very carelessly copied, or the scribe's source must have been an interim copy in what was probably a cursive script that was most difficult to read. I am inclined to the latter view, for few late-medieval scribes would have butchered their text so fiercely if they had been able to read it.

[33] In this, I follow the example set by Brown, *Franks, Burgundians, and Aquitanians*, 102.

The scribes of F, G_1, J, and O sometimes omitted the second of doubled letters (e.g., *ampula* instead of *ampulla*)[34]; these spellings are retained only if they appear in a variant for other reasons. Variants are not retained from MSS K, L, M, and N.

ORDO XXII A

A E I	D H	C F G_1 J O
1. [fol. 121r] Ordo[35] ad inungendum et coronandum regem[a] in ecclesia Remensi.	1. Incipit ordo ad consecrandum et coronandum regem in Francia[b].	1. Ordo ad inungendum et coronandum regem[c].

1. [a] Francorum *add.* E. —[b] Francie D H. —[c] Francie *add.* C.

2. Primo paratur[a] solium in[b] modum eschafaudi[c], aliquantulum eminens, contiguum exterius choro ecclesie inter utrumque chorum[d], positum in medio, in quo per gradus ascenditur et in quo possint pares regni, et aliqui[e] si necesse fuerit, cum rege[f] consistere[g]. Rex autem, die quo ad coronandum venerit, debet processionaliter recipi, tam a canonicis quam a ceteris [fol. 121v] ecclesiis conventualibus.

2. [a] in ecclesia Remensi *add.* C. —[b] ad F H. —[c] eschaphaudi E, eschaufaudi F G_1, escafaudi I, eschaffaudi O. —[d] chorum *om.* J O. —[e] alii H; et *add.* D. — [f] cum rege] cum eo C F G_1 O, cum eis J. —[g] constistere F, consistere *om.* D.

3. Sabbato[a] precedente diem dominicam in qua rex est consecrandus et coronandus[b], post completorium[c] expletum[d], committitur ecclesie custodia custodibus a rege deputatis cum propriis custodibus ecclesie, et debet rex in tempestive[e] noctis silentio venire in ecclesiam orationem facturus et ibidem in oratione aliquantulum, si voluerit[f], vigilaturus. Cum pulsatur[g] ad matutinas, debent esse parati custodes regis, introitum ecclesie observantes, qui aliis hostiis[h] ecclesie obseratis firmius[i] et munitis[j]; canonicos ac[k] clericos ecclesie debent honorifice ac diligenter[l] intromittere[m] quociescumque[n] opus fuerit eis. Matutine more [fol. 122r]

---

[34] This was doubtless a feature of lost manuscript x^6. The scribe of C must have corrected these to the normal spelling along with his many other changes.

[35] The title is preceded in J by a reference to its source: "Du mesme livre ✠ fol. ix^xx.xix. et ii^c.xiii." The references are to the original *Croix* (lost manuscript *4*) and to *Nouveau Croix* (lost manuscript *5*). Manuscript O's source is noted in the upper left corner of p. 1290: "Registre Croix fol. ~~199~~ [199 *crossed out*] 205"; "fol. 205" is incorrect and should read "fol. 213" (see also n. 24 above). The title is preceded by "Sacre et Couronnement des Rois et Reines" in a hand different from that of the ordo. In C a miniature in the bottom margin (fol. 72r) depicts the seated archbishop blessing the kneeling king, while a lay peer, accompanied by a bishop, supports his crown.

solito decantantur[o]; quibus expletis[p], pulsatur ad primam, que cantari debet in aurora diei. Post primam cantatam, debet rex,

A D E F H G$_1$ I J O	C
	indutus ad carnem camisia, et desuper tunica serica apertis profundius ante et retro in pectore, videlicet et inter scapulas aperturis tunice sibi invicem connexis ansulis argenteis, et desuper roba communi,

cum archiepiscopis et[q] episcopis et[q] baronibus et aliis quos intromittere voluerit in ecclesiam venire[r] antequam fiat aqua benedicta[s], et debent esse sedes disposite[t] circa altare hinc et inde, ubi archiepiscopi et episcopi honorifice[u] sedeant. Episcopis paribus,

A E	C D F G$_1$ H I J O
	videlicet primo Laudunensi[v], postea Belvacensi[w], deinde Lingonensi[x], postea Cathalanensi[y], ultimum vero Noviomensi[z],

cum[a] aliis episcopis istius[b] archiepiscopatus Remensis; sedentibus seorsum inter[c] altare et regem ab oppositis altaris, non longe a rege, nec multis[d] indecenter interpositis[e].

3. [a] Et sabbatho J O. —[b] et coronandus *om.* H. —[c] complectorium F G$_1$ J. —[d] expletum *om.* G$_1$ J O. —[e] intempeste F J O, in tempeste C G$_1$, intempestive I. —[f] si voluerit *om.* I. —[g] autem *add.* C F J; Cum pulsatur] Cum autem vero pulsatur E, cum compulsatur autem O. —[h] ostiis D G$_1$ H I. —[i] firmius obseratis C F G$_1$, firmius observatis J O. —[j] munitus E. —[k] et J O. —[l] ac diligenter *om.* H. —[m] honorifice intromittere ac diligenter C F G$_1$ J O. —[n] quotienscumque E, quociens G$_1$, quotiescumque I J O. —[o] decantur E. —[p] explettis F. —[q] et *om.* G$_1$. —[r] veniet E. —[s] in ecclesiam ... benedicta] in ecclesiam antequam fiat aqua benedicta venire I. —[t] deposite I. —[u] honorifice *om.* H. —[v] Laudunensis D H. —[w] Belvacensis D H. —[x] Lingonensis D, Lingonienensis H, Magonensis I, Lengonensi O. —[y] Cathalanensis D H, Castalanensis I, Catalanensi O. —[z] Ultimum vero Noviomensi] ultimo Noviomensis D H I, ultimo vero Noviomensi J. —[a] cum *om.* C. —[b] illius E; istius *om.* F G$_1$ J O; cum ... istius] aliis episcopis C. —[c] ante J. —[d] multum H. —[e] oppositis E.

A D E H I	C	F G$_1$ J O
4. Quomodo[a] sacra ampulla debeat venire[b].	4. Sciendum est autem quod rex debet de baronibus suis nobilioribus et fortioribus accipere et eos	4. Quomodo sacra ampulla debet venire. Sciendum est autem[c] quod rex debet accipere de baronibus suis nobilioribus et fortioribus et eos in

A D E H I	C	F G$_1$ J O
	in aurora diei mittere apud sanctum Remigium pro sancta ampulla. Et isti debent iurare abbati et ecclesie quod dictam sanctam ampullam bona fide ducent et reducent ad ipsam ecclesiam beati Remigii. Quo facto,	aurora diei mittere apud sanctum Remigium pro sacra^d ampulla. Et isti debent iurare abbati et ecclesie quod dictam sanctam ampullam bona fide ducent et reducent ad istam^e ecclesiam beati Remigii. Quo
Inter primam	inter primam	facto, inter primam

et terciam debent venire monachi beati Remigii [fol. 122v] processionaliter cum^f crucibus et cereis cum sacrosancta^g ampulla, quam debet abbas reverentissime^h deferre sub cortina^i serica^j quatuor perticis^k a quatuor monachis albis indutis^l sublevata^m. Rex autem debet mittere^n de baronibus qui eam secure conducant et, cum venerit^o ad ecclesiam beati Dyonisii vel usque ad maiorem ianuam ecclesie propter turbam comprimentem, debet archiepiscopus cum ceteris archiepiscopis^p et episcopis^q, baronibus necnon et canonicis, si fieri potest, occurrere sancte ampulle, et eam de manu abbatis recipere cum pollicitatione de reddendo bona fide, et sic ad altare cum magna populi^r reverentia deferre^s, abbate^t et^u aliquibus [fol. 123r] de^v monachis pariter^w comitando^x. Ceteri^y monachi^z debent expectare in ecclesia beati Dyonisii vel in^a capella beati Nicholai^b, donec omnia peracta fuerint, et^c quoad usque sacra^d ampulla^e fuerit reportata^f.

4. ^{a} Quando D, Qua hora H. —^{b} ampulla venire debeat H. —^{c} autem *om*. J O. —
^{d} sancta G$_1$ O. —^{e} ipsam G$_1$ J O. —^{f} cum *om*. I. —^{g} sancta H, sacra sancta I,
sacrasancta O. —^{h} reverendissime G$_1$ H J. —^{i} sacra *add*. E. —^{j} cerica O. —
^{k} particis E G$_1$, partitis J O. —^{l} induti E, indutis *om*. I. —^{m} Hoc fiebat antiquitus nunc vero quatuor vassali monasterii sancti Remigii deferunt quatuor
ipsas perticas *add*. I. —^{n} munere H. —^{o} Rex autem ... venerit] et cum venerint
C F G$_1$ J O. —^{p} archiepiscipis ceteris I. —^{q} et episcopis] episcopis et C F G$_1$
J O. —^{r} populi *om*. I. —^{s} defferre O; deferre *om*. E, *but add. in a blank space
in another hand*. —^{t} abbati J. —^{u} et *repeated* C. —^{v} baronibus *add*. E. —
^{w} pariter *om*. I. —^{x} cum comitantibus C, commitendo I, concomitantibus F G$_1$
J O. —^{y} vero *add*. C F G$_1$ J O. —^{z} revestiti de cappis cericeis *add*. I. —^{a} alia
add. I . —^{b} Nicholay C, Nicolay E G$_1$, Nicolai F J O; Nicholai *om*. I. —^{c} et *om*.
E. —^{d} sancta J O. —^{e} ad eos *add*. C. —^{f} deportata E; una cum monachis predictis quia suscepta ampulla agendum *add*. I.

5. Quid suscepta^a ampulla agendum sit.^{b}

Archiepiscopus[c] ad missam se preparat[d] cum dyaconibus et subdyaconibus, vestimentis insignioribus et pallio induendus[e]. In hunc modum
indutus, venit[f] processionaliter ad altare more solito; cui venienti, rex
debet[g] assurgere reverenter. Cum autem[h] venerit archiepiscopus ad
altare[i], debet pro omnibus ecclesiis sibi subditis a rege hec[j] petere.

> 5. [a] sacra *add.* F. —[b] Quid ... sit] Qua suscepta C; Quid ... sit *om.* I. —[c] dum
> cantatur tercia, facta aqua benedicta *add.* D H I. —[d] parat F. —[e] et *add.* C D F
> G₁ H J O. —[f] inductus venit F, venit indutus I. —[g] debet rex I O. —[h] autem *om.*
> H. —[i] ad altare *om.* D. —[j] hoc C E O.

A C D E F G₁ G₂ H I J O *Meurier*[36]

6. Admonitio[a] ad regem dicendo ita[b].

[fol. 123v] A[c] *vobis*[d] *perdonari*[e] *petimus, ut*[f] *unicuique*[g] *de nobis et
ecclesiis nobis*[h] *commissis canonicum privilegium ac*[i] *debitam legem
atque*[j] *iusticiam conservetis*[k] *et defensionem*[l] *exhibeatis*[m], *sicut rex in
suo regno*[n] *debet unicuique episcopo et ecclesie*[o] *sibi commisse.*

> 6. [a] Amonicio F G₁ O. —[b] dicenda ita O; ita *om.* I, dicendo ita *om.* J, Admoni-
> tio ... ita *om.* C; Admonitio ... ita] Serement du roy a son sacre. Et primo
> sequitur admonicio archiepiscopi Remensi G₂. —[c] A] Ita a I. —[d] nobis I O. —
> [e] personari E. —[f] et F J. —[g] ubiquique I. —[h] nobis *om.* G₂. —[i] et I J. —[j] ac C. —
> [k] conservet H, consuetis I. —[l] deffensionem O. —[m] exhibentis E. —[n] in regno
> suo G₂ H. —[o] episcopo et ecclesie] episcopo, ecclesie J.

7. Responsio regis ad episcopos[a].

Promitto[b] *vobis et perdono*[c], *quod*[d] *unicuique*[e] *de vobis*[f] *et*[g] *ecclesiis vobis commissis canonicum privilegium et debitam legem atque
iusticiam servabo, et defensionem*[h], *quantum potero, adiuvante
Domino, exhibebo*[i], *sicut rex in suo regno unicuique episcopo et
ecclesie sibi commisse per rectum exhibere debet.*

> 7. [a] Responsio ... episcopos] Regis responsio G₂. —[b] Promicto G₂. —[c] id est
> perfecte dono *add.* I. —[d] quia C G₁ J O. —[e] ubiquique I. —[f] nobis I. —[g] et *om.*
> *Meurier.* —[h] deffensionem O. —[i] quantum potuero (potero G₂) exhibebo
> Domino adiuvante C F G₁ G₂ J O.

8. Item[a] hec[b] dicit rex, et promittit[c] et firmat iuramento[d].

[fol. 124r] *Hec*[e] *populo christiano et*[f] *michi*[g] *subdito in Christi nomine promitto*[h]. *In primis*[i], *ut*[j] *ecclesie Dei omnis populus christianus*[k] *veram pacem vestro*[l][37] *arbitrio in*[m] *omni tempore servet*[n].

---

36 Hubert Meurier (= Hubertus Morus), *De sacris unctionibus libri tres* (Paris:
Apud Guillielmum Bichonium, 1593), 225–26, quoted the oaths (here nos. 6–8) from
the *livre bleu* (lost MS 2), so I retain the variants from his book; see Jackson, "The
livres bleu and *rouge*," 181.

37 MS D and Meurier, *De sacris unctionibus*, 226, also read *vestro*, as does the

*Item[o], ut[p] omnes rapacitates[q] et omnes iniquitates[r] omnibus gradibus[s]
interdicam. Item, ut[t] in omnibus iudiciis equitatem et[u] misericordiam
precipiam[v], ut michi[w] et vobis[x] indulgeat[y] suam misericordiam
clemens et misericors Deus[z]. Item[a], de[b] terra mea ac iuriditione[c]
michi[d] subdita universos hereticos[e] ab ecclesia denotatos pro viribus
bona fide exterminare[f] studebo. Hec omnia supradicta[g] firmo[h] iuramento.* Tunc manum apponat[i] libro[j].

8. [a] Item *om.* D H. —[b] hoc E. —[c] promictit G$_1$. —[d] Item ... iuramento] Hoc
etiam dicit rex et firmat proprio iuramento G$_2$. —[e] Hoc G$_2$. —[f] et *om.* G$_2$. —
[g] mihi I J *Meurier,* michi *corr. to* mihi O. —[h] promicto G$_1$; promitto nomine D
H, promicto in Christi nomine G$_2$. —[i] Imprimis I, In primis *om.* J. —[j] in O. —
[k] Dei et omni populo christiano H. —[l] nostro C E F G$_1$ G$_2$ J O, meo H, vero I. —
[m] in *om.* H. —[n] servabo H; servet in omni tempore E G$_2$. —[o] Item *om.* H. —
[p] Et E. —[q] capacitates E. —[r] et omnes iniquitates *om.* O. —[s] gradibus *om.* I. —
[t] Et E, quod *Meurier;* ut *om.* G$_2$. —[u] et *om.* F. —[v] preceptam O. —[w] mihi J
Meurier, michi *corr. to* mihi O. —[x] et vobis *om.* H. —[y] per *add.* H. —[z] Dominus C F G$_1$ G$_2$ J O. —[a] quod *add. Meurier.* —[b] Ee E, *leading to Gatticus's
erroneous reading,* Item è terra. —[c] iuridictione C D, iurisdictione G$_2$ H I J O
Meurier, iuridicione G$_1$. —[d] mihi I J *Meurier,* michi *corr. to* mihi O. —[e] et
add. G$_2$. —[f] exterminari J. —[g] supra dicta O *Meurier,* supradicta *om.* I. —
[h] firmat J. —[i] opponit *corr. to* apponat A, apponit J. —[j] supradicta firmo ...
libro] firmo proprio iuramento G$_2$.

A C D E F G$_1$ H I J O

9. Hiis[a] factis[b] promis [fol. 124v] sionibus, statim incipitur[c] "Te
Deum laudamus," et duo archiepiscopi vel episcopi ducunt regem per
manus ante altare, qui prosternit se ante altare usque in[d] finem[e] "Te[f]
Deum laudamus[g]." Postmodum surgit, iam antea preparatis et positis
super[h] altare corona[38] regia, gladio[i] in vagina[j] incluso, calcaribus aureis,
sceptro deaurato, et virga ad mensuram unius[k] cubiti vel amplius
habente desuper manum eburneam. Item, caligis sericis[l] et iacinctinis
intextis per totum[m] liliis aureis, et tunica eiusdem coloris et operis in
modum tunicalis[n] quo[o] induuntur subdyaconi ad missam, necnon et
socco prorsus eiusdem coloris et operis[p], qui [fol. 125r] est factus fere in
modum cappe[q] serice[r] absque caperone[s], que omnia abbas beati[t] Dyonisii in Francia de monasterio suo[u] debet Remis[v] afferre, et stans ad

---

oath that Louis XI sent to the Parlement of Paris to be registered there (Ordo XXIV, n.
21). The misreading must have been in the original version of the ordo; the scribes of
H and *I*, seeing that was wrong, then made their peculiar corrections of the error (this
part of the ordo is missing in *B*). See Jackson, "The *livres bleu* and *rouge*," 181–82.

[38] *aurea* add. after *corona* in *A*, but crossed out with a red line (the text here is
black), apparently by the scribe; cf. n. 43.

altare custodire. Tunc primo rex stans ante[w] altare deponit vestes suas preter tunicam sericam[x] et camisiam, apertas profundius[y] ante et retro, in[z] pectore videlicet et[a] inter scapulas, aperturis[b] tunice sibi invicem conexis[c] ansulis[d] argenteis[e]. Tunc[f] in primis[g] ibi a magno camerario Francie[h] regi dicte calige calciantur[i], et postmodum a duce Burgundie[j] calcaria eius pedibus astringuntur et statim tolluntur[k]. Postmodum rex[l] a solo archiepiscopo gladio accingitur, quo accincto statim

A E I	C F G_1 J O	D H
[fol. 125v] idem gladius[m] e vagina ab archiepiscopo[n] extrahitur, vagina super altare reposita[o], et datur ei[p] ab archiepiscopo in manibus cum ista oratione[q].	idem gladius discingitur[r] ab archiepiscopo et e vagina[s] extrahitur. Vagina super altare reposita; et datur ei ab archiepiscopo in manibus cum ista oratione. Oratio[t].	idem gladius discingitur et e vagina[u] ab archiepiscopo extrahitur. Vagina super altare posita, et datur ab archiepiscopo[v] in manibus cum ista oratione dicendo. Alia oratio[w].

9. [a] His J O. — [b] finitis E. — [c] incipiatur C F G_1 J O. — [d] ad J O. — [e] de add. G_1. — [f] Ee E. — [g] laudamus om. C F G_1 O. — [h] super] ante super C. — [i] gladi E. — [j] vaginam I. — [k] huius I. — [l] cerisis O. — [m] et iacinctinis (iacintinis F G_1 J, iacentinis O) per totum in textis (intextis F G_1 J O) C F G_1 J O. — [n] tunicellis E. — [o] qua I. — [p] opus E. — [q] cape E F H. — [r] cerice O. — [s] caparone C F G_1 O, caperono H, capparone J. — [t] sancti D J. — [u] beati … suo om. H. — [v] Remis om. E J. — [w] a: I. — [x] cericam O. — [y] apertas profunditus E, appertas profundius F. — [z] et I. — [a] et om. E. — [b] apperturis F. — [c] connexis F G_1 H I J O. — [d] Ensulis O. — [e] apertas profundius … argenteis om. C. — [f] Tunc] Et tunc C F G_1 J O. — [g] imprimis J. — [h] a magno camerario Francie ibi C. — [i] calceante J. — [j] Burgondie D F. — [k] astringantur et statim tollantur J. — [l] rex om. H. — [m] discingitur add. I. — [n] evagina ab archiepiscopo e vagina E. — [o] posita E. — [p] ei om. I. — [q] Hic datur gladius add. E. — [r] distinguitur G_1, distringitur J, destringitur O. — [s] evagina F G_1 O. — [t] Oratio] Oratio in datione gladii F G_1 O, gratiae in donatione gladii J. — [u] evagina D — [v] extrahitur … ab archiepiscopo om. H. — [w] Alia oratio om. H.

10. *Accipe hunc gladium cum Dei benedictione tibi collatum*[a], *in quo, per virtutem sancti Spiritus*[b] *resistere et eicere*[c] *omnes inimicos tuos valeas, et cunctos sancte Dei ecclesie*[d] *adversarios regnumque tibi commissum tutari*[e] *atque protegere castra*[f] *Dei, per auxilium invictissimi triumphatoris*[g] *domini nostri Iesu*[h] *Christi. Qui cum Patre.*[i]

10. [a] tibi colla / tibi collatum E. — [b] Spiritus sancti D F H. — [c] eiicere J O. — [d] sancte ecclesie Dei H, Dei sancte ecclesie O. — [e] tueari E. — [f] castro H. — [g] triomphatoris F O. — [h] IHESU H, Ihesu G_1. — [i] et spiritu sancto vivit et regnat Deus per omnia secula seculorum. Amen add. D H.

11. Hic cantatur ista[a] antifona[b].

Confortare[39] *et esto vir, et observa custodias*[c] *Domini Dei tui, ut ambules in viis*[d] *eius, et custodias cerimonias*[e] *eius, et precepta*[f] *eius, et testimonia*[g] *et iu* [fol. 126r] *dicia, et quocumque*[h] *te vertaris*[i] *confirmet te Deus.*[40]

11. [a] ista *om.* E I. —[b] antiphona C D F G₁ H I J O; Antiphona *add. as rubric* H. —[c] custodias observa J. —[d] vuis E. —[e] sermones H, sermonias *corr. to* sermonia O. —[f] precepta *a corr. by scribe* F. —[g] eius *add.* H. —[h] quocunque E J. —[i] verteris C G₁ H J O.

12. Dum cantatur ista[a] antifona[b], dicitur ista oratio post dationem gladii[c].

Deus qui providentia tua celestia[d] *simul*[e] *et terrena*[f]

A B C D E F G₁ H I J O

moderaris,[41] *propitiare christianissimo*[g] *regi nostro, ut omnis*[h] *hostium suorum fortitudo*[i]*, virtute gladii spiritualis frangatur*[j] *ac*[k] *te pro illo pugnante penitus conteratur. Per dominum*[l]*.*

12. [a] ista *om.* E. —[b] antiphona C D G₁ H I J O. —[c] Oratio *add.* C E. —[d] ecclesiae O. —[e] simul celestia H. —[f] terrestria H. —[g] christianissimum E. — [h] omnes O; incursus *add.* B H. —[i] fortitudoque B H. —[j] frangantur I. —[k] a: F. — [l] nostrum Iesum Christum filium tuum qui tecum vivit et regnat in unitate spiritu sancti Deus. Per omnia secula seculorum *add.* D; Sequitur *add.* E; Per dominum *om.* J.

13. Gladium[a] [42] debet rex humiliter recipere[b] de manu archiepiscopi,

---

[39] *C* has four-line staves for musical notation that was never entered. *D* gives the musical notation for the antiphon (conventional square notation on a four-line staff — see Plate 25). *E* has space for the notation, but neither staves nor notation were entered.

[40] In *D* (and *K*) the antiphon ends with *Euouae.* These letters do not form a word, but a *differentia*, a set of vowels that indicate the notes on which the last six syllables of the antiphon's concluding words, "Et in secula *seculorum* amen," are to be sung. I am grateful to Anne Walters Robertson for her help with this.

[41] Fol. 1r of manuscript *B*, the first six folios (twelve pages) of which are missing, begins with the letters *deraris* of *moderaris.* I calculated the average amount of text per page and concluded that one of the missing pages contained a miniature that occupied one-half of the page, which must explain why this part of the manuscript is missing.

[42] Many of the initials in *B* are illuminated, and nineteen of these are historiated with narrative scenes. They are all briefly described, and some were published, by Anne D. Hedeman, "The Commemoration of Jeanne d'Evreux's Coronation," 13–28. Rather than unnecessarily multiply the number of notes with a reference to each of these initials, the reader is referred to Hedeman's study.

et offerre ad altare et statim resumere de manu archiepiscopic[43] et incontinenti dare senescallod Francie, si senescallume habuerit, sinf autem, cui voluerit de baronibus ad portandum ante se etg in ecclesia usque ad finem misse, et post missam usqueh ad palatium.

13. a Hunc gladium J. —b resumere F. —c et offerre ... archiepiscopi *om.* F. — d senescalo C, seneschalo J. —e seneschalum J. —f sui O. —g et *om.* C. — h usque *om.* I.

ABDEHI	CFG₁JO
14. Huc usque de gladio. Post hec preparatur unctio [fol. 126v] in hunc modum.	14. Post hec vero prepararia debet unctio in hunc modum.

Crisma in altari ponitur super patenamb consecratam et archiepiscopus sacrosanctam ampullam, quamc abbas beatid Remigiie attulit, super altare debet aperire, et inde cum acu aureaf aliquantulum de oleo celitusg misso attrahere, et, crismati paratoh in patenai, diligentiusj immiscerek ad inungendum regem, qui solus inter universos reges terre hoc glorioso prefulget privilegio,

ACEFG₁JO	BDHI
ut oleo celitus misso singulariter inungaturl.	ut crismate mixto cum oleo celitus misso modo alio quamm ceteri reges singulariter inungaturn. Alii enimo reges inunguntur solum in humero. Iste vero in capite, et in aliis membris sicut inferius distinguetur.

14. a prepari O. —b pathenam H. —c quas C, qua I. —d sancti D B H. — e Remensis *add.* B H. —f cum acu aurea] cum aurea virgula C F G₁ J O. — g aliquantulum de oleo celitus] aliquantulum celitis E. —h peracto C, parati J O. —i pathena H. —j cum digito *add.* B C D F G₁ J O. —k inmiscere E F O; cum digito *add.* H. —l inunguatur C. —m qua I. —n inungantur H. — o reges singulariter inungatur alii enim *om.* I.

15. Parataa unctione qua rex debet inungi ab archiepiscopo, debent dissolvi ansule aperturarumb vestimentorum regis ante et retro, et, genibus regisc in terram posi [fol. 127r] tisd,

---

[43] *et offerre ... archiepiscopi et*, add. in margin in *A*; because *et* was already in the text, it is repeated in *A*. The addition is in the text in *B, C, D, E, G₁, H, I, J,* and *O,* which do not have the superfluous *et*; the passage is omitted in *F*. The addition (in black in *A*) was made by the scribe himself and is surrounded by a red triangle. It appears, therefore, that the other passages crossed out in red were crossed out by the scribe.

A E	B D H	C F G₁ J O	I
archiepiscopus debet super eumᵉ dicere has orationesᶠ antequam eum inungat.⁴⁴	duo archiepiscopi vel episcopi dicant letaniam que sequitur.	duo archiepiscopi vel episcopi incipiunt letaniamᵍ.	

15. ᵃ Peracta E J. —ᵇ aptarum E, apperturarum J. —ᶜ flexis *add.* H. —ᵈ positis *om.* H. —ᵉ super eum debet E. —ᶠ omnes *add.* E. —ᵍ litaniam J.

A C E F G₁ I J O	B D H⁴⁵
	16. [fol. 188r] *Kyrieleyson.*
	*Christeleyson*ᵃ.
	Kyrieleyson.
	Christe, audi nos.
	Sancta Maria, *ora pro nobis*ᵇ.
	[fol. 188v] *Sancte Michael*ᶜ, *ora pro nobis*ᵈ.
	Sancte Gabriel, *ora.*
	Sancte Raphael, *ora.*
	Sancte chorus angelorum, *ora.*
	Sancte Iohannes Baptista, *ora.*
	Sancte Petre, *ora.*
	Sancte Paule, *ora.*
	Sancte Andrea, *ora.*
	Sancte Iacobe, *ora.*
	*Sancte Iohannes*ᵉ, *ora.*
	Sancte Thoma, *ora.*
	Sancte Philippe, *ora.*
	Sancte Iacobe, *ora.*
	Sancte Bartholomee, *ora.*
	Sancte Matthee, *ora.*
	Sancte Symon, *ora.*
	*Sancte Thaddee*ᶠ, *ora*ᵍ.
	Sancte Mathia, *ora.*
	Sancte Barnaba, *ora.*
	Sancte chorus apostolorum, *ora.*
	[fol. 189r] *Sancte Stephane,* *ora*ʰ.

⁴⁴ See no. 21 below for the last part of this passage in other manuscripts.

⁴⁵ The entire litany is omitted in *A C E F G₁ I J O*, and the last part of it is missing from *B*. The one that follows is from *D* (which is relatively correct), with variants from *H* and the extant part of *B*.

A C E F
G$_1$ I J O

	B D H
Sancte Clemens,	*ora.*
Sancte Calixte,	*ora.*
Sancte Marcelle,	*ora.*
Sancte Laurenti,	*ora.*
Sancte Dyonisi cum sociis tuis,	*orate.*
Sancte Nichasi cum sociis suis,	*orate.*
Sancte Maurici cum sociis suis,	*orate.*[i]
Sancte Gervasi,	*ora.*
Sancte Prothasi,	*ora.*
Sancte Tymothee[j]*,*	*ora.*
Sancte Appollinaris[k]*,*	*ora.*
[fol. 3v] *Sanctus chorus martirum,*	*ora.*
Sancte Silvester,	*ora.*
Sancte Remigi,	*ora*[l]*.*
Sancte Augustine,	*ora.*
Sancte Iheromine[m]*,*	*ora.*
Sancte Ambrosi,	*ora.*
Sancte Gregori,	*ora.*
Sancte Syxte,	*ora.*
[fol. 189r] *Sancte Sinici*[n]	*ora.*
Sancte Rigoberte,	*ora.*
Sancte Martine,	*ora.*
Sancte Maurili,	*ora.*
Sancte Nicholae,	*ora*[o]*.*
Sancte chorus confessorum,	*ora.*

16. [a] Christe eleyson B. — [b] pro nobis *om.* H. — [c] Michahel B. — [d] pro nobis *om.* B H. — [e] evangelista *add.* H. — [f] Thadee B. — [g] Sancte Symon ... Thaddee, ora *om.* H. — [h] Sancte Stephane, ora *om.* H. — [i] Sancte Calixte ... Maurici ... orate] Sancte Kalixte (Calixte H), ora. Sancte Marcelle, ora. Sancte Nichasi cum sociis tuis, orate, orate pro nobis (orate, orate pro nobis *om.* H), orate. Sancte Laurenti, ora. Sancte Quintine, ora. Sancte Dyonisi cum sociis tuis, orate pro nobis (pro nobis *om.* H). Sancte Maurici cum sociis tuis, orate pro nobis (orate pro nobis *om.* H), orate B H. — [j] Thimothee H. — [k] Apollinaris B. — [l] Sancte Nicholae, ora *add.* B H. — [m] Ieromine B H. — [n] Siniti H. — [o] Sancte Nicholae, ora *om.* B H.

17. *Sancta Maria Magdalena*[a]*,*	*ora.*
Sancta Maria Egyptiaca[b]*,*	*ora.*
Sancta Felicitas,	*ora.*
Sancta Perpetua,	*ora.*
Sancta Agatha,	*ora.*

A C E F		
G₁ I J O	**B D H**	
	Sancta Agnes,	*ora.*
	Sancta Cecilia,	*ora.*
	Sancta Eutropia,	*ora.*
	Sancta Genovefa,	*ora.*
	Sancta Columba,	*ora.*
	Sancta Scolastica,	*ora.*
	Sancta Petronilla,	*ora.*
	Sancta Katherina,	*ora.*
	Sancte chorus virginum,	*ora.*
	[fol. 190r] *Omnes sancti*ᶜ,	*orate*ᵈ.

17. ᵃ Magdalene B D H. —ᵇ Egyptiacha B, Egipciaca H. —ᶜ et sancte *add.*
B H. —ᵈ pro nobis *add.* B H.

18. *Propicius esto, parce nobis Domine, ora*ᵃ.
*Propicius esto, libera nos Domine, ora*ᵃ.
*Ab insidiis dyaboli, libera nos Domine*ᵇ.
A dampnatione perpetua, libera.
*Per misterium sancte*ᶜ *incarnationis tue, libera.*
Per passionem et crucem tuam, libera.
Per graciam sancti Spiritus paracliti, libera.
*In die iudicii, libera*ᵈ.

18. ᵃ ora *om.* B H. —ᵇ nos Domine *om.* B. —ᶜ sancte *om.* H. —ᵈ nos Domine
add. H.

19. *Peccatores, te rogamus, audi nos.*
Ut pacem nobis dones, te rogamus.
*Ut misericordia et pietas*ᵃ *tua nos custodiat, te rogamus*ᵇ.
*Ut graciam sancti Spiritus cordibus nostris clementer*ᶜ
    *infundere digneris, te rogamus*ᵈ.
*Ut ecclesiam tuam regere et defendere*ᵉ *digneris, te roga-*
    mus.[46]

A C E F		
G₁ I J O	**D H**	
	Ut domnum apostolicum et omnes[47] *gradus ecclesie in*	
	sancta religione conservare digneris, te rogamus.	
	Ut regibus et principibus christianis pacem et concordiam	
	*donare digneris, te rogamus*ᶠ.	

---

[46] From this point *B* is missing two folios (four pages) between fols. 4v and 5r. The average amount of text per page indicates that one of the missing pages contained a miniature that occupied one-third of the page; see also n. 41 above.

[47] The scribe of *H* wrote *Ut omnes apostolicum omnes,* but the letters *omnes apostolicum om* were partially erased, and nothing was written in their place.

A C E F

G₁ I J O | D H

Ut hunc famulum tuum N. in regem eli [fol. 190v] gere digneris, te rogamus, audi nos^g.

Ut eum benedicere et sublimare digneris, te rogamus^f.

Ut eum ad regni fastigium perducere digneris, te rogamus^f.

Ut cunctum populum christianum precioso sanguine tuo redemptum conservare digneris, te rogamus.

Ut cunctis fidelibus defunctis requiem eternam donare digneris, te rogamus^f.

Ut nos exaudire digneris, te rogamus^f.

Fili Dei, te rogamus, audi nos.

19. ^{a} pietas et misericordia H. —^{b} rogamus om. B, audi nos add. H. —^{c} clementer om. H. —^{d} rogamus om. B. —^{e} defensare H. —^{f} audi nos add. H. — ^{g} audi nos om. H.

20. Agnus Dei qui tollis peccata mundi, parce nobis Domine.

Agnus Dei, qui tollis peccata mundi, exaudi nos Domine.

Agnus Dei, qui tollis peccata mundi, miserere nobis.

Christe, audi nos.

Kyrieleyson.

Christeleyson^a.

Kyrieleyson.

20. ^{a} Christe eleison H.

A E	D H I	C F G₁ J O
	21. Archiepiscopus debet super regem dicere^a has orationes antequam eum inunguat^b, et^c debet sedere sicut sedet quando consecrat episcopos^d.	21. Qua^e finita, archiepiscopus debet super eum dicere has orationes antequam eum inungat. Debet autem sedere sicut sedet cum^f consecrat episcopos.

21. ^{a} dicere super regem H. —^{b} inungat H I. —^{c} et om. I. —^{d} sedere ... episcopos] sedere archiepiscopus sicut sedet quando episcopos consecrat I. — ^{e} Que J. —^{f} quando F.

22. [Oratio^a.]

Te invocamus^b, sancte Pater omnipotens, eterne^c Deus, ut hunc famulum tuum N.^{d}, quem tue divine dispensationis^e providentia^f in primordio plasmatum usque in^g hunc^h presentem diem iuvenili flore letantem crescere concessisti, eum^i tue pietatis^j dono ditatum^k

plenumque gracia veritatis de die in diem coram Deo et hominibus ad
meliora semper proficere facias^l, ut^m summi^n regiminis^o solium^p
gracie superne largitate gaudens^q suscipiat, et misericordie^r tue muro
ab hostium adversitate undique munitus, plebem sibi [fol. 127v] *com-*
missam cum pace propitiationis et virtute^s victorie^t feliciter regere
mereatur. Per^u.

22. ^{a} Oratio *om.* A, *but in no other MS*; Oratio *repeated* E. —^{b} domine *add.* C
F G$_1$ J O . —^{c} sempiterne I. —^{d} H.: J. —^{e} divine dispensationis] defensionis J. —
^{f} providenta D. —^{g} ad E. —^{h} hunc *om.* F. —^{i} cum E H. —^{j} pitatis D. —^{k} dica-
tum F J O. —^{l} valeat H. —^{m} et *add.* H. —^{n} sanctum E. —^{o} regis I. —^{p} solum
O. —^{q} congaudens C. —^{r} misericordie *om.* I. —^{s} virtutibus H. —^{t} victorie *om.*
O. —^{u} Per. *om.* I; Iesum Christum dominum nostrum. Amen. *add.* H.

23. Alia^a oratio^b.

Deus, qui populis tuis virtute^c consulis et amore^d dominaris^e, da
huic^f famulo tuo spiritum sapiencie tue cum regimine discipline, ut
tibi toto^g corde devotus in regni^h regimine semper maneat ydoneus^i,
tuoque^j munere ipsius temporibus^k ecclesie^l securitas^m dirigatur, et in
tranquillitate^n devotio ecclesiastica permaneat, ut^o, in bonis
operibus

A B C D E F G$_1$ H I J O

perseverans^p,^{48} ad eternum regnum te duce valeat pervenire. Per^q.

23. ^{a} Alia *om.* E I. —^{b} Alia oratio *om.* D H. —^{c} virtuti J. —^{d} amori J. —
^{e} domineris H. —^{f} da huic] te hunc E. —^{g} toto *om.* H. —^{h} regni *om.* C E, in
regni *om.* I. —^{i} maneat ydoneus] manere ac idoneus I. —^{j} tueque E, hocque
O. —^{k} temporibus serenitas ecclesie A, *but* serenitas *crossed out in red ink*
by scribe. —^{l} ecclesie *om.* J. —^{m} securitas ecclesie C D F G$_1$ O. —^{n} transquillitate C F G$_1$, tranquilita J. —^{o} et C. —^{p} perseveres et I. —^{q} Per. *om.* I; Christum dominum nostrum. Amen. (Amen *om.* B) *add.* B H.

24. Alia oratio^a.

In diebus eius^b oriatur omnibus^c equitas et iusticia^d, amicis adiu-
torium, inimicis obstaculum, humi [fol. 128r] *libus solatium, elatis*
correctio, divitibus doctrina, pauperibus pietas, peregrinis pacifica-
tio, propriis in patria pax et securitas, unumquemque secundum
suam mensuram^e moderate^f gubernans, seipsum^g sedulus discat^h, ut
tua irrigatus^i compunctione toto^j populo tibi placita prebere vite possit
exempla^k, et per viam veritatis cum grege^l gradiens sibi subdito opes
frugales habundantur^m acquirat^n, simulque ad salutem non solum
corporum^o, set^p eciam^q cordium a te concessam^r, cuncta accipiat^s;

---

^{48} *B*, which has two missing folios, continues on fol. 5r with *perseverans*.

sicque in te^t cogitatum animi consiliumque^u omne componens^v,
plebis^w gubernacula cum pace simul et sapiencia^x semper invenire
videatur, teque auxilian [fol. 128v] *te, presentis vite prosperitatem et*
prolixitatem percipiat, et per tempora^{49} bona usque ad summam
senectutem perveniat, huiusque fragilitatis finem^y perfectum, ab
omnibus viciorum vinculis tue largitate^{50} pietatis^z liberatus^a, et infi-
nite prosperitatis premia perpetua^b angelorumque eterna commercia
consequatur. Per^c.

24. ^{a} Alia oratio *om.* I. —^{b} illis C. —^{c} oriatur in omnibus C, ciriatur omnis E. —
^{d} iudicia C. —^{e} suam mensuram *om.* G$_1$. —^{f} moderare H. —^{g} regere *add. in a*
14th century hand B. —^{h} sedulus regere discat G$_1$ J, sedutus regere discat O. —
^{i} gratia *add.* I. —^{j} toti C F G$_1$ J O. —^{k} exemplo J. —^{l} rege I. —^{m} habundanter C
E G$_1$, abundanter J, abundantes O. —^{n} adquirat B H. —^{o} corporis H; habundantur ... corporum *om.* I. —^{p} sed B C D E G$_1$ I J O. —^{q} eciam *om.* H. —^{r} concessa J O. —^{s} recipiat J. —^{t} in te *om.* G$_1$; sicque in te] sitque iuste J. —
^{u} consilium H. —^{v} omnes compunctiones I. —^{w} plebis *om.* D. —^{x} paciencia
H. —^{y} fine E. —^{z} pietatis largitate C F G$_1$ J O. —^{a} liberatis E. —^{b} perpetua premia J. —^{c} dominum nostrum Iesum Christum filium tuum qui tecum vivit et
regnat in unitate spiritus sancti Deus. Per omnia secula seculorum. *Clerus.*
Amen. *add.* D.

25. Consecratio regis.

Omnipotens sempiterne Deus, creator ac^a gubernator celi et terre,
conditor et dispositor angelorum et hominum, rex regum et dominus
dominorum^b, qui Abraham^c fidelem^d famulum tuum^e de hostibus tri-
umphare fecisti, Moysi et Iosue populo tuo^f prelatis multiplicem victo-
riam tribuisti, humilem quoque puerum^g [fol. 129r] *David regni*
fastigio sublimasti, eumque de ore leonis et de manu bestie atque
Golie, set^h et de gladio maligno Saul et omnium inimicorum eius^i
liberasti, et Salomonem sapiencie pacisque ineffabili^j munere ditasti,
respice propitius^k ad preces nostre humilitatis^l, et super hunc^m famu-
lum tuum N.^{n}, quem supplici devotione in regnum^{51} pariter eligimus,
benedictionum^o tuarum dona multiplica, eumque dextera^p tue
potentie^q semper^r ubique circundas^s. Quatinus^{t52} predicti Abrahe

---

^{49} Written *temporalia* in *A*, but the letters *lia* were crossed out by the scribe with
a red line as above, n. 38; cf. also n. 43. In addition, the three letters are underlined in a
slightly brown ink, so apparently that was done in another hand (the ink in the text is
very black).

^{50} In *A* there is an erasure the width of an interword space, and the brown-ink
hand added what looks like quotation marks around *largitate*.

^{51} *regem* written in margin in a medieval hand in *B*.

^{52} In *E* an abbreviated marginal note in a different hand reads *Quatinus*, apparently as a way of drawing attention to the beginning of a new sentence.

fidelitate[u] *firmatus, Moysi mansuetudine*[v] *fretus,*[53] *Iosue fortitudine munitus, David humilitate exaltatus, Salomonis sapiencia decoratus, tibi in omnibus complaceat, et* [fol. 129v] *per tramitem iusticie in offenso*[w] *gressu semper incedat, et totius regni ecclesiam deinceps cum plebibus sibi annexis, ita enutriat ac doceat, muniat ac*[x] *instruat, contraque*[y] *omnes visibiles et invisibiles*[z] *hostes idem*[a] *potenter regaliterque*[b] *tue virtutis regimen*[c] *administret, ut*[d] *regale solium videlicet Saxonum, Mertiorum, Nordan, Chymbrorum*[e],[54] *sceptra*[f] *non deserat, set*[g] *ad pristine fidei pacisque concordiam eorum animos, te opitulante, reformet,*[55] *ut*[h], *utrorumque horum populorum debita subiectione fultus, condigno*[i] *amore glorificatus per longum vite spacium*[j] *paterne*[k] *apicem glorie tua miseratione unatim*[l] *stabilire*[m] *et gubernare mereatur, tue quoque*[56] *protectio* [fol. 130r] *nis galea*[n] *munitus et scuto insuperabili iugiter protectus, armisque*[o] *celestibus circundatus*[p], *obtabilis*[q] *victorie*[r] *triumphum de hostibus feliciter*[s] *capiat, terroremque sue potentie*[t] *infidelibus inferat, et pacem tibi*[u] *militantibus letanter reportet*[v]; *virtutibus*[w],[57] *necnon quibus prefatos fideles tuos decorasti, multiplici honoris*[x] *benedictione*[y][58] *condecora*[z], *et in regimine regni sublimiter colloca, et oleo gracie Spiritus sancti perunge*[a].[59]

---

[53] In this case Gatticus's misreading of *C* (*fixus* instead of *fretus*) is excuseable because *C* reads *frrus*, which is obviously an impossible reading.

[54] In *E* passage is written "saxorū. in etate. normā. cymbro[rum]" (*rum* is expanded from the normal abbreviation, which I cannot reproduce in print), proving that the manuscript's scribe (or its source) displayed even less than normal understanding of the peoples' unexpected names.

[55] According to Meurier, *De sacris unctionibus,* 175, both the *livre bleu* and the *livre rouge* read "Ut regale solium Saxonum, Noriciorum, Normanorum, Danorum, et Cimbrorum sceptra non deserat, sed ad pristinae fidei pacisque concordiam corum animos te opitulante reformet," and he then drew some erroneous conclusions. According to M. de la Salle (Reims, MS 1485, no. 4, p. 2), this was a misquotation: "Mais ... on remarquera seulement que les livres bleu et rouge portent *Saxonum, Merciorum Nordan Cimbrorum* et qu'au livre rouge il est ecrit a la marge d'une main nouvelle *Normanorum Danorum,* mais qu'on ne trouve aucun MS qui rapporte cette priere comme Meurier.... Les MSS de la Bibl. du Roy et de Sens (apud Martene to. 3 p. 203 et 215) rapportent cette priere en memes termes que les MSS bleu et rouge de l'Eglise de Reims."

[56] In *E* an abbreviated marginal note in another hand looks something like *uŏ′*; I was not able to resolve the abbreviation (see also n. 62 below).

[57] A marginal note in Ordo XXIII, MS *L* (Reims 1485, no. 3, p. 19), reads, "Les Mss violete et rouge de la Cathedrale ... mettent un point avant *virtutibus*"; MSS *C* and *F* do also, but *E* and *G₁* do not.

[58] A space was left for a cross in *G₁*, but it was never inserted.

[59] *Per dominum nostrum* added in the margin in a fourteenth-century hand in *B,*

25. [a] et C E O; creator ac *om.* D B H I. —[b] dominantium E, dominancium H. —
[c] Habraham C, Abraam E. —[d] fidelem *repeated* J. —[e] tuum famulum E. —
[f] tuo *om.* C. —[g] tuum *add.* C F G_1 H J O. —[h] sed B C D E G_1 I J O. —[i] eius *om.*
C H. —[j] inefabili I. —[k] propitius *om.* I. —[l] humilitatis nostre C. —[m] et super
hunc] et semper in hunc I. —[n] H.: J . —[o] ✠ *add.* B G_1. —[p] dexterra E. —
[q] potencie tue C F G_1 J O. —[r] et *add.* C F G_1 I J O. —[s] circumda *corr. to* circunda O. —[t] quatenus J O. —[u] fidelitati J . —[v] mansuetudini J. —[w] inofenso
F. —[x] et C F G_1 J O. —[y] contra H. —[z] et invisibiles *om.* F. —[a] ita C. —[b] idem
add. C. —[c] regium H. —[d] et I. —[e] Nordam Cymbrorum B, Nordam Chimbrorum C F, Nordan Cimbrorum D, Nordam Cimbrorum H, Nordan Chimbrorum
O; Saxorum, in etate, Norman [*or* Normam], Cymbrorum E; Saxonium Mertiorum Cordancymbrorum I; Saxonum et Mertiorum, Nordamchimbro-
rumque J. —[f] dextra J . —[g] sed B C D E G_1 I J O. —[h] ut *om.* D. —[i] et condigno
F, et cum digno C G_1 I J O. —[j] spacia H. —[k] paterne] per active E. —[l] una cum
I, unatin O; unatim *om.* J . —[m] stabiliri H J; unatim stabilire] una cum
stabilitate E. —[n] galea *om.* I. —[o] eternisque E, animisque J. —[p] circumdatus O. —[q] optabilis B C D F G_1 H J O, optabilem I. —[r] victorie *om.* I. —
[s] fidelis H. —[t] potentie tue I. —[u] tibi *om.* C F G_1 J O. —[v] reportet] te portet E. —
[w] virtutibus *om.* J. —[x] honoris *om.* I. —[y] ✠ *add.* B. —[z] cumdecora C, eum
decora I. —[a] Qui vivis *add.* C.

26. Hic inungatur[a] untione[b] crismatis et olei de celo missi prius ab
archiepiscopo confecti in patena[c], sicut superius dictum est[d]. Inungat
autem archiepiscopus eum[e] primo in[f] summitate capitis de dicta[g]
unctione, secundo[h] in pectore, tercio inter[i] [fol. 130v] scapulas, quarto in
ipsis[j] scapulis, quinto in campagibus[k] brachiorum, et dicat cuilibet
inunctioni[l].

26. [a] ungatur B H. —[b] unctione B C D H I, inunctione F G_1 J O. —[c] pathena B. —
[d] est *om.* J. —[e] eum *om.* H. —[f] in *om.* O. —[g] sancta C. —[h] Secondo C. —[i] tertio
in I. —[j] ipsis *om.* I. —[k] compage C F G_1 J O, copagibus E. —[l] unctioni D B H,
unctione I; cuilibet inunctioni] dans unctio. unctio E.

27. Ungo[a] te in regem de oleo sanctificato[b]. In nomine Patris[c] et
Filii[c] et Spiritus sancti[d],
et[e] dicant omnes "Amen[f]." Dum hec[g] unctio agitur cantant[h] assistentes[i]
hanc antifonam[j].

27. [a] Unguo D. —[b] sanctissimo H; ✠ *add.* G_1 I. —[c] ✠ *add.* B F G_1 I. —[d] ✠ *add.*
B F; Amen *add.* E I. —[e] et *om.* C F G_1 J O. —[f] Amen *om.* I. —[g] hec *om.* I. —
[h] cantent C G_1 J. —[i] assistantes O. —[j] Antiphona *add. as rubric* C; et Spiritus
sancti et dicant ... antifonam] et Spiritus sancti. Amen. Et dicant omnes
Amen. Finita unctione cantatur antiphona E.

which also adds in the bottom margin: *Qui virtute cruxis tartara destruxit, regnoque*
diaboli superato ad celos victor ascendit. In quo potestas omnis regnumque consis-
tit et victoria. Qui est gloria humilium et vita salusque populorum. Qui tecum etc.

28. *Uncxerunt*[a] *Salomonem Sadoch*[b] *sacerdos et Nathan*[c] *propheta regem in Gyon*[d], *et accedentes*[e] *leti dixerunt, "Vivat rex in eternum."*[60]

28. [a] Unxerunt C F G₁, Dixerunt E, Uncti sunt J, Unctionem O. —[b] Sadohc E F. —[c] Natham H. —[d] Gyin J. —[e] accedens E, accendentes O.

29. Facta unctione[a], cantata antifona[b], dicat archiepiscopus hanc orationem[c].

Christe, perunge hunc regem in regimen[d], *unde unxisti sacerdotes, reges ac*[e] *prophetas et*[f] *martires, qui per fidem vicerunt*[g] *regna, operati*[h] *sunt iusticiam atque adepti sunt promissiones*[i]. *Tua sacratissima*[j] *unctio super* [fol. 131r] *capud*[k] *eius defluat atque ad*[l] *interiora descendat, et cordis illius*[m] *intima penetret*[n], *et promissionibus quas adepti sunt victoriosissimi reges, gracia tua dignus efficiatur, quatinus et*[o] *in presenti seculo*[p] *feliciter regnet et ad eorum consortium in celesti regno perveniat*[q]. *Per dominum nostrum Iesum*[r] *Christum filium tuum, qui unctus est*[s] *oleo leticie*[t] *pre consortibus suis, et virtute crucis potestates*[u] *aerias*[v] *debellavit, tartara*[w] *destruxit, regnumque*[x] *dyaboli superavit, et ad celos victor ascendit. In cuius manu victoria*[y] *omnis*[z] *gloria et potestas consistunt, et tecum vivit et regnat Deus*[a] *in unitate*[b] *Spiritus sancti Deus. Per omnia secula seculorum*[c].

29. [a] et *add.* B C F G₁ H J O. —[b] antiphona B C D F H G₁ I J O; Facta ... antifona] Finita antiphona' E. —[c] Oratio *add. as rubric* C E G₁ O. —[d] regimmem E, regem J. —[e] et I; ac *om.* C. —[f] ac C G₁ O. —[g] vinxerunt C, vixerunt F J. —[h] optati J. —[i] repromissiones B D H I, missiones J. —[j] sanctissima J. —[k] caput B C D F G₁ I J O. —[l] ad *om.* H. —[m] allius O. —[n] intima penetret] pene / netret G₁. —[o] quatinus et] quatenus J O. —[p] seculo *om.* I. —[q] proveniat L. —[r] Ihesum G₁. —[s] de *add.* J O. —[t] leticie *om.* C. —[u] potentialiter J. —[v] aereas C F G₁ H I O, aacies E, areas J. —[w] tantam H. —[x] regimenque O. —[y] manu victoria] victoria et manu C F G₁ J O. —[z] eius J O. —[a] Deus *om.* B C D F G₁ H J O. —[b] in uninitate E. —[c] Amen *add.* B C E F G₁ I O.

30. Alia[a] oratio[b].

Deus[c] *electorum fortitudo et humi* [fol. 131v] *lium celsitudo, qui in primordio per effusionem*[d] *diluvii mundi crimina castigare voluisti et per columbam ramum olive portantem pacem terris redditam demonstrasti. Iterumque*[e] *Aaron famulum tuum per unctionem olei sacerdotem*[f] *sanxisti, et postea per huius unguenti infusionem ad regendum populum Israeliticum*[g] *sacerdotes, reges ac*[h] *prophetas perfecisti, vultumque*[i] *ecclesie*[j] *in oleo exhilarandum*[k] *per propheticam*

---

[60] *B* gives the musical notation for this antiphon, as does *C* (conventional square notation on a four-line staff in both cases). *E* leaves space for the notation, but neither staves nor notation were added.

famuli tui vocem David esse predixisti; ita quesumus, omnipotens Pater[l], *ut per huius*[m] *creature*[n] *pinguedinem, hunc servum tuum*[o] *sanctificare*[p] *tua benedictione*[q] *digneris, eumque in*[r] *similitudine columbe pacem simplicitatis*[s] *populo sibi*[t] *commisso presta-* [fol. 132r] *re*[u]*, et exempla Aaron*[v] *in Dei servitio diligenter imitari, regnique fastigia in consiliis scientie et equitate iudicii semper assequi, vultumque hylaritatis*[w] *per hanc olei unctionem*[x] *tuamque benedictionem*[y]*, te*[z] *adiuvante, toti plebi paratum*[a] *habere facias. Per dominum nostrum*[b]*.*

30. [a] alia *om.* B H. —[b] Alia oratio *om.* J. —[c] qui *add.* I. —[d] infusionem B D E H I, *but corr. in a medieval hand to* effusionem *in* B. —[e] iterum D H. —[f] iterumque Aaron ... sacerdotem] Iterum Aaron famulum tuum sacerdotem (sacerdotem Aaron famulum tuum F G$_1$) per unctionem olei sacerdotem C F G$_1$, iterum sacerdotem J O. —[g] Israheliticum B, Ysraheliticum G$_1$. —[h] et F J. —[i] vultum H, introitumque J. —[j] ecclesie] et elesit E, *corr. in another hand to (apparently)* ecclesie. —[k] exhilarendum O. —[l] omnipotens Deus Pater C F G$_1$ J O. —[m] eius O. —[n] cantare I. —[o] ✠ *later add. in space left for it* H. —[p] ✠ *add.* B. —[q] ✠ *add.* D F G$_1$. —[r] in *om.* I. —[s] simplicitas I. —[t] suo J O. —[u] perstare E, pretare L. —[v] antem E. —[w] hylaritas C, hillaritatis F H. —[x] inunctionem O. —[y] ✠ *add.* F G$_1$. —[z] et D. —[a] toto plebi peractum I. —[b] Iesum Christum filium tuum *add.* D.

31. Alia oratio[a].

Deus Dei filius, dominus noster Iesus[b] *Christus, qui a Patre oleo exultationis unctus est pre participibus suis, ipse per*[c] *presentem sacri*[d] *unguinis*[e] *infusionem*[f] *Spiritus paracliti super capud*[g] *tuum infundat benedictionem*[h] *eandemque*[i] *usque ad interiora cordis tui penetrare*[j] *faciat, quatinus*[k] *hoc*[l] *visibili et tractabili dono, invisibilia percipere, et temporali*[m] *regno iustis* [fol. 132v] *moderaminibus*[n] *executo*[o]*, eternaliter cum eo regnare merearis. Per*[p]*.*

31. [a] Alia oratio *om.* I. —[b] Ihesus G$_1$ O, IHESUS H. —[c] per *om.* C. —[d] sacre J. —[e] unguentis E, unctionis H J, unguenti I. —[f] effusionem J. —[g] caput B D E H I, corpus C F G$_1$ J O. —[h] ✠ *add.* B F G$_1$ H. —[i] eamdemque J. —[j] penare D. —[k] quatenus D B H J O. —[l] hec E. —[m] corporali E. —[n] iustis moderamibus E, moderationibus iustis J, iustis moderationibus O. —[o] exequuto I. —[p] dominum nostrum Iesum Christum filium tuum *add.* D; eumdem dominum nostrum Iesum Christum *add.* E; Per] qui vivit et regnat B, qui vivit et regnat Deus per omnia secula seculorum. Amen. H; dominum *add.* I; etc. *add.* O; Per *om.* J.

32. Hiis[a] dictis orationibus, connectuntur

A E	B D H I	C F G$_1$ J O
ansule^b aperturarum^c vestimenti^d regis propter inunctionem,	ab archiepiscopo vel sacerdotibus vel saltem^e dyachonibus^f propter mundiciam consecrationis ansule aperturarum vestimentorum^g regis propter inunctionem,	ansule aperturarum vestimenti regis ab archiepiscopo vel sacerdotibus vel dyaconibus propter inunctionem,

et tunc a camerario Francie induitur tunica iacinctina^h, et^i desuper socco^j, ita quod^k dextram manum habet^l liberam^m in apertura^n soccio^o, et super sinistram soccum^p elevatum^q sicut elevatur casula sacerdoti^r. Deinde datur ei^s ab archiepiscopo

<table>
<tr><td align="center">A E F G$_1$ J O</td><td>B C D H I^{61}</td></tr>
<tr><td>sceptrum in manu dextra^t et virga in sinistra, et in datione sceptri et virge, dicuntur iste^u orationes. Set^v notandum^w quod^x antequam dentur sceptrum et virga, datur^y</td><td></td></tr>
</table>

A B C D E F G$_1$ H I J O

anulus^z, et in datione anuli^a dicitur hec oratio^b.

32. ^{a} His I, Post his J — ^{b} connectuntur ansule] convercuntur ansules E. — ^{c} aperte I. — ^{d} vestimentorum B H. — ^{e} satem I. — ^{f} dyaconum D, diaconibus H I. — ^{g} vestimenti D, aperte vestimenti I. — ^{h} iacintina D E G$_1$ I, hyacintina J, iacentina O. — ^{i} et *om.* B H. — ^{j} sacco E. — ^{k} itaque C E. — ^{l} dexteram manum habet B C E F, dexteram manum habeat G$_1$ H J O. — ^{m} et *add.* E. — ^{n} appertura F I. — ^{o} sccci E. — ^{p} sacum E. — ^{q} elevatum *om.* H. — ^{r} sacerdoci F, sacerdotis G$_1$. — ^{s} ei *om.* I. — ^{t} dextera E F G$_1$ J. — ^{u} hec J. — ^{v} Sed E F G$_1$ J O. — ^{w} est *add.* F. — ^{x} quod *om.* E. — ^{y} detur E. — ^{z} annulus J. — ^{a} anulli I, annuli J. — ^{b} Oratio *add. as rubric* C; Hic datur anulus et dicitur *add.* F; Hic detur anulus (annulus J) et dicatur hanc oracionem (hanc oracionem *om.* J O) *add.* G$_1$ J O.

33. *Accipe anulum^a, signaculum vide* [fol. 132v] *licet^b fidei sancte, soliditatem regni, augmentum potentie, per que^c scias triumphali^d potentia hostes repellere^e, hereses^f destruere, subditos* ^{62} *coadunare^g et^h catholice fidei perseverabilitati connecti^i.*

---

^{61} The concordance of *C* with *B*, *D*, *H*, and *I* in this instance appears to be entirely fortuitous and in no way affects *C*'s place in the stemma (p. 377), for *C* cannot otherwise be grouped with *B*, *D*, *H*, and *I*. Manuscript *C* revised the rubrics in several places in order to render them more sensible than in earlier manuscripts of the ordo, and here *C*, like the stemma's lost MS *x^9*, simply omits a passage that was out of order in the earliest form of the ordo.

^{62} As in no. 25, something like $\hat{u}$/ was added in the margin of *E* in a different hand, perhaps at *subditos*; see n. 56 above.

33. ᵃ annulum J. —ᵇ videlicet *om.* H. —ᶜ quem B H.—ᵈ triumphari H. —
ᵉ replere I. —ᶠ herises H. —ᵍ coadiunare J. —ʰ ecclesie *add.* F. —ⁱ perseverabilitati connecti] perseverabilitate connecti G_1, per severitatem connectere I,
perseverare utilitate connecti J, perseverare veritate connecti O.

34. Oratio post annulumᵃ.

Deus, cuius est omnis potestas et dignitas, da famulo tuo prosperum
sue dignitatis effectum, in qua, te remunerante, permaneat semperque
*timeat*ᵇ *tibique iugiter placere contendat. Per dominum*ᶜ.

34. ᵃ anulum C F G_1 O; Oratio ...annulum] Post dationem anuli. Oratio B, Post
dacionem anuli. Oracio H. —ᵇ te timeat B H. —ᶜ nostrum Iesum Christum
filium tuum *add.* D.

35. Dato anuloᵃ, statim postᵇ deturᶜ sceptrumᵈ, et dicatur hec
oratioᵉ.

*Accipe sceptrum regie*ᶠ *potestatis insigne, virgam scilicet regni rec-*
*tam*ᵍ, *virgam virtutis qua te ipsum bene*[63] *regas*ʰ, *sanc* [fol. 133v] *tam*
*ecclesiam populumque videlicet*ⁱ *christianum tibi a Deo commissum*
*regia virtute ab improbis defendas*ʲ, *pravos corrigas, rectos pacifices,*
*et*ᵏ, *ut viam rectam*ˡ *tenere possint*ᵐ *tuo iuvamine*ⁿ *dirigas, quatinus*ᵒ
*de temporali regno ad eternum regnum*ᵖ *pervenias. Ipso adiuvante*
cuius regnum et imperiumۚq *sine fine*ʳ *permanet*ˢ *in secula seculorum*ᵗ.

35. ᵃ anullo I, annulo J O. —ᵇ post *om.* E. —ᶜ ei *add.* H. —ᵈ in manu dextra
(dextera C F G_1 H J O) *add.* B C F G_1 H I J O. —ᵉ oratio *om.* E; que sequitur
add. G_1; Oratio *add. as rubric* C E. —ᶠ regis E. —ᵍ recta E; virgam ... rectam
om. H. —ʰ regis J. —ⁱ videlicet *om.* E. —ʲ deffendas H I O. —ᵏ et *om.* I. —ˡ rectam
viam H. —ᵐ possent O. —ⁿ munimine E. —ᵒ quatenus J O. —ᵖ regnum *om.* I. —
ۚq manet *add., then expuncted* F. —ʳ sine fine *om.* H. —ˢ permaneat B D H. —
ᵗ Amen. *add.* B E H.

36. Oratio post sceptrumᵃ datumᵇ.

*Omnium, Domine, fons bonorum cunctorumque*ᶜ *Deus institutor*ᵈ
*profectuum*ᵉ,[64] *tribue, quesumus, famulo tuo N.*ᶠ *adeptam bene regere*
*dignitatem, et a te sibi prestitum honorem*ᵍ *dignare corroborare*ʰ; *hono-*
*rifica*ⁱ *eum*ʲ *pre cunctis regibus terre; uberi eum*ᵏ *benedictione*ˡ [fol.
134r] *locupleta*ᵐ, *et in solio regni firma stabilitate consolida. Visita*
*eum*ⁿ *in sobole, presta ei prolixitatem*ᵒ *vite, in diebus eius semper*

---

[63] As in nos. 25 and 33, an abbreviation that looks something like *uō* was added in
the margin of *E* in a different hand at the line beginning *bene regas*; see also nn. 56 and
62 above.

[64] In *E* the passage is written something like *cunctoru₃ deus institor profectun₃*,
and there is a marginal correction *tii*) at *profectun₃*. The only way that I can make
sense of it is to read the original text as *cunctorumque Deus instuitor profectunque*,
in which case the correction changes *profectunque* to *profectum*.

oriatur iusticia[p], *ut*[q] *cum iocunditate*[r] *et leticia eterno*[s] *glorietur in regno. Per.*

36. [a] ceptrum C. — [b] Oratio ... datum *om.* I. — [c] cunctorum B C F G₁ H J O, cunctorumque *or* cunctorum E. — [d] institor *corr. by scribe to* institutor E. — [e] profectum O. — [f] H.: J. — [g] honorifice D. — [h] roborare D B H, corrobore O; corroborare *om.* I; dignitate coroborare E. — [i] honorificata E, honorofica O. — [j] cum E; cum I, *followed by a blank space about the length of* cunctis. — [k] terre uberi eum] terre tueri eum E, terre uberiori eum H, terram uberem J, uberi cum O. — [l] ℞ *add.* B. — [m] locupletta F. — [n] eum *om.* E. — [o] probitatem *corr. in marg. to* prolixitatem E. — [p] semper oriatur iustitia] semper oriatur E, *with corr. in marg. in another hand to* pax semper oriatur. — [q] et B E H I. — [r] iucunditate O. — [s] eterne J O.

37. Post statim datur ei[a] virga[b], et dicitur[c].

Accipe virgam virtutis atque equitatis, qua intelligas[65] *mulcere pios et terrere*[d] *reprobos, errantibus viam doce*[66] *lapsisque*[e] *manum porrige, disperdasque*[f] *superbos et*[g] *releves humiles, ut aperiat tibi hostium*[h] *Iesus Christus*[i] *dominus noster*[j]*, qui de se ipso ait, 'Ego sum hostium*[k]*; per me si quis introierit salvabitur;' et ipse, qui est*[l] *clavis David et sceptrum*[m] *domus Israel*[n]*, 'qui aperit, et* [fol. 134v] *nemo claudit, claudit, et nemo aperit'*[o]*; sit tibi adiutor, qui eduxit 'vinctum de domo carceris, sedentem in tenebris*[p] *et*[q] *umbra mortis,' ut in omnibus sequi*[r] *merearis eum*[s]*, de quo propheta David cecinit*[t]*, 'Sedes tua, Deus, in seculum seculi; virga equitatis*[u] *virga regni tui.' Et imiteris eum qui dicit, 'Diligas iusticiam et odio habeas*[v] *iniquitatem; propterea unxit te Deus, Deus*[w] *tuus*[x]*, oleo leticie,' ad exemplum illius*[y] *quem ante secula unxerat*[z] *'pre*[a] *participibus suis,' Iesum Christum dominum nostrum*[b]*.*

37. [a] et I. — [b] in manu sinistra *add.* B C D F H I J O. — [c] dicitur] dicatur hec oratio. Oratio C, dicatur. Oratio H; virga dicitur] virga in manu sinistra et dicatur hanc oracionem G₁. — [d] tenere E. — [e] orantes viam doce lapsis J. — [f] dispergasque F. — [g] et *om.* O. — [h] ostium B D G₁ H I J O. — [i] Christus Iesus B, Ihesus Christus G₁, Christus IHESUS H, IESUS Christus J, Ihesus Christus O. — [j] Iesus Christus dominus noster] Deus Iesus noster I. — [k] ostium D B G₁ H I J O. — [l] est qui E. — [m] septrum O. — [n] Israhel B. — [o] et nemo claudit ... aperit] et nemo claudit et nemo I, et claudit, claudit et nemo aperit J, et nemo claudit et nemo aperit O. — [p] in tenebris [*fol. 65r*] et in tenebris E. — [q] et in

---

[65] The letter *t* by itself at the end of the line expuncted in *A*.

[66] Manuscript *E* is difficult here. Gatticus thought there was a lacuna in the manuscript (his note reads, "Lacunam Codicis implevimus ex editis"), and he incorrectly edited "(*errantibus docere*) *viam vitae*." *E* looks something like *cia'dē / tibus viam doce* at a line break, so it should be something like *cia_den / tibus viam doce* (although the first word could read *erante / tibus*).

H. —^{r} sequi] si quidem J, si qui O. —^{s} cum E O. —^{t} propheta David cecinit]
propheta cecinit dicens H. —^{u} virga equitatis *add. in marg. in what appears*
to be another contemporary hand O. —^{v} habebis E. —^{w} Deus *om.* H. —^{x} tuus
om. G$_1$ O, Deus tuus *om.* C I J. —^{y} illius *om.* G$_1$. —^{z} miserat J. —^{a} pro O. —
^{b} dominum nostrum Iesum Christum E, Ihesum Christum dominum nostrum
etc. O.

38. Post istam orationem convocantur pares ex nomine^a a^b cancel-
lario^c, si presens est, sin autem ab archiepiscopo.

A E	B D H	C F G$_1$ J O	I
	et vocantur	Primo laici,	Et vocantur primo laici duces:
	primo layci,	postea^f clerici	Primo dux Normanie, dux
	postea clerici,		Acquitanie, dux Burgundie.
	et clerici^d		Comites: Comes Campanie
	vocantur eo		palatinus, comes Remensis
	ordine quo		palatinus, comes Flandrie.
	dictum est		Postea vocantur clerici: Primo
	superius de		archiepiscopus Remensis,
	sedendo^e.		postea episcopus Laudunensis,
			Episcopus Belvacensis, Lingo-
			nensis, Cathalanensis,
			Noviomensis.

Quibus vocatis et circumstantibus^g, archi [fol. 135r] episcopus accipit de
altari coronam regiam, et solus imponit eam capiti regis, qua imposita,
omnes pares, tam^h clerici^i quam laici^j, manum apponunt^k corone et^l eam
undique sustentant^m, et soli pares; tunc archiepiscopus dicit istam^n ora-
tionem^o.

38. ^{a} ex nomine] nomine suo C F G$_1$ J L O. —^{b} et O. —^{c} suo *add.* C F G$_1$ I J O. —
^{d} et clerici *om.* H. —^{e} sendendo H. —^{f} secundo J. —^{g} circunstantibus B E G$_1$
J, circonstantibus F. —^{h} cum E. —^{i} quibus vocatis ... omnes pares tam clerici
repeated O. —^{j} tam laici quam clerici J. —^{k} apponant E O. —^{l} et *om.* E. —
^{m} sustentent E. —^{n} hanc B E H. —^{o} Oratio *add. as rubric* C F G$_1$ O.

39. *Coronet te Deus corona glorie atque iusticie, honore et^a opere*
fortitudinis, ut per officium nostre benedictionis^b^{67} cum fide recta^c et
multiplici bonorum operum fructu ad coronam pervenias^d regni per-
petui. Ipso largiente cuius regnum et imperium^e permanet in secula
seculorum^f.

39. ^{a} honore et] honoret E. —^{b} ✠ *add.* B H. —^{c} certa E. —^{d} perveniat E J. —
^{e} sine fine *add.* C. —^{f} Amen *add.* E.

---

^{67} A space was left for a cross in *G$_1$*, but it was never written.

40. Oratio post coronam[a].

Deus perpetuitatis, dux virtutum, cunctorum hostium victor, bene-
[fol. 135v] *dic[b] hunc famulum tuum tibi capud[c] suum inclinantem, et prolixa[d] sanitate[e] et prospera felicitate eum conserva, et ubicumque, pro quibus tuum auxilium[f] invocaverit[g], cito assis[h] et[i] protegas ac[j] defendas; tribue ei[k], quesumus Domine, divicias glorie tue, comple in bonis desiderium eius, corona eum in[l] miseratione et misericordia, tibique[m], Deo, pia devotione iugiter famuletur. Per dominum.*

40. [a] Oratio post coronam *om.* I. —[b] ✠ *add.* B D F G₁ H. —[c] caput B C D E G₁ H I J O. —[d] pro leta E, prolixi I. —[e] prolixa sanctitate C, prolixat sanctitate O. —[f] auxilium tuum C F G₁ J O. —[g] provocavit *corr. to* vocavit B, vocaverit H. —[h] adsis B J O. —[i] cito assis et *om.* I. —[j] et E. —[k] deffendas tribue et O. — [l] in *om.* J. —[m] ubique E.

41. Statim post istam orationem dicatur ista benedictio[a].

Extendat[b] omnipotens Deus dexteram sue benedictionis[c], et circundet[d] te muro felicitatis[e], ac custodia sue protectionis sancte Marie ac beati[f] Petri, apostolorum principis, sanctique Dyonisii[g], atque[h] omnium sanctorum intercedentibus[i] meritis[j]. Amen[k].

41. [a] Benedictio *add. as rubric* C. —[b] Concedat E. —[c] ✠ *add.* B D G₁ H. — [d] circondit F, circumdet O. —[e] felicitas O. —[f] beata O. —[g] sancti Dionisii I. — [h] beati Remigii et *add.* B D H. —[i] interdentibus E, intercedentibus *om.* I. — [j] Resp. *add.* C. —[k] Alia benedictio *add.* F, Alia oracio *add.* G₁.

42. Indulgeat tibi [fol. 136r] *Dominus omnia peccata que gessisti[a], et tribuat[b] tibi[c] graciam et misericordiam quam[d] humiliter ab eo[e] deposcis, et liberet te[f] ab adversitatibus cunctis et ab omnibus inimicorum[g] visibilium et invisibilium[h] insidiis[i]. Amen[j].*

42. [a] fecisti E. —[b] tribuat *repeated* O. —[c] tibi *om.* B D H. —[d] qua I. —[e] ab eo humiliter B D H, ab eo similiter J. —[f] te *om.* I. —[g] omnium *add.* C F G₁ J O. — [h] invisibilium *om.* I. —[i] Clerus *add. as rubric* D. —[j] Alia benedictio *add.* F, Alia oracio *add.* G₁.

43. Angelos suos bonos, *qui te semper[a] et ubique precedant[b], comitentur et subsequantur[c], ad custodiam tui ponat et[d] a peccato seu[e] gladio[f] et ab[g] omnium[h] periculorum discrimine sua potentia liberet[i]. Amen[j].*

43. [a] sempeii E. —[b] praecedunt *corr. by scribe to* praecedant J. —[c] comittentur et subsequentur B, comitantur et subsequentur C, comitentur et subsequentur D H, comitantur et subsequantur G₁ J O, committantur et subsequentur I. —[d] te *add.* B H. —[e] sive C F G₁ O. —[f] seu gladio *om.* J. —[g] ab *om.* I. —[h] se gladio et ab omni E. —[i] Clerus *add. as rubric* D. —[j] Alia benedictio *add.* F, Alia oracio *add.* G₁.

44. *Inimicos*[a] *tuos ad pacis caritatisque*[b] *benignitatem*[c] *convertat, et bonis omnibus*[d] *te graciosum et amabilem faciat, pertinaces quoque in tui insectatione*[e] *et odio*[f] *confusione salutari induat, super te autem*[g] *participatio et sanctificatio*[h] *sempiterna flo* [fol. 136v] *reat*[i]. *Amen*[j].

44. [a] Rimicos H. —[b] charitatisque I O. —[c] benignitatemque E. —[d] operibus B C D E H I. —[e] inseoratione F, miseracione G_1 J O, sectatione I. —[f] hodio E. — [g] ante O. —[h] ✠ *add.* B D H. —[i] Clerus *add. as rubric* D. —[j] Alia benedictio *add.* F, Alia oracio *add.* G_1.

45. *Victoriosum te atque triumphatorem*[a] *de*[b] *invisibilibus atque visibilibus*[c] *hostibus semper efficiat, et sancti nominis sui*[d] *timorem pariter et amorem*[e] *continuum cordi tuo*[f] *infundat, et*[g] *in fide recta ac bonis operibus*[h] *perseverabilem reddat, et pace in*[i] *diebus tuis concessa, cum palma victorie te ad perpetuum regnum perducat*[j]. *Amen*[k].

45. [a] triumphantem J. —[b] de *om.* H. —[c] visibilibus atque invisibilibus B H. — [d] tui H I. —[e] clamorem A, *but* cl *crossed out in the brown ink hand.* —[f] cordis tui C. —[g] et *om.* G_1. —[h] te *add.* B H; operibus *repeated but apparently crossed out on second occurrence* O. —[i] in *om.* E. —[j] Clerus *add. as rubric* D. —[k] Alia benedictio *add.* F, Oracio alia *add.* G_1.

46. *Et qui te voluit super populum suum*[a] *constituere regem*[b], *et*[c] *in presenti seculo felicem*[d], *eterne felicitatis tribuat*[e] *esse consortem*[f]. *Amen.*

Quod ipse prestare dignetur[g].

46. [a] tuum I. —[b] regem constituere B H. —[c] et *om.* J. —[d] et *add.* B H. —[e] te *add.* B H. —[f] consortium E. —[g] Qui vivit et regnat *add.* B D; Quod ipse prestare dignetur *om.* J.

47. Alia benedictio statim dicenda[a] super eum[b].

Benedic[c], *Domine, hunc preelectum principem, qui regna omnium regum a seculo moderaris*[d]. *Amen*[e].

Et tali [fol. 137r] *eum*[f] *benedictione*[g] *glorifica, ut Davitica*[h] *teneat sublimitate sceptrum salutis et sanctifice*[i] *propitiationis, munere reperiatur locupletatus*[j]. *Amen*[k].

Da ei a[l] *tuo spiramine regere*[m] *populum, sicut Salomonem fecisti regnum obtinere*[n] *pacificum*[o]. *Amen*[p].

Quod ipse prestare[q].

47. [a] dicenda *om.* B D H. —[b] Alia benedictio ... eum *om.* I; Benedictio *add. as rubric* C. —[c] ✠ *add.* B D H. —[d] Clerus *add. as rubric* D. —[e] Alia benedictio *add.* F, Oracio *add.* G_1. —[f] cum O. —[g] ✠ *add.* B D H. —[h] locupleta ut Davidica J, glorifica et Davidica O. —[i] sanctifica C. —[j] locuplettatus F; Clerus *add. as rubric* D. —[k] Alia benedictio *add.* F, Oracio *add.* G_1. —[l] a *om.* C F G_1 J O. —

^m regem G₁. —ⁿ optinere C. —^o Clerus *add. as rubric* D. —^p Da ei ... Amen *om.* I. —^q dignetur, qui vivit et regnat *add.* B.

48. Regis status ^{a 68} designatur.

*Sta*⁶⁹ *et retine amodo*^b *statum, quem hucusque paterna sugges-tione*^{c 70} *tenuisti, hereditario*^d *iure*^e *tibi delegatum per auctoritatem*^f *Dei*^g *omnipotentis et per*^h *presentem traditionem nostram, omnium*ⁱ *scilicet episcoporum, ceterorumque Dei*^j *servorum*^k. *Et quanto clerum propinquiorem sacris altaribus prospicis*^l, *tanto ei potiorem*^m *in locis congruentibus honorem impen* [fol. 137v] *dere memineris, quatinus*ⁿ *mediator Dei et hominum te mediatorem cleri et plebis in hoc regni solio confirmet*^o, *et in regno eterno secum*^p *regnare faciat, Iesus*^q *Christus dominus noster, rex regum et dominus dominantium. Qui cum Deo Patre*^r.

48. ^a Status regis H I. —^b ammodo H. —^c paterna suggestione] paterna suc-cessione B C F G₁ H J O, paterna vel successione D. —^d hereditacionis H. — ^e vite E. —^f actoritatem A. —^g patris *add.* I. —^h per *om.* I. —ⁱ omniumque H. — ^j ceterorum Deique I. —^k servorum Dei C E F G₁ J O. —^l conspicis F. —^m ei potiorem] et peccatorem H, et potiorem J O. —ⁿ quatenus J O. —^o consumet E —^p situm J. —^q IHESUS H, Ihesus O. —^r et Spirito sancto vivit et regnat Deus. Per omnia secula seculorum. Amen *add.* B H.

49. Alia ^a oratio ^b.

Omnipotens Deus 'det tibi de rore celi et de pinguedine terre habundantiam^c *frumenti, vini*^d *et olei, et serviant tibi populi*^e *et adorent te tribus*^f; *esto dominus fratrum tuorum, et incurventur ante te filii*^g *matris tue, et qui benedixerit*^h *tibi*ⁱ *benedictionibus*^j *replea-tur,'*⁷¹ *et Deus erit adiutor tuus*^k. *'Omnipotens*^l *benedicat*^m *tibi*ⁿ *bene-dictionibus celi desuper*^o *in montibus*^p *et in*^q *collibus, benedictionibus abyssi*^r [fol. 138r] *iacentibus deorsum, benedictionibus*^s *uberum et*

---

⁶⁸ The scribe of *J* got confused in copying his source. He initially wrote *Quod ipse prestare dignetur*; then he crossed out *dignetur* and wrote *dignum Regis / statum designatur* (fol. 17r–v).

⁶⁹ *Sta* with a decorated *O* rather than *S* in manuscript *E*; Gatticus wrongly read *Diu.*

⁷⁰ According to M. de la Salle (Reims, MS 1485, no. 4, p. 3), "Dans un MS de S. Remy de 1285 [= lost manuscript *1*] on lit *paterna suggestione* et au dessus est ecrit d'une main tres ancienne *vel successione*." The variant from *D* here therefore suggests that *D* was copied from lost manuscript *1*. This evidence is also important in that it provides a date for lost manuscript *1*; farther down on the same page, though, La Salle gives the date of the Saint-Remi manuscript as 1286. See also Ordo XXII B-C, n. 21, and Ordo XXIII, n. 131.

⁷¹ Gen. 27: 28–29. I failed to note this in Ordo XV,35.

uvarum pomorumque. Benedictiones[72] *patrum antiquorum, Abraham*[t]
et[u] *Ysaac et Iacob confortate sint*[v] *super te. Per dominum.'*[73]

49. [a] Alia *om.* B D H. —[b] Alia oratio *om.* I. —[c] abundantiam J. —[d] frumenti,
vini] frumentum H; habundantiam frumenti, vini] abundantiam frumenti una
I. —[e] et servientibus populi I. —[f] et adorent te tribus *om.* H. —[g] genua J; filii
om. O. —[h] benedicerit O. —[i] tebi E. —[j] benedictione J. —[k] Alia oratio *add. as
rubric* C F G$_1$ J O, *which begin a new prayer with the following, as does* H. —
[l] Deus *add.* C G$_1$ O. —[m] ⊕ *add.* B F G$_1$ H. —[n] tuus omnipotens. Benedicat tibi
I. —[o] desuper celi E. —[p] in montibus] inontibus O. —[q] in *om.* B D H I. —
[r] abbissi H. —[s] abyssi ... benedictionibus *om.* D. —[t] Abraam E. —[u] et *om.* C F
H J O. —[v] sunt E I.

50. Alia oratio[a].

Benedic[b], *Domine, fortitudinem principis, et opera manuum illius
suscipe, et benedictione tua terra eius de pomis repleatur de fructu*[c]
celi[d] *et rore atque abyssi subiacentis, de fructu*[c] *solis et lune*[e], *de vertice*[f] *antiquorum montium, de pomis eternorum collium, et de
frugibus*[g] *terre et*[h] *plenitudine eius; benedictio illius qui apparuit in
rubo*[i] *veniat super*[j] *capud*[k] *eius, et plena sit*[l] *benedictio Domini in filiis
eius, et tingat*[m] *in oleo pedem suum*[n], *cornua rinocerontis*[o] [fol. 138v]
*cornua illius, in ipsis ventilabit gentes usque ad terminos terre, quia
ascensor*[p] *celi auxiliator suus in sempiternum fiat*[q]. *Per dominum
nostrum.*

50. [a] Alia oratio *om.* I. —[b] ⊕ *add.* F G$_1$. —[c] fructi O. —[d] celesti D B H. —[e] et
add. B C F G$_1$ H J O. —[f] virtute B D H, *but corr. to* virtice *in a fourteenth-
century hand in* B. —[g] fructibus I. —[h] de *add.* C F G$_1$ J O. —[i] rubro G$_1$ I. —
[j] me *add.* I. —[k] caput B C D E F G$_1$ H I J O. —[l] sit *om.* I. —[m] tinguat C, unguat
E, intingat I. —[n] eius I. —[o] rinoceruntis C G$_1$ O, renoventis I, rinocerotis J. —
[p] assensor O. —[q] fiet B H.

51. Hiis[a] expletis, archiepiscopus cum paribus coronam[b] sustentantibus[c], regem taliter insignitum deducit[d] in solium sibi preparatum, sericis stratum et ornatum[e], ubi collocat[f] eum in sede eminenti, unde[g] ab
omnibus possit videri; quem in sede sua[h] taliter residentem, mox
archiepiscopus, mitra deposita, osculatur, dicens, "Vivat Rex in eternum," et post eum episcopi et laici pares, qui eius[i] coronam sustentant,

---

[72] In *E*, a marginal addition in a different hand reads something like *uō* at the line
"morumque. Benedictiones patrum." Although there is an identical addition at the line
"scipe et benedictione tua terra" near the beginning of no. 50, I do not think that this
indicates the sign of the Cross. See also nn. 56, 62, and 63.

[73] The latter part of no. 49 is modified from Gen. 49: 25–26. I failed to note this in
Ordo XV,35.

hoc idem dicentes[j][74]; hiis[k] expletis, missa primo a cantore[l] et succentore[m], chorum servantibus, inchoetur[n] et suo ordine decantetur[o].

51. [a] His I J. —[b] coronam cum paribus I. —[c] sustantibus H. —[d] ducit F, deducunt H. —[e] coronatum E, ornant I. —[f] collocet I. —[g] usque I. —[h] sua sede C F
G_1 J O. —[i] eius om. I. —[j] Nota (Et notandum H) quod regina debet consecrari
et coronari ante missam, statim post regem add. B H. —[k] Et his I, His J. —
[l] a cantore primo C F G_1 J O. —[m] et succentore] succintore O. —[n] incoetur I. —
[o] in qua cum principali oratione misse dicatur pro rege hec oratio add. C.

52. Oratio pro rege[a].

Quesumus, omnipotens Deus[b], *rex noster* [fol. 139r] *N.*[c],[75] *qui tua
miseratione regni suscepit*[d] *gubernacula, virtutum eciam omnium
percipiat incrementa*[e], *quibus decenter ornatus, et vitiorum*[f] *monstra
devitare*[g], *et*[h] *hostes superare*[i], *et ad te qui*[j] 'via*[k], veritas*[l] *et vita' es*[m],
graciosus valeat pervenire. Per.

52. [a] pro rege om. B C H. —[b] ut famulus tuus (tuus om. J) add. B C D F G_1 J O;
ut supra, add. H, *which omits the remainder of the prayer*; ut add. I. —
[c] Henricus I, N. om. J. —[d] suscepit regni I; suscep *apparently later corr. to*
suscepit C. —[e] percipiant incrementum E. —[f] nostrorum add. J. —[g] davitice
E, devittare F, evitare J. —[h] et om. B. —[i] et hostes superare om. D. —[j] quia
G_1. —[k] et add. C. —[l] veritatis F. —[m] es om. I.

| A B D E F | C |
| G₁ H I J O | |

A B D E F G_1 H I J O	55. Quando[76] legitur ewangelium, rex et regina debent deponere coronas suas. Notandum quod lecto evangelio, maior inter archiepiscopos et episcopos accipit librum evangelii et defert domino regi et regine ad deosculandum. Et postea domino archiepiscopo missam celebranti. Post offertorium pares deducunt regem ad altare coronam eius sustinentes; rex autem debet offerre panem unum,[77] vinum in urceo argenteo. Tredecim bisantes

---

[74] Variant *j* is a marginal addition in *B*, but is incorporated into the text in *H*.

[75] *Henricus* for *N* in manuscript *I* is the result of having misread the gothic *N* as
an *H*; wishing to spell out all abbreviations, the scribe then transformed the *H* into an
appropriate name. He repeated his error below, nos. 53, var. *d*, and 54, var. *d*. The
scribe of manuscript *J* misread the letter in the same way in two places, but at least he
left it as an *H*.

[76] The scribe of *C* (or of *C*'s source) moved text around so as to order the text
more rationally than in the normal ordo. No. 55 largely reproduces the *F G_1 J O* version of no. 55.

[77] *C* reads *uinum* rather than *unum* (the scribe distinguished between the initial
v and the initial *u*); the scribe simply put one minim too many in *unum*.

aureos. Et regina similiter. In eundo autem et redeundo gladius nudus defertur coram eo.

Secreta dicenda est cum principali secreta misse.

A B C D E F G₁ H J O

53. Secreta[a].

*Munera, quesumus Domine, oblata sanctifica, ut et[b] nobis unige-
niti tui corpus et sanguis[c] fiant, et N.[d] [78] regi nostro ad optinendam[e]
anime corporisque[f] salutem, et ad peragendum iniunctum officium,
te[g] largiente, usquequaque proficiant[h]. Per.*

53. [a] Secreta] Alia oracio G₁. —[b] et *om.* I. —[c] corporis et sanguinis J. —[d] fiant
et N.] fiant Henrici I, fiat et N. E, fiant et huic J. —[e] obtinendam H J, obtinendum I, optinandam *corr. to* obtinendam O. —[f] animeque corporis H. —[g] te
om. H. —[h] perficiant I.

| A B D E F | C |
| G₁ H I J O | |

56. Antequam [79] vero archiepiscopus dicat "Pax
domini," debet dicere hanc benedictionem super regem et
super populum.[80]

71. Sequitur benedictio.

*Benedicat tibi Dominus custodiensque te, sicut voluit
te super populum suum constituere regem, ita quod in
presenti seculo felicem et eterne felicitati tribuat esse
consortem. Amen.*

72. *Clerum ac populum, quem sua voluit opitulatione
[tua sanctione congregari, sua dispensatione et[a]] tua
administratione faciat per diuturna tempora feliciter
gubernari. Amen.*

72. [a] tua sanctione congregari sua dispensatione et *om.* C, *apparently by
mistake.*

73. *Quatinus divinis monitis parentes, adversitatibus omnibus carentes, bonis omnibus exuberantes, tuo
ministerio fideli amore obsequentes, et in presenti seculo
pacis transquillitate fruantur et tecum eternorum civium
consortio potiri mereantur. Amen.*

Quod ipse prestare etc.

---

[78] See n. 75 above on the reading of *I.*

[79] Nos. 55–58 in *C* contain part of the rubrics of no. 56 in the *G₁ J O* version and
the formulas of nos. 71–73 in the *G₁ J O* version. See the Synoptic Table, p. 371.

[80] A miniature in the bottom margin of *C*, fol. 84r, depicts a club-wielding youth
doing battle with a lion. This must refer to David's victory over the lion in no. 25.

A B D E F G_1 H I J O	C
	Sequitur. *Et pax eius.* 56. Dicto autem "Agnus Dei," ille qui detulit evangelium accipiens ab archiepiscopo pacem, eam defert regi cum oris osculo. Et regine in libro. Et post eum omnes archepiscopi et episcopi regi dant osculum pacis, unus post alium in suo solio residenti. Postcommunio dicenda cum principali postcommunione misse.

A B C D E F G_1 H I J O

54. Postcommunio[a].

Hec, Domine[b], *oratio*[c] *salutaris famulum tuum N.*[d][81] *regem nostrum ab omnibus tueatur*[e] *adversis, quatinus*[f] *et ecclesiastice pacis*[g] *obtineat transquillitatem*[h], *et post* [fol. 139v] *istius*[i] *temporis decursum, ad eternam perveniat hereditatem. Per.*

54. [a] Post communionem E F I; Postcommunio] Alia oracio G_1, Postmodum O; Postcommunio *om.* J. —[b] Domine *om.* J. —[c] oblatio C. —[d] Henricum I; N. *om.* J. —[e] tueatur *om.* H. —[f] quatenus J O; quatinus *om.* E. —[g] ecclesie pacis E J, ecclesiastice puppis J. —[h] tranquillitatem E H, transquilitatem G_1 I, tranquilitatem J, tranquillitatem O; transquillitatem obtineat C F. —[i] ipsius C, illius E.

A E	B D H I	F G_1 J O	C
55. Notandum quod	55. Notandum quod[a] legitur Evangelium[b], rex et regina debent deponere coronas suas, et	55. Quando legitur Ewangelium[c], rex et regina debent deponere coronas suas. Notandum quod	

A B D E F G_1 H I J O

lecto Evangelio[d], maior inter archiepiscopos[82] et episcopos[e] accipit librum Evangelii[f] et defert[g] domino[h] regi ad deosculandum[i], et postea domino[j] archiepiscopo missam celebranti. Post offertorium pares deducunt regem ad altare coronam eius sustinentes[k]. Rex autem debet offerre[l] panem unum[m],[83] vinum in urceo[n] argenteo, tredecim bisentios aureos[o]; in eundo[p] et redeundo[q], gladius nudus defertur[r] coram eos[s].

---

[81] See n. 75 above on the reading of *I*.

[82] *archiepiscopos* added later in a blank space *A*.

[83] As above, n. 77, the scribe of *E* wrote *unum* with one minim too many, turning the word into *vinum*. The scribe of *C* did likewise here.

55. ^aquando I. —^b Ewangelium D. —^c Evangelium J O. —^d Ewangelio F G_1. —
^e et episcopos *om.* B H. —^f Evangeliorum E, Ewangelii F G_1. —^g debet E. —
^h domino *om.* F. —ⁱ osculandum I; et postea regine *add.* B D H. —^j domino
om. F. —^k coronam eius sustinentes *om.* I. —^l debet offere] offerat B H. —
^m vinum E, unum *om.* J. —ⁿ vinumque in vitro I. —^o tresdecim bisancios
aureos B H, tredecim bisantios aureos D, tredecim bisentios argenteos E,
tresdecim besantes aureos F, tresdecim bisantos aureos G_1 O, tridecim bisancios aureos I, tredecim bisantos aureos J; et regina similiter, et (et *om.* F G_1 J
O) *add.* B D F G_1 H J O. —^p in eundo] In eundo autem F G_1 J O. —^q reddeundo
G_1. —^r deferatur H; gladius nudus defertur] gladius acutus deferent E. —
^s coram rege B H.

A B D E F H I	G_1 J O	C
	71. Notandum [84] quod antequam archiepisco- pus dicat "Pax Domini sit semper vobiscum," debet dicere hanc [fol. 323v] benedictionem super regem et super populum sic^a. *Benedicat tibi*^b *Dominus custodiensque*^c *te,* *sicut voluit te super populum suum constituere* *regem, itaque*^d *in presenti seculo felicem et eterne* *felicitati tribuat esse consortem. Amen.*	

71. ^a sic *om.* J. —^b te J. —^c custodiatque J. —^d ita quod J O.

| | 72. *Clerum ac populum, quem sua voluit*
opitulacione tua sanctione congregari, sua dis-
pensacione et tua administracione per diuturna
tempora faciat feliciter gubernari. Amen.
73. Alia oracio^a.
Quatinus^b *divinis monitis parentes, adversi-*
tatibus omnibus carentes, bonis omnibus exube-
rantes, tuo ministerio fideli amore obsequentes,
et in^c *presenti seculo pacis transquillitate*^d *fruan-*
tur^e *et tecum eternorum civium consorcio potiri*
mereantur. Amen.
Quod ipse prestare^f. | |

73. ^a Alia oracio *om.* J O. —^b Quatenus J. —^c in *om.* J. —^d tranquilitate J, tranquillitate O. —^e fruatur J. —^f dignetur *add.* J.

---

[84] Nos. 71–73 in the *G_1 J O* group were moved to a location that is more rational
than the original location in *A, B, D, E, F, H,* and *I.*

A B D E F G_1 H I J O   C

56. Finita[85] missa, iterum pares adducunt regem coram[a] altare[b], et[c] ibi communicat corpus et sanguinem Domini[d] de manu[e] archiepiscopi missam celebrantis; set[f] notandum est quod ille qui dedit ei Evangelium[g] ad [fol. 140r] deosculandum debet post "Pax Domini" accipere pacem ab archiepiscopo missam celebrante[h] et deferre regi[i], et post eum omnes archiepiscopi et episcopi[j] dant osculum pacis regi[k] unus[l] post alium in suo solio residenti. Missa finita, deponit archiepiscopus coronam de capite regis, et[m] expoliato rege de insignioribus vestimentis et aliis indutis[n], iterum imponit capiti suo archiepiscopus aliam coronam minorem, et sic vadit ad palatium, nudo gladio precedente; et sciendum[o] quod eius camisia propter sanctam unctionem debet comburi.

56. [a] coram *om.* H. — [b] altari B D E F G_1 H J O. — [c] et *om.* O. — [d] Domini *om.* H. — [e] domini *add.* F G_1 J O. — [f] sed B D E F G_1 I J O. — [g] Ewangelium F G_1. — [h] celebranti I. — [i] et regine cum libro *add.* B D H; cum oris osculo, et regine in libro *add.* F G_1 J O. — [j] archiepiscopi et episcopi] archiepiscopi E, episcopi et archiepiscopi I. — [k] dant regi osculum pacis B H, regi dant osculum pacis F G_1 J O. — [l] unum O. — [m] et *om.* I. — [n] inductis F, induto I. — [o] est *add.* O.

A B D E H I	F G_1 J O	C
57. De reductione ampulle.	57. De ampulle reductione[f].	
Sciendum quod rex debet accipere de baronibus suis nobilioribus et fortioribus in die coronationis sue in aurora diei, et mittere apud sanctum Re [fol. 140v] migium pro sancta ampulla, et illi debent iurare[a] abbati et ecclesie quod dictam sanctam ampullam bona fide ducent[b] et reducent ad sanctam ecclesiam beati Remigii; abbas autem, hoc facto, debet sanctam ampullam afferre, sicut superius est notatum. Finita consecratione et missa, debent iterum iidem[c] barones reducere sanctam ampullam		
	Finita consecratione et missa, debent iterum iidem[g] barones reducere[h]	

---

[85] B, D, and E (and apparently F) begin a new paragraph with *Finita*, although A, H, and I do not (no. 56 is not rubricated in A). I adopt the paragraphing of B, D, and E.

| usque ad sanctum Remigium^d hon- orifice et secure, et eam restituere loco suo^e. | sanctam ampullam usque ad sanctum Remigium honorifice et secure, et eam restituere loco suoⁱ. |

57. ^aiure A. — ^badducent E. — ^chiidem E, idem H I. — ^dreducere ... Remigium] reducere usque ad sanctum Remigium sanctam ampullam H. — ^erestituere in loco suo D B, reducere in suo loco I; Et sic finis de rege. Sequitur de coronatione regine Francie et de eius consecracione etc. *add.* H. —^fredducione G_1; De ampulle reducione *om.* J. —^gidem O. —^hredducere G_1. —ⁱhonorifice ... suo] honorifice et restituere loco suo J.

A E	B D F G_1 H J O	C	I
58. Ordo ad reginam benedicen- dam.⁸⁶	58. Ordo ad regi- nam benedicendam que debet benedici sive coronari et^a con- secrari. Statim post factam consecra- tionem regis hoc modo^b.	58. Consecratio regine.⁸⁷ Sequitur ordo ad reginam benedicendam, que debet consecrari statim post factam con- secrationem regis.	

58. ^abenedici sive coronari et *om.* D F G_1 J O. —^bhoc modo *om.* F G_1 J O.

59. Debet parari ei^a solium in modum solii regis, debet tamen^b ali- quantulum minus esse. Debet autem regina adduci in ecclesiam^c et rex in suo solio parari in omnibus ornamentis^d regiis, sicuti^e in solio residebat post inunctionem^f et^g coronationem suam^h, [fol. 141r] superius anno- tatamⁱ. Regina autem^j, adducta in^k ecclesiam, debet prosterni ante altare et, prostrata, debet orare; qua^l elevata ab^m oratione ab episcopisⁿ, debet iterum capud^o inclinare, et archiepiscopus hanc orationem dicere^p.

59. ^aei parari C F G_1 J O; ei *om.* I. —^btamen *om.* I. —^cecclesia D B H I. — ^dsuis *add.* C F G_1 J O. —^eregiis sicut F J, regis sicut I. —^functionem E, inuc- cionem G_1. —^gpost *add.* I. —^hsuam *om.* J. —ⁱadnetatam J. —^jautem *om.* C. — ^kadducta in] ducta ad H. —^lque H. —^mab *om.* I. —ⁿarchiepiscopis E. — ^oiterum caput B C D E G_1 I J O, caput iterum H. —^pOratio *add. as rubric* B C D F G_1 H; sic. Oremus *add.* C; sic *add.* F G_1; Sic. Oratio *add.* O.

---

⁸⁶ In *A* the brown-ink hand added in the margin at "Ordo ad reginam" an abbrevia- tion (a rather elaborate letter *C* followed by a long curving upright line) that appar- ently means *Capitulum* and is intended to mark the beginning of a section. It appears elsewhere in the manuscript also, and it probably dates from the fourteenth century.

⁸⁷ A miniature in the bottom margin of fol. 84v in *C* depicts two barons holding the crown upon the head of the kneeling queen as the archbishop administers a blessing. See Plate 24.

60. *Adesto, Domine, supplicationibus*[a] *nostris, et quod humilitatis*[b] *nostre*[c] *gerendum est, misterio*[d] *tue virtutis impleatur effectu. Per.*

60. [a] suplicationibus O. —[b] humilitati J. —[c] nostre *om.* G_1. —[d] ministerio E.

61. Notandum quod tunica regine et camisia[a] debent esse aperte usque ad corrigiam, et dominus[b] archiepiscopus debet inungere eam de[c] oleo sancto in capite et in pectore, et dicere dum inungit:

In nomine[d] *Patris*[e] *et Filiiis*[e] *et Spiritus*[f] *sancti, prosit tibi hec unctio olei*[g] *in honorem et confirmationem eternam*[h].

61. [a] regine et camisia] et camisia regine E. —[b] dominus *om.* F. —[c] de *om.* C F G_1 J O. —[d] ✠ *add.* D G_1. —[e] ✠ *add.* F G_1. —[f] ✠ *add.* F. —[g] olei inunctio I. — [h] Amen *add.* I.

62. Sequitur hec[a] oratio[b] post inunctionem[c].

Omnipotens sempiterne [fol. 141v] *Deus, affluentem spiritum tue benedictionis*[d] *super famulam*[e] *tuam nobis orantibus propitiatus infunde, ut que per manus nostre impositionem hodie regina instituitur, sanctificatione*[f] *tua digna et electa permaneat, ut*[g] *nunquam*[h] *postmodum de*[i] *tua gracia*[j] *separetur indigna. Per*[k].

62. [a] Sequitur hec *om.* E. —[b] H oracio. —[c] unctionem B H; post inunctionem hec oratio C F G_1 J O, *and* Oratio *add. as rubric* C; Sequitur ... inunctionem *om.* I. —[d] infunde *add.* H, *so repeated seven words later.* —[e] familiam I. — [f] sanctificationis E. —[g] et B D E H. —[h] numquam H O. —[i] a: B H. —[j] de tua gratia postmodum C. —[k] Per *om.* F.

63. Post istam orationem[a] datur regine[b] ab archiepiscopo[c] sceptrum modicum alterius modi quam[d] sceptrum regium et virga consimilis virge regie[e], absque orationibus. Tunc debet anulus[f] inmitti[g] digito et dicere[h].

63. [a] unccionem G_1. —[b] regine *om.* C F G_1 J O. —[c] episcopo I. —[d] quem I; modi quam] modicam D. —[e] virge regie] virge. Regis I. —[f] annulus J. — [g] inmitti in C, immitti I, iungi J, inungi O; anulum imminere B H. —[h] dicere] dici sic F G_1 J O; dicere] sic *and* Sequitur oratio *add. as rubric* C.

64. *Accipe anulum*[a] *fidei, signaculum sancte trinitatis, quo possis*[b] *omnes hereticas pravitates*[c] *devitare, et barbaras gentes virtute tibi*[d] *prestita ad agnitionem veritatis*[e] *advocare*[f].

64. [a] anullum I, annulum J. —[b] que possit J O. —[c] pravitates hereticas C. — [d] tibi *om.* I. —[e] virtutis J. —[f] Per *add.* E.

65. Sequitur[a] oratio[b].

[fol. 142r] *Deus, cuius est omnis potestas et dignitas, da famule tue signo tue fidei*[c] *prosperum*[d] *sue dignitatis effectum, in qua tibi semper firma maneat*[e], *tibique iugiter placere contendat*[f]. *Per.*

65. [a] Alia C. —[b] Sequitur oratio *om.* G[1]; Oratio *add. as rubric* I. —[c] fidei tue C. —[d] da famule ... prosperum] da familiae tuae signa tuae fidei, ut prosperum J. —[e] permaneat B D H. —[f] concedat O.

66. Tunc debet ei imponi a solo archiepiscopo corona in capite ipsius, quam impositam, sustentare[a] debent undique barones[b]; archiepiscopus autem[c] debet[d] dicere in impositione[e].

Accipe coronam glorie, honorem iocunditatis, ut splendida fulgeas et eterna exultatione[f] coroneris[g].

66. [a] sustetare E. —[b] barones sustentare undique debent J. —[c] autem *om.* I. — [d] debet *om.* H. —[e] corone orationem *add.* E, hanc oracionem *add.* F, oracionem *add.* G[1] J O. —[f] exaltatione I. —[g] Per *add.* E.

67. Alia[a] oratio[b].

Omnium, Domine, fons[c] bonorum et cunctorum dator provectuum[d], tribue famule tue N. adeptam bene regere dignitatem, et a te sibi prestitam in ea bonis operibus corrobora[e] gloriam. Per.

67. [a] Sequitur B C H. —[b] Accipe coronam glorie ... Alia oratio *om.* G[1]. —[c] fons Domine I. —[d] provectuuum B. —[e] corobora E.

68. Post istam orationem [fol. 142v] barones qui coronam eius sustentant deducunt eam ad solium, ubi[a] in sede parata collocatur, circumstantibus[b] eam baronibus[c] et matroniis[d] nobilioribus;

| A B D E F G[1] H I J O | C |

in oblatione, in[e] pace ferenda[f], in communione[g], penitus est ordo regis superius annotatus[h] observandus.

68. [a] ubi *om.* H. —[b] circunstantibus B C G[1] J, circonstantibus F. —[c] baronis I. —[d] matronis E F G[1]. —[e] et H. —[f] et *add.* B G[1] H J; in pace ferenda *om.* J. — [g] communicatione J O. —[h] adnotatus J.

69. Benedictio[a] vexilli[b].

Inclina, Domine, aurem tuam ad preces nostre[c] humilitatis, et per interventum beati Michaelis archangeli tui[d] omniumque celestium[e] virtutum, presta nobis auxilium dextere tue, ut[f] sicut benedixisti Abraham adversus quinque reges triumphantem, atque David regem in tui nominis laude triumphales[g] congressus exercentem, ita bene✠dicere[h] et[i] sanctifi✠care[j] digneris vexillum hoc quod ob de- [fol. 143r] fensionem[k] sancte ecclesie contra hostilem rabiem[l] defertur[m], quatinus[n] in nomine tuo[o] fideles et defensores[p] populi Dei[q] illud[r] consequentes per virtutem sancte crucis triumphum et victoriam se ex hostibus adquisisse[s] letetur[t]. Qui cum Patre et Spiritu sancto[u].

69. [a] Sequitur benedictio H. —[b] Oracio *add.* G_1 J O. —[c] nostras G_1 J O; nostre *om.* E. —[d] et beati Dionisii martiris *add.* G_1 J O. —[e] celestiumque J. —[f] et D B H I. —[g] triumphantes J. —[h] ✠ *om.* E I J O. —[i] ac B D H. —[j] ✠ *om.* D E F G_1 I J O. —[k] deffensionem I. —[l] rabiem *om.* I. —[m] deferturum H. —[n] quatenus J O. — [o] in tuo nomine B H; tuo *om.* D. —[p] deffensores I. —[q] tui F. —[r] Dei illud] Dei N. Illud H. —[s] acquisisse D F G_1 I J, aquisisse O. —[t] letentur B G_1 H I J O; victoriam ... adquisisse] victoriam se de hostibus acquisse letetur E. —[u] vivit et regnat *add.* D; et spiritu sancto *om.* F G_1 O; Qui cum ... sancto] Per dominum nostrum Iesum Christum filium tuum qui tecum vivit et regnat B; Qui cum ... sancto] Per dominum nostrum Ihesum Christum H, Qui cum Patre etc. J.

A B D E F H I	G_1 J O	C
	70. Ad[88] tradendum autem vexillii[a] domino regi dicitur sic[b].	
	Diex[c] par sa grace et par les prieres de[d] vostre[e] glorieux patron monseigneur saint Denis vous doint[f] avoir noble[g] victoire de tous voz[h] ennemis. Amen[i].[89]	

70. [a] vexillum J O. —[b] dicitur sic] dicas ita J O. —[c] Dieu J. —[d] de *om.* J O. — [e] nostre O. —[f] donne J, doient O. —[g] bonne J. —[h] vos J O. —[i] Amen *om.* J.

A B D E F H I		C G_1 J O

71. Notandum[a] quod antequam[b] archiepiscopus dicat[c] "Pax Domini sit semper vobiscum,"[d] debet dicere hanc benedictionem[e] super regem et super populum[f].

Benedicat tibi Dominus custodiensque te, sicut te[g] voluit[h] super populum suum[i] constituere regem, ita et[j] in presenti seculo felicem et eterne felicitatis[k] tribuat esse consortem. Amen[l].

71. [a] est *add.* I. —[b] quando I —[c] dicat archiepiscopus D, archiepiscopus dicit I; archiepiscopus dicat *om.* B H. —[d] dicatur archiepiscopus *add.* B H. —[e] oracionem H. —[f] sic *add.* F, astantem *add.* H. —[g] te sicut te sicut E. —[h] voluit te F. —[i] tuum I. —[j] ut E. —[k] felicitati F. —[l] Alia benedictio *add.* F.

72. *Clerum ac populum, quem sua voluit opitulatione[a]* | *tua sanctione[b] congregari, sua dispensatione[c] et tua* [fol.

---

[88] This text that concludes *G₁, J, L, M, N,* and *O* obviously belongs to the coronation ceremony no more than does the *Benedictio vexilli* (no. 69), although the latter was at least a traditional formula in the ordines ever since the Ratold Ordo (Ordo XV).

[89] *O* adds, "Collationé par nous Conseiller Maitre a ce Commise. [signed] Lourdet."

ABDEFHI   C G$_1$ J O

143v] *administratione*[d] *per diuturna tempora faciat feliciter gubernari*[e]. *Amen*[f].

72. [a] opitulante H. —[b] tua sanctione *om*. E. —[c] dispensacione H. —[d] administracione H. —[e] gubernare I. —[f] Alia benedictio *add*. F.

73. *Quatinus divinis monitis parentes, adversitatibus omnibus carentes, bonis omnibus exuberantes, tuo ministerio fideli amore obsequentes, et in presenti seculo*[a] *pacis tranquillitate*[b] *fruantur et tecum eternorum civium consortio potiri mereantur. Amen.*

Quod[c] *ipse*[d] *prestare dignetur, qui vivit.*

73. [a] in seculo presenti B H. —[b] transquillitate F. —[c] et *add*. E. —[d] ipse *om*. B.

A B C D E   H
F G$_1$ I J O 74. *Nomina XII parium Francie.*

Archiepiscopus Remensis
Episcopus Laudunensis ——> *duces*
Episcopus Lingonensis
 Laici duces.

Burgundie
Acquitanie ——> *duces laici*
Normannie
 Clerici comites.

Episcopus Noviomensis[a]
Episcopus Belvacensis ——> *comites*
Episcopus Cathalanensis
 Laici comites.

Tolosanus
Campanie ——> *comites laici*
Flandrie
 Unde versus.

Lingonensis, Remis, Laudunensis, Normannia, Acquitania, Burgundia sunt duces.

Noviomensis, Belvacensis, Cathalanensis, Tholosa, Campania, Flandria sunt comites.

 Explicit.

74. [a] Novionensis H.

A B D E F
G₁ H I J O

C

75. Finita⁹⁰ missa, iterum pares adducunt regem. Et barones reginam coram altari. Et ibi communicant corpus et sanguinem Domini de manu domini archiepiscopi missam celebrantis.

Deinde deponit archiepiscopus coronam de capite regis. Et expoliato rege de insignioribus vestimentis et aliis indutis, iterum imponit capiti suo archiepiscopus aliam coronam minorem, et sic vadit ad palatium, nudo gladio precedente.

Et sciendum quod eius camisia propter sanctam unctionem debet comburi. Tunica vero serica reservetur quia in ea debet rex sepeliri. Et idem debet fieri de camisia et tunica regine. Regina eciam deposita corona, aliam leviorem accipit et sic redit ad palatium.

Finita consecratione et missa, debent iidem barones reducere sanctam ampullam usque ad sanctum Remigium honorifice, et secure eam restituere loco suo.

A B C D E
F G₁ H J O

I

76. [fol. 9v] Finita⁹¹ autem letania, erigant se. Sublatus vero princeps, interrogetur a domino metropolitano hoc modo.

Vis fidem sanctam a catholicis viris tibi traditam tenere et operibus iustis observare? [Resp.ᵃ] *Volo.*

Interrogetur. *Vis sanctis ecclesiis ecclesiarumᵇ ministris tutor et deffensor esse?* [Resp.ᵃ] *Volo.*

Interrogetur. *Vis regnum tuum a Deo concessum secundum iusticiam patrum tuorum regere ac deffendere?* [Resp.ᵃ] *Volo. Et in quantum* [fol. 10r] *divino fultus adiutorio ac solatio omnium suorum valuero, ita me per omnia fideliter acturumᶜ promitto.*

76. ᵃ Resp. *om.* I; *here add. from Ordo XIX,15 for the sake of clarity.* — ᵇ ęcclesiarumque *Ordo XIX,15.* —ᶜ esse *add. Ordo XIX,15.*

⁹⁰ No. 75 in *C* was compiled partly from nos. 56 and 57 in the other manuscripts.

⁹¹ Added at the end of the ordo in the same hand as the remainder of the manuscript. Nos. 76–77 are from Ordo XIX,15–16 from that ordo's MS *A* (Reims, Bibl. mun., MS 343); nos. 78–80 are from Ordo XIX,37–39. Upon reexamining Reims 343, I cannot tell whether *I* was copied directly or indirectly from it — I think that the latter is likely. Minor differences between Reims 343 and *I* are not noted, but the major ones are indicated as variants from Ordo XIX.

A B C D E
F G₁ H J O

I

77. Queratur ab eoᵃ si sanctas Dei ecclesias ac rectores ecclesiarum necnonᵇ cunctum populum sibi subditumᶜ iuste ac religiose regali providentia iuxta morem patrum suorum deffendere ac regere velit. Illo autem proferenteᵈ in quantum divino fultus adiutorio ac solatio omnium suorum valuerit, itaᵉ se per omnia fideliter esse acturum, ipse episcopus affatur populum, si tali principi ac rectori se subicere ipsiusque reginiᶠ firma fide stabilire atque iussionibus illius obtemperare velint iuxta apostolum, 'Omnis anima potestatibus sublimioribus subdita sit,' regi quasi precellenti. Tunc ergo a circunstante clero et populo unanimiter dicatur, "Fiat. Fiat. Amen."

77. ᵃ Queratur ab eo *om. Ordo XIX,16.* —ᵇ et *add. Ordo XIX,16.* —ᶜ subiectum *Ordo XIX,16.* —ᵈ profitente *Ordo XIX,16.* —ᵉ Ita I, *beginning a new sentence.* —ᶠ regnum *Ordo XIX,16.*

78. In hoc loco dominus metropolitanus sedere eum faciat super sedem dicendo.

In hoc regni solio te confirmet, et in regno eterno secum regnare faciat, Iesus Christus dominus noster, rex regum et dominus dominantium. Qui cum Deo Patre vivit et regnat.

79. Professio regis ante solium coram Deo, [clero et populo.

Profiteor et promitto coram Deoᵃ] et angelis eius amodo et deinceps legem et iusticiam pacemque sancte Dei ecclesie populo michiqueᵇ subiecto, pro posse et nosse facere et conservare salvo condito misericordie respectu, sicut in consilio fidelium nostrorum melius etᶜ invenire poterimus.

Pontificibus quoque ecclesiarum Dei condignum et canonicum honorem exhibere, atque ea, que ab imperatoribus et regibus ecclesiis sibi commissis collata et reddita sunt, inviolabiliter conservare abbatibus etiam et vasisᵈ dominicis nostris congruum honorem secundum consilium fidelium nostrorumᵉ. Amen.

79. ᵃ clero ... Deo *om.* I; *here add. from Ordo XIX,38.* —ᵇ populoque michi *Ordo XIX,38.* —ᶜ et *om. Ordo XIX,38.* —ᵈ etiam comitibus et vassis *Ordo XIX,38.* —ᵉ prestare *add. Ordo XIX,38.*

A B C D E
F G₁ H J O

I

80. [fol. 10v] Tunc det illis oscula pacis. Cunctus autem cetus clericorum tali rectore gratulans, sonantibus campanis, alta voce concinat, "Te Deum laudamus."

ORDO XXII B AND ORDO XXII C

French Translations of the Last Capetian Ordo

Dates: ca. 1350, 1555–66.

Other names for Ordo XXII C: Ordo of Louis VII (Du Tillet, Godefroy, Buchner), Ordo of Louis VIII (Dom Brial), Ordo of Du Tillet or French Translation of the Ordo of Sens (Schreuer)[1]

Introduction

There are two translations of the Last Capetian Ordo. Following the example set by the French translations of Ordo XX A, and in order to make future references to these texts as clear as possible, I labeled them Ordo XXII B and Ordo XXII C, and I identified the paragraph numbers similarly.

The first, Ordo XXII B, is previously unpublished and has had no influence upon the development of either the ceremony or the scholarship concerning it. Nonetheless, it is an important early example of a translated liturgical text. On linguistic grounds the translation, which shows traces of the Picard dialect, could have been made as early as 1340, and it is certainly not later than 1360. It was based upon a lost manuscript much like Ordo XXII A's manuscript *A E* group, although it was copied from neither of those two manuscripts because the translation contains a few words that are not in either of them. The translations's manuscript *A*, which has been dated 1380–1400, contains not the original translation, but a copy of it. The translation predates the important series of translations commissioned by Charles V, but the manuscript postdates that series.[2] The reference to the collects of the Mass in no. 52b and to the Agnus Dei in no. 71b, neither of which is in any surviving Latin manuscript of the ordo, show that the translator is likely to have been a priest familiar with the Mass.

---

[1] [Michel-Jean-Jacques] B[rial], "Auteur du formulaire pour le sacre de Philippe-Auguste," *Histoire littéraire de la France*, 14 (1817), 22–26. For the citations of Schreuer's and Buchner's studies, see Vol. I: 4, n. 7.

[2] Hans Erich Keller kindly advised me on the dating of the translation, and Sylvie Lefèvre provided me with information concerning the date of manuscript *A*. Lefèvre's dating was confirmed by François Avril on the basis of filigrees, etc. The manuscript contains three poems, Nicole Oresme's French treatise against judicial astrology, a translation of an ordo for the ordination of a priest, and Ordo XXII B. Copied by a single scribe, it is a very fair manuscript written in an unusually legible Gothic book script on carefully ruled lines in two columns (see Plate 27).

The second translation (Ordo XXII C) was inserted by Jean du Tillet into his *Recueil des roys de France*, the presentation manuscript of which (MS *B*) dates from 1566. If Du Tillet himself did not make the translation, it was certainly done under his supervision, for its language and style are consistent with his other writing. Du Tillet himself identified his source as the ordo in the Chambre des comptes's register *Croix* (Ordo XXII A, lost manuscript *4*).[3] For reasons that are entirely unknown, Du Tillet asserted that the ordo had been written at the order of Louis VII for the coronation of Philip Augustus in 1179, and that is the attribution that was adopted for some two centuries.[4]

Neither translation is very faithful to its source. In manuscript *A*, for example, the puzzling names of the kingdoms in no. 25b, the prayer of consecration, were simply omitted and replaced with the words "the lordship of believers and nonbelievers." It alters the order of some of the liturgical formulas near the end of the king's ordo so as to present them more rationally than the Latin text does. The order of Du Tillet's text proves that he did, in fact, base it upon a manuscript belonging to the G_1 *J O* group of the Latin text, i.e., the original *Croix*. Nevertheless, he occasionally changed the order of the text, he added explanatory material that was not in his source, or he simply omitted text, particularly the shorter rubrics.[5] Ordo XXII B is generally closer to the Latin source as far as the rubrics are concerned, but Du Tillet usually presented more accurate translations of the liturgical formulas in Ordo XXII C.

---

[3] Quoted by Brown, *Franks, Burgundians, and Aquitanians*, p. 56 (from which I quote, standardizing the quotation), from Paris, Bibl. nat., MS fran. 2854 (the copy of the *Recueil des roys* presented to Henry II), fol. 144r: "La forme et ceremonie des sacre et couronnement des roy et royne est registré en papier intitulé, double de plusieurs lettres, extraictz et autres choses, assemblees de diverses matieres et [*read* és] Chambre des comptes livre cotté ✠ feuillet ixˣˣ. xix. soubz tel signe V." The printed editions (e.g., Du Tillet, *Receuil des roys* [1607 ed.], 275) rendered the description senseless by replacing "✠" with a nonexistent "4." Until Brown published the description correctly, it was not certain which manuscript, Ordo XX B, lost MS *1* or lost MS *5* (and Ordo XXII A, lost MS *4* or lost MS *5*), was the manuscript of the original *Croix*; the folio number given by Du Tillet, before *Nouveau Croix* was copied, proves that the manuscript in which the Last Capetian Ordo began on fol. 213 was *Nouveau Croix*. It is worth noting that, in *Croix*, the ordo was copied on paper, whereas the remainder of the volume was presumably parchment, as is *Noster*, the surviving *mémorial* of the Chambre des comptes.

Brown's study contains much information concerning the ordo and Du Tillet's version of it. I am deeply indebted to the book and its author, although very little of what Brown has discovered will be repeated here.

[4] For details, see Brown, *Franks, Burgundians, and Aquitanians*, 54–68.

[5] Brown, *Franks, Burgundians, and Aquitanians*, 68–80, presents a detailed survey of Du Tillet's modifications.

Manuscripts

Ordo XXII B

A—Paris, Bibl. nat., MS fran. 994, no. 5, pp. 93–100. Formerly MS Colbert 1849, then MS fran. 7310³. Fourteenth century, last quarter. Description: *Catalogue des manuscrits français: Ancien fonds*, vol. 1 (Paris, 1868), 171–72. See Plate 27.

Editions

None.

Ordo XXII C

B—Paris, Bibl. nat., MS fran. 2848, fols. 168r–178r. 1566. Translated from Ordo XXII A, lost manuscript *4*. This manuscript of Jean du Tillet's *Recueil des roys de France*, with its stunning, full-page portraits of the French kings, was presented to Charles IX. Description: see Ordo XVII B, MS *A*, and Brown, *Franks, Burgundians, and Aquitanians*, 55–59, 117.⁶

C—Saint Petersburg, National Library of Russia at Saint Petersburg (formerly Saltykov-Shchedrin State Public Library), MS Fr. F. v. IV, no. 9, fols. 166v–177r. Ca. 1566. Another copy of Du Tillet's *Recueil des roys de France*. Not examined, but collated by E. A. R. Brown, who suggested that *B* might be the prototype of *A*. Description: see Ordo XVII B, MS *B*.

D—Geneva, Bibl. publique et universitaire, MS fr. 84, fols. 207r–220r. Ca. 1566. Another copy of Du Tillet's *Recueil des roys de France*, apparently copied from *B* for Du Tillet before his death in 1570. Not examined, but collated by E. A. R. Brown. Description: see Ordo XVII B, MS *C*.

E—Paris, Bibl. de l'Institut de France, MS Godefroy 380, pp. 351–84. Mid-seventeenth century. Source not stated. Not collated.

Editions

a—Jean du Tillet. Several editions, of which a_1 and a_2 are pirated (see Ordo XVII B, ed. *a*).

---

⁶ We can expect detailed information about this manuscript and manuscripts *C* and *D* when E. A. R. Brown completes her study, *Jean du Tillet and his* Recueils *for the Kings of France*. In the meantime, see Elizabeth A. R. Brown and Myra Orth, "Jean du Tillet et les illustrations du grand *Recueil des Roys*," *Revue de l'Art*, 115 (1997): 8–24, which touches on some of the issues and discusses the relationship between MSS *B* and *D*.

a_1—*Les mémoires et recerches* (Rouen: Philippe de Tours, 1578), 147–57.

a_2—*Les mémoires et recerches* (Troyes: Philippe des Chams, 1578), fols. 155v–166r.

a_3—*Recueil des roys, leurs couronne et maison* (Paris: Jacques du Puys, 1580; reprinted 1586, 1587, and 1588xxxx, 187–98.

a_4—*Recueil des roys, leurs couronne et maison* (Paris: Jean Houzé; Jamet and Pierre Metayer; Barthelemy Macé, 1602), 189–99;

a_5—*Recueil des roys, leurs couronne et maison* (Paris: Abel l'Angelier; Barthelemy Macé; Pierre Matayer, 1607; reprinted Paris: Pierre Metayer, 1618), 265–74. From *B*.[7]

b—Godefroy, 1–12, from *a* or a manuscript copy of *a*, with some modifications.[8]

c—Brown, *Franks, Burgundians, and Aquitanians*, 117–35, from *B* with numerous variants from *C* and *D*.

Principles of the Edition

Ordo XXII B is from manuscript *A*. In most cases, I retained its sentence breaks to the extent that I could identify them, but occasionally the syntax required that I ignore them. It is often impossible to determine whether the scribe intended a construction like *qu'on* or *lequel* to be one or two words; these are reproduced in accordance with generally accepted modern editorial procedures. The scribe wrote, apparently indiscriminately, either *u* or *n* in a number of words (e.g., *convenables* or *couvenables*, *diliganment* or *diligaument*); I retained this scribal peculiarity. In a few instances I corrected the text, but always give the manuscript's reading in a variant. Otherwise, I reproduce the manuscript's reading rather than render words as they would appear in modern French; this results in some inconsistancies. I sometimes could not tell whether the scribe wrote *c* or *t*, particularly when the two letters come together; thus, *promectre* could read *promettre*. In all instances except one, *Nostre Seigneur* is abbreviated; in that one instance it is written as two words, so I expanded all abbreviations as two words.

Manuscript *B*, the base manuscript of Ordo XXII C, contains a fair

---

[7] Bévy, *Histoire des inaugurations*, 198–224, published a version of ed. *a*, but it consists of paraphrases and quotations from a_4, so it cannot be counted as a separate edition. On a translation of Du Tillet's text back into Latin, see Ordo XXII A, n. 25.

[8] The source and the modifications are discussed by Brown, *Franks, Burgundians, and Aquitanians*, 80–85. The Godefroys' alterations were a primary source of the otherwise unnecessary dispute between Schreuer and Buchner early in the twentieth century; see Vol. I: 4, n. 7.

amount of punctuation, but it does not accord with the sixteenth-century printed editions or with modern usage, and it is not always easy to follow its sense. The scribe normally used a diagonal line (/) to indicate a period; I render this as a period. He often indicated the beginning of a phrase or clause with a capital letter without any preceeding punctuation; in most such instances I added a comma and began the phrase or clause with a lowercase letter, although in some cases I began a new sentence instead, but only if the context called for one. I made no attempt to modernize the punctuation fully, but in a few other instances I sought to make the text more readily comprehensible to modern readers, mostly by adding a comma, usually to separate elements in a series, to set off parenthetical expressions or explanatory material, or to set off the vocative (which is almost never punctuated), and without noting my addition. Otherwise, my punctuation closely follows that of the manuscript, and its sentences are retained to the extent permitted by the sense of the translation. I added apostrophes, acute accents, and cedillas in accordance with the General Principles of the Edition. The manuscript's y for i and x or z for s are retained, although they were usually changed in the printed editions of the Du Tillet's *Recueil des roys*. The manuscript's capitalization is standardized. I do not note the scribe's two corrections over erasures.[9]

Neither A nor B has many paragraph divisions. I added the paragraphs so that they accord with those in the Latin text. Where possible, the two translations are given identical paragraph numbers, which are distinguished by the addition of b or c (to accord with the translations' labels), and the numbers are always the same as the those of Ordo XXII A. This was done in order to facilitate cross-references and to avoid ambiguity in future references. Ordo XXII B and Ordo XXII C have separate variant letters, although there is one set of notes for both translations. Where the scribe of A or B obviously omitted letters or, occasionally, a word, I supply the missing text in square brackets.

---

[9] Brown's (ed. c's) variants from manuscripts C and D are not repeated here.

Ordo XXII B

Paris, Bibl. nat., MS fran. 994

1b. [p. 93] Comment on couronne le roy en l'eglise de Reins.

2b. Premierement on appa-
reille un siege par maniere d'e-
chauffaut[a] entre le cuer et l'autel,
ou quel on monte par degrés, et ou
quel les pers du royaume et aucuns
autres, s'il est nectessité, puissent
estre avec le roy. Et le jour que le
roy vient a estre couronné[b], il doit
estre receuz a procession des
chanoines et des autres eglises
conventuaux.

2b. [a] de chauffaut A. —[b]couron-
nés A.

3b. Le samedi devant le
dymenche que le roy doit estre
consacrés et couronnés, apres
complies chantees, on commet la
garde de l'eglise aux garde[s]
deputés du roy avec les propres
gardes de l'eglise, et doit le roy en
la silence de mienuit venir en
l'eglise pour aourer et illeuc, s'il
veult, par l'espasse d'aucune heure
veiller. A l'eure que on sonne
matines doivent estre prestes lé
gardes du roy et garder l'entree de

Ordo XXII C

Du Tillet, *Recueil des roys*

2c. [fol. 168r] Premierement[10]
soit preparé ung trosne en maniere
d'escharfauld aucunement eminent,
joignant par dehors au choeur de
l'eglise, mis ou mylieu entre l'un et
l'autre, ouquel soit monté par
degrés et y puissent estre avec le
roy les pairs du royaume et autres,
si mestier est. Ou jour que ledict
roy viendra pour estre couronné,
soit receu a procession tant des
chanoines que autres eglises con-
ventueles.

3c. Le samedy precedent le
dimenche du sacre et couronnement dudict roy, a l'issue de
complyes, la garde de ladicte eglise
soit commise aux gardes deputés
par icelluy roy avecques les propres gardes de ladicte eglise, en
laquelle ledict roy ou silence de
celle nuict vienne faire son oraison
et selon sa devotion y veille une
piece en prieres. Quant matines
sonnent, les gardes dudict roy
soient appareillés pour garder

---

[10] Du Tillet preceded this with the statement (fol. 167v), "Parce que le vray office
des roy et royne est declairé par les oraisons et ceremonies de leurs sacres et couron-
nemens, ne sera impertinent inserer l'ordre commandé par ledict roy Loys le Jeune
jusques a present observé avecques sumptuosités plus grandes. Car le dire de sainct
Jehan Crisostome est certain que les roys complaisans a Dieu ont prosperé longue-
ment et leurs ennemys ont esté humiliés soubz eulx. Ceulx qui ont mal regné ont esté
humiliés soubz leurs ennemys et chastiés en leurs personnes et estat." Cf. Brown,
Franks, Burgundians, and Aquitanians, 118, n. 2, concerning the reference to John
Chrysostom; Brown concluded (pp. 4–5, 67–68) that nothing really shows why Du
Tillet attributed the ordo to Louis VII.

l'eglise et les autres huis de l'eglise fermés et diligaument gardés, et les chanoines et les clers de l'eglise doivent entroduire en l'eglise honnourablement et reverenment toutesfoyz qu'il appartient. Matines doivent estre chantees selon la maniere acoustumee, les quelles chantees on doit sonner prime en telle maniere que on la chante au point du jour. Prime chantee, le roy doit, avec les archevesques et evesques et barons et autres les quelz il voudra, venir en l'eglise avant que on face l'eaue benoite, et doivent estre sieges disposés et ordenés environ l'autel, ou les archevesques et les evesques honnourablement se puissent seoir, en tel maniere toutesvoies que les evesques pers et les autres de l'archevesché soient entre l'autel et le roy et nenne trop loing du roy, en telle maniere qu'entre eulz et le roy n'aie mie mont de personnes entreposees.

l'entree de ladicte eglise, et les autres portes d'icelle bien fermees et garnyes, mettre ens honnorablement et diligemment les chanoynes et clercz de ladicte eglise toutes les foys qu'il leur sera besoing. Les matines soient chantees ainsi qu'il est accoustumé. Lesquelles achevees, soit prime sonnee et chantee a l'aulbe du jour. Apres vienne ledict roy en l'eglise avecques les archevesques, evesques, barons et autres qu'il vouldra qui y entrent, et ce avant que l'eaue beniste soit faicte. Les sieges soient disposés environ l'autel d'une part et d'autre, esquelx les archevesques et evesques soient assis par honneur. Les evesques pairs, celluy de Laon le premier, puis celluy de Langres, apres celluy de Beauvoys, puis celluy de Chaalons, et le dernier celluy de Noyon, avecques les autres evesques suffragans de l'archevesché de Reins estans assis a part entre l'autel et le roy a l'opposite dudict autel, non loing dudict roy, [fol. 168v] sans qu'il y ait entre eulx gueres de personnes pour eviter l'indecence.

4b.   Comme la sainte ampolle doit estre aportee.

Entre prime et tierce doivent venir les moi- [p. 94] nes de Saint Remi a procession avec la sainte ampoule, laquelle doit li abbes reveraument porter dessoubz une courtine de soye par quatre perches tenues de quatre moines revestus

4c.   Convient sçavoir que le roy doit choisir de ses plus nobles et puissans barons et les envoyer a la poincte du jour a Sainct Remy pour avoir la saincte empoule. Et ilx doyvent jurer aux abbé et eglise[11] que de bonne foy ilx conduiront et

---

[11] The plural *aux* here refers to the abbot and to the church. This grammatical peculiarity appears elsewhere in this text.

en aubes, en haut eslevee, et le roy doit envoier de ses barons qui seurement la conduissent, et quant elle est porté jusqu'a l'eglise de Saint Denis ou jusques a la grant porte de la grant eglise pour la presse, l'arcevesque de Rains avec les autres archevesques et barons et avec les chanoines, se ce peut estre fait, doit aler en l'encontre de la sainte ampole et la recevoir de la main de l'abbé, en promectant par bonne foy de la rendre, et ainsi a l'autel en grant reverence doit estre portee, l'abbé acompaignent et aucuns de ses moines ; les autres moines doivent attendre en l'eglise Saint Denis ou en la chapelle Saint Nicolas jusques atant que tout soit parfait et jusques atant que la sacree ampole devra estre raportee.

reconduiront ladicte saincte empoule a ladicte eglise Sainct Remy. Ce faict, entre prime et tierce les moynes dudict Sainct Remy viennent en procession avecques les croix et cierges et ladicte saincte empoule, laquelle soit portee par l'abbé tresreveremment soubz ung poisle de soye, duquel les quatre bastons soient portés par quatre religieux vestuz en aulbes. Et quant ilx seront arrivés a l'eglise Sainct Denis, ou pour la presse si elle estoit trop grande, jusques a la grande porte d'icelle, [12] l'archevesque accompaigné des autres archevesques, evesques et barons et des chanoines, si faire se peult, aille au devant de ladicte saincte empoule, la reçoive de la main dudict abbé et luy promecte de la luy rendre de bonne foy. Ainsi la porte a l'autel avecques grande reverence du peuple, ledicte abbé et aucuns desdictz moynes l'accompaignans. Semblablement les autres moynes attendent en ladicte eglise Sainct Denys ou en la chappelle Sainct Nicolas, jusques a ce que tout soit parfaict et que ladicte saincte empoule soit rapportee.

5b. L'ampole receue, l'archevesque se doit appareiller a chanter la messe et les autres menistres, qui doivent estre vestus

5c. L'archevesque lors s'appareille a la messe, vestu des plus insignes vestemens et de palle, avecques les diacres et soubzdi-

---

[12] Du Tillet mistranslated the Latin text here (the earlier translator interpreted the passage correctly). Buchner, "Zur Datierung und Charakteristik," 381, 394, did not know the Latin text. He argued, wrongly, that Du Tillet's text translated an ordo composed in 1171 on the orders of Louis VII and that this [mis]translation proved that Philip Augustus was to have been crowned in the abbey church of Saint-Denis in Reims rather than in the cathedral of Notre-Dame.

des plus nobles et precieux vestemens. Et en ceste maniere doit
venir avec la procession de ses
menistres a l'autel, encontre lequel
venant le roy se doit reveraument
lever, et quant il est a l'autel venus,
il doit pour toutes les eglises a lui
subgetens et au roy demander.

6b. *Nous demandons que vous
nous octroiés que a chascun de
nous*[13] *et aux eglises qui nous
sont commises, que le regulier
privilege, deue loy et justice vous
gardez et deffense donnés, si come
le roy en son royaume doit faire a
chascun evesque et a l'eglise qui
lui est commise.*

7b. La responce du roy.

*Je vous promet et octroie que
a chascun de vous et aux eglises
qui vous sont commises, regulier
privilege, deue loy et justice je
garderoy, et, selon ce que je pou-
ray a l'aide de Dieu deffense je
donray*[a], *si comme le roy en son
royaume a chascun evesque et
l'eglise qui lui est commise selon
droit doit faire.*

7b. [a] douray A.

8b. *De rechief au peuple
crestien, qui m'est*[a] *subget, ou non
de Dieu je promet que a l'Eglise de
Dieu tout le peuple des crestiens,
ai vostre*[b] *jugement, vraie paix en
tous temps garderoy. De rechief
que toutes rapines et iniquités a*

acres, et en ceste maniere vestu
vienne a l'autel en procession
selon qu'il est accoustumé, et le
roy se lieve et le revere venant.
Quand ledict archevesque sera a
l'autel, demande au roy pour toutes
les eglises a luy subjectes ce qui
ensuit.

6c. [fol. 169r] *Nous te
requerons nous octroyer que, a
nous et aux eglises a nous commises, conserves le privilege canonique, loy et justice deue, nous
gardes et defendes comme roy est
tenu en son royaume a chacun
evesque et eglise a luy commise.*

7c. Et ledict roy responde aux
evesques.

*Je vous promectz et octroye
que a chacun de vous et aux
eglises a vous commises je
garderay le privilege canonique,
loy, et justice deue, et a mon pouvoir (Dieu aydant) vous
defendray comme roy est tenu par
droict en son royaume a chacun
evesque et a l'eglise a luy commise.*

8c. Aussi ledict roy promette
et jure par serment ce qui ensuyt.
*Je promectz ou nom de
Jesuschriste au peuple crestien a
moy subject ces choses. Premierement, que tout le peuple crestien
gardera[y] a l'Eglise de Dieu en
tout tempz la vraye paix par vostre
advys. Item, que je defendray*

---

[13] *vous* written, then crossed out in red ink and replaced with *nous*.

*toutes gens de quelque condicion
ou estat qu'ilz soient, je deffen-
droy. De rechief en tous jugemens,
equité et misericorde je commen-
deroy, a celle fin que a moy et a
vous li debonnaires et misericors
Diex face indulgence. De rechief
de ma terre et juridicion a moy
subgete tous herites de l'Eglise a
moy comdempnés a mon povoir
en bonne foy je extermineroy.*

Tout ce doit promectre par
serement, la main mise sur le livre.

8b. ᵃ met A. —ᵇ ai vostre *is
Claude Buridant's reasonable
reading of* aiñe *in* A.

9b. Ces promesses faites, tantost on commence « Te Deum laudamus », et deux archevesques ou
evesques mainent par la main le
roy a l'autel, qui se met a coudes et
a genous jusques a la fin du Te
Deum. Et lors il se lieve, tenant
appareillés et mis sur l'autel la
couronne d'or, le glaive enclos en
sa gayne, les esperons dorés, le
ceptre doré et la verge a la mesure
d'un coude ou de plus, qui a par
dessus une main d'iv[o]ire, et les
chose texues de soie, par tout semé
de fleur de liz dorees, et une cote
de tel oeuvre et de telle couleur
faite a la maniere d'une tunique de
quoy est vestus li soubzdyacres a
la messe. De rechief un autre
aournement de tel oeuvre et de tel
couleur qui est a la maniere d'une
chape de soye sanz chaperon, les
quelles choses toutes doit li abbés

*toutes rapines et iniquités de tous
degrés. Item, que en tous jugemens
je commanderay equité et misericorde, affin que Dieu clement et
misericordieux m'octroye et a
vous sa misericorde. Item, que de
bonne foy je travailleray a mon
pouvoir mettre hors de ma terre et
jurisdiction a moy commise tous
les heretiques declairés par l'E-
glise. Toutes les choses susdictes
je confirme par serment.*

Mette lors la main sur le livre
des Evangiles.

9c. Ces promesses faictes, soit
incontinant commencé a chanter le
Te Deum, et deux archevesques ou
evesques maynent ledict roy par
les mains a l'autel, devant lequel il
se prosterne jusques a la fin dudict
Te Deum. Apres se lieve. Auparavant doivent avoir esté mises sur
ledict autel les couronne royale,
son espee enclose dedans le fourreau, ses esperons d'or, le sceptre
doré et la verge a la mesure d'une
couldee [fol. 169v] ou plus, ayant
au dessus une main d'ivoire. Aussi
les chausses appellees sendales ou
botines de soye de couleur de bleu
azuré semees par tout de fleurs de
lys d'or et la tunique ou dalmatique
de mesmes couleur et euvre, faict
en la maniere de chazuble de laquelle les soubzdiacres sont vestuz
a la messe. Et avec ce le surcot qui
est le manteau royal, totalement de

de Saint Denis en France de s'abbaye a Rains aporter et sur l'autel garder. Lors le roy, qui est en estant devant l'autel, doit desvetir ses robes, excepté la cote de soye et chemise, [en] laquelle cote et chemise soient grans et parfons ouvertures devant et derriere, c'est a dire ou piz et entre les espaules, jointes ensemble par anses d'argent. Lors les chausses dessus dictes doivent estre chaussies au roy du grant chambelain de France. Apres, le duc de Bourgoigne li doit chaussier les esperons, lesquelz doivent estre tantost ostés. Apres, le roy doit estre ceint du glaive d'un seul archevesque, lequel ceint, tantost li arcevesques trait hors le glaive de sa gaine, la gaine sur l'autel remise, et le donne es mains du roy en disant ceste oroison.

semblables couleur et euvre, faict a bien prés en maniere d'une chappe sans chaperon. Toutes lesquelles choses l'abbé de Sainct Denys en France doit de son monastere apporter a Reins et estre a l'autel pour les garder. Lors le roy estant devant l'autel despouille premierement ses vestemens, fors la camisole de soye et sa chemise, qui soient ouvertes bien a val[14] devant et derriere, sçavoir est a la poictrine et entre les espaules, les ouvertures de ladicte camisole estans recloses et rejoinctes ensemble par attaches d'argent. Adonc tout premier le grand chambellan de France chausse au roy lesdictes botines que ledict abbé de Sainct Denis luy aura baillees. Et apres le duc de Bourgoigne luy attache les esperons et incontinent les luy oste. Puys l'archevesque seul luy ceigne son espee, et aussitost la luy desceigne et la tire hors du fourreau qui soit mis sur l'autel, et ladicte espee nue mise par ledict archevesque en la main du roy en disant l'oraison qui ensuyt.

10b. *Pren ce glaive qui t'est donné avec la benei-* [p. 95] *çon de Dieu, duquel par la vertu de Jhesucrist tu puisses resister et hors getter touz tes anemis et tous les adversaires de Sainte Eglise, ton royaume garder et les chastiaux de Dieu deffendre par l'aide du*

10c. *Prens ce glaive a toy donné avecques la benediction de Dieu, par lequel en la vertu du Sainct Esperit tu puisse[s] resister et repoulser tous tes ennemys et les adversaires de la saincte Eglise, defendre le royaume a toy commis, et garder*

---

[14] The manuscript reads "a val" ("à val" is the reading of the printed editions), but the French translation of the Ordo of Reims (Ordo XX B,10) reads "ouvertes bien aval devant et derrieres."

non vaincu victorien Nostre
Seigneur Jhesucrist. Qui cum
Patre.

11b. Lors on chante une telle antienne.

Soies confortés et homs
virtueux et soies sur les gardes de
*Dieu ton*ᵃ *Seigneur et va en ses*
voies, et gardes cerimonies et ses
commandemens et ses tesmoi-
gnages et jugemens, a celle fin
que, en quelque lieu tu te tornes,
Dieu te conferme.

11b. ᵃ com A.

12b. Quant ceste antienne est chantee, on dit ceste oroison.

Dieu, par laquelle pourveance
les choses celestes et terriennes
sont ordenement atrempees, soyes
propices a nostre trescrestien roy,
a celle fin que toute la force de ses
anemis par la vertu du glaive
esperituel soit brisee, et toy pour
lui combatent, toute acraventee.[15]

13b. Le glaive doit li roys humblement penre de la main de
l'archevesque et offrir a l'autel, et
tantost de rechief de la main de
l'archevesque le reprenre et incontinent le bailler au seneschal de
France ; s'il en y a point, il doit
bailler a un des barons, auquel qui
voudra, a porter devant soy en l'e-
glise jusques a la fin de la messe et
apres jusques au palais.

l'armee de Dieu par l'aide de Nostre
Seigneur Jesuscrist, triumphateur
invincible, lequel regne [fol. 170r]
avec le Pere, et cetera.

11c. Lors par le choeur soit chantee ceste anteyne.

Soye conforté et virile, observe
les enseignemens du Seigneur ton
Dieu affin que tu chemynes en ses
voyes et gardes ses ceremonies,
commandemens, tesmoignages et
jugemens, et qu'il te confirme en
quelque endroict que tu te
tournes.

12c. Et l'archevesque dye cest oraison.

Dieu, qui par ta providence
gouverne[s] les choses celestes et
terriennes ensemble, soys propice
a nostre roy trescrestien, a ce que
par la vertu du glaive spirituel
toute la force de ses ennemys soit
rompue, et toy bataillant pour
luy, entierement brisee par Nostre
Seigneur Jesuschrist, et cetera.

13c. A l'heure ledict roy
reçoyve en humilité ladicte espee
de la main dudict archevesque et
l'offre a l'autel, puys la repreigne
de la main dudict archevesque et
sans demeure la baille au connestable de France s'il en a. Et s'il
n'en a, a celluy de ses barons qu'il
luy plaira, pour la porter devant
luy tant en l'eglise jusques a la fin
de la messe, que aprés la messe
jusques au palays.

---

[15] "acravantee" = "écrasée"

14b. De la preparacion du cresme de quoy il doit estre enoings.

Li cresmes doit estre mis sur l'autel en la patene et li arcevesques la sainte ampole que li abbes de Saint Remi a portee, doit ouvrir et a une esguille d'or un pou de l'uille qui du ciel fu envoié, atraire et diligaument mesler avec le cresme qui est en la patene pour en oindre le roy, lequel roy entre les autres terriens est de ce privilege ahourés,[16] que en son sacre il est oings de l'uille du ciel envoiee.

15b. Appareillé l'ointure de quoy le roy doit estre oings, les ances des ouvertures de ses robes doivent estre deslacies devant et derriere, et le roy agenoillié. Li arcevesques sur li doit dire ces oroisons avant ce que il l'oigne.

22b. *Nous t'appellons, Pere tout puissant, pardurables Diex que ton sergent cy N., lequel par la pourveance de ta dispensacion de son commencement tu as fourmé, et jusques a ceste journee en la fleur de sa jeunesce*[a] *acroissement as donné, du don de ta pitié anrichiz et plain de grace de verité, de jour en jour devant toy et*

14c. Cela faict, l'unction soit preparee en ceste maniere.

Le cresme estant mys a l'autel sur une patene consacree, l'archevesque ouvre la saincte empoule apportee par l'abbé Sainct Remy, et estant sur ledict autel et en tire avec une petite verge d'or ung peu de l'huille envoyé du ciel, et diligemment avec le doigt le mesle ou cresme preparé en la patene pour oindre le roy, lequel seul entre tous les roys de la terre resplendit de ce glorieux privilege qu'il est singulierement oinct de l'huille envoyé du ciel.

15c. Ladicte unction preparee soient par ledict archevesque deffermees lesdicts attaches des ouvertures des vestemens du roy devant et derriere et, ledict roy mis a genoux, [fol. 170v] deux archevesques ou evesques commencent la letanye ;

21c. laquelle finye l'archevesque, assys comme il syet quand il consacre les evesques, dye sur luy avant que l'oindre les troys oraisons qui ensuyvent.

22c. *Nous t'invoquons, Seigneur, sainct Pere tout puissant, Dieu eternel, qu'il te plaise cestuy ton serviteur (soit nommé), auquel par la providence de ta divine dispensation creé dés le commencement as donné croistre jusques a ce present jour resjouy de la fleur de jeunesse, enrichy du don de ta pieté et plain de la grace*

---

[16] "ahourés" = "aourné" (= "orné," "éclatant"); the Latin reads "prefulget privilegio."

*devant les hommes fay le de bien
en mieulx tousjours pourfiter, a
celle fin que, la chaire de souverain gouvernement par la largesse de ta grace joieusement
retenue et du mur de ta misericorde encontre tes adversaires
environ guarnis, son peuple en
paix et en vertus de victoire glorieusement puisse gouverner.*

22b. ᵃjennesce A.

23b. *Diex, qui tes peuples par
vertus conseilles, par amour
seigneuris donne a ton sergent cy
l'esperit de sapience avec le gouvernement de discipline, a celle
fin que*¹⁷ *ce dont son cuer a toy
devot ou gouvernement du royaume et en bonnes euvres perseverans puisse pervenir au royaume
pardurable.*

24b. *En ces jours a toutes
gens nesce*ᵃ *equité et justice, a ses
amis aide, a ses a[ne]mis ostacle,
aux humbles solaz, aux orgueillex
correpcion, aux riches doctrine,
aux povres pitié, aux pelerins
paix, aux propres en leur paix*

*de verité, faire de jour en jour
tousjours proffiter en myeulx
devant Dieu et les hommes, affin
que par la largesse de la grace
superieure il preigne en grande
lyesse le trosne du supreme gouvernement et par le mur de ta
misericorde couvert de toutes parts
de l'adversité des ennemys, il
puisse eureusement gouverner le
peuple a luy commis en la paix de
propiciation et vertu de victoire.
Par Nostre Seigneur Jesuschrist,*
et cetera.

23c. *Dieu, qui par vertu con-
seille tes peuples et par amour les
domine, donne a cestuy ton serviteur l'esperit de ta sapience avec
la reigle de discipline, a ce que a
toy devot de tout son cueur il soit
tousjours idoyne ou gouvernement du royaume et par ton don
en son tempz la seurté de l'Eglise
soit adressee et que la devotion
ecclesiastique soit permanente en
tranquillité. Et que luy perseverant
en bonnes oeuvres puisse par ta
conduicte parvenir au royaume
eternel. Par Nostre Seigneur
Jesuschrist* etc.

24c. *En ses jours naisse a
tous equité et justice, aux amys
secours, aux ennemys obstacle,
aux affligés consolation, aux
eslevez correction, aux riches
enseignement, aux pauvres pityé,
aux pelerins* [fol. 171r] *pacifica-*

---

¹⁷ The text of this formula is incomplete after "a celle fin que," and does not make
a great deal of sense; one cannot know whether the translator or the scribe of *A* was
responsible for the defect.

seurté, en gouvernant chascun atrempeement selon sa mesure, soy meismes apreigne et congnoisse, a celle fin que, de ta compuncion arousés, a tout le peuple exemple de vie a toy plaisanz puisse donner, en alant par la voie de verité, a son peuple attrempees richesses habondaument, acquerre a la senté des cuers et des corps de toy octroyé toutes choses couvenables retenue; et en ceste maniere la pensé de son cuer et tout son conseil en toy, ordenant li peuples, gouvernement en paix et en sapience puisse tousjours trouver et il, toy aidant, prosperité et longueur de ceste presente vie retenue jusques a la viellesce, et en la fin de ceste fragilité par la largesce de ta pitié de touz lians de pechies delivrés, les pardurables joies des anges puisse faire et aconsuivre.

24b. ª veste A.

25b. C'est la consecracion.

[p. 96] Tout puissant pardurable Diex, creeur et gouverneur de ciel et de terre, faiseur et disposeur des anges et des homes, roy des roys, sire des seigneurs, qui ton loyal sergent Abraham ses ennemis fais vaincre et surmonter, qui a Moyse et Josué, princes de

tion, aux pauvres subjectz paix et seurté en la patrie. Apreigne continuellement a se commander soy mesmes et moderement gouverner ung chacun selon son estat, affin que, arrousé de ta compunction, il puisse donner a tout le peuple exemples de vye a toy agreables, et chemynant par la voye de verité avec le trouppeau a luy subject, acquiere en abondance frugales richesses, et perçoyve ensemble tout ce qui est par toy concedé pour le salut des ames et des corpz. Et ainsi mettant en toy la cogitation de sa pensee et tout conseil, soit veu inventer tousjours les gouvernacles du peuple en paix et sapience assemblees, et par ton ayde ait la prolixité et prosperité de la presente vye et par tempz bons parvienne a grande vieillesse, et delivre des lyens de tous vices par la largesse de ta pieté, obtienne parfaicte fin de ceste fragilité et les perpetuelles recompenses de la felicité infinye et societés eternelles des anges. Par Nostre Seigneur Jesuschrist etc.

25c. Lesdictes trois oraisons achevees, dye ledict archevesque celle de la consecration du roy qui ensuyt.

Dieu eternel, tout puissant createur et gouverneur du ciel et de la terre, facteur et dispositeur des anges et des hommes, roy des roys et seigneur des seigneurs, qui feys Abraham ton fidele serviteur triumpher de ses ennemys, a Moyse et Josué preposés a ton

ton peuple mont de nobles victoires
as voulu octroier, qui l'umble
enfant David a la hautesse du
royaume tu voulsis eslever et de la
bouche du lyon et de la main de la
beste et de Golie, et avec ce du
maligne glaive de Saül et de tous
ses anemis t'a pleu a delivrer, et
Salemon du souverain don de
paix et sapience as voulu donner,
regarde propices aux preces de
nostre humilité et sur ton sergent
cy, lequel par humble devocion du
commun accort en roy nous eslisons, multiplie[a] les dons de tes
beneiçons, et de la destre de ta
puissance en tous temps et en
tous lieux l'environne, a celle fin
que de la loyauté du devant dit
Abraham confermés, de la debon-
nereté Moyse aenforciés[b], de la
force Josué guarnis, de humilité
de David exauciés, de la sapience
Salemon aornez, a toy en toutes
choses puisse plaire et par le
santier[c] de justice sanz offense
aler, et de tout le royaume l'eglise
desormaiz avecques les peuples
subgiés en telle maniere nourrisse
et enseigne, garde et entroduisse,
et encontre tous ses anemis visibles et non visibles puissaument
et royalment le gouvernement de
ta vertus administre, que le royal
siege[d], le ceptre et la seigneurie
des creans et mescreans ne
delaisse, mais leurs courages a
l'unité et l'acordance de paix et de
foy par t'ayde renforme, a celle
fin que, de deue subjection de l'un
et de l'autre peuple environnés et

peuple as donné plusieurs victoires, as elevé a la haultesse du
royaume David ton humble serviteur et l'as delivré de la gueule du
lyon et de la main de la beste et de
Golyas et du maling glaive de
Saül et de tous ses ennemys, as
enrichy Salomon de don indicible
de sapience et paix, apaisé
regarde aux prieres de nostre
humilité et multiplye les dons
[fol. 171v] de tes benedictions sur
cestuy ton serviteur (soit nommé)
lequel par humble devotion nous
eslisons par ensemble ou royaume, et l'environne tousjours et
en tous lieux de la dextre de ta
puissance, a ce que confirmé de la
fidelité dudict Abraham, joyssant
de la mansuetude de Moyse, garny
de la fortitude de Josué, exalté de
l'humilité de David, decoré de la
sapience de Salomon, il te soit en
toutes choses complaisant, et
marche tousjours de pas sans
chopper par la voye de justice et
tellement nourisse, enseigne, garde
et instruise d'oresenavant l'eglise
de tout le royaume et les peuples y
annexés, administre puissam-
ment et regalement le regiment de
ta vertu contre tous ennemys visibles et invisibles, qu'il ne delaisse
le trosne royal, sçavoir est les
sceptres des Françoys, Bourgui-
gnons, et Aquitaniens, mais
reforme par ton ayde leurs volun-
tés a la concorde des premiere foy
et paix, affin que, clarifié de la
deue subjection de tous ses peuples
et glorifié de l'amour condigne, il

de digne honneur glorifiez, par
longue espace de vie la hautesce
de paterne gloire par ta miseracion
assambler, establir et gouverner
deserve, ou du heaume de ta pro-
tection garnis et de ton escu invin-
cible couvers, et des armes du ciel
environnez, la gloyre de desirable
victoire beneureusement de ses
anemis preingne, la paour de sa
puissance aus mescreans demon-
stre, et paix a ses sergens liement
par ses vertus raporte; et des ver-
tus desquelles tes loyaux sergens
dessus diz aornas par honneur de
digne beneiçon l'en orne, et en
gouvernement du royaume haute-
ment assiés et confermés, et le
*paroings*e *de l'uille et unction de*
la grace du Saint Esperit.

puisse par ta miseration establir
et gouverner en unyon le sommet
de la gloire paternelle par long
espace de vye, et garny du
heaulme de ta protection, tousjours
couvert du bouclier invincible,
environné des armes celestes, il
preigne eureusement le triumphe
de la victoire desirable de ses
ennemys, face crainte de sa puis-
sance aux infideles, et rapporte
en joye la paix a ceulx qui mili-
tent soubz toy, et le decore par
multipliee benediction d'honneur
des vertus desquelles as decoré tes
fideles susdictz, le colloque haulte-
ment ou gouvernement du roy-
aume et l'oingz de l'huille de la
grace du Sainct Esperit.

25b. ª multiplier A. —ᵇ Moyse a
enforciés A. —ᶜ sautier A. —
ᵈ cierge A. —ᵉ par oings A.

26b. Lors le doit oindre li arcevesques de l'onction devant dicte
et meslee sur la patene et le doit
oindre premierement ou sommet
du chief, secondement ou piz,
tiercement entre les espaules,
quartement sur les espaules, quintement es jointures des bras, et a
chascune unction doit dire :

26c. Ladicte oraison finye face
ledict archevesque l'onction des
cresme et huille [fol. 172r] envoyé
du ciel, par luy meslé auparavant
en la patene comme dict a esté, et
ce en cinq endroictz de la personne
du roy, le premier au dessus du
chief, le second en la poictrine, le
tiers entre les espaules, le quart
esdictes deux espaules, le quinct
es joinctures des deux bras, disant
a chacun endroict :

27b. *Je te oings en roy de*
l'uille sanctifié, ou non du Pere et
du Filz et du Saint Esperit.

27c. *Je t'oingz*[18] *de l'huille*
sanctifié ou nom du Pere, du Filx
et du Sainct Esperit.

---

[18] *Loingz,* the reading of *B,* although grammatically possible, is either a mistranslation or a scribal error.

Et tuit doivent dire « Amen. » Quant un fait ceste unction, les assistens doivent chanter ceste antienne.

28b. *Sadoch li prestres et Nathan le prophete oygnyrent en Gyon Salemon en roy, et liement disoient : « Vive le roy pardurablement ».*

29b. Parfaite l'unction, l'antienne chantee, l'archevesque doit dire ceste oroison.

Jhesucrist, paroing[a] ce roy en gouvernement de l'ointure de quoy tu oygnis les prestres, les roys et les prophetes et les martirs qui pour la foy ont vaincu les royaumes, ont parfait justice et ont prises les promissions ; ta tressacree unction sur son chief dequeure, par dedans descende et les entrailles du cuer trespasse, et par ta grace soit fait dignes des promissions, lesquelles les tres victoriaux roys ont eues, a celle fin que en ce siecle glorieusement il vive et regne, et a leur compaignie ou royaume du ciel parmaine, par Nostre Seigneur Jhesucrist ton filz, qui est oings de l'uille de leesce et de joie par dessus touz hommes, et par la vertu de la croiz a les puissances a l'ennemi vaincues, enfer destruit, le royaume du dyable supedité, et sur tous les cielx victoriaux glorieux est montez, en laquelle maint toute gloire, toute puissance sont, et vit et regne Diex en l'unité du Saint Esperit pardurablement.

29b. [a] par oing A.

Et tous respondent « Ainsi soit-il. » A prendre les espaules pour deux et bras pour deux, l'onction seroit faicte en sept endroictz. Pendant que ledict archevesque la faict, soit chantee l'anteyne.

28c. *Le presbtre Sadoch et le prophete Nathan oignirent Salomon roy en Hierusalem, et venans joyeulx deyrent : « Vive le roy eternellement ».*

29c. Laquelle achevee ledict archevesque dye les oraisons qui ensuivent.

Seigneur Dieu, oingtz ce roy ou gouvernement de ce que as oingtz les presbtres, roys, prophetes et martirs qui par foy ont vaincu les royaumes, ouvré la justice et obtenu les promissions. Ta tressacree unction descoule sur son chief, descende jusques au dedans, penetre le profond de son cueur et soit par ta grace faict digne des promesses qu'ont obtenues les tresvictorieux roys, affin qu'il regne eureusement ou siecle present et parvienne a leur compaignee ou regne celeste, par Nostre Seigneur Jesuschrist ton filx, qui a esté oinct de l'huille de joye pardessus tous ses consors et en vertu de la croix a debellé les puissances de l'air, destruict les enfers, vaincu le royaume du diable, et victeur est monté aux cieulx, en la main duquel consistent victoire toute gloire et puissance, vit avec toy, et regne Dieu en unité du Sainct Esperit par tous les siecles des siecles.

30b. Une autre oroison.

Diex, force des esleuz, la hautesce des humbles, qui des le commencement du monde par l'abondance du deluge les pechiés dudit monde chastias et par la colombe le rainsiau d'olive por- [p. 97] *tant paix a la terre rendue demonstras, de rechief Aaron ton sergent par l'unction d'uille en prestre saintifias, et apres par l'effusion de cest oignement pour gouverner le peuple d'Israel les prestres, les roys et les prophetes ordenas et la face de l'Eglise*ª *par l'uille en joie estre esclarcie par la voiz de ton prophete David anonças, ainsi, tout puissant Pere, par la grace de ceste creature ton sergent cy daignes de ta beneiçon sanctifier et lui en la semblance de la colombe paix a son peuple suppliant li faiz annoncier et ou service de Dieu les exemples de Aaron diligaument ensuivre et les hautesces de son royaume en conseil de science et equité de jugement tousjours gouverner, et par ceste sainte unction et ta beneiçon vout plus de leesce et d'ilarité a tout son peuple li faiz demonstrer. Per dominum.*

30b. ª teglise A.

31b. *Diex, filz de Dieu, Nostre Seigneur Jhesucrist, qui de Dieu le Pere de l'uille de exultacion es oings par dessus tous hommes parçonniers de ta gloyre issis par ceste presente infusion de oingture, la beneiçon du Saint Esperit sur ton*

30c. *Dieu, fortitude des eleuz et haultesse des humbles, qui as ou commencement voulu* [fol. 172v] *chastier les pechés du monde par effusion du deluge, et as demonstré par la columbe portant le rameau d'olive la paix estre rendue aux terres, et apres par unction d'huille as ordonné presbtre Aaron ton serviteur, et puis par infusion de cest unguent as renduz parfaictz les presbtres, roys et prophetes pour regir le peuple d'Israel, et as par la voix prophetique de David ton serviteur predict que la face de l'Eglise seroit joyeuse en huylle. Ainsi nous te supplyons, Pere tout puissant, que ton plaisir soit sanctifier de ta benediction cestuy ton serviteur par la gresse de ceste creature, a ce qu'il apporte a la semblance de la columbe la paix de simplicité au peuple a luy commis, qu'il imite diligemment ou service de Dieu les exemples d'Aaron, et qu'il atteigne tousjours les haultesses du royaume en conseilx de science et equité de jugement, et le faictz avoir par ceste unction d'huille (toy aydant) la face preparee a joye a tout le peuple. Par Jesuschrist Nostre Seigneur etc.*

31c. *Jesuschrist Nostre Seigneur Dieu, filx de Dieu, qui par le Pere a esté oinct de l'huille d'exultation pardessus tous ses participans, par la presente infusion du sacré unguent du Sainct Esperit infonde sur ton chief la chief espande, et les entrailles de ton cuer face trespercier, a celle fin que par ce don visible et traitable les dons invisibles reçoives et le temporel royaume par justes atrempences gouverner, et avecque lui pardurablement deserves a regner.*

32b. Ces oroisons dictes, on met les ances des ouvertures au[x] robes du roy pour cause de l'uncion, et lors du chambellan de France il est vestus de la cote de soy[e] devant dicte et de l'autre aournement, lequel est en maniere de mantel ou de chappe de soye, en telle maniere que la main destre ait franche ouverture de ce vestement, et sur la senestre l'autre pan est eslevez en maniere de chasuble de prestre. Et apres ce, l'archevesque lui baille le ceptre en la main destre et la verge en la senestre, maiz avant lui est baillés l'annel, et en lui baillant, ceste oroison on dit qui s'ensuit.

33b. *Pren l'annel, cenacle de la sainte foy, la fermeté du royaume, acroissement de puissance par quoy tu saches par victorieuse puissance les anemis debouter, les heresies debouter et destruire, les subgiz assembler et a la commune et crestienne foy en perseverence conjoindre.*

34b. L'oroison apres l'annel.

benediction et la face penetrer jusques a l'interieur de ton cueur, affin que tu puisse[s] par ce don visible et traictable percevoir les choses invisibles, et apres avoir par justes moderations accomply le regne temporel, regner avec luy eternellement. Par Jesuschrist Nostre Seigneur etc.

32c. Lesdictes oraisons achevees, soient par ledict archevesque, presbtres ou diacres les attaches des ouvertures des vestemens du roy refermees a cause l'unction[a]. Et lors ledict grand chambellan de France veste audict roy la[b] dalmatique de bleu azuré et par dessus le manteau [fol. 173r] royal de façon que la main dextre soit a delivre devers l'ouverture dudict manteau, lequel sur la senestre main soit elevé comme la chazuble d'un presbtre. Et apres ledict archevesque luy mette l'anneau ou doigt medicinal de la main dextre, disant :

32c. [a]l'unction *corr. from* l'onction B. —[b] les B.

33c. *Prens l'anneau, signacle de la saincte foy, solidité du royaume, augmentation de puissance, par lesquelles choses tu sache[s] chasser les ennemys par puissance triumphale, exterminer les heresies, reunir les subjectz et les annexer a la perseverance de la foy catholique. Par Jesuschrist Nostre Seigneur etc.*

34c. Apres ledict anneau baillé, dye ledict archevesque l'oraison qui ensuyt.

*Dieu, de qui vient toute dig-
nité et toute puissance, donne a
ton sergent sa dignité et euvre en
prosperité, en laquelle, toy donnant, il demeure et tousjours te
doubte et continuement a plaire
s'esforce.*

35b. Donné l'annel, tantost
apres l'archevesque lui donne le
ceptre en la main destre, et est
dicte ceste oroison.

*Pren le noble ceptre de royal
puissance, c'est assavoir verge
droite de royaume, verge de vertus par laquelle toy meismes bien
te gouvernes, Sainte Eglise et le
peuple des crestiens a toy de Dieu
commis par vertu royal des
envaiseurs deffendes, les mauvais
corriges[a], droituriers appaisier,
et que droite voie puisse tenir, par
t'ayde les adresces, a celle fin que
du temporel royaume au pardurable parvenir par l'ayde de
celui de quoy le royaume et l'empire dure pardurablement.*

35b. [a] corrigeurs A.

36b. L'oroison apres le ceptre.

*Sire de tous, fontaine de tous
biens, establisseurs de prouffiz,
donne a ton sergent N. la dignité
receue[19] bien gouverner, et l'onneur de toy a lui donnee daignes
confermer ; sur tous roys
crestiens et autres l'onneure,
enrichis le de habondant, et ou*

*Dieu, duquel est toute puis-
sance et dignité, donne a ton
serviteur l'eureux effect de sa dignité, en laquelle toy remunerant il
soit permanent, te craigne tousjours et s'efforce complaire. Par
Jesuschrist Nostre Seigneur etc.*

35c. Puis ledict archevesque
mette le sceptre en la main dextre
dudict roy en disant :

*Prens le sceptre, enseigne de
la puissance royale, sçavoir est la
droicte verge du royaume, verge
de vertu, par laquelle gouverne
bien toy mesmes, defendz des
meschans par royale puissance
saincte Eglise, qui est le peuple
crestien a toy commis de Dieu,
corrige les mauvais, pacifie les
droicturiers, addresse les qu'ilx
puissent par ta grace tenir la
droicte voye, affin que du royaume temporel tu parvienne[s] au
royaume eternel, aydant celuy
duquel le regne et empire est sans
fin, permanent es siecles des*

36c. Apres ledict sceptre
baillé, dye l'oraison qui ensuyt.

*Seigneur fontayne de tous
biens, Dieu aucteur de tous bons
effectz, donne (nous te supplyons)
a ton serviteur bien gouverner
celle dignité qu'il a apprehendee,
te plaise luy corroborer l'honneur
ouquel l'as constitué, honorifie le
pardessus [fol. 173v] tous les roys*

---

[19] *Retenue* in *A*. Also, one expects the preposition *de* at this point and below in no.
67b, but it was not impossible to construct the infinitive without a preposition (information that I owe to Claude Buridant).

siege du royaume fermement l'establis, en lignie le visite, longeur de vie li octrie, et en son temps tousjours nesce[a] justice, a celle fin que en joie et en leesce soit glorifiés ou royaume pardurable.

36b. [a] leesce A.

37b. Apres celui est donnee la verge, et est dit :

Pren la verge de vertus et de equité, par laquelle tu entendes les bons amer, les mauvaiz espouenter, aux desvoiés voie enseigner, au cheuz la main estent et les humbles relieve, a celle fin que Jhesucrist Nostre Seigneur l'uys si te veille ouvrir, qui dit de soy meismes : 'Je sui l'uys ; cil qui par moy entrera, sauvez sera,' et cilz qui est la clef de David et le ceptre de la maison d'Israel, 'qui euvre et nulz ne clot, qui clot et nul ne euvre,' te [p. 98] soit aideur, qui mist hors 'le prisonnier lié et saint en tenebres et en ombre de mort de la maison de chartre,' et en toutes choses ensives, de quoy David li prophetes par prophecie chante : 'Tes sieges, Diex, pardurablement dure et la verge de ton royaume est verge de equité.' Et de rechief que tu ensuivez celui qui dit : 'Tu as amé justice et haÿ iniquité, et pour ce ton Dieu t'a oingt de l'uille de leesce et de exultacion' par dessur[20] touz

de la terre, enrichis le de benediction abondante, consolide le de ferme stabilité ou trosne du royaume, visite le en lignee, donne luy prolixité de vye, en ses jours naisse tousjours justice, affin que en joye et liesse il ait gloire ou royaume eternel. Par Jesuschrist etc.

37c. Consequemment ledict archevesque mette la main de justice en la main senestre dudict roy en disant :

Prens la verge de vertu et equité par laquelle tu saches asseurer les bons et faire craindre les mauvais, enseigne le chemyn aux desvoyés, tendz la main aux tumbés, rabaisse les orguilleux, eleve les humbles, affin que Nostre Seigneur Jesuschrist t'ouvre l'huys, ayant de luy mesmes prononcé : 'Je suis l'huys, par lequel qui entrera sera sauvé,' et luy qui est la clef de David et le sceptre de la maison d'Israel, 'qui ouvre, et nul ferme, qui ferme et nul ouvre,' celluy qui mect hors 'de la maison de prison l'enchesné seant es tenebres et umbre de mort' te soit aydant, a ce que tu puisse[s] ensuyvre en toutes choses celluy duquel le prophete David a chanté : 'Dieu ton siege est ou siecle du siecle, la verge d'equité est la verge de ton regne,' et imiter celluy qui dict : 'Ayme justice et hay iniquité pource Dieu, ton Dieu, t'a oingt de l'huille de lyesse' a l'exemple de celluy qu'il avoit oingt devant les

---

[20] "dessur" = "au-dessus de."

hommes qui par toy sont parçon-niers de la vie de gloyre.

38b. Apres ceste unction les pers par nom sont appelés[a] du chancelier de France ou de l'archevesque se le chancelier n'est present, lesquelz appelés et venus, l'archevesque prent sur l'autel la couronne royal, et il mesmes la met sur le chief du roy, laquelle mise tuit li pers, tant clers comme lays, mettent la main a la couronne et de toutes parties la soustiennent, et lors li archevesques dit ceste oroison.

38b. [a] appelees A.

39b. *Diex te couronne de la couronne de gloire et de justice, d'onneur et d'euvre de force, a celle fin que par l'office de nostre beneiçon, en droite foy et en habondant fruit de bonnes euvres puisses parvenir a la couronne du royaume pardurable.*

40b. L'oroison apres la cou-ronne.

Diex de pardurableté, duc de vertus, de tous adversaires victo-riaus, beneys ton sergent cy, son chief a toy enclinant, et en longue santé et habondant felicité le garde, et en quelque lieu et pour quelques besongnes t'ayde deman-dera, hastivement l'essausses et gardes et deffendes, et te requerons

siecles pardessus tous ses partici-pans, Jesuschrist Nostre Seigneur.

38c. Ladicte main de justice baillee audict roy, le chancellier de France, s'il y est, synon ledict archevesque, appelle par leurs noms et selon leur ordre les pairs de France, les laiz les premiers, puys les clercz, lesquelz estans a l'entour, preigne ledict arche-vesque la couronne royale de dessus l'autel et la mette seul sur le chief du roy, et aussi tost tous lesdictz pairs tant clercz que [fol. 174r] lays y mectent les mains et eux seulx la soustiennent de tous costés, disant ledict archevesque :

39c. *Dieu te couronne de la couronne de gloire et justice, hon-neur et oeuvre de constance, affin que par l'office de nostre benedic-tion avecques droicte foy et fruict multiplié de bonnes euvres tu parvienne[s] au royaume per-petuel par la largesse de celluy duquel le regne et empire est per-manent es siecles des siecles.*

40c. Ladicte couronne assize sur ledict chief du roy, soustenue par lesdictz pairs, ledict arche-vesque dye les oraison et benedic-tion suyvantes.

Dieu d'eternité, duc des ver-tuz, victeur de tous ennemys, beneys cestuy ton serviteur a toy inclinant son chief, conserve le en longue santé et prospere felicité, en quelque endroict qu'il invoque ton ayde assiste luy aussi tost, le garde et defendz, octroye luy (nous te supplyons, Seigneur) les que tu lui donnes les richesses de ta gloyre et acomplis en biens son desir et le couronne en ta miseracion et misericorde, et a toy, Dieu, serve continuement par sainte devocion.

41b. Tantost apres ceste oroison doit estre dicte ceste beneiçon.

Li tous puissans Diex estande sa destre de sa beneiçon et t'environne du mur de debonnaireté, de la guarde de sa protection, par les merites de la benoite Vierge Marie, de saint Pere le prince des apostres et de tous les saints de paradis. Amen.

42b. *Dieu te pardoint les pechiés que tu as faiz et te doint grace et misericorde que humblement tu requieres, et te delivrez de toutes aversités et de tous les agués de tes anemis visibles et non visibles. Amen.*

43b. *Les bons anges, qui tous temps et en tous lieux t'adreicent, t'acompaignent pour toy garder envoie*[a] *et de tout pechié et glaive de touz perilz par sa puissance te delivre. Amen.*

43b. [a] euuore A.

44b. *Tes anemis a benignité de paix et de charité convertisse et en tous biens gracieus et aimable te face, les pertinens en toy poursuivre et hair de confusion ordenee a leur sauveté reveste, et sur toy florisse la sanctificacion pardurable. Amen.*

richesses de ta grace, accomplys en biens son desir, la couronne luy soit en miseration et misericorde et a toy Seigneur serve continuellement en bonne devotion. Par Nostre Seigneur Jesuschrist etc.

41c. *Le Dieu tout puissant estende la dextre de sa benediction et infunde sur toy le don de sa protection, t'environne du mur de felicité, et garde de sa propiciation par l'intercession des merites de la Saincte Vierge Marie, des benoist sainct Pierre prince des apostres, sainct Gregoire et tous les sainctz. Ainsi soit il.*

42c. *Le Seigneur te pardonne tous les maulx que tu as faictz, t'octroye la grace et misericorde que humblement tu luy demande[s], et te delivre de toutes adversités et de toutes embusches des ennemys visibles et invisibles. Ainsi soit il.*

43c. *Commette a ta garde ses bons anges, lesquelx tousjours et en tous lieux te precedent, accompaignent et suyvent* [fol. 174v] *et sa puissance te delivre de peché, de glaive et de malaventure de tous perilx. Ainsi soit il.*

44c. *Convertisse tes ennemys a la benignité de paix et charité, te face gracieux et aymable a tous les bons, remplisse de confusion a toy salutaire[s] ceulx qui seront obstinés a te hayr et persecuter, et sur toy florisse sanctification eternelle. Ainsi soit il.*

45b. *Victorieux et glorieux seurmonter de tes anemis visibles et non visibles te face, et son saintisme nom la paour ensemble et l'amour dedans ton cuer espande et en droite foy et en bonnes euvres perseverable te rende, et paix en tous temps octroie, avec la paume de victoire au royaume pardurable te conduise. Amen.*

46b. *Et qui t'a voulu son peuple establir et constituer, et en ce present siecle beneureux ordener, en la beneurté pardurable te veille acompaigner. Amen.*

47b. Autre beneiçon.
Sire, beneys cest esleu prince, qui les royaumes de tous roys des le commencement gouvernes. Amen.

Et de celle fin le glorifie, qui en la hautesce de David le cept[r]e de royaume il tiengne, et du don de ta sainte propiciacion soit trouvés plains et riches. Amen.

Donnes lui par ton inspiracion bien gouverner son peuple, si come a Salemon tu fais avoir royaume paisible. Amen.

48b. Cy est descript l'estat du roy.

Soies fermes et establez et retieng desormaiz l'estat que par paterne succession tu as tenu, et qui par droit d'eritage est a toy

45c. *Te face tousjours victorieux et triumphateur de tes ennemys visibles et invisibles, infunde continuellement en ton cueur les craincte et amour conjoinctes de son sainct nom, te rende perseverant en droicte foy et bonnes euvres, et la paix concedee en tes jours te conduise avec la palme de victoire ou regne perpetuel. Ainsi soit il.*

46c. *Et celluy qui t'a voulu constituer roy sur son peuple t'ayant faict eureux en ce present siecle, t'octroye participation de la felicité eternelle, ce que veuille donner celluy qui regne, etc.*

47c. *Seigneur, qui de tout tempz gouvernes les regnes de tous roys, benys ce present prince. Ainsi soit il.*

Et de telle benediction le glorifie qu'il tienne le sceptre de salut avec la sublimité de David et soit enrichy du don de saincte propiciation. Ainsi soit il.

Octroy luy par ton inspiration gouverner le peuple comme as donné a Salomon le regne pacifique, ce que veuille donner celluy qui regne, etc.

48c. Apres ledict archevesque addressant sa parolle audict roy luy dye :
Soye stable et retiens d'oresenavant l'estat lequel as tenu jusques a present par la suggestion[21] de ton pere de droict hereditaire

---

[21] Du Tillet's translation, "suggestion" instead of "succession," would seem to show that Du Tillet consulted a manuscript like the Latin manuscripts *A* and *E*, both of

venus par l'auctorité de Dieu le tout puissant et par nostre tradicion, c'est a dire de touz les evesques et de touz les autres sergens de Dieu ; et de tant que le clergié tu [p. 99] *voiz des sains et sacrés anciens plus aprochier, de tant te souvienge convenablement a lui plus grant honneur porter, a celle fin que li moyannerres*[a] *de Dieu et des hommes moyannerre*[b] *du clergié et du peuple ou siege du royaume te conferme, et en son royaume pardurable regner te face Nostre Seigneur Jhesucrist, roy des roys, sire des seigneurs.*

48b. [a] moyanierres A. —[b] moyanierre A.

delegué par l'auctorité du Dieu tout puissant et par nostre presente tradition, sçavoir est de tous les evesques et autres serviteurs de Dieu, et aye souvenance de partir en lieux convenables autant plus grand honneur [fol. 175r] *au clergé que tu le voy[s] estre plus proche des sacrés autelx, affin que le mediateur de Dieu et des hommes te confirme mediateur du clergé et du peuple en ce trosne du royaume et que Nostre Seigneur Jesuscrist, roy des roys et seigneur des seigneurs, qui regne avec Dieu, etc., te face avec luy regner ou royaume eternel.*

49b. Oratio cum Deo Patre.[22]

49c. Et adjouste ledict archevesque les oraisons ou benedictions suyvantes.

Dieu le tout puissant te doint de la rousee du ciel et de la gresse de la terre, habondance de vin et fourment et huille, et te serve le peuple et t'aourent les lengues et les lignies, et soies sires de tes freres, et s'agenoullent devant toy

Le Dieu tout puissant te donne de la rosee du ciel et gresse de la terre, abondance de froment, vin et huille. Les peuples te servent et les lignees te reverent. Soye seigneur de tes freres, et les filx de ta mere s'agenoillent devant toy.

---

which read "paterna suggestione," but Brown, *Franks, Burgundians, and Aquitanians,* 74–75, suggested, probably correctly, that Du Tillet consciously altered his translation on the basis of Ordo XV,34, MS *C,* which likewise reads "paterna suggestione." See also Ordo XXII A, n. 70 and Ordo XXIII, n. 131.

"Succession" in no. 48b is not found in either Latin manuscript *A* or *E,* which are the two that most closely resemble the translated text. The Latin text's MS *B* (ca. 1330) does read "paterna successione."

[22] The odd rubric of no. 49b derives from the tendency of some scribes to write the concluding words of a liturgical formula at the right end of one or more lines that contain the beginning of the next formula. In this case, "cum Deo Patre" concludes no. 48 in the Latin text, and "Oratio" is the rubric for no. 49, the following text. This suggests that the rubric occupied only the first part of the line, and it gives a slight clue as to the appearance of *A*'s source.

le filz de ta mere, et qui te beneis-
tra si soit de beneiçon raempliz,
Diex sera tes aidierres. Le tout
puissant te beneisse des beneiçons
du ciel pardessus et des beneiçons
de l'abisme parfont par dessoubz,
de la beneiçon de lignie de grapez
et de fruiz, et les beneiçons de nos
anciens peres Abraham, Ysaac et
Jacob, soient sur toy confortés.
Per dominum.

Quiconques te benira soit remply
de benedictions, et Dieu soit a ton
ayde par Nostre Seigneur Jesus-
christ etc. Le Dieu tout puissant
te benye des benedictions du ciel
en hault, es montaignes et collines,
et des benedictions de l'abisme
estans ça bas, benedictions des
mamelles, raisins et pommes, les
benedictions des anciens peres
Abraham, Isaac et Jacob soient
confortees sur toy. Par Nostre
Seigneur Jesuschrist etc.

50b. Oroison.

Sire Diex, beneis la force de
nostre prince et reçoy les euvres
de ses mains, et par ta beneiçon
sa terre soit raemplie de fruis, du
fruit de l'abysme gisant par des-
soubz, du fruit du soleil et du
fruit de la lune, et du forment des
anciennes montaignes, et des
fruiz des pardurables, et des mois-
sons de terre et de sa planté ; et la
beneiçon de celui qui apparut ou
bisson viengne sur ton chief, et
parfaite beneiçon soient sur tes
enfans, et tiengne en huille ton
pié, et tes cornes soient si comme
la corne de l'unicorne, esquelles il
en chacera les paiens et mescre-
ans jusques a la fin de terre, car
cilz qui est ou ciel montés lui sera
aydierres pardurablement.

50c. *Seigneur, beney la forti-*
tude du prince, reçoy les euvres de
ses mains, sa terre par ta bene-
diction soit remplye de pommes,
du fruict du ciel rosee et abisme
qui est dessoubz, du fruict des
soleil et lune et du sommet des
anciennes montaignes, des
pommes des collines eternelles,
des bledz de la terre et de sa pleni-
tude. La benediction de celluy qui
apparut ou buisson vienne sur
son chief et la plaine benediction
du Seigneur soit en ses filx. Son
pied soit teinct en huille, ses
corn[e]s soient comme les cornes
du rinoceron, en eulx il dechas-
sera les gentilx jusques [fol. 175v]
aux limites de la terre, car celluy
qui est monté[a] *au Ciel sera a tous-*
jours son ayde.

50c. [a] a monté B.

51b. Ces choses acomplies, li
archevesques, avec les pers qui
soustiennent la couronne, le roy en
telle maniere noblement aournés

51c. Lesdictes oraisons ou
benedictions achevees, ledict
archevesque, accompaigné desdictz pairs soustenans ladicte

et sacrez mene en la chaiere de paremens de soye couverte et aournee, et l'assient en siege haut et eslevez, ouquel il puisse estre veu de tous ; lequel ainssi en son siege seant, li archevesques doit baisier, et die : « Vive le roy pardurablement ». Et apres lui les evesques et les lays pers qui la couronne soustiennent doivent ainsi faire et ainsi dire. Ces choses acomplies, li chantre et li soubzchantre encommençant[a] la messe, la quelle doit estre en son ordre chantee ;

51b. [a] en commencant A.

couronne, mene ledict roy ainsi aorné ou trosne a luy preparé et le assiee en sa chaise si eminente qu'il puisse estre veu de tous. Ce faict sa mitre ostee l'aille baiser ainsi seant et dye : « Vive le roy eternellement ». Apres luy, les autres pairs evesques et lays soustenans sadicte couronne facent le semblable, disans mesmes parolles. Et les premier chantre et soubzchantre gardans le choeur commencent la messe, qui soit chantee en son ordre et dicte l'oraison speciale pour ledict roy, qui ensuyt.

52c. *Nous te requerons, Dieu tout puissant, que nostre roy (soit nommé) ton serviteur, lequel par ta miseration a receu le gouvernement du royaume, perçoyve aussi l'accroissement de toutes vertus, desquelles decemment aorné il puisse eviter les monstres des vices, vaincre les ennemys et parvenir agreable a toy qui es la voye, verité et vie. Par Nostre Seigneur Jesuscrist etc.*

55b. et leue l'Evangille, le plus grant entre les archevesques doit prenre le livre des Evangiles et

55c. Lors[23] que l'Evangile est chanté, ledict roy se leve de sa chaise et luy soit ostee sa couronne

---

[23] Excepting the penultimate sentence, no. 55c is close to the reading of no. 55 in the *F G₁ J O* manuscript group of the Latin text, but it should be here associated with the Latin text's no. 55 from manuscript *C* because 1) the latter is the only surviving one that contains the sentence referring to the Secret and because 2) Du Tillet's translation, like Ordo XXII A, MS *C*, places no. 55 before no. 53. Nonetheless, the similarity here between Ordo XXII A, MS *C*, and Du Tillet's translation might be purely fortuitous because the text of Du Tillet's translation otherwise follows the order in *Croix*, which is known from the *G₁ J O* group of the Latin manuscripts. Brown, *Franks, Burgundians, and Aquitanians*, identified slight evidence that at some point, Du Tillet might have consulted another manuscript.

presenter au roy pour baisier, puis a l'archevesque qui celebre la messe. Apres l'offrande, li pers menent le roy a l'autel. Et le roy doit offrir pain et vin en un vaissiau d'argent et XIII besans d'or, et en alant et venant li glaives tout nu doit estre devant lui portés, et a l'Agnus Dei cilz qui a porté l'Evangile au roy pour baisier lui doit la paiz prise de l'archevesque porter, et apres lui tous les archevesques et evesques l'un apres l'autre donnent la paiz au roy en son siege.

de dessus la teste. Apres l'Evangile, le plus grand des archevesques et evesques preigne le livre des Evangiles et le porte a baiser audict roy, puys audict archevesque celebrant la messe. A l'offrande soient portés ung pain, ung barril d'argent plain de vin et treize besans d'or. Et ledict roy y soit conduict et ramené par lesdictz pairs soustenans sadicte couronne, son espee nue portee devant luy allant a ladicte offrende[a] et retournant. En ses secretz dye ledict archevesque ce qui ensuyt.

55c. [a] *The first* e *in* offrende *written over an erasure* B.

53c. *Nous te supplyons,* [fol. 176r] *Seigneur, qu'il te plaise sanctifier les presens offertz et que par ta largesse ilx proffictent a nostre roy (soit nommé) pour obtenir le salut de l'ame et du corpz et parachever l'office enjoinct. Par Nostre Seigneur Jhesuschrist* etc.

54c. *Seigneur, ceste oraison salutaire preserve nostre roy (soit nommé) ton serviteur de toutes adversités affin qu'il obtienne la tranquilité de la paix ecclesiastique, et apres le decours de ce tempz parvienne a l'heritage eternel. Par Nostre Seigneur Jesuschrist* etc.

56b. Fenie la messe, les pers emmenent le roy devant l'autel, et commenie du sanc et corps de Nostre Seigneur Jhesucrist de la main l'archevesque. Et lors la messe chantee, li archevesques desmet la couronne du chief au roy et lui despoulle des premieres robes, et revestus d'autres li archevesques li remet ou chief une autre couronne mendre, et ainsi s'en va au palaiz, devant lui le glaive denué ; et est assavoir que sa chemise pour la sainte unction doit estre brulee.

71b. Les beneiçons que li archevesques doit dire sur le roy et sur le peuple devant ce que on die Agnus Dei.

Nostre Sire te beneisse et ainsi come il t'a voulu sur son peuple establir, ainsi en ce present siecle beneureux et de la pardurable beneurté compaings et parçonnier te face. Amen.

72b. *Le clergié et le peuple, que par s'ayde et t'ordenance a voulu assembler par sa dispensacion et par ta ministracion par tres lonc temps te face beneurement gouverner. Amen.*

73b. *A celle fin que eulz aux divins commandemens obediens, et de toutes adversitez defaillans, et en toutes euvres habondans et en ce present siecle de transquilité de paix user, et avecques toy en la compaignie des pardurables bourgoiz du ciel glorieusement se puissent delicier. Amen.*

71c. Avant que ledict archevesque chante « Pax Domini sit semper vobiscum », il dye sur ledict roy et son peuple les benedictions suyvantes.

Le Seigneur te benye et garde, et ainsi que il luy a pleu te constituer roy sur son peuple, ainsi il te face eureux en ce present siecle et compaignon de l'eternelle felicité. Ainsi soit il.

72c. *Les clergé et peuple, qu'il a voulu par sa grace et ton commandement estre assemblés, face estre eureusement gouvernés moyennant ta dispensation et son administration.[24] Ainsi soit il.*

73c. *Affin que obeissans aux divins admonestemens, vuydes de toutes adversités, abondans de tous biens, servans a ton ministere, par amour fidele ilx joyssent en ce present siecle de la tranquilité de paix, et apres avec toy de la societé des cytoiens eternelx, ce que veuille donner celluy qui regne. Ainsi soit il.*

---

[24] Du Tillet reversed the ownership of the two substantives: Ordo XXII A,72 reads "sua dispensatione et tua administratione."

56c. Apres ledict Pax Domini, celluy qui aura porté baiser audict roy le livre des Evangiles, preigne la paix dudict archevesque le baisant en la joue, et la presente par le baiser audict roy. Et apres luy tous les autres archevesques et evesques en leur ordre aillent baiser icelluy roy seant en son trosne, et la messe achevee, lesdictz pairs derechef l'amenent devant le grand autel, ou il [fol. 176v] reçoive par la main dudict archevesque la communion des corps et sang de Nostre Seigneur. Ce faict, ledict archevesque luy oste la grande couronne qu'il avoit sur la teste et a luy, despouillé de ses plus insignes habillemens et revestu d'autres, mecte sur son chief une autre couronne plus petite, et ainsi ledict roy s'en aille au palays, sadicte espee estant portee nue devant luy, et soit sa chemise brullee a cause de la saincte unction.

57c. Apres lesdictz sacre et messe lesdictz barons reconduisent la saincte empoule jusques a Sainct Remy honorablement et seurement, et soit remise en son lieu.[25]

---

[25] Before the queen's ordo Du Tillet inserts the following, which is not from Ordo XXII A:

"[fol. 176v] Monsieur Jehan de France, filx du roy Jehan, duc de Berry, ostaige en Angleterre delivré a tempz le premier fevrier M.III^c.LXV. feyt promesse de retourner en foy de vray filx de roy sacré, qui monstre que le sacre du roy trescrestien honnoroit ses filx et tesmoignoit leur foy et loyaulté plus grande que de ceulx qui estoient filx de roys non sacrés.

Au partir de Reins ledict roy a accoustumé aller a sainct Marcol et y faire faire sa neufeine. Apres et non plus tost il touche les malades des escruelles qui est chose ancienne. Le roy Philippes le Bel approchant de sa mort feyt appeler le roy Loys Hutin son filx aisné, l'instruisit et apprint la maniere de toucher lesdictz malades, luy

52b. Cy sont les troiz collectes de la messe.

[p. 100] *Sire Diex tous puissans, nous te requerons que nostre roy N., qui par ta miseracion a receu les gouvernemens du royaume de toutez vertus, avec ce recoive il acroissement, desquelz convenablement aournés et les desordenances des pechiés eschiver et ses anemis surmonter, et a toy qui es voie, verité et vie gracieusement puisse paraler.*

53b. Le secret.

Les dons, Sire, qui te sont[a] *offers, sainctefie, a celle fin que nous soient faiz le corps et le sanc de ton seul filz Jhesucrist et au salut de l'ame*[b] *et du corps de nostre roy N., et a parfaire*[c] *l'office a lui envoié, par ta largesse en toutes manieres profitent.*

---

enseignant sainctes et devotes paroles qu'il avoit accoustumé dire en les touchant, le prescha de saincteté de vye pour faire cest attouchement, luy remonstrant que selon l'escripture Dieu ne oyt ne exaulce les vicieux et par eulx ne faict miracles.

Witikind en l'hystoire saxonique recite le sacre d'Othon, premier empereur, faict a Aix la Chappelle par Hildebert archevesque [fol. 177r] de Maience assisté de ceulx de Treves et Coloigne et qu'il print les insignes imperiaulx de dessus l'autel, luy baillant l'espee luy deit,

Prens ce glaive par lequel tu dechasses tous les barbares ennemys de Jesuscrist et mauvays crestiens de tout l'empire des Françoys par l'auctorité divine et puissance a toy donnee pour tresferme paix de tous les crestiens.

Luy vestant le manteau luy deit,

Soye admonesté par ces cornes demises jusques aux espaules de quel zele de foy tu doy ardoir et te conduire jusques a la fin a garder la paix.

Luy donnant les sceptre et main de justice luy deyt,

Par ces insignes tu soye admonesté corriger tes subjectz de chastiement paternel et tendre la main de misericorde, premierement aux ministres de Dieu, puys aux vefves et pupilles et que l'huille de miseration jamais ne defaille de ton chief affin que soy ou present et future siecles de premiation sempiternelle couronné.

Les ceremonies dudict sacre sont significatives de l'office du prince."

Du Tillet got the formulas from Widukind, *Res gestae Saxonicae*, 56, which Brown (ed. *c*) quotes in her apparatus. The formulas are Widukind's invention, for none of them is in Vogel-Elze or in Elze.

53b. ª sons A. —ᵇ delame A —
ᶜ apparfaire A.

54b. Post communionem.
*Ceste oroison de salut, sire
Diex, ton sergent N. nostre roy de
toutes aversités deffende, a celle
fin que la transquilité de paix
commune il tiengne, et apres le
decours de ce temps au pardurable heritage parviengne.*

58b. Pour couronner la royne.

58c. [fol. 177r] Quand la royne
est sacree et couronnee avec le roy
audict Reins,

59b. L'en doit appareiller un
siege en la maniere de celui du roy,
un pou mendre, et doit estre amenee la royne a l'eglise ; et li roys en
son siege et throne doit estre
appareillez de tous aournemens de
roy en la maniere qu'il estoit aournés
en son throne. Apres son unction
dessus notee, et la royne amenee a
l'eglise, se doit agenoiller devant
l'autel a coudes et a genous et doit
aourer ; laquelle oroison parfaite,
des evesques eslevee, elle doit son
chief rencliner, et li archevesques
sur li ceste oroison doit dire :

59c. luy soit preparé ung trosne
moindre aucunement que celluy
dudict roy, lequel y seant ja sacré
et couronné, la royne soit amenee
en l'eglise et se prosterne devant
l'autel pour faire son oraison. Laquelle achevee, soit relevee par les
evesques sur ses genoux et encline
son chef pendant que ledict archevesque dira l'oraison qui ensuyt.

60b. *Sire, soies presens a nos
supplicacions, et ce que par le
ministre et office de nostre humilité est a faire et par le fait et
force de ta vertu soient acomplis.*

60c. *Seigneur, entendz a noz
supplications, et ce qui est a faire
par le ministere de nostre humilité soit remply de l'effect de ta
vertu.*

61b. Et est assavoir que la cote
de la royne et sa chemise doivent
estre ouvertes jusques a la couroie.
Et li archevesques la doit oindre de
l'uille sainte ou chief et ou piz et
dire en oingnant :

Ou nom du Pere et du Filz et

61c. Les tunique et chemise de
la royne doyvent estre ouvertes
jusques a la ceincture. Et ledict
archevesque l'oigne du sainct [fol.
177v] huille ou chief et en la poictrine, disant :

Ou nom du Pere et du Filx et

du Saint Esperit. Ceste unction d'uille te profite a honneur et confirmacion pardurable.

62b.   Ceste oroison s'ensuit.

Tout puissant et pardurable Dieu, l'abondant esperit de ta beneiçon sur t'ancelle par noz humbles oroisons propices respans, et laquelle par l'imposicion de noz mains au jour d'ui est royne establie par ta sanctificacion digne esleue, persevere, a celle fin que de ta grace desormais ja ne soit dessevree.

63b.   Apres ceste oroison est donné de la main de l'archevesque un petit ceptre en guise que le ceptre au roy et une verge semblable a la verge du roy, sanz oroisons. Et lors l'annel doit estre mis en son doit, et dire.

64b.   *Pren l'annel de la foy, signacle de la Saincte Trinité, ouquel tu puisses toutes manieres de heresies eschiver, et les estranges nacions par la vertu a toy donnee a la congnoissance de verité appeller.*

65b.   Et s'ensuit l'oroison.

Dieu, de qui est toute puissance et toute dignité, donne a t'ancelle par le signe de ta foy convenable fait de la dignité, en laquelle, a toy tousjours ferme et estable, persevere et a toy plaire continuement s'esforce. Per dominum.

66b.   Lors li doit estre mise

du Sainct Esperit, ceste unction d'huille te proffite en honneur et confirmation eternelle.

62c.   Apres ladicte unction, dye l'oraison qui ensuit.

Dieu eternel tout puissant, apaisé par noz prieres, infunde l'abondant esprit de ta benediction sur ta servante, affin qu'elle, ce jourd'huy instituee royne par l'imposition de nostre main, demeure par ta sanctification digne et esleue et que jamais cy apres elle comme indigne ne soit separee de ta grace. Par Nostre Seigneur Jhesuscrist etc.

63c.   Puis ledict archevesque sans oraisons mette es mains de ladicte royne le sceptre moindre et d'autre maniere que celluy du roy, et la main de justice semblable a celle d'icelluy roy. Et lors luy mette l'anneau ou doigt luy disant :

64c.   *Prens l'anneau de la foy, signacle de la Sainct Trinité, par lequel tu puisse[s] eviter toutes malices heretiques, et par la vertu qui t'est donnee appeler les nations barbares a la cognoissance de la verité.*

65c.   Apres dye l'oraison suyvante.

Dieu, duquel est toute puissance et dignité, donne a ta servante par ce signe de ta foy l'effect prospere de sa dignité, en laquelle foy elle demeure tousjours ferme, et continuellement elle s'efforce de te plaire. Par Nostre Seigneur Jesuscrist etc.

66c.   Soit puys apres par le seul

d'un seul archevesque la couronne ou chief, laquelle de toutes parties doivent soustenir les barons. Et doit dire li archevesques en lui mettant :

Pren couronne de gloyre, honneur de joie, a celle fin que en resplendissant tu reluises et de pardurable exultacion tu soies couronné.

67b. Et s'ensuit l'oroison.

Sire, fontaine de tous biens et donneur de touz proffiz et acroissemens, donne a t'ancelle N. la dignité receue bien gouverner, et en li par bonnes euvres sa gloyre de toy donnee enforcis et confermes. Per dominum.

68b. Apres ceste oroison les barons qui la couronne soustiennent la doivent ou siege et throne qui li est appareillé mener, et doit estre environnee des barons et des plus nobles dames ; en l'offrende, en la paix porter, en la communion, l'ordenance[26] du roy dessus nommee doit estre gardee.

archevesque imposee la couronne sur le chief de ladicte royne, laquelle couronne soit soustenue de toutes partz par les barons, et la mectant dye ledict archevesque.

Prens la couronne de gloire, honneur de liesse, affin que tu reluyse splendide et soye coronnee de joye pardurable.

67c. Apres avoir mise ladicte couronne adjoute, ledict archevesque [dye] l'oraison [fol. 178r] qui ensuyt.

Seigneur, fontaine de tous biens et donneur de tous honneurs, octroye a ta servante bien regir celle dignité qu'elle a prinse, et fortifie en elle par bonnes euvres la gloire que luy as donnee. Par Nostre Seigneur Jesuscrist etc.

68c. Ce faict, les barons soustenans sa couronne la menent et colloquent en son trosne, estans lesdictz barons et les plus grandes et nobles dames joignant elle. A l'offrande de la messe la paix et la communion l'ordre du sacre du roy soit observé en celluy de la royne, et l'ordre susdict est gardé quant elle est sacree et couronnee ailleurs que audict Reins.[27]

---

[26] The scribe of *A* incorrectly began a new sentence with *L'ordenance.*

[27] Du Tillet adds, "Ceulx dudict feu roy Henry second et de la royne Catherine sa femme ont esté amplement escriptz et publyés par impression, par iceulx sera cogneu qu'il y a eu petite diversité." Neither translation contains the benediction of the banner from the Latin text (Ordo XXII A,69), although it was certainly at the end of the ordo in Du Tillet's source, and Du Tillet translated it later in his *Recueil des roys* (MS *B*, fols. 208v–209v; MS *C*, fols. 207v–208v; and MS *D*, fols. 259v–260v), along with the French prayer that follows in the $G_1 J O$ group of manuscripts of the Last Capetian Ordo (Ordo XXII A,70). These versions of Ordo XXII A,69–70 were edited by Brown (ed. *c*), 135–38.

ORDO XXIII

The Ordo of Charles V

Date: 19 May 1364
Other names: none

Introduction

The Ordo of Charles V is unusual in a number of ways. The production of its manuscript *A* was personally supervised by the king, who signed and added it to his own library less than two years after his coronation. The manuscript's famous, highly detailed miniatures provide the best example we have of an illustrated coronation text from medieval France, and the king's impatience to possess this prescriptive text is demonstrated by the remarkable speed with which the work was completed.[1] Charles's interest extended to having several copies made for the royal library, and in 1380 he ordered one copy (lost manuscript *3*) deposited at the abbey of Saint-Denis for use at future coronations. Several marginal corrections in *A*, now unfortunately erased, may have been made by the king himself (or one of his secretaries)—E. S. Dewick thought so when he prepared his edition of the ordo (ed. *g*), and I am inclined to agree.

The ordo's liturgy is the longest of all French ordines, and no other ordo reflects current political circumstances as clearly as it does. The English king had claimed to be the legitimate heir to the French throne. Charles V's father, king John, had died in England less than six weeks before the coronation and had previously been a prisoner of the English for several years. The Treaty of Calais, signed in late 1360, had imposed a heavy ransom and severe territorial losses upon France, and two of Charles V's brothers had had to go to England as hostages to ensure that the treaty's provisions would be respected. Under the circumstances, it is no wonder that the liturgy, which improves and enlarges upon the Last

---

[1] It might not seem possible for so many miniatures of this manuscript's quality to have been produced so quickly, but François Avril informed me in conversation that the Parisian workshop that executed them was indeed capable of completing them in the available time. The illustrations are not just decoration: they are what one might term a "mirror of coronation," an illustrative program to be followed at future coronations. This intent was fulfilled when Charles VI took the manuscript to Reims for his coronation; see Richard A. Jackson, "Les manuscrits des *ordines* de couronnement de la bibliothèque de Charles V, roi de France," *Le Moyen Age* (1976), 76.

Capetian Ordo's liturgy, should incorporate texts appropriate to the situation. These emphasized the divine nature of French kingship, and they called repeatedly upon God to aid the king in strengthening his army and in overcoming his enemies, additions that make this more warlike than any previous French ordo. The ordo's clause of inalienability in the coronation oath was the result of a specific provision in the act that united Burgundy (almost immediately after the death of the last Capetian duke of Burgundy), Normandy, Champagne, and Toulouse to the Crown in 1363. The ordo for the queen is also longer than any previous or succeeding queen's ordo. Its additions emphasize the queen's fecundity at a time, rather late in Charles V's and Jeanne de Bourbon's lives, when there was still no heir apparent to the throne.[2]

The ordo contains nineteen formulas that do not previously appear in texts in this collection: nos. 9, 11, 15, 26, 33–34, 45, 50–51, 53–55, 61, 64–65, 99, 101, 106 (twice), and 117. Some of the novelties are drawn from the local liturgy (e.g., nos. 33–34), some seem to have been devised for the occasion (e.g., no. 15), and at least one was borrowed from the imperial coronation ceremony (no. 117). Number 80 demonstrates that the sources were examined in detail because it appears only once before, in Ordo III,2.[3] Many of the innovations in the Ordo of Charles V were retained in later ceremonies.

This ordo appears not only to reflect fairly well the ceremony of 19 May 1364, but also to have formed the core of Charles VI's coronation ceremony in 1380. In 1429, on the other hand, the manuscripts that contained the ordo were not available for Charles VII's coronation in Reims: manuscript *A* and its cognate manuscripts, lost manuscripts *1* and *2* (either of which might have been MS *A*'s unidentifiable source), were either in Rouen or already in England,[4] and lost manuscript *3* was in

---

[2] For details of this and the preceeding paragraph, see Jackson, *Vive le roi*, 26–34, 72–81 (= *Vivat rex*, 31–37, 69–78), and Jackson, "Les manuscrits des *ordines*," 67–68. The evidence of manuscripts *B* and *D*, both of which contain the clause of inalienability (in no. 19), shows that some of my statements in *Vive le roi* now need to be modified.

[3] Schramm, "Ordines-Studien II," 45–47, discussed the sources of the ordo, but that material needs to be entirely reviewed because nearly all the formulas were in manuscripts in Reims. The three main sources were Ordo XXII A; Ordo XV, MS *G*; and Ordo XIX, MS *A*. Nos. 32 and 94, *Deus Pater eterne glorie sit adiutor tuus*, apparently did come from a Spanish source, as Schramm suggested (see also Ordo XIV, n. 16), and a few other formulas were drawn from scattered texts.

[4] The recently published inventory of the Duke of Bedford's estate is most disappointing because it refers only to "the grete librarie that cam owte of France." See Richard A. Rouse's and Mary A. Rouse's review of Jenny Stratford, *The Bedford Inven-*

Saint-Denis, i.e., in that part of France that was under English control. There does not seem to have been a copy of the ordo in Reims in 1429, when, it appears, the Last Capetian Ordo (Ordo XXII) was again called into service for the coronation of Charles VII. In 1461 lost manuscript *3* could again be consulted, with the result that Louis XI's ceremony was a mixture of the Last Capetian Ordo and its successor. A somewhat modified version of the Ordo of Charles V was produced and deposited in the cathedral treasury in Reims, perhaps in 1478; that manuscript, known as the *livre rouge* (lost manuscript *4*), contained nearly all the coronation liturgy in Charles VIII's ordo of 1484. It was by way of the *livre rouge* and the ceremony devised in 1484 that the Charles V's ordo would exert its permanent influence upon the French ceremony.[5]

Apart from the four manuscripts in the royal library, there seem to have been remarkably few manuscript copies of the ordo. Manuscript *B* had been given to the Sainte-Chapelle in Bourges by the Duc de Berry, and it was from *B* that manuscript *E* was copied and illuminated in Bourges.[6] It was truly unexpected to discover that the Duke of Berry's manuscript (*B*) was not copied from his brother's manuscript (*A*), but that they descended from a common source. Initially, it seemed likely that *D*, which was copied in England, was copied from *A*, which was part of the royal library when the Duke of Bedford acquired it. Collation of the manuscripts proved that this was not the case and that *D* and *A* were not so closely related. I did not initially realize that two copies of the ordo (lost MSS *1* and *2*) had probably gone to England along with *A* in the Duke of Bedford's collection. Only when I recognized this did I understand that *D* must have been copied from lost manuscript *1* or *2*; for the stemma I arbitrarily assume that *D* was copied from *2*.

Still more important was the discovery that both *F* and *G* were copied from the *livre rouge*, which was considered most authoritative and was regularly consulted at later coronations. The recognition of the contents of the *livre rouge* in *F* and *G* would not have been possible if Hubert Meurier had not quoted extensively from the lost Reims manuscript in the study of royal anointing that he published in 1593.[7] Meurier's

---

tories: The Worldly Goods of John, Duke of Bedford, Regent of France (1389–1435), Reports of the Research Committee of the Society of Antiquaries of London 49 (London: Society of Antiquaries of London, 1993), in *Speculum* 72 (1997), 226–28.

[5] For details of this paragraph, see Jackson, *Vive le roi,* 34–40 (= *Vivat rex,* 38–43), and "The *livres bleu* and *rouge.*"

[6] See Ordo XX B, n. 10.

[7] Meurier, *De sacris unctionibus,* is cited in full in Ordo XXII A, n. 36. See also n. 16 below.

readings and sequence of texts accord very well with the readings and the sequence of texts in F and G. As we shall see, F was recollated with the *livre rouge*, so its readings and the sequence of its rubrics and formulas surely reflect quite accurately the contents of the *livre rouge*. Furthermore, in 1511 Guillaume Eustache published an edition of Charles V's ordo (edition a, which omits the queen's ordo); it is the first printed edition of any French coronation ordo. The concordance of F and G with edition a proves that Eustache's edition likewise was copied from the *livre rouge* (not from F), so it is an independent witness to the contents of the *livre rouge*.[8]

Manuscript F, which belonged to the bishops of Noyon, peers of France, is extremely interesting for another reason: it contains a large number of additions and corrections. The readings of MS G and ed. a prove that many of these were copied from marginal additions in the *livre rouge*, although some are to be found nowhere else. The approximate date of F suggests that those additions that were copied from the *livre rouge* were not yet in the manuscript in the Reims cathedral when F was copied, but they certainly were there by the time ed. a was published in 1511. Manuscript F was indubitably collated with the *livre rouge* sometime after F was originally written. (The additions in the *livre rouge* were normally copied into the margin in G, although the scribe of G sometimes incorporated them into the text.)

Manuscript F was corrected not just once, however. The modifications are written in at least four different hands, none of which belonged to professional scribes. 1) The most extensive corrections were made by one person who wrote both a late medieval semi-cursive script and a cursive book script; this is the hand that added most of the marginal additions from the *livre rouge*.[9] 2) A few corrections were printed in a rather course, late fifteenth-century hand that could be described as a semi-humanistic miniscule.[10] 3) The second most common corrections are written in a humanistic cursive book script that probably dates from the

---

[8] Several of Meurier's readings differ from both F and a. Some of these differences might be simply the result of careless editing on Meurier's part, but others (e.g., vars. 113d–e) probably reflect additions and corrections to the *livre rouge* after the publication of Eustache's edition. I carefully examined the possibility that Meurier might have copied from Eustache's edition (ed. a), but, although the evidence is slender, rejected it in favor of the *livre rouge* as his source.

[9] When writing the addition in the bottom margin of fol. 60r, this person wrote everything (no. 14) up to the prayer *Omnipotens sempiterne Deus* in an ordinary cursive, but he wrote the prayer (no. 15) in a cursive book script.

[10] There may be two such hands, but I could not distinguish them with certainty.

early sixteenth century. Finally, 4) there are some marginal additions in a typically nearly illegible sixteenth-century cursive hand. In the variants and notes these are identified as hand 1, 2, 3, or 4 if it was possible to distinguish them.[11]

I long thought that G was copied from F rather than from the *livre rouge*. I did consider the possibility that G was copied from edition a, but a could not have been G's source because a incorporates into its text the marginal additions in the *livre rouge*, and the scribe of G could not possibly have known which of them to place in the margin; furthermore, variants 10i, 13x, and 38u exclude a as G's source. In most variants, manuscripts F and G and edition a agree with each other, but in many cases only G and a agree with each other, but differ from F. Some of the most striking instances of the agreement of G and a against F are found in variants 21a, 39n, 40g, and 78b — the last variant alone is almost sufficient to prove that G was copied from the *livre rouge* rather than from F.

Guillaume Eustache (ed. a) printed only the king's ordo from the *livre rouge*, and the scribe of G did likewise; this similarity between the two copies from the *livre rouge* is not accidental because the custom of crowning the queens at Saint-Denis had become so well entrenched by the early decades of the sixteenth century that there was no longer any need for a queen's ordo for a Reims coronation. Therefore, F is the only original copy of the queen's ordo from that lost manuscript. Some of F's readings are clearly erroneous and reflect the carelessness with which F was copied, but others (corrections to grammatical errors, above all) could well reflect the many similar corrections to the king's ordo in the *livre rouge*. Excepting its locations of the *livre rouge*'s marginal additions, edition a is a more accurate copy of the *livre rouge* than MS F, but G is the best copy of the three.

I have argued elsewhere that the *livre rouge* was composed between 1461 and 1484, and I suggested a precise date of 1478 for the manuscript. I based my argument upon three considerations. First, the sequence of formulas in the Ordo of Louis XI reflects the sequence in the Last Capetian Ordo (Ordo XXII A) rather than the one in the *livre rouge*, and some

---

[11] I am very confident of my identifications of hand 4 and quite confident of hand 1 when written in semi-cursive script. I am far less confident of the distinction between hand 1 in cursive book script, hand 2, and hand 3, and it is even possible that there is no hand 3, but only a variation of hand 1's cursive book script. All corrections in the queen's ordo were made in the same hand, but I was not able to identify it with any one of the others. Someone who has access to documents written by the bishops of Noyon or their secretaries might be able to identify precisely who wrote the additions and corrections in each of the four hands.

of the formulas in the *livre rouge* are not in the Ordo of Louis XI. Second, with one minor exception, the sequence in Charles VIII's ordo, on the other hand, is exactly that of the *livre rouge*, but of no other manuscript of any other ordo (see the Synoptic Table of the late medieval ordines [Appendix II, pp. 621–24]). Third, the year 1478 is the one in which Jehan Foulquart wrote his treatise on coronations (see Ordo XXIV), and there was a copy of Charles V's ordo, also dated 1478, in the library of the abbey of Saint-Remi.[12]

Strictly speaking only manuscripts *A*, *B*, *D*, and *E* may be called manuscripts of the Ordo of Charles V. They contain identical formulas and rubrics, except that some rubrics were altered or removed because they became superfluous when the litany or something else was moved. The cathedral's *livre rouge* and its manuscript copies, MSS *F* and *G*, should be regarded as marking the transition to a new ordo, although they built upon the Ordo of Charles V to take the next step in the development of the rite. The Synoptic Table outlines the differences between the copies of Charles V's Ordo and between that and the ordo in the *livre rouge*.

A number of *A*'s rubrics that were originally omitted in manuscript *D* were later added. Judging from the hand, these very brief additions were made before the end of the fifteenth century. They appear to demonstrate that *D* was then collated with *A*.

Lost manuscripts

1—Manuscript lost from the royal library after the death of Charles VI.[13]

2—Manuscript lost from the royal library after the death of Charles VI.[14]

3—On 7 May 1380 Charles V deposited in the abbey of Saint-Denis a

---

[12] For further details concerning the *livre rouge*, see Jackson, "The *livres bleu* and *rouge*," as well as the introductions to Ordines XXIV and XXV. Several problems relating to these texts have yet to be resolved, but this is not the place to address those issues. For example, some of the liturgical differences between Ordo XXIII's MS *A* and the *livre rouge* are in both the Ordo of Louis XI and the Ordo of Charles VIII, but others are not.

[13] Delisle's no. 229; see Jackson, "Les manuscrits des *ordines*," 74–75. Except that they did not contain the various oaths after the coronation ordo (see n. 16 below), I am now convinced that Delisle's nos. 229 and 231 contained the same texts as Tiberius B.viii (see MS *A*), so that a copy of the Ordo of Charles V was in each, as was a copy of Ordo XX B (lost MSS *7* and *8*). An inventory of the royal library gives the explicit of no. 229 as "Domine aspirando"; these words are found only in the prayer *Actiones nostras* (no. 118), which appears in the later medieval ceremony for the first time in this ordo.

[14] Delisle's no. 231; see Jackson, "Les manuscrits des *ordines*," 74–76. An inventory of the royal library gives the explicit as "Ut hunc presentem"; the first appearance of these words in the ceremony is in the litany of Charles V's ordo (no. 113). Lost manuscript *2* was probably copied from lost manuscript *1*, or vice versa.

Synoptic Table of Ordo XXIII						
A Tiberius B.viii	C* Latin 9479	B Latin 8886	D Additional 32097	E Dupuy 365	F Saint-Sulpice	G** Latin 13314
1–10		1–10	1–10	1–10	1–10	1–10
11		11	11	11		
12–13		12–13	12–13	12–13	12–13	12–13
					14–15	14–15
16–34		16–34	16–34	16–34	16–34	16–34
35 incipit		35 incipit	35 incipit	35 incipit	35 incipit	35 incipit
				109–118	109–118	109–118
35 explicit		35 explicit	35 explicit	35 explicit	35 explicit	35 explicit
36–44		36–44	36–44	36–44	36–44	36–44
45 rubric		45 rubric	45 rubric	45 rubric	45 rubric	45 rubric
45 formula		45 formula	45 formula	45 formula		
46–53		46–53	46–53	46–53	46–53	46–53
54–55		54–55	54–55	54–55		
56–60		56–60	56–60	56–60	56–60	56–60
61		61	61	61		
		103–104	103–104	103–104		
62–83		62–83	62–83	62–83	62–83	62–83
					103–106	103–106
					108	108
84–86		84–86	84–86	84–86	84–86	84–86
87–102	87–102	87–102	87–102	87–102	87–102	
103–104	103–104	103–104		103–104		
105–108	105–108	105–108	105–108	105–108		
109–118		109–118	109–118			

* Manuscript C is placed immediately after MS A because it was copied from A.
** Edition a is identical to G and likewise omits the queen's ordo (nos. 87–102).

manuscript that he prescribed for the coronations of his successors; it was kept in the abbey treasury with the coronation insignia. Probably copied from lost manuscript *1* or *2*. This seems to have been the manuscript that furnished the first part of the Ordo of Louis XI. Given its location with the coronation insignia, it is likely to have been consulted for several other ceremonies before the manuscript disappeared during the later part of the Wars of Religion in the sixteenth century.[15]

4—Reims, Trésor de la cathèdrale, MS known as the *livre rouge*.[16] 1478? Probably copied from lost manuscript *3*, the other three manuscripts in the royal library having been taken to England. Readings of manuscript *F* and edition *a*, both copied from the *livre rouge*, show that the entire ceremony was carefully reviewed when composing the manuscript because, in addition to altering the order of some of the liturgical formulas, it corrected a number of grammatical errors, some of which were centuries old.

5—Reims, Bibl. de l'abbaye de Saint-Remi. A manuscript dating from 1478.[17] Probably copied from lost manuscript *4*.

---

[15] This is Léopold Delisle's no. 228; for details, see Jackson, *Vive le roi*, 34–40 (= *Vivat rex*, 38–43), and Jackson, "Les manuscrits des *ordines*," 67–88, particularly 78–87. Like MSS *A*, *B*, and *E*, lost MS *3* contained the oaths of the peers and various royal officers (see n. 153 below).

[16] Variants from the *livre rouge* from Meurier are given with the variants, if possible, or in notes, but most of Meurier's modernized orthography is not retained. Meurier did not state which manuscript was his source in his description of the ceremony on pp. 243–56, but the quotations prove that it was the *livre rouge* rather than the *livre bleu*. Meurier somewhat paraphrased the rubrics, so only his readings of the formulas are retained.

Reims, Bibl. mun., MS 1485 is a collection of miscellaneous eighteenth-century manuscripts on coronations. No. 4 in the collection is a four-page piece entitled "Remarques sur les livres et prieres du sacre des roys." Written, according to Loriquet, *Reims*, 2,1: 692, by M. de la Salle, it quotes some passages from the *livre rouge*; I present them in appropriate footnotes. (Loriquet did not identify which M. de la Salle wrote the manuscript.)

[17] La Salle noted (Reims, MS 1485, no. 4, p. 3) "les deux MSS de S. Remy, l'un de 1286, l'autre de 1478." It is not certain that the latter manuscript contained the Ordo of Charles V, although it does seems likely from its date that it contained the revised version of the *livre rouge*. The author's precise dates suggest that at least some of the Saint-Remi manuscripts were dated.

The only manuscript described by Lelong, *Bibliothèque historique*, 2: 704, that could possibly be this manuscript is his no. 25949:

"MS. Ordo ad inungendum et coronadum Regem Franciae : *in-4*.

Ce Manuscrit est conservé dans la Bibliotheque de l'Abbaye de S. Remy de Reims,

Manuscripts

A—London, British Library, MS Cotton, Tiberius B.viii, fols. 43r–74v (foliation in pencil). 1365 (i.e., 13 April 1365–4 April 1366). The manuscript, which bears the king's signature on fol. 74v (see n. 161), is sumptuously illuminated with over forty high-quality miniatures and is the third of the three medieval French coronation manuscripts that contain an entire cycle of miniatures (the others are Ordo XXI, MS *A*, and Ordo XXII A, MS *B*). The manuscript is incomplete in that leaves between fols. 48v–49r and 53v–54r have disappeared since the seventeenth century. The text of the ordo was later corrected at several points, but most of the corrections were eventually erased and are no longer legible. In this manuscript, now commonly called the Coronation Book (*Livre du sacre*) of Charles V, the Ordo of Charles V is preceded by 1) a French translation of the Ordo of Reims (Ordo XX B, MS *B*), 2) the texts of the coronation oaths (Ordo XX B, nos. 20b–22b), and 3) lists of the Peers of France (Ordo XX B, nos. 23b–34b); 4) the Ordo of Charles V is followed by 5) a collection of oaths to the king. The Duke of Bedford acquired the manuscript when he purchased the royal library in 1427; it was taken to England, either during the duke's lifetime, or shortly after his death, and there it has apparently remained ever since. Base manuscript for this edition. Description: Dewick, *Coronation Book*, xi–xii; Claire Richter Sherman, "The Queen in Charles V's 'Coronation Book': Jeanne de Bourbon and the 'Ordo ad reginam benedicendam'," *Viator*, 8 (1977), 255–68.[18] See Plate 28.

---

num. 64, S.7. Il est moins ancien que l'*Ordo ad consecrandum et coronandum Regem Franciae*, etc. qui a environ 500 ans [i.e., Ordo XXII A]. Le commencement de ces Cérémonies, et une partie de ce qui suit, est semblable à l'*Ordo VI* (du P. Martenne) *ad coronandum Regem Franciae* [i.e., Ordo XXI, the Ordo of 1250]. Le reste est comme dans l'*Ordo VII. ad coronandum eumdem Regem*, (du même Martenne) [i.e., Ordo XXII A]."

    The incipit given by Lelong is very similar to the incipit of Ordo XXII A, MS *C*, but is identical only to the incipit of Ordo XXIII, MSS *F* and *G* (i.e., the revised version in the *livre rouge*). Lelong did not identify this text as identical with his no. 25947 (see Ordo XXII A, n. 13), so it does not appear to have been a copy of Ordo XXII A. I can think of only two explanations for Lelong's statement that the beginning of his no. 25949 was similar to the beginning of the Ordo of 1250: 1) either Lelong saw that there are a number of similarities in the first parts of Ordines XXI and XXII A, but carelessly failed to note the significant differences, or 2) there was an ordo that Lelong's description accurately describes, but it has left no further trace of its contents. In the latter case, no. 25949 was not a copy of the ordo in the *livre rouge*.

    [18] See also Jackson, "Les manuscrits des *ordines*," 69–72.

B—Paris, Bibl. nat., MS lat. 8886, fols. 62v–83v (foliation in pencil). Early
fifteenth century. Although this magnificent pontifical was copied
from Bayeux, Bibl. de la Chapitre, MS 61, for Jean, Duke of Berry, it
also contains the Ordo of Charles V copied from a now-lost manuscript (but not from lost MS *1* or *2*, neither of which contained a
series of officials' oaths after the ordo)[19]; this ordo is not in the
Bayeux manuscript. The manuscript was given to the Sainte-
Chapelle in Bourges in 1405–1407. Description: see Ordo XXB, MS *C*.

C—Paris, Bibl. nat., MS lat. 9479, fols. 213r–219r. Early fifteenth-century
addition to a stunning fourteenth-century pontifical of Arles. Copied
from *A*, which establishes a *terminus ad quem* of 1427 (when the
Duke of Bedford purchased the royal library) or, at the latest, 1435
(death of the Dule of Bedford). This incomplete text contains only
nos. 87–108, the queen's ordo and the benediction of the banner.[20]
Description: Leroquais, *Pontificaux*, 2: 154–57, no. 141.

D—London, British Library, MS Additional 32097, fols. 150v–161v. Fifteenth century. Copied from lost manuscript *1* or *2* (either is an arbitrary assumption).[21] Description: see Ordo XXB, MS *D*.

E—Paris, Bibl. nat., MS Dupuy 365, fols. 28r–54r. Fifteenth century, third
quarter. Copied from *B*. Description: see Ordo XXB, MS *E*.

F—Paris, Archives de la Compagnie des prêtres de Saint-Sulpice, MS
1928, fols. 57r–98r.[22] Ca. 1480. This attractive manuscript, which consists of extracts from a pontifical, was copied for Guillaume de
Marafin (or Maraffin), bishop of Noyon from 1473 to 1501. Copied
from the *livre rouge* (lost MS *4*), it is fortunate that the manuscript
was compared with the *livre rouge* before the end of the century,

[19] I wrongly stated in "Les manuscrits des *ordines*," 75, n. 26, that MS *B* was
copied from MS *A*.

The full-page color plate of fol. 46r (the beginning of an ordo for the coronation of
an emperor in Rome) in Sclafer and Lafitte, *Catalogue général des manuscrits latins,
n⁰ 8823–8921*, Planche F, gives some idea of the high quality of manuscript *B*; see also
Plates 17 and 18.

[20] The addition also contains non-French coronation texts taken from the Roman
pontifical: "Ordo romanus ad benedicendum regem et reginam imperatorem vel
imperatricem coronando" (fols. 117r–129r); "De benedictione et coronacione reginam
imperatricem" (fols. 129r–132v); "De benedictione et coronatione aliorum regem et
reginarum" (fols. 133r–140v); and "De benedictione et coronatione regine" (fols.
140v–146r).

[21] I asserted incorrectly in "Les manuscrits des *ordines*," 75, n. 27, that MS *D* was
copied from MS *A*.

[22] I am truly grateful to the Abbé Jean Goy for having brought the manuscript to
my attention at the kind request of its discoverer, Raymond Etaix.

perhaps at the time of Charles VIII's coronation in 1484, and almost certainly when Louis XII was crowned in 1498; the errors of transcription were then corrected, and marginal notes were added from the *livre rouge* and other sources. Description: none. See Plates 29–30.

G—Paris, Bibl. nat., MS lat. 13314, fols. 3r–44r. Ordo copied from the *livre rouge* (lost MS *4*) for Charles de Villiers-de-l'Isle Adam, Bishop of Beauvais from 1530 to 1535. This very carefully written manuscript (with an excellent frontispiece and decorated border around the first page of text) contains only the king's ordo of Charles V. Three texts added later (on fols. 45r–54r) provide some details concerning the coronations of Henri II, Francis II, and Charles IX. Description: Leroquais, *Pontificaux*, 1: 179, no. 152.

H—Paris, Bibl. de l'Institut de France, MS Godefroy 380, pp. 263–334. Mid-seventeenth century. Copied from ed. *d₁*. Not collated.

I—Paris, Bibl. de l'Institut de France, MS Godefroy 382, pp. 135–180. Mid-seventeenth century. Copied from *E*. Not collated.

J—Reims, Bibl. mun., MS 1492, fols. 21r–36r. Eighteenth century. An anonymous note on fol. 21 says, "Copie d'un Cérémonial latin du Sacre de nos rois imprimé en 1510 [i.e., edition *a*], lequel est au chartrier de Saint Remy." It contains the same marginal additions as *L*, but the latter is more recent, so *L* is copied from *J*. Description: Loriquet, *Reims*, 2: 699–704. Not collated.

K—Reims, Bibl. mun., MS 1489 (nouv. fonds), no. 7, pp. 1–40. Eighteenth century. Copied from *e*. Nos. 1–106. Description: see Ordo XVII A, MS *H*. Not collated.

L—Reims, Bibl. mun., MS 1485 (nouv. fonds), no. 3, pp. 1–35. Eighteenth century. Copied from *J*. Description: Loriquet, *Reims*, 2: 692. Not collated.

Editions

a—*Consecratio et coronatio regis Francie* (Paris: Guillaume Eustache, 1510 [o.s.]), from lost manuscript *4*, the cathedral's *livre rouge*.[23] (Paris, Bibl. nat., Rés. Li²⁵.1) See Plate 33.

---

[23] On fol. 20v Eustache prints a notice of his privilege: "Et a donné le roy nostre syre audit Guillaume Eustache, libraire et relieur de livres, iuré de l'université de Paris, lettre de privilege et terme de deux ans pour vendre et distribuer lesditz livres, affin de soy rembourser de ses fraitz et mises. Et defend ledict seigneur a tous imprimeurs et libraires de ce royaulme de non imprimer ledict livre, jusques au temps dessusdit, sur peine de confiscation desdictz livres et d'amende arbitraire. Fait le xx. de mars. Mil. ccccc. et. x. / Ainsi signé des Landes." This was before Easter, so the privilege dates from 1511 if 1 January is taken to begin the new year.

b—*L'ordre et les cérémonies du sacre et couronnement du tres-chrestien roy de France* (Paris: Nicolas Chesneau, 1575), from *a*, with a French translation by René Benoist.

c— Bouchel, *Decreta ecclesiae Gallicanae*, 701–716, from *a*.[24]

d—John Selden, *Titles of Honor*. Several editions, all of which print the litany at its proper place in the ceremony rather than at the end of the ordo, its location in *A*:

d_1— 2nd ed. (London: R. Whitakers, 1631), 222–55, from *A* with variants from *c*.[25]

d_2—3rd ed. (London: T. Dring, 1672), 177–206.

d_3— *Tituli honorum ... juxta editionem Londinensem anni 1672*, trans. Simon Johannes Arnold (Frankfurt: impressis Jeremiae Schrey, et Henrici Johannes Meyeri haered., literis Goderitschianis, 1696), Part 1: 236–75.

e— Godefroy, 1: 31–51, from d_1.[26]

f— William Prynne, *Signal Loyalty and Devotion of Gods True Saints and Pious Christians (as also of Idolatrous Pagans) towards their Kings* (London: [no publisher], 1660), 194–224, from d_1.

g—Dewick, cols. 15–54, from *A* and d_1. This is by far the best of all previous editions.[27]

---

[24] Schramm, "Ordines-Studien II," 283, erred in asserting that this is an edition of the Last Capetian Ordo.

[25] Martimort, no. 777, p. 387, states that this is also printed in the first edition of 1614, but Charles V's ordo is not there.

[26] Godefroy lists his source as *Titres d'honneur*, but that must be his translation, for National Union Catalog and the catalogs of the Bibliothèque nationale de France and the British Library show no such title. It must have been the importance of Selden's source (MS *A*) that induced Godefroy to reprint Selden's edition rather than to use MS *E* (Dupuy 365) which was copied from *B*; MS Dupuy 365 was, on the other hand, Godefroy's source for Ordo XX B, ed. *a*.

[27] Roland Delachenal, *Histoire de Charles V*, 5 vols. (Paris: A. Picard et fils, 1909–31), 1: 65–97, discusses the coronation of Charles V and prints numerous extracts from Dewick and other printed editions, but does not present the entire text, so this is not an edition.

Le sacre et couronnement du roy de France (Reims: Jean de Foigny, 1575), which was printed in anticipation of Henry III's coronation, presents the ordo's liturgical formulas in Latin, but the rubrics are in French, so it is not an edition of the ordo. Quick collation of a number of the formulas show that the formulas were copied from the *livre rouge* (lost manuscript *4*) rather than from ed. *a*, so any attempt to reconstruct the readings of the *livre rouge* would need to take this work into account.

The Stemma

As is often the case, the evidence for the relationship between manuscripts can be slender. Only seven medieval and sixteenth-century manuscripts of the Ordo of Charles V survive, but the stemma can only be tentative because five important manuscripts have disappeared. The readings of MSS *F* and *G* and edition *a* do provide us with a number of useful clues, however, because they preserve the contents of Charles V's ordo in lost MS *4*, the *livre rouge* (except that *G* and *a* omit the queen's ordo). Manuscript *A* was one of four similar manuscripts in the royal library; the other three were lost MSS *1*, *2*, and *3*. Manuscript *A* could have been copied from lost MS *1*, or *A*, *1*, *2*, and *3* could all have been copied from a common source (which is not shown on the stemma). Manuscript *A* and lost MSS *1* and *2* were taken to England by 1435 at the latest as part of the Duke of Bedford's possessions; lost MS *3* was, therefore, the only one of the original four to remain in France. This made it the source of the *livre rouge*, a conclusion that is supported by var. 20u, which substitutes *sancti Dyonisii* for *beati Dyonisii*.

Manuscript *F* and edition *a*, both independently copied from the *livre rouge*, display a number of readings in common with *B* and *D*, but not with *A*. Therefore, *A*'s source was not the immediate source of *B*, *D*, and

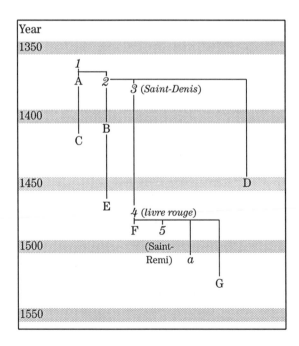

lost MS *3*. For the sake of simplicity, the stemma arbitrarily assigns the role of *A*'s source to *1*. Equally arbitrarily, the stemma assumes that *1* was considered authoritative and that *2* was copied from it, and it arbitrarily depicts lost MS *2* as the source of *B*, *D*, and *3*. In reality, the roles of *1* and *2* might have been reversed, but one's choice here is of little significance because both sources have disappeared.

Although the queen's ordo in *C* was copied either from *A* or from *A*'s source, it has in common with *A* a number of peculiarities that make *A* itself *C*'s probable source. That means that *C* was copied before 1427 because in that year the duke of Bedford purchased the royal library and apparently soon moved it to Rouen, whence it was taken to England; MS *C* was probably copied before the death of Charles VI in 1422.

Manuscript *D* was copied in England in the late fifteenth century, after the French royal library had gone to that country. It was not copied from *A* though, so it must have been copied from either lost MS *1* or lost MS *2*.[28]

Lost MS *5* is likely to have been copied for the library of the abbey of Saint Remi as part of the initial production of the *livre rouge*, but the stemma cannot show that it was contemporary with the *livre rouge* any more than it can show that the four manuscripts in the royal library were probably contemporary.

Principles of the Edition

Manuscript *A*'s official sanction makes it the logical base text for this edition. The paragraphing is usually added (*A*'s rubrics tend not to show any division, no matter how long they are). The sentences are normally from *A* (as designated by an initial capital letter), but sometimes *A*'s capitals break a sentence incorrectly; in those instances *A*'s readings are given in variants. In a few places the scribe copied a word incorrectly or omitted a word; when he did so, and all other manuscripts have the correct reading, the correct reading is given in the text and the erroneous one from *A* in a variant. It is sometimes impossible to determine whether the scribe wrote *c* or *t* (for example, the manuscript appears to read *eciam* or *etiam* indiscriminately); I have reproduced his readings to the best of my ability, and they do not always agree with those of Dewick (ed. *g*). Many abbreviated words could be expanded with either *cum* or *cun* (e.g., *cuiuscumque/cuiuscunque*, *circumstantibus/circunstantibus*),

---

[28] It is possible, of course, that *D* was copied indirectly from *2*, but I have found no evidence, whether internal or external, for the existence of an intermediate manuscript between *2* and *D*. Although a number of *D*'s readings were corrected from its source, these could easily have been independent corrections made by the scribe when he copied the manuscript.

but when the scribe wrote such words out, he always spelled them with the letter *n*, so I expand them likewise. This does not apply to the preposition *cum*, however, which is always spelled with an *m*. (Scribes varied considerably in spelling such words, and variants of these spellings are not retained unless there is another reason for a variant.) *Ihesus* is the spelling the scribe uses when the name is written in full, and its abbreviations are so expanded; variants of that spelling are not retained unless for another reason. The manuscript and its miniatures have been much discussed in the literature, and they were reproduced by Dewick, so it did not seem necessary to burden the notes with a description of each miniature. The punctuation has been standardized.

The scribe of *B* usually wrote a double *t* as *ct* (e.g., *promicto*); he wrote *sceptrum* and so forth without a *c*; and when he wrote out the name *Jesus* he wrote it *ihesus*. Manuscript *E* follows *B* in the spelling of *ihesus*, but not of *septrum*. These variants are not retained.

Manuscript *C* was copied in a neat Gothic book script. There are several later corrections, all made by the same person, in a fifteenth-century cursive script.

The scribe of *D* sometimes employed a double lowercase *ff* for capital *F*, but he was not consistent. These variants are not retained.

The scribe of *E* usually wrote the upper curve of the letter *c* with a horizontal stroke, with the result that the letter sometimes looks like *t*, or sometimes the *t* looks like *c*. Those peculiarities are not retained if a word does not otherwise differ from *B*, the scribe's source.

The large number of corrections and additions in *F* made it necessary to treat this text differently from the others. The complex nature of these alterations requires that many of them be explained in footnotes, rather than given as variants, so there are more footnotes for this ordo than for any other ordo. Although some of the *livre rouge*'s additions in *F* were incorporated into the text in *G*, most of them were written in *G*'s margin when *G* was copied. This presented a peculiar problem in that the marginal note is not always at the same location in each manuscript, and it is not always clear to what the addition referred. Therefore, working partly from the context, I have attempted to show the location of these additions in both *F* and *G*. If an addition is in the margin in both *F* and *G*, it is given in a footnote. If it is a variant in the text in both *F* and *G*, or if it is a correction within the text in *F* that was incorporated into the text in *G*, or if it is a marginal correction in *F* that was incorporated into the text in *G*, it is given as a variant. Breathing marks were also added to a number of the liturgical formulas in *F*; these are not retained.

Several of the manuscripts, *E*, *F*, and *G* in particular, shifted rubrics and formulas from their original location. Their location in each manuscript is shown by means of parallel columns, but the paragraph numbers of *A* are retained in each instance in order to show what was moved from where. The Synoptic Table (p. 460) makes the sequences very clear.

The word *Oremus* is rubricated in every instance in *G*, even though it was to pronounced by the officiant and should not have been rubricated; these rubrications are not retained as variants. Also the scribe of *G* always spelled *Cristus* and *cristian* ... without an *h* when he wrote these words in their various forms; these variants are not retained unless they are part of a variant retained for other reasons.

Edition *a* was copied from lost manuscript *4*, so its variants are retained, excepting a few obvious typographical errors. I also retain the variants from the liturgical formulas in those passages quoted by Meurier (see n. 16) from lost manuscript *4*. Editions *b* and *c* were independently copied from *a*, so their variants are not retained, although their sigla are given (for nos. 1–19 only) for a few of the most striking examples of affiliation with *a*.

As an aid to understanding the text, most of Dewick's (ed. *g*'s) corrections or suggestions for corrections to manuscript *A* are retained unless the correction had already been made in another manuscript.

ORDO XXIII

A B D E F G *a*

1. [fol. 43r] Ordo[29] ad inungendum[a] et coronandum regem[b].

1. [a] ungendum E. — [b] regem *om.* B E; Ordo ... regem] Incipit ordo ad consecrandum et coronandum regem Francie F G *a b c.*

2. Primo paratur solium[a] in modum eschafaudi,[b] aliquantulum eminens,[c] contiguum exterius choro ecclesie inter utrumque chorum, positum in medio, in quo per gradus ascenditur et in quo possint pares regni, et aliqui si necesse fuerit, cum eo[d] consistere. Rex autem, die quo ad coronandum venerit, debet processionaliter recipi, tam a canonicis quam a ceteris ecclesiis conventualibus.

2. [a] solium *om.* F, *later add. in marg. in hand 1.* — [b] eschaufaudi D E *a b c.* — [c] exeminens E. — [d] rege F G *a b c.*

3. Sabbato precedente diem dominicam [fol. 43v] in qua rex est consecrandus et coronandus[a], post complectorium[b] expletum, committitur

---

[29] In *a*, the incipit is preceded by a title, "Consecratio regis Francie," which was presumably added by the publisher.

ecclesie custodia custodibus a rege deputatis cum propriis custodibus
ecclesie. Et debet rex in tempeste noctis silencio venire in[c] ecclesiam
orationem facturus et ibidem[d] in oratione aliquantulum, si voluerit, vigilaturus[e]. Cum pulsatur autem[f] ad matutinas, debent esse parati custodes
regis, introitum[g] ecclesie observantes, qui aliis hostiis[h] ecclesie firmius
obseratis[i] et munitis. Canonicos et[j] clericos ecclesie debent honorifice
intromittere ac diligenter[k] quocienscunque opus fuerit eis. Matutine
more solito decantentur[l]. Quibus expletis, pulsatur ad primam, que cantari debet in aurora diei.

3. [a] et coronandus om. B D E. —[b] completorium D E F G. —[c] ad F G a b c. —
[d] ibidem om. F G a b c. —[e] ibidem ... vigilaturus] ibidem aliquantulum vigilaturus si voluerit D. —[f] autem om. F G a b c. —[g] in introitum E. —[h] ostiis
G. —[i] observatis B D E; firmius obseratis] obseratis firmius F, obseratis firmis
G a b c. —[j] ac F G a b c. —[k] intromittere ac diligenter] ac diligenter intromittere F G a b c. —[l] decantetur E.

4. Post primam cantatam, debet rex cum archiepiscopis et episcopis
et baronibus et aliis quos intromittere voluerit in ecclesiam venire antequam fiat aqua benedicta, et debent esse sedes disposite[a] circa altare
hinc et inde, ubi archiepiscopi et episcopi honorifice sedeant, episcopis[b]
paribus,[30] videlicet primo Laudunensi[c], postea[d] Belvacensi, deinde Lingonensi[e], postea[d] Cathalanensi[f], ulti [fol. 44r] mum[g] Noviomensi[h] cum
aliis episcopis[i] archiepiscopatus Remensis, sedentibus seorsum inter
altare et regem ab[j] oppositis altaris, non longe a rege, nec multis indecenter interpositis[k]. Et debent canonici ecclesie Remensis[l] processionaliter cum duabus crucibus, cereis et[m] thuribulo cum incenso ire ad
palatium archipiscopale. Et episcopi[n] Laudunensis[o] et Belvacensis, qui
sunt primi pares de episcopis, debent esse in predicta processione
habentes sanctorum reliquias colo[p] pendentes. Et in camera magna
debent reperire[q] principem in regem consecrandum sedentem et quasi
iacentem supra thalamum decenter ornatum[r]. Et cum ad dicti principis
presentiam applicaverint. Dicat Laudunensis[o] episcopus hanc orationem.

4. [a] deposite B E F a b c. —[b] Episcopis A; honorifice sedeant episcopis]
sedeant honorifice de episcopis B E. —[c] Landunensi a. —[d] post ea A. —[e] Lin-
guonensi F. —[f] Catalanensi D. —[g] ultimo F G a b c. —[h] Noviemensi D,
Novioniensi a. —[i] istius add. F G a b c. —[j] ob D. —[k] interpositis a later corr.
over erasure F. —[l] Remansis D. —[m] et om. D. —[n] ipsi F G a. —[o] Landunensis
a. —[p] collo D F G a b c. —[q] repperire B. —[r] ordinatum A.

---

[30] episcopis paribus is part of the previous sentence in B, F, and G; manuscript F
begins a new sentence, and B and G a new clause with videlicet.

5. *Omnipotens sempiterne Deus, qui famulum tuum N.*ª *fastigio*
*dignatus es sublimare, tribue quesumus ei, ut ita in*ᵇ *huius seculi*
*cursu multorum in commune salutem disponat, quatenus*ᶜ *a veritatis*
*tue tramite non recedat. Per dominum*ᵈ.

5. ª regis *add.* F G *a b c*, regni *add. in brackets Dewick (ed. g).* —ᵇ in *om. a*
b c. —ᶜ quatinus E F *a c.* —ᵈ nostrum Iesum Christum filium tuum. Qui tecum
vivit et regnat etc. *add. a b c.*

6. Qua oratione dictaª, sta [fol 44v] tim suscipiant eum duo predicti
episcopi dextera levaqueᵇ honorifice et ipsum reverenter ducant ad
ecclesiam canentesᶜ hoc responsorium cum canonicis predictisᵈ.

Ecce mitto angelum meum, qui precedat te et custodiat semper.
Observa et audi vocem meam, et inimicus ero inimicis tuis et affli-
*gentes te*ᵉ *affligam, et precedet te angelus meus.*

6. ª completa F G *a b c.* —ᵇ levantque B D E. —ᶜ cantantes B E. —ᵈ Resp. *add.*
as rubric E F G *a c.* —ᵉ afflige̅ / tes te affligentes te E.

7. Finito responsorio, canteturª versusᵇ.

Israel, si me audieris, non erit in te deus recens neque adorabis
*deum alienum, ego enim Dominus. Observa*ᶜ.

7. ª sequens *add.* F G *a b c*; Finito ... cantetur *om.* E. —ᵇ versus *om.* E; Finito
... versus *om.* B; Vers. *add. as rubric* E F *a.* —ᶜ et audi vocem meam et inimicus ero inimicis etc. *add. a b c.*

8. Cunctoque eumª ³¹ populo [fol. 45r] sequente ad hostiumᵇ ecclesie
clerus subsistat. Et alterᶜ episcopus, scilicet Belvacensis, si presens
fuerit, dicat hanc orationem qui sequiturᵈ.

*Deus, qui scis humanum genus*ᵉ *nulla*ᶠ *virtute posse subsistere*ᵍ,
concede propicius, ut famulus tuus N., quem populo tuo voluisti pre-
*ferri, ita tuo*ʰ *fulciatur adiutorio, quatenus*ⁱ *quibus*ʲ *potuit preesse*
*valeat et prodesse. Per dominum*ᵏ.

8. ª Cuncto enim B, Cuncto cum D, Cunctoque cum F, Cuncto eum E. —
ᵇ ostium B E G *a b c.* —ᶜ alter *om.* D. —ᵈ qui sequitur *om.* B E F G *a b c*; Oratio *add. as rubric* E F *a b c*; Oremus *add.* G. —ᵉ humanum genus] genus
humanum F G *a b c.* —ᶠ multa E. —ᵍ sustinere D. —ʰ quo F, *later corr. in*
hand 1 to tuo. —ⁱ quatinus E F G, quanto *a b c.* —ʲ quibus *om.* E. —ᵏ nostrum
Iesum Christum filium tuum *add. a b c.*

9. Introeuntes autem ecclesiam, precedentes canonici dicant usque
ad introitum chori hanc antiphonamª.

Domine, in virtute tua letabitur rex.

---

³¹ *B*'s reading, *Cuncto enim,* apparently came about because the word *enim,* only
four words earlier, is on the line just above.

9. ᵃ Antiphona *add. as rubric* F.

10. Finitaᵃ antiphonaᵇ, metropolitanus, cuiᶜ in ecclesia expectanti ante altare, per predictosᵈ episcopos rex consecrandus presentabiturᵉ dicat hanc orationem sequentemᶠ.

*Omnipotens*³² *Deus, celestium*ᵍ *moderator*ʰ, *qui famulum tuum N. ad regni fastigium dignatus es provehere, concede, quesumus, ut a cunctis adversitatibus liberatus*ⁱ, *et*ʲ *ecclesiastice pacis dono muniatur et ad eterne pacis gaudia te donante pervenire mereatur*ᵏ. *Per dominum*ˡ.

10. ᵃ autem *add.* B E. —ᵇ anthiphona D. —ᶜ cui *om.* B E. —ᵈ dictos G. —ᵉ reverenter *add.* F G *a b c.* —ᶠ dicat ... sequentem] dicat oracionem B E; Oratio *add.* E, Oremus *add.* G. —ᵍ celestiumque B D E F, *later corr. to* celestium F. —ʰ mediator G. —ⁱ liberatus *om. a b c.* —ʲ ab *add.* B E, ad *add.* D. —ᵏ mereamur B D E. —ˡ Alia oratio *add. as rubric* D E.

ABDE   FG*a*

11. *Deus*³³ *humilium visitator, qui nos sancti Spiritus illustracione consolaris, pretende*ᵃ *super hunc famulum tuum N. graciam tuam, ut per eum tuum nobis*ᵇ *adesse senciamus adventum*ᶜ.

11. ᵃ prende B, pende E. —ᵇ nobis tuum E. —ᶜ adesse senciamus adventum] senciamus adventum adesse. Per dominum B.

ABDEFG*a*

12. Qua oratione [fol. 45v] dictaᵃ, ducant predicti episcopi regem consecrandum ad sedendum in cathedra sibi preparata³⁴ in conspectu cathedre archiepiscopi, et ibi sedebit donec archiepiscopus veniat cum sancta ampullaᵇ, cui venienti assurget rex reverenter.

12. ᵃ oratione [fol. 45v] oratione dicta A —ᵇ ampula F G *a b c.*

---

³² *Metropolitanus super regem orat ante altare* later add. in left marg. at *Omnipotens* in hand 1 in *F*, add. in marg. in *G*, add. in text after *Oremus* and before *Omnipotens Deus* in *a*. In the same hand *Oremus* later add. in top marg. above *Omnipotens* in hand 1 in *F*, add. in text before *Omnipotens* in *G*, add. in text before *Metropolitanus ... altare* in *a*.

³³ This prayer is added in the margin in *A* by the scribe who copied the remainder of the manuscript, and it appears as though he intended it to precede the prayer in no. 10. It is in the text in *B D E* after no. 10, however, so that must have been its location in *A*'s source.

³⁴ *Rex sedet in cathedra expectans* later add. in marg. at *sedebit* in hand 1 in *F*, add. in marg. at *preparata* in *G*, add. in parentheses in text before *in conspectu* in *a b c*.

13. Quando[35] sacra[a] ampulla[b] debeat[c] venire.[36]

Inter primam et terciam debent venire monachi beati Remigii processionaliter cum crucibus et cereis cum[d] sacrosancta ampulla[e], quam debet
abbas reverentissime[f] deferre[g] sub[h] cortina[i] serica, quatuor particis[j] [37] a
quatuor monachis albis indutis sublevata. Rex autem debet mittere de
baronibus qui eam secure conducant, et cum venerit ad ecclesiam beati
Dyonisii[k] vel usque ad maiorem ianuam ecclesie propter turbam[l] comprimentem[m]. Debet[38] archiepiscopus superpilitio[n] stola et capa[o] sollempni[p]
indutus cum mitra[q] et baculo pastorali sua cruce precedente[r] cum ceteris
archiepiscopis et episcopis, baronibus[s] necnon et canonicis, si fieri potest,
occurrere sancte ampulle[t], et eam[u] de manu abbatis recipere cum pollicitatione de reddendo bona fide, et sic ad[v] altare[39] [fol. 46r] cum magna
populi reverentia defferre[w], abbate et aliquibus de monachis pariter cum
comitantibus[x].[40] Ceteri vero[y] monachi debent expectare in ecclesia beati
Dyonisii[z] vel in capella beati Nicolai[a], donec omnia peracta[b] fuerint, et
quousque[c] sacra ampulla[d] fuerit reportata[e].

13. [a] sancta B E. —[b] ampula E F G _a c._ —[c] debet D. —[d] et F G _a b c._ —
[e] ampula F G _a b c._ —[f] reverendissime D G. —[g] defferre B E. —[h] cum D. —
[i] courtina F G _a b c._ —[j] partitis E. —[k] beati Dyonisii] Remensem B E. —[l] turbam _om._ D. —[m] comprimantem F, _later corr._ to comprimentem. —[n] super-
cilio B E, superpellicio D, superlicio F G _a b c._ —[o] cappa B E F G _a b c._ —
[p] solenni E F G _a b c._ —[q] mittra F G. —[r] procedente B E. —[s] Baronibus A —
[t] ampule F G _a b c._ —[u] reverenter _add._ F G _a b c._ —[v] de B E. —[w] deferre B D
E _a b c._ —[x] cum comitantibus] cum commitantibus B E, cum comitatibus D,
committendo F _a_, comitendo G. —[y] vero _om._ F G _a b c._ —[z] Remigii B E. —
[a] Nicholai D F _a_, cappella (capela E) beati Nicholay B E. —[b] parata B E. —
[c] quo adusque F G, quoadusque _a b c._ —[d] ampula G _a b c._ —[e] Quid suscepta
ampula agendum sit _add. a b c._

---

[35] _Nota de sancta ampulla_ (_Nota de ampula_ F G _a b c_) later add. in marg. _A_, add.
in marg. at _Inter primam_ in _F G_ (in hand 4 in _F_), add. in text before _Inter primam_ in
_a b c._

[36] In D E F G _a b c_ this sentence is treated as the conclusion of the sentence in no.
12.

[37] Read _perticis_, according to Dewick (ed. _g_, col. 18, n. 1); _perticis_ or _particis_
(abbreviated) in _B F_; _particis_ written out _D G_; _partitis_ E.

[38] _Quomodo_ (_Quomodo_] _Nota a b c_) _metropolitanus recipit sacram ampullam_
(_ampulam_ G _a b c_) _in porta ecclesie, et in quo habitu ei cum quibus_ later add. in
marg. in hand 1 in _F_, add. in marg. at _pastorali sua cruce_ in _G_, add. in parentheses in
text before _pastorali sua cruce_ in _a b c._

[39] _Abbas sancti Remigii_ (_Dionisii G a_) _stat ad dextram_ (_dexteram G_) _altaris
servans ampullam_ (_ampulam G a b c_) later add. in marg. in hand 1 in _F_, add. in marg.
_G_, add. in parentheses in text before _et sic ad altare_ in _a b c._

[40] Dewick's note (ed. _g_, col. 18, n. 3) reads, "_sic_ probably for _eum_, or perhaps we
should read _concomitantibus_."

A B D E

F G *a*

14. In[41] susceptione ampulle[a] sacre ad portam ecclesie maioris, cantatur hec antiphona.

O preciosum munus, o preciosa gemma, que pro unctione Francorum regum in ministerio angelico celitus est emissa.
Vers. *Inveni David servum meum.*
Resp. *Oleo sancto meo unxi eum.*[42]
Oremus.

14. [a] ampule G *a b c.*

15. *Omnipotens sempiterne Deus, qui pietatis tue dono genus regum Francorum oleo perungi decrevisti, presta quesumus, ut famulus tuus rex noster perunctus hac sacra et presenti unctione, sancto pontifici[a] Remigio emissa divinitus, et in tuo servicio semper dirigatur, et ab omni infirmitate misericorditer liberetur. Per dominum.*

15. [a] pontifice *a.*

A B D E

16. Quid suscepta ampulla agendum sit.

Archiepiscopus ad missam se preparat cum dyaconibus et subdyaconibus, vestimentis insignioribus et pallio induendus, et, in hunc modum indutus[a], venit processionaliter

F G *a*

16. Quid suscepta ampula agendum sit[b].

Archiepiscopus dum cantatur tercia,[43] facta aqua benedicta, ad missam se preparat cum diaconibus et subdiaconibus, vestimentis insignioribus et pallio et

---

[41] Nos. 14–15 were later added in the bottom margin in in hand 1 in *F* (no. 14 is in a semi-cursive script and no. 15 in a book miniscule) with no indication as to where they should be inserted, although it appears that it was intended that they should precede *Ceteri monachi debent expectare* in no. 13 (see Plate 29). I place them in their location in *G* and *a*. They first appear in the ceremony at the coronation of Charles VIII in 1484 (Ordo XXV,56–57), and they might have been copied into *F* at that time.

[42] The versicle and response are Ps. 88: 21.

[43] *Dum cantatur tercia, facta aqua benedicta, archiepiscopus ad missam se preparat cum diacono et subdiacono in sacristia* later add. in marg. at *tercia* in hand 1 in *F*, add. in marg. at *Archiepiscopus* in *G*. Editions *a*, *b*, and *c* incorporate both the original reading of the *livre rouge* and the marginal addition, so they read quite redundantly: *Dum cantatur tertia facta aqua benedicta archiepiscopus ad missam se preparat cum diacono et subdiacono in sacristia. Archiepiscopus dum cantatur tertia facta aqua benedicta ad missam se preparat....*

A B D E

ad altare more solito; cui venienti, rex debet assurgere reverenter.

F G *a*

racionali desuper induendus et in hunc modum indutus. Venit duobus suis suffraganeis asociatis[c] processionaliter ad altare more solito; cui venienti, rex debet asurgere reverenter.

A B D E F G *a*

Cum autem venerit archiepiscopus ad altare, debet pro[d] omnibus ecclesiis sibi subditis a rege hec petere.

16. [a] Indutus A. —[b] Quid ... sit *om. a b c because add. before no. 14 above (in var. 13d₂).* —[c] *later corr. to* asociatiis *F,* associatus G *a.* —[d] pro *om.* B E.

17. Ammonitio[a] ad regem dicendo ita.

A[44] *vobis perdonari petimus, ut unicuique de nobis et ecclesiis nobis commissis canonicum privilegium ac*[b] *debitam legem atque*[c] *iusticiam conservetis et*[d] *deffensionem*[e] *exhibeatis*[f]*, sicut rex in regno suo*[g] *debet unicuique episcopo et ecclesie sibi com* [fol. 46v] *misse.*

17. [a] Amonicio F, Amonitio G *a.* —[b] privilegium et B E G *a b c,* previlegium et F. —[c] ac B E. —[d] conservetis et] consuetudinem B E. —[e] defencionem D, defensionem F *a b c.* —[f] exibeatis F. —[g] in suo regno F G *a b c.*

18. Responsio regis ad episcopos[a].

Promitto[45] *vobis et perdono, quia unicuique de vobis et ecclesiis vobis commissis canonicum privilegium*[b] *et debitam legem atque iusticiam conservabo*[c]*, et deffensionem*[d]*, quantum potuero*[e]*, exhibebo*[f]*, Domino adiuvante*[g]*, sicut rex in suo regno unicuique episcopo et ecclesie sibi commisse per rectum exhibere*[h] *debet.*

18. [a] episcopum F *a c.* —[b] previlegium F. —[c] conservabo *om.* F, *but* servabo *later add. in marg. in hand 1;* servabo G *a b c.* —[d] defencionem D, defensionem *a b c.* —[e] potero F G *a.* —[f] potuero exhibebo] potero potuero B, *then* potero *crossed out by scribe;* potuero exhibebo] potuero E. —[g] adiuvante Domino exhibebo F G *a b c* —[h] exibere F.

19. Item[a] hec dicit rex, et promittit et firmat iuramento[b].

Hec[46] *populo christiano et michi subdito in Christi nomine*

---

[44] *Amonicio (Amonitio G) later add. in marg. F in hand 4, add. in marg. G.*

[45] *Promissio regis later add. in marg. in hand 1 in F, add. in marg. in G, and in text before responsio in a c; Promissio et add. in text before responsio in b.*

[46] *Iuramentum regis later add. in marg. in hand 1 in F, add. in marg. at Hec dicit in G, and in text before Hec populo in a b c.*

*promitto*c: *in primis, ut ecclesie Dei omnis populus christianus veram pacem nostro arbitrio in omni*47 *tempore servet, et superioritatem, iura et nobilitates corone Francie inviolabiliter custodiam et illa nec transportabo nec alienabo*d. *Item, ut omnes rapacitates et omnes iniquitates omnibus gradibus interdicam. Item*e, *ut*f *in omnibus iudiciis equitatem et misericordiam precipiam, ut michi et vobis indulgeat per*g *suam misericordiam clemens et misericors Dominus*h. *Item*i, *de terra mea ac iuridicione*j *michi sub* [fol. 47r] *dita universos hereticos ab ecclesia denotatos pro viribus bona fide exterminare studebo*k. *Hec omnia supradicta firmo iuramento.* Tunc manum apponat*l* libro et librum osculetur*m.*48

19. a Item *om.* F G *a b c.* —b Item ... iuramento] Hec dicit rex promittit et firmat cum iuramento E. —c promitto nomine F G *a b c.* —d et superioritatem ... alienabo *om.* F G *a b.* —e Iterum F G *a.* —f ut *om.* E. —g per *om.* F G *a b c.* — h Deus F G *a.* —i Iterum F G *a.* —j iurisditione G, iurisdictione *a b c.* — k faciam B, *but crossed out by scribe and replaced with* studebo. —l apponat *om.* E. —m et librum osculetur] et osculetur eum F G *a.*

20. Hiis factis processionibusa, statim incipiaturb "Te Deum laudamusc."49 Sed secundum usum Romanumd et aliquorum regnorum non dicitur "Te Deume" usque post intronizationem, que est post orationem "Sta et retine," et videtur melius ibif dici quam hic. Et duo predicti episcopi ducunt regem per manus ante altare, qui prosternit se ante altare usque in finem "Te Deumg"; postmodum 50 surgit, iamh antea preparatis eti positis super altare corona regia, gladio in vagina incluso, carcaribusj aureis, sceptrok deaurato, et virga ad mensuraml unius cubiti vel amplius habente desuperm manum eburneam. Item, caligis sericisn et iacinctinis per totum intextiso liliis aureis, et tunica eiusdem coloris et operis in modum tunicalis quo induuntur subdyaconip ad missam, nec nonq et [fol.

---

47 From here to the end of the oath in *A* the original oath was erased and replaced with the present text by the scribe himself; see Plate 28. T. Julian Brown very carefully checked the manuscript's script for me and was convinced that the correction was not made "in a later and coarser hand" as Dewick thought (ed. *g*, col. 19, n. 1), but was either made by the scribe of the rest of the ordo or, less likely, by someone else, and that it was part of the original production of the manuscript (letter of 17 August 1976). I wish to express my gratitude to the late Julian Brown for his kind help.

48 *Apponit rex manum super evangelia* (*evangelio b*) *et osculatur* later add. in marg. in hand 1 in *F*, add. in marg. in *G*, and in text before *Tunc manum apponat libro et osculetur eum* in *a*.

49 *Dicitur in fine Te Deum et non hic* later add. in marg. in hand 1 in *F*, add. in marg. in *G*, and add. in text in *a*.

50 *Preparatio insignium* (*insignitum a*) *et ornamentorum regalium* later add. in marg. in hand 1 in *F*, add. in marg. in *G*, and add. in text before *Postmodum* in *a*.

47v] socco[r] prorsus eiusdem coloris et operis[s], qui est factus fere in modum cappe serice[t] absque caperone, que omnia abbas beati[u] Dyonisii in Francia de monasterio suo debet Remis afferre, et stans ad altare custodire. Tunc primo[v] rex stans ante altare deponit vestes suas[w] preter tunicam sericam[x] et camisiam, apertas[y] profundius ante et retro, in pectore videlicet et inter scapulas, aperturis tunice sibi invicem connexis ansulis argenteis. Et[z] tunc in primis dicatur ab archiepiscopo oratio sequens[a].

20. [a] promissionibus F G a. —[b] incipitur F G a; Psalmus add. as rubric E. —[c] te dominum confitemur add. E. —[d] Romanorum F a. —[e] laudamus add. B E F G a. —[f] ibi melius B, tibi melius E. —[g] laudamus add. F G a. —[h] in add. F G a. —[i] et / et E. —[j] calcaribus F G a. —[k] Sceptro A, septro B F G. —[l] mensura A. —[m] de super A. —[n] cericis G. —[o] intextis per totum F G a. —[p] subdyachoni E. —[q] nec non om. B E. —[r] sacco a. —[s] in modum tunicalis ... operis om. G. —[t] serile E. —[u] sancti F G a. —[v] premio E. —[w] Exuitur rex later add. in marg. in hand 1 in F. —[x] sericam om. B D E. —[y] appertas B, apertasque E. —[z] Et om. F G a. —[a] oratio sequens om. B, sequens om. E, and Oratio add. as rubric B E; archiepiscopo oratio sequens] archiepiscopo. Oremus F G a.

21. *Deus inenarrabilis auctor mundi, conditor generis humani, gubernator imperii, confirmator regni, qui ex utero fidelis amici tui patriarche nostri Abrahe preelegisti regem seculis[a] profuturum. Tu[b] presentem regem hunc[c] N. cum exercitu[d] suo per intercessionem omnium sanctorum uberi[e] benedic✠tione locupleta et in solium regni firma stabilitate connecta[f].[51] Visita eum sicut[g] Moysem[h] in Rubro[i], Ihesum Nave[j] in prelio, Gedeon in agro, Samuelem in templo. Et illa cum[k] benedicti [fol. 48r] ✠one[l] syderea ac[m] sapiencie tue rore perfunde, quam[n] beatus David in psalterio, Salomon[o] filius eius te remunerante[p] percepit[q] e celo. Sis ei contra acies inimicorum lorica, in adversis galea, in prosperis[r] paciencia, in protectione clipeus sempiternus. Et presta, ut gentes illis[s] teneant fidem, proceres sui habeant pacem, diligant caritatem, abstineant se a cupiditate, loquantur[t] iusticiam, custodiant veritatem. Et ita populus iste pululet[u] coalitus benedictione[v] eternitatis, ut semper maneant tripudiantes in pace victores.*

Quod ipse prestare etc.[52]

21. [a] seculi G a. —[b] tunc B E. —[c] hunc om. E. —[d] excercitu B F G a. —[e] ubi D. —[f] connecte F G a. —[g] visitasti add. B E. —[h] Moysen B E. —[i] Rubo B E F G a —[j] Neve B, Nene E. —[k] cum om. F G a. —[l] ✠ om. B E. —[m] a D. —[n] quem

[51] *connect* with a space for the remainder of the word in *D* (i.e., the scribe probably noticed the error, but was hesitant to disregard his source and correct it).

[52] *etc.*] *dignetur, qui tecum et cum Spiritu sancto sine fine permanet in secula seculorum. Amen* later add. in text and in marg. in hand 2 in *F*, add. in text in *G a.*

B D E. —[o] Psalmon B, Psalmum E. —[p] remunerance A. —[q] precepit E. —[r] prosperiis E. —[s] illius F G *a*. —[t] loquentur *a*. —[u] pullulet *a*. —[v] ✠ *add.* F G *a*.

22. Qua oratione dicta, statim ibi a magno camerario Francie regi dicte calige[a] calciantur.[53] Et post modum[b] a duce Burgondie[c] calcaria eius pedibus astringuntur[d] et statim tolluntur.

22. [a] regi dicte calige] dantur ei regi dicte calige et D. —[b] postmodum E. —[c] Burgundie D F G *a*. —[d] astriguntur B E F.

23. Benedictio super gladium.[54]

Exaudi, Domine quesumus[a], *preces nostras, et hunc gladium quo famulus tuus N. se accingi desiderat, maiestatis tue dextera bene-* [fol. 48v] *dicere* ✠ *dignare, quatinus*[b] *deffensio*[c] *atque protectio possit esse ecclesiarum, viduarum, orphanorum, omniumque Deo servientium contra sevitiam*[d] *paganorum, aliisque insidiantibus sit pavor*[e], *terror et formido*[f].

23. [a] super gladium ... quesumus] super gladium regi dandum. Exaudi Domine quesumus B D E, super gladium regi dandum. Exaudi quesumus Domine F, super gladium regi dandum. Oremus. Exaudi quesumus Domine G, super gladium regi dandum. Benedicitur ensis. Oremus. Exaudi quesumus Domine *a*. —[b] quanto *a*. —[c] defensio B E *a*; deffenso F, *later corr. to* deffensio. —[d] sevicciam D. —[e] potior *a*. —[f] Per Christum *add.* F *a*, Per Christum dominum nostrum *add.* G.

24. Postmodum rex a solo archiepiscopo gladio[a] accingitur[55]; quo accincto[b], statim[c] idem[d] gladius discingitur[e] e vagina[f], et ab archiepiscopo extrahitur, vagina super altare reposita[g], et datur ei[h] ab archiepiscopo in manibus cum ista oratione dicendo, quem rex in manu sua[i] teneat cuspide elevato donec[j] antiphona[k] "Confortare" etc. fuerit cantata et oratio sequens dicta[l] per archiepiscopum[m].

24. [a] gladio *om.* B E. —[b] accinto F. —[c] statim *om.* F G *a*. —[d] ibidem E. —[e] distingitur B E. —[f] e vagina et] a vagina et E, et e vagina F G *a*. —[g] posita F G *a*. —[h] ei *om.* F G *a*. —[i] sua *om.* F G *a*; rex in manu sua] in manu sua rex D. —[j] cantatur *add.* E. —[k] anthiphona *a*. —[l] dicta *om.* B. —[m] Oremus *add.* F G; fuerit ... archiepiscopum] antiphona cantatur et oratio sequens per archiepiscopum. Oratio E.

---

[53] *Ibi* (*Hic G*) *debent calige poni et post* (*postea G*) *a duce Burgundie calcaria pedibus astringi* later add. in marg. in hand 4 in *F*, add. in marg. in *G*, add. in text before *Qua oratione dicta* in *a b*.

[54] *Dominus vobiscum. Oremus* later add. in marg. in hand 1 in *F*. A second addition, *Benedicitur ensis* was also later add. in marg. in hand 1 in *F*, add. in marg. at *Exaudi quesumus* in *G*.

[55] *Rex accingitur gladio a solo archiepiscopo* later add. in marg. in hand 1 in *F*, add. in marg. in *G*, add. in text before *Postmodum rex* in *a*.

25. *Accipe*[56] *hunc gladium cum*[a] *Dei benedictione*[b] *tibi collatum, in quo, per virtutem sancti Spiritus*[c] *resistere et eicere*[d] *omnes inimicos tuos valeas, et cunctos sancte Dei ecclesie*[e] *adversarios regnumque tibi commissum tutari atque protegere castra Dei, per auxilium*[f] *invictissimi*[g] *triumphatoris domini nostri Ihesu Christi*[h].

25. [a] tuum *a.* — [b] ✠ *add.* F G *a.* — [c] Spiritus sancti F G *a.* — [d] eiecere E, eiicere *a.* — [e] Dei ecclesie] ecclesie Dei F, ecclesie G *a.* — [f] auxilium *om.* D. — [g] invictissimum B E. — [h] auxilium *add.* D.

B D E F G *a* d_1[57]

26. *Accipe*[58] *inquam hunc gladium per manus nostras vice et auctoritate*[a] *sanctorum apostolorum consecratas*[b], *tibi regaliter impositum nostreque*[c] *bene✠dictionis officio in defensione*[d] *sancte Dei ecclesie ordinatum divinitus. Et esto memor de quo psalmista prophetavit dicens, 'Accingere gladio tuo super femur tuum, potentissime,' ut in hoc per eundem vim equitatis exerceas*[e], *molam*[f] *iniquitatis potenter destruas et sanctam Dei ecclesiam, eiusque fideles propugnes et*[g] *protegas, nec minus sub fide falsos quam christiani nominis*[h] *hostes execreris*[i] *ac*[j] *destruas, viduas et pupillos*[k] *clementer adiuves ac defendas*[l], *desolata restaures, restaurata conserves, ulciscaris*[m] *iniusta, confirmes bene disposita, quatinus hec in agendo virtutum*[n] *triumpho gloriosus, iusticieque cultor egregius cum mundi salvatore cuius typum geris in nomine, sine fine merearis regnare. Qui cum*[o] *Patre* etc.[p]

26. [a] authoritate d_1. — [b] consecras D. — [c] nostre E F, *later corr. to* nostreque *in hand 1 in* F. — [d] deffensionem F G, defensionem *a.* — [e] excerceas F G. — [f] *Read* molem. — [g] ac F G *a.* — [h] nomini B D E F, *later corr. to* nominis F. — [i] exsecreris B D F G *a, but the first* s *later erased* G; excecreris E. — [j] et B E. — [k] pupilos G. — [l] deffendas D F G. — [m] usciscaris B E. — [n] virtutem E. — [o] Deo *add.* F G *a.* — [p] etc.] et Spiritu sancto vivit et regnat Deus. Per omnia secula seculorum. Amen F G *a.*

---

[56] *Traditio gladii, quem rex tenet erectum et nudum (nudum om. G) usque ad finem orationis sequentis antiphone "Confortare"* later add. in marg. at *Accipe* in a cursive hand (which differs from the cursive hand so far noted) in *F*, add. in marg. in *G*, add. in text before *Accipe hunc gladium* in *a*.

[57] Beginning with this prayer a folio leaf in *A* has disappeared since the seventeenth century. It is here reproduced from the edition of Selden (ed. d_1, p. 228); nevertheless, following Dewick's example (ed. *g*) when he reproduced the missing text from Selden, the orthography is put into the same form as in the remainder of the manuscript, and all variants of all other manuscripts are given.

[58] *F G a* do not treat this as a separate text. The other manuscripts do, which is correct because nos. 26 and 27 are formulas from different sources.

27. Hic cantatur ista[a] antiphona antifona[b].

Confortare et esto vir, et observa custodias Domini Dei tui, ut ambules[c] in viis eius, et custodias[d] cerimonias eius, et precepta eius, et testimonia et iudicia[e], quocunque te verteris[f] confirmet te Deus.

27. [a] sequens *add.* E. —[b] anthiphona D. —[c] ambulas D. —[d] observa custodias ... custodias] observa custodias Domini et G. —[e] et *add.* F G *a.* —[f] verteus, vertens *or* verteiis D.

28. Cantata ista antiphona, dicitur ista[a] oratio post dationem gladii[b].

Deus, qui providentia tua celestia simul et[c] terrena[d] moderaris, propitiare christianissimo regi nostro, ut omnis hostium suorum

A B D E F G *a*

[fol. 49r] *fortitudo,*[59] *virtute gladii spiritualis frangatur, a te[e] pro illo pugnante penitus conteratur. Per[f].*

28. [a] Cantata ... ista] Cantata antiphona, dicitur E. —[b] Oremus *add.* F G *a.* — [c] et *om. a.* —[d] terena F. —[e] ate B, ac te F G *a.* —[f] dominum nostrum Iesum Christum filium tuum. Qui tecum vivit et regnat in unitate Spiritus sancti Deus. Per omnia secula seculorum *add. a.*

29. Gladium debet rex humiliter recipere de manu archiepiscopi et, devote flexis genibus, offerre[60] ad altare et, statim genibus regis in terram positis, resumere[61] de manu archiepiscopi et incontinentia[a] dare senescallo[b] Francie, si senescallum[c] habuerit. Sin autem, cui voluerit de baronibus ad portandum ante se et in ecclesia usque in finem[d] misse, et[e]

---

[59] *fortitudo* is the first word after the missing leaf in *A*. Most of the manuscript's miniatures are in the wide bottom margins, and there is little difference between the amount of text on those leaves with miniatures and ones without miniatures: they contain about 230–270 words (1475–1690 characters). Leaves with miniatures in the middle of a page contain about 195–205 words (1110–1240 characters). The missing leaf here contained 179 words (1108 characters), so it clearly had a miniature in the middle of the page, which is surely why it was removed from the manuscript. The context suggests that the miniature must have dealt with the sword in some way, although it is difficult to surmise what it was because four surviving miniatures depict a complete series of acts concerning the sword: the king placing the sword on the altar; receiving the sword from the archbishop; handing the sword to the designated sword-bearer; and kneeling at his faldstool, while the archbishop prepares the chrism, and the sword-bearer holds the sword with its point upright.

[60] *Rex offert gladium* later add. in marg. in hand 1 in *F*, add. in marg. at *Gladium debet* in *G*, add. in text before *Gladium debet rex* in *a b.*

[61] *Resumit genibus flexis de manu archiepiscopi et dat cui vult* later add. in marg. at *resumere* in hand 1 in *F*, add. in marg. at *resumere* in *G*, add. in parentheses in text before *et statim genibus* in *a.*

post missam usque ad palatium. Tradito per regem gladio[f], ut dictum est, dicat archiepiscopus hanc[g] orationem[h].

29. [a] statim F G *a.* —[b] senescalo G. —[c] senescallon E, senescalum G. —[d] in fine D, ad finem F G *a.* —[e] Et A. —[f] per regem gladio] autem gladio, per regem D. —[g] hanc *om.* E. —[h] Oremus *add.* F G *a.*

30. *Prospice,*[62] *omnipotens Deus, serenis obtutibus*[a] *hunc glorio- sum regem N. Et sicut*[b] *benedixisti Abraham, Ysaac et Iacob, et*[c] *sic illum largis benedictionibus spiritualis gracie cum omni plenitudine*[d] *potentie irrigare atque perfundere*[e] *dignare. Tribue ei de rore celi et de pinguedine terre habundantiam*[f] *frumenti*[g], *vini*[h] *et olei et omnium frugum opulentiam, ex largitate divini muneris* [fol. 49v] *longa per tempora, ut illo*[i] *regnante sit sanitas corporum*[j] *in patria, et pax in- violata sit in regno, et dignitas gloriosa regalis palacii*[k] *maximo splendore regie potestatis*[l] *oculis omnium fulgeat, luce clarissima choruscare*[m] *atque splendere quasi splendidissima*[n] *fulgura, maximo perfusa lumine videatur. Tribue ei, omnipotens Deus*[o], *ut sit fortis- simus protector patrie et consolator ecclesiarum atque cenobiorum sanctorum, maxima cum pietate regalis munificencie, atque ut sit fortissimus regum, triumphator hostium, ad opprimendas*[p] *rebelles et paganas*[q] *nationes. Sitque suis inimicis satis terribilis pre maxima fortitudine regalis potentie, optimatibus quoque atque precelsis, pro- ceribus*[r] *ac fidelibus sui regni sit munificus et amabilis et pius, ut ab omnibus timeatur atque diligatur. Reges quoque de lumbis eius per successiones*[s] *temporum futurorum egredian* [fol. 50r] *tur*[t], *regnum hoc regere totum. Et post gloriosa tempora atque felicia presentis vite gaudia sempiterna, in perpetua beatitudine habere mereatur.*
Quod ipse prestare dignetur et cetera[u].[63]

30. [a] obtulibus D. —[b] sic F, *later corr. to* sicut. —[c] et *om.* F G *a.* —[d] tue *add.* F G *a.* —[e] perfundare D. —[f] abundantiam G. —[g] et *add.* B E. —[h] vini *om.* D. — [i] ille D. —[j] corporis F G *a.* —[k] palacii *om.* F G *a.* —[l] potestatis D. —[m] chorus- cante F G *a.* —[n] splendissima F *a*, splendidississima E. —[o] Deus *om.* D. — [p] opprimendos F G *a.* —[q] pravas D, paganorum F G *a.* —[r] proceribusque B D E. —[s] sussessiones F . —[t] egredientur E. —[u] prestare dignetur et cetera *om.* B E.

31. Alia benedictio[a].

---

[62] *Super regem genuflexum* later add. in marg. at *Prospice* in hand 1 in *F*, add. in marg. in *G*, add. in text before *Oremus* in *a*.

[63] *digneris qui cum unigenito filio tuo domino nostro Hiesu (Iesu G a) Christo et Spiritu sancto vivis et regnas Deus per omnia secula seculorum (Amen add. G a)* later add. in marg. in hand 3 with an arrow inserted between *prestare* and *et cetera* F, add. in text in *G a* (which omit *dignetur et cetera*).

Bene✠dic, Domine, quesumus, hunc[b] *principem nostrum quem ad salutem populi nobis*[c] *a te credimus esse concessum; fac eum esse annis multiplicem, vigenti*[d] *atque salubri corporis robore vigentem, et ad senectutem optatam*[e] *atque demum ad finem pervenire felicem. Sit nobis fiducia eum obtinere*[f] *gratiam pro populo*[g], *quam*[h] *Aaron in tabernaculo, Helyseus*[i] *in fluvio, Ezechias in lectulo, Zacharias vetulus*[j] *imperavit*[k] *in templo, sit illi regendi virtus atque auctoritas, qualem Iosue suscepit in castris, Gedeon sumpsit in preliis*[l], *Petrus accepit in clave, Paulus est usus in dogmate. Et ita pastorum cura tuum profici* [fol. 50v] *at in ovile, sicut Ysaac profecit in fruge et Iacob dilatatus est in grege.*

Quod ipse etc.[m]

31. [a] et cetera *add.* F *a,* Alia benedictio *om.* E. —[b] huic *a.* —[c] ad salutem populi nobis *om.* E. —[d] in genti E, ingenti G *a;* genti *with a space before the word* F, *later corr. to* Ingenti. —[e] optatem D. —[f] optinere B E. —[g] pro populo] propulo B, populo E. —[h] quem D. —[i] Heliseus B D. —[j] veculus E. —[k] impetravit F G *a.* —[l] castris B, *then crossed out by scribe and* preliis *add.* —[m] ut supra *later add.* F; etc.] prestare digneris, qui cum unigenito Filio tuo domino nostro Iesu Cristo et Spiritu sancto vivis et regnas Deus. Per omnia secula seculorum. Amen G

32. Oratio[a].

Deus, Pater eterne glorie, sit adiutor tuus et protector, et omnipotens bene✠dicat[b] *tibi, preces tuas in cunctis exaudiat, et vitam tuam longitudinem*[c] *dierum adimpleat, thronum*[d] *regni tui iugiter firmet, et gentem populumque*[64] *tuum in eternum conservet, et inimicos tuos confusione induat, et super te sanctifi✠catio*[e] *Christi floreat*[f], *ut qui tibi tribuit in terris imperium, ipse in celis conferat premium. Qui vivit etc.*[65]

32. [a] Oremus F G *a,* Oratio *om.* D E. —[b] ✠ *om.* F, *but later add. both in text and in marg.* —[c] longitudine F G *a.* —[d] tronum D. —[e] ✠ *om.* B E. —[f] floreat Christi D.

33. Huc usque de gladio. Post hec preparatur[a] unctio in hunc modum.[66] Sed quamdiu ab archiepiscopo paratur[b] incipit cantor responsorium.

---

[64] In *F* fol. 67v begins with *que,* which was later crossed out, and *que* was added to *populum* at the end of fol. 67r.

[65] *et regnat trinus et unus Deus per omnia secula seculorum (Amen add. G a)* later add. in marg. in hand 2 in *F,* add. in text *G a.*

[66] *Hic preparatur unctio* later add. in marg. in hand 1 in *F,* add. in marg. in *G,* and add. in text before *Post hec preparatur* in *a.*

A B D E F G *a Meurier*[67]

Gentem Francorum inclitam simul cum rege nobili, beatus Remigius sumpto celitus crismate[c] *sacro, sanctificavit gurgite, atque Spiritus sancti plene ditavit munere.*

Vers. *Qui dono singularis gracie in columba apparuit et divinum crisma*[d] *celitus ponti* [fol. 51r] *fici ministravit.*

Vers[e].[68] *Ora pro nobis, beate Remigi*[f].

Resp[g]. *Ut digni efficiamur promissionibus*[h] *Christi*[i].

Oremus[j].

33. [a] paratur G. — [b] paratur *om.* F, *but later add. in hand 3.* — [c] chrismate *Meurier.* — [d] chrisma *Meurier.* — [e] Vers. *om.* F *a.* — [f] Remigii *a.* — [g] Resp. *om.* D E F *a.* — [h] promissione F G. — [i] Christi *om.* F. — [j] Oremus *later add. in marg. in hand 1 in* F; Resp. Ut digni ... Christi *om. Meurier.*

34. Oratio[a].

Deus, qui[b] *populo tuo eterne salutis beatum Remigium ministrum tribuisti, presta, quesumus, ut quem doctorem vite habuimus in terris, intercessorem* [*semper*[c]] *habere mereamur in celis. Per Christum*[d].

34. [a] Oratio *om.* D. — [b] pro *add.* B. — [c] semper *om.* A *only.* — [d] dominum nostrum. Amen *add.* G.

A B D E F G *a*

35. Crisma in altari ponitur[a] super patenam consecratam; et archiepiscopus sacro sanctam ampullam[b], quam abbas beati[c] Remigii attulit, super altare debet aperire, et inde cum acu aurea[69] aliquantulum de oleo celitus misso attrahere, et, crismati parato[d] in patena, diligentius cum digito immiscere ad inungendum regem, qui solus inter universos reges terre hoc glorioso prefulget privilegio[e], ut oleo celitus misso singulariter[f] inungatur[g]. Parata unctione[h] qua rex debet inungi ab archiepiscopo, debent dissolvi ansule aperturarum[i] vestimentorum[70] regis ante et retro, et, genibus regis in terram positis[j],[71] prostrato super faldistorium, archiepiscopo eciam con [fol. 51v] similiter prostrato.[72]

---

[67] Meurier, 244.

[68] *dicit archiepiscopus later add. in marg. in hand 1 in* F, *add. in marg. in* G.

[69] *Hic debet fieri mistio* (*mixtio* G) *de crismate et oleo celitus misso later add. in marg. in hand 4 in* F, *add. in marg. in* G, *add. in text before* Crisma ponitur in altari *in* a.

[70] *Dissolvuntur ansule aperturarum vestimentorum regis later add. in marg. in hand 1 in* F, *add. in marg. at* qua debet rex *in* G, *add. in parentheses in text before* Parata unctione *in* a.

[71] *Rex genuflectit et prosternitur super tapetum later add. in marg. in hand 1 in* F, *add. in marg. at* faldistorium *in* G, *add. in parentheses after* ante et retro *in* a.

[72] *Et* (*Et om.* a) *archiepiscopus super faldistorium later add. in marg. in hand 1*

A B D	E F G a
Duo archiepiscopi vel episcopi incipiunt letaniam. Quere letaniam[k] in fine huius libri[l].	duo[73] archiepiscopi vel episcopi incipiant[m] letaniam sequentem[n].

    109. *Kyrieleyson*[74] ... *Sancte chorus confessorum, ora.*

    110. *Sancta Maria Magdalena ... Omnes sancti, orate.*

    111. *Propitius esto ... In die iudicii, libera.*

    112. *Peccatores ... Ut obsequium servitutis nostre rationabile facias, te rogamus, audi nos.*

    113. Tunc archiepiscopus ... integre repetente. *Ut hunc famulum ... Benedi✠cere, sublimare et consecrare digneris.*

    114. Quo dicto ... prosequentibus letaniam. *Ut regibus ... Fili Dei, te rogamus, audi nos.*

    115. *Agnus Dei ... Kyrieleyson.*

    116. Letania finita ... annunciat. *Pater noster ... Et cum spiritu tuo.*

    117. *Oremus. Pretende ... mereatur. Per dominum.*

    118. *Attiones nostras ... finiatur. Per dominum.*

A B D E F G a

Archiepiscopus[o] debet super eum[p] dicere has orationes antequam eum inunguat[q], debet autem[r] sedere sicut[s] sedet cum[t] consecrat episcopos.[75]

   35. [a] ponitur in altari F G a. —[b] ampulam F G a; De ampulla *later add. in marg.* A. —[c] sancti F G a. —[d] peracto E. —[e] previlegio F. —[f] singularite A. —

---

in *F,* add. in marg. at *super faldistorium* in *G,* add. in parentheses in text immediately after *super tapetum* (the preceding addition) in *a.*

  [73] *F G a* treat this as the conclusion of the previous sentence.

  [74] The variants in nos. 109–118 in *E, F, G,* and *a* are given at their location in *A* at the end of the ordo. Selden (ed. *d₁*), 231–33, also moved the litany from the end of the ordo to here with the statement, "but because it properly should follow here, I have so placed it."

  [75] *Archiepiscopus sedens, orat super regem consecrandum* later add. in marg. at *episcopos* in hand 1 in *F,* add. in marg. at *Item archiepiscopus* in *G,* add. in text after *Oratio* in *a.*

^g ut oleo ... inungatur] ut crismate mixto cum oleo celitus misso modo alio quam ceteri reges singulariter inungatur. Alii enim reges inunguntur solum in humero, iste vero in capite et in aliis membris sicut inferius distinguetur F G *a.* —^h unctio B E. —ⁱ apperturarum B F, appertuarum E. —^j et *add.* F G *a.* — ^k Quere letaniam *om.* D. —^l huius libri *om.* B. —^m dicant F G *a.* —ⁿ sequentem] que sequitur. Incipit letania (Incipit letania *om.* G) F G *a.* —^o Item archiepiscopus F G *a.* —^p regem F G *a.* —^q inungat B E. —^r debet autem] et debet F G *a.* —^s sicut *repeated* B. —^t quando F G *a.*

36. Oratio^a.⁷⁶

Te invocamus, Domine^b sancte Pater omnipotens, eterne Deus, ut hunc famulum tuum N., quem tue^c divine^d dispensationis providentia in primordio plasmatum usque in^e hunc presentem diem iuvenili flore letantem crescere concessisti^f, eum tue pietatis dono ditatum plenumque gracia veritatis de die in diem coram Deo et hominibus^g ad meliora semper proficere facias, ut summi regiminis solium^h gracie superne largitate gaudens suscipiat, etⁱ misericordie tue muro ab hostium adversitate undique munitus, plebem sibi commissam cum pace^j propiciationis et virtute victorie^k regere mereatur. Per^l dominum^m.

36. ^a Sequitur oratio B; Oratio *om.* D, *but add. in another hand;* Oratio *om.* E. —^b Domine *om.* F G *a.* —^c tue *om.* F, *but later add. in hand 1.* —^d divine tue B E. —^e in *om.* F, *but later add. in hand 1.* —^f concessissi D. —^g et *add.* F, *but later crossed out.* —^h solum B. —ⁱ et *om.* F, *but later add. in hand 1.* — ^j cum pace *om. a.* —^k feliciter *add.* F G *a.* —^l Christum *add.* G. —^m Per dominum *om.* F, *but* Per Christum dominum nostrum. Amen *later add. in marg. in hand 3.*

37. Alia^a oratio^b.

[fol. 52r] *Deus, qui populis tuis^c virtute consulis et amore dominaris, da huic famulo tuo^d spiritum sapiencie^e tue cum regimine discipline, ut tibi toto corde devotus in regni regimine semper maneat ydoneus, tuoque munere ipsius temporibus securitas ecclesie^f dirigatur et^g in tranquillitate^h devotio ecclesiastica permaneat, ut, in bonisⁱ operibus perseverans, ad eternum regnum^j te duce valeat pervenire. Per.*

37. ^a Alia *om.* B. —^b Alia oratio *om.* D E F G *a;* Oremus *add.* F G *a.* —^c populus tuus B E. —^d N. *add.* E F G *a.* —^e sapienti / cie G. —^f ecclesie securitas F G *a.* —^g et *om.* G *a.* —^h transquillitate B E, transquilitate F G. —ⁱ omnibus *a.* — ^j regnum eternum E.

38. Alia oratio^a.

---

⁷⁶ *Oremus later add. in marg. in hand 1 in F.*

In diebus eius oriatur omnibus equitas et iusticia, amicis adiuto-rium, inimicis obstaculum, humilibus solatium, elatis correctio[b], divitibus doctrina, pauperibus pietas, peregrinis pacificatio, propriis in patria pax et[c] securitas, unumquemque secundum suam mensuram moderate gubernans, seipsum sedulus[d] discat[e], ut tua irrigatus com-punctione[f] toto[g] populo tibi[h] placita[i] prebere vite possit exempla, et per viam veritatis cum grege gradiens sibi [fol. 52v] subdito opes frugales habundanter[j] acquirat[k], simulque ad salutem non solum corporum[l], sed eciam cordium a te concessam[m], cuncta accipiat. Sicque[n] in te cogi-tatum[o] animi consiliumque omne componens[p], plebis gubernacula cum pace simul, et sapientia semper invenire videatur. Teque auxili-ante, presentis[q] vite prosperitatem et prolixitatem percipiat, et[r] per tempora bona usque ad summam senectutem perveniat, huiusque fragilitatis finem perfectum, ab omnibus viciorum vinculis tue pietatis largitate[s] liberatus, et infinite[t] prosperitatis premia perpetua angelorumque eterna commercia consequatur[u]. Per dominum.

38. [a] Alia oratio *om.* D, *but add. in another hand;* Alia oratio *om.* E; Alia ora-tio] Oratio B, Oremus F G *a.* —[b] correptio E. —[c] et *om.* F, *but later add. in marg.* —[d] regere *later add. in marg. in hand 1 in* F, add. in text in G *a.* —[e] distat E. —[f] conpunctione B. —[g] toti F G *a.* —[h] tibi *om.* G. —[i] placita *om.* B E. —[j] abundanter G *a.* —[k] acquiras B E. —[l] corporum non solum F G *a.* —[m] con-cessa E, concessum *a.* —[n] Sitque B D E. —[o] gogitatum D. —[p] et *add.* B E. —[q] prentis A. —[r] ut F G *a.* —[s] largitate pietatis F G *a.* —[t] in fine D. —[u] conse-quantur F G, *later corr. to* consequatur F.

39. Consecratio regis[a].

Omnipotens sempiterne Deus, creator ac[b] gubernator celi et terre, conditor et dispositor angelorum et hominum, rex regum et dominus dominorum, qui Abraham[c] fidelem famulum tuum de hostibus tri-umphare[d] fecisti, Moysi et Iosue populo tuo pre [fol. 53r] latis multi-plicem victoriam tribuisti, humilem quoque puerum tuum[e] David regni fastigio[f] sublimasti, eumque de ore leonis et de manu bestie atque Golie, sed et de gladio maligno Saul et omnium inimicorum eius liberasti, et Salomonem sapientie pacisque[g] ineffabili munere ditasti[h], respice propicius ad preces nostre humilitatis, et super hunc famulum tuum N., quem supplici[i] devocione in huius regni regem[j] pariter eligimus, benedic✠tionum[k] tuarum[l] dona multiplica, eumque dextera potentie tue[m] semper[n] ubique circunda, quatinus predicti Abrahe fidelitate[o] firmatus, Moysi mansuetudine fretus, Iosue fortitudine munitus, David humilitate exaltatus, Salomonis[p] sapiencia[q] decora-tus, tibi in omnibus complaceat, et per tramitem[r] iusticie in offenso[s] gressu semper incedat, et tocius regni ecclesiam deinceps cum plebibus sibi annexis, ita enutriat ac[t] *doceat, muni* [fol. 53v] *at et instruat, con-traque*[u] *omnes visibiles et invisibiles hostes idem potenter regaliterque tue virtutis regimen administret, ut regale solium*[v] *videlicet Saxonum, Merciorum, Nordan*[w]*, Chimbrorum*[x] *sceptra non deserat, sed ad pristine*[y] *fidei pacisque concordiam eorum animos, te opitulante, reformet,*[77] *ut, utrorumque horum populorum debita subiectione ful-tus, cum digno*[z] *amore glorificatus per longum vite spatium paterne apicem glorie tua miseratione unatim stabilire et gubernare mereatur, tue quoque protectionis galea munitus et scuto insuperabili iugiter protectus, armisque*[78] *celestibus circundatus, optabilis victorie trium-phum de hostibus feliciter*[a] *capiat, terroremque sue potentie infi-delibus inferat, et pacem*[b] *militantibus letanter reportet,*[79] *virtutibus necnon quibus*[c] *prefatos fideles tuos decorasti, multiplici honoris benedicti✠one condecora, et in regimine regni sublimiter colloca*[d]*, et oleo gracie*

B D E F G a d[1][80]

Spiritus sancti[e] *perunge. Per dominum nostrum*[f]*, qui virtute crucis tartara destruxit, regnoque dyaboli superato ad celos victor ascendit, in quo potestas omnis regnumque*[g] *consistit et victoria, qui est gloria humilium et vita salusque populorum. Qui tecum etc.*

39. [a] Oremus *add.* F G a. — [b] creator ac *om.* F G a. — [c] Habraham F, Abrahan G. — [d] triumphale D. — [e] tuum *om.* F G a. — [f] fastidio B E. — [g] pacis et B E. — [h] dicasti B E. — [i] suplici E. — [j] regere B E. — [k] bene✠dittionum E. — [l] tua cum D. — [m] potencie sue B E, tue potentie F G a. — [n] super G a. — [o] felicitate B E. — [p] Samonis A. — [q] sapiencie D. — [r] tramittem F. — [s] in officio B E. — [t] et B E; ac *om.* F G a. — [u] contra F, *later corr. in hand 1 to* contraque. — [v] solacium B E. — [w] Nordam F G a. — [x] Cymborum F, *later corr. to* Cymbro-rum; Cimbrorum G a. — [y] prestine B E. — [z] condigno F G a. — [a] fideliter E. — [b] tibi *add.* F G a. — [c] preest *add.* D. — [d] collata B E; collocata F, *later corr. to* colloca. — [e] et oleo ... sancti] et oleo Spiritus sancti gracie (gracia G a) F G a. — [f] ih (*for* Ihesum) *begun, then crossed out by scribe* B. — [g] regumque G a.

---

[77] On this passage in the *livre rouge*, see Ordo XXII A, n. 55.

[78] *armis* abbreviated ar̄īs in *F*, and later crossed out and *armis* written out in marg. in hand 2.

[79] An eighteenth-century marginal note in MS *J*, p. 19, reads, "Les Mss violet et rouge de la Cathedrale ... mettent un point avant *virtutibus*." *F* does also, although neither *G* nor *a* does.

[80] After *gracie* a folio leaf in *A* has disappeared since the seventeenth century. As above, it is here reproduced from the edition of Selden, p. 236; nevertheless, the orthography is put into the same form as in the remainder of the manuscript, and all variants of all other manuscripts are given.

40. Hic inungatur inunctione[a] crismatis[b] et olei de celo missi prius[c] ab archiepiscopo confecti in patena[d] sicut in[e] superius[f] dictum est. Inungat autem archiepiscopus eum primo in summitate capitis de dicta[g] unctione, secundo in pectore, tertio inter scapulas, quarto [in ipsis scapulis, quinto[h]] in campagine[i] brachiorum, et dicat cuilibet unctioni.[81]

Ungo te in regem de oleo sanctificato, in nomine Patris[j] et Filii[k] et Spiritus[k] sancti. Dicant[l] omnes[m]. Amen.

40. [a] unctione B F G *a*, in unctione D. — [b] inungatur inunctione crismatis] unguatur unctione carismatis E. — [c] prius *om.* D; primus F, *later corr. to* prius. — [d] pathena D. — [e] in *om.* D F G *a*. — [f] in superius] prius B E, in su- / superius *d₁*. — [g] sancta G *a*. — [h] in ... quinto *om.* A *only.* — [i] campage B D E, compagibus F G *a*. — [j] ✠ *add.* E F G *a*. — [k] ✠ *add.* F G *a*. — [l] Et dicant F G *a*. — [m] Dicant omnes *om.* B E.

41. Dum hec unctio[82] agitur, cantent assistentes[a] hanc[b] antiphonam[c].

Unxerunt[83] Salomonem Sadoch sacerdos et Nathan propheta regem in Gyon, et accedentes leti dixerunt, "Vivat rex in eternum."

41. [a] cantant assistentes F *a*, cantant assistantes G. — [b] agitur ... hanc] agatur cantent omnes istam B E. — [c] anthiphonam D G.

42. Facta unctione et[a] cantata antiphona, dicat archiepiscopus hanc orationem[b].

Christe, perunge hunc regem in regimen, unde unxisti sacerdotes, reges ac[c] prophetas ac[d] martyres, qui per fidem vicerunt regna, operati sunt iusticiam atque[e] adepti sunt promissiones[f]. Tua sacratissima unctio super caput eius[g] defluat[h] atque ad interiora descendat, et cordis illius intima penetret, et promissionibus quas adepti sunt victoriosissimi[i] reges, tua[j] gracia[k] dignus efficiatur, quatenus et in presenti seculo feliciter re-

---

[81] *forma consecrationis* later add. in right marg. at *unctioni* hand 1 in F (but not G *a*), and *Hic inungatur in capite, secundo in pectore, tercio inter (in* ed. *a) scapulas (scapulis* ed. *a), quarto in ipsis scapulis, quinto in compagibus brachiorum (brachiorum om.* G) later add. in hand 4 in left marg. at *Ungo te* in F, add. in marg. at *primo in summitate capitis* in G; add. in parentheses in text before *Primo in summitate capitis* in *a*. Meurier, 245, quoted the formula of anointing and the antiphon in nos. 40–41.

[82] *unctio* repeated F, but later crossed out at second occurrence, perhaps by scribe.

[83] *cantatur hec antiphona* later add. in marg. in hand 1 in F, add. in marg. at *dum hec unctio* in G, but not add. in *a*.

A B D E F G *a*

[fol. 54r] *gnet*[84] *et ad eorum consortium in celesti*[l] *regno perveniat. Per dominum nostrum Ihesum Christum filium tuum. Qui unctus est oleo leticie pre consortibus suis*[m]*, et virtute crucis potestates aerias*[n] *debellavit, tartara destruxit, regnumque dyaboli superavit, et ad celos victor ascendit, in cuius victoria manu*[o] *omnis gloria et potestas consistunt, et tecum vivit et regnat in unitate Spiritus sancti Deus per omnia secula seculorum. Amen.*

42. [a] Facta unctione et *om.* F G *a.* —[b] Oremus *add.* F G *a.* —[c] et F G *a*; ac *om.* D. —[d] et F G *a.* —[e] atque *om.* B E. —[f] repromissiones F G *a* —[g] eius *om.* B E. — [h] fluat F, *later corr. in hand 1 to* defluat. —[i] victorissimi D E; victorissimi F, *corr. to* victoriossimi. —[j] tua *om.* F, *later add. in hand 1 after* gracia. —[k] gracia *om.* E; tua gracia] gratia tua G *a.* —[l] celisti A. —[m] tuis E. —[n] aeries A. —[o] manu victoria F G *a.*

43. Alia oratio[a].[85]

Deus, electorum fortitudo et humilium celsitudo[b]*, qui in primordio per effusionem diluvii mundi crimina castigare voluisti et per*[c] *columbam ramum olive portantem pacem terris*[d] *redditam demonstrasti. Iterumque*[e] *sacerdotem Aaron famulum tuum per unctionem olei sacerdotem*[f] *sanxisti, et post eas*[g] *per huius unguenti infusionem ad regendum populum Israeliticum*[h] *sacerdotes, reges ac prophetas perfecisti, vultumque*[i] *ecclesie in oleo ex* [fol. 54v] *hylarandum per propheticam*[j] *famuli tui vocem David esse predixisti; ita quesumus, omnipotens Deus*[k] *Pater, ut per huius creature pinguedinem hunc servum tuum sanctificare*[l] *tua bene✠dictione digneris, eumque in similitudinem*[m] *columbe pacem simplicitatis populo sibi commisso prestare, et exempla Aaron in Dei servicio diligenter imitari, regnique*[n] *fastigia in consiliis*[o] *sciencie et equitate iudicii semper assequi, vultumque*[p] *hylaritatis per hanc olei unctionem tuamque*[q] *benedicti✠onem, te adiuvante, toti*[r] *plebi paratum habere facias. Per dominum.*

43. [a] Alia oratio *om.* D E, *but add. in another hand* D. —[b] alstitudo *corr. by scribe to* celcitudo D. —[c] per *om.* D. —[d] terre B E; ad *add.* D. —[e] Iterum D. — [f] sacerdotalem E. —[g] postea B D E, preterea F G *a.* —[h] Israheliticum E;

---

[84] *gnet* is the first text after the missing leaf in *A*. It contained 199 words (1179 characters), so, like the other missing leaf, it contained a miniature in the middle of one of its pages (see n. 59 above). In this case the miniature surely depicted the anointing because the context demands an illustration of that act, and there is none in the manuscript.

[85] *Oremus* later add. in marg. in hand 1 in *F*, add. in text in *G a*.

Israelicum F, *later corr. to* Israeliticum. —[i] multumque B, multum E. —
[j] prophecam B F, *later corr. (in hand 2 or 3) to* propheticam *in* F. —[k] Deus /
Deus E, *then the first* Deus *crossed out.* —[l] *apparently* sanctificatione F,
later corr. to sanctificare. —[m] similitudine F G *a.* —[n] regni F, *later corr. to*
regnique. —[o] conciliis G *a.* —[p] multumque E. —[q] tuam F, *later corr. to*
tuamque. —[r] toto E.

44. Alia[a] oratio[b].

*Deus Dei filius, dominus noster Ihesus Christus, qui a Patre oleo
exultationis unctus est pre participibus suis, ipse per presentem sacri
unguinis[c] infusionem Spiritus paracliti super caput[d] tuum infundat
bene✠dictionem[e] eamdemque[f] usque ad interiora cordis tui penetrare
faciat, quatinus[g] hoc visibili et tracta* [fol. 55r] *bili dono invisibilia
percipere, et temporali regno iustis moderaminibus executo[h], eternaliter cum eo regnare merearis. Qui solus sine peccato rex regum
vivit et gloriatur cum Deo Patre. In unitate eiusdem Spiritus sancti
Deus. Per[i].*

44. [a] Alia *om.* B. —[b] Oremus *add.* F G *a;* Alia oratio *om.* D E, *but add. in
another hand in* D. —[c] unguenti F G *a.* —[d] capud D. —[e] ✠ *om.* D. —[f] eandemque D E G. —[g] quatenus F G *a.* —[h] execute G *a.* —[i] omnia secula *add.* B;
omnia secula seculorum. Amen *add.* E F G *a.*

A B D E	F G *a*
45. Hiis dictis orationibus, connectuntur ansule aperturarum[a] vestimenti regis ab archiepiscopo vel sacerdotibus vel dyaconibus propter inunctionem[b].	45. Hiis dictis orationibus, connectuntur ab archiepiscopo vel[f] sacerdotibus vel saltem diaconem[87] propter mundiciam consecrationis ansule apperturarum[g] vestimenti regis propter inunctionem,
Benedictio[c] [86] cuiuscunque regalis ornamenti[d].	
Deus, rex regum et dominus dominancium, per quem reges	

---

[86] This rubric and prayer were added in the margin in *A* by the scribe who copied
the remainder of the manuscript. They are in the text in *B, D,* and *E.*

[87] *connectuntur ansule aperturarum vestimentorum regis per diaconem vel* (*vel*
om. *G a*) later add. in marg. in hand 1 in *F,* add. in marg. at *connectuntur* in *G,* add. in
parentheses in text before *His dictis orationibus* in *a.* The word *dioconem* is abbreviated *diocoñ* in the text in *F, G,* and *a* and in the marginal addition in *F,* but it is
spelled out *dioconem* in *G,* so I have chosen to expand it to this alternative form rather
than to the normal *diaconum* (which one would expect to be abbreviated *diaconū*).
The word *vel* is redundant in *F* and is omitted in *G* and *a.*

regnant et legum conditores iura
decernunt, dignare propicius
bene✠dicere hoc regale ornamen-
tum, et presta, ut famulus tuus
rex noster, qui illud portaturus
est, ornamento bonorum morum
et sanctarum actionum[e] in con-
spectu tuo fulgeat, et post tempo-
ralem vitam eternam gloriam que
tempus non habet sine fine pos-
sideat. Per Christum.

45. [a] apperturarum B E. —[b] unctionem B D E. —[c] Sequitur benedictio B E. —
[d] vestimenti D. —[e] attionum E. —[f] ve F, *later corr. to* vel. —[g] appertuarum F,
later corr. to apperturarum.

A B D E F G *a*

46. Et tunc[a] a camerario Francie induitur[88] tunica iacinctina, et de
super[b] socco[c], ita quod[d] dexteram manum habet liberam in apertura[e]
socci[f], et super[g] soccum[h] elevatum sicut elevatur casula sacerdoti[i]. Tunc
ab archiepiscopo unguantur[j] sibi manus de[k] predicto oleo celitus misso[l],
ut supra, et dicat archiepiscopus.[89]

46. [a] Et tunc] Tunc B E. —[b] desuper B D E. —[c] sacco B E. —[d] ita quod] itaque
E. —[e] appertura B E F G, copertura *a.* —[f] sacci B D E. —[g] sinistram *add.* F G
a. —[h] saccum B D E. —[i] sacerdotis G. —[j] ab archiepiscopo ungantur]
archiepiscopus inungat D. —[k] de *om.* B E. —[l] emisso G.

A B D E F G *a Meurier* [90]

47. *Unguantur[a] manus iste de oleo sanctificato, unde uncti[b] fuerunt*
reges et prophete[c], et sicut unxit Samuel David in regem, ut sis[d] bene-
dictus et constitutus rex in regno isto, quem[e] [91] *dominus Deus tuus*
dedit tibi ad regendum et gubernandum.

Quod [fol. 55v] *ipse prestare[f].*

47. [a] Unguantur E F *a.* —[b] ducti *a.* —[c] prophhete *a.* —[d] sit B E. —[e] quo F, *later*

---

[88] *Hic induitur tunica iacinctina, et de super socco ponatur a camerario Fran-*
cie later add. in marg. in hand 4 in *F*, add. in marg. at *Et tunc* in *G*, add. in parentheses
in text before *et tunc a camerario* in *a*.

[89] *Hic unguantur manus* later add. in marg. in hand 4 in *F*, add. in marg. at *Tunc*
ab archiepiscopo in *G*, add. in text before *Unguantur manus* in *a*.

[90] Meurier, 246.

[91] Dewick (ed. *g*, col. 31, n. 1) noted that this text omits the words *super populum*
istum, but that it then failed to correct the relative pronoun from *quem* to *quod*.

corr. to quod; quod G *a Meurier.* —ᶠ etc. *later add. in another hand* D; Quod
ipse prestare *om.* F G *a Meurier.*

ABDEFG*a*

48. Deinde dicat archiepiscopus hanc[a] orationem[b].

*Deus, qui es iustorum gloria et misericordia peccatorum, qui
misisti Filium tuum*[c] *preciosissimo*[d] *sanguine suo genus humanum
redimere, qui conteris bella et pugnator es*[e] *in te sperantium, et sub
cuius arbitrio*[f] *omnium regnorum continetur potestas, te humiliter
deprecamur, ut presentem famulum tuum N. in tua misericordia confidentem in presenti sede regali bene⊹dicas eique*[g] *propitius adesse
digneris, ut qui tua expetit protectione deffendi*[h]*, omnibus hostibus
sis*[i] *fortior; fac eum, Domine, beatum esse et victorem de inimicis
suis. Corona eum corona iusticie et pietatis, ut ex toto corde et*[j] *tota
mente in te credens tibi deserviat, sanctam ecclesiam tuam*[k] *deffendat*[l]
et sublimet, populumque a te sibi commissum iuste regat; et[m] *nullis
insidiantibus malis cum in iusticia*[n] *convertat. Accende, Domine,
cor* [fol. 56r] *eius ad amorem gracie tue per hoc unctionis oleum, unde
unxisti sacerdotes, reges et prophetas, quatinus iusticiam diligens per
tramitem similiter incedens*[o] *iusticie, post peracta a te disposita*[p]*, in
regali excellencia annorum curricula pervenire ad eterna gaudia*[q]
mereatur. Per eundem etc.

48. [a] hanc *om.* F G *a.* —[b] hanc orationem archiepiscopus E; sequentem. Oremus *add.* G. —[c] tuum *om.* B E. —[d] precioso F G *a.* —[e] pugnatores [*sic*] B E. —
[f] arcibrio D. —[g] atque B E, eidemque F G *a.* —[h] defendi B D E *a.* —[i] sit F G *a.* —
[j] ex *add.* E F G *a.* —[k] sanctam tuam ecclesiam F G *a.* —[l] defendat B D *a.* —
[m] et *om.* F G *a.* —[n] malis cum in iusticia] malis cum in iusticiam B, malis
eum in iniusticia eum D, malis eum in iusticiam E, eum malis in iusticiam
(*later corr. in hand 1 to* in iniusticiam) F, eum malis in iniusticiam G *a, corr.
to* malis eum in iniusticiam *g.* —[o] insedens B E. —[p] tempora *add.* E. —[q] gaudia
eterna F G *a.*

49. Facta[92] autem manuum unctione, iungat rex manus ante pectus.
Post ea[a] si voluerit rex[b] cirotecas[c] subtiles induere, sicut faciunt episcopi
dum consecrantur, ob[d] reverenciam sancte unctionis ne manibus nudis
aliquid tangant[e], primo[f] ab archiepiscopo benedicentur cyroteces[g] in hec
verba sequentia.

49. [a] postea D E F G *a.* —[b] rex *om.* F G *a.* —[c] sirotecas B E, cirothecas F G *a.* —
[d] ad F G *a.* —[e] tangat F G *a.* —[f] primo *om.* F G *a.* —[g] cirotece B D E, cirothece
F G *a.*

---

[92] *Iungit rex manus ante pectus* later add. in marg. in hand 1 in *F*, add. in marg. at
Facta autem in *G*, add. in text before *Facta autem* in *a.*

50. Oratio[a].

Omnipotens[93] *Creator, qui homini ad ymaginem tuam creato manus digitis discretionis insignitas tanquam*[b] *organum intelligentem*[c] *ad recte operandum dedisti*[d]*, quas servari mundas precepisti, ut in eis anima digna portaretur, et tua in eis digne contractarentur*[e] *misteria, benedi✠ceret*[f] *et sancti✠ficares*[g] *di* [fol. 56v] *gneris hec manuum tegumenta, ut quicunque reges hiis cum humilitate manus suas velare voluerint, tam cordis quam operis mundiciam, tua*[h] *misericordia subministret. Per Christum.*

50. [a] Oremus F G *a.* —[b] tamquam B. —[c] intelligentie F G *a.* —[d] dedisti *om.* F G *a.* —[e] *hyphenated* contra- / ctarentur *at end of line* F, *later corr. to* contre- / ctarentur; contrectarentur *a.* —[f] ✠ *om.* B D E. —[g] ✠ *om.* B E. —[h] tuam E.

51. Et aspergantur cyrotece[a] aqua benedicta[b], deinde imponuntur manibus regis per archiepiscopum, dicentem.

Circunda,[94] *Domine, manus huius*[c] *famuli tui N. mundicia novi hominis, qui de celo descendit, ut quemadmodum Iacob dilectus*[d] *tuus pelliculis edorum*[e] *opertis manibus paternam benedictionem oblato patri cibo potuque gratissimo impetravit, sic et iste gracie tue benedicti✠onem*[f] *impetrare mereatur. Per eundem dominum nostrum Ihesum Christum*[g]*, qui in similitudinem carnis peccati*[h] *tibi obtulit semetipsum*[i]*. Amen.*

51. [a] cirothece F G *a.* —[b] aqua benedicta cirotece B E. —[c] huius *om.* D. —[d] dilectus / tus E. —[e] edorum F, *later corr. to* hedorum; hedorum G *a.* —[f] ✠ *om.* B D E. —[g] filium tuum *add.* E F G *a.* —[h] tui *add.* F, *but crossed out, apparently by scribe.* —[i] semet ipsum A.

52. Vel si rex maluerit cyrotecas[a] non habere, tunc facta manuum[b] unctione dictisque orationibus ad eam spectantibus, episcopi absistentes[c] cum cotone[d] [95] manus regis abstergant, et mica[e] panis vel cum sale fricent[f], [fol. 57r] deinde lavent sibi manus quibus lotis, et manibus etiam[g] archiepiscopi, benedicat archiepiscopus anulum[h] sic[i] dicens.

Oremus[j]*.*

52. [a] cirothecas F G *a.* —[b] manum B E. —[c] assistentes B E F G *a.* —[d] cottone

---

[93] *Benedictio cirotecarum* (*cyrothecarum* G, *cirothecarum a*) later add. in marg. in hand 4 in *F*, add. in marg. at *Oremus* in *G*, add. in text before *Oremus* in *a*.

[94] *Hic ponatur cyrothece* (*ponuntur cyrothece* G, *ponuntur cirothece* ed. *a*) *in manibus regis* later add. in marg. in hand 4 in *F*, add. in marg. at *Circunda* in *G*, add. in parentheses in text before *Circunda* in *a*.

[95] *Si rex non capiat cirothecas* (*cyrothecas* G) *manus eius, abstergantur cum cottone* (*cotone* G) *per episcopos et laventur* later add. in marg. in hand 1 in *F*, add. in marg. at *Vel si rex* in *G*.

F G *a.* —[e] mia F, *later corr. to* mica. —[f] ritent E. —[g] manibus et eciam E. —
[h] annulum G. —[i] sic *om.* B E. —[j] Oremus *om.* B E.

53. Oratio[a].

Deus,[96] *tocius*[b] *creature principium et finis, creator et consecrator*[c]
humani generis[d], *dator*[e] *gracie spiritualis, largitor eterne salutis, in*
quo clausa sunt omnia, tu, Domine, tuam emitte benedicti✠onem[f]
super hunc anulum[g], *ipsumque benedi✠cere*[h] *et sanctifi✠care*[i]
digneris, ut qui per eum famulo tuo honoris insignia concedis, virtu-
tum premia largiaris, quo discretionis habitum semper retineat, et
vere fidei fulgore prefulgeat, sancte quoque Trinitatis armatus
munimine miles inexpugnabilis acies dyaboli constanter evincat[j] *et*
sibi ad veram salutem mentis et corporis proficiat. Per Christum.

53. [a] Oratio *om.* B D E F G *a, but add. in another hand* D. —[b] tocius *om.* B E. —
[c] conservator A. —[d] generis humani G *a.* —[e] doctor B E. —[f] ✠ *om.* F G *a.* —
[g] famulum G *a.* —[h] ✠ *om.* B E. —[i] ✠ *om.* D E F G *a.* —[j] evncat E, emicat *a.*

A B D E	F G *a*

54. Benedictio[97] anuli.

Deus, celestium terrestriumque[a] *conditor creatu-*
rarum atque humani generis benignissimus[b]
reparator, dator spiritualis gracie omniumque bene-
dictionum largitor, qui iusticiam tue legis in cordi-
bus credencium[c] *digito tuo*[d], *id est unigenito tuo*
scribis, tui[e] *magi in Egipti*[f] *resistere non valentes*
continuabant dicentes, 'Digitus Dei hic est.'[98]
Immitte Spiritum sanctum tuum[g] *paraclitum de*
celis super hunc anulum arte fabrili[h] *decoratum, et*
sublimitatis tue potencia ita eum emundare dig-
neris, ac[i] *omni nequicia lividi venenosique serpen-*
tis procul expulsa, metallum a te bono conditore

---

[96] *Benedictio anuli* (*anulli* G) later add. in marg. in hand 4 in *F*, add. in marg. at
Oremus in *G*, add. in text before *Oremus* in *a*.

[97] Nos. 54–55 were added in the margin in *A*. Dewick (ed. *g*) thought that the addition was made in a later hand, but script, decoration, and punctuation are those of the
scribe who wrote the remainder of the manuscript. Nos. 54–55 are in the text in *B*, *D*,
and *E*. Dewick erred in placing the location of these formulas before the beginning of
no. 53, but only because the scribe indicated that the additions were to be made both
before and after no. 53; perhaps he intended that they should replace no. 53, although
that does not seem likely because all three formulas are in *B*, *D*, and *E* in the sequence
given here.

[98] Ex. 8: 19.

ABDE   FG*a*

*creatum munimine^j a cunctis sordibus inimici
maneat. Amen.*

54. ^a terrestrium D. —^b benignissi B, benigni E. —^c credendum E. —^d et *add.*
B D E. —^e cui B E. —^f Egypto B E. —^g tuum sanctum B E. —^h fabricali E. —
^i ac *corr. to* ut *Dewick (ed. g).* —^j munimine *corr.* to immune *Dewick (ed. g).*

55. Alia oracio^a.

*Bene✠dic, Domine, et sancti✠fica^b anulum
istum et mitte super eum septiformem^c Spiritum
tuum, quo famulus tuus eo fruens, anulo fidei sub-
arratus, virtute altissimi sine peccato custodiatur,
et omnes benedictiones que in scripturis divinis
reperiuntur super eum copiose descendant, ut quecunque sanctificaverit sanctificata permaneant, et
quecunque benedixerit, spirituali benedictione
benedicantur. Per.*

55. ^a Alia oracio] Benedictio E. —^b sancti✠ E. —^c septiformam E.

56. Deinde datur ei ab archiepiscopo sceptrum in
manu dextera et virga in sinistra, et in datione sceptri
et virge dicentur iste orationes. Sed notandum ante-
[fol. 57v] quam dantur sceptrum et^a virga, datur anulus, et in dacione anuli^b dicitur hec oratio. Hic detur
anulus et dicatur^c.

56. Deinde
datur ei ab
archiepiscopo
anulus, et in
datione anuli
dicitur oratio^d.

A B D E F G *a Meurier*[99]

Accipe[100] *anulum^e, signaculum videlicet^f fidei sancte, soliditatem
regni, augmentum potentie. Per que^g scias triumphali potentia hostes
repellere, hereses destruere, subditos coadunere^h, et catholice fidei^i per-
severabilitati^j connecti.*

56. ^a et *om.* D. —^b dcu *add.* B, *then crossed out by scribe.* —^c Hic detur ...
dicatur *om.* E. —^d sequens *add.* G. —^e annulum *Meurier.* —^f videlicet signaculum B E. —^g q̄ F, *later expanded in hand 2 to* quem; quam G, quem *a
Meurier;* que *corr. to* quem *Dewick (ed. g).* —^h coadunare B F G *a Meurier.* —
^i Dei E. —^j perseverabilitate F G *a.*

---

[99] Meurier, 246.
[100] *Hic datur anulus et ponitur in quarto digito dextre manus* later add. in
marg. in hand 4 in *F*, add. in marg. at *Accipe anulum* in *G*, add. in text before *Accipe
anulum* in *a*.

ABDEFG*a*

57. Oratio post annulum[a].

Deus, cuius est omnis potestas[b] *et dignitas, da*[c] *famulo tuo prosperum sue dignitatis effectum, in qua, te remunerante, permaneat semperque*[d] *timeat tibique iugiter placere contendat. Per*[e] *dominum.*

57. [a] anulum F G *a;* Oremus *later add. in marg. in hand 1* F. —[b] potestas *om.*
E. —[c] de D. —[d] semper F, *later corr. in hand 2 to* semperque te; semperque
te G *a.* —[e] Christum *add.* F G *a.*

58. Dato anulo, statim post detur sceptrum in manu dextera, et dicatur hec oratio[a].

A B D E F G *a Meurier*[101]

Accipe[102] *sceptrum regie potestatis*[b] *insigne, virgam scilicet regni
rectam, virgam virtutis, qua te ipsum*[c] *bene regas*[d]*, sanctam ecclesiam
populumque videlicet*[e] *christianum tibi a Deo commissum regia virtute*[f] *ab impro* [fol. 58r] *bis defendas*[g]*, pravos*[h] *corrigas, rectos pacifices, et, ut*[i] *viam rectam tenere possint tuo iuvamine dirigas,
quatinus*[j] *de temporali regno ad eternum regnum pervenias,*[103] *ipso
adiuvante cuius regnum et imperium sine fine permanet*[k] *in secula
seculorum*[l]*.*

58. [a] Oremus *add.* F, *but later crossed out.* —[b] dignitatis *Meurier.* —[c] teipsum
G *a Meurier.* —[d] reges *Meurier.* —[e] videlicet *om.* B E. —[f] christianum ... virtute *om. Meurier.* —[g] deffendas D F G. —[h] pvos *later corr. to* pravos F. —[i] in
add. D. —[j] quanto *a,* quatenus *Meurier.* —[k] permaneat F, *later corr. to* permanet; permanent G *a.* —[l] Amen *add.* B E *Meurier.*

A B D E F G *a*

59. Oratio post sceptrum datum[a].[104]

*Omnium, Domine, fons bonorum cunctorum Deus institutor pro-
fectuum*[b]*, tribue, quesumus, famulo tuo N. adeptam bene regere*[c] *digni* [fol. 58v] *tatem et a te sibi prestitum honorem dignare corroborare*[d]*;
honorifica eum pre cunctis regibus terre, uberi eum benedictione*[e]
*locupleta, et in solio regni firma stabilitate consolida; visita eum in
sobole, presta ei prolixitatem vite, in diebus eius* [semper[f]] *oriatur iusticia, ut*[g] *cum iocunditate et leticia eterno glorietur in regno. Per
dominum.*

---

[101] Meurier, 247.

[102] *Hic detur sceptrum in manu dextera* later add. in marg. in hand 4 in *F,* add. in
marg. at *Accipe* in *G,* add. in text before *Accipe* in *a.*

[103] *as* repeated by mistake at the beginning of the next folio *F,* but crossed out.

[104] *Oremus* later add. in marg. in hand 1 in *F,* add. in text after *datum* in *G.*

59. [a] datum *om.* E —[b] institutorum perfectum E. —[c] agere F G *a.* —[d] roborare F G *a.* —[e] ✠ *add.* F G *a.* —[f] semper *om.* A *only.* —[g] et B E F G *a.*

60. Post statim datur ei virga in manu sinistra, et dicitur[a].

Accipe[105] *virgam virtutis atque equitatis, quia*[b] *intelligas mulcere pios et terrere reprobos, errantibus viam doce*[c] *lapsisque manum porrige, disperdasque superbos et releves humiles, ut aperiat tibi hostium*[d] *Ihesus Christus dominus noster, qui de se ipso*[e] *ait, 'Ego sum hostium*[f]*; per me si quis introierit salvabitur'; et ipse qui est clavis David et sceptrum domus Israel, 'qui aperit, et nemo claudit, claudit, et nemo aperit.' Sit tibi adiutor, qui eduxit 'vinctum de*[g] *domo carceris, sedentem in tenebris*[106] *et umbra mortis,' ut in* [fol. 59r] *omnibus sequi merearis eum, de quo propheta David*[h] *cecinit, 'Sedes tua, Deus, in seculum seculi, virga equitatis virga regni tui,' et imiteris*[i] *eum qui dixit*[j]*, 'Diligas iusticiam et odio habeas iniquitatem; propterea unxit te Deus, Deus tuus, oleo leticie,' ad exemplum illius quem ante secula unxerat 'pre participibus suis,' Ihesum Christum dominum nostrum*[k].

60. [a] Post ... dicitur] Postea detur ei virga in manu sinistra dicens E. —[b] quas B E, qua D F G *a.* —[c] dare *a.* —[d] ostium B E G *a.* —[e] seipso G *a.* —[f] ostium B E G *a.* —[g] et D. —[h] David propheta D, prophetha David E. —[i] imiteris E. — [j] dicit F G *a.* —[k] Amen *add.* B E.

A B D E

F G *a*

61. Benedictio corone.[107]

Deus tuorum corona fidelium, qui in capitibus eorum ponis coronam de lapide precioso[a]*, bene*✠*dic et sancti*✠*fica coronam istam, quatinus sicut ipsa*[b] *diversis preciosisque lapidibus adornatur, sic famula tua*[c] *largiente gracia repleatur. Per.*

61. [a] preciopo E. —[b] ipsam B E. —[c] te *add. in brackets as corr.* Dewick (*ed. g*); famula tua] famulus tuus tua D.

---

[105] *Hic detur virga in manu sinistra* later add. in marg. in hand 4 in *F*, add. in marg. at *Accipe* in *G*, add. in text before *Accipe* in *a*. Meurier, 247, quotes only the incipit, *Accipe virgam virtutis atque equitatis, qua intelligas mulcere pios, et terrere reprobos.*

[106] The letters *ene* in *tenebris* are written as a correction over erasure in *F*, but it is impossible to read what was originally written.

[107] No. 61 was added in the margin in *A* by the scribe who copied the remainder of the manuscript (not in a later hand, as Dewick [ed. *g*] thought). It is in the text in *B*, *D*, and *E*. The uncorrected feminine forms prove that this was copied from an ordo for a queen, but it is from no surviving French ordo, and I have not been able to determine its source.

A F G *a*

B D E

103. Benedictio super regem.[108]

Benedi✠*cat te Dominus custodiatque te, et sicut te voluit super populum*[a] *esse regem, ita in presenti seculo felicem et eterne felicitatis tribuat*[b] *esse consortem*[c].

103. [a] te add. D. —[b] tribue D —[c] Amen. Oracio *add.* D.

104. *Clerum et*[a] *populum, quem sua voluit opitulacione tua sanctione congregari, sua dispensacione et*[b] *tua administracione per diuturna tempora faciat feliciter gubernari. Amen.*

104. [a] ac D. —[b] ut D.

A B D E

62. Post istam orationem convocantur pares nomine suo a cancellario[a] suo, si presens est. Sin autem ab archiepiscopo, primo laici, post ea[b] clerici; quibus vocatis et circunstantibus, archiepiscopus accipit de altari coronam regiam[c], et solus imponit eam[d] capiti regis. Qua posita, omnes pares, tam clerici quam laici, manum apponunt[e] coronam[f] et eam undique sustentant[g], et soli pares. Tunc archiepiscopus dicit[h] istam orationem antequam coronam situet in capite, sed eam tenet satis alte ante caput regis[i].

F G *a*

62. Post[109] istam orationem convocantur pares ex nomine a cancellario, si presens est, sinautem ab archiepiscopo, et vocantur primo laici, postea clerici, et clerici vocantur eo ordine quo dictum est superius de sedendo. Quibus vocatis et circunstantibus, archiepiscopus accipit de altari coronam regiam,[110] et solus imponit eam capiti regis; qua imposita, omnes pares tam clerici quam laici manum apponunt corone et eam undique sustentant, et soli pares; tunc archiepiscopus dicit istam orationem antequam coronam situet in capite, sed eam tenet[j] satis alte ante caput regis.

62. [a] domino *add.* D. —[b] postea B D E. —[c] regiam *om.* B E. —[d] ea D. —[e] super *add.* B E. —[f] corone D. —[g] substentant B E, sustentent D. —[h] dicat E. —[i] eius B E. —[j] tenent G *a*.

---

[108] Nos. 103–104 are also located in their proper location near the end of the ordo in *B, D,* and *E.*

[109] *Hic debent* (*debet G a*) *vocari pares* later add. in marg. in hand 4 in *F*, add. in marg. at *Post istam* in *G*, add. in parentheses in text before *Post istam* in *a*.

[110] *Archiepiscopus accipit de altari coronam regiam* later add. in marg. in hand

A B D E F G *a Meurier*[111]

63. Oratio[a].

Coronet[112] *te Deus corona glorie atque iusticie, honore et opere fortitudinis, ut* [fol. 59v] *per officium nostre benedictionis* ✠[b] *cum fide recta et multiplici bonorum operum fructu*[c] *ad coronam pervenias*[d] *regni perpetui*[e]*, ipso*[f] *largiente cuius regnum et imperium permanet in secula seculorum*[g].

63. [a] Oratio *om.* B D E F G *a Meurier.* —[b] ✠ *om.* B E. —[c] fructu *om.* B E. — [d] venias F, *corr. to* pervenias. —[e] perpetui regni B E. —[f] te *add.* D. —[g] Amen *add.* B D E *Meurier.*

64. Qua oratione dicta, ponendo coronam in capite[a] dicat archiepiscopus.

Accipe[113] *coronam regni, in nomine Pa*✠*tris et Fi*✠*lii*[b] *et Spiri*✠*tus sancti* ✠[c]*, ut spreto antiquo hoste spretisque contagiis viciorum*[d] *omnium sic iusticiam, misericordiam* [fol. 60r] *et iudicium diligas*[e]*, et ita iuste*[f] *et*[g] *misericorditer et pie vivas, ut ab ipso domino nostro Ihesu Christo in consortio sanctorum eterni regni coronam percipias*[h].

64. [a] regis *add.* D. —[b] ✠ *om.* F, *but later add.* —[c] ✠ *om.* B E F G *a.* —[d] victorum A. —[e] dirigas *Meurier.* —[f] iuste *om.* F, *but later add. in hand 2.* —[g] et *om.* F G *a Meurier.* —[h] percias D, accipias E.

A B D E F G *a*

65. *Accipe*[114] *inquam coronam, quam sanctitatis gloriam et honorem, et opus fortitudinis intelligas*[a] *signare, et per hanc te participem ministerii nostri non ignores, ita ut sicut nos in interioribus pastores rectoresque animarum intelligimur*[b]*, ita ut*[c] *contra omnes adversitates ecclesie*[d] *Christi deffensor*[e] *assistas, regnique*[f] *tibi a Deo dati, et per officium nostre bene*✠*dictionis*[g] *invice*[h] [115] *apostolorum, omniumque sanctorum regimini tuo commissi utilis executor*[i]*,*

---

3 in *F*, add. in marg. at *Quibus vocatis* in *G*, add. in parentheses in text before *Quibus vocatis* in *a*.

[111] Meurier, 247–48.

[112] *Teneat metropolitanus coronam alte primo duabus manibus, postea sinistra tantum quando benedicit* later add. in marg. in hand 1 in *F*, add. in marg. at *Coronet te Deus* in *G*, add. in parentheses in text before *Coronet te Deus* in *a*.

[113] *Hic ponat coronam in capite quam semper teneat manu sinistra* later add. in marg. in hand 1 in *F*, add. in marg. at *Accipe coronam* in *G*, add. in parentheses in text before *Accipe coronam* in *a*. Meurier paraphrased the rubric in no. 64.

[114] *F*, *G*, and *a* treat no. 65 as a continuation of no. 64.

[115] *F* omitted *vice*, but later it was added twice in hand 3: in the text and in the margin, but (perhaps still later) *vice* in the margin was crossed out.

perspicuusque regnator semper appareas, ut inter gloriosos athle-
tas[j],[116] *virtutum gemmis ornatus, et premio sempiterne*[k] *felicitatis*
coronatus, cum redemptore ac salvatore nostro[l] *Christo, cuius nomen*
vicemque gestare crederis, sine fine glorieris[m]*. Qui vivit*[n] *et imperat*
Deus cum Deo[o] *Patre in secula seculorum.* [fol. 60v] *Amen.*

65. [a] incellas B E. —[b] intelliguntur B E. —[c] Ita tu, *beginning a new sentence* F
G a. —[d] ecclesi B, ecclesiis E. —[e] defensor B D E a. —[f] tui *add.* D. —[g] ✠ *om.*
F G a. —[h] in vice B D E; invice] in voce exultationis vice (vice *om.* F) F G a. —
[i] exequutor B E. —[j] athlethas E. —[k] sempiterne *om.* E. —[l] Ihesu *add.* B D E. —
[m] gestare F, *later corr. in hand 3 to* glorieris. —[n] et regnat *add.* D. —[o] Deo
om. D.

66. Oratio post coronam.[117]

A B D E F G *a Meurier*[118]

Deus perpetuitatis, dux virtutum, cunctorum hostium victor,
benedic[a] *hunc famulum tuum*[b] *tibi caput suum*[c] *inclinantem, et pro-*
lixa sanitate et prospera felicitate eum conserva, et ubicunque[d] *pro*
quibus auxilium tuum[e] *invocaverit, cito assis*[f] *et protegas ac*[g] *def-*
fendas[h]*; tribue ei, quesumus Domine*[i]*, divicias glorie tue, comple in*
bonis desiderium eius, corona eum in miseratione et misericordia,
tibique, Deo, pia devotione iugiter[j] *famuletur. Per*[k] *dominum.*

66. [a] ✠ *add.* B D E F G *a Meurier.* —[b] tuum *om.* F G a. —[c] suum *om.* B E. —
[d] ut ubicumque B E, et ubicumque D. —[e] tuum auxilium F G *a Meurier.* —
[f] adsis B E. —[g] et B D E. —[h] defendas B E a. —[i] Domine *om.* F, *but later add.*
in hand 3. —[j] iugiter *om. Meurier.* —[k] Christum *add.* F G *a Meurier.*

67. Statim post istam orationem dicatur ista benedictio[a].

Extendat[119] *omnipotens Deus dexteram sue benedictionis*[b]*, et cir-*
cundet te muro felicitatis, ac custodia tua[c] *protectionis sancte Marie*
ac[d] *beati Petri*[e]*, apostolorum principis, sanctique*[f] *Dyonisii, atque*[g]
omnium sanctorum[h] *intercedentibus meritis. Amen.*

67. [a] Statim ... benedictio] Statim post orationem dicatur benedictio sequens
E. —[b] ✠ *add.* F G *a Meurier.* —[c] tue D, sue F G *a Meurier.* —[d] et E. —[e] et

---

[116] Hyphenated *a-* / *thletas* F, but the *a* at the end of the line was later crossed out
and *a* was added on the following line.

[117] *Oremus* later *add. in marg. in hand 1 in* F, *add. in text before* Deus perpetuitatis *in* G a.

[118] Meurier, 248–52, slightly modified the rubrics in nos. 66–74; his renderings of
them are not retained.

[119] *Benedictio* later *add. in marg. in hand 3 in* F, *add. in marg. at* Extendat *in* G,
add. in text before Extendat *in* a.

Pauli *add.* F, *but later crossed out.* —ᶠ sancti E F G *a.* —ᵍ beati Remigii et *add.*
F G *a Meurier.* —ʰ sanctorum omnium E.

68. Alia benedictio ᵃ.

Indulgeat tibi Dominus omnia peccata [fol. 61r] *que gessisti, et*
*tribuat*ᵇ *tibi*ᶜ *graciam et misericordiam quam humiliter ab eo*ᵈ
deposcis, et liberet te ab adversitatibus cunctis et ab omnibus inimico-
*rum omnium*ᵉ *visibilium et invisibilium insidiis. Amen.*

68. ᵃ Alia benedictio *om.* F G *a.* —ᵇ tribuat *om.* E. —ᶜ tibi *om.* F G *a Meurier.* —
ᵈ ab eo humiliter F G *a Meurier.* —ᵉ omnium *om.* F G *a.*

69. Alia benedictio ᵃ.

*Angelos suos bonos, qui te semper et ubique precedant,*ᵇ *commit-*
*tentur*ᶜ *et subsequantur,*ᵈ *ad custodiam tui ponat et a peccato sive*
*gladio*ᵉ ¹²⁰ *et ab omnium*ᶠ *periculorum discrimine sua potencia*
*liberet*ᵍ. *Amen*ʰ.

69. ᵃ Alia benedictio *om.* F G *a.* — ᵇ procedant E. — ᶜ commitentur F, *later*
corr. to comitentur; comitentur G *a Meurier.* —ᵈ subsiquentur B E. —ᵉ et te a
peccato seu gladio F G *a Meurier.* —ᶠ omni *a.* —ᵍ liberet *om.* F, *but later add.*
in hand 3. —ʰ Amen *om.* E.

70. Alia benedictio ᵃ.

*Inimicos tuos ad pacis caritatisque*ᵇ *benignitatem convertat, et*
*bonis omnibus*ᶜ *te graciosum et amabilem faciat, pertinaces quoque in*
*tui insectatione*ᵈ *et odio confusione salutari induat, super te autem*ᵉ
*participatio et*ᶠ *sancti*✠*ficatio*ᵍ *sempiterna floreat. Amen.*

70. ᵃ Alia benedictio *om.* F G *a.* —ᵇ charitatisque *Meurier.* —ᶜ operibus F G *a*
Meurier. —ᵈ infestacione D —ᵉ autem *om. Meurier.* —ᶠ et *om.* F, *but later*
add. in hand 3. —ᵍ ✠ *om.* D *Meurier.*

71. Alia benedictio ᵃ.

*Victoriosum*ᵇ *te*ᶜ *atque triumphatorem de*ᵈ *invisibilibus atque visibili-*
*bus*ᵉ *hostibus*ᶠ *semper efficiat, et sancti nominis sui*ᵍ *timo-* [fol. 61v]
*rem pariter et*ʰ *amorem continuum cordi tuo infundat, et in fide recta*
*ac bonis operibus perseverabilem reddat, et pace*ⁱ *in*ʲ *diebus tuis con-*
cessa, cum palma victorie te ad perpetuum regnum perducat. Amen.

71. ᵃ Alia benedictio *om.* E F G. —ᵇ Victorisum F, *later corr. to* Victoriosum. —
ᶜ te *om.* G *a.* —ᵈ te D. —ᵉ atque visibilibus *om.* B D E. —ᶠ hostiis B E. —ᵍ tui
D. —ʰ ac *Meurier* —ⁱ pacem D; pacem F, *later corr. to* pace. —ʲ *om.* E.

72. Alia benedictio ᵃ.

*Et*ᵇ *qui te voluit super*ᶜ *populum suum*ᵈ *constituere regem, et in*ᵉ

---

¹²⁰ *te a* was later added over an erasure in *F*; the original is illegible.

presenti seculo felicem eterne felicitatis tribuat esse consortem. Amen[f].
Quod ipse prestare.[121]

72. [a] Alia benedictio *om.* F G *a.* —[b] Ut F (*with a decorated initial* U), *later corr. in hand 2 to* Et. —[c] te *add.* F, *but crossed out.* —[d] omnium D. —[e] in *om.* F, *but later add.* —[f] Amen *om.* B E *Meurier.*

73. Alia benedictio dicenda[a] super eum[b].

Benedic[c],[122] *Domine, hunc*[d] *regem nostrum, qui regna omnium regum a*[e] *seculo moderaris. Amen.*

Alia benedictio[f].

Et tali eum benedicti✠one[g] *glorifica*[h]*, ut Davitica*[i] *teneat sublimitate sceptrum salutis et sanctifice propiciationis, munere reperiatur*[j] *locupletatus. Amen.*

Alia benedictio[k].

Da ei tuo spiramine[l] *cum mansuetudine ita regere populum, sicut Salomonem fecisti regnum obtinere pacificum.* [fol. 62r] *Amen.*

Alia benedictio[m].

Tibi cum timore sit subditus tibique militet[n] *cum quiete; sit tuo*[o] *clipeo protectus, cum proceribus et ubique gracia tua victor existat. Amen.*

Alia benedictio[p].

Honorifica eum pre cunctis regibus gencium, felix populis[q] *dominetur, et feliciter eum nationes adornent*[r]*; vivat inter gentium nationes magnanimes*[s]*. Amen.*

Alia benedictio[t].

Sit in iudiciis equitatis singularis; locuplet[u] *eum tua predives dextera; frugiferam obtineant*[v] *patriam, et eius liberis tribuas profutura. Amen.*

Alia benedictio[t].

Presta ei prolixitatem vite per tempora, ut[w] *in diebus eius oriatur iusticia*[x]*; a te robustum teneat regiminis solium, et cum iocunditate et iudicia*[y] *eterno glorietur regno. Amen.*

Quod ipse prestare dignetur etc.[z][123]

73. [a] dicenda *om.* F G *a.* —[b] dicenda super eum *om.* B E. —[c] ✠ *add.* F G *a Meurier.* —[d] hunc *om.* F G *a Meurier.* —[e] e: *Meurier.* —[f] Alia benedictio *om.* F G *a.* —[g] ✠ *om.* B E *a.* —[h] gloriosa D. —[i] Davidica *Meurier Dewick* (*ed. g*). —

[121] *dignetur cuius regnum et imperium sine fine permanet in secula seculorum. Amen later add. in marg. in hand 1 in* F*, add. in text in* G *a.*

[122] *Statim fiat ista secunda benedictio later add. in marg. in hand 1 in* F*, add. in marg. at* super eum *in* G*, add. in parentheses in text before* Benedic *in* a.

[123] *ut supra later add. in* F*, add. in text after* etc. *in* a.

[j] reparatur B, reparetur E; repleatur F, *later corr. in hand 2 to* reperiatur. —[k] Alia benedictio *om.* E F G *a*. —[l] Da ei a spiramine tuo F G *a*, Da ei a tuo spiramine *Meurier*. —[m] Alia benedictio *om.* E F G *a*. —[n] milites *Meurier*. —[o] tuo *om.* B E. —[p] Alia benedictio *om.* E F G *a*. —[q] populus B. —[r] adorant B E, adorent *Meurier*. —[s] magnimes B D E, magnanimus F G *a Meurier*. —[t] Alia benedictio *om.* B E F G *a*. —[u] locupletet F G *a Meurier*. —[v] optineat F, obtineat D G *a Meurier*. —[w] et *Meurier*. —[x] iusticiam A (*the* m *is partially erased*). —[y] iusticia B D E, leticia F G *a Meurier*. —[z] etc.] cuius regnum et imperium sine fine permanet in secula seculorum. Amen G.

74. Alia oratio[a].[124]

Omnipotens Deus 'det tibi de rore celi et de pinguedine terre habundanciam[b] [fol. 62v] *frumenti, vini et olei, et*[c] *serviant*[d] *tibi populi et adorent te*[e] *tribus; esto dominus fratrum tuorum, et*[f] *incurventur ante te filii matris tue, et qui benedixerit tibi benedictionibus repleatur,'* [*et qui maledixerit tibi*[g] *maledictionibus repleatur*[h],]*' et Deus erit adiutor tuus.*

Alia oratio[i].[125]

'Omnipotens bene✠dicat[j] *tibi benedictionibus celi de super*[k] *in montibus et collibus, benedictionibus abyssi iacentibus deorsum, benedictionibus uberum' et*[l] *uvarum pomorumque; benedictiones*[m] *patrum antiquorum, Abraham*[n], *Ysaac et Iacob, confortate*[o] *sint super te. Per*[126] *dominum.*

74. [a] Alia oratio *om.* B E. —[b] abundantiam G *a Meurier*. —[c] et *om. Meurier*. —[d] servant F, *later corr. to* serviant. —[e] de D. —[f] et *om.* F G *a*. —[g] tibi maledixerit B D E. —[h] et qui ... repleatur *om.* A F G *a Meurier, but add. in marg. by scribe* A. —[i] Alia oratio *om.* B E F G *a*. —[j] ✠ *om.* B E F, *but later add.* F. —[k] desuper B D E *a Meurier*. —[l] et *om. Meurier*. —[m] uberum ... benedictiones *om.* D. —[n] et *add.* F G *a*. —[o] confortare D.

A B D E F G *a*

75. Alia oratio[a].[127]

Benedic, Domine, fortitudinem principis, et opera manuum illius suscipe, et benedictione tua terra eius de pomis repleatur de fructu celi[b] *et rore atque abyssi subiacentis, de fructu solis*[c] *et lune, et de vertice antiquorum montium, de pomis eternorum collium, et de frugibus terre et de*[d] *plenitudine eius; benedictio illius qui apparuit in rubo*[e]

[124] *Oremus* later add. in marg. in hand 1 in *F*, add. in text *G a*.

[125] *F*, *G*, and *a* do not separate the two parts of this benediction (*a* does not even have any punctuation beween *tuus* and *omnipotens*), although *B* and *E* do separate them, but without a rubric.

[126] *Christum* later add. in *F*, add. in text in *G a*.

[127] *Oremus* later add. in hand 1 in marg. in *F*, add. in text in *G a*.

veniat super [fol. 63r] *caput*[f] *eius, et plena sit benedictio Domini in filiis eius, et tingat in oleo pedem suum, cornua rinoceruntis*[g] *cornua illius, in ipsis ventilabit gentes*[h] *usque ad terminos terre, quia ascensor celi auxiliator suus*[i] *in sempiternum fiat. Per dominum.*

75. [a] Alia oratio *om.* B E. —[b] celesti F G *a.* —[c] soli A. —[d] de *om.* F G *a.* — [e] rubro B. —[f] capud D. —[g] rinoceruntis *om.* F, *but* cornua *later crossed out and* cornua rinocerontis *add. in marg. in hand 3*; rinocerontis G *a.* — [h] gentes ventilabit B E. —[i] auxiliator suus accensor celi B.

76. Deinde[128] coronatus rex et[a] ducatur per manum ab archiepiscopo, concomitantibus[b] paribus tam prelatis quam laicis, de altari per chorum usque ad solium[c] iam antea[d] preparatum[e]. Et dum rex ad solium venerit, archiepiscopus ipsum collocet in sede[f]. Et hic regis status designatur et dicat archiepiscopus.

76. [a] et *om.* B E F G *a.* —[b] cum committantibus F, *but the first* m *is crossed out*; cum comitantibus B E G. —[c] vel *add.* F, *but crossed out.* —[d] ante B D E; solemniter *add.* F, solenniter *add.* G *a.* —[e] paratum B E. —[f] sedem F G *a.*

A B D E F G *a Meurier*[129]

77. *Sta*[130] *et retine a modo*[a] *statum, quem huc* [*usque*[b]] *paterna*[c] *successione*[131] *tenuisti, hereditario iure tibi*[d] *delegatum per auctoritatem*[e] *Dei*[f] *omnipotentis et per presentem traditionem nostram, omnium scilicet episcoporum ceterorumque servorum Dei*[g]. *Et quanto*

[128] *Hic ducitur rex ad solium* later add. in marg. in hand 4 in *F*, add. in marg. at *Deinde* in *G*, add. in parentheses in text before *Deinde* in *a*.

[129] Meurier, 252.

[130] *Archiepiscopus loquitur* later add. in hand 1 in marg. *F*, add. in marg. at *Sta et retine* in *G*, add. in parentheses in text before *Sta et retine* in *a*.

[131] La Salle wrote (Reims MS 1485, no. 4, p. 3), "Meurier l. 3, c. 11, rapporte la forme du couronnement en ces terms, *Sta et retine amodo statum qum hucusque paterna traditione tenuisti*, pretendant conclure des paroles suivantes que le sacre donne le caractere de la Royauté par le choix et consentement des Pairs. Mais sans entrer dans l'examen de ce point, il suffit de remarquer que le livre bleu porte comme tous les imprimés *quem hucusque paterna successione tenuisti*. Le MS rouge ajoute *vel successione*, mais ce *vel* est manifestement inutile.... Dans un MS de S. Remy de 1285 [= Ordo XXII A, lost manuscript *1*] on lit *paterna suggestione*, et au dessus est ecrit d'une main tres ancienne *vel successione*, ce qui a donné lieu de conjecturer que ces mots *paterna suggestione* avoient este employés au sacre de quelque Roy sacré du vivant de son pere comme Louis 7 du temps de Louis le Gros et Philippe Auguste du vivent de Louis 7, et que comme ces mots ne pourroient servir dans les occasions ordinaires ou les Roys sont sacrés apres la mort de leurs predecesseurs, on ajouta au dessus ou a costé *vel successione*, ce que les copistes ne comprenant pas, ils ont ecrit l'lun ou l'autre de ces mots seulement laissant le *vel* quoyqu'inutile." See also Ordo XXII A, n. 70, and Ordo XXII B-C, n. 20.

*clerum propinquiorem sacris altaribus prospicis, tanto ei pociorem in
locis congruentibus honorem impen* [fol. 63v] *dere memineris, quatinus*[h] *mediator Dei et hominum te mediatorem cleri*[i] *et plebis*[132] (hic
faciat eum sedere, archiepiscopus tenendo eum per manum[j]) *in hoc
regni solio confirmet, et in regno eterno*[k] *secum regnare faciat, Ihesus
Christus dominus noster, rex regum et dominus dominantium. Qui
cum Deo*[l].

77. [a] amodo B D a. —[b] usque *om.* A *only.* —[c] vel *add.* F G a. —[d] tibi iure
Meurier. —[e] authoritatem *Meurier.* —[f] Patris *add.* F, *but later crossed out.* —
[g] Dei servorum F G a *Meurier.* —[h] quatenus *Meurier.* —[i] celi G a —[j] tenendo
eum per manum] illum manu tenens *Meurier.* —[k] eterno *om.* E. —[l] Patre et
Spiritu sancto vivit et regnat. Per omnia secula seculorum (secula seculorum
om. F) *add.* F G a.

A B D E F G a

78. Secundum usum aliquorum[a], maxime secundum usum Romanorum, post intronizationem et non ante, metropolitanus inchoat, canonicis
prosequentibus,[133] "Te Deum laudamus[b]." Quo finito dicit super regem.

78. [a] aliorum E. —[b] laudamus *om.* D; non dicitur nisi post orationem
sequentem *add.* G a.

79. Vers. *Firmetur manus tua et exaltetur*[a] *dextera tua.*
Resp[b]. *Iusticia et iudicium preparatio sedis tue.*
Domine[c], *exaudi*[d].
Et clamor[e].
Dominus vobiscum.
Et cum spiritu tuo[f].
Oremus.

79. [a] exaltatetur E. —[b] Resp. *om.* E. —[c] Domine] Vers. Domine G. —[d] orationem meam *add.* B D E G a. —[e] Et clamor *om.* F; meus ad te veniat *add.* B
D E, meus *add.* G. —[f] Dominus vobiscum ... tuo *om.* B E; Et cum spiritu tuo
om. F G a.

80. Oratio[a].
Deus, qui victrices Moysi manus[b] *in oratione firmasti*[c], *qui, quamvis etate latesceret*[d], *infatigabili sanctitate*[e] *pugnabat, ut dum Amalech
iniquus vincitur, dum prophanus nationum populus subiugatur,
exterminatis alienigenis hereditati tue possessio*[f] *copiosa serviret*[g],
opus manuum nostrarum [fol. 64r] *pia mater*[h] *orationis exauditione*

---

132 *co[n]stituat* later add. in marg. in hand 3 in *F*, add. in text in *G a.*
133 *Dicetur Te Deum post orationem sequentem* later add. in marg. in hand 1 in *F*,
add. in marg. at *Te Deum* in *G*, add. in parentheses in text before *Te Deum* in *a*.

confirma. Habemus et[i] *nos apud te, sancte Pater, dominum salvatorem, qui pro nobis manus suas tetendit*[j] *in cruce, per quem eciam precamur, Altissime, ut eius potencia suffragante, universorum hostium frangatur impietas populusque tuus, cessante formidine, te solum timere*[k] *consistat*[l]*. Per eundem* etc.

> 80. [a] Oratio *om.* B D F G *a.* —[b] manus Moysi D. —[c] formasti B E. —[d] lacesceret F G *a.* —[e] sanctate B. —[f] processio D. —[g] serviet E. —[h] mater F, *later corr. in hand 2 to* nostre; nostre G *a.* —[i] et *om.* E. —[j] tetedit A, extendit E. — [k] temere B E. —[l] condiscat F G *a.*

81. Hiis[a] expletis, archiepiscopus cum paribus coronam sustentantibus, regem taliter insignitum et deductum[b] in[c] solium sibi preparatum, sericis[d] stratum[e] et ornatum,[134] ubi collocavit[f] eum in sede [fol. 64v] eminenti, unde ab omnibus possit videri. Quem in sede sua taliter residentem, mox archiepiscopus, mittra[g] deposita, osculatur[h], dicens, "Vivat rex in eternum." Et[135] post eum episcopi et laici pares, qui eius coronam sustentant, hoc idem dicentes.[136] Hiis expletis, manebit[i] rex sedens in suo solio[j], donec regina fuerit consecrata, qua consecrata et ad suam sedem[k] reducta, missa a cantore primo et succantore[l], chorum servantibus, inchoetur et suo ordine decantetur[m].

> 81. [a] His *a.* —[b] dedutum F, *later corr. to* deductum. —[c] in *om.* B D E. —[d] preparatum sericis] preparatum sericis preparatum F G *a.* —[e] statum B E. — [f] collocavit *corr. to* collocabit *Dewick (ed. g).* —[g] mitra B E G *a.* —[h] eum *add.* F G *a.* —[i] expletis manebit] expletis non se movebit F G *a.* —[j] in solio suo B E. —[k] sedem *om.* B E. —[l] subcantore B D E; missa primo a cantore et succentore F G *a.* —[m] et suo ordine decantetur *om.* D.

82. Oratio pro rege[a].

Quesumus, omnipotens Deus, ut famulus tuus rex noster N., qui tua miseratione regni suscepit gubernacula, virtutum eciam omnium percipiat incrementa, quibus decenter ornatus, et vitiorum monstra devitare, et[b] *hostes*[c] *superare*[d]*, et ad te qui 'via veritas et vita' es, graciosus valeat pervenire. Per dominum.*

---

[134] *In ordinario sancti Dionisii, post inthronisacionem* (*intronizationem* G *a*) *regis, ponitur professio eius ante osculum parium* later add. in marg. in hand 1 in *F*, add. in marg. at *Hiis expletis* in *G*, add. in parentheses in text before *His expletis* in *a*. The ordinary here was doubtless lost manuscript *3*.

[135] *Hic pares debent osculari regem post* (*sicut* ed. *a*) *archiepiscopus* (*post archiepiscopus om.* G) later add. in marg. in hand 4 in *F*, add. in marg. at *Et post eum* in *G*, add. in parentheses in text before *Vivat rex* in *a*.

[136] *Hic incipiet archiepiscopus Te Deum. Quo incepto, recedat* later add. in marg. in hand 1 in *F*, add. in text *G a*. The addition appears twice in *G*, which also adds it in the margin at *Hic incipiet* in the text.

82. ᵃpro rege *om.* B E. —ᵇet *om.* G *a.* —ᶜhospes E. —ᵈet hostes superare *om.* D F, *but later add. in marg.* (*in hand 3?*) F.

83. Secreta.

*Munera, quesumus Domine, oblata sanctifica, et ut*ᵃ *nobis unige-niti tui corpus et sanguis fiant*ᵇ, *et N.*[137] *regi nostro ad obtinendam*ᶜ *anime corporisque salutem, et ad*ᵈ *peragendum iniunctum*ᵉ [fol. 65r] *officium, te largiente, usquequaque proficiant*ᶠ. *Per.*

83. ᵃet ut] ut et F G *a.* —ᵇfiat G *a.* —ᶜoptinendam B E F. —ᵈad *repeated* B E; ad *om.* F, *but later add.* (*in hand 3?*). —ᵉsibi *add.* B D E. —ᶠperficiat B E, proficiat G.

A B D E | F G *a Meurier*[138]

103. [fol. 89v] Notandum quod antequam "Pax Domini sit semper vobiscum" dicatur, archiepiscopus debet dicere hanc benedictionem super regem et super populum.

Benedicat[139] ✠ᵃ *tibi Dominus custodiensque te, sicut te voluit super populum suum constituere regem, ita et in presenti seculo felicem et eterne felicitatis tribuat esse consortem. Amen.*

103. ᵃ✠ *om. Meurier.*

104. *Clerum ac populum, quem sua voluit opitula-tione tua voluit sanctione*ᵃ *congregari, sua dispensatione et tua administratione per diuturna tempora faciat feliciter gubernari. Amen.*

104. ᵃtua voluit sanctione *later corr. in hand 3 to* et tua sanctione F; et tua sanctione G *a Meurier.*

105. *Quatinus*ᵃ *divinis monitis parentes, adversitati-bus omnibus carentes, bonis* [fol. 90r] *omnibus exuberan-tes, tuo ministerio fideli amore obsequentes, et in presenti seculo pacis transquilitate*ᵇ *fruantur et tecum eternorum civium consortio potiri*ᶜ *mereantur. Amen.*

*Quod ipse prestare dignetur, cuius regnum et impe-rium sine fine permanet in secula seculorum. Amen*ᵈ.

---

[137] *ludovico* later add. in hand 2 above *N.* in *F* (see Plate 30). This would seem to prove that the corrections to *F* in this hand were made at the time of Louis XII's coro-nation in 1498.

[138] Meurier, 253–55.

[139] *Benedictio super regem* later add. in marg. in hand 3 in *F*, add. in marg. at *Benedicat* in *G*, add. in parentheses in text before *Benedicat* in *a*.

105. [a] Quatenus *Meurier*. —[b] tranquillitate *a Meurier*. —[c] petiri G. —[d] Amen *om.* G *a*.

A B D E	F G *a Meurier*
	106. *Et benedictio Dei Patris*[a] *omnipotentis, Pa✠tris et Fi✠lii et Spiritus ✠ sancti super vos descendat*[b] *et maneat semper. Amen.*

106. [a] Patris *later crossed out* F; Patris *om.* G *a Meurier*. —[b] descendat super vos G *a*.

108. Benedictio[140] vexilli.
Inclina, Domine ... quinque reges [fol. 90v] *triumphantem ... acquisisse letentur. Qui cum Patre.*

A B D E F G *a*

84. Post communionem[a].
Hec, Domine, oratio salutaris famulum tuum N. regem nostrum[b] *ab omnibus tueatur adversis, quatinus*[c] *et ecclesiastice pacis obtineat*[d] *tranquillitatem*[e]*, post istius temporis decursum ad eternam perveniat hereditatem. Per dominum.*

84. [a] Postcommunionem B E, Postcommunio F G *a*. —[b] nostrum *om.* F G *a*. —[c] quatenus D. —[d] optineat F. —[e] transquillitatem B E, transquilitatem F G; et *add.* F G *a*.

85. Quando[a] legitur[b] Ewangelium[c], rex et regina debent deponere coronas suas. Notandum quod[d], lecto Ewangelio[e], maior inter archiepiscopos et episcopos accipit librum ewangelii[f] et deffert[g] domino[h] regi ad deosculandum, et post ea[i] regine, et post ea[j] domino archiepiscopo missam celebranti. Post offertorium[k] pares deducunt regem ad altare coronam eius sustinentes. Rex autem debet[l] offerre panem unum[m], vinum in urceo[n] argenteo, tresdecim bisantos[o] aureos, et regina similiter. In eundo autem[p] et redeundo, gladius nudus defertur[q] coram eo[r]. Finita missa, iterum pares adducunt regem coram altari, et[s] communicat corpus et sanguinem Domini[t] de manu[u] archiepiscopi missam celebrantis. Sed notandum est quod ille qui [fol. 65v] dedit ei Ewangelium[v] ad deosculandum[w] debet post "pax[141] Domini" accipere pacem ab archiepiscopo missam celebrante et defferre[x] regi cum oris osculo, et regine in[y] libro, et post eum omnes archiepiscopi et episcopi, unus post alium, dant osculum pacis regi[z] in suo solio residenti. Missa finita, deponit archiepiscopus

[140] Variants from *F, G, a,* and *Meurier* in no. 108 are given below at their location in *A*.

[141] *Pax* later add. in marg. (in hand 3?) in *F*, add. in marg. at *pax* in *G*.

coronam de capite regis, et[a], expoliato rege de insignioribus vestimentis et aliis indutis, iterum imponit capiti suo[b] archiepiscopus aliam[c] coronam minorem, et sic vadit ad palatium, nudo gladio[142] precedente. Et sciendum[d] quod eius camisia propter sanctam[e] unctionem debet comburi.

85. [a] Quando] Notandum quando dum F G *a.* —[b] legetur B E. —[c] Evangelium B D E G *a.* —[d] post *add.* D; Notandum quod] et F G *a.* —[e] Evangelio B D E G *a.* —[f] evangelii B D E G *a.* —[g] defert D *a,* defer G. —[h] domino *om.* F G *a.* —[i] postea D F G *a.* —[j] postea D E F G *a.* —[k] affertorium D. —[l] debet autem G *a.* —[m] unum *om.* D. —[n] vitro G. —[o] tridecim bisancios F G *a.* —[p] In eundo autem] et in eundo F G *a.* —[q] deffertur B E F; nudus offertur deffertur B. —[r] rege F G *a.* —[s] ibi *add.* F G *a.* —[t] Domini *om.* E. —[u] domini *add.* D. —[v] Evangelium B D E G *a.* —[w] osculandum B E. —[x] deferre D E F G *a.* —[y] cum F G *a.* —[z] unus post ... regi] dant osculum pacis regi unus post alium F G *a.* —[a] et *om.* F G *a.* —[b] aliam coronam *add.* B, *then crossed out by scribe.* —[c] archiepiscopus aliam *om.* F G *a.* —[d] est *add.* E F G *a.* —[e] sanctam *om.* G.

86. De[143] ampulle reductione[a], sciendum[b] quod rex debet accipere de baronibus suis nobilioribus et[c] forcioribus in die coronationis sue in aurora diei[d] mittere apud sanctum Remigium pro sancta ampulla[e], et illi debent iurare abbati et ecclesie quod dictam sanctam[f] ampullam[g] bona fide ducent et reducent ad sanctam ecclesiam beati Remigii[h]. Abbas autem, hoc facto, debet sanctam ampullam[i] afferre, sicut[j] superius est notatum[k]. Finita consecratione et missa, de [fol. 66r] bent iterum hiidem[l] barones reducere sanctam ampullam[m] usque ad sanctum Remigium honorifice et secure, et eam restituere [in[n]] loco suo[o].[144]

86. [a] reductione ampule F G *a.* —[b] est *add.* E G. —[c] et *om.* F G *a.* —[d] et *add.* F G *a.* —[e] ampula F G *a.* —[f] sanctam *om.* G *a.* —[g] ampulam F G *a.* —[h] Remigi E. —[i] ampulam F G *a.* —[j] sic F, *later corr. to* sicut. —[k] notandum B E. —[l] idem D F G *a,* hiisdem E. —[m] ampulam F G *a.* —[n] in *om.* A only. —[o] et cetera *add.* F G *a.*

ABCDEF

87. Ordo[a] [145] ad reginam benedicendam[b], que debet consecrari statim[c] post factam[d] consecrationem regis[e]; debet ei parari[f] solium in

---

[142] Apparently originally *nudum gladium F*, but corr. to *nudo gladio.*

[143] *De ampulle reduccione* later add. in marg. *A*, but then partially erased. *A* does not actually begin a new paragraph here, but logic demands one.

[144] Manuscript *G* ends with no. 86, as does edition *a*, although, as in *F*, nos. 109–118 and nos. 103–106 and 108 had been inserted earlier. In *G* the ordo is followed by three later texts (see the description of MS *G*, p. 464). Edition *a* adds (fol. 20v) "Explicit consecratio et coronatio regis Francie," which is followed by the privilege (quoted above, n. 23).

[145] *C* contains only the ordo for the queen, beginning on fol. 213r, and the benediction of the banner. "Incipit ordo ad reginam" was later added at the bottom of fol. 212v in the same hand as the other additions and corrections (as a guide for binding).

modum solii regis[g], debet tamen aliquantulum minus[146] esse; debet autem regina adduci a duobus episcopis[h] in ecclesiam[i] et rex in suo solio[j] sedere in omnibus ornamentis suis regiis, [fol. 66v] sicuti[k] in solio residebat post inunctionem[l] et coronationem suam[m], superius annotatam[n]. Regina autem[o], adducta in ecclesiam, debet prosterni ante altare et, prostrata, debet orare; qua elevata ab oratione ab episcopis, debet iterum caput inclinare, et archiepiscopus hanc orationem dicere[p].

> 87. [a] Incipit ordo C. —[b] benedicendum reginam B E; ad reginam benedicen-
> dam] ad reginam Francie benedicendam et consecrandam F. —[c] statim *om.*
> D. —[d] sanctam B D E F. —[e] hoc modo *add.* F. —[f] parari ei F, ei parare E. —
> [g] regis solii F. —[h] a duobus episcopis adduci F. —[i] crine soluto *add.* F. —
> [j] solio suo F. —[k] ornamentis suis regiis sicuti] ornamentis regis sicut F. —
> [l] unctionem F. —[m] suam *om.* B D E. —[n] annotatem E. —[o] autem *om.* F. —[p] sic
> *add.* B D E.

88. Oratio[a].

Adesto, Domine[b], supplicationibus nostris, et quod humilitatis nostre gerendum est, misterio[c] [147] tue virtutis impleatur effectu[d]. Per dominum.

> 88. [a] Oremus D. —[b] Domine *om.* F. —[c] misterio *corr. to* mi[ni]sterio *Dewick*
> (*ed. g*). —[d] effectu *om.* B D E.

89. Deinde dicat archiepiscopus[a] hanc[b] orationem[c].

Omnipotens eterne[d] Deus, fons et origo totius bonitatis, qui feminei sexus fragilitatem[e] nequaquam reprobando adversaris, sed[f] dignanter comprobando pocius eligis. Et qui infirma mundi eligendo forcia queque confundere decrevisti, quique etiam glorie virtutisque tue triumphum in manu Iudich[g] femine olim Iudaice plebi de hoste sevissimo designare[h] voluisti; respice, quesumus, ad preces humilitatis nostre. Et super hanc famulam tuam [fol. 67r] N., quam supplici devotione in reginam[i] eligimus, benedicti❦onum tuarum dona multiplica, eamque[j] dextera tue potencie semper et ubique circunda; sitque[k] et[l] bone[m] muniminis tui undique[n] firmiter protecta, quatinus[o] visibilis seu invisibilis hostis nequicias triumphaliter[p] expugnare valeat. Et una cum Sarra atque Rebecca, Lya et Rachel, beatis[q] reverendisque feminabus[r], fructu uteri sui fecundari seu gratulari mereatur, ad totius decorem regni statumque sancte Dei ecclesie regendum necnon protegendum. Per Christum dominum nostrum. Qui ex intemerato[s] beate Marie virginis alvo nasci, visitare ac[t] renovare dignatus est mundum. Qui tecum vivit etc.

---

[146] There is one minum too many in *minus* in *C*.

[147] *ministerio* in Ordines XIII,25, XV,47, and perhaps XXIV,69, but *misterio* in Ordo XXII A,60.

89. [a] archiepiscopus dicat E. —[b] hanc *om.* B E. —[c] Oratio *add. as rubric* E F. —[d] eterne *om.* B E. —[e] fragilitati F. —[f] se F, *later corr. to* sed. —[g] Iudith D. —[h] resignare F —[i] regina F. —[j] Eamque A C F. —[k] sicque C. —[l] et *crossed out* A. —[m] et bone] bone B C D E; ut umerbone *corr. to* ut umbone F. —[n] setus *add.* F, *but crossed out.* —[o] quatinus *om.* F. —[p] triumphanter F. —[q] bis F. —[r] feminis F. —[s] temerato B E. —[t] et B E.

90. Alia oratio[a].

Deus, qui solus habes immortalitem[b] *lucemque inhabitas*[c] *inaccessibilem*[d], *cuius providencia in sui disposicione non fallitur, qui fecisti*[e] *que futura sunt et vocas ea que non sunt, tanquam*[f] *ea que* [fol. 67v] *sunt, qui superbos equo moderamine de principatu deicis atque humiles in sublime*[g] *dignanter provehis. Ineffabilem*[h] *misericordiam tuam supplices exoramus, ut sicut Hester reginam Israelis*[i] *causa salutis de captivitatis sue*[j] *compede solutam*[k] *ad regis Assueri thalamum regnique sui*[l] *consortium transire fecisti*[m]. *Ita hanc famulam tuam N. humilitatis nostre benedicti✠one*[n] *christiane plebis gracia salutis ad dignam, sublimemque*[o] *copulam regis*[p] *nostri misericorditer transire concedas*[q]. *Et ut in regalis federe coniugii semper manens pudica, proximam virginitatis*[r] *palmam continere queat*[s], *tibique Deo vivo et vero in omnibus et*[t] *super omnia iugiter placere desideret. Et te inspirante que*[u] *tibi placita sunt*[v] *toto corde perficiat. Per dominum nostrum* etc.

90. [a] Alia oratio] Item alia benedictio B D F, Alia benedictio E. —[b] immortalitatem B C D F. —[c] habitas F. —[d] accessitabilem E. —[e] ea *later add.* C. —[f] tamquam B. —[g] dignitatis *later add.* C. —[h] inestabilem E. —[i] regina Israel F. —[j] tue D. —[k] et *add.* F. —[l] sui *om.* E. —[m] *festi F*, later corr. to *fecisti*. —[n] benedi✠ctionis F; ✠ *om.* B E. —[o] sublimamque E, sublimenque F. —[p] regis vel imperatoris misericorditer *later add. in marg.* C. —[q] conedas F, *later corr. to* concedas. —[r] virginitatis *corr. to* virginitati *Dewick (ed. g)*. —[s] valeat F. —[t] et *om.* E. —[u] que *om.* B D E. —[v] sint B E.

91. Alia oratio[a].

Omnipotens sempiterne Deus, hanc famulam tuam celesti bene✠dictione sancti✠fica[b], *et quam in adiutorio regni reginam eligi* [fol. 68r] *mus, tua ubique sapientia doceat atque*[c] *confortet et*[d] *ecclesia tua fidelem famulam semper*[e] *agnoscat. Per*[f] *Christum*[g] *dominum nostrum.*

91. [a] benedictio E; Alia oratio *om.* B. —[b] ✠ *om.* B E F. —[c] ac F —[d] in D; confortet et C, *later corr. to* conformet ut. —[e] tua fidelem famulam semper] tua semper fidelem famulam semper B, tua sancta fidelem famulam semper E. —[f] eundem *later add.* C. —[g] Christum *om.* B E.

92. Notandum[a] quod tunica regine et camisia debent esse aperte

usque ad corrigiam, et dominus archipiscopus debet inungere eam[b] oleo sancto in capite et in pectore, et dicere dum inungit in qualibet unctione. *In nomine Pa✠tris et Fi✠lii et Spiri✠tus sancti, prosit tibi hec unctio olei in honorem et confirmationem eternam [in secula seculorum. Amen[c].]*

> 92. [a] est *add.* B E. —[b] de *add.* F. —[c] in secula seculorum. Amen *om.* A F, *but add. in marg. by scribe* A, *and add. in text* B C D E.

93. Facta unctione, dicat archiepiscopus.

Oratio[a].

Spiritus sancti[b], gracia humilitatis nostre officio in te copiosa descendat, ut sicut manibus nostris[c] indignis oleo materiali[d] oblita[e] pinguescis exterius, ita eius invisibili[f] unguine delibuta[g] impinguari[h] merearis[i] in terris[j], eius[k] spirituali[l] unctione perfectissime semper imbuta, et illicita declinare tota mente, et spernere[m] discas seu valeas, et utilia[n] anime tue iugiter cogitare[o], optare atque operari queas.

> 93. [a] Oratio *om.* B D F. —[b] Sancti spiritus F. —[c] licet *later add.* C. —[d] materialis E. —[e] oblita C, *later corr. to* oblinita; ollita D; es *add.* F. —[f] invisibile D. —[g] pinguescis ... delibuta *om.* F. —[h] impingari D. —[i] mereari A. —[j] interius B D E; *corr. over erasure to* interius F. —[k] eius *later corr. to* eiusque C. —[l] spiritua B E. —[m] sperne A. —[n] ultima F. —[o] cogitare *om.* F; et *later add.* C.

94. Alia oratio.

Deus Pater eterne glorie sit tibi adiu [fol. 68v] *tor. Et omnipotens bene✠dicat[a] tibi, preces tuas exaudiat, vitam tuam longitudinem[b] dierum adimpleat, bene✠dictionem[c] tuam iugiter confirmet, te cum omni populo in eternum conservet, inimicos tuos confusione induat, et super te Christi sanctificatio ac huius olei infusio floreat, ut[d] qui tibi in terris tribuit benedictionem, ipse in celis conferat meritum angelorum[e]. Benedi✠cat[a] te[f] et custodiat in[g] vitam eternam Ihesus Christus dominus noster. Qui vivit.*

> 94. [a] ✠ *om.* B E. —[b] longitudine D F. —[c] ✠ *om.* B E F. —[d] Ut A C. —[e] et *add.* D. —[f] te *om.* F, *but later add.* —[g] in *om.* F, *but later add.*

95. Tunc debet ab archiepiscopo anulus immitti[a] digito[b] et dicere[c].

Accipe anulum fidei, signaculum sancte trinitatis, quo possis omnes hereticas pravitates devitare, et barbaras gentes virtute tibi prestita ad[d] agnitionem veritatis advocare[e].

> 95. [a] ei *add.* F. —[b] regine *add.* D. —[c] et dicere] dicens. Oratio E. —[d] ad *om.* E. —[e] advocate E.

96. Sequitur oratio[a].

Dominus vobiscum.

Oremus[b].

Deus, cuius est omnis potestas et dignitas, da famule tue signo tue fidei[c] *prosperum sue dignitatis effectum, in qua tibi semper firma maneat*[d]*, tibique iugiter* [fol. 69r] *placere contendat. Per dominum.*

96. [a] Sequitur oratio *om.* E. —[b] Dominus vobiscum. Oremus] Dominus vobiscum. Et (cum spiritu tuo *add.* E). Oremus (Oratio *add. as rubric* E) B E; Dominus vobiscum. Oremus *om.* F. —[c] fideli F. —[d] permaneat F.

97. Post istam orationem datur[a] ab archiepiscopo sceptrum modicum alterius modi quam sceptrum regium[b] et virga consimilis virge regie. Et in[c] tradendo dicat archiepiscopus.

Accipe virgam virtutis et equitatis, et esto pauperibus misericors[d] *et affabilis, viduis, pupillis*[e] *et orphanis diligentissimam curam*[f] *exhibeas, ut omnipotens Deus augeat tibi*[g] *graciam suam. Qui vivit et regnat.*

97. [a] regine *add.* F. —[b] regum F. —[c] in *om.* E. —[d] misericors pauperibus E. — [e] pupillis *om.* F. —[f] cum E. —[g] misericordiam tuam et *add.* F, *but later crossed out.*

98. Sequitur post dationem sceptri et virge hec oratio[a].

Omnipotens sempiterne Deus, affluentem spiritum tue benedictionis super famulam tuam nobis orantibus propiciatus infunde, ut que per manus nostre impositionem hodie regina instituitur[b]*, sanctificatione tua digna*[c] *et electa permaneat, ut*[d] *nunquam post modum de tua gracia separetur indigna. Per dominum.*

98. [a] sequens *add.* D; Sequitur ... oratio] Sequitur post oracionem septri et virge hec oracio B, Post orationem sceptri et virge dicitur hec oratio E, In datione sceptri et virge oratio F. —[b] instituisti B E. —[c] divina B E. —[d] Et F.

99. Tunc debet ei[a] imponi a solo archiepiscopo corona in capite ipsius, quam impositam, sustentare debent undique barones[b]; archiepiscopus autem[c] debet dicere in impositione orationem[d].

[fol. 69v] *Accipe coronam glorie et regalis excellentie, honorem iocunditatis, ut splendida fulgeas et eterna exultatione coroneris. Ut scias te esse consortem regni populoque Dei semper prospere consulas, et quanto plus exaltaris, tanto amplius*[e] *humilitatem diligas atque custodias. Unde*[f] *sicut exterius auro et gemmis redimita evites*[g]*, ita et interius*[h] *auro sapientie virtutumque gemmis decorari contendas, quatinus post occasum huius seculi cum prudentibus virginibus sponso perhenni domino nostro Ihesu Christo digne et laudabiliter occurrens*[i] *regiam*[j] *celestis aule merearis ingredi ianuam. Auxiliante*

domino nostro Ihesu Christo. Qui cum Patre et Spiritu sancto vivit et
regnat. Per infinita secula seculorum. Amen[k].

99. [a] ei *om.* F. —[b] barones undique D. —[c] antem F. —[d] orationem *om.* F. —
[e] plus F. —[f] ut *add.* F. —[g] enites B D E. —[h] ita et inte [fol. 52v] ita et interius *at*
page break E. —[i] occurrens *om.* F. —[j] regina F, *later corr. to* regiam. —[k] Ihesu
Christo ... Amen *om.* A, *but add. in marg. by scribe, and in text* B C D E;
Auxiliante domino ... Amen] Qui cum Deo F.

100. Post impositam coronam dicat archiepiscopus[a].

Omnium, Domine, fons bonorum et cunctorum dator provectuum[b],
tribue famule tue N. adeptam bene regere dignitatem, et a te sibi
prestitam in ea[c] *bonis operibus corrobora*[d] *gloriam. Per dominum*[e].

100. [a] Oratio *add.* E, hanc orationem *add.* F. —[b] provectum F. —[c] prestitam in
ea] prescitam in ea B, prescitam E. —[d] corobora D. —[e] Alia oratio *add.* E F.

101. [fol. 70r] *Domine sancte Pater omnipotens, eterne*[a] *Deus, hono-*
ris[b] *cunctorum auctor ac*[c] *distributor, benedictionumque omnium*[d]
largus infusor, tribue[e] *super hanc famulam tuam*[f] *reginam bene✠dic-*
tionis[g] *gracie tue copiam, et quam humana sibi*[h] *electio preesse*
gaudet, tua[i] *superne electionis ac bene✠dictionis*[g] *infusio accumulet.*
Concede ei, Domine, auctoritatem regiminis, consilii magnitudinem,
sapientie, prudencie et intellectus habundantiam, religionis ac
pietatis custodiam, quatinus mereatur[j] *bene✠dicis et augmentari in*
nomine ut Sara[k], *visitari et fecundari ut Rebecca, contra omnium*
muniri[l] *monstra viciorum ut Iudich*[m], *in*[n] *regni regimine eligi ut Hes-*
ter, ut[o] *quam humana nititur fragilitas bene✠dicere celestis potius*
intimi roris et sacri olei repleat infusio. Et que a nobis[p] *coronatur et*
bene✠dicitur[g] *in reginam a te mereatur*[q] *obtinere*[r] *in premio*[s] *eterni-*
tatis [fol. 70v] *perpetue. Et sicut ab hominibus sublimatur in nomine,*
ita a te sublimetur fide et operatione. Illo etiam sapientie[t] *tue cum*[u]
rore perfunde[v], *quem beatus David in repromissione et filius eius*
Salomon[w] *percepit in locupletatione. Sis ei, Domine, contra cunctorum*
ictus inimicorum lorica, in adversis galea, in[x] *prosperis*[y] *sapientia,*
in protectione clipeus sempiternus. Sequatur pacem, diligat caritatem,
abstineat se ab omni impietate, loquatur iusticiam, custodiat veri-
tatem. Sit cultrix iusticie et pietatis, amatrix religionis. Vigeatque
presenti bene✠dictione[g] *in hoc evo annis plurimis et in sempiterno*
sine fine eternis.[z] *Prestante domino nostro Ihesu Christo, qui cum*
Patre et Spiritu sancto vivit et regnat Deus. Per omnia secula seculo-
rum. Amen.

101. [a] eterne *om.* F. —[b] honorum F, honoris *corr. to* honorum *Dewick (ed. g).* —
[c] et B E. —[d] omnium C, *later corr. to* omniumque. —[e] Tribue A —[f] tuam N.: E. —

^g ✠ *om.* B E. —^h sibi] sit D. —ⁱ tua *corr. to* tue *Dewick (ed. g).* —^j mereatur
om. F. —^k Sarra B D E F. —^l et *later add.* C. —^m Iudith D. —ⁿ In A. —^o Ut A. —
^p eligitur *later add.* C. —^q mereat F, *later corr. to* mereatur. —^r obtineri F. —
^s in premio] premium D. —^t fide *add.* B, *but crossed out by scribe.* —^u eam C
F. —^v profunde B E. —^w Salmon B, Psalmon E. —^x adversis autem *add.* F, *but
later crossed out.* —^y galea *add.* F, *but crossed out.* —^z *corr. over erasure to*
eternis *F.*

102. Post istam orationem barones qui coronam eius sustentant^a
deducunt^b eam ad solium, ubi in sede parata^c collocatur, cir- [fol. 71r]
cunstantibus^d eam baronibus et^e matronis nobilioribus; in oblatione, in
pace ferenda, in communione, penitus est ordo regis superius annotatus
observandus^f.¹⁴⁸

102. ^a coronam eius sustentant] coronam substentant F. —^b deducant B D E
F. —^c paratur D. —^d circumstantibus D. —^e maternis vel *add.* D. —^f penitus ...
observandus] Finitus est ordo regis superius et cetera F.

A B C E	D

103. Notandum¹⁴⁹ quod antequam archiepiscopus dicat
"Pax Domini" etc.^a, debet dicere hanc benedictionem^b
super regem et super populum sic^c.

*Benedicat tibi^d Dominus custodiatque te, et sicut
voluit te super populum suum constituere regem^e, ita¹⁵⁰
in presenti seculo felicem et eterne felicitatis tribuat esse
consortem. Amen.*

103. ^a etc. *om.* E. —^b oracionem B E. —^c et super populum sic] et populum sic
B, et populum dicens. Benedictio E. —^d te B E. —^e reginam C.

104. Alia benedictio.
*Clerum ac populum, quem sua voluit opitulatione^a
tua sanctione^b congregari, sua dispensatione^c et tua
administratione per diuturna^d tempora facias^e feliciter
gubernari. Amen.*

---

¹⁴⁸ F ends here (fol. 98r), but all the texts that follow (except no. 107, which is
omitted in both *F* and *G*) were already intercalated in *F* (see the Synoptic Table, p.
460).

¹⁴⁹ Nos. 103–104 appear twice in *B*, *D*, and *E* (here on fol. 81r–v in *B*, fol. 160v in *D*,
and fol. 53v in *E*), for they are also inserted between nos. 61–62 (fol. 74r in *B*, fol. 156v
in *D*, and fol. 44v in *E*). There are slight differences between the copies. Nos. 103–106
and no. 108 are between nos. 83 and 84 in *F* and *G*.

¹⁵⁰ *quod*, written in error after *ita* in *A*, is crossed out by a red line, apparently by
the scribe.

104. ᵃ et *add. in brackets Dewick (ed. g).* —ᵇ sanctificatione E. —ᶜ tua sanctificatione congregari sua dispensatione congregari, sua dispensatione E. —ᵈ diurturna E. —ᵉ facias *om.* D.

A B C D E

105. Alia benedictio.

Quatinus divinis monitis parentes, adversitatibus omnibus carentes, bonis omnibus exuberantes, tuo ministerio fideli amore obsequentes, et in presenti seculo [fol. 71v] *pacis tranquillitate*ᵃ *fruentur, et tecum eternorum civium consortio potiri mereantur*ᵇ. *Amen.*

Quod ipse prestare dignetur, cuius regnum et imperium sine fine permanet in secula seculorum. Amen.

105. ᵃ transquillitate B D E. —ᵇ mereamur B E.

106. *Et*¹⁵¹ *bene✠dictio*ᵃ *Dei*ᵇ *omnipotentis, Pa✠tris*ᵃ, *et Fi✠lii*ᵃ, *et Spiritus ✠*ᵃ *sancti super vos descendat*ᶜ *et maneat semper*ᵈ. *Amen*ᵉ.

106. ᵃ ✠ *om.* B E. —ᵇ Patris *add.* F, *but later crossed out.* —ᶜ descendat *later crossed out* C. —ᵈ super vos ... semper *om.* D. —ᵉ super vos... Amen] etc. B, descendat etc. E.

107. Explicit ordo et officium inᵃ consecrationeᵇ regis et regine.

107. ᵃ in *om.* C. —ᵇ in consecratione] consecrationis E.

A B C D E *Meurier*

108. Benedictioᵃ ¹⁵² vexilliᵇ.

*Inclina, Domine, aurem tuam ad preces nostre humilitatis*ᶜ, *et per interventum beati Michaelis archangeli tui omniumque*ᵈ *celestium*ᵉ *virtutum, sed et beatorum martyrum Dyonisii, Rustici et Eleutherii omniumque sanctorum tuorum*ᶠ, *presta nobis*ᵍ *auxilium dextere tue, ut*ʰ *sicut benedixisti Abraham adversus quinque reges triumphantem, atque David regem in tui nominis laude triumphales*ⁱ *congressus*ʲ *exercentem*ᵏ, *ita benedicere*ˡ *et sanctificare*ᵐ *digneris hoc vexillum*ⁿ *quod ob deffensionem*ᵒ *regni et*ᵖ *sancte ecclesie contra hostilem rabiem defertur* q, *quatinus*ʳ *in nomine tuo*ˢ *fideles et* [fol. 72r] *defensores*ᵗ *populi Dei illud consequentes per virtutem sancte crucis triumphum et victoriam se ex hostibus acquisisse*ᵘ *letentur*ᵛ. *Qui cum Patre* etc.¹⁵³

---

¹⁵¹ This addition to no. 105 is assigned its own number because it is not in ordines XXII A and XXIV (at nos. 73 and 83 respectively), although it is in Ordo XXV, 151.

¹⁵² No. 108 is located before no. 84 in *F*, *G*, *a*, and *Meurier* (pp. 254–55); their variants are given here, however.

¹⁵³ *C* ends here. *E* adds the rubric *S'ensuit le serment que les pers de France font au roy* (fol. 54r) then the series of oaths (fols. 54v–59v) that are in MS *A*, fols. 75r–80r,

108. ^aSequitur benedictio D. — ^bOratio *add.* E. — ^chumilitatis nostre *Meurier.* —^d omniumue F, *later corr. to* omniumque. —^e celestium *om.* G. — ^fsed et ... tuorum *om.* F G *a Meurier.* —^gnobis *om.* D. —^h et F G *a Meurier.* — ⁱin tui nominis laude triumphales] in tui nominis triumphales F G, in tui nomine triumphales *a,* in tuo nomine triumphales *Meurier.* —^j egressus D. — ^kexcercentem C. —^l ✠ *add.* B E F G *a Meurier.* —^m ✠ *add.* B E *Meurier.* — ⁿvexillum hoc F G *a.* —^o defensionem B *a Meurier,* deffensione E; *abbreviated* deffēonem F, *later expanded (in hand 3?) to* deffensionem. —^p regni et *om.* F G *a Meurier.* —^q deffertur D. —^r quatenus *Meurier.* —^s in nomine tuo] in Christi nomine F G *a,* in nomine Christi *Meurier.* —^t deffensores F G. — ^u acquississe F, acquisiisse *Meurier.* —^v letentur *om.* D.

A B D

109. *Kyrieleyson.*[154]
Christeleyson.
Kyrieleyson^a.
Christe, audi nos^b.

Sancta Maria^c,	*ora pro nobis.*
Sancte Michael^d,	*ora.*
Sancte Gabriel,	*ora*^e.
Sancte Raphael,	*ora.*
Sancte chorus angelorum,	*ora.*
Sancte Iohannes Baptista,	*ora.*
Sancte Petre,	*ora*^f.
Sancte Paule,	*ora.*
Sancte Andrea,	*ora.*
Sancte Iacobe,	*ora.*
Sancte Iohannes,	*ora.*
Sancte Thoma,	*ora.*
Sancte Philippe,	*ora.*
Sancte Iacobe,	*ora*^g.
Sancte Bartholome^h,	*ora.*
Sancte Matthee,	*ora.*
Sancte Symon,	*ora.*

and in MS *B,* fols. 83v–87r. They are printed in Dewick (ed. *g,* 55–60) from *A,* but I do not include them here because they have no bearing on the coronation ceremony. There are three large miniatures with these oaths in *E* (although none in *B*), and a note on fol. 59v in the seventeenth-century hand of Théodore Godefroy reads, "Ce livre a esté escript en l'an 1378 du regne du roy Charles V." Godefroy may have worked out the date from the list of peers in Ordo XX B,24.

[154] For the location of the litany and succeeding prayers (nos. 109–118) in *E, F, G,* and *a* (the variants from which are given here), see no. 35.

Sancte Thadee,	*ora*[i].
Sancte Mathia,	*ora.*
Sancte Barnaba,	*ora.*
Sancte chorus apostolorum,	*ora.*
Sancte Stephane,	*ora.*
Sancte Clemens,	*ora.*
[fol. 72v] *Sancte Calixte,*	*ora.*
Sancte Marcelle,	*ora.*
Sancte Nichasi[j] *cum sociis suis*[k],	*orate*[l].
Sancte Laurenti,	*ora.*
Sancte Dyonisii cum sociis suis[k],	*orate*[m].
Sancte Mauricii[n] *cum sociis suis*[k],	*orate*[o].
Sancte Gervasi,	*ora.*
Sancte Prothasi[p],	*ora.*
Sancte Tymothee[q],	*ora.*
Sancte Apollinaris[r],	*ora.*
Sancte chorus martyrum,	*ora.*
Sancte Silvester,	*ora*[s].
Sancte Remigi[t],	*ora.*
Bis et alciori voce cantetur[u].	
Sancte Augustine,	*ora.*
Sancte Ieromine[v],	*ora.*
Sancte Ambrosi,	*ora.*
Sancte Gregori,	*ora.*
Sancte Syxte[w],	*ora.*
Sancte Sinici[x],	*ora.*
Sancte Rigoberte,	*ora.*
Sancte Martine,	*ora.*
Sancte Maurili[y],	*ora.*
Sancte Nicolae[z],	*ora.*
Sancte chorus confessorum,	*ora.*

109. [a] Kyrieleyson *om.* B D E. — [b] Kyrieleyson ... audi nos] Kyrie eleyson. Respondeat chorus, deinde episcopi. Christe eleyson. Kyrie eleyson (Kyrie eleyson *om.* G). Respondeat chorus, deinde episcopi. Kyrieleyson. Respondeat chorus, deinde episcopi. Christe audi nos. Respondeat chorus. Deinde episcopi F G *a.* — [c] Respondeat chorus *add.* F G *a.* — [d] Chorus *add.* F G *a.* — [e] Sancte Gabriel, ora. *om.* B D E. — [f] Sancte Petre, ora *repeated* A. — [g] Sancte Iohannes ... Sancte Iacobe, ora. *om.* F G *a.* — [h] Bartholomee B D F G *a.* — [i] Sancte Mathee ... Thadee, ora] Sancte Symon, ora. Sancte Thadee, ora. Sancte Mathee, ora B D E. — [j] Nichasii B E. — [k] tuis F G *a.* — [l] Sancte Maurici cum sociis suis, orate *add.* D. — [m] Sancte Laurenti ... orate *om.* B E. —

[n] Maurici B E F *a*. —[o] Sancte Mauricii ... orate *om.* D. —[p] Prothasii G. —[q] Thimotee B, Thymothee D G. —[r] Appollinaris B, Appolinaris D E F G. —[s] Sancte Silvester, ora *om.* E G. —[t] Remigii B. —[u] Sancte Remigi ... cantetur] Sancte Remigii II (Remigii II] Remigi nomen *a*) bis (bis *om.* G) et alciori voce dicitur. Ora F G *a*. —[v] Iheromine B E F G, Hieronyme *a*. —[w] Xiste B. —[x] Funci F G *a*. —[y] Maurilli G *a*; Sancte Martine ... Maurili] Sancte Maurili, ora. Sancte Martine B E. —[z] Nicholae B F *a*, Nichoale D, Nycholae E.

110. *Sancta Maria Magdalena,*	*ora*[a].
Sancta Maria Egypciaca[b],	*ora.*
Sancta Felicitas,	*ora.*
Sancta Perpetua,	*ora.*
Sancta Agatha,	*ora.*
Sancta Agnes,	*ora.*
Sancta Cecilia[c],	*ora.*
Sancta Eutropia,	*ora*[d].
Sancta Genovefa[e],	*ora.*
Sancta Columba,	*ora.*
[fol. 73r] *Sancta Scolastica*[f],	*ora.*
Sancta Petronilla,	*ora.*
Sancta Katherina[g],	*ora.*
Sancte chorus virginum,	*ora pro nobis.*
Omnes sancti,	*orate pro.*

110. [a] ora] ora pro nobis, ora E. —[b] Egipciaca D, Egiptiaca F G *a*. —[c] Lucia B E. —[d] Sancta Eutropia, ora *om.* E. —[e] Genofefa D. —[f] Stolastica F. —[g] Katerina B.

111. *Propicius esto, parce nobis Domine.*
Propicius esto, libera nos[a] *Domine*[b].
Ab insidiis dyaboli, libera.
A dampnatione perpetua, libera.
Per misterium sancte incarnationis tue, libera.
Per passionem et crucem tuam, libera.
Per graciam sancti Spiritus paracliti, libera.
In die iudicii, libera.

111. [a] parce nobis B E F G *a*. —[b] Ab omni malo, libera nos Domine *add.* E.

112. *Peccatores, te rogamus, audi nos.*
Ut pacem nobis dones, te rogamus.
Ut misericordia et pietas tua nos custodiat, te rogamus.
Ut graciam sancti Spiritus[a] *cordibus nostris clementer infundere digneris, te rogamus.*
Ut ecclesiam tuam regere et deffendere[b] *digneris, te rogamus*[c].

Ut dompnum[d] *apostolicum et omnes gradus ecclesie in sancta religione*[e] *conservare digneris, te rogamus*[f].

Ut archiepiscopum nostrum N. cum omni grege sibi commisso in tuo sancto servicio confortare et conservare di [fol. 73v] *gneris, te rogamus.*

Et[g] dicitur bis[h].

A B D Meurier[155]

Ut obsequium servitutis nostre racionabile facias, te rogamus.

112. [a] Spiritus sancti F G *a.* —[b] deffensare F G, defensare *a.* —[c] Ut ecclesiam ... rogamus *om.* B D E. —[d] domum E. —[e] religione *om.* B. —[f] Ut dompnum ... rogamus *om.* F G *a.* —[g] Et *om.* F G *a.* —[h] Et dicitur bis *om.* D.

113. Tunc[156] archiepiscopus ab accubitu surgens et, ad regem consecrandum se[a] volvens, baculum pastoralem cum sinistra tenens, dicat hos versus, choro post eum quemlibet integre repetente[b].

Ut[157] *hunc presentem famulum tuum*[c] *N. in regem coronandum bene✠dicere digneris, te rogamus, audi nos.*

Secundo dicit.

Bene✠dicere et sublimare[d] *digneris, te rogamus.*

Tercio dicit.

Bene✠dicere[e], *sub✠limare*[f] *et conse✠crare*[g] *digneris, te rogamus.*

113. [a] se *om.* D. —[b] repente A, repetendo F G *a.* —[c] famulum tuum presentem B E. —[d] Bene✠dicere et sublimare] Ut hunc presentem famulum tuum N. in regem coronandum bene✠dicere et subli✠mare *Meurier.* —[e] et *add.* B; Benedicere] Ut hunc presentem famulum tuum N. in regem coronandum bene✠dicere *Meurier.* —[f] ✠ *om.* B E F G *a.* —[g] ✠ *om.* B D E F G *a.*

---

[155] Meurier, 244–45.

[156] *Surgat archiepiscopus* later add. in marg. in hand 3 in *F*, add. in text in parentheses before *Tunc archiepiscopus* in *a.*

Meurier, 244–45, omitted the rubrics in no. 113. His additions in the second and third of these benedictions are not pure invention on his part. They must have come from his Reims source, for they are the readings of Ordo XXV,91 and all later ordines that print the complete text. If they were to be found in the *livre rouge* (lost manuscript *4*), it is difficult to explain why they do not appear in *F*, *G*, and *a*. Perhaps Meurier did not work from the *livre rouge* itself, but from a copy of it, or perhaps there had been further additions to the *livre rouge* after the publication of edition *a*; so many manuscripts have disappeared that it is impossible to achieve certainty in such matters.

[157] *Cantat metropolitanus* later add. in marg. in hand 1 in *F*, add. in marg. in *G*, add. in text in parentheses before *Ut hunc presentem* in *a.*

A B D

114. Quo dicto et a choro responso, redit[a] ad accubitum, episcopis resumentibus et prosequentibus letaniam.

Ut regibus et principibus christianis pacem et concordiam donare[b] digneris[c], te rogamus.

Ut cunctum populum christianum precioso sanguine tuo[d] redemptum conservare digneris, te rogamus.

Ut cunctis fidelibus defunctis[e] requiem eternam donare digneris, te rogamus.

Ut nos exaudire di [fol. 74r] *gneris, te rogamus[f].*

Fili[g] Dei,[158] *te rogamus.*

114. [a] reddit F G a. — [b] dignare D. — [c] dig' (*a scribal error for* Te rogamus) *add.* B. — [d] tuo *om.* G a. — [e] deffunctis B. — [f] Ut nos exaudire digneris, te rogamus audi nos *repeated* E. — [g] Filii F.

115. *Agnus Dei, qui tollis peccata mundi, parce nobis Domine.*

Agnus Dei, qui tollis peccata mundi, exaudi nos Domine.

Agnus Dei, qui tollis peccata mundi, miserere nobis[a].

Christe, audi nos.

Kyrieleyson.

Christeleyson.

Kyrieleyson.

115. [a] miserere nobis] dona nobis pacem B E.

116. Letania finita, metropolitanus surgens, rege et episcopis prostratis manentibus, annunciat.

Pater[159] *noster.*

Et ne nos[a].

Salvum fac servum tuum[b].

Deus meus sperantem in te.

Esto ei, Domine, turris fortitudinis[c].

A facie inimici.

Nichil[d] proficiat inimicus in eo.

Et filius iniquitatis non apponat[e] nocere ei.

Domine, exaudi[f].

Et clamor[g].

Dominus vobiscum.

Et cum spiritu tuo.

Oremus.

---

[158] *E* adds *ii.* after *Dei*; perhaps this was meant to be *bis*, i.e., repeated.

[159] *Dicat metropolitanus* later add. in marg. in hand 3 in *F*, add. in marg. *G*, add. in text in parentheses before *Pater noster* in *a*.

116. ª inducas *add.* B E, inducas etc. *add.* D; Sed libera *add. as response* G. —
ᵇ Domine *add.* E. —ᶜ inimici *add.* F, *but crossed out by scribe.* —ᵈ Nihil *a* —
ᵉ ultra *add.* E. —ᶠ oracionem meam *add.* B D E G. —ᵍ meus ad te veniat *add.*
B D E G.

117. Oratio ª.

*Pretende, quesumus Domine ᵇ, huic ᶜ famulo tuo N. dexteram celestis
auxilii, ut te toto corde perquirat ᵈ et que digne postulat assequi mereatur. Per dominum ᵉ. Resp ᶠ. Amen ᵍ.*

117. ª Oratio *om.* B D E F G *a, but add. in another hand* D. —ᵇ Domine quesumus D. —ᶜ huc F, *corr. to* huic (*apparently by scribe*). —ᵈ perquirant G. —
ᵉ nostrum Iesum Cristum filium tuum. Qui tecum vivit et regnat in unitate
Spiritus sancti Deus. Per omnia secula seculorum *add.* G. —ᶠ Resp. *om.* D G. —
ᵍ Resp. Amen *om.* B E F *a.*

118. [fol. 74v] Alia oratio ª.[160]

*Actiones ᵇ nostras, quesumus Domine, aspirando preveni et adiu-
vando ᶜ prosequere, ut cuncta nostra operatio et oratio ᵈ a ᵉ te semper
incipiat et per te cepta finiatur. Per dominum ᶠ.*[161]

118. ª Alia oratio *om.* B E. —ᵇ attiones E, acciones F. —ᶜ adiurando *a.* —
ᵈ operatio et oratio] operaris et omnis nostra actio D. —ᵉ ad *a.* —ᶠ nostrum
Iesum Cristum filium tuum. Qui tecum vivit et regnat *add.* G.

---

[160] *Oremus* later add. in marg. in hand 1 in *F*, and as part of the rubric in *G*, but not
add. in *a*.

[161] Charles V's autograph signature follows in *A*: "Ce livre du sacre dez rois de
France est a nous, Charles le Ve de notre nom, roy de France, et le fimes coriger,
ordener, escrire et istorier l'an MCCCLXV. Charles" (reproduced in Dewick, Plate 39,
and elsewhere). This is followed (fols. 74v–80r) by the oaths of sundry royal officers
(fols. 83v–87r in *B* and fols. 161v–163v in *D*). Dewick, in publishing them (ed. *g*, col.
54–62), noted (col. 91) that they are in a different hand from the two coronation
ordines, but T. Julian Brown, although initially thinking that these additions were written in a hand different from that of the remainder of the manuscript, concluded that
the entire manuscript was copied by a single scribe (letter of 17 August 1976). In *D*,
they are followed by a list of the places in the basilica of Saint-Denis where the tombs
of saints buried in that church are located.

Ordo of Louis XI

Date: 15 August 1461 and 1478
Other names: Treatise of Jean Foulquart (Schramm)

Introduction

Jean Foulquart, who was a municipal official of the city of Reims, *procureur syndic de l'échevinage*, wrote in 1478 a brief treatise on the obligations of the *échevins* of Reims at the time of various ceremonies.[1] His work contains many details concerning the coronation of Louis XI on 15 August 1461, including the whole of an ordo that is indubitably the ordo followed on that occasion.[2] He translated the rubrics, but left the formulas in Latin. Pierre Varin published Foulquart's treatise in 1843 (edition *a*). Varin omitted all but the incipits of the liturgical texts, however, so the full text of the ordo has never been published previously.

The ordo is an amalgam of the Last Capetian Ordo (Ordo XXII A) and the Ordo of Charles V (Ordo XXIII); all its formulas figure in one of those two ordines.[3] The liturgy is basically that of the Last Capetian Ordo, to which are added two series of rubrics and formulas from the Ordo of Charles V: nos. 7–17 at the beginning of the ordo (= Ordo XXIII,1–10), and nos. 28 and 34 (= Ordo XXIII,23 and 33). The formulas in the queen's ordo mirror the Last Capetian Ordo exactly; the ordo omits all the additions made for the coronation of Jeanne de Bourbon in 1364. Taking into account the changes necessitated by the omission of many prayers in Charles V's ordo, Foulquart's translations of the rubrics up through the prayers that follow the consecration, i.e., nos. 7–45, closely match the rubrics in Charles V's ordo. Thereafter, the ordo's rubrics tend to be drawn primarily from the Last Capetian Ordo, although here, too, some of the readings were taken from the Ordo of Charles V—the two ordines

---

[1] Pierre Varin (ed. *a*, p. 559), referred to Foulquart as a "clerc de l'échevinage," which is the term that Foulquart himself uses (MS *A*, fol. 22r), but Reims, Bibl. mun., MS 1490, no. 5, p. 16, called him a "procureur sindic de l'echevinage," as does a seventeenth-century marginal note in manuscript *A*, fol. 22r. There is a manuscript biography of Foulquart in Reims, Bibl. mun., MS 1648, fols. 1–14.

[2] A text published by Godefroy, 1: 172–75, gives some additional information about this coronation, mostly details concerning the participants.

[3] The Synoptic Table of Ordines XXII–XXV (pp. 621–24) provides a quick survey of the liturgical content of Foulquart's ordo.

were interwoven in ways that are far too complex to describe in detail here.[4]

Identifying the manuscript sources of the ordo is no easy matter, for they are nearly all lost. The rubrics are of no help because in this ordo they are in French rather than in the Latin of its sources. Therefore, only differences in the liturgical formulas can help identify the source manuscripts. Knowing the history of some lost manuscripts does help, nonetheless, and this history makes it likely that the two major sources were the *livre bleu*, the Reims cathedral's authoritative copy of the Last Capetian Ordo (Ordo XXII A, lost MS *2*), and the Saint-Denis copy of Charles V's ordo (Ordo XXIII, lost MS *3*). Still, the problem is compounded by the likelihood that the Ordo of Charles V was itself taken in part from the *livre bleu*. Where the readings of Louis XI's ordo are identical with those in Charles V's ordo, they tend to be those of the cathedral's *livre rouge* (Ordo XXIII, lost MS *4*), which, as I have explained elsewhere, had to have been based upon the Saint-Denis copy of Charles V's ordo (Ordo XXIII, lost MS *3*).[5] If the readings are in both the Last Capetian Ordo and the Ordo of Charles V, they are usually the readings of the Last Capetian Ordo's $C\ F\ G_1\ J\ O$ group, i.e., of those manuscripts descended from that ordo's lost MS x^6.[6] This is, indeed, one reason for believing that that lost manuscript x^6 was the *livre bleu*.

One piece of evidence that the Last Capetian Ordo largely defined Louis XI's ordo is in the prayer of consecration, *Omnipotens sempiterne Deus creator et gubernator*, where Louis XI's ordo reads "in regem eligimus." All manuscripts of the Last Capetian Ordo read "in regnum pariter eligimus" (Ordo XXIIA,25), but a late medieval hand wrote "regem" in the margin at this passage, showing that the word "regnum" was changed to "regem" at some time.[6] Both readings are very different

---

[4] Foulquart's translation sometimes adds details to the rubrics and sometimes omits parts of them. Foulquart was surely responsible for many of these differences, but others may have been in his Latin source.

[5] Jackson, "The *livres bleu* and *rouge*." I checked some of the readings from the *livre rouge* group of Charles V's ordo against those in Foulquart's ordo to see if the *livre rouge* was in use already in 1461, and the outcome of my investigation was negative. Some of the formulas in the *livre rouge* are not in the Ordo of Louis XI. I argue in "The *livres bleu* and *rouge*" that the *livre rouge* was contemporary with Foulquart's text (i.e., 1478). Even if my argument there is correct, the *livre rouge* did not provide the text of the ordo in Foulquart's treatise. Some passages that are in the *livre rouge*, but not in other manuscripts of Charles V's ordo, are in Foulquart's ordo, but others are not. Either those passages were in marginal additions in a source of Foulquart's ordo, or they were added to the *livre rouge* from Foulquart's ordo.

[6] Ordo XXII A, n. 51.

from the reading in Charles V's ordo (no. 39), "in huius regni regem pariter eligimus" (two manuscripts substitute "regere" for "regni"). Number 61 adopts the readings of the Last Capetian Ordo rather than the Ordo of Charles V, and the instruction added in no. 76 in Charles V's ordo is omitted here in no. 62.

Confirmation that the *livre bleu* was the copy of the Last Capetian Ordo used in preparing Louis XI's ordo is provided by the prayer, *Omnipotens Deus det tibi* (no. 63). The prayer first appears in the French ceremony in a marginal addition to MS *G* (which was in the Reims cathedral) of Ordo XV,35; it is there presented in two paragraphs, the second beginning with the words "Omnipotens benedicat tibi." It is a single paragraph in the Last Capetian ordo (Ordo XXII A,49) and in Charles VIII's ordo (Ordo XXV,133), but Charles V's ordo treats it as two separate prayers (Ordo XXIII,74). Louis XI's ordo is the only ordo that does not have the second paragraph (or part). A marginal note after the words "Deus erit adiutor tuus," on an eighteenth-century copy of Charles V's ordo (Ordo XXIII, MS *L*) explains why. The note states that "in the cathedral's *livre bleu* this prayer ends here." This not only explains this peculiarity of Louis XI's ordo, but also it provides almost certain proof that the *livre bleu* was consulted during the preparation of this ceremony.[7]

The ordo's text was put together from more than two sources, though. Some differences (e.g., the omission or transposition of words) between Louis XI's ordo and the two earlier ordines can be explained by scribal error, but others prove that other manuscripts were consulted in 1461. For example, Louis XI's ordo adds the words "per rectum exhibere debet" to the end of the episcopal *petitio* and the royal *promissio* (nos. 21–22). The phrase is found in no surviving manuscript of either the Last Capetian Ordo or Charles V's ordo. On the other hand, it is in the *promissio* of all manuscripts of both the Ratold Ordo (Ordo XV,3) and the Ordo of 1250 (Ordo XXI,10, which was probably copied from a lost Reims manuscript), as well as in the *petitio* of some of the Ratold Ordo's manuscripts (Ordo XV,2). The Ordo of Louis XI was, therefore, very carefully put together, and the selection of texts strongly suggests that the work was done by clerics. The effort expended in producing it was surely occasioned by Louis XI's coronation in 1461, not by Jehan Foulquart's desire to produce a complete coronation ordo.

The original manuscript of Foulquart's treatise has been lost, and manuscript *A* is an early seventeenth-century copy of it. The manuscript

---

[7] Reims, Bibl. mun., MS 1485, no. 3, p. 28: "dans le Livre bleu de la Cathedrale cette Oraison finit ici."

does contain all the liturgical texts of the ordo, but they are somewhat faulty, for the scribe made a number of obvious errors.

Manuscripts *B*, *C*, and *D* omit most of Foulquart's text. Manuscript *B* is the source of both *C* and *D*. Manuscript *D* was copied either from *C* or directly from *B*. The copyist of *B* modernized almost all the spelling and some of the language of the three manuscripts, and there would be no reason to retain the readings of any of these three manuscripts if *B* did not appear to be derived, independently of *A*, from lost manuscript *1*.

This is not an edition of Foulquart's entire treatise. I begin at that point in Foulquart's treatise that treats of the city's immediate preparations for the coronation of Louis XI. The translation of the ordo's rubrics begins with no. 7. The edition concludes with the addition concerning the peers at the end of the ordo.

Lost manuscripts

1—Reims, repository unknown, but probably the municipal archives. 1478.

Manuscripts

A—Paris, Bibl. nat., MS fran. 8334, fols. 47r–70v (Foulquart's entire treatise is on fols. 22r–77r). Formerly anc. suppl. fran. 1515². 1626. Copied from lost manuscript *1*. This is the only surviving manuscript that contains all the liturgical texts. The manuscript, along with MS 8335, is a collection of copies of pieces intended for a history of Reims, sent to André Duchesne by Jean Rogier l'Aîné. Description: Omont, *Catalogue général de l'ancien supplément français*, 1: 222. See Plate 31.

B—Reims, Bibl. mun., MS 1651 (nouv. fonds), fols. 11v–14r. Nos. 1 to middle of no. 11, 67–81, and 84–87 only. Eighteenth century. Copied from lost manuscript *1*. Description: Loriquet, *Reims*, 2: 822.

C—Reims, Bibl. mun., MS 1489 (nouv. fonds), no. 9, fols. 193v–197v. Eighteenth century. Nos. 1 to middle of no. 11, 67–81, and 84–87 only. Copied from *B*. Description: Loriquet, *Reims*, 2: 694.

D—Reims, Bibl. mun., MS 1490 (nouv. fonds), no. 5, pp. 16–23 (preceded by some introductory comments concerning preparations for the ceremony). Eighteenth century. Nos. 5 to middle of no. 11, 67–81, and 84–87. Copied from *B* or *C*. Description: Loriquet, *Reims*, 2: 695–96.

Editions

a—Pierre Varin, *Archives administratives de la ville de Reims: Collection de pièces inédites pouvant servir à l'histoire des institutions dans l'intérieur de la cité,* Collection de documents inédits sur l'histoire de France: Première série: Histoire politique, 3 vols. (Paris: Crapelet, 1839–1848), 2, part 1: 566–75, from *A.* Nearly the whole of Foulquart's treatise is on pp. 559–79.

Principles of the Edition

The text is from manuscript *A,* the only surviving manuscript that contains the complete text. The paragraphing and sentences are from the manuscript. The manuscript is almost entirely without punctuation; I retain much of Varin's punctuation (although I do delete a number of his excessive commas), but not his sentences (he sometimes divided the manuscript's sentences). The scribe of *A* had much difficulty reading his source, and there are a number of errors in his transcription of both the Latin and the French texts. Many of his abbreviations are like none other that I have seen and appear to have been traced from the source; in expanding these abbreviations, I simply provide the correct text if the manuscript appeared to permit that. If letters or words were omitted, I supplied them between square brackets, at the same time noting *B*'s reading in those passages that are in *B.* I corrected other errors, giving the original in each case in a variant, if possible, or in a footnote. Some of the erroneous readings do appear in manuscripts of other *ordines,* nonetheless, and it is possible that *A*'s source was faulty, and it is even more likely that it was difficult to read. (Also, an erroneous reading sometimes provides a clue as to the appearance of a scribe's manuscript source; see n. 23 below for an instance where the scribe apparently traced his source.) The copyist did modernize some of the spellings, particularly in the Latin texts; his modernizations are retained, but not his occasional accents. He always wrote *atout* (= *avec*) as two words (*a tout*), and he wrote *apres* as one or two words (*apres* or *a pres*); both *atout* and *apres* have always been rendered as one word. The scribe corrected his copy in a number of places; few of these corrections are noted. Both *sainct* and *saint* etc. are found in the manuscript, but *sainct* is far more common, so abbreviations are expanded with *c.* Likewise, there is only a single instance of *autre,* but many of *aultre,* so abbreviations of this word are expanded with *l.* In some nouns the scribe appears to have omitted the letters *ti* so that, for example, *sanctificatione* in no. 71 looks like *sanctificaone,* but this is only a scribal peculiarity, and I spell the words out. The word *quesumus* is abbreviated in all except three instances, when it is spelled out once as *quesumus* and twice as *quaesumus;* I expand the abbreviations without the diphthong because that is the common fifteenth-century spelling.

The original manuscript of Foulquart's treatise was presumably still in Reims in the eighteenth century, and *B* is an independent copy of it. Some of *B*'s readings supply evidence of the original reading of the text, thus correcting a few errors in *A*. In most cases *B* gives only the incipit of liturgical texts; these are noted. The scribe of *B* often modernized spelling; these modernizations are not noted. No variants are retained from *C* or *D* because they are descended from *B*.

ORDO XXIV

A B C

1. [fol. 47r] Avant[8] que le roy vienne pour soy sacrer, et de la plus tost apres qu'on est adverty du trespas de son predecesseur roy, ceulx qui sont commis a l'office de fruiterie, doivent a chacune porte de la ville renouveller et faire respendre de neuf les armes du roy ; et a celle au moings par ou il doibt entrer doibt estre faict, et mis tout en hault, un grand estandart desdictes armes.

2. On faict aussy volontiers aucuns misteres, [fol. 47v] sans parler, qu'on penst[a] debvoir estre plaisant au roy, de[9] lieux plus convenables en la ville, par ou il doibt passer le jour qu'il faict son entree pour estre sacré ; lesquelz se font aux despens du sacre[10] ; et ainsy fust faict audict sacre du roy Loys [XI] ; et fust advancé argent par le recepveur du sacre a ceulx qui se firent, en promettant de leur restituer le surplus qu'ilz y frairoient.

2. [a] peust A.

3. Cedict jour qu'il[a] faict son entree, il doibt avoir quatres des plus notables hommes[b] de la ville, et esleuz par lesdictes eschevins, a leur conseil, dont le prevost de l'eschevinage doibt estre l'ung, qui luy vont au devant, a la porte par laquelle il faict sadicte entree, portent le poesles[11] sur luy depuis ladicte porte jusques en l'eglise de[c] Nostre Dame, ou il va

---

[8] Foulquart's text does not have a title or subtitles. The coronaton text is preceded (fols. 35v–47r) by the first part of Foulquart's treatise on the obligations of the *échevins* of Reims at the time of a coronation ceremony (printed in Varin, ed. *a*, 559–67). Fols. 22r–35v are devoted to the *échevins*' duties at other ceremonies.

[9] Varin (ed. *a*) suggested that *de* should be read *ès*.

[10] *se font aux despens du sacre* underlined in *A*.

[11] The word appears to be written *presles*, which could be a scribal error, although sometimes the scribe's *o* does look like an *r*. The letter *l* is a correction that renders illegible what the scribe originally wrote. Varin (ed. *a*) saw that the word's fifth letter had been corrected, and he read *prestes*, which I think is wrong; he suggested correcting it to *poëles*. The word is spelled *pale* at the beginning of no. 4, and MS *B* reads *pale*.

descendre ; et ainsy fust faicte audict sacre dudict roy Loys [XI] ; et furent le[s] IIII qui le porterent, Anthoine de Zelandre[d], lors cappitaine de Reims, maistre Jehan Chardon, bailly de Reims, maistre Nicol Sanguiun[e], bailly de chappitre, et Raulde du Molins[f], prevost de l'eschevinage.

3. [a] que le B. —[b] hommes *om.* B. —[c] de *om.* B. —[d] Holande B. —[e] Jacquemin B. —[f] Baulde du Moulinet B, Rauldé du Molins *a* (*read* Baude du Molinet).

4. [fol. 48r] Ledicte pale qu'ils portent[a] sur luy avoit esté emprunté en l'eglize de Reims ; et en icelle eglize fust pris par aulcuns des gens du roy, qui l'emporterent ; et en paierent les commis a la fruiterie, XIII livres tournois[b] a ladicte eglize ; et pour eviter telz empructz, que ne semble pas estre fortz honnestes pour telz choses, il m'est advis, soubz correction, que bon seroit que messieurs les eschevins, quant ils auroient[c] le conte de la recepte de la taille dudict sacre, qui encore n'est rendu, s'il y a aulcuns deniers de reste, en fissent faire ung bel[d] et honnestes, qui serviroit a plusieurs sacres, si mestier estoit, et se garderoit en l'eschevinage ; et serois d'opinion, soubz correction qui[e] vouldroit faire a mon advis, qu'il fust faict[f] de beau velours pers, semee[g] de petite fleurs de lis, comme sont les chappes du roy Charles quinte, qu'il donna a ladicte[h] eglize de Reims ; et que les quatre bastons en fussent aussy vestuz et couvertz[i], de moings peinctz, en ceste forme ; et que sur chacun[j] desdictz bastons y eust ung ange[k] portant[12] les deux les armes du roy, [fol. 48v] et les deux[l] aultres les armes de la ville ; si en soit faict au bon plaisir de messieurs les eschevins[m], auxquelz en est l'auctorité.[13]

4. [a] porterent B. —[b] tournois *om.* B. —[c] auroient *corr. from* auroit *by scribe* A; ovront B, auront *a.* —[d] fassent faire ung bel B. —[e] en *add.* B. —[f] faict *om.* B. —[g] parsemé B. —[h] ladicte *om.* B. —[i] couverts et vetus B. —[j] chacuns A. —[k] angel B. —[l] deux *om.* B. —[m] au bon plaisir de mesdits seigneurs les echevins B.

A B C D

5. Le[14] roy ainsy conduict et mené, comme dict est, soubz ledict pasle, jusques audict lieu de l'eglize de Reims, doibt illecq descendre et

---

[12] Corrected from *ange__ port* (the first word is partly illegible) to *ange portant* in *A*; *B* reads *angel*, and that must have been what the scribe of *A* wrote originally.

[13] Foulquart's proposal for the poles supporting the canopy is particularly attractive because the cathedral of Reims is *sui generis* in that it is surrounded by famous statues of guardian angels and also because the four angels would visually depict the prayer that calls upon them to surround and protect the king (no. 57). The *échevins* apparently liked the idea, for it was implemented at Charles VIII's coronation (Ordo XXV,10), but, unfortunately, the king's men also liked it (Ordo XXV,21).

[14] Varin (ed. *a*) here added a subtitle, "S'ensuit le cérémonial du sacre." Schramm,

estre receu processionnellement, tant des chanoines, comme des autres eglizes conventuelles, et conduict au coeur d'icelle eglize, au devant de[a] grand aultel, la[b] ou il doibt faire son oraison ; et icelle faict doibt aller au palais archiepiscopal, en la[c] chambre qui luy est preparé[d], et illecq soy tenir et disposer a faire, pour son sainct sacre et couronnement recepvoir, selon que le mistere le requiert, et comme dict et declarez sera cy apres[e] ; et se son[f] plaisir est de soupper, ou de faire collation, dont luy doibt estre appresté[g] comme il appartient.

5. [a] du B. —[b] la *om.* B. —[c] sa B. —[d] preparee B. —[e] et comme dict et declarez sera cy apres *om.* B. —[f] bon *add.* B. —[g] à pret B.

6. Assçavoir est, que ledict sacre et couronnement se doibt faire ung jour de dimanche, ou ung jour de feste [fol. 49r] solannelle, pour tant de[a] grande saincteté du mistere ; duquel, et des circonstans, depuis que le roy est venu, receu et conduict au pallais archiepiscopal, comme dict est, la declaration s'ensuit.[15]

6. [a] tant de] cause de la B.

7. Premierement, doibt estre preparé ung siege en façon d'eschafaut, aussez hault, contige ou[a] joignant du coeur de l'eglize[b], par deshors, assis tout au milieu, entre les deux coeurs, auquel on monte par degrez et montee qui y sont faictz par dedans ledict coeur ; et y a en pavé[c] d'iceluy coeur certaines petites pierres qui ce lieuvent, pour y ficher et mettre au[d] [16] pieces de bois portantz ladicte montee ; lesquelles pier[r]es se peuvent facilement cognoistre, pour ce que audict coeur n'en y a nulz semblables, ne ainsy petites[e] ; et iceluy eschafaultz sont tenuz de faire faire[f] messieurs du chappistre de ladicte eglize, en[g] leurs despence, ou de la fabricque d'icelle eglize, et les defaire, et preparer[h] les aultres apres ledict sacre ; et doibt estre sy grand ledict siege, ou eschafault, que le[s][i] pairs de France y puissent estre, et seoir avec le roy[j], si besoing est.

7. [a] contigu et B. —[b] de l'eglize] de laditte eglise B. —[c] en pavé] au pied B. — [d] au] au sus les B. —[e] n'y en a nulles semblables ni aussi petites B. —[f] faire *om.* B. —[g] a B. —[h] et les defaire et preparer] et de le faire et de reparer B. — [i] le A B. —[j] avec le roy *om.* B.

8. [fol. 49v] Doibvent aussy lesdictz de chappistre, ou leurdicte fabricque, faire mettre sablon a suffisance dedans ladicte eglize, pour y

---

"Ordines-Studien II," 51, who did not see many of the manuscripts, was misled by Varin's manufactured titles. *D* omits all the text to this point, and summarizes it in a single paragraph.

[15] Everything up to here is Foulquart's text. His translation of the ordo follows.

[16] Varin (ed. *a*), who did not know *B*'s reading (*au sus les*), suggested that this should read *aulcunes.*

pouvoir porter a cheval la saincte ampolle, si[a] mestier est, jusques a
l'entree du coeur.[17]

8. [a] se B.

9. Le samedy, vueille du dimanche, ou aultre jour veuille de la feste
solennelle que le roy doibt estre sacré, apres complie[a], la garde de ladicte
eglize se bail et commet[b] aux gardes qu'il plaist au roy d'y commettre,
avec les propres coustres, clercs et laiz d'icelle eglize, et doibt le roy, sans
bruict, ou plus grande[c] silence de la nuict, venir en ladicte eglise faire son
oraison, et la, s'il luy plaist, veiller ung peu de temps en oraisons[d].

9. [a] complies B. —[b] se commet et baille B. —[c] grand B. —[d] un peu de tems en
oraison B.

10. Quand on sonne les matines, les gardes mises de par le roy, qui
gardent l'entree de l'eglize, toutz les aultres portaux et entrees d'icelle
fermees et bien barees, doivent estre prestz a honnorablement et diligemment[a] mettre dedans les chanoinnes et[b] chappelains et clerz de l'e-
glize, toutefois[c] que besoing leur sera.

[fol. 50r] Les matines cestuy[d] jour se chantent en[e] la maniere accoustumé, et tantost qu'elles sont dictes, on doibt sonner prime, qui se doibt
chanter des le poing[f] du jour.

10. [a] et diligemment *om.* B. —[b] et *om.* B. —[c] toutes les fois B. —[d] celui B. —
[e] a: B. —[f] point B.

11. Apres que prime est chantee, et avant que l'eau beneiste se face,
le roy doibt venir a l'eglize avec les archevesques, evesques, princes et
barrons, et aultres qu'il luy plaira mettre, et faire entrer dedans ladicte
eglize[a] ; et doibvent estre les sieges preparés et disposez entour l'aultel,
d'une part et d'aultre, ou les archevesques et evesques doibvent seoir
honnorablement, et premiers les pairs de France, selon cest ordre : c'est
assçavoir, premierement l'evesque de Laon ; apres[b] l'evesque de Beauvais[c] ; apres, l'evesque de Langres ; apres[b], celuy de Chaalons ; et le
dernier celuy de Noyon. Et les aultres evesques de la province de Reims
doibvent seoir au dessoubz, entre l'hostel et le roy, a l'opposite de l'hostel, et non pas arriere du roy, ne trop serees, ne trop arriere l'ung de
l'aultre ;[18]

---

[17] I do not know of any coronation at which a horse was ridden into the church;
the custom was for the consecrator to meet the ampulla's bearer at the cathedral's
main portal.

[18] Before skipping to the beginning of the queen's ordo, *B* adds:
"Le reste des ceremonies, prieres et oraisons du sacre et couronnement du roi,
ainsi que le tout est amplement contenu au livre intitulé Ordo ad consecrandum et

A

et doibvent les chanoinnes de l'eglize de Reims, en belle procession, atout deux croix, les cierges, [fol. 50v] l'encensoir et l'encens, aller querir le roy au palais archepiscopal, pour venir a l'eglize, comme dict est; et doivent estre en ladicte procession l'evesque de Laon et l'evesque de Beauvais, qui sont les deux premiers pairs de France evesques, ayantz des reliquaires de sainct pendant a leurs col; et en la grande chambre dudict palais doivent recepvoir le prince, en roy, pour consacrer; lequel il doibvent trouver assiz, et comme couché sur le lict qui doibt estre paré decentement, comme il apartient; et quand ilz sont venuz et appliquez a la presence du prince, l'evesque de Laon doibt dire l'oraison qui s'en-suict.

11. ᵃ avec les archevesques ... ladicte eglize *om.* B. —ᵇ en apres B. —ᶜ et *add.* B.

12. Oratio.

Omnipotens sempiterne Deus, qui famulum tuum N. regis fasti-gioᵃ dignatus es sublimareᵇ, tribue quesumus ei, ut ita in huius seculi cursu multorum in commune salutem disponat, quatenus a veritatis tue tramitae non recedat. Per dominumᶜ nostrum etc.

12. ᵃ fastidio A. —ᵇ sublimere A. —ᶜ dominum] Annum A.

13. [fol. 51r] Tantost que ladicte oraison est dicte, lesdictz deux evesques doivent prendre le roy honnorablement, l'ung a la dextre et l'aultre a la senestre, et le doivent mener reveremment a l'eglize, chan-tant avec lesdictz chanoinne[s] le respond qui s'ensuict.

Respond.

Ecce ego mitto angelum meum, qui precedat te et custodiat semper.

Observa et audi vocem meam, et inimicus eroᵃ inimicis tuis et affligentes te affligam, et precedet te angelus meus.

13. ᵃ inimicis oro A.

---

coronadum regem Franciae in ecclesiae Remensis, nous ne les avons pas transcrites ici, parce qu'elles se trouvent audit livre imprimé qui commence par ces mots : Primo quod paratur solium, in modum eschafaudi, aliquantulum eminens contiguum exterius chori [*read* choro] ecclesie." The printed edition in question is doubtless Ordo XXIII, ed. *a*, which was copied from the cathedral's *livre rouge*.

The writer then jumps to no. 66 below and slightly paraphrases it before copying no. 67:

"Ces ceremonies et prieres du sacre du roi etant achevees, avant qu'on chante l'yntroite de la messe, si la reine est illec presente, pour etre ointe et benie comme le roi, auquel cas, avant que chanter ledit introite, l'archeveque de Reims doit vacquer a ladite onction et benediction de la reine en la maniere qui s'ensuit."

14. Vers. *Israel, si me audieris, non erit in te deus recens [neque adorabis] deum alienum, ego enim Dominus.*

Observa etc.

15. Ce dict, tout le peuple suyvant le roy derriere ; quand ilz viennent a l'huys de l'eglize, ladicte procession y doibt arrester, et doibt dire l'evesque de Beauvais, s'il est present, l'oraison qui s'ensuict.

Oratio.

[fol. 51v] *Deus, qui scis genus humanum nulla virtute posse subsistere, concede propitius, ut famulus tuus N., quem populo tuo voluisti praeferri, ita tuo fulciatur adiutorio, quatenus quibus potuit praeesse valeat et prodesse. Per dominum* etc.

16. Ladicte oraison achevee, ilz entrent[a] dedans l'eglize, et doibvent les chanoinnes precedentz chanter, jusques a l'huis du coeur, l'antienne qui s'ensuict.

Antiphona.

Domine, in virtute tua laetabitur rex etc.

16. [a] entient A.

17. Et celle anthiesne dicte et finie, l'archevesque de Reims, attendant devant l'austel en ladicte eglize, a qui le roy doibt estre presenté reveremment par lesdictz evesques, pour consacrer en roy, doibt dire ou il est attendant devant ladicte aultel, l'oraison qui s'ensuict.

[fol. 52r] Oratio.

Omnipotens sempiterne Deus, coelestium terrestriumque moderator, qui famulum tuum N. ad regni fastig[i]um dignatus es provehere, concede, quesumus, ut a cunctis adversitatibus liberatus, et ecclesiasticae pacis dono muniatur, et ad aeternae pacis gaudia te donante pervenire mereatur. Per dominum etc.

18. Et ladicte oraison parfaicte, les dessusdictz evesques doivent mener le roy, pour consacrer, en la chaire qui luy est preparé au devant de la chaire dudict archevesque. En icelle chaire doit seoir jusques a ce que ledict archevesque vienne apres, atout la saincte ampolle, comme dict sera cy apres, devant lequel, quant il l'apporte, le roy se doibt lever en grande reverence.

Quand le roy est en ladicte chaire, avant que l'abbé de Sainct Remy ait apporté la saincte ampolle et avant que les archevesques luy voize au devant, on a accoustumé de faire l'eau beneiste, en attendant ; laquelle [fol. 52v] faicte, ledict archevesque en donne au roy et aux prelatz d'entour.

19. Comment on doibt aporter la saincte ampolle.

Assçavoir est que le roy doibt prendre et eslire de ses barons, des meilleurs et plus soitz,[19] et des plus seurs, loyaulx aussy, jusques au nombre de quatre au moings, et des le poinct du jour les envoyer en l'eglize de Sainct Remy de Reims pour avoir la saincte ampolle qui se y garde empres le precieux corps dudict sainct Remy ; lesquelz barons doivent faire serment, jurer et promettre[a] a l'abbé et a l'eglize dudict Sainct Remy, que ladicte saincte ampolle, de bonne foy, ilz conduiront et reconduiront en ladicte eglize de Sainct Remy ; et ce faict, entre prime et tierce, doibvent venir les moinnes dudict Sainct Remy processionnellement, atout les croix et les cierges, avec ladicte saincte ampolle, laquelle l'abbé dudict lieu doibt porter en tresgrande reverence, soubz une courtine ou paesler de soye, [fol. 53r] eslevé sur quatre perches et porteez de IIII moines vestuz d'aubes ; et eulx venuz au devant de l'eglize Sainct Denys, ou jusques au grand portail de l'eglize, pour la compression de la tourbe du peuple, l'archevesque de Reims, accompagné des aultres archevesques et evesques et barons et aussy des chanoinnes de l'eglize, se faire se peult, vestuz [d']ung surplis, d'une estolle dessus et d'une chappe solenne, atout sa mytre et sa crosse, la croix precedente, doibt aller au devant de ladicte saincte ampolle et la recepvoir de la main dudict abbé, en luy promettant de bonne foy de luy rendre apres ledict sacre ; et en ceste estat la doibt, en grande reverence du peuple, porter a l'aultel, ledict abbé et aulcuns de ses moyennes le compagnant aussy ; et les aultres moyennes doibvent attendre en l'eglize de Sainct Denys, ou en la chappelle de Sainct Nicolas en l'Hostel[b] Dieu, jusques a ce que ledict sacre soit parfaict, et tant qu'on rapporte ladicte saincte ampolle.

19. [a] permettre A. —[b] l'Aultel A.

20. [fol. 53v] A ladicte saincte ampolle ainsy receue et porte[e] par ledict archevesque audict grand hostel, iceluy archevesque se doibt preparer a la messe avec ses diacres et soubdiacres, et vestir les plus notables et riches ornementz de l'eglize, et son pallion dessus ; et en estat pontifical[a], accompagné de deulx de ses suffragantz, venir processionellement a l'aultel, en la maniere accoustumé ; et quant il vient pres, le roy se doibt lever de sadicte chaire et luy faire la reverence.

20. [a] pontificat A.

21. Quand ledict archevesque est ainsy venu a l'autel que dict est, il doibt requerir et demander au roy, pour toutes les eglize[s] qui luy sont subgectes, ce qui s'ensuict en latin.

A vobis perdonari petimus, ut unicuique de nobis, et ecclesiis

---

[19] *soitz* is very clear ; Varin (ed. *a*) suggested, doubtless correctly, that the word should be *fortz*.

nobis commissis canonicis,[20] *previlegium ac debitam legem atque ius-*
ticiam conservetis et defensionem exhibeatis, sicut rex in suo regno
unicuique episcopo et ecclesiae sibi commissae peb rectum exhibere
debet.

22. [fol. 54r] A ceste requeste le roy doibt respondre en la maniere
qui s'ensuit, en addressant sa parolle audict archevesque et aux aultres
prelatz de sa province illecq pressentz.

*Promitto vobis et perdono, quia*ᵃ *unicuique de vobis, et ecclesiis*
vobis commissis canonicis, previlegium et debitam legem atque ius-
ticiam servabo, et defensionem, quantum potero, exhibebo, Domino
adiuvante, sicut rex in suo regno unicuique episcopo et ecclesiae sibi
commissae per rectum exhibere debet.

22. ᵃquae A.

23. Apres que le roy a faict ladicte promesse et serment, il faict
encor[e] et jure es presence desdictz prelatz et des pairs et barrons de
France illecq presens a tout le peuple de son royaulme, ce qui s'ensuict.

Haec populo christiano et mihi subdito in Christi nomine
promitto: in primis, ut ecclesiae Dei omnis populus christianus veram
*pacem nostro arbitrio in omni tempore servet. Item, ut omnes*ᵃ *rapaci-*
tates et omnes iniquitates omnibus gradibus interdicam. Item, [ut] in
omnibus iudiciis aequitatem et misericordiam praecipiam, ut [fol.
54v] mihi et vobis indulgeat suam misericordiam clemens et miseri-
cors Dominus. Item, [ut] de terra mea ac iurisdictione mihi subdita
*universos hereticos ab ecclesia denotatos*ᵇ *pro viribus bona fide exter-*
minare studebo. Haec omnia supradicta firmo iuramento.[21]

---

[20] All other ordines read *canonicum*, both here and below in no. 22. Someone
doubtless misread the source; given the other errors in MS *A*, that person is more
likely to have been the seventeenth-century copyist than Foulquart.

[21] On 14 April 1482, Louis XI, who was then at Tournus, sent a copy of this oath to
the Parlement of Paris to be recorded in its registers. Louis XI's copy and original
cover letter survive in Paris, Arch. nat., X¹ᴬ 9318, nos. 152 (the letter) and 153 (the
oath). The letter was published by Joseph Vaesen and Etienne Charvay, *Lettres de
Louis XI publiée pour la Société de l'Histoire de France*, 11 vols. (Paris: Librairie
Renouard, 1883–1909), 9: 206–207, and the oath in 9: 207–208, n. 2. Because there are
some errors in that transcription of the oath, I reproduce it here from the manuscript,
retaining its capitalization, but adding punctuation (there is none):

"Hec populo Christiano michi subdito in christi nomine promicto, Ut ecclesie dei
omnis populus christianus veram pacem vestro arbitrio servet omni tempore.

Item, ut omnes Rapacitates et Iniquitates ab omnibus gradibus Interdicam.

Item, ut in omnibus Iudiciis equitatem et misericordiam precipiam, Ut michi et
Vobis indulgeat suam misericordiam clemens et misericors deus.

Et en disant ces motz et faisant ledict serment, il doibt mettre la main sur le livre aux Evangiles et les baiser.

23. ᵃ eos A. —ᵇ deniatos A.

24. Les professions et sermentz dessusdictz faictz et jurez, comme dict est, on doibt incontinent commencer a chanter le cantique « Te Deum laudamus, » et tantost qu'il est commencé, deux archevesques ou evesques puis doibvent prendre le roy par les mains, et du lieu ou il a faict ledict serment, le mener devant ledict aultel, le plus pres que faire se peult bonnement ; et la se doibt le roy prosterner et tenir par terre jusques a la fin dudict cantique.

25. Il fault assçavoir sur ce pas que l'abbé de Sainct Denis en France doibt apporter audict sacre, de sadicte abbaye, les choses qui s'ensuivent, pour y servir comme sy [fol. 55r] apres sera dict, c'est assçavoir la couronne royal[e], l'espeeᵃ estant en son fourreau, les esperons dorez, le septre d'or aussy, et une vergette d'une coudee de longueur, ou environ, au sommet de laquelle y a une main d'ivoyr; semblablement des chausses de soye de couleur jacynthe, semees tout du long de fleurs de liz d'or, la robbe de semblable couleur, et semees comme lesdictes chausses, qui doibte estre en façon d'une tunicque que vest ung soubdiacre quant il veust servir a la messe.

25. ᵃ l'espés A.

26. Et ung manteau de semblable couleur et seinure²² aussy, qui est faict comme en la façon d'une chappe de soye, sans chapperon derriere ; toutes lesquelles choses iceluy abbé doibt preparer et mettre sur l'aultel,

---

Item, de terra mea ac Iuriditione michi subdita universos hereticos ab ecclesia denotatos pro viribus bona fide exterminare studebo.

Hec omnia supradicta firmo Iuramento."

Noteworthy here is the reading "vestro arbitrio servet omni tempore," every word of which is found only in one manuscript or another of Ordo XXII A,8. This is one of the proofs that Louis XI's ceremony was based in part upon the Last Capetian Ordo.

Copies of the oath that Louis XI sent to the Parlement of Paris are to be found in Paris, Bibl. nat. MS nouv. acq. fran. 7232, fol. 45r (and in manuscripts copied from that, e.g., Paris, Bibl. de l'Arsenal, MS 4227, fol. 38r); in Paris, Arch. nat. KK 1442, fol. 55r–v; and elsewhere. It was printed (with some errors) by Pierre Dupuy, *Traité de la majorité de nos rois et des régences du royaume* (Paris: Chez la Veuve Mathurin du Puis et Edme Martin, 1655), 232–33, whence it was reprinted (with an additional error) in François André Isambert et al., eds., *Recueil général des anciennes lois françaises*, 29 vols. (Paris: Belin-le-Prieur, 1822–33), 10: 458, no. 42 (which incorrectly states that the source was p. 354 rather than pp. 232–33). See also Jackson, *Vive le Roi*, 79 (= *Vivat rex*, 76).

²² Probably *seigniere*, "une sorte d'étoffe réticulée" (Godefroy, *Dictionnaire*, 7: 359).

tandis qu'on chante ledict canticque, se prepare, ne les a auparavant, soy tenir illecques les gardant.

27. Et ledict canticque chanté, le roy se lieve et despouille et met jus devant ledict autel toutz ses habitz, excepté une robbe de soye, qu'il a sur sa chemise [fol. 55v] aussy, et sadicte chemise aussy, qu'il retient; lesquelles robbes et chemises sont ouvertes et despinsees parfondement, et bien bas, devant et derriere, c'est assçavoir tenantz et fermantz a la poitrine et entre deux espaulle[s] a aurletz ou crapins d'argent.

Apres que le roy est ainssy despouillé que dict est, le grand et premier chambellan de France luy doibt mettre et chausser lesdictes chausses.

En apres le duc de Bourgoigne, comme premier pair de France lay, luy seinct et astreinct a ses piedz les esperons dessusdictz, et tantost apres les luy oste. Et avant que l'archevesque luy baille l'espee, il faict la benediction dessus et dict l'oraison qui s'ensuict.

28. Oratio.

Exaudi, quesumus Domine, preces nostras, et hunc gladium quo famulus tuus N. se accingi desiderat, maiestatis tuae dextera benedicere dignare, quatenus defensio atque protectio possit esse[a] *ecclesiarum, viduarum, orphanorum omniumque Deo servientium contra saevitiam paganorum, aliisque insidiantibus sit pavor,* [fol. 56r] *terror et formido. Per dominum.*

28. [a] possit esse] sit A.

29. La benediction faicte, ledict archevesque seul, et non aultre, doibt rendre au roy ladicte espee; et tantost qu'il l'a seinct, iceluy archevesque la deseinct et oste aussy, et la tire nue hors de sa gayne, met ladicte gaigne sur ledict aultel, et ladicte espee nue donne au roy en sa main, en disant ce qui s'ensuict.

30. Oratio.

Accipe hunc gladium cum Dei benedictione tibi collatum, in quo, per virtutem sancti Spiritus resistere et eicere[a] *omnes inimicos tuos valeas, et cunctos sanctae Dei ecclesiae adversarios regnumque tibi commissum tutari atque protegere castra Dei, per auxilium invictissimi triumphatoris*[b] *domini nostri Iesu Christi, qui cum Patre et Spiritu sancto vivit et regnat Deus per omnia secula etc.*

30. [a] et eicere] contra A. — [b] invictissime triumphatoris] invictissime triumphatores A.

31. En baillant au roy ladicte espee nue, apres que ledict archevesque a dict ce que dessus, le cuer[23] [chante] l'anthiesne qui s'ensuict.

---

[23] The reading *cuer* is not certain (the word looks like *crue*), but it is the most

[fol. 56v] Anthiesne.

Confortare et esto vir, et observa custodias Domini Dei tui, ut ambules in viis eius, et custodias ceremonias eius, et testimonia et iudic[i]a, et quocumque te verteris confirmet te Deus.

32. Apres que l'archevesque a baillé au roy l'espee, comme dict est, et qu'on chante ladicte anthiesne, iceluy archevesque dict l'oraison qui s'ensuict.

Oratio.

Deus qui providentia tua coelestia simul et terrena moderaris, propitiare christianissimo regi nostro, ut omnis hostium suorum fortitudo, virtute gladii spiritualis frangatur, ac te pro illo pugnante penitus conteratur. Per dominum.

33. Le roy doibt honnorablement recepvoir ladicte espee de la main dudict archevesque, apres la offrir et mettre sur l'aultel, sur lequel les archevesque la doibt reprendre, et rebaillir derechef au roy, qui incontinent la doibt reprendre et la bailler au senechal ou connestable de France, s'il est present, sinon a quelque baron qu'il luy plaist ; lequel depuis la en avant, tout au long du sacre et du service, et en [fol. 57r] retournant apres au palais archepiscopal pour disner, la doibt porter toute nue devant le roy.

34. Apres ces choses, l'archevesque doibt preparer l'onction en la maniere que je diray tantost ; et tandis qu'il la prepare sur l'aultel, le chantre de l'eglize doibt commencer a chanter, et le coeur doibt achever l'anthiesne qui s'ensuist.

Anthiesne.

Gentem Francorum inclitam simul cum rege nobili, beatus Remigius sumpto coelitus chrismate sacro, sanctificavit gurgite, atque Spiritus sancti plene ditavit munere.

35. La maniere de preparer l'onction.

Le chresme se met premierement de sur l'aultel, et puis l'archevesque doibt prendre sur ledict aultel la saincte ampolle que l'abbé de Sainct Remy a apporté, et d'icelle, atout une verjette d'or, tirer un peu de l'huille envoiee du ciel divinement, et incontinent le mesler de son doict avec le chresme preparé sur ladicte patene pour enoindre et consacrer le roy, qui seul entre toutz les aultres roys [fol. 57v] de la terre resplendist de ses glorieux privileges qu'il est singulierement enoinct et consacré d'huille envoyee des sainctz cieux divinement.

---

likely possibility. The scribe was probably unable to read his source and just traced it; if so, and if his tracing is fairly exact, the source must have been extremely difficult to read.

36. La sacree et saincte onction dont le roy doibt estre enoinct, preparee par l'archevesque, comme dict est, on doibt delasser les anneletz ou agrappins des vestemens du roy, devant et derrier, et se doibt mettre le roy a deux genoulx; et lors deux[a] archevesques doivent commencer la letanie et la dire jusques a ce pas, *Ut hunc famulum tuum*, et la cesser, et adoncque l'archevesque de Reims doibt dire sur le roy, devant qu'il l'oindre et sacre, les oraysons qui s'ensuivent, et doibt estre assiz ledict archevesque, aynsy qu'il est quand il sacre ung evesque.

36. [a] deusx A.

37. Oratio.

Te invocamus, Domine sancte Pater omnipotens, sempiterne Deus, ut hunc famulum tuum, quem tuae divinae animae dispensationis providentia in primordio plasmatum[a] usque in hunc presentem diem, iuvenili flore laetantem crescere concessisti, eum tuae pietatis dono ditatum plenumque gracia veritatis de die in diem coram Deo et hominibus ad meliora semper proficere facias, ut summi regiminis solium, graciae supernae largitate gaudens suscipiat, et misericordie tue muro ab hostium adversitate undique munitus, plebem sibi commissam cum[b] pace propitionis et virtute victoriae[c] foeliciter [fol. 58r] *regere mereatur. Per dominum.*

37. [a] peasmatum A. —[b] tum A. —[c] virtute victoriae] virtutis vigore A.

38. Oratio.

Deus, qui populis tuis virtute co[n]sulis et amore dominaris, da huic[a] famulo tuo N. spiritum sapientiae tuae cum regimine disciplinae, ut tibi toto corde devotus in regni regimine maneat semper idoneus, tuoque munere[b] ipsius temporibus securitas ecclesiae dirigatur et in tranquillitate devotio ecclesiastica permaneat, ut, in bonis operibus perseverans, ad aeternum regnum te duce valeat pervenire. Per dominum nostrum etc.

38. [a] hinc A. —[b] tuorumque numere A.

39. Oratio.

In diebus eius oriatur omnibus et aequitas et iusticia, amicis adiutorium, inimicis obstaculum, humilibus solatium, elatis correctio, divitibus doctrina, pauperibus pietas, peregrinis pacificatio, propriis in patria pax et securitas, unumquemque secundum suam mensuram moderate gubernans, seipsum sedulus regere discat, ut tua irrigatus compunctione toto[a] populo tibi placita prebere possit vitae exempla, et per [viam] veritatis cum grege gradiens sibi subdito opes frugales habundantur[b] *acquirat, simulque ad salutem non solum corporum, sed etiam cordium a te concessam, cuncta accipiat. Sicque*[c] *in te cogitatum animi*[24] *consiliumque*[d] *omne componens, plebis* [fol. 58v] *gubernacula cum pace simul*[e], *et sapientia semper invenire videatur. Teque auxilliante, presentis vitae prosperitatem et prolixitatem percipiat, et per temporalia*[25] *bona usque*[f] *ad summam senectutem perveniat, huiusque fragilitatis finem perfectum*[g], *ab omnibus vitiorum vinculis tuae pietatis largitate liberatus, et infinitae prosperitatis praemia perpetua angelorumque aeterna commercia*[h] *consequatur. Etc.*

> 39. [a] toti A. —[b] habundantur] huius autem A. —[c] concessam cuncta accipiat. Sicque] concessem cunctam accipiat seque A. —[d] conselumque A. —[e] scilicet A. —[f] usue A. —[g] finem perfectum] sine perfecta A. —[h] convercia A.

40. La consecracion du roy.
Oratio.

Omnipotens sempiterne Deus, creator et gubernator coeli et terrae, conditor [et] dispositor angelorum et hominem, rex regum et dominus dominantium, qui Abraham fidelem famulum tuum de hostibus triumphare fecisti, Moysi et Iosue[a] *populo tuo praelatis multiplicem victoriam tribuisti, humilem quoque*[b] *puerum tuum David regni fastigio sublimasti, eumque de ore leonis et de manu bestiae atque Goliae, sed et de gladio maligno Saul et omnium inimicorum eius liberasti, et Salomonem sapientiae pacisque ineffabili*[26] *munere ditasti, respice propitius* [fol. 59r] *ad preces nostrae humilitatis, et super hunc famulum tuum N., quem devotione supplici in regem elegimus*[c], *benedictionum tuarum dona multiplica, eumque dextera potentiae tuae semper et ubique circunda, quatenus praedicti Abrahae fidelitate firmatus*[d], *Moysi mansuetudine fretus, Iosue fortitudine munitus, David humilitate exaltatus, Salomonis sapientia decoratus, tibi in omnibus complaceat, et per tramitem iusticiae in offenso gressu semper incedat, et totius [regni] ecclesiam deinceps cum plebibus sibi annexis, ita enutriat*[e] *ac doceat, muniat et instruat, contraque omnes visibiles et invisibiles hostes idem potenter regaliterque tuae virtutis regimen administret,*[27] *ut regale solium videlicet Saxonum, Merciorum, Nordam, Chimbrorum*[f] *sceptra non deserat, sed ad pristinae fidei pacisque*

---

[24] *animi* is illegible in *A* and is probably traced from the source.

[25] On the reading *temporalia*, see n. 49 on manuscript *A* at this point in Ordo XXII A,24. The reading is also found in manuscripts of Ordo XV,8.

[26] In *A* the word *ineffabili* looks like *iudiffabili* with an abbreviation mark over the *d*.

[27] The manuscript's reading is uncertain, but *administret* is what it should read.

concordiam eorum animos, te opitulante, reformet, ut, utrorumque[g]
horum populorum debita subiectione fultus, et cum digno amore
glorificatus per longum vitae spatium paternae apicem gloriae tua[h]
miseracione unatim[i] *stabilire et gubernare mereatur, tuae quoque*
protectionis galaea[j] *munitus et scuto insuperabili iugiter protectus,*
armisque celestibus circundatus, optabilis[k] *victoriae* [fol. 59v] *trium-*
phum de hostibus foeliciter capiat, terroremque potentiae suae infi-
delibus[l] *inferat, et pacem militantibus laetanter reportet, virtutibus*
nec non quibus prefatos[m] *fideles tuos decorasti, multiplici honoris*
benedictione condecora, et in regimine regni sublimiter colloca, et
oleo graciae[n] *Spiritus sancti perunge. Per dominum* etc.

40. [a] Moysi et Josue] Moysias Iosiae A. —[b] quorum A. —[c] eleguims A. —[d] for-
matus A. —[e] erudiat A. —[f] Chombrorum A. —[g] utrorumsque A. —[h] gloriae
tua] ecclesiae tuae A. —[i] unatum A. —[j] a *add.* A. —[k] obtabilem A. —[l] infer-
tibus A. —[m] profatos A. —[n] colloca et oleo graciae] collocutur oleo quae A.

41. Quand ledict archevesque a dict ceste oraison, il doibt enoyndre
le roy de la saincte onction du chresme et de l'huille aportee divinement
des cieulz, ainsy preparé sur ladicte patene que dict est dessus, et le doibt
oindre premierement au sommet de la teste, secondement en la poitrine,
tiercement entre les espaulles, quartement les espaules en la compage et
liure des bras, et doibt dire a chacune desdictes onction[s] ce qui s'ensuict.

Ungo te in regem de oleo sanctificato, in nomine Pa✠tris et Filii et
Spiritus ✠ sancti.

Et a ce toutz les assistans doibvent respondre, *Amen.*

42. Tandis aussy que ladicte unction se faict, les assistans doivent
chanter l'anthiesne qui s'ensuict.

Anthiesne.

[fol. 60r] *Unxerunt Salomonem Sadoch sacerdos et Nathan pro-*
pheta[a] *regem in Gyon*[b]*, et accedentes laeti dixerunt, "Vivat rex in aeter-*
num."

42. [a] prophetam A. —[b] Gyon] quem A.

43. Ladicte onction faicte et ladicte anthiene chantee, ledict archevesque doibt dire l'oraison qui s'ensuit.

Christe, perunge hunc regem in regimen[a]*, unde unxisti sacerdotes,*
reges ac prophetas ac martyres, qui per fidem vicerunt regna, operati
sunt iusticiam [atque] adepti sunt promissione[s]; tua sacratis-
sima unctio super caput eius defluat atque ad interiora descendat, et
cordis [illius] intima penetret, et promissionibus quas adepti sunt

victoriosissimi reges[b], *gracia tua dignus efficiatur, quatenus et in presenti seculo feliciter regnet et ad eorum consortium in caelesti regno perveniat. Per dominum nostrum Ihesum Christum filium tuum, qui unctus est oleo laetitiae prae*[c] *consortibus suis, et virtute crucis potestates aereas debellavit, tartara destruxit, regnumque diaboli superavit, et ad caelos victor ascendit, in* [fol. 60v] *cuius victoria et manu omnis gloria et potestas consistunt, et [tecum] vivit et regnat in unitate Spiritus sancti Deus per omnia secula seculorum. Amen.*

43. [a] reginem A. — [b] victoriosissimi reges] victoriosissime rege A. — [c] prae crossed out A.

44. Alia oratio.

Deus, electorum fortitudo et humilium celsitudo[a], *qui in primordio per effusionem diluvii mundi crimina castigare voluisti et per columbam ramum olivae portantem pacem terris redditam demonstra[s]ti. Iterum sacerdotem Aaron famulum tuum per unctionem olei sacerdotem sanxisti, et postea per huius unguenti infusionem ad regendum populum*[b] *Israeliticum sacerdotes, reges ac pro[phetas per]fecisti, vultumque ecclesiae in oleo exhilarandum per propheticam famuli tui vocem David esse predixisti; ita quesumus, omnipotens Deus Pater*[c], *ut per huius creaturae pinguedinem hunc servum tuum sanctificare tua benedictione digneris, eumque in similitudinem*[d] *columbae pacem simplicitatis populo sibi commisso praestare, et exempla Aaron in Dei servitio diligenter imitari, regnique fastigia in consiliis scienciae et equitate iudicii semper assequi, vultumque hylaritatis, per hanc olei unctionem tuamque*[e] *benedictionem,* [fol. 61r] *te adiuvante, toti plebi paratum habere facias. Per dominum etc.*

44. [a] celsituto A. — [b] popolum A. — [c] Pater] presta A. — [d] similitudinae A. — [e] tuamque] tuam quam A.

45. Aultre oraison.

Deus Dei filius, dominus noster Iesus Christus, qui a Patre[a] *oleo exultationis unctus est prae participibus suis, ipse*[b] *per presentem sacri unguinis*[c] *infusionem Spiritus paracliti super caput*[d] *tuum infundat benedictionem ea[m]demque usque ad interiora cordis tui penetrare*[e] *faciat, quatenus hoc visibili et tractabili dono, invisibilia percipere, et temporali regno iustis moderaminibus exequuto, eternaliter cum eo regnare merearis, qui cum eodem Patre vivit et regnat in unitate eiusdem Spiritus sancti Deus. Per omnia secula seculorum. Amen.*

45. [a] patie A. — [b] respice A. — [c] unguimis A. — [d] paracliti super caput] paracleti sanctus corpus A. — [e] penetrari A.

46. Les oraisons ainsy dictes, les aneeletz ou aggrapins des[a] ouvertures des vestemenz du roy se relassent et se rejoindent par l'archevesque, ou par prebstres ou diacre[s], a cause de l'onction; et adoncq le grand chambellan de France luy veste la robbe de coulleur jacynthe, et le manteau dont dessus est parlé, de telle [fol. 61v] façon qu'il ayt la main dextre a delivre la fente, ou le troupt dudict manteau, et le manteau levé sur la senestre, comme on lieve la chasuble a ung prebstre ; et lors l'archevesque luy donne l'anneau au doigt et dict ce qui s'ensuit.

46. ᵃ aggrapins des / aggrapins des A.

47. *Accipe anulum, signaculum videlicet fidei sanctae, soliditatem regni, augmentum potentiae, per quem scias triumphari*[28] *potentia hostes repellere, haereses destruere, subditos coadiunare et catholicae*ᵃ *fidei perseverabilitate connecti.*

47. ᵃ chatolicae A.

48. Apres que l'annel luy est baillé, se dict ceste orayson.
Oratio.
*Deus, cuius est omnis potestas et dignitas, da famulo tuo prosperum*ᵃ *suae dignitatis effectum, in qua, te remunerante*ᵇ*, permaneat semperque timeat tibique [iugiter] placere contendat. Per dominum.*

48. ᵃ presperum A. —ᵇ remmerante A.

49. Quand cest orayson est dicte, et que l'annel luy est baillé, comme dist est, l'archevesque luy baille le sceptre a la main dextre et dist ce qui s'ensuyt.
[fol. 62r] *Accipe sceptrum regiae potestatis insignae, virgam scilicet regni rectam, virgam virtutis, qua teipsum bene regas, sanctam*ᵃ *ecclesiam et populum videlicet christianum tibi a Deo commissum*ᵇ *regia virtute ab improbis defendas, pravos corrigas, rectos pacifices, et, ut viam rectam tenere possint*ᶜ *tuo iuvamine dirigas, quatinus de temporali regno ad eternum regnum pervenias*ᵈ*, ipso adiuvante cuius regnum et imperium sine fine permanet in secula seculorum. Amen.*

49. ᵃ sanctam] stanigts (*or something similar*) A. —ᵇ commissam A. —ᶜ possunt A. —ᵈ perveniat A.

50. Apres qu'il luy a baillé ledict scheptre, il a dict l'oraison qui s'ensuit.
Oratio.
*Omnium, Domine, fons bonorum cunctorumque Deus institutor*ᵃ *profectuum, tribue, quesumus, famulo tuo N. adeptam bene regere*ᵇ

---

[28] Ordo XXII A,33, MS *H*, also reads *triumphari* rather than *triumphali*.

dignitatem, et a te sibi praestitum honorem dignare coroborare;
honorifica eum prae cunctis regibus terrae, uberi^c *eum benedictione*
locupleta, et in solio^d *regni firma stabilitate consolida; visita eum in*
sobole, praesta ei prolixitatem^e *vitae, in diebus eius semper oriatur*
iusticia, ut^f *cum iocunditate et laetitia aeterno [glorietur in regno].*
Per dominum nostrum etc.

> 50. ^a institorum A. — ^b bene regere] regem A. — ^c deberi A. — ^d latupleta et in
> solo A. — ^e prelixitatem A. — ^f et A.

51. [fol. 62v] Ce dist, l'archevesque luy donne la verge dont dessus
est parlé, a la main senestre, et dict ce qui s'ensuit.

Accipe virgam virtutis et aequitatis, qua intelligas mulcere pios et
terrere reprobos, errantibus viam doce lapsisque^a *manum porrige,*
disperdasque superbos et releves humiles, ut aperiat tibi hostium Iesus
Christus dominus noster, qui de se ipso ait, 'Ego sum ostium; per me
si quis introierit salvabitur'; et ipse qui est clavis David et sceptrum
domus Israel, 'qui aperit, et nemo claudit, et claudit, et nemo aperit';
sit tibi adiutor, qui eduxit 'vinctum de domo carceris, sedentem in
tenebris et umbra mortis,' ut in omnibus sequi merearis eum^b*, de quo*
propheta David cecinit, 'Sedes tua, [Deus,] in seculum seculi, virga
aequitatis virga regni tui,' et imiteris eum qui dixit^c*, 'Diligas iusti-*
tiam et odio habeas iniquitatem; propterea unxit te Deus, Deus [tuus],
oleo laetitiae,' ad exemplum illius quem ante secula unxerat 'prae par-
ticipibus suis,' Ihesum Christum dominum nostrum.

> 51. ^a labsisque A. — ^b eumque A. — ^c imitaris eum qui dicit A.

52. [fol. 63r] Quand ledict archevesque a dict ceste oraison, le chancelier de France, s'il est present, appelle toutz les pairs de France par
leurs noms et les faict assembler, premierement les pairs lays, et apres
les clercs; et s'il n'est present, ledict archevesque les doibt convocquer;
et eux assemblez^a et estantz a l'entour du roy, iceluy archevesque prend
la couronne royale dessus l'aultel, et luy seul l'impose sur la teste du roy,
laquelle ainsy mises, tous lesdictz pairs, tant clercs que lays, y doivent
mettre la main et la soubstenir de toutes pars, et non aultres; et adoncq
ledict archevesque dict ceste oraison qui s'ensuit.

> 52. ^a assembleez A.

53. *Coronet te Deus corona gloriae*^a *atque iusticiae, honore et opere*
fortitudinis, ut^b *per officium nostre benedictionis cum fide recta et*
multiplici bonorum operum fructu ad coronam pervenias regni perpe-
tui, ipso^c *largiente cuius regnum et imperium permanet in secula*
seculorum. Amen.

53. ᵃ gloria A. —ᵇ et A. —ᶜ ipse A.

54. Apres ladicte coronation, se dist ceste orayson.
[fol. 63v] Oratio.

Deus perpetuitatis, dux virtutum, cunctorum hostium victor, benedic hunc famulum tuum tibi caput suum inclinantem, et prolixa sanitate et prospera foelicitate eum conserva, et ubicunque pro quibus auxilium tuum invocaverit, cito assis et protegas et deffendas; tribue ei, quesumus Domine, divitias gloriae tuae, comple in bonis desiderium eius, corona eum in miseratione et misericordia, tibique, Deoᵃ, pia devotione iugiter famuletur. Per dominum nostrum.

54. ᵃ Deus A.

55. Apres ceste oraison, soit incontinent dicte la benediction qui s'ensuit par ledict archevesque.
Benedictio.

Extendat omnipotens Deus dexteram suae benedictionis, et circumdet te muro foelicitatis, ac custodia suae protectionis sanctae Mariae ac beati Petri, apostolorum principis, sanctique Dionisii atque omnium sanctorum intercedentibus meritis. Amen.

56. *Indulgeat tibi Dominus omnia peccata quae gessisti, et tribuat tibi graciam et misericordiam quam humiliter ab eo deposcis, et liberet te ab adversitatibus cunctis et ab omnibus inimicorum omnium visibilium et invisibilium insidiis. Amen.*

57. [fol. 64r] *Angelos suos bonos, qui te semper et ubique precedant, [committentur] et subsequantur, ad custodiam tui ponat et a peccato seu²⁹ gladio et ab omnium periculorum discrimine sua potentia liberet. Per dominum. Amen.*

58. *Inimicos tuos ad pacis charitatisque benignitatem convertat, et bonis omnibus te graciosum et amabilem faciat, pertinaces quoqueᵃ in tui miseratione³⁰ et odio confusione salutari induat, super te autem participatio et sanctificatio sempiterna floreat. Amen.*

58. ᵃ quos A.

59. *Victoriosum [te] atque triumphatorem de invisibilibus atque visibilibus hostibus semper efficiat, et sancti nominis sui timorem pariter et amorem continuum cordi tuo infundat, et in fide recta ac*

---

²⁹ *sui*, the reading of *A*, is obviously incorrect; the source could have read either *seu* or *sive*—both are found in manuscripts of Ordines XXII A,43 and XXIII,69.

³⁰ Ordo XXII A,44, MSS *G, J*, and *O* also read *miseratione* rather than *insectatione*, which is the reading of most manuscripts.

bonis operibus perseverabilem reddat, et pace in diebus tuis concessa,
cum palma victoriae te ad perpetuum regnum perducat. Amen.

60. *Et qui te voluit super populum tuum*[31] *constituere regem, et in*
presenti seculo foelicem aeternae foelicitatis tribuat esse consortem.
Amen.

Quod ipse prestare[a] *dignetur, cuius regnum et imperium sine fine*
perveniat in secula seculorum. Amen.

60. [a] preparare A.

61. [fol. 64v] Aultre benediction a dire sur le roy incontinent apres la
precedente.

Benedic, Domine, hunc praeelectum principem, qui regna omnium
regum a seculo moderaris. Amen.

Et tali eum benedictione glorifica, ut Davidica[a] *teneat sublimitate*
sceptrum salutis et sanctificae propitiacionis, munere reperiatur
locupletatus. Amen.

Da ei tuo spiramine regere populum, sicut Salomonem fecisti
obtinere regnum pacificum. Amen.

Quod ipse prestare[b] *dignetur, cuius regnum et imperium sine fine*
permanet in secula seculorum. Amen.

61. [a] Davitica *corr. to* Davidica A. —[b] parare A.

62. L'estat du roy est designé en ce qui s'ensuit, que luy dict l'archevesque.

Sta et retine amodo statum[a], *quem huc usque*[b] *paterna successione*
tenuisti, hereditario iure tibi delegatum[c] *per auctoritatem Dei*
omnipotentis et per presentem traditionem nostram, omnium scilicet
episcoporum ceterorumque servorum Dei.[32] *Et quanto* [fol. 65r]
[clerum] propinquiorem sacris altaribus prospicis, tanto ei potiorem[d]
in locis congruentibus honorem impendere memineris, quatenus
mediator Dei et hominum te mediatorem cleri et plebis in hoc regni
solio confirmet,[33] *et in regno aeterno secum regnare faciat, Ihesus*

---

[31] Ordo XXII A,45, MS *I* also reads *tuum,* but most manuscripts of most ordines
read *suum.*

[32] I give the text as in Ordo XXII A,48 and Ordo XXIII,77. The manuscript is complex and incorrect here. As written, it reads "omnium propinquiorem sacris altaribus
scilicet temporibus coeteromque servorum Dei"; "propinquiorem sacris altaribus" was
crossed out, and "coeteromque" was corrected to "coeterorumque" so that it now
reads "omnium scilicet temporibus coeterorumque servorum Dei," a reading found in
no other manuscript of this formula.

[33] *conservet* in *A,* where there is an erasure and correction at the beginning of the
word; the original is illegible.

*Chrystus dominus noster, rex regum et dominus dominantium. Qui
cum Deo Patre* etc. *Amen.*

62. ᵃstatium *corr. (apparently later) to* statum A. —ᵇhunc usque A. —ᶜdele-
gatium *corr. (apparently later) to* delegatum A. —ᵈpotiore A.

63. Oratio.

*Omnipotens Deus, 'det tibi de rore coeli et de pinguedine terrae
habundantiam*ᵃ *frumenti, vini et olei, et serviant tibi populi et
adorent*ᵇ *te tribus; esto dominus fratrum tuorum, et incurventur ante
te*ᶜ *filii matris tuae, et qui benedixerit tibi benedictionibus repleatur,'
et Deus erit adiutor tuus.*[34]

63. ᵃhabundatia A. —ᵇadorant A. —ᶜse A.

64. Alia oratio.

*Benedic, Domine, fortitudinem principis, et opera manuum illius
suscipe, et benedictione tua terra eius de pomis repleatur de fructu
coeli et rore atque abissy subiacentis, de fructu solis et lunae, et de vertice antiquorum montium, de pomis aeternorum collium, et de
frugibus terrae et de plenitudine eius. Benedictio illius*ᵃ *qui apparuit
in rubro veniat super caput eius, et plena sit* [fol. 65v] *benedictio
Domini in filiis eius, et tingat in oleo pedem suum.*

Cornua rinoceruntis [*cornua illius, in ipsis ventilabit gentes
usque ad terminos terre, quia ascensor celi auxiliator*[35]] *suus in sempiternum fiat. Qui cum Deo Patre et Spiritu sancto vivit et regnat
Deus per omnia secula seculorum. Amen.*

63. ᵃeius A.

65. Les oraisons et benedictions dessusdictes achevees et finies,
ledict archevesque, avec les aultres pairs de France, soubstenantz la
couronne du roy, doibt mener ledict seigneur aynsy vestu et couronné,
que dict est, portant le sceptre et la verge, au siege qui lui est preparé au
bout du coeur, comme dict est au commencement, qui doibt estre toute
tendue et pavee de soye et de tapisserie, et en icelluy siege ou chaire, qui
doibt estre haulte eslevé, affin que chacun le puisse veoir et regarder,
ledict archevesque le collecque et assiet, et apres qu'il y est assis, tantost
apres ledict archevesque oste sa mytre et le va baiser en la bouche, en

[34] This ordo does not have the second part of the prayer, *Omnipotens benedicat
tibi benedictionibus.* See the Introduction, p. 525.

[35] The manuscript begins a new paragraph with *Cornua rinoceruntis*; someone
then apparently skipped two lines (here add. from Ordo XXII A,50) when copying his
source — whether it was Foulquart or the seventeenth-century copyist cannot be
known.

disant ce qui s'ensuict : « Vivat rex in aeternum. » [fol. 66r] Apres luy font[a] ainsy les evesques pairs et apres eulx les pairs laiz, qui soubstiennent ladicte couronne, disant comme ledict archevesque : « Vivat rex in aeternum. »

65. [a] sont A.

66.   Ces choses ainsy faictes, ledict archevesque s'en retourne a l'aultel dire son confiteor, et le chantre et le soubchantre gardent le coeur commencent a chanter l'introite de la messe, qui se chante honorificquement et solempnellement ; sy ce n'estoit que la reyne[a] fust illecque presente pour estre oincte et benie comme le roy ; auquel cas, tantost que l'archevesque est retourné d'aupres le roy, avant qu'on chante la messe, il doibt vacquer a ladicte onction et benediction en la maniere qui s'ensuyt.

66. [a] regne A.

A B C D

67.   Premier[a], son siege ou[b] tribunal doibt estre preparé comme celuy du roy, sauf tant[c] qu'il doibt estre ung petit plus bas et doibt estre a costier[d] de celuy du roy, du costé senestre du coeur ; et ce doibt faire une montee comme a celuy du roy ; et sont les petites pierres au pavé, comme du costé d'iceluy du roy ; et si doibt estre paré et tapissé comme celuy du roy[e].

67. [a] Premierement B. —[b] et B. —[c] sauf pourtant B. —[d] doibt estre a costier] a coté B. —[e] comme du costé d'iceluy ... du roy] pareillement et se doit etre paré et tapissé de même B.

68.   Le roy estant en son tribunal, habitué[a] de toutz les [fol. 66v] ornementz dessusdictz, comme l'archevesque luy[b] a laissé apres sa coronation et consecration[c] dessusdictes declaré[d], on doibt amener la reyne en l'eglise, et la doibvent compagner[e] les barons et nobles dames du royaulme ; et celles venues[f] en l'eglize, se doibt prosterner et agenouiller devant le grand aultel de ladicte eglize[g], et en cest estat faire son oraison ; et apres que elle a faict sadicte orayson[h] et qu'elle [s'est[i]] rellevee, les evesques la doivent prendre et la faire ragenouiller[j] et incliner sa teste devant l'archevesque de Reims, qui doibt dire sur elle l'oraison qui s'ensuict[k].

68. [a] habillé B. —[b] l'y B. —[c] sa consecration et son couronnement B. —[d] dessudictes declaré om. B. —[e] accompagner B. —[f] elle venue B. —[g] de ladicte eglize om. B. —[h] apres que elle ... oraison] apres qu'elle est faite B. —[i] s'est om. A, here add. from B. —[j] réagenouiller B. —[k] doibt dire ... s'ensuict] dira sur elle cette oraison B.

69. Oratio[a].

Adesto, Domine, supplicationibus nostris, et quod humilitatis nos-
trae gerendum est, ministerio[36] tuae virtutis[b] impleatur effectu. Per
dominum[c].

69. [a] Oratio *om.* B. —[b] veritatis A, virtutis B. —[c] etc. *add.* B.

70. Sur ce pas, faict[a] a notter que la robbe et [la[37]] chemise de la
reyne doivent estre ouverte[b] jusques a la ceinture. Et l'archevesque la
doibt oindre de la saincte huille en faisant le signe de la croix comme au
roy, au chief et en la poitrine, et dire ce qui s'ensuit quand il a oint, et a
chacune fois[c].

In nomine Patris[d] et Filii[d] et Spiritus sancti[d], prosit tibi haec unctio
olei in honorem et confirmationem aeternam. Amen.

70. [a] Sur ce pas faict a notter] Sur ce est à noter B. —[b] ouvertes B. —[c] ce qui
s'ensuit ... fois] chacune fois qu'il l'oint ce qui s'ensuit B. —[d] ✠ *add.* B.

71. [fol. 67r] Apres que ladicte unction est faicte, il[a] doibt dire l'oraison qui s'ensuict[b].

Omnipotens sempiterne Deus, affluentem spiritum tuae be✠nedic-
tionis[c] super famulam tuam nobis orantibus propitiatus[d] infunde, ut
que per manus nostrae impositionem hodie regina instituitur, sancti-
ficatione tua digna et electa permaneat, ut nunquam post modum de
tua gracia separetur indigna. Per dominum[e].

71. [a] il] l'archeveque de Reims B. —[b] qui s'ensuict *om.* B. —[c] ✠ *om.* B. —[d] pro-
pitiatis A. —[e] super famulam ... dominum] etc. B.

72. Quand ceste oraison est dicte, ledict[a] archevesque luy donne ung
sceptre en la main[b] dextre, ung peu plus petit que celuy du roy, et une
verge[38] au bout de laquelle y[c] est une main d'ivoire, comme a celle du roy,
en la main[b] senestre sans rien dire ; puis apres il luy doibt bailler l'annel
au doigt et dire ce qui s'ensuict[d].

Accipe annulum fidei, signaculum sancte trinitatis, quo possis
omnes hereticas pravitates devitare, et barbaras gentes virtute tibi
praestita ad agnitionem veritatis advocare[e].

---

[36] Varin (ed. *a*) read *misterio*, which is correct if the word is not abbreviated. I
think, though, that a loop on the word, perhaps traced from the source, indicates an
abbreviation. Manuscript *B* reads *ministerio*, which is the reading of Ordo XIII,25,
Ordo XV,47, and Ordo XXII A, MS *E*, so it is more likely that the word is *ministerio*.

[37] If *la* is in *A*, it is now hidden in the binding, as is the termination of several
words on fol. 66v; *la* is here added from *B*.

[38] *verge* is illegible in *A*. It was traced from the source, another proof of the
source's illegibility.

72. ᵃ ledict *om.* B. — ᵇ en sa main B. — ᶜ y *om.* B. — ᵈ s'ensuict] suit B. — ᵉ signaculum ... advocare] etc. B.

73. Oratioᵃ.

*Deus, cuius est*ᵇ *omnis potestas et dignitas, da famulae tuae signo tuae fidei prosperum suae dignitatis effectum, in qua tibi semper firma permaneat, tibique* [fol. 67v] *iugiter placere contendat. Per dominum*ᶜ.

73. ᵃ Oratio] Et puis l'oraison B. — ᵇ est *om.* B. — ᶜ da famulae ... dominum] etc. B.

74. Ce faict, l'archevesque seul luy doibt mettre la couronne sur la teste, et la doivent les barons soubstenir de toutes pars³⁹ ; et enᵃ la luy mettant doibt ledict archevesque dire l'oraison qui s'ensuictᵇ.

Accipe coronam gloriae, honorem iocunditatis, ut splendida fulgeas et aeterna exultatione corroneris.

74. ᵃ en *om.* B. — ᵇ qui s'ensuict] suivante B.

75. Alia oratio.

Ceste oraison se doibt puis direᵃ.

*Omnium, Domine, fons bonorum et cunctorum dator provectuum, tribue famulae tuae adeptam bene regere dignitatem, et a te sibi praestitam in ea bonis operibus corrobora*ᵇ *gloriam. Per*ᶜ.

75. ᵃ Accipe coronam gloriae ... puis dire *om.* B. — ᵇ omnibus coroborare B. — ᶜ dominum etc. *add.* B.

76. Apres ceste oraison, les barons et princes du royaulme presens, qui soubstiennent la couronne, laᵃ mennent et conduisentᵇ en ceste estat au siege ou tribunal preparé pour elle, comme dict est dessusᶜ ; et la doivent compaigner et estre entour elleᵈ les barons et les nobles dames et princesses du royaulme ; et elle ainsy colloquee, lesdicts chantre et soubchantreᵉ commencent la messe, qui se doibt chanter solempnelle-ment, comme dict est dessusᶠ ; et se doibtᵍ dire [fol. 68r] par l'archevesque pour orayson devant l'Espistre celle qui s'ensuictʰ.

76. ᵃ la *om.* B. — ᵇ la reine *add.* B. — ᶜ dessus *om.* B. — ᵈ accompagner et estre au tour d'elle B. — ᵉ lesdicts chantre et soubchantre] les chantres et souschantres qui tiennent le choeur B. — ᶠ comme dict est dessus *om.* B. — ᵍ dibt A. — ʰ celle qui s'ensuict *om.* B.

77. Oratioᵃ.

---

³⁹ *A* does not read *pars*, but something like *cher* (it is simply traced from the source, and the *r* is a correction), which makes no sense, so one must read it as *pars* (as Varin did in ed. *a*). *B* reads *parts*.

Quaesumus, omnipotens Deus, ut famulus tuus rex noster N., qui tua miseratione suscepit regni gubernacula, virtutum etiam omnium percipiat incrementa, quibus decenter ornatus, et vitiorum monstra devitare, et hostes superare, et ad te qui 'via veritas et vita' es, gratiosus valeat pervenire. Per dominum nostrum Iesum Christum etc.[b]

76. [a] Oratio *om*. B. —[b] N. qui ... etc.] etc. B.

78. Quand l'Evangile se lict, le roy et la royne se doivent lever et mettre jus leurs corones [de[a]] dessus leur teste[b] tant que ladicte[c] Evangile soit dicte; et apres qu'elle est leue[d], le plus grand de tous les archevesques et evesques presentz[e] doibt prendre le livre aux[f] Evangiles et le porter baiser au roy, et apres a l'archevesque qui dict la messe.

78. [a] de *om*. A, *here add from* B. —[b] leurs têtes B. —[c] ledit B. —[d] qu'il est lu B. —[e] et evesques presentz *om*. B. —[f] des B.

79. A l'offertoire, les pairs de France menent et compaignent[a] le roy tenantz la main a sa coronne a aller offrir, et apres la royne, et doibvent offrir le roy et la royne[b] chacun ung pain, ung flascon d'argent plain[c] de vin et treize besans[d] d'or; et ces[e] choses offertes, lesdictz pairs et barons les remennent[f] en leurs sieges comme devant; [fol. 68v] et est assçavoir que en allant et retournant de ladicte offrande, ledict[g] seneschal ou connestable de France doibt porter tousjours l'espee nue devant le roy, et semblablement a la fin de la messe et a retourner au palais.

79. [a] accompagnent B. —[b] et doibvent ... royne *om*. B. —[c] d'argent plain *om*. B. —[d] batons B. —[e] ses A. —[f] remeirent B. —[g] le B.

80. S'ensuict l'oraison secrete que l'archevesque dict a la messe. Oratio secreta[a].

Munera, quaesumus Domine, oblata sanctifica, ut et nobis unigeniti tui corpus et sanguis fiant, et N. regi nostro ad obtinendum animae corporisque salutem, et ad peragendum iniunctum officium, te largiente, usquequaque proficiat. Per eundem dominum nostrum[b].

80. [a] a la messe. Oratio secreta *om*. B. —[b] ut et nobis ... nostrum] etc. B.

81. Apres que ledict archevesque[a] a dict l'orayson dominicalle, et avant qu'il dict : « Pax Domini sit semper vobiscum[b] », il doibt faire sur le roy et sur le peuple la benediction qui s'ensuict[c].

Benedicat tibi Dominus custodiensque[40] *te, sicut voluit te super populum suum*[d] *constituere regem, itaque in presenti seculo felicem et aeternae felicitatis tribuat esse consortem. Amen*[e].

---

[40] *custodiensque* is the reading of the Last Capetian Ordo (Ordo XXII A,55, 61, and 79) also. Manuscript *B* correctly reads *custodiatque*, as do most ordines.

81. ᵃque ledict archevesque] qu'il B. —ᵇsit semper vobiscum *om.* B. —ᶜs'ensuict] suit B. —ᵈtuum B. —ᵉitaque in presenti ... Amen] etc. B.

82. [fol. 69r] *Clerum ac populum, quem sua voluit opitulatione tua sanctione congregari, sua dispensatione et tua administratione*ᵃ *per diuturna tempora faciat foeliciter gubernari. Amen.*

82. ᵃtua administratione] ministratione A.

83. *Quatenus divinis monitis parentes, adversitatibus omnibus carentes, bonis omnibus exuberantes, tuo ministerio fideli amore obsequentes*ᵃ, *et in presenti seculo pacis tranquillitate fruantur, et tecum aeternorum civium consortio potiri mereantur. Amen.*

*Quod ipse praestare dignetur, cuius regnum et imperium sine fine permanet in secula seculorum. Amen*ᵇ.

83. ᵃobsequentibus A. — ᵇClerum ac populum ... Amen *om.* B.

84. Assçavoir est que l'archevesque, ou aultre prelat qui a baillé au roy l'evangeliaire a baiser, apres la lecture de l'Evangille, doibt prendre la paix de l'archevesque celebrant la messe apres qu'il a dict : « Pax Domini sit semper vobiscum », en le baisant en la boucheᵃ, et la doibt porter au roy, en leᵇ baisant semblablement, et apres luy toutz les aultres archevesques et evesques presentz baisentᶜ pareillement le royᵈ ; et ledict archevesque qui [fol. 69v] la premier baiséeᵉ, porte la paix a la royne, en luy baillant baiser le livre auxᶠ Evangilles.

84. ᵃen la baisant a la bouche B. — ᵇla B. — ᶜbaisant B. — ᵈle roy *om.* B. — ᵉla premier baisé] la le premier baisé B. — ᶠdes B.

85. Oraison que dict l'archevesque apres la perceptionᵃ. Oratioᵇ.

*Haec, Domine, oratio*ᶜ *salutaris famulum tuum N. regem nostrum ab omnibus tueatur adversis, quatenus et ecclesiasticae pacis obtineat tranquillitatem, et post istius temporis decursum perveniat ad aeternam hereditatem. Per dominum nostrum*ᵈ.

85. ᵃcommunion B. —ᵇOratio *om.* B. —ᶜperceptio B. —ᵈet ecclesiasticae pacis ... nostrum] etc. B.

86. Quand la messe est finie, les pairs de France mennent le roy et la royne devant l'aultel, et la ilz reçoivent de la main de l'archevesque qui a dict la messe, et communient, le precieulx corps etᵃ sang de Jesus Christ, comme faict le prestre a la messe ; et apres ce faict, ledict archevesque de Reims oste au roy la coronne dessusᵇ sa teste, et les aultres vestementz apportez de Sainct Denys en France, comme dict est devantᶜ, qui se rendent a l'abbé dudict lieu, pour yᵈ reporter et garder pour les aultres

sacres; et luy ainsy despouillé et tantost[e] revestu d'aultres habitz, et luy doibt remettre ledict archevesque une nouvelle[f] [fol. 70r] couronne plus petite sur la teste, et en cest estat[g] s'en va au palais, le seneschal et connestable precede[h] qui porte l'espee nue devant luy et la royne aussy[i], accompagnee[j] comme dessus.

Et est a noter que la chemise du roy se doibt brusler apres, a cause de la saincte unction; et si faict celle de la royne[k].

86. [a] le *add.* B. —[b] dessus] de sur B. —[c] comme dict est devant *om.* B. —[d] l'y B. —[e] est aussitot B. —[f] nouvelle *om.* B. —[g] il *add.* B. —[h] le senechal ou connetable le precedant B. —[i] qui est *add.* B. —[j] accompagnee] qui est accompagnee B. —[k] pour cause de la sainte onction; et si fait aussi la reine B.

87. Quand le roy retourne au palais pour disner, les barons qui ont esté querir la sainte ampolle a Sainct Remy, la doivent reconduire aussy, selon leur[s] promesses cy dessus registré[a], et doibt estre reporté honorablement et en procession, comme elle a esté apportee, ainsy que dict est cy dessus, et remise[b] et restitué en son lieu empres[c] le glorieux corps de monsieur saint Remy, apostre de France.

87. [a] leurs promesses cy dessus registré] la promesse qu'ils en ont faite B. —[b] ainsy que dict est ... remise] en l'eglise Notre Dame, et doit etre remise B. —[c] en pres B.

A

88. Assçavoir est aussy que anciennement[a] y avoit douze pairs en France, VI prelatz et VI laitz, six ducz et VI contes, dont les prelatz ne se muent, desquelz les noms s'ensuivent.

L'archevesque duc de Reims.

L'evesque duc de Laon.

L'evesque duc de Langres.

L'evesque conte de Beauvais.

L'evesque conte de Chaalons.

L'evesque conte de Noyon.

Ces pairs sont en ordres comme ilz doibvent seoir, a la senestre du roy, quand il tient le lict de justice.

88. [a] aucunement A.

89. [fol. 70v] Le duc de Bourgongne.

Le duc de Normendie.

Le duc d'Aquitaine.

Le conte de Toulouze.

Le conte de Flandres.

Le conte de Champaigne.

Toutz lesquels pairs laiz sont de presentz en la main du roy et uniz a la coronne, excepté Flandres qui est en guerre, au moings en treuve pour le present; et si il tient Artoys qui estoit des nouvelles parries. Et les nouveaulx pairs sont :

Le duc d'Alençon.
Le duc de Bourbon.
Le duc de Bretaigne.
Le conte d'Estampes.
Le conte d'Artoys, en la main du roy.
Le conte de Clermont, le conte de Reteloys.[41]

---

[41] After the ordo Foulquart continues his treatise on the obligations of the *échevins* of Reims at a coronation (fols. 70v–77r); it is printed in Varin (ed. *a*), 575–79.

ORDO XXV

The Ordo of Charles VIII

Date: 29 May–2 June 1484
Other names: none

Introduction

The Ordo of Charles VIII differs markedly from all previous texts. Like many of them, it contains the entire liturgy of the coronation ceremony, and it incorporates many of the rubrics and instructions that had become increasingly longer with the passage of time. It goes far beyond them, though, with its long description of the events preceding the coronation ceremony, its extensive particulars concerning the king's formal entry into Reims, its wealth of local detail, its careful record of the active participants, and its insertion of a specific king's name into the liturgical formulas at the appropriate places. This is not a generic coronation ordo, but a precise and full description of a specific event, and that is something unprecedented in the history of the ceremony. Although the coronation of Louis XII in 1498 and some sixteenth-century ceremonies are not as well documented as this one, the Ordo of Charles VIII set the standard for reporting future coronations. It is a fitting conclusion to a history that began in the eighth century, as well as to this edition of the texts that are the foundation of our knowledge of that history.

The narrative was written by a cleric who appears to have been in the entourage of the Archbishop of Reims. He was doubtless deeply involved in the events he described. The many details, the exact knowledge of the liturgy, the several references to the consecration of a bishop, and the full quotation of the welcoming address by Dr. Brice Bobille (see no. 4), all suggest that the cathedral's Dean was himself the text's author. The text's references to "mondit sieur l'archevesque" exclude the archbishop himself as the author.

The primary source of the ceremony's liturgy was certainly the cathedral's *livre rouge* (Ordo XXIII, lost manuscript 4). The ordo omits the first occurrence of the *livre rouge*'s nos. 103–104, and it inverts the *livre rouge*'s nos. 82–83 and 103–106 (see the synoptic table, Appendix II). The only new formulas in this ordo are nos. 26 and 28, both drawn from the local liturgy of the Reims cathedral. Otherwise, the ordo's sequence of formulas follows exactly their order in the *livre rouge*. No previous ordo possesses the same sequence of formulas as the *livre rouge* and Charles

VIII's ordo. Within the formulas themselves, a number of the text's readings accord with those of our three surviving copies of the *livre rouge* (Ordo XXIII, MSS *F* and *G* and ed. *a*), as well as with Meurier's extracts from the *livre rouge*. These readings provide additional evidence that the *livre rouge* was consulted in preparing this ceremony. Nevertheless, other manuscripts were also examined in 1484, as the ordo itself explains in no. 34, and some readings in a few liturgical formulas were not drawn from the *livre rouge*.

Manuscripts *B* and *C* were independently copied from the original manuscript in the seventeenth century; the fifteenth-century manuscript of the ordo disappeared thereafter. Manuscript *B* is probably slightly older than manuscript *C*; when the latter was copied and published, it may be that the source manuscript was regarded as no longer possessing any value and was discarded, a common procedure in the early-modern period.[1]

Manuscript *B* was part of a collection of materials that formed the Brienne collection. Its copies of earlier ordines has figured prominently in the editions of several earlier ordines (see the Index of Manuscripts).

Manuscript *C* was copied for the publication of the Godefroys' *Cérémonial françois* in 1648. This copy was corrected in many places prior to publication, and some of those corrections suggest that the text was collated either with manuscript *B* or with lost manuscript *1* after *C* was copied, probably fairly soon thereafter.

I associate with this ordo two unpublished extracts from manuscript *A*. The British Library's manuscript Arundel 149 is not a particularly pretty manuscript and is not remarkable as a manuscript. The entire manuscript is a collection of royal and imperial coronation materials from various sources. Its copy of the Last Capetian Ordo (Ordo XXII A, MS *H*), which is the last text in the manuscript, is of some significance because it appears to have been copied from one of the lost manuscripts in the royal library and because it helped to establish that ordo's stemma. A peculiar feature of the manuscript appears on fol. 23r, on which the Last Capetian Ordo begins. After an ornate capital *D* in *Die* at the very beginning of the page, the scribe copied a passage, in Latin, concerning the king's reception at the cathedral on the day preceding his coronation, followed immediately without a break, by a passage concerning the reception of the Holy Ampulla at the church. Again without a break, this

---

[1] The late Father Leonard Boyle († 1999), former Prefect of the Biblioteca Apostolica Vaticana, explained in a recent lecture that it was from such discards that a significant part of that library's enormous manuscript holdings was constituted.

is followed by the text of the Last Capetian Ordo. These two passages are in no manuscript of either the Last Capetian Ordo or the Ordo of Charles V, but they are in Charles VIII's ordo, where their rubrics are in French. It is not absolutely certain that they belong with the Ordo of Charles VIII, for they might have been composed for the coronation of either Louis XI or Louis XII. Had they been part of the former ceremony, though, Foulquart would surely have quoted them when he discussed the king's arrival in the city (Ordo XXIV,3–5). There is no detailed description of Louis XII's coronation, so it makes sense to present the two passages in parallel columns with Charles VIII's ordo. It is likely that the two passages were extracted from the very text that was composed for Charles VIII's coronation; if nothing else, they demonstrate that an ordo like the present one was based upon a Latin text.[2]

Théodore and Denis Godefroy, in preparing their edition, the only previous edition of this description and ordo, made a copy (MS *C*) of the entire manuscript. When *Le cérémonial françois* was published, however, only the incipits of the liturgical formulas were normally printed, so the text has not previously been printed in full.

Lost manuscripts

1—Location unknown, but doubtless Reims, and probably the cathedral's archives or library. Manuscript entitled *Cy apres s'ensuit la venue du roy Charles VIIIᵉ de ce nom, a Reyms, pour recepvoir son sacre et couronnement.* The manuscript appears to have been the source of both manuscripts *B* and *C*.

Manuscripts

A—London, British Library, MS Arundel 149, fol. 23r. Extracts from a Latin text of the ordo. Nos. 23–30, 83–84 only. Description: see Ordo XXII A, MS *H*.

B—Paris, Bibl. nat., MS nouv. acq. fran. 7232, fols. 47r–89v. Formerly MS Brienne 263. Seventeenth century, first half. Description: see Ordo XX B, MS *H*. See Plate 32.

C—Paris, Bibl. de l'Institut de France, MS fonds Godefroy 381, pp. 53–147ᴮ.[3] Seventeenth century, first half. Description: none.

---

[2] I suggest that Arundel 149 was copied at a time when there would have been an intense interest in coronations, that is, around the time of Henry VII's coronation at Westminster on 30 October 1485, less than a year and a half after Charles VIII's coronation at Reims.

[3] The pagination of the last part of this text is rather confusing. The sequence of pages is 146, 147ᴬ, 148ᴬ, 147ᴮ, 148ᴮ.

D—Paris, Bibl. de l'Arsenal, MS 4227, fols. 39r–84v. Seventeenth century. Copied indirectly from *B*. Description: see Ordo XX B, MS *K*. Not collated.

E—Paris, Bibl. de l'Assemblée nationale, MS 195, fols. 46r–84r. Formerly MS B.105ⁱ, tome 68. Late seventeenth or early eighteenth century. Apparently copied from *D*. Description: see Ordo XVII B, MS *G*. Not collated.

F—Paris, Arch. nat., KK 1442, fols. 56r–114r. Eighteenth century. Copied, apparently indirectly, from *B*. Description: see Ordo XVII B, MS *I*. Not collated.[4]

Editions

a—Godefroy, 1:184–208. From *C*.[5]

Principles of the Edition

Both manuscripts *B* and *C*, seventeenth-century copies of lost manuscript *1*, are faulty. In each case the scribe modernized the source's fifteenth-century orthography, but neither is fully consistent. Because *B* retains the older spellings to a much larger degree than *C*, I selected *B* as the base text for this edition, and the paragraphs are those of *B*. Many paragraphs are short, however, and it did not seem necessary to assign a separate number to each of them, but rather to each group of topically related paragraphs. Liturgical formulas and rubrics are printed as separate paragraphs even if *B* presents them as a single paragraph.

There is little punctuation in *B*, so almost all punctuation has been added. The want of punctuation has made it difficult to delineate sentences. The scribe often began a phrase, a clause, or what might be a sentence with a capital letter without any preceeding punctuation. I have rendered that letter either as an uppercase or a lowercase one, as the context appeared to require, preceeding it by the appropriate punctuation mark. I ignored the fairly extensive punctuation of MS *C* on the assumption that it was added by the Godefroys.

---

[4] There may be other seventeenth- or eighteenth-century manuscripts copied directly or indirectly from *B*. I did not look for them.

[5] This text is not in Théodore Godefroy, *Le cérémonial de France* (Paris: Abraham Pacard, 1619). Manuscript *C* appears to have been recollated with its source or MS *B*, for a number of its initial errors were corrected. In most cases only the incipits of the liturgical formulas were printed.

Alexandre Le Noble, *Histoire du sacre et du couronnement des rois et reines de France* (Paris: Gaultier-Laguionie, 1825), presented a version of Charles VIII's ordo that is a rather free adaption, so it is not an edition.

Judging from some of the erroneous readings, lost manuscript *1* must have been quite difficult to read—it was probably written in a late-medieval cursive script. Manuscript *B*'s readings, in particular, are therefore sometimes utter nonsense. In turn, *B* is itself most difficult to read; it is often impossible to distinguish between the letters *a* and *e* and between *o* and *u*. I render *B*'s readings to the best of my ability, occasionally supplying missing letters in square brackets. Where *C* gives a correct reading (this includes text omitted in *B*), that reading is given in the text and *B*'s incorrect one in a variant. If letters are missing in a variant from *C*, they are simply supplied in square brackets. Where neither *B* nor *C* has a correct reading, but apparently reproduces an error in the source, I often suggest a correct reading by means of a reference to the appropriate text in another ordo (usually Ordo XXIII, the Ordo of Charles V). A few variants from edition *a* are also given in order to facilitate understanding the text.[6]

The scribe of *B* usually (though not always) wrote *dict* (*ledict*, etc.) with a *c*, so abbreviations of these words are expanded with the *c*. Manuscript *C* usually renders words like *lesdictes* as two words (*les dictes*); where *C*'s readings are retained, these are here written as one word.

In *B* the name of the coronation city sometimes appears to have been written *Reins* rather than *Reims*, but that is not certain, and all such instances are here rendered with *m*.

The scribe of *B* sometimes wrote *eut* as *eu*. This scribal peculiarity is simply ignored, and the word is spelled out.

Where *B* reads *sieur* and *seigneur*, *C* normally (but not always) has *monsieur* and *monseigneur*. This suggests that, where *C* differs from *B*, the word was abbreviated in the source, but that, where both manuscripts have the same word, it was spelled out in the source. This being the case, it was unfortunately necessary to retain variants of these words.

Manuscript *C* was copied for preparation of the printed edition, and it is very clearly hand-lettered, but it does share some of the peculiarities of the seventeenth-century practice for printing Latin texts. Both the Latin *ae* and *oe* diphthongs (æ and œ) are normally written *oe* as two separate letters, but sometimes they are written as a diphthong; these are usually (but not always) *e* in manuscript *B*. Manuscript *B*'s readings better reflect fifteenth-century usage and are doubtless the readings of the

---

[6] Ed. *a* corrects a number of errors that remained in *C* after *C* had been corrected (see the previous note). This suggests that *a* was recollated with lost manuscript *1* before its publication.

source. The readings of *C* are here retained and are rendered either *ae* (e.g., *sœculum* becomes *saeculum*) or *oe* (e.g., *fœmina* becomes *foemina*) only if they appear in a variant for other reasons.

Because the scribe of *C* modernized the text much more than the scribe of *B* did, there is little reason to retain many variants from *C*. The normal spellings of the following words in *B* and *C* are respectively: *ampole* or *ampolle* or *empoule/ampoule* or *ampoulle*; *chaiere/chaire*; *cueur/coeur*; *coulleur/couleur*; *eglise* or *eglize/esglise*[7] or (rarely) *eglise*; *oroison/oraison*; *pers/pairs*; *Reims/Rheims*; *robbe/robe*; *sainct/saint*; *ung/un*. Where *B* has *conte* instead of *comte*, *C* invariably has *comte*, so these variants are not retained. Also not normally retained are variants of the ultimate *z* if *C* spells the word with *s* (*soubz/soubs*). On the other hand, variant spellings from *C* are retained if they appear to preserve the spellings of the source, or if they correct what seem to be *B*'s scribal errors. Obvious scribal errors in *C* are not retained, nor are most instances of *y* for *i*. Deleting the many modernizations and some scribal errors greatly reduces what would otherwise be a very large number of uninteresting and uninformative variants.

The two extracts in *A* are printed in columns parallel to the text in *B* and *C*—to the extent that that is possible where the Latin rubrics are so different from the French description. The paragraph numbers from *A* are identified by the addition of the letter *a* so that ambiguity may be avoided in future references.

ORDO XXV

B C

1. [fol. 47r] Cy apres s'ensuit la venue du roy Charles VIII[e a] de ce nom, a Reyms, pour recepvoir son[b] sacre et couronnement; et les choses qui y furent faictes. Ensemble le mistere du sainct sacre et couronnement des roys de France.

1. [a] huictiesme C. —[b] saint *add.* C.

2. Le sabmedy XXIX[e a] jour du mois de may, l'an mil quatre cens quatre vingt quatre[b], apres disner, le treschrestien roy de France Charles VIII[me c] de ce nom, aagé de[d] pres de quatorze ans, filz du feu roy Louis XI[me e] de ce nom et de la feue royne Charlotte, fille de Savoye, se partit[f] du chasteau de Gueux distant[g] de la cité de Reyms de deux lieues, auquel il estoit arrivé des le jeudy devant et jour de l'Ascension, pour aller audict Reyms

---

[7] One instance of *esglize* in no. 63, and *C*'s normal spelling *esglise*, suggest that something like that may have been the source's normal spelling.

prendre et recevoir son sainct sacre et couronnement, comme avoient faictz[h] ses predecesseurs roys de France.

2. [a] vint-neufiesme C. —[b] mille quatre cent quatre vingts et quatre C. —[c] huic-tiesme C. —[d] et C. —[e] unsiesme C —[f] partist C. —[g] gisant C. —[h] faict C.

3. Et environ une heure apres midy de ce jour, [fol. 47v] se partirent pour aller au devant du[a] roy, les gens d'eglise, eschevins, nobles, bourgeois et habitans de ladicte ville de Reyms, jusques au[b] nombre de soixante, bien montez et honnestement habillez, avec et en la compaignie[c] de Charles de la Ramee, cappitaine de Reyms, lesquels chevaucherent jusques a la descente de Muyre[d], ou ils trouverent li[e] roy vestu d'une robbe courte de drap d'or, ayant ung bonnet noir sur sa teste, ung chappeau viollet dessus et une plume d'autriche[f] blanche par dessus, monté sur ung cheval de poil moreau fort esveillé, accompaigné de tres haultz et puissans princes et barons et seigneurs[g]. Messeigneurs :

Louis, duc d'Orleans, de Vallois et de Milan[h];

René, duc d'Allençon[i];

Pierre de Bourbon, conte de Clermont, de la Marche, sieur de Beaujeu et d'Armignac;

Phelippes[j] de Savoye, conte de Bresse;

François de Bourbon, comte de Vandosme[k];

François d'Orleans, conte de Dunoys;

Louis[l] de Bourbon, comte daulphin d'Auvergne;

François de Laval, comte de Montfort;

Jean, comte de Roussy;

[fol. 48r] Robert de Sarrebruche[m], comte de Braine;

Jehan d'Armignac, }
Louys d'Armignac[n], } contes de Guise et de Mayenne;[8]

Philippes de Croy, conte de Porcien[o];

Louys de Luxembourg;

Guy Pot, conte de Sainct Pol, qui estoit prochain du roy;

et de plusieurs autres seigneurs, comtes, chevalliers[p] et escuyers.

3. [a] dudict C. —[b] audit B, *corr. to* au. —[c] compagnie C. —[d] Muire C. —[e] le C. — [f] d'autruche C. —[g] puissants princes, barons et seigneurs C. —[i] Millan C. —

---

[8] *et de Mayenne*] etc. *d'humaine* in *B*; the source must have been difficult to read here. On these two sons of Jacques d'Armagnac, duc de Nemours (who was beheaded in 1477), see Anselme de Sainte-Marie (or Anselme de la Vierge Marie [Pierre Guibours]), *Histoire généalogique et chronologique de la maison royale de France*, 3rd ed., 9 vols. (Paris: La Compagnie des Libraires, 1726–1733), 3: 407–10, 429–31. I owe this reference to the kindness of Hervé Pinoteau.

[i] d'Alençon C. —[j] Philippes C. —[k] Vendosme C. —[l] Louys C. —[m] Sarebruche
C. —[n] Je[a]n d'Armignac, Louis d'Armignac, comtes de Guyse et de Maienne
C. —[o] Philippes de Croüy comte de Portien C. —[p] chevaliers C.

4. En presence desquelz et de plusieurs autres qui estoient illecquez
arrivez de toutes parts, le roy s'arresta[a] tout court au devant desdicts
habitans, qui le saluerent par la bouche de messire Brice[b] Bobille, docteur en Decret, chanoine et doyen de l'eglise de Reyms, en la maniere qui
s'ensuit.

«Nostre souverain Seigneur. Vos treshumbles et tresobeis-
sans chappelains et sujestz[c], les gens d'eglise, eschevins, nobles,
bourgeois et tout le peuple de vostre noble et ancienne cité de
Reims, sachant[d] vostre tres glorieuse venue, en ensuivant le Psal-
miste, qui dict : «Filiae Sion exultent in rege suo»,[9] et pour
accomplir ce qui est escript 1. P. ii : «Regem honorificate»[10] en
feste et[e] joye et en liesse, envoyent ceste compaignie[f] au devant
[fol. 48v] de vostre royalle Majesté, en toute humilité et obedi-
ence, pour vous recevoir et obeir, vous offrant[g], comme autres
fois par moy vous ont faict offrir, leurs corps, leurs biens, leurs
cueurs et tout ce qu'ils ont, pour du tout faire et disposer a vostre
bon plaisir et obeir a vos commandemens, comme vos bons,
vrays et loyaulx soubgetz[h], jusques a la mort inclusivement.
Chantans en grand[i] joye ce qui est escript, Math. 21o[j] : «Benedictus qui venit in nomine Domini»,[11] Sire, benit soyés[k] vous et le
bien venu, qui venez au nom de Dieu.

Sire, vous venez au nom de Dieu, qui venez en vostre jeune
aage, vierge, pur et net, pour recepvoir vostre sainct sacre de la
divine unction[l] envoyee de Dieu le createur pour les treschres-
tiens roys de France, et non pour autres. Parquoy ils ont, et au
plaisir de Dieu, vous arez[m] grace et pouvoir de guerir et alleger
les pauvres mallades[n] de la douloureuse malladie[o] que chascun
scet[p] qui est don celeste et divin. Et pour ce vous pouvons dire :
«Benedictus qui venit in nomine Domini». Vous soiez le tresbien
venu, avec[q] vostre tresnoble et tresexcellente compaignie, qui
venez ou nom[r] de Dieu.

Au surplus, Sire et nostre souverain Seigneur, [fol. 49r] pour
ce que ceulx[s] de vostredicte ville vous seroient vollontiers aulcunes[t] petites remonstrances, et que l'heure est importune, vous

---

[9] Ps. 149: 2.
[10] I Petr. 2: 17
[11] Mt. 21: 9.

supplient tres humblement[u] que vostre bon plaisir soict[v], apres la
reception de vostre sainct sacre, leur donner un petit mot de
vostre benigne audience, et vous soyez le tres bien venu « in
nomine Domini. »

4. [a] ilec arrivez de toutes pars, le roy s'aresta C. —[b] Boice B. —[c] sujects C. —
[d] sçachants C, *corr. from* sachants. —[e] en C. —[f] compagnie C. —[g] offrans C. —
[h] subjets C. —[i] par grande C. —[j] Matth. XXI[o] C. —[k] soyez C. —[l] onction C —
[m] aurez C. —[n] malades C. —[o] la loureuze maladie C. —[p] chacun sçait C (sçait
is a correction). —[q] avecques C. —[r] compagnie qui venez au nom C. —[s] ceux
C. —[t] volontiers aucunes C. —[u] trehumblement C. —[v] soit C.

5. A la fin de laquelle proposition fut[a] honorablement et doulcement
prononcee par ledit[b] doyen, le roy mit la main au chappeau et dit[c] :
« Grand mercy, Messieurs », et tenant[d] lors et tout au long de ladite
proposition une tres bonne gravité et ung tres honneste maintien, autant
qu'il eust peu faire en l'aage de cinquante ans. Et ce dit, les dictz[e] habitans se retirerent[f] devant ledict sieur roy en ladicte ville, excepté ledict
capitaine, ses gens et les deux sergeans[g] d'icelle ville qui demourerent[h]
derriere.

Lequel cappitaine presenta au[i] roy les clefz des portes dudit Reyms,
qui les delaissa en sa charge, en luy disant qu'il les avoit bien gardees
auparavant et que s'il avoit bien faict, il fit[j] encores mieulx, ainsi qu'il en
avoit bonne fiance en luy.

5. [a] fut] qui fust C. —[b] ledict C. —[c] meit la main au chapeau et dist C. —[d] et
tenant] Entenant C. —[e] dict lesdicts C. —[f] retirent B. —[g] sergens C. —
[h] demeurerent C. —[i] capitaine presenta au dict C. —[j] feit C.

6. Ces choses ainsi faictes et dictes, le roy print a marcher et
chevaucher avant, avecques lesdicts [fol. 49r] princes, ducs, contes,
barons, sieurs, chevalliers, seigneurs escuiers[a] estans entour et avec luy.
Et tout aupres d'illec, trouva les freres des quatre ordres des mandians[b],
les relligieux du Val des Escolliers[c], qui en procession luy estoient allez
au devant atout leurs croix, et bien quatre cens jeunes hommes compaignons et enfans portans[d] torches de cire allumees et ardentes comme
sy[e] c'eust esté de nuict, qui luy estoyent venus au devant avec lesdicts
freres et religieux. Tous lesquels apres leur salut faict[f] au roy, s'en
retournerent en ladicte ville, chantans joyeusement : « Noel! Vive le roy ! »

6. [a] seigneurs, chevaliers, escuyers C, *corr. from* chevalliers, escuyers. —
[b] mandiens C. —[c] Escholiers C. —[d] portant C. —[e] si C, *corr. from* ci. —[f] faict C.

7. Et marcha ledict seigneur roy apres eulx accompaigné[a] comme
dessus, jusques empres[b] une chappelle de saincte Geneviefve estant aux

champs, aupres de laquelle estoient les gentilz hommes de l'Hostel du
roy, les archers de la garde, les prevostz de l'Hostel et des mareschaulx,
atout leurs archers en armes, et plusieurs autres seigneurs et capitaines,
qui se minrent[c] [12] illec tous en bel ordre et conduite[d] et convoyerent le
roy dela en avant, sans le habandonner[e] ne delaisser jusques a ce qu'il
eust faict son entree en l'eglise et qu'il fust ou pallais[f] archiepiscopal, qui
luy estoit [fol. 50r] preparé pour reposer, comme dict sera cy apres, lesdictz archers de la garde estans a pied depuis la premiere porte jusques
audict palais.

7. [a] eux accompag[n]é C. —[b] enpres C. —[c] meirent C, *corr. from* miirent. —
[d] tous illec en bel ordre et conduicte C. —[e] l'abandonner C. —[f] feust au palais C.

8. Quand le roy veint au devant l'eglise[a] Sainct Eloy, du coste de la
porte a Vesle, par laquelle il faisoit son entree en ladicte ville, il trouva
illec le convers[b] dudict lieu, qui avoit preparé un table bien honnestement, sur laquelle estoient[c] pain, pommes, poires et autres fruictz, et vin
a grand largesse, qui[d] presentoit et donnoit a tous passans.

8. [a] vient devant l'esglise C. —[b] couvers C. —[c] estoyent C. —[d] qu'il C.

9. Dela en tirant outre pour entrer en ladicte ville, quand le roy vint[a]
a la premiere porte, ou les portiers et gardes de la ville ont accoustumé
de eulx tenir, il trouva illec une belle jeune[b] fille, ayant les cheveux de
couleur d'or pendans jusques sur les reins, sur son chef ung chappeau[c]
d'argent doré, et ung de fleurs, vestue d'une robbe de drap de soye, de
laquelle le corps et les manches estoyent de coulleur d'azur, semez de
fleurs de lis d'or, et le bas de coulleur blanche, et ung rainseau[13] de soye
verte par dessus tout au long, tenant en ses mains les clefs des portes de
ladite ville, laquelle subtillement par engin secret descendit[d] du hault de
ladicte porte au bas au devant du roy, et le salua en luy presentant [fol.
50v] lesdictes clefs, disant les motz qui s'ensuivent.

> Nostre roy, prince et souverain Seigneur,
> Treschrestien nommé par excellence,
> A qui sont deubz gloire, louange, honneur,
> Subjection, amour et reverence.
> Vostre cité de Reims obeissance
> Vous fait[e] par moy, qui cy la represente,
> Et de franc cueur, en vraye confidence,
> Les clefs des portes humblement vous presente.

---

[12] This word looks like *midrent* in *B*, but I assume that what looks like *d* is a
scribal peculiarity for *in* as in *rainseau* (n. 13 below).

[13] This word looks like *radseau* in *B*, but see the scribal peculiarity above, n. 12.

Desquels mots, offre et present le roy fut bien comptant[f] et joyeulx, comme il sembloit a le regarder, et ordonna a ung de ses gens estans[g] entour luy, qu'il prit[h] lesdictes clefs. Ce qu'il feist[i], et les emporta en son logis au pallais. Et ladicte fille, par ledict engin remonta au lieu d'ou[j] elle estoit descendue.

9. [a] veint C. —[b] jeune *om.* C. —[c] un chapeau C. —[d] descendict C. —[e] faict C. — [f] fust bien content C. —[g] a l'un de ses gens estant C. —[h] prist C. —[i] feit C. — [j] dont C.

10. En ceslieu[a], droict au devant de ladicte porte, estoit le palion preparé a porter sur[b] le roy, lequel estoit de damas pers semé de fleurs de lis d'or, eslevé sur quatre lances, au sommet desquelles avoit quatre angles[c], dont les deux tenoient les armes du roy, et les deux autres les armes de la ville de Reims,[14] que soustenoient et portoyent Philippes de Bezannes[d], eschevin et prevost[e] de l'eschevinage ; maistre Jehan Bourguet[f], eschevin ; maistre Jehan Cauchon le Jeune, lieutenant du cappitaine ; et maistre Jehan de Reims, bailly du [fol. 51r] chapitre de Reims, a ce faire esleuz[g] et ordonnez par les eschevins dudict Reims.

10. [a] En cedict lieu C. —[b] sus C. —[c] anglez C. —[d] Besannes C. —[e] et prevost *om.* C. —[f] Jean Bourgnet C, *corr. from* Jean Boingnet. —[g] eslus C.

11. Soubz lequel palion, avant que le roy s'y mit[a], messire Pierre de Refert[b], chevalier, comme grand escuier qui chevauchoit devant luy, portant l'espee en escharpe, fut[c], et se teint une espace, avant que le roy venst jusques audit lieu[d], la face tournee devers le roy. Quand le roy approcha[e], il en saillit par costiere du costé destre[f]. Et les quatre portans ledict pallion[g] l'approcherent du roy, qui entra dessoubs[h] et fut dela en avant conduict soubz icelluy jusques au portail de l'eglise[i] de Reims ; le peuple qui en grand[j] multitude estoit, et avoict[k] esté depuis ledict lieu de Muyre jusques a ladicte eglise, chantans[l] a haulte voix quand il passoit : « Vive le roy! Noel! Vive le roy ! »

11. [a] meit C. —[b] Pierre Dursé C. —[c] feut C. —[d] veint jusques au dict lieu C. — [e] aprocha C. —[f] dextre C. —[g] palion C. —[h] dessoubz C. —[i] l'esglise C. — [j] grande C. —[k] avoit C. —[l] esglise chantant C.

12. Des incontinent que le roy fut entré en ladicte premiere porte de ladicte ville, il eust la riviere de Vesle au descouvert jusques au boullevert[a], sur laquelle y avoit en trois nascelles[b] des jeunes compaignons, qui jouxtoyent en la quittance et en eut[c] deux ou trois cheuz dans[d] l'eaue.

---

[14] This shows that the *échevins* had adopted Jean Foulquart's proposal for the canopy's supports; cf. Ordo XXIV,4.

12. ᵃ a descouvert jusques au boulevert C. —ᵇ nacelles C. —ᶜ quintaine et y en eut C. —ᵈ dedans C.

13. Contre ledit boulevertᵃ estoit la fontaine de jouvent, qui sans cesser jettetᵇ eaue, en laquelle se baignoient gens de divers estatz pour rajeunir. Et au dessus estoient les personnages de Cupidoᶜ [fol. 51v] tout nudz, les yeux bandez, tenant ung dartᵈ, et de Venus habituee en dame. Et au front de ladicte fontaine par hault estoit escript ce qui s'ensuit.

> C'est la fontaine de jouvent,
> Ou les vieulx se baignent souvent,
> Dont rajeunissent aussy beaux,
> Comme font jeunes jouvenceauxᵉ.

13. ᵃ ledict boulevert C. —ᵇ jectoit C, *perhaps corr. to* jetoit. —ᶜ Cupidon C. — ᵈ un dard, *corr. from* un dart C. —ᵉ jouveneaux C.

14. Au dessus de la grosse porte jumelle de la porte a Vesle estoyent les armes du roy et une grande baniereᵃ aux armes de France.

Item, et aussy tost que le roy eust passé ladicte porte et entré en laᵇ ville, on commença a sonner les cloches par toutes les eglises sans cesser jusques a ce qu'il fust au palais archiepiscopal a luy preparé.

14. ᵃ banniere C. —ᵇ ladicte C.

15. Au coing de la Magdaleneᵃ, au devant de la croix, sur ung eschaffault, y avoit deux jeunes enfans tous nudz allaictansᵇ une louve, ayans chacun un escriteau lié au bras, ou estoit escript a l'un Reims ou Remus, et a l'autre Romulus; et apres eulx ung pasteurᶜ gardant des brebis, ayant un escriteau, nommé Faustulus, et sa femme aupres de luyᵈ, nommee Lorence, a qui ledict pasteur porta garder et [fol. 52r] nourrir lesdictz enfans quand il les eut trouvéᵉ. Et au front dudict eschaffault estoit escript en grosse lettre ce qui s'ensuit.

> Deulx filz jumeaulx, Remus et Romulus,
> Nez de Reaᶠ, d'une louve alaitezᵍ,
> Par ung pasteur appellé Faustulus,
> Et par sa femme gardez et bien traictez,
> Furent depuis sy hautementʰ montez,
> Qui firent comme dominantz sur tous hommes,
> Les gens Reimz hors de Rome bout<i>ᵢ,
> Fonderent Reims la cité ou nous sommes.¹⁵

---

¹⁵ The fiction of the founding of and naming of Reims by and after Remus was fostered by the image of the she-wolf nursing Romulus and Remus in one of the vaults of the Roman arch in Reims (known as the Porte Mars). I find the image no longer discernible, although older drawings show its outline clearly.

15. ª Magdelaine C. —ᵇ alaictans C. —ᶜ aupres d'eux un pasteur C. —ᵈ empres luy C. —ᵉ trouvez C. —ᶠ Rhea C. —ᵍ alaictez C. —ʰ si haultement C. —ⁱ Qu'ils feirent Rome dominant sur tous hommes / Les gens Remus hors de Rome boutez C.

16. Item, et droitª devant Sainct Fiacre sur ung autre eschaffault avoit ung roy portant grandᵇ barbe et grande chevelure, assis en une chaire, tenant en l'une des mains une espee nue et en l'autre ung sceptre royal, ayant ung brevet contenant « Pharamond premier roy des François », entour lequel estoyent plusieurs personnages a grand barbeᶜ et chevelures, qui le couronnoyent et tenoient une couronne d'or sur sa teste, qui estoient habillez comme Turcz et Sarrasinsᵈ, les uns armez, les autres non. Et au devant dudit roy estoient quatre grandz barbus habituez comme en docteurs, qui tenoient une grande lettre devant luy, faisans semblant de lire et ne [fol. 51v] disoient mot, portans chacun son nom par escript attaché chacun a son affeublureᵉ, qui sont telz : Salagast, Wisogast, Bosogast, Widagast. Et au front dudict eschafault estoit escript en grosse lettre ce qui ensuit.

> Les Françoys extraicts des Troyansᶠ,
> Payens nommez Sicambriansᵍ,
> Font Pharamond leur premier roy,
> Qui leur fit la salicque loyʰ,
> Et les affranchist des Romains,
> Lors regnans sur tous les humains.
> On contoit quand ce cas advint,
> L'an de grace quatre cens vingt.¹⁶

16. ª droict C. —ᵇ grande C. —ᶜ grandes barbes C. —ᵈ Turcs et Sarazins C. — ᵉ affublure C. —ᶠ Troyens C. —ᵍ Sicambriens C. —ʰ feit salique loy C.

17. Depuis ledict Sainct Fiacre, tout au long de la rue jusquesª a la croix Sainct Victor, et depuis ladicte croix en retournant pardevant Sainct Denis, estoient ardantes les grandes torches des mestiers qu'on porte a la Feste Dieu, qui sont fort grandes et grosses ; et telles y aᵇ plus de quarante piedz de haulteur et bien soixante livres de cire ; et les rues bien parees par contre les maisons, les unes de rainseaulx d'arbres, les autres de linge fin, les autres de tapisserye, les autres de painctures ; et [fol. 53r] au devant de la chappelle de Clermarest y avoit ung petit eschaffault, sur lequel estoient plusieurs sainctz relicquaires et cierges ardensᶜ, et ung moyne de l'abbaye de Signy auprezᵈ, qui faisoit grand debvoir de

---

¹⁶ On these last two tableaux, see Jackson, *Vive le roi*, 178–79 (= *Vivat rex*, 166–67).

crier : «Vive le roy», et tout au long aux fenestres et par la rue tant de gens que c'estoit merveilles, crians semblablement : «Noel ! Vive le roy !»

17. [a] jusques *om.* C. —[b] de *add.* C. —[c] ardans C. —[d] empres C.

18. Joindant de la croix Sainct Victor, sur ung eschaffault bien[a] tendu de tapisserye[b], estoit le mistere du baptistere[c] et sacre du roy Clovis, premier roy chrestien des François, par personnaiges, et la mission de la sainct empoule[d]. Et au front dudict eschaffault estoit escript ce qui ensuict[e].

> L'an de grace cinq cens, le roy Clovis
> Receut a Reims par saint Remy baptesme,
> Couronne et sacre de l'ampolle pour cresme,
> Que Dieu des cieulx par son angle[f] a transmis.

Quand le roy perceut[g] ledit mistere[h], il arresta ung petit et demanda que c'estoit; a quoy luy fut respondu que c'estoit le mistere du sacre qu'il debvoit recepvoir, et lors il se desseuba et mit[i] jus son chappeau et passa outre, en tirant pardevant[j] l'abbaye de Saint Denis.

18. [a] ung B. —[b] tappisserie C. —[c] baptistaire C. —[d] sainte ampoule C. — [e] s'ensuict C. —[f] ange C. —[g] ape[r]ceut C. —[h] ledict mystere C. —[i] se desubla et meit C. —[j] par devers C.

19. Contre l'aumosne dudit Sainct Denis avoit ung [fol. 53v] autre[a] eschaffault, sur lequel estoit ung jeune filz vestus[b] d'une robbe d'asure[c], semee de fleurs de lis de couleur d'or, ayant une couronne d'or sur sa teste, entour luy ses serviteurs, comme le roy, en luy baillant[d] a laver quand il guarit des escrouelles; et devant luy personnages[e] comme gens malades de ladicte maladie, lesquelz il guarissoit[f], en les touchant en signe de la croix. Et au front dudict eschaffault estoit escript ce qui s'ensuit.

> En la vertu de la saincte unction[g],
> Qu'a Reims reçoit le noble roy de France,
> Dieu par ses mains confere guarison[h]
> D'escroelles[i], voicy la demonstrance.

19. [a] aultre C. —[b] vestu C. —[c] robe d'asur C. —[d] a luy baillant B. —[e] personnages *om.* C. —[f] guerissoit C. —[g] sainte onction C. —[h] guerison C. —[i] D'escrouellez C.

20. En passant pardevant ladicte histoire, plusieurs non regardans les vers dessus escriptz, cuidoient que ce fut[a] ung miracle de sainct Marcoud[b], et ainsy le dict on au roy, lequel, sans gueres arrester[c], passa outre pour tirer en l'eglise[d] de Reims, qui luy estoit en plain regard devant ses yeulx, ou devant de laquelle, a la descente du portail, et[e] tirant dedans le

parvis, estoient les religieux de Sainct Remy revestus d'aubes et chappes de drap d'or et de soye, qui estoyent venus, cuidans estre procession-nellement avecq messieurs les dignitez et chanoines de l'eglize de Reims a la reception du roy, comme il [fol. 54r] fault[f] es autres processions generalles. Mais supposé que les anciens livres ordinaires et registres de ladicte reception portent que les eglises collegialles et conventuelles du-dict Reims soyent a ladicte reception avec lesdictz chanoines, neantmoings on les fit[g] tenir au dehors de ladicte eglise ; et entre eulx, au devant du portail d'icelle esglize, descendit le roy.

20. [a] fust C. —[b] Marcoul C. —[c] arester C. —[d] l'esglize C. —[e] en *add.* C. —[f] il fault] ils sont C. —[g] feit C.

21. Incontinent qu'il fut descendu, les maistres de son Hostel firent[a] prendre et emporter le palion qui avoit esté porté sur luy, duquel les gens du prevost de l'Hostel prindrent et eurent les lances et les angles qui estoient dessus.[17]

21. [a] feirent C.

22. Tout au milieu[a] dudict portail avoict une chaere paree et ung coussin de drap d'or au dessus, sur lequel le roy se mit[b] a genoux, et la luy fut baillé a baisier le livre aux Evangiles[c] par monsieur de Reims, qui illec l'attendoit en habit pontifical, sa croix et sa crosse devant luy, accompaignié[d] de reverendz pairs les evesques de Laon, Langres, Chaalons, Noyon[e], pairs de France ; Amiens, Lombars, Sez[f], Perigueux, Alby et Sainct Pons[g] ; et des dessusdicts chanoynes et chappellains de ladicte eglize, revestus en chappes de drap d'or, velours[h], damas et soye.

22. [a] millieu C. —[b] au devant sur lequel le roy se meit C. —[c] a baiser le livre aux Evangilles C. —[d] accompaigné C. —[e] Noion C. —[f] Lombais Seez C. — [g] Sainct Pour C. —[h] veloux C.

B C	A
23. Apres que le roy eust baisié le livre aux Evangiles[a], [fol. 54v] l'archevesque de Reims le mit et introniza[b] en ladicte eglize, et ce faict, les evesques de Laon a destre[c] et de Langres[d] a senestre, estably et ordonné par ledict archevesque de Reims a officier audit sacre, pour et au lieu de l'evesque de	23a. [fol. 23r] Die sabbati ad vesperas dum rex recipitur in ecclesia beate Marie. In die recep-cionis sue debent ire processiona-liter archiepiscopus et episcopi ac canonici predicte ecclesie et alie ecclesie conventuales ob viam regi. Archiepiscopus debet dare regi ad osculandum textum Evangeliorum.

[17] Thus was frustrated Jean Foulquart's intention that the canopy and its supports should be used for several coronations; see Ordo XXIV,4 and n. 14 above.

B C	A
Beauvais, absent et excusé par maladie, fut conduit[e] ledict roy jusques dedans le coeur, au devant du grand autel, non pas que lesdicts evesques teinssent le roy, mais alloient pas a pas apres luy, et monsieur[f] de Dumois et autres seigneurs[g] le tenoient et supportoient[h] pour la tres grande foule et presse du peuple qui y estoit, desirant le veoir, et depuis ledict portail jusques audict cueur, ne eut le roy que son bonnet noir sur sa teste ; et quand il fut arrivé pres du grand autel, se mit a genoulx et y fut tandis qu'on chantoit les antesnes[i] qui s'ensuivent, que commencerent a chanter lesdictz chanoines, chappellains[j] et vicaires en conduisant le roy depuis ledit portail et jusques au grand autel. Et premier le respond qui s'ensuit.	Tunc debet cantari istud responsorium.

23. [a] eut baisé le livre aux Evangilles C. —[b] meit et intronisa C. —[c] dextre C. —[d] d'Amiens *a.* —[e] conduict C. —[f] monseigneur C. —[g] seigneurs *om.* C. —[h] surpportoient C. —[i] se meit a genous et fut tandis que l'on chantoit les antiennes C. —[j] chappelains C.

24. Responsorium. *Ecce ego mitto angelum meum, qui praecedat te et custodiat semper. Observa et audi vocem meam, et inimicus ero tuus[a] et affligentes te afligam[b], et precedet te angelus meus.*

24a. *Ecce ego mitto angelum meum, qui precedat te et custodiat semper. Observa et audi vocem meam, et inimicus ero inimicis tuis et affligentes te[c] affligam. Et precedet te angelus meus.*

24. [a] tuus] tuis inimicis C. —[b] affligam C. —[c] te / te A.

25. [fol. 55r] Versus[a]. *Israel si me audieris, non erit in te deus recens neque adorabis deum alienum, ego enim Dominus. Observa et audi vocem meam[b]* etc.

25a. Versus. *Israel, si me audieris, non erit in te deus recens neque adorabis deum alienum, ego enim Dominus. Et precedet.*

25. [a] Verset C. —[b] etc. *om.* C.

B C | A

26. En^a la fin dudict respond, chanterent l'antisne^b de Nostre Dame, qui s'ensuit.

Antiphona. *Beata Dei genitrix Maria, virgo perpetua, templum Domini, sacrarium Spiritus sancti, sola sine exemplo placuisti foemina Iesu^c Christo, ora pro populo, interveni pro clero, intercede pro devoto femineo sexu.*

26a. Finito responso, debet incipi antiphona de beata virgine. Tunc rex debet se prosternere ante altare,

26. ^a Et en C. —^b l'antienne C. —^c feliciam Iesum B.

27. Quand ladicte antesne^a fut chantee, le roy fut levé de son oraison par les evesques de Laon et de Langres^b, et apres qu'il fut levé, monsieur^c l'archevesque de Reims dict.
Ora pro nobis, sancta Dei genitrix.
Et le cueur respondit.
Ut digni efficiamur promissionibus Christi.

27a. et duo episcopi vel archiepiscopi debent eum surgere. Post orationem factam, archiepiscopus vero debet dicere versiculum.

Ora pro nobis, sancta Dei genitrix.

27. ^a antienne C. —^b d'Amiens *a*. —^c monseigneur C.

28. Puis ledit archevesque dict^a l'oraison qui s'ensuit.
Oracio.
Concede nos famulos tuos, quesumus Domine Deus, perpetua mentis et corporis sanitate et^b gaudere, et gloriosa beate Marie virginis intercessione [fol. 55v] *a praesenti liberari tristitia, et aeterna perfrui leticia. Per dominum nostrum Ihesum Christum^c, qui tecum vivit et regnat. In unitate [Spiritus^d] sancti Deus. Per omnia secula seculorum.*
Et le coeur respondit: *Amen.*

28a. Et postea oratio, *Concede nos,* vel alia secundum quod tempus exigit.

28. ^a dist C. —^b et *om.* C. —^c filium tuum *add.* C. —^d Spiritus *om.* B, *here add. from* C.

B C	A
29. Puis apres mondict sieur^a de Reims dit^b.	
29a. Iterum dicat versus pro rege.	
Domine, salvum fac regem^c.	*Domine, salvum fac regem,*
Et le cueur respondit.	
Et exaudi nos in die qua invocaverimus te.	

29. ^a seigneur C. —^b dict C. —^c regem fac B.

30. Et puis il dict^a l'oraison qui s'ensuit.	30a. et orationem.
Oracio.	
Quesumus, omnipotens Deus, ut famulus tuus rex noster Carolus, qui tua miseracione suscepit regni gubernacula, virtutum eciam [*omnium*^b] *percipiat*[18] *incrementa, quibus decenter ornatus, et vitiorum monstra devitare, et hostes superare, et ad te qui 'via, veritas et vita' es, graciosus valeat pervenire. Per dominum nostrum Ihesum* etc.^c	*Quesumus, omnipotens Deus, ut famulus tuus rex noster, qui tua miseracione suscepit regni gubernacula, virtutum eciam omnium percipiat incrementa, quibus decenter ornatus, et viciorum monstra devitare, et hostes supernare, et ad te qui 'via, veritas et vita' es, graciosus valeat pervenire. Per Christum* etc., vel alia si placet.
Et le cueur respondit: *Amen.*	

30. ^a dist C. —^b omnium *om.* B C, *but later add.* C. —^c Ihesum etc.] Iesum Christum etc. C.

B C

31. Quant lesdictes oraisons furent dictes et achevees, lesdictz evesques^a de Laon et de Langres^b menerent le roy baisier^c le grand autel et faire son oblacion. Et ce faict, il fut conduit^d et mené par les princes et seigneurs estans avec luy ou^e palais archiepiscopal en la chambre a luy preparee pour reposer.

---

[18] *percipiat* is a correction in *B*, and it might read (incorrectly) *praecipiat*. Apparently the source was difficult to read here, which might account for *B*'s omission of *omnium* and *C*'s initial omission of *omnium*. The conclusion of the following word, *incrementa*, was also corrected in *B*.

Et environ une heure apres, le roy, qui avoit changé d'habit, retourna en ladicte eglize[f], vestu d'une robbe longue de damas blanc forree de martes sablines[g], pour ouir les vespres, ou il fut tout au [fol. 56r] long d'icelles, lesquelles furent tenues par mondit sieur[h] l'archevesque en habit pontifical, en la fin desquelles ledit roy retourna audit palais.

31. [a] evesque B. —[b] d'Amiens *a*. —[c] baiser C. —[d] conduict C. —[e] au C. — [f] esglise C. —[g] damars blanc fourree de martres sabelines C. —[h] seigneur C.

32. Depuis que le roy fut party de ladicte eglise, on y dict[a] et acheva complies en la maniere accoustumee[b]. Et incontinent apres on sonna les matines qui furent dictes et chantees de ce jour pour le lendemain.

Et apres qu'on eut tout chanté, monsieur de Dumois[c] alla en ladicte eglise ordonner qu'on y feist une closture en maniere de barrieres[d] au devant du grand autel, a l'entour du lieu ou le roy debvoit recevoir son sainct sacre et couronnement, afin que le lendemain en le recevant la foule du peuple assistant ne luy peust nuire, ne aux princes, prelats et seigneurs d'entour luy, laquelle closture fut incontinent faite et eschevée[e].

Entre huict et neuf au soir de ce jour, les archers de la garde du roy furent envoiez en ladicte esglize pour la garder avec les coustres d'icelle, pour y demeurer toute la nuict, et le lendemain jusques apres le sacre et service faict.

32. [a] dist C. —[b] acoustumee C. —[c] monseigneur de Dunois C. —[d] barriere C. — [e] faicte et achevee C.

33. Et environ ung quart d'heure apres, le roy alla en ladicte eglise faire son oraison, pour ce que l'ordinaire du sacre porte que, de nuict en [fol. 56v] grand[19] silence et sans bruict, le roy doibt aller en ladicte eglise faire son oraison et en icelle veiller une espace de temps, s'il luy ploit[a], en prieres et oraisons. Et assez tost aprés s'en retourna oudit palais, ou il dormit et fut depuis toute la nuict et[b] jusques au lendemain que on le fut querir pour sacrer et couronner, comme dict sera[c] cy apres.

33. [a] plaist C. —[b] et *om*. C. —[c] sera dict C.

34. Le soir, apres que l'eglise fut close, on prepara tous les sieges requis pour le mistere dudict sacre, et le[s] para-t-on[a] de tapisserie.

Des avant la venue du roy on avoit preparé son throsne et les sieges des pers, ainsy que les anciens livres et ordinaires du mistere portent que faire se doibt a chacun sacre, lesquels ont esté pour ce veus[b] et concordez

---

[19] Beginning with this page, *B* is written in a different hand, one that is somewhat more legible than the hand that wrote the first part of the ordo. Both hands are far more difficult to read than the one that copied Ordines XX B and XXII A in this manuscript.

par monsieur[c] l'archevesque de Reims et les autres pers ecclesiastiques, et par autres avec eulx ; et en a esté faict et partout (en tant que touche le mistere et les ceremonies du sacre et couronnement) entierement, ainsy que faire se doibt selon lesdictz livres et ordonnances[d]. Parquoy ne fault plus querir ne chercher pour sçavoir comment on[e] doibt faire en tel cas, car tout a esté [fol. 57r] accomply[f] a celuy cy.

34. [a] les para on C. —[b] veuz C. —[c] monseigneur C. —[d] ordinaires C. —[e] en C. — [f] acomply C.

35. Et pour monstrer la forme du trosne, est assavoir que au pulpitre, droict au milieu[a] au dessoubz de l'arche qui porte le crucifix,[20] y avoit une chayere haulte[b] eslevee sur ung siege, a laquelle et a costier[c] d'icelle on montoit a trois pas, qui estoit le trosne[d] du roy ; et aux deux costez par bas sur ledict pulpitre deux bancs, qui estoient les sieges des pers ecclesiasticques et seculiers, comme [sera dict cy apres ; et au costé dextre contre la closture dudict pulpitre, du costé vers le choeur, y avoit un autel paré, sur lequel furent dictes les messes du roy, comme[e]] il sera cy apres[f] declaré ; et montoit on audict pulpitre par un large montee de bois faicte tout propre, de laquelle les boutz des montants se arrestoyent et boutoyent[g] en trois trous[h], dont les pierres, qui sont petites, avoient esté levees[i] du pavé du costé destre, auprins l'entré[j] moyenne des chayerez. Et en approchant[k] dudict pulpitre, par dessoubz ladicte montee, y avoit des[l] semblables pierres levees ; et en leurs trous estoyent mits[m] debout les tresteaulx[n] qui portoient et soustenoient ladicte montee, de laquelle les marches estoyent closes. Et sy y avoit barrieres et appoyes aux deux costez. Et sy estoit de largeur pour[o] monter et descendre a l'aise trois hommes de front. Le tout paré hault et bas de tapisserye[p] le plus honnestement que faire se peult.

35. [a] a sçavoir que au pupitre droict au millieu C. —[b] hault C. —[c] a costé C. — [d] throsne C. —[e] sera dit cy apres ... comme om. B, *here add. from* C. — [f] comme cy apres sera C. —[g] bouts des montans s'arrestoient et boutoient C. —[h] dans le choeur *add.* a. —[i] levez B. —[j] dextre empres l'entree C. — [k] aprochant C. —[l] de C. —[m] estoient mis C. —[n] treteaux C. —[o] y *add.* C. — [p] tappisserie C.

36. [fol. 57v] Ce mesme soir, monsieur de Lombais, abbé de Sainct Denis en France, envoya au roy la robbe de couleur jacinte en façon d'une tunicque a soubdiacre, pour luy vestir le lendemain sur la[a] chemise.

---

[20] Such a crucifix is called a rood in English, giving rise to the term rood-screen (or rood-loft) for the entire architectural feature (the *jubé* in French). Referring to the rood-screen here as a *pulpitre* certainly implies that it was commonly used for preaching. See Jackson, "Le pouvoir monarchique," 237–51.

36. [a] sa C.

37. Le dimanche[a] trentiesme et penultiesme jour du mois de may oudict an mil quatre cens quatre vingtz[b] quatre, qui fut le jour du sainct sacre et couronnement, environ cinq heures du matin, le roy envoia le comte de Roussy, le grand seneschal de Normandye, messire Hardouin, sieur[c] de Mailly, et messire Jacques de Luxembourg en l'eglise de Sainct Remy, par devers l'abbé et les relligieulx[d], pour avoir la saincte ampole ; lesquels sieurs[e], arrivez audict Sainct Remy, requierent a maistre Robert de Lenoncourt, commandataire et administrateur perpetuel de ladicte abbaye, et aux relligieux[f] pour ce assemblez, d'avoir ladicte saincte ampole, et leur jurerent et promisrent[g] en presence de Jehan Vauchelet et Jehan Joffre[h], notaires de la cour de Reims, qui en firent l'instrument[i], que de bonne foy ils la conduiroient jusques en l'eglise de Reims, et apres le sacre et service fait[j], la reconduiroient en ladicte eglise de Saint[k] Remy, et si bailleroient en ladicte eglise en signe de [fol. 58r] ce les banieres de leurs armes.

37. [a] dimenche C. —[b] et *add.* C. —[c] seigneur C. —[d] religieux C. —[e] seigneurs C. —[f] religieux C. —[g] promirent C. —[h] Joffrin C. —[i] firent instrument C. — [j] faict C. —[k] Sainct C.

38. A ladicte heure de cinq heures ou environ, le roy envoia audict commandataire une hacquenee de poil blanc pour luy monter a aporter et reporter ladicte saincte ampole. Et sy envoya ung palion de damas[a] blanc broché d'or pour porter sur icelle saincte ampole.

38. [a] de damars C.

39. Entre cinq et six heures du matin que prime estoit desja sonnee et chantee, l'archevesque de Reims ; et les evesques de Laon, Langres, Chaalons et Noyon, pers de France (celuy d'Amiens commis a representer l'evesque de Beauvais, pair de France, absent et excusé par malladye) ; les evesques de Lombars[a] (abbé de Sainct Denis en France), de Sez[b], de Perigueux, d'Albi[c] et de Sainct Ponts ; alerent au cueur de ladicte eglise de Reims, tous et chascuns d'eulx en estat et habit pontifical, pour proceder au mistere dudict sainct sacre et couronnement.

39. [a] Lombais C. —[b] Says C. —[c] d'Alby C.

40. Quand ils furent en iceluy cueur ledict archevesque de Reims alla seoir en une chaiere qui luy estoit preparee, le dos contre le grand autel, et les evesques pers de France sur ung banc preparé du costé destre au lieu, et [fol. 58v] ainsy que on a accoustumé[a] de faire pour seoir les diacres et soubdiacres en jours solenpnelz[b], et furent assis en l'ordre que s'ensuit.

L'evesque de Laon, le premier, au bout vers l'autel.

L'evesque de Langres[c], le second.

L'evesque de Chalon[d], le tiers, pour ce que celuy de Beauvais n'y estoit pas, qui l'eut preceddé[e] s'il y eust esté en personne.

L'evesque de Noyon, le quart, qui eust esté le quint.

L'evesque d'Amiens, commis pour Beauvais, le cinquiesme.

40. [a] qu'on a acoustumé C. —[b] solemnels C. —[c] Langre C. —[d] Chaalons C. — [e] l'eust precedé C.

41. L'evesque de Lombais[a], abbé de Saint Denis en France, se tint au coing sinistre[b] de l'autel, gardant les habitz royaulx qu'il avoit apporté[c] de sadicte abbaie pour ledict sacre, lesquelz il mit[d] sur ledict autel, c'est assavoir la couronne royalle; l'espee atout sa gaine ou foreau[e]; les esperons d'or ou dorez, qui ont des boullettes[f] rondes assez[g] grosses sur les boutz des verges; le sceptre roial d'or ou doré; la verge longue d'environ une coudé,[h] ayant une main d'yvoire au bout d'enhault; les chausses; et le soc ou mantel en [fol. 59r] façon de chappe sans chapperon derriere, de couleur jacinte[i], qui est entre jaune, rous[j] et bleu, semé de fleurs de lis[k] d'or. Et les autres evesques estoient debout et tous droicts.

41. [a] Lonbais C. —[b] senestre C. —[c] aporté C. —[d] mist C. —[e] foureau C. — [f] boulettes C. —[g] assés C —[h] environ d'une coudee C. —[i] hyacinte *a*. —[j] roux C. —[k] lys C.

42. Environ six heures du matin, les six pers de France seculiers, commiz et ordonnez par le roy nostre sire a estre et officier audict sacre, se partirent de la chambre dudict sieur[a], ou ilz estoient tous assemblez pour aller en ladicte eglize, vestus de manteaulx ou socques de pairie[b], renversez sur les espales[c] comme ung espitoge ou chappe[d] de docteur, et fourrez de hermines, ayans sur leurs testes des cercles[e] d'or, le[s] ducs a demi[f] fleurons[21] et les comtes tous simples; et s'en allerent ensemble au cueur de ladicte eglize, ouquel ilz furent assis du costé senestre sur ung banc semblable a celuy des pers ecclesiasticques[g], et en l'ordre qui s'ensuit, c'est a sçavoir.

Le premier au bout pres de l'autel, monsieur Loys[h], duc d'Orleans, representant le duc de Bourgongne.

Le second apres, monsieur[i] René, duc d'Alençon, representant le duc de Normandye.

Le tiers, monsieur[i] Pierre de Bourbon, comte de Clermont et de la

---

[21] A marginal note in *C* reads, "Les cercles des pairs ducs differens de ceux des pairs comtes." This and the succeeding marginal notes were usually placed in the margin of the printed edition (ed. *a*), although they were often slightly altered or amplified in *a*.

Marche, que le roy fist duc [fol. 59v] quant a ce, representant le duc d'Acquitaine.

Le quart, monsieur Louis, conte d'Ausny d'Auvergne de Bourbon[j], representant le comte de Flandres vivant, qui par ce precedda[k] celuy de Champaigne, qui devoit[l] estre le quatriesme.

Le quint, monsieur Philippe[m] de Savoye, comte de Bresse, representant le conte de Champaigne.

Le sixiesme, monsieur[i] François de Bourbon, comte de Vendosme, representant le conte de Thoulouse.

42. [a] seigneur C. —[b] parie C. —[c] espaules C. —[d] chappes C. —[e] cules B. — [f] les ducs a demy C. —[g] ecclesiastiques C. —[h] monseigneur Louys C. —[i] monseigneur C. —[j] monseigneur Loüis de Bourbon comte daulphin d'Auvergne C. —[k] preceda C. —[l] Champagne qui debvoit C. —[m] monseigneur Philippes C.

43. Audict mistere furent presens, monsieur[a] François de Laval, comte de Montfort, seigneur du Gavre[22] grand maistre d'Hostel de France, portant cercle et habitué comme lesdicts pers comtes.

Et messire Guillaume de Rochefort, chevalier, docteur en lois[b] et en Decret, chancelier de France, ayant sur sa teste ung mortier de drap d'or.

43. [a] presents monseigneur C. —[b] loix C.

44. Cedict jour, environ sept heures du matin, mesdicts sieurs[a] les evesques de Laon et de Langres (commis pour Beauvais quand[b] a ce), accompagnez des chanoines, vicaires et chappellains de ladicte esglise, se partirent d'icelle et allerent processionnellement [a tout les deux[c]] crois[d] que portoient messire Nicolle Le Bourgeois[e] et messire Thomas Mayreau[f], coustres clercz[g] de ladicte eglize; de l'eaue [fol. 60r] benoite[h] que portoit messire Pierre Bourgeois, chappellain d'icelle esglise; [de[i]] deux cierges[j] allumez et deux ensansoires[k], que portoient quatre enfans de cueur, querir le roy oudit palais archiepiscopal, qui estoit lors en la premiere chambre haute[l] sur le jardin, en montant par la grande salle par le bout de la salle[m] basse, assis ou accoudé[n], a demy couché sur le lict de parement illec preparé. Et monterent seullement en ladicte chambre lesdictz evesques de Laon et Langres, leurs clers portans leurs crosses, les dessusdictz coustres portans lesdites[o] croix, le chappelain portant l'eaue beniste, et lesdictz enfans portans les cierges et ensansoires[p], et peu d'autres, avecq messire[q] Jehan Encher, docteur en theologie, chantre, et messire Nicolle Coullemois[r], chanoine et soubzchantre [de ladicte

---

[22] *de* (corr. from *du*) *Gavre* C; *du Guaure* a. Anselme de Sainte-Marie, *Histoire généalogique*, 8: 383, gives a brief biography of François de Laval, sire de Gavre, Grand-Maître de France.

esglise. Et eulx arrivez en ladicte chambre[s], quand ils perceurent[t] le roy sur ledict lict, l'evesque de Laon dict[u] l'oroison qui s'ensuit.

44. [a] seigneurs C. —[b] quant C. —[c] a tout les deux *om.* B, *here add. from* C. — [d] croix C. —[e] maistre (*corr. from* maistere) Nicolle Bourgeois C. —[f] Nayreau C. —[g] clers C. —[h] beniste C. —[i] de *om.* B C, *here add. because the context requires it.* —[j] sierges C. —[k] encensoirs C. —[l] haulte C. —[m] sale C. — [n] acoudé C. —[o] lesdictes C. —[p] ensensoirs C. —[q] maistre C. —[r] Nicole Coulemois C. —[s] de ladicte ... chambre *om.* B, *here add. from* C. —[t] parçurent C, apperceurent *a.* —[u] dist C.

45. Oracio.

Omnipotens sempiterne Deus, qui famulum tuum Carolum regis fastigio dignatus es sublimare, tribue quesumus ei, ut ita in huius seculi cursu multorum in commune[a] salutem disponat, quatenus a veritatis tuae tramitae non recedat. Per dominum nostrum Ihesum Christum filium tuum, qui tecum vivit et regnat in unitate Spiritus sancti Deus. [fol. 60v] *Per omnia secula seculorum. Amen.*

45. [a] communem B.

46. Apres que ladicte oraison fut achevee, lesditz evesques de Laon a destre et de Langres a senestre leverent reveremment le roy de dessus ledict lict. Et le menerent avecq ladicte procession en l'eglise pour sacrer et couronner[a] roy de France. Et en alant fut chanté le respond[b] qui s'ensuit, qui fut commencé par ledict chantre[c] et soubschantre en saillant de ladicte chambre.

46. [a] pour estre sacré et couronné *a.* —[b] en allant fut chanté le respons C. — [c] commancé par les dicts chantres C.

47. Responsorium.

Ecce ego mitto angelum meum, qui praecedat[a] te et custodiat semper. Observa et audi vocem meam, et inimicus ero inimicis tuis et affligentes te affligam, et precedet te angelus meus[b].

Israel, si me audieris, non erit in te deus recens neque adorabis deum alienum, ego enim Dominus. Observa et audi vocem meam etc.

47. [a] precedat, *corr. from* proecedat C. —[b] Versus *add.* C.

48. Quand le roy partit de sa chambre en allant a l'eglize, il estoit vestu d'une chemise de soye au nud sur sa cher[a], et dessus d'une robbe [de soye[b]] de couleur jacinte, qui est en façon d'une tunique a soubdiacre[c], fendue et fermee a bouttons par devant et par derriere[d], apporté de Saint[e] Denis en France, et au par dessus d'une longue robbe de damara blanc forree de martres[f], ung bonnet noir sur [fol. 61r] sa teste ; et aloit[g] en grande devocion, comme on pouvoit congnoistre a le regarder.

48. ᵃ chair C. —ᵇ de soye *om.* B, *here add. from* C. —ᶜ soubsdiacre C. —
ᵈ derier B. —ᵉ Sainct C. —ᶠ de damars blanc fourré de martres C. —ᵍ alloit C.

49. A l'entrée de ladicte esglize, au portail de la croisee du costé des
fons, quand il fut illec parvenu, on arresta ; et a ce lieu dict l'evesque de
Langres, commis pour celuyᵃ de Beauvaisᵇ, l'oroison qui s'ensuit.

Oracio.

Deus, qui scis humanum genus nulla virtute posse subsistere, con-
cede propicius, ut famulus tuus Carolus, quem populo tuo voluisti pre-
ferri, ita tuo fulciatur adiutorio, quatenus quibus potuit preesse valeat
et prodesse. Per dominum nostrum Ihesum Christum filium tuum, qui
tecum etc.

49. ᵃ celluy C. —ᵇ dist *add.* C.

50. Et apres que ladicte oraison fut dicte, ilz entrerent en l'eglise en
chantant l'antienne qui s'ensuit, qui fut commancéᵃ par lesdicts chantre
et soubschantre.

Antiphona.

Domine, in virtute tua laetabitur rex etc.

Et tantost que ladite antesneᵇ fut dicte, on commança a sonner les
orgues jusques a ce que le roy fut entré dedans le cueur par l'huis de
devant les fons.

50. ᵃ commencee C. —ᵇ ladicte anthiene C.

51. Le roy entré oudict cueur, lesdicts evesques [fol. 61v] de Laon et
Langres le menerent et presenterent reveremment pour [leᵃ] consacrer
en roy audict archevesque assis en sa chaiere, le dos contre l'autel, qui
l'attendoit ; sur lequel tantost qu'il luy fut presenté, il dictᵇ l'oroison qui
s'ensuit.

Oracio.

Omnipotens sempiterne Deus, celestium terrestriumque moderator,
qui famulum tuum Carolum ad regni fastigium dignatus es pro-
vehere, concede, quesumus, ut a cunctis adversitatibus liberatus et
ecclesiasticae pacis dono muniatur et ad aeterneᶜ pacis gaudia te
donante pervenireᵈ mereatur. Per dominum nostrum Ihesum Chris-
tum filium tuum, qui tecum vivit et regnat in unitate Spiritus sancti
Deus, per omnia secula seculorum. Amen.

51. ᵃ le *om.* B, *here add. from* C. —ᵇ dist C. —ᶜ aeterna C. —ᵈ provenire B.

52. Enᵃ la fin de ladicte oraison, lesdicts evesques de Laon et Langres
leverent le roy et le menerent seoir en une chaiere qui luy estoit prepareeᵇ,
ainsy comme a l'opposite de celle dudict archevesque, au pres du lieu ou

on met le seau a eau benoite quant on la fais[c] en ladicte esglize ; en[d] laquelle chaiere il fut jusques a ce que on apporta ladicte saincte ampolle de Sainct Remy.

52. [a] Et en C. —[b] preparé B. —[c] mect le seau a eau beniste quand on la faict C. — [d] en] et en C.

53. Et en attendant la venue de ladicte saincte ampole, monsieur de Reims print[a] de l'eaue benoiste, qui [fol. 62r] avoict esté faicte a la premiere messe au poinct du jour, et en donna au roy, pour ce que le chanoine sepmainier qui la debvoit faire ne peut avoir entree au cueur pour la faire au lieu accoustumé, pour la presse des gens, et la fit[b] a la fin de tout le service, au lieu ou elle est ordinairement chacun jour derrier[e][c] le grant autel au devant de l'autel de la Magdelaine[d].

53. [a] monseigneur de Rheims prist C. —[b] fist C. —[c] derriere C. —[d] le grand autel au devant de l'Hostel de la Magdelaine C.

54. Avant la venue d'icelle saincte ampole, on chanta tierce, le roy estant assis tousjours en sa chaire.

55. Entre sept et huict[a] heures au matin de ce jour [vint[b]] maistre Robert de Lenoncourt, commandataire[c] et administrateur perpetuel de l'abbaye dudict Sainct Remy, vestu d'un surplis[d] et d'une chappe de drap d'or dessus, ung bonnet noir sur sa teste, et monté sur la hacquenee, et soubz le palion que le roy luy avoit envoié, que porterent sur luy a quatre bastons au partir du lieu ou elle fut prinse jusques au dehors de l'eglise, outre[e] les avant loges, quatre relligieux[f] de ladicte abbaie, revestus d'aubbes[g], lesquelz chanterent, en la prenant et portant, les antienne et oraison qui feust[h].

55. [a] Entre les sept a huict C. —[b] vint om. B C, here add. from a. —[c] commendateur C. —[d] surpelis C. —[e] oultres C. —[f] religieux C. —[g] abbaye revestuz d'aulbes C. —[h] s'ensuit C, s'ensuivent a.

56. Antiphona.

O preciosum munus, o preciosa[a] gemma, quae pro unctione Francorum regum misterio[b] angelico caelitus est emissa.

[fol. 62v] Vers. *Inveni David servum meum.*

Resp. *Oleo sancto unxi eum.*

56. [a] spreciosa B. —[b] ministerio C, in ministerio *Ordo XXIII,14.*

57. Oracio.

Omnipotens sempiterne Deus, qui[a] pietatis tuae dono genus regio[b] Francorum oleo perungi decrevisti, praesta quesumus, ut famulus tuus rex noster Carolus pe018ctus hac sacra et presenti unctione, sancto pontifici Remigio emissa divinitus, et in tuo servicio semper diri-gatur, et ab omni infirmitate misericorditer liberetur. Per dominum nostrum etc.

57. [a] qui *om.* C. —[b] regium C, regum *Ordo XXIII,15.*

58. Et depuis lesdictz avant loges jusques au portail de l'eglise de Reims, combien que selon tous les livres anciens lesdictz relligieux deussent avoir porté ledict palion tousjours[a], neantmoins il fut porté depuis lesdictz avant loges, et jusques audict portail de l'eglise par maistre Jehan Cauchon[b] le Jeune, Jehan de Secaneuel, Jacques des Champs et[c] Claude Toguel[d], feodaux dudict Sainct Remy, accompagnés[e] des dessus-dictz Jehan, comte de Roussi, Jacques de Brese[f], comte de Maleurié[g], seneschal de Normandie, Messire Hardouin, sieur[h] de Mailly, et Jacques de Luxembourg[i], qui estoient a la gardes[j], comme dict est dessus ; [ledit de Lenoncourt[k]] apporta ladicte saincte ampolle pendant a son col, les relligieux de ladicte abbaye allans[l] processionnellement [fol. 63r] devant, jusques au devant du portail de ladicte eglize de Reims, auquel lieu il descendit de dessus ladicte hacquenee, et eut oudict voiage[m], avec les dessusdictz, vingt quatre hommes, arbalestriers du Chesne le Populeux, en hocquetons de livrée, portans[n] chacun l'arbalestre sur l'espaule, pour conduire et raconduire ladicte saincte ampole.[23]

58. [a] toursjours B. —[b] Caunchon C. —[c] et *om.* C. —[d] Lognel C. —[e] accompa-gné C. —[f] Bere C. —[g] Maleurier C, Moleurier *a.* —[h] seigneur C. —[i] Leuxem-bourg C. —[j] qui l'estoient allé querir C. —[k] ledit de Lenoncourt *om.* B C, *here add. from a.* —[l] allants C. —[m] audict voyage C. —[n] portants C.

59. Et laquelle ainsy apportee[a], estant devant ledit[b] portail, mondit sieur[c] l'archevesque en habit pontifical, accompagné d'aulcuns des evesques dessus nommez, et d'aulcuns chanoynes, aussy atout sa crosse, et la croix devant, alla processionnellement sur ledict portail prendre et recevoir ladite[d] saincte ampolle des mains dudit[e] commandataire, qui l'avoit apporté[f] ; et avant de la recepvoir, promet[g] de bonne foy a icelluy[h] commandataire de la luy rendre et restituer apres le sacre du roy et le service faict, en la presence de Jehan Joffrin et Jehan Vauchelet, not-taires[i], ausquelz ledict commandataire en requit[j] instrument. Et apres ladicte promesse, la print et receut et tres reveremment la porta sur le grand autel, ledict commandataire, aulcuns des relligieux dudit[e] Sainct Remy, les evesques et chanoines le accompagnans[k], qui chanterent en la

---

[23] At several coronations the inhabitants of Le Chesne, a village some sixty kilo-meters northeast of Reims, were involved in a protracted, vicious, and sometimes riotous dispute concerning their rights at the ceremony. The story has never been told in full, although in Reims there is ample material for it.

recevant et portant sur ledit[b] autel les antienne[l] et oroison dessus escriptz[m].

O preciosum[n] munus, o preciosa gemma etc.

Omnipotens sempiterne Deus, qui pietatis [fol. 63v] *tuae dono genus regio[o] Francorum oleo* etc., ut supra.

59. [a] aportee C. —[b] ledict C. —[c] mondict seigneur C. —[d] ladicte C. —[e] dudict C. —[f] aportee C. —[g] avant que la recevoir promist C. —[h] iceluy C. —[i] Jehan Loffrin et Jehan Vochelin notaires C. —[j] requist C. —[k] les acompagnants C. —[l] antiene C. —[m] escriptes C. —[n] presiosum C. —[o] regium C.

60. Apres que monsieur de Reims eut mis ladicte saincte ampolle[a] sur le grand autel, le dessusdit[b] commandataire de Sainct Remy qui l'avoit apporté[c], comme dict est, se mit[d] au coing destre dudict autel et s'y tint au long du mistere gardant icelle saincte[e] ampole.

60. [a] ampolle *corr. from* ampoulle B. —[b] dessusdict C. —[c] apportee C. —[d] mist C. —[e] saincte C.

61. Ces choses ainsy faictes, ledict archevesque et les evesques et chanoines commis a faire offices de diacre et soubdiacre, assistans et procedans a la messe, allerent ou revestiaire ou sacraire de ladicte eglize, eulx preparer et revestir pour le sainct sacre et service divin faire[a].

61. [a] pour faire le sainct sacre et service divin C.

62. Et combien que par les ordinaires et anciens livres dudict mistere soit expressement dict que deux des evesques de la province de Reims doivent[a] faire office, l'un de diacre, l'autre de soubzdiacre, neantmoings pource que d'iceulx n'estoient venus[b] sinon ceulx de Laon, Chaalons et Noyon, qui sont pairs de France et officioyent audict mistere comme pers, et celuy d'Amiens, qui fut commis a tenir lieu de per pour celuy de Beauvais absent, mondit sieur l'archevesque commit[c] et ordonna l'evesque de Sainct Pons a faire office de diacre et l'evesque de Sez[d] a faire [celuy de[e]] souzdiacre, qui le [fol. 64r] firent[f] en habit pontifical, chacun d'eulx la mittre[g] sur la teste.

62. [a] doibvent C. —[b] venuz C. —[c] mondict seigneur l'archevesque commist C. —[d] Says C. —[e] celuy de *om.* B C, *here add. from* a. —[f] soubsdiacre qui le feirent C. —[g] la mythre C.

63. Monsieur[a] l'archevesque revestu en habit pontifical comme pour dire messe, de la chasuble que le roy Charles Quint donna a ladicte eglize, qui est de velours per[b] semé de petites fleurs de lis[c] d'or, ayant son palion et le racional dessus ; lesdicts evesques de Sainct Pons et de Sez, revestus[d] de tunicques et dalmaticques pareilles a ladicte chasuble, et aussy du don dudit roy Charles Quint[e] ; avec douze des chanoines de

ladicte esglize assistans et proceddans, revestus[f] d'autres tunicques et dalmactiques de divers draps[g] de velours, damas et soye de couleur[h], s'en vint au devant du grand[i] autel, et en passant par pres de[j] roy pour aprocher ledit[k] autel. Quand le roy le vit[l], il se leva reveremmant devant luy, et puis se rasseit[m] en sadicte chayere.

63. [a] Monseigneur C. —[b] pers C. —[c] lys C. —[d] Says revestuz C. —[e] du dict roy Charles le Quint C. —[f] assistants et procedants revestuz C. —[g] drap C. — [h] damars et soye de couleurs C. —[i] grant C. —[j] du C. —[k] ledict C. —[l] veit C. — [m] rasseist C.

64. Le roy estant en sadicte chayere assis, ledict archevesque s'approcha de luy et luy feit[a] pour toutes les eglises a luy subgettes les requestes et petitions qui s'ensuit[b].

64. [a] fist C. —[b] s'ensuivent C.

65. Petitio archiepiscopi pro omnibus ecclesiis sibi subditis.

A vobis perdonari petimus, ut unicuique de nobis et ecclesiis nobis commissis canonicum [fol. 64v] *privilegium ac debitam legem atque iustitiam conservetis, et defensionem[a] exhibeatis, sicut rex in suo regno unicuique episcopo et ecclesiae sibi commissae per[b] rectum exhibere debet.*

65. [a] deffensionem *corr. from* defensionem C. —[b] pro B.

66. A laquelle requeste et peticion, le roy respondit en cette[a] maniere.

Responsio regis.

Promitto vobis et perdono, quod unicuique de nobis et ecclesiis vobis commissis canonicum privilegium [ac[b]] *debitam legem atque iusticiam servabo, et deffensionem, quantum potero, exhibebo, Domino adiuvante, sicut rex in suo regno unicuique[c] episcopo et ecclesiae sibi commissae per rectum exhibere debet.*

66. [a] ceste C. —[b] ac *om.* B, *here add. from* C. —[c] uniquique C.

67. Puis fit[a] les autres promesses qui s'ensuivent.

Haec populo christiano et michi[b] subdito in Christi nomine promitto.

In primis, ut ecclesiae Dei omnipotentis populus christianus veram pacem nostro arbitrio in omni tempore servet.

Item, ut omnes rapacitates et omnes iniquitates omnibus interdicam.

Item, ut in omnibus iudiciis equitatem et misericordiam precipiam, ut michi[b] et vobis indulgeat suam misericordiam clemens et misericors [fol. 65r] *Dominus.*

Item, de terra mea ac iuridictione^c michi^b subdita universos here-
ticos ab ecclesia denotatos pro viribus bona fide exterminare studebo.
Haec omnia supradicta firmo iuramento.
Et en disant les mots et juremens, il mit^d les deux mains sur le livre
aux Evangiles, et puis le baisa.

> 67. ^a fist C. —^b mihi C. —^c iurisdictione C. —^d mist C.

68. Quand le roy eut faict lesdictes promesses et juremens, ainsy que
dict est^a, il se leva de sa chaiere et fut devestu devant le grand autel de sa
robbe de damara^b fourree de martres et de ses autres habitz, excepté sa
chemise et la robbe en façon de tunicque qu'il avoit dessus, lesquelles
estoient fendues bien avant devant et derriere^c entre les espaulles, et fer-
mees^d a boutons d'argent. Et lors l'archevesque de Reims dit^e sur luy
l'oroison qui s'ensuit.

> 68. ^a ainsi que dist est C. —^b damars C. —^c derier B. —^d fermés B. —^e dist C.

69. Oracio.

Deus, inenarrabilis^a auctor mundi, conditor generis^b humani,
gubernator imperii, confirmator regni, qui ex utero fidelis amici tui
patriarche nostri Abrahe preelegisti regem seculi profuturum. Tu pre-
sentem [regem^c] hunc Carolum cum exercitu suo per intercessionem
omnium sanctorum uberi^d benedictione locupleta et in solium regni
firma stabilitate connecta. Visita eum sicut Moysem in rubro^e, Iesum
Nave^f in prelio, Gedeon [fol. 65v] in agro, Samuelem in templo. Et illa
eum benedictione siderea aut^g sapiencie tue rore perfunde, quem bea-
tus David in psalterio, Salomon filius eius^h te remunerante percepitⁱ
e celo. Sis ei contra acies inimicorum lorica, in adversis galea, in
prosperis paciencia, in protectione clipeus^j sempiternus. Et presta, ut
gentes illi teneant fidem, proceres sui habeant pacem, diligant cari-
tatem, abstineant se a cupiditate, loquantur iusticiam^k, custodiant
veritatem. Et ita populus iste pullulet^l coalitus benedictione aeterni-
tatis, ut semper maneant tripudientes^m in pace victores.

Quod ipse praestare dignetur, qui tecum et Spiritu sancto sine fine
permanet in secula seculorum. Amen.

> 69. ^a inexorabilis B. —^b genus B. —^c regem *om.* B C, here add. *from Ordo*
> *XXIII,21.* —^d ubere B. —^e Moysen in rubo C, *corr. from* Moysen in rubro. —
> ^f ave C. —^g syderea ac C. —^h eius filius B. —ⁱ praecipit B. —^j clypeus C. —^k et
> *add.* C. —^l populo iste pulula B. —^m trepudiantes B.

70. Aprés que ladicte oraison fut dicte, ledit comte de Dumois^a,
comme grand ou premier chambellan de France, chaussa au roy les
chausses apportees de Sainct Denis en France.

70. ª Dunois C.

71. Et apres monsieurª d'Orleans, faisant office de per de France, mitᵇ et ferma aux piedz du roy les esperons apportez dudit Sainct Denis, et ung peu apres les luy osta. Et ce faict, ledict archevesque de Reims fit [fol. 66r] sur l'espee apporteeᶜ dudict Sainct Denis la benediction qui s'ensuit.

71. ª monseigneur C. — ᵇ mist C. — ᶜ fist sur l'espee aportee C.

72. Benedictio super gladium regi dandum.

Exaudi, quesumus Domine, praecesª nostras, et huncᵇ gladium quo famulus tuus Carolus seᶜ accingi desiderat, maiestatis tue dextera benedicere dignare, quatinusᵈ deffensio atque protecctioᵉ possit [esseᶠ] ecclesiarum, viduarum, orfanorumᵍ, omniumque Deo servientium contra seviciam paganorum, aliisque insidiantibusʰ sit terror et formido. Per dominum nostrum etc.

72. ª preces C. — ᵇ famulum *add.* B. — ᶜ se *om.* C. — ᵈ quatenus C. — ᵉ protecctio *is* C's *reading;* B *reads* proxetico, *or something similar.* — ᶠ esse *om.* B, *here add. from* C. — ᵍ orphanorum C. — ʰ insidientibus B.

73. Quand ladicte benediction fut faicte, l'archevesque print ladicte espee avec la gaine et la saindilᵃ au roy, et ung peu apres la luy dessaindilᵇ, et la tira hors de ladicte gaine, et mit ladicte gaineᶜ sur l'autel, et puis bailla ladicte espee toute nue au roy en ses mains, en disant l'oraison qui s'ensuit ; laquelle espee le roy receut humblement des mains dudict archevesque, et durant ladicte oraison la tinteᵈ toute droicte, la poincte en hault, et aussy tandis que on chanta le responteᵉ apres, et l'oraison ensuitᶠ.

73. ª sa gaisne et la ceignit C. — ᵇ deceignit C. — ᶜ gaisne et mist la dicte gaine C. — ᵈ tint C. — ᵉ qu'on chanta le respons C. — ᶠ ensuivant C.

74. Oracio.

Accipe hunc gladium cum Dei benedictione [fol. 66v] tibi collatum, in quo per virtutem Spiritus sancti resistere et eicere omnes inimicos tuos valeas, et cunctos sanctaeª Dei ecclesiae adversarios regnumque tibi commissum tueariᵇ atque protegere castra Dei, per auxilium invictissimi triumphatoris domini nostri Ihesu Christi.

Accipe²⁴ inquam hunc gladium per manus nostras vice et auctoritateᶜ sanctorum apostolorum consecratas, tibi regaliter impositum nostreque benedictionis officio in deffensionem sancte Dei ecclesiae ordinatum divinitus. Et esto memor de quo psalmista prophetavit dicens,

---

²⁴ Manuscripts *B* and *C* are like Ordo XXIII,26, MSS *F* and *G*, in that they do not treat this as a separate text.

'Accingere[d] *gladio tuo super femur tuum, potentissime,' ut in hoc per eundem*[e] *vim equitatis exerceas, molam iniquitatis potenter destruas et sanctam Dei ecclesiam, eiusque fideles propugnes et*[f] *protegas, nec minus sub fide falsos quam christiani nominis*[g] *hostes execreris ac destruas, viduas et pupillos clementer adiuves ac deffendas, desolata restaures,* [*restaurata conserves, ulciscaris iniusta, confirmes*[h]] *bene disposita, quatinus*[i] *hoc in agendo virtutum triumpho gloriosus, iusticieque cultor egregius cum mundi salvatore cuius tipum geris in nomine sine fine merearis regnare, qui cum Deo Patre et Spiritu sancto vivit et regnat Deus, per omnia secula seculorum. Amen.*

74. [a] sanctos C. —[b] tueri C, tutari *in most other ordines.* —[c] auctore B. — [d] Accinge B. —[e] eumdem C. —[f] ac C. —[g] christianos novos *corr. to* christianis novos C. —[h] restaurata ... confirmes *om.* B, *here add. from* C. —[i] quatenus C.

75. [fol. 67r] Ladicte oraison achevee, lesdicts chantre et soubchantre commencerent[a] a chanter, et le cueur escheva l'antesne[b] qui s'ensuit. Antiphona.

Confortare et esto vir, et observa custodias Domini Dei tui, ut ambules in viis eius, et custodias cerimonias eius, et precepta eius, et testimonia et iudicia, et quocumque te verteris confirmet te Deus.

75. [a] cha[n]tres et soubschantre commancerent C. —[b] acheva l'antienne C.

76. Apres laquelle ledict archevesque dict[a] l'oroison qui s'ensuit. Oracio.

Deus, qui providentia tua celestia simul et terrena moderaris, propiciare christianissimo regi nostro, ut omnis hostium suorum fortitudo, virtute gladii spiritualiter frangatur, ac te pro illo pugnante penitus conteratur. Per dominum nostrum etc.

76. [a] dist C.

77. En la fin de ladicte oroison, le roy, tenant l'espee nue en la maniere dessusdicte, se mit[a] devotement a genoux[b], et ce fait[c], la rendit audict archevesque, qui la luy rendit de rechef; et apres qu'il l'eut receu[d], le roy la bailla a monsieur Pierre de Rohan, sieur de Gié[e], mareschal de France, lequel la porta nue devant le roy [fol. 67v] depuis lors, et jusques en fin du sacre et service faict en l'eglize, et depuis en retournant au palais et durant tout le disner.

77. [a] mist C. —[b] genoulx C. —[c] faict C. —[d] receue C. —[e] monseigneur Pierre de Rohan siegneur de Gié C.

78. Et apres que le roy, estant a genoulx, eut baillié[a] ladicte espee audict sieur de Gié[b], ledict archevesque dict[c] sur luy les trois oroisons cy apres ensuivant.

Prima oracio.

Prospice, omnipotens Deus, serenis obtutibus hunc gloriosum regem Carolum; et sicut tu benedixisti Abraham, Ysaac[d] et Iacob, sic illum largis benedictionibus spiritualis gracie cum omni[e] plenitudine tuae potentiae irrigare atque perfundere[f] dignare; tribue ei de rore celi et de pinguedine terre habundanciam frumenti, vini et olei et omnium frugum opulentiam[g], ex[h] largitate divini muneris longa per tempora, ut illo regnante sit sanitas corpori[s][i] in patria, et pax inviolata sit in regno, et dignitas gloriosa regalis palacii maximo splendore regiae potestatis occulis[j] omnium fulgeat, luce clarissima coruscare atque splendere[k] quasi splendidissima fulgura, maximo perfusa lumine videatur; tribue ei, omnipotens Deus, ut sit fortissimus protector patriae et consolator ecclesiarum atque cenobiorum sanctorum, maxima [fol. 68r] cum potestate regalis munificentiae, atque ut sit fortissimus regum, triumphator hostium, ad oprimendas rebelles et paganas nationes. Sitque suis inimicis satis terribilis pre maxima fortitudine regalis potencie, obtimatibus[l] quoque atque procelsis, proceribusque[m] ac fidelibus sui regni sit munificus et amabilis et pius, ut[n] ab omnibus timeatur atque diligatur; reges quoque de lumbis eius per successiones futurorum temporum egrediantur, regnum hoc regere totum. Et post gloriosa tempora atque felicia praesentis vitae gaudia sempiterna, in perpetua beatitudine habere mereatur.

Quod ipse prestare dignetur[o], qui cum unigenito filio tuo domino nostro Ihesu Christo et Spiritu sancto vivis et regnas Deus. Per omnia secula seculorum. Amen.

78. [a] baillé C. — [b] seigneur de Gié C. — [c] dist C. — [d] Isaac C. — [e] spiritualiter gracie cum omnium B. — [f] profundere C. — [g] oppulantiam B. — [h] ea C. — [i] corporum C *and Ordo XXIII,30, but* corporis *Ordo XXIII,30, var. j.* — [j] regio potestatis oculis C. — [k] coruscare atque splendore C. — [l] optimatibus C. — [m] praecelsis proceribusque C, precelsis proceribus *Ordo XXIII,30.* — [n] et C. — [o] digneris C.

79. Secunda oracio.

Benedic, ✠ Domine quesumus,[a] hunc principem nostrum quem ad salutem populi nobis a te credimus esse concessum; fac eum esse annis multiplicem, vigenti atque salubri[b] corporis robore vigentem, et ad senectutem optatam atque demum ad finem pervenire felicem. Sit nobis fiducia eum obtinere gratiam pro populo, quam Aaron in tabernaculo, Eliseus in fluvio, Ezechias in lectulo, Zacarias[c] vetulus impetravit in templo, sit illi[d] regendi virtus [fol. 68v] atque auctoritas, qualem Iosue suscepit in castris, Gedeon sumpsit in preliis, Petrus accepit in clave, Paulus est usus in dogmate. Et ita pastorum cura tuis[e] proficiat in ovile, sicut Isaac profecit in fruge et Iacob est dilatatus in grege.

Quod ipse prestare dignetur[f], qui cum unigenito filio tuo domino nostro Ihesu Christo et Spiritu sancto vivis et regnas Deus. Per omnia secula seculorum. Amen.

79. [a] Benedic quaesumus Domine C. —[b] salubris B. —[c] Zacharias C. —[d] tibi C. —[e] tuum *Ordo XXIII,31.* —[f] digneris C.

80. Tertia oratio.

Deus Pater aeterne gloriae sit adiutor tuus et protector, et omnipotens benedicat ✠[a] tibi, preces tuas in cunctis exaudiat et vitam tuam longitudine dierum adimpleat, tronum[b] regni tui iugiter[c] firmet, et gentem populumque tuum in aeternum conservet, et inimicos tuos confusione induat, et super te sanctificatio Christi floreat, ut qui tibi tribuit in terris imperium, ipse[d] in caelis conferat premium. Qui vivit et regnat trinus et unus Deus, per omnia secula seculorum. Amen.

80. [a] ✠ *om.* C. —[b] thronum C. —[c] iungit B. —[d] et *later add.* C.

81. Quand lesdictes oraisons furent dictes et achevees, monsieur[a] l'archevesque se retourna devers l'autel, et sur icelluy prepara la tres sacree onction pour enoindre et consacrer le roy, qui est seul, entre tous les rois[b] et princes du monde, enoint[c] [fol. 69r] et consacré de onction[d] divine. Et la prepara en la maniere qui ensuite[e].

81. [a] monseigneur C. —[b] roys C. —[c] enoinct C. —[d] d'unction C. —[e] s'ensuit C.

82. Premierement, il print la patene[a] du calice Saint[b] Remy, qui est fort grande,[25] et sur icelle mit[c] du sainct cresme, ainsy comme pour sacrer ung evesque ou ung autre roy, et la mit[c] sur ledict autel.

Et en apres il print la saincte ampole apporté[d] de Sainct Remy, comme dict est, et la ouvrit. Et en une esguille ou espingle d'or pendant a icelle tira dedans[e] environ le gros d'un pois de l'uille[f] divinement envoyee, dont les roys de France singulierement[g] entre tous les autres roys de la terre, et nuls autres, soyent enoings[h] et consacrez, et en plusieurs lieux comme dict sera cy apres[i] ; car les autres roys le sont seulement en la teste, et ceulx de France le sont en neuf places[j], comme le roy Charles present l'a esté. Et icelle tiree, print[k] et mesla au doigt tres bien avec ledict cresme. Et puis restoupa et reclouit ladicte saincte ampole comme elle estoit auparavant.

82. [a] platene C. —[b] Sainct C. —[c] mist C. —[d] aportee C. —[e] de dedans *a.* — [f] l'huile C. —[g] singulirement C. —[h] sont enoincts C. —[i] aprez C. —[j] en mesme place B. —[k] prist C.

---

[25] The beautiful and justly famous late twelfth-century chalice "of Saint Remi" is now on display in the palatine chapel, part of the *Musée du sacre* in the former archiepiscopal palace.

B C

83. Et tandis que ledict archevesque preparoit ladite^a unction,
lesdictz chantre et soubzchantre
commencerent^b a chanter, et le
cueur et les assistans respondirent
et acheverent, l'antesne^c qui s'ensuit.

Antiphona.

*Gentem Francorum inclitam
simul cum rege nobili, beatus
Remigius sumpto celitus crismate
sacro,* [fol. 69v] *sanctificavit gurgite, atque Spiritus sancti plene
ditavit munere*^d.

*Qui dono singularis gratiae
in columba apparuit*^e *et divinum*^f
*crisma celitus pontifici minis-
travit.*

Puis ledict archevesque dict^g.

Ora pro nobis, beate Remigi.

Et le cueur respondit.

*Ut digni efficiamur promis-
sionibus Christi.*

A

83a. In recepcione sancte
ampulle debet cantari hec antiphona.

*Gentem Francorum inclitam
simul cum rege nobili. Beatus
Remigius, sumpto celitus crismate sacro, sanctificavit gurgite,
atque Spiritus sancti plene ditavit munere.*

Versus. *Qui dono singularis
gracie in columba apparuit et
divinum crisma celitus pontifici
ministravit.*

83. ^a ladicte C. — ^b commancerent C. — ^c l'anthiene C. — ^d Versus *add.* C. — ^e
appararuit C. — ^f divini B. — ^g dist C.

84. Et apres dit ledict archevesque l'oroison^a qui s'ensuit.

Oracio.

*Deus, qui populo tuo aeterne
salutis beatum Remigium minis-
trum*^b *tribuisti, praesta, quesumus,
ut quem doctorem vitae habuimus
in terris, intercessorem semper
habere mereamur in celis. Per
Christum dominum nostrum.
Amen.*

84a. Oratio.

Deus, qui salutis eterne etc.

84. ^a et puis apres ledict archevesque dist l'oraison C. — ^b mistrum B.

B C

85. Ladicte unction preparee, et les antesnes[a], verset et oraison achevez, les boutons d'argent, dont la robbe du roy estoit fermee devant et derriere, furent deffermez, et ladicte robbe et sa chemise avallez[b] bien bas.

85. [a] anthienes C. — [b] avallee C.

86. Et ce faict, le roy se mit[a] a genoux et se prosterna sur ung tapis et un coussin preparez devant ledict autel, et aussy feit[b] semblablement ledict archevesque. Et eulx estans ainsy prosternés[c], les evesques de Chaalons et Noyon commencerent[d] a chanter la letanie qui s'ensuit, le cueur [fol. 70r] disant comme eulx et apres eulx, jusques a « Sancta Maria », que le coeur dela en avant respondit « Ora pro nobis » jusques en la fin, puis « Libera nos Domine », « Miserere nobis[e] », et « te rogamus audi nos », « Parce nobis Domine », « Exaudi nos Domine », « Miserere nobis », excepté en d'aulcuns lieux que l'archevesque chanta, et tous les autres ensemble dirent apres luy comme il avoit dict, ainsy que dict sera[f] sur le pas.

86. [a] mist C. — [b] fist C. — [c] ainsi prosternez C — [d] commancerent C. — [e] Miserere nobis *om.* C. — [f] sera dict C.

87. Letania.
Kyrie eleison.
Christe eleison.
Kyrie eleison.
Christe, audi nos.

Sancta Maria,	*ora pro nobis.*
Sancte Michael,	*ora pro nobis.*
Sancte Gabriel,	*ora pro nobis.*
Sancte Raphael,	*ora.*
Sancte chorus[a] angelorum,	*orate pro nobis.*
Sancte Iohannes Baptista,	*ora.*
Sancte Petre,	*ora.*
Sancte Paule,	*ora.*
Sancte Andrea,	*ora.*
Sancte Iacobe,	*ora.*
Sancte Iohannes,	*ora.*
Sancte Thoma,	*ora.*
Sancte Philippe,	*ora.*
Sancte Bartolome[b],	*ora.*
Sancte Mathee,	*ora.*

Sancte Simon,	*ora.*
Sancte Thadee,	*ora.*
Sancte Mathia,	*ora.*
Sancte Barnaba,	*ora.*
Sancte Iude[c]*,*	*ora.*
Sancte chorus[a] *apostolorum,*	*ora.*
Sancte Stephane,	*ora.*
Sancte Clemens,	*ora.*
Sancte Calixte,	*ora.*
Sancte Marcelle,	*ora.*
Sancte Nicasi cum sociis tuis,	*orate*[d].
Sancte Maurici,	*ora.*
Sancte Gervasi,	*ora.*
Sancte Protasi,	*ora.*
Sancte Thimothee[e]*,*	*ora.*
Sancte Apolinaris[f]*,*	*ora.*
Sancte chorus[a] *martirum,*	*ora.*
Sancte Silvester[g]*,*	*ora.*
[fol. 70v] *Sancte Remigi,*	*ora.*
Sancte Remigi,	*ora*[h].
Nota quod bis[i] cantatur et altiori voce.	
Sancte Augustine,	*ora.*
Sancte Iheromine[j]*,*	*ora.*
Sancte Ambrosi,	*ora.*
Sancte Georgi[k]*,*	*ora.*
Sancte Sanson[l]*,*[26]	*ora.*
Sancte Sixte,	*ora.*
Sancte Rigoberte,	*ora.*
Sancte Martine,	*ora.*
Sancte Nicolae,	*ora.*
Sancte Maurile[m]*,*	*ora.*
Sancte chorus[a] *confessorum,*	*ora.*

87. [a] corus B. — [b] Bartholomae C. — [c] Iuda C. — [d] Sancte Calixte ... Sancte Nicasi ... orate] Sancte Marcelle, ora. Sancte Calixte, ora. Sancte Nicasie cum sociis tuis, orate. Sancte Laurenti, ora. Sancte Dionisi cum sociis tuis, orate C. — [e] Thimotee B. — [f] Apollinaris C. — [g] Sylvester C. — [h] Sancte Remigi, ora *om. at second instance* C. — [i] per bis C. — [j] Heronyme C. — [k] Gregori *Ordo XXIII,109.* — [l] Sinici *Ordo XXIII,109* — [m] Maurili C.

88. *Sancte Maria Magdalena*[a]*,*	*ora.*
Sancta Maria Egiptiaca,	*ora.*

[26] Both *B* and *C* have the erroneous readings *Georgi ... Sanson.*

Sancta Felicitas,	*ora.*
Sancta Perpetua,	*ora.*
Sancta Agatha,	*ora.*
Sancta Agnes,	*ora.*
Sancta Cecilia,	*ora.*
Sancta Eutropia,	*ora.*
Sancta Genovefa,	*ora.*
Sancta Columba,	*ora.*
Sancta Scolastica[b],	*ora.*
Sancta Petronilla,	*ora.*
Sancta Catherina,	*ora.*
Sancta Margareta[c],	*ora.*
Sancta Christiana,	*ora.*
Sancte chorus[d] *virginum,*	*ora.*
Omnes sancti,	*orate*[e].

88. [a] Magdalene C. — [b] Scholastica C. — [c] Sancta Chatarina, ora. Sancta Marguarita C. — [d] corus B. — [e] Omnes sanctae, orate *add.* C.

89. *Propicius esto, parce nobis Domine*[a].
Ab insidiis diaboli, libera nos Domine.
A dampnatione perpetua, libera nos Domine.
Per misterium sanctae incarnationis tuae, libera nos Domine.
Per passionem et crucem tuam, libera etc.[b]
Per gratiam sancti Spiritus paracliti, libera.
In die iudicii, libera.

89. [a] Propitius esto, libera nos Domine *add.* C. — [b] etc.] nos Domine C.

90. *Peccatores, te rogamus, audi nos.*
Ut pacem nobis dones, te rogamus, audi nos.
Ut misericordia et pietas tua nos custodiant[a], *te rogamus*[b].
Ut gratiam sancti Spiritus cordibus nostris clementer infundere[c] *digneris*[d].
Ut domnum[e] *apostolicum et omnes gradus ecclesie in sancta religione conservare digneris, te rogamus etc.*[f]
Ut archiepiscopum nostrum Petrum[27] *cum omni*[g] *grege sibi commisso*

---

[27] The consecrating archbishop of Reims in 1484 was Pierre de Laval, a second cousin of Charles VIII (Charles VI was their common great-grandfather). See Anselme de Sainte-Marie, *Histoire généalogique*, 2: 47, and, above all, Pierre Desportes et al., *Diocèse de Reims*, Fasti ecclesiae Gallicanae, 1200–1500, vol. 3 (Turnhout: Brepols, 1998), 211–15. Desportes's work is most useful for the prosopography of Reims, and I would have referred to it often throughout this volume if it had been available before I sent the manuscript to the press for copyediting.

in tuo[h] [fol. 71r] *servicio confortare et conservare*[i] *digneris, te rogamus.*

Nota bis cantatur[j].

Ut obsequium servitutis nostrae racionabile facias, te rogamus[b].

90. [a] custodiat C. —[b] audi nos *add.* C. —[c] confundere B. —[d] te rogamus audi nos *add.* C; Ut ecclesiam tuam regere et deffendere digneris, te rogamus *add. Ordo XXIII,112.* —[e] dominum C. —[f] etc.] audi nos C. —[g] cum omni] una cum C. —[h] sancto *add. Ordo XXIII,112.* —[i] conservare et confortare C. —[j] Nota bis cantatur *om.* C.

91. Quand la letanie fut dicte jusques a ce pas, monsieur[a] l'archevesque se leva et se tourna vers le roy a consacrer, print le baston pastoral, c'est asçavoir la crosse, a la main[b] senestre, et dict[e] les vers qui s'ensuivent.

Lesquels le cueur reprint et dict[c] entierement apres luy en la maniere qui s'ensuit.

Ut hunc famulum tuum Carolum[d] *in regem coronandum benedicere*
    digneris, te rogamus, audi nos.

Chorus[e]. *Ut hunc famulum tuum Carolum*[f] *in regem*[g], ut supra.

[*Ut hunc famulum Charolum in regem coronandum benedicere et sub-*
    limare digneris, te rogamus, audi nos.

Chorus. *Ut hunc famulum tuum Charolum in regem*[h] [28]]

Ut hunc[i] *famulum tuum Carolum*[f] *in regem coronandum benedicere,*
    sublimare et conservare digneris, te rogamus, audi nos.

Chorus[g]. *Ut hunc famulum tuum,* ut supra.

91. [a] monseigneur C. —[b] le baston pastorial, c'est a sçavoir la crosse en la main C. —[c] dist C. —[d] Carolum *corr. from* Charolum C. —[e] Corus B. —[f] Charolum C. —[g] etc. *add.* C. —[h] Ut hunc ... in regem *om.* B, *here add. from* C. —[i] hunc *om.* C.

92. Apres que mondict sieur[a] l'archevesque eut dict, et le cueur respondu, les trois vers dessusdicts, il s'en retourna mettre pres[b] le roy en prosternacion comme devant, et lesdicts evesques de Chalons[c] et Noyon acheverent la letanie, et le cueur respondent[d] en la maniere qui s'ensuit.

Ut regibus et principibus christianis pacem et concordiam donare
    digneris, te rogamus, audi nos.

[fol. 71v] Chorus[e]. *Te rogamus* etc.

Ut hunc famulum tuum Carolum[f] *in regem eligere* [*digneris*[g]], *te roga-*
    mus, audi nos.

---

[28] *regem* is the last word on p. 105 in *C*, and at the top of p. 106 the scribe failed either to add the words "ut supra" or to complete the formula with the words "coronandum benedicere et sublimare digneris, te rogamus audi nos."

Ut eum benedicere digneris, te rogamus, audi nos.

Ut eum sublimare digneris, te rogamus, audi nos.

Ut eum ad regni fastigium perducere digneris, te rogamus, audi nos[h].

Ut cunctum populum christianum precioso sanguine tuo redemptum consecrare[i] *digneris, te rogamus, audi nos*[h].

Ut cunctis fidelibus defunctis requiem aeternam donare digneris, te rogamus etc.

Ut nos exaudire digneris, te rogamus, audi nos[h].

Fili Dei, te rogamus etc.[j]

> 92. [a] seigneur C. —[b] empres C. —[c] Chaalons C. —[d] et le cueur respondent] le choeur respondant C. —[e] Corus B. —[f] Charolum C. —[g] digneris *om.* B, *here* add. *from* C. —[h] audi nos] etc. C. —[i] conservare C. —[j] etc.] audi nos C.

93. *Agnus Dei, qui tollis peccata mundi, parce nobis Domine.*

Agnus Dei, qui tollis peccata mundi, exaudi nos[a] *Domine.*

Agnus Dei, qui tollis peccata[b] *mundi, miserere nobis.*

Christe, audi nos.

Kyrie eleyson.

Christe eleyson.

Kyrie eleyson.

> 93. [a] parce nobis B. —[b] pecata B.

94. Ladicte letanie achevee, comme dict[a] est, mondit [fol. 72r] sieur[b] l'archevesque se leva de rechief, et dict[c], *Pater noster,* laquelle il dit[a] tout bas, et en fin d'icelle dict[a].

Et ne nos inducas in tentationem.

Chorus[d]. *Sed libera nos a malo.*

Salvum fac servum tuum.

Chorus[d]. *Deus meus speranteme*[e] *in te.*

Esto ei, Domine, turris fortitudinis.

Chorus. *A facie inimici.*

Nichil proficiat inimicus in nobis[f].

Chorus. *Et non aponat ultra nocere ei.*

Domine, exaudi orationem meam.

Chorus. *Et clamor meus etc.*

Dominus vobiscum.

[Chorus[g].] *Et cum spiritu tuo.*

> 94. [a] dist C. —[b] mon dict seigneur C. —[c] de rechef et dist C. —[d] Corus B. —[e] sperantes C. —[f] Nihil proficiat inimicus in eum C. —[g] Chorus *om.* B, *here* add. *from* C.

95. *Oremus.*

Oracio.

Praetende, quesumus Domine, huic famulo tuo Carolo, dexteram[a] *coelestis auxilii, ut te toto corde perquirat et que digne postulat assequi mereatur. Per dominum nostrum* etc.

95. [a] Charolo, dextram C.

96. Alia oracio.

Actiones nostras, quaesumus Domine, aspirando preveni et adiuvando prosequere, ut cuncta nostra operacio et oracio a te semper incipiat et per te cepta finiatur. Per dominum nostrum etc.

97. En fin desdictes oraisons, ledict archevesque se asseit[a] devant le roy sur une chayere preparee[b] en façon comme s'il voulloit consacrer ung evesque. Et dict sur le roy estant a genoux[c] devant luy les oroisons qui s'ensuivent, avant qu'il le sacrat[d].

Oracio.

Te invocamus, sancte Pater, omnipotens sempiterne Deus, [fol. 72v] *ut*[e] *hunc famulum tuum Carolum*[f]*, quem tuae divinae dispensationis providentia in primordio plasmatum usque in hunc presentem diem iuvenili flore letantem*[g] *crescere concessisti, eum tuae pietatis dono ditatum plenumque*[29] *gratia veritatis de die in diem coram Deo et hominibus ad meliora semper proficere facias, ut summi regiminis solium*[h] *gratiae supernae largitate gaudens suscipiat, et misericordiae tuae muro ab hostium adversitate undique munitus, plebem sibi commissam cum pace propiciacionis et virtute victorie feliciter regere*[i] *mereatur. Per Christum dominum nostrum. Amen.*

97. [a] assist C. — [b] preparé B. — [c] dist sur le roy estans a genoulx C. — [d] consacrast C, sacrast *a*. — [e] et C. — [f] Charolum C. — [g] latentem C. — [h] suum regimine solum B. — [i] rege B.

98. Alia oracio.

Deus, qui populis tuis virtute consulis et amore dominaris, da huic famulo tuo Carolo[a] *spiritum sapiencie tuae cum regimine disciplinae, ut tibi toto corde devotus in regni regimine*[b] *semper maneat ydoneus, tuoque munere ipsius temporibus ecclesiae securitas dirigatur et in tranquilitate devocio ecclesiastica permaneat, ut*[c]*, in bonis operibus perseverans, ad eternum regnum te duce valeat pervenire. Per dominum nostrum Ihesum Christum* etc.

98. [a] Charolo C. — [b] regimen C. — [c] et C.

99. Alia oracio.

---

[29] *B* reads *pernuique*, or something similarly nonsensical. I reproduce *C*'s reading.

In diebus eius oriatur omnibus[a] *equitas et iusticia, amicis adiuto-*
rium, inimicis obstaculum, humilibus solacium, elatis correctio,
divitibus doctrina, pauperibus pietas, peregrinis pacificatio, propriis
in patria pax [fol. 73r] *et securitas, unicuique*[b] *secundum suam men-*
suram moderate gubernans, se ipsum sedulus regem discat, ut tua
irrigatus compunctione toto populo tibi placita praebere vitae possit
exempla, et per viam veritatis cum grege gradiens sibi subdito, opes
frugales habundanter acquirat, simulque ad salutem non solum corpo-
rum, sed eciam cordium a te concessam, cuncta[c] *accipiat. Sitque in te*
cogitatum animi consiliumque omne componens[d] *plebis gubernacula*
cum pace simul et patientia semper[e] *invenire videatur. Teque auxili-*
ante, presentis vitae prosperitatem et prolixitatem percipiat, et per
tempora bona usque ad summam senectutem perveniat, huiusque
fragilitatis fine[f] *perfecta, ab omnibus vitiorum vinculis tuae largitate*
pietatis liberatus, et infinite[g] *prosperitatis praemia*[h] *perpetua angelo-*
rumque aeterna commercia consequatur. Per dominum nostrum Ihe-
sum Christum etc.

99. [a] omnis C. —[b] unumquemque C. —[c] cunctam B. —[d] compositionem B. —
[e] semper *om.* C. —[f] fragilitate fiat C. —[g] infinita C. —[h] pura B.

100. Alia oracio quae est consecratio regis.

Omnipotens sempiterne Deus, gubernator celi et terre, conditor et
dispositor angelorum et hominum, rex regum et dominus dominorum,
qui Abraham fidelem famulum tuum de hostibus triumphare fecisti,
Moysi et Iosue populo tuo prelatis multiplicem victoriam tribuisti,
humilem quoque puerum David regni fastigio sublimasti, eumque de
ore leonis et [fol. 73v] *de manu bestie atque Golie, sed et de gladio*
maligno Saul et omnium inimicorum eius liberasti, et Salomonem
sapienciae pacisque ineffabili munere ditasti, respice propicius ad
preces nostre[a] *humilitatis, et super hunc famulum tuum Carolum,*
quem supplici[b] *devotione in huius regni regem pariter eligimus*[c]*,*
benedictionum tuarum dona multiplica, eumque dextrae[d] *tue poten-*
tiae semper ubique circunda, quatenus predicti Abrahe fidelitate fir-
matus, Moisi[e] *mansuetudine fretus, Iosue fortitudine munitus, David*[f]
humilitate exaltatus, Salomonis sapiencia decoratus, tibi in omnibus
complaceat, et per tramitem[g] *iustitiae inoffenso gressu semper ince-*
dat, et tocius regni ecclesiam deinceps cum plebibus sibi annexis, ita
enutriat ac doceat, muniat ac instruat, contraque omnes visibiles et
invisibiles hostes idem potenter regaliterque tue virtutis regimine
administret, ut regale solium videlicet Saxonum, Merciorum, Nordam,
Chubrorum[h] *sceptra non deserat, sed ad pristinae fidei pacisque*

concordiam eorum animos te opitulante reformet, ut, utrorumque horum populorum debita subiectione fultus, et cum digno[i] amore glorificatus per longum vitae spacium paterne apicem glorie[j] tua miseracione unatim stabilire et gubernare mereatur, tuae quoque protectionis galea munitus, et scuto insuperabili[k] iugiter protectus, armisque celestibus [fol. 74r] *circundatus, optabilem[l] victoriae triumphum de hostibus feliciter capiat, terroremque[m] suae potenciae infidelibus inferat, et pacem militantibus letenter[n] reportet, virtutibus necnon quibus prefatos fideles tuos decorasti, multiplici honoris benedictione ✠[o] condecora[p], et in regimine[q] regni sublimiter collocatum[r], oleo gratiae Spiritus sancti perunge. Per dominum nostrum, qui virtute crucis tartara detruxisti[s], regnoque diaboli superato ad celos victor ascendit, in quo potestas omnis regnumque consistit et victoria, quae[t] est gloria humilium et vita salusque populorum. Qui tecum vivit et regnat [in unitate[u]] eiusdem Spiritus sancti Deus, per omnia secula seculorum. Amen.*

100. [a] nostra C. —[b] Charolum quem suplici C. —[c] elegimus C. —[d] dextra C. —[e] Moisis C. —[f] Davidis C. —[g] Ramitem B. —[h] Nordanhimbrorumque *corr. from* Nordanumbrorumque C; Nordan Chimbrorum *Ordo XXIII,39.* —[i] cum divino C. —[j] gloria B. —[k] insuperabile B. —[l] optabilis *Ordo XXIII,39 and nearly all MSS of all other ordines.* —[m] teremque B. —[n] latanter C, *but* letanter *Ordo XXIII,39.* —[o] ✠ *om.* C. —[p] cum decora B. —[q] regimen C. —[r] collocatum] colloca et *Ordo XXIII,39.* —[s] dextruxit C, destruxit *Ordo XXIII,39.* —[t] qui *Ordines XIX,26 and XXIII,39.* —[u] in unitate *om.* B, *here add. from* C.

101. Quand ladicte oroison fut dicte, ledict archevesque de Reims print la patene[a] sur laquelle il avoit preparé l'unction, comme dessus est devisé, et d'icelle oindit[b] et sacra le roy en neuf places.

Premierement, ou sommet de la teste.

Secondement, en la poictrine.

Tiercement, entre[c] deux espaules[d].

Quartement, en l'espaulle destre.

Quintement, en l'espaulle senestre.

Sextement, au plis du bras dextre.

Septiesmement, au plis du bras senestre.

Huictiesmement, en la paulme et au long de la main dextre.

Neufiesmement, en la main senestre.

101. [a] platine C. —[b] et de celle oignit C. —[c] les *add. a.* —[d] espaulles C.

102. Et a chacune onction[a], excepté celle des mains, dit [fol. 74v] l'archevesque[b] ce qui s'ensuit.

Ungo te in regem de oleo sanctificato, in nomine Patris et Filii et Spiritus sancti.

Et les assistans a chacune fois respondirent, *Amen.*

102. [a] unction C. —[b] dit l'archevesque] ledict archevesque dict C.

103. Tandis qu'il faisoit lesdictes unctions, lesdictz chantre et soubz-chantre commancerent[a] a chanter, et le cueur et les assistans acheverent, l'antesne[b] qui s'ensuit.

Antiphona.

Unxerunt Salomonem Sadoch sacerdos et Nat[h]an[c] propheta regem in Gyon, et accedentes leti dixerunt, "Vivat rex in aeternum."

103. [a] commencerent C. —[b] l'anthienne C. —[c] Natan B C, *but corr. to* Nathan C.

104. Lesdictes unctions faictes et ladicte antesne[a] chantee, ledit monsieur[b] l'archevesque dict[c] sur le roy les oroisons qui s'ensuivent.

Oracio.

Christe, perunge hunc regem [in regimen[d]], unde unxisti sacerdotes, reges ac prophetas et martires, qui fide vicerunt regna, operati sunt iusticiam atque adepti sunt repromissiones; tua sacratissima unctio super caput eius defluat atque ad interiora descendat, et cordis illius intima penetret, et promissionibus quas adepti sunt victoriosissimi reges, gracia tua dignus efficiatur, quatinus[e] et in presenti seculo feliciter regnet et ad eorum consorsium[f] in celesti regno perveniat. Per dominum nostrum Ihesum Christum [fol. 75r] filium tuum, qui unctus est oleo leticie pre consortibus suis, et virtute crucis potestates aereas debellavit, tartara dextruxit[g], regnumque diaboli superavit, et ad celos victor ascendit, in cuius manu victoria, omnis gloria et potestas consistunt, et tecum vivit et regnat in unitate Spiritus sancti Deus per omnia secula seculorum. Amen.

104. [a] anthienne C. —[b] monseigneur C. —[c] dist C. —[d] in regimen *om.* B, *here add. from* C. —[e] quatenus C. —[f] consortium C. —[g] destruxit C.

105. Alia oracio.

Deus, electorum fortitudo et humilium celsitudo, qui in primordio per infusionem[a] diluvii mundi crimina castigare voluisti et[b] columbam ramum olive portantem pacem terris redditam demonstrasti. Iterumque sacerdotem Aaron famulum tuum per unctionem olei[c] sacerdotem sanxisti, et postea per huius unguenti infusionem ad regendum populum[d] Israeliticum sacerdotes, reges et prophetas perfecisti, vultumque ecclesie in oleo exhilarendum[e] per propheticam famuli tui vocem David esse predixisti, ita quesumus, omnipotens Deus Pater, ut per huius creaturae pinguedinem hunc servum tuum sanctificare tua benedictione digneris, eumque[f] in similitudine columba[g] pacem simplicitatis populo sibi commisso praestare, et exempla Aaron in Dei servicio diligenter[h] *imitari, regnique fastigia in conciliis*[i] *scientiae*[j] *et equitate iudicii semper assequi, vultumque hilaritatis per hanc olei unctionem tuamque benedictionem, te adiuvante, toti plebi paratum habere facias. Per dominum nostrum Ihesum filium tuum etc.*

105. [a] effusionem *Ordo XXIII,43.* —[b] per *add. Ordo XXIII,43.* —[c] dei C. — [d] populum *om.* C. —[e] exilarendum *corr. to* exilarandum C. —[f] cumque C. — [g] columbae C, columbe *Ordo XXIII,43.* —[h] diligentur B. —[i] consiliis C. — [j] sanctis B.

106. [fol. 75v] Alia oracio.

Deus Dei filius, dominus noster Ihesus Christus, qui a Patre oleo exultationis unctus est prae participibus suis, ipse per presentem sacri unguinis infusionem Spiritus paracliti super caput tuum infundat benedictionem eandemque[a] *usque ad interiora cordis tui penetrare faciat, quatinus*[b] *hoc visibili et tractabili dono invisibilia percipere, et temporali regno iustis moderationibus*[c] *exequuto*[d]*, eternaliter cum eo regnare merearis, qui solus sine peccato rex regum vivit et gloriatur cum Deo Patre. In unitate eiusdem*[e] *Spiritus sancti Deus. Per omnia secula seculorum. Amen.*

106. [a] eandamque B. —[b] quatenus C. —[c] moderaminibus C. —[d] executo *corr. to* exequuto C. —[e] eiusdem *om.* C.

107. Lesdites oroisons achevees, monsieur[a] l'archevesque et les prelats estans[b] entour le roy releverent sa chemise et sa robbe de couleur jacinte[c], et la refermerent aux boutons qui [y[d]] estoient, comme dessus est dict, pour la neteté[e] et pureté de la sacree unction par luy receue.

107. [a] monsieur] mondict seigneur C. —[b] estants C. —[c] jacinthe C. —[d] y *om.* B, *here add. from* C. —[e] netteté C.

108. Et ce faict monsieur de Dumois[a] comme grand, ou premier chambellan de France, luy vestit la robbe jacinte[b], et par dessus le socq, qui est en façon d'une chappe d'eglise, non aiant chapperon derriere, du costé destre[c] duquel il eut le bras a delivre, et sur le bras senestre ledict soc[d] fut levé, comme on liesve la chasuble a un presbre[e], et puis apres mondict sieur[f] l'archevesque luy oindit[g] les mains, comme dessus est dict, de ladicte unction estant sur la patene[h], et en luy oignant [fol. 76r] dict[i] ce qui s'ensuit.

108. [a] monseigneur de Dunois C. —[b] jacinthe C. —[c] dextre C. —[d] socq C. — [e] on leve la chasuble comme a un prestre C. —[f] seigneur C. —[g] oignit C. — [h] platene C. —[i] dist C.

109. *Ungantur manus istae de oleo sanctificato, unde uncti fuerunt reges et prophetae, et sicut unxit Samuel David in regem, ut*

sis benedictus et constitutus rex in regno isto, quod dominus Deus tuus dedit tibi ad regendum et gubernandum.

Quod ipse praestare dignetur, qui in Trinitate perfecta vivit et regnat unus Deus per omnia [secula[a]*] seculorum. Amen.*

109. [a] secula *om.* B, *here add. from* C.

110. En apres mondict sieur[a] l'archevesque dit[b] l'oroison qui s'ensuit. Oracio.

Deus, qui es iustorum gloria et misericordia peccatorum, qui misisti filium tuum preciosissimo sanguine suo genus humanum redimere, qui conteris bella et pugnator es in te sperantium, et sub cuius[c] *arbitrio omnium regnorum continetur potestas, te humiliter deprecamur, ut famulum tuum presentem Carolum*[d] *in tua misericordia confidentem in presenti sede regali benedicas, eique propicius adesse digneris, ut qui tua expetit protectione deffendi, omnibus*[e] *hostibus sit fortior; fac eum, Domine, beatum esse et victorem de inimicis suis. Corona eum corona iusticie et pietatis, ut ex toto corde et tota mente*[f] *deserviat, sanctam tuam ecclesiam deffendat et sublimet, populumque a te sibi commissum iuste regat nullis insidiantibus malis eum in iusticiam convertat*[g]*. Accende, Domine, cor eius ad amorem gratie tue per hoc unctionis oleum, unde unxisti sacerdotes, reges et prophetas, quatinus*[h] *iusticiam diligens per* [fol. 76v] *tramitem similiter incedatur iusticiae*[i]*, post peracta a te*[j] *disposita, in regali excellentia annorum curricula pervenire ad gaudia aeterna mereatur. Per eundem*[k] *dominum nostrum Ihesum Christum etc.*

110. [a] seigneur C. — [b] dist C. — [c] et *add.* B. — [d] ut presentem famulum tuum Charolum C. — [e] hominibus B. — [f] in te credens tibi *add. Ordo XXIII,48.* — [g] conducat B. — [h] quatenus C. — [i] similiter iustitiae incedens C. — [j] a te] atque C. — [k] eundem *om.* C.

111. Quand lesdictes mains furent enoinctes[a] et sacrees, comme dict est, le roy les joindit[b] ensemble devant sa poitrine[c].

Et print on une paire de gans, que ledict archevesque benit en la forme qui s'ensuict.

Oracio.

Omnipotens Creator, qui homini ad ymaginem tuam creato[d] *manus digitis discretionis insignitas tanquam organum intelligencie ad recte operandum dedisti, quas servari mundas precepisti, ut in eis anima digna portaretur, et tua in*[e] *eis digne contractarentur*[f] *misteria, benedicere et sanctificare digneris hec manuum tegumenta, ut quicunque*[g] *reges hiis*[h] *cum humilitate manus suas velare voluerint, tam cordis quam operis mundiciam, tua misericordia subministret*[j]. *Per Christum dominum. Amen*[j].

111. [a] oinctes C. —[b] joignit C. —[c] poictrine C. —[d] creator B. —[e] in *om.* C. — [f] contractaretur B. —[g] quamque B. —[h] his C. —[i] subministrat B. —[j] per ... Amen] Per Dominum nostrum Iesum Christum filium tuum, etc. C.

112. Puis jetta de l'eau benoiste[a] dessus et les mit[b] es mains du roy pour la saincteté de l'onction, comme on fait[c] a ung evesque quand on le sacre, et en les luy mettant dict[d] l'oraison qui s'ensuit.

[fol. 77r] Oracio.

Circunda, Domine, manus huius famuli tui Caroli[e] *mundicia novi hominis, qui de celo descendit, ut quemadmodum Iacob dilectus tuus pelliculis edorum*[f] *opertis*[g] *manibus paternam benedictionem oblato Patri cibo potuque gratissimo impetravit, sic et iste gracie tue benedictionem impetrare*[h] *mereatur. Per eundem dominum*[i] *Ihesum Christum, qui in similitudinem*[j] *carnis peccati tibi*[k] *obtulit semetipsum. Amen.*

112. [a] beniste C. —[b] mist C. —[c] sanctité de l'unction comme on faict C. — [d] dist C. —[e] Charoli C. —[f] haedorum C. —[g] apertis B. —[h] impetrari B. —[i] nostrum *add.* C. —[j] similitudine B. —[k] tibi *om.* B.

113. Lesdictes choses faictes et achevees, mondict sieur[a] l'archevesque print l'anel du roy et sur iceluy fit[b] la benediction qui s'ensuit.

Oracio[c].

Deus, tocius creaturae principium et finis, creator et conservator humani generis, dator gratie spiritualis, largitor aeterne salutis, in quo clausa sunt omnia, tu, Domine, tuam mitte[d] *benedictionem super hunc annullum*[e], *ipsumque benedicere et sanctificare digneris, ut qui per eum famulo tuo honoris insignia concedis, virtutum premia largiaris, quo discretionis*[f] *habitum semper retineat*[g], *et vero ali*[h] *fulgore prefulgeat, sancte quoque Trinitatis armatus munimine miles inexpugnabilis acies diaboli constanter evincat et sibi ad veram salutem mentis*[i] *et corporis* [fol. 77v] *proficiat. Per Christum dominum nostrum. Amen.*

113. [a] seigneur C. —[b] fist C. —[c] Oracio *om.* C. —[d] emitte *Ordo XXIII,53.* — [e] annulum C. —[f] que distionis B. —[g] retinet B. —[h] vere Dei C, vere fidei *Ordo XXIII,53.* —[i] meritis B.

114. Ladicte benediction faicte, mondict sieur[a] l'archevesque print ledict anel et le mit au doit[b] medicinal de la main destre[c] du roy, en disant[d] ce qui s'ensuit.

Accipe anullum[e], *signaculum videlicet fidei sancte, soliditatem regni, augmentum potenciae, per quem*[f] *scias triumphali potencia hostes repellere, hereses destruere, subditos coadiunere*[g], *et catholice fidei*[h] *perseverabilitate connecti.*

> 114. [a] seigneur C. —[b] mist au doigt C. —[c] dextre C. —[d] et disant B. —[e] annulum C. —[f] per quae C. —[g] coadunere *Ordo XXIII,56.* —[h] fidae B.

115. Apres dict[a] l'oroison qui s'ensuit.

Oracio post annullum[b].

Deus, cuius est omnis potestas et dignitas, da famulo tuo prosperum suae dignitatis effectum, in qua, te remunerante, permaneat semperque timeat tibique iugiter placere contendat. Per dominum nostrum Ihesum Christum filium tuum, qui tecum vivit[c] *etc.*

> 115. [a] dist C. —[b] annulum C. —[c] vivit *om.* C.

116. En apres ledict archevesque print le sceptre et le bailla au roy en sa main dextre, en disant l'oroison qui s'ensuit.

Oratio.

Accipe sceptrum regiae potestatis insigne, virgam scilicet regni rectam, virgam virtutis, qua te ipsum bene regas, sanctamque ecclesiam et populum videlicet christianum tibi a Deo commissum regia virtute ab [fol. 78r] *improbis deffendas*[a], *pravos corrigas, rectos pacifices, et, ut viam rectam tenere possint tuo iuvamine dirigas, quatinus*[b] *de temporali regno ad eternum regnum pervenias*[c], *ipso adiuvante, cuius regnum et imperium sine fine permanet in secula seculorum. Amen.*

> 116. [a] defendas C. —[b] quatenus C. —[c] perveniat C.

117. Apres dict[a] l'oroison qui s'ensuit.

Oracio post sceptrum datum.

Omnium, Domine, fons bonorum cunctorum Deus institutor profectuum[b], *tribue, quesumus, famulo tuo Carolo*[c] *adeptam bene regere dignitatem, et a te sibi prestitum*[d] *honorem dignare coroborare*[e]; *honorifica eum prae cunctis regibus terre, uberi eum*[f] *benedictione* ✠[g] *locupleta, et in solio regni firma stabilitate consolida. Visita eum in sobole*[h], *presta ei prolixitatem vitae, in diebus eius semper oriatur iusticia, et*[i] *cum iocunditate*[j] *et leticia eterno glorietur in regno. Per Christum*[k] *dominum nostrum etc.*

> 117. [a] dist C. —[b] perfectuum B. —[c] famulo tuo Carolo] tuo Charolo C. —
> [d] praepositum C. —[e] corroborare C. —[f] cum C. —[g] ✠ *om.* C. —[h] soble C. —
> [i] ut *Ordo XXIII,59.* —[j] iucunditate C. —[k] Christum *om.* C.

118. Ladicte oraison achevee, mondict sieur[a] l'archevesque print la verge, au sommet de laquelle [y[b]] a une main d'yvoire, et la bailla au roy en sa main senestre, en disant ce qui s'ensuit.

Oracio.

Accipe virgam virtutis atque equitatis, qua intelligas mulcere pios et terrere reprobos[c], *errantibus viam doce*[d], *lapsisque manum porrige, disperdasque* [fol. 78v] *superbos et releves humiles*[e], *ut aperiat tibi hostium*[f] *Ihesus Christus dominus noster, qui de se ipso ait, 'Ego sum hostium*[f]*; per me si quis introierit salvabitur;' et ipse qui est clavis David et sceptrum domus Israel, 'qui aperit, et nemo claudit, [claudit*[g]*,] et nemo aperit.' Sit tibi adiutor, qui eduxit 'vinctum de domo carceris, sedentem in tenebris et umbra mortis,' ut in omnibus sequi merearis eumque*[h] *de quo propheta David cecinit, 'Sedes tua, Deus, in seculum seculi, virga equitatis virga regni tui,' et imiteris*[i] *eum qui dicit, 'Diligas iusticiam et odio habeas iniquitatem; propterea unxit te Deus*[j]*, Deus tuus, oleo leticie,' ad exemplum illius quem ante secula unxerat 'prae participibus*[k] *suis' Ihesum Christum dominum nostrum*[l]*.*

118. [a] seigneur C. —[b] y *om.* B C, *here add. from a.* —[c] improbos C. —[d] docere B. —[e] humiles *om.* C. —[f] ostium C. —[g] claudit *om.* B C, *here add. from Ordo XXIII,60.* —[h] cumque C, eum *Ordo XXIII,60.* —[i] immitabis B. —[j] Deus *erroneously crossed out* C. —[k] particibus B. —[l] etc. *later add.* C.

119. Apres[30] ladicte oroison, monsieur[a] messire Guillaume de Rochefort chevalier, docteur en Loix et en Decret, chancelier de France, illec present, appella les pers de France en l'ordre qui s'ensuit. C'est a sçavoir :

Le[31] duc de Bourgongne, pour lequel se presenta le duc d'Orleans.

Le[32] duc de Normandye, pour lequel se presenta le duc d'Allençon[b].

Le duc d'Acquitaine[c], pour lequel se presenta le comte de Clermont.

[fol. 79r] Le comte de Flandres, pour lequel se presenta le comte Daufin[d].

Le compte de Champaigne, pour lequel se presenta le comte de Bresse.

Le comte de Toulouse[e], pour lequel se presenta le comte de Vandosme[f].

119. [a] monseigneur C. —[b] d'Alençon C. —[c] d'Aquitaine C. —[d] Daulphin C. — [e] Thoulouse C. —[f] Vandosme *corr. to* Vendosme C.

120. L'archevesque[33] duc de Reims present, qui faisoit le sacre. L'evesque duc de Laon, present.

[30] A marginal note in *C* reads, "Le chancelier de France appelle les pairs de France pour assister au couronnement du roy."

[31] A marginal note at the bottom of p. 124 in *C* reads, "Les pairs laics appellés au couronnement du roy, premier que les pairs clercs."

[32] A marginal note at the top of p. 125 in *C* reads, "Le rang des pairs."

[33] A marginal note in *C* reads, "Rang des pairs ecclesiastiques."

L'evesque duc de Langres, present.

L'evesque comte de Beauvais, pour lequel se presenta l'evesque d'Amiens.

L'evesque comte de Chaalons, present.

L'evesque comte de Noyon, present.

121. Et sy ledict chancellier de France n'eust esté present audict sacre, ledict archevesque de Reims eust appellé lesdictz pers en l'ordre dessusdict.

122. Apres ladicte evocation, ledict archevesque de Reims se leva de sa chaere, et alla prendre sur l'autel la couronne royalle apportee[34] de sainct Denis en France, et la mist seul dessus sur le chief[a] du roy sans la asseoir[b].

A laquelle, tantost les pers seculiers et ecclesiasticques meirent la main pour la soustenir avecq ledict archevesque, qui dict[c] adoncques l'oroison qui s'ensuict.

122. [a] la mist seul dessus sur le chief] la mist dessus le chef C. —[b] l'asseoir C. — [c] dist C.

123. [fol. 79v] Oracio.

Coronet te Deus corona gloriae atque iustitiae, honore et opere fortitudinis, ut per officium nostre benedictionis ✠ cum fide recta et multiplici bonorum operum fructu ad coronam pervenias regni perpetui, ipso largiente cuius regnum et imperium permanet in secula seculorum. Amen.

124. Puis[35] ledict archevesque seul assit[a], et imposa ladicte couronne sur le chef du roy, et tantost lesdictz pers y midrent la main et la soustindrent[b] de toute pars, et puis ledict archevesque dict[c] l'oroison qui s'ensuit.

Oracio.

Accipe coronam regni, in nomine Patris ✠ et Filii ✠ et Spiritus sancti ✠, ut spreto antiquo hoste spretisque contagiis viciorum omnium sic iusticiam, misericordiam et iudicium diligas, et ita iuste, misericorditer, et pie vivas, ut ab ipso domino nostro Ihesu Christo in consorcio sanctorum eterni regis[d] coronam percipias.

Accipe[36] inquam coronam, quam sanctitatis gloriam et honorem, et opus fortitudinis intelligas signare, et per hanc te participem

---

[34] A marginal note in *C* reads, "L'archevesque de Rheims prend sur l'autel la couronne royale et la met dessus le chef du roy sans l'asseoir."

[35] A marginal note in *C* reads, "L'archevesque de Rheims assiet et impose seul la couronne sur le chef du roy. Et les autres pairs y mectent la main et la soustiennent de toutes parts."

[36] These two paragraphs are treated as single prayer in one paragraph in *B* and *C*,

ministerii[e] *nostri non ignores,*[37] *ita ut sicut nos in*[f] *interioribus pastores rectoresque animarum intelligimur*[g]*, ita tu contra omnes adversitates ecclesiae* [fol. 80r] *Christi defensor assistas, regnique tibi a Deo dati, et per officium nostrae benedictionis* ✠ *in vice*[h] *apostolorum, omniumque sanctorum regimini*[i] *tuo commissi utilis executor, perspicuusque*[j] *regnator semper apareas, ut inter gloriosos athletas, virtutum gemmis ornatus, et praemio sempiternae foelicitatis coronatus, cum redemptore ac salvatore nostro Ihesu Christo, cuius nomen vicemque gestare crederis, sine fine glorieris, qui vivit et imperat Deus cum Deo Patre in secula seculorum.* [fol. 60v] *Amen.*

124. [a] assist C. — [b] mirent la main et la soustinrent C. — [c] dist C. — [d] regni *Ordo XXIII,64.* — [e] misterii B. — [f] in *om.* C. — [g] illigunntur B. — [h] in vicem C. — [i] regum B. — [j] prespicunimsque (*or something similar*) B.

125. Alia oracio.

Deus perpetuitatis, dux virtutum, cunctorum hostium victor, benedic hunc famulum tuum tibi caput suum inclinantem, et prolixa sanitate et prospera foelicitate eum conserva, et ubicumque[a] *pro quibus tuum auxilium invocaverit, cito assis*[b] *ac protegas et deffendas; tribue ei, quesumus Domine, divitias*[c] *glorie tuae, comple in bonis desiderium eius, corona eum in miseracione et misericordia, tibique Deo pia devotione iugiter famuletur. Per dominum nostrum Ihesum Christum filium tuum etc.*

125. [a] ubicunque C. — [b] adsis C. — [c] ditias B.

126. Apres que lesdictes oroisons furent achevees, ledict archevesque fit[a] sur le roy la benediction en la maniere qui s'ensuit.

[fol. 80v] Benedictio.

Extendat omnipotens Deus dexteram suae benedictionis ✠, *et circundet*[b] *te muro felicitatis, ac custodia sue protectionis sanctae Mariae ac beati Petri, apostolorum principis, sanctique Dionisii, atque beati Remigii, et omnium sanctorum intercedentibus meritis. Amen.*

126. [a] fist C. — [b] circundet *corr.* to circumdet C.

127. *Indulgeat tibi Dominus omnia peccata quae gessisti, et tribuat tibi misericordiam et gratiam quam ab eo*[a] *humiliter deposcis, et liberet te ab adversitatibus cunctis, et ab omnibus inimicorum omnium visibilium et invisibilium insidiis. Amen.*

---

but they are separate prayers in Ordo XXIII,64–65. Therefore, I here assign a single number to the prayer, but separate it into two paragraphs.

[37] A marginal note in *C* reads, "Le roy est participant du ministere ecclesiastique avec les evesques."

127. ^a ab eo] a Deo C.

128. [*Angelos suos bonos, qui te semper et ubique praecedant, comitentur et subsequantur, ad custodiam tui ponat et a peccato seu gladio et ab omnium^a periculorum discrimine sua potentia liberet. Amen^b.*]

128. ^a omniu C. —^b Angelos suos ... Amen *om.* B, *here add. from* C.

129. *Inimicos tuos ad pacis caritatisque benignitatem convertat, et bonis operibus te graciosum et amabilem faciat, pertinaces quoque in tui miseracione^a et odio confusione salutari induat, super te autem participatio et sanctificatio sempiterna^b floreat. Amen.*

129. ^a insectatione *Ordo XXIII,70.* —^b perpetua C.

130. *Victoriosissimum^a atque triumphatorem de visibilibus atque invisibilibus^b hostibus semper efficiat, et sancti nominis sui^c timorem pariter et amorem continuum cordi tuo infundat, et in fide recta ac bonis operibus perseverabilem reddat, et pace^d in diebus tuis concessa, cum palma victoriae te ad perpetuum regnum perducat. Amen.*

130. ^a Victoriosum C; Victoriosum te *a and most MSS of Ordo XXIII,71.* — ^b atque invisibilibus *om.* C. —^c tui B. —^d pacem C.

131. [fol. 81r] *Et qui te voluit super populum suum constituere regem, et in presenti seculo felicem, aeternae felicitatis tribuat esse consortem. Amen.*

Quod ipse^a praestare dignetur, cuius regnum et imperium sine fine permanet in secula seculorum. Amen.

131. ^a Qui ipsi B.

132. Et incontinent^a apres fit ladicte^b benediction qui s'ensuit. Benedictio.

Benedic Domine hunc regem nostrum preelectum principem, qui regna omnium regum a seculo moderaris. Amen.

Et tali eum^c benedictione glorifica, ut Davitica^d teneat sublimitate sceptrum salutis et sanctificae propiciationis, munere reperiatur locupletatus. Amen.

Da ei tuo spiramine cum mansuetudine ita regere populum, sicut Salomonem fecisti regnum obtinere pacificum. Amen.

Tibi cum timore sit subditus tibique^e militet cum quiete; sit tuo clipeo^f protectus, cum proceribus et ubique gratia tua victor existat. Amen.

Honorifica eum prae cunctis regibus gencium, felix populis dominetur^g, et feliciter eum nationes adornent; vivat inter gencium nationes magnanimus. Amen.

Sit in iudiciis aequitatis singularis; locuplet[h] [fol. 81v] *eum tua providens*[i] *dextera; frugiferam obtineat patriam, et*[j] *eius liberis tribuas profuturam*[k]. *Amen.*

Presta ei prolixitatem vitae per tempora, ut in diebus eius oriatur iusticia, a te robustum teneat regiminis solium, et cum iocunditate[l] *et iusticia aeterno glorietur regno. Amen.*

Quod ipse praestare dignetur cuius regnum et imperium sine fine permanet in secula seculorum. Amen.

132. [a] incontinant B. —[b] fist l'autre C. —[c] cum C. —[d] Davidica C. —[e] tibique *om.* C. —[f] clypeo C. —[g] populus dualitur B. —[h] locuplet et C, *corr. to* locupletatus et. —[i] predives *Ordo XXIII,73.* —[j] et *om.* C. —[k] profutura *Ordo XXIII,73.* —[l] incunditate *corr. to* iucunditate C.

133. Puis apres dit[a] les autres oraisons et les[b] benedictions qui s'ensuivent.

Benedictio.

Omnipotens Deus 'det tibi de rore coeli, et de pinguedine terrae habundanciam frumenti, vini et olei, et serviant tibi populi, et adorent te tribus; esto dominus fratrum tuorum, et incurventur ante te filii matris tuae, et qui benedixerit tibi benedictionibus repleatur,' et Deus erit adiutor tuus. 'Omnipotens[38] *benedicat tibi benedictionibus celi desuper in montibus et collibus*[c], *benedictionibus abissi iacentibus deorsum, benedictionibus uberum' et uvarum pomorumque; benedictiones patrum antiquorum Abraham, Isaac et Iacob, confortate sint super te.* [fol. 82r] *Per Christum dominum nostrum. Amen.*

133. [a] dist C. —[b] les *om.* C. —[c] colibus B.

134. Alia benedictio.

Benedic, Domine, fortitudinem principis, et opera manuum illius[a] *suscipe, et benedictione tua terra eius de pomis repleatur de fructu celesti et rore atque abissi subiacentis, de fructu solis et lune*[b], *et de vertice antiquorum montium*[c], *de pommis*[d] *eternorum collium, et de frugibus terrae et de*[e] *plenitudine eius; benedictio illius qui apparuit in rubo veniat super caput eius, et plena sit benedictio domini in filiis eius, et tingat in oleo pedem suum, cornua rinocerontis cornua illius, in ipsis ventilabit gentes usque ad terminos terrae, quia ascensor*[f] *coeli auxiliator suus [in sempiternum fiat. Per dominum nostrum Ihesum Christum*[g],] *qui tecum vivit et regnat in unitate Spiritus sancti Deus per omnia secula seculorum. Amen.*

---

[38] This second part is treated as a continuation of the previous paragraph in both *B* and *C*, as well as in Ordo XXII A,49. No. 133 is two paragraphs in Ordo XV,35 and two prayers in Ordo XXIII,74; only the first part is in Ordo XXIV,63.

134. ᵃipsius B. —ᵇlumine C. —ᶜnostrorum B. —ᵈpomis C. —ᵉde *om.* C. —
ᶠassensor B. —ᵍin sempiternum ... Christum *om.* B C, *here add. from Ordo
XXIII,75.*

135. Les quatre benedictions et oroisons dessusdictes achevees et
ditzᵃ par ledict archevesque, il printᵇ le roy par la main et le mena,
accompagnéᶜ des pers soustenansᵈ sa couronne, de devant l'autel parmy
le cueur ouᵉ pulpitre, entre les deux cueurs, au lieu ou son siege ou trosneᶠ
luy estoit preparé, comme dessusᵍ est declaré. Et quant ils furent illec
arrivez,³⁹ le roy estant tout debout, le dos contre son siege prest a soy
seoirʰ [fol. 82v] en iceluy, qui estoict fort hault [etⁱ] eslevé, tellement
qu'on le pouvoit veoir du dehors de l'eglize. Avant qu'il asseitʲ, ledict
archevesque luy dictᵏ ce qui s'ensuit, en le tenant tousjours par la main
jusques a ce que enˡ disant les mots : « In hoc regni solio confirmet », il le
fitᵐ seoir et ne le tint plus.

135. ᵃdictes C. —ᵇprist C. —ᶜacompagné C. —ᵈsoustenants *corr. to* soustenans C. —ᵉau C. —ᶠthrosne C. —ᵍcomme cy dessus C. —ʰa soy soir B. —ⁱet
om. B, *here add. from* C. —ʲs'assist C. —ᵏdist C. —ˡen *om.* C. —ᵐfist C.

136. *Sta et retine amodo statum, quam*ᵃ *huc usque paterna successione tenuisti, hereditario iure*⁴⁰ *tibi delegatum per auctoritatem Dei
omnipotentis et per presentem traditionem nostram, omnium scilicet*ᵇ
*episcoporum, ceterorumque Dei servorum; et quanto clerum propin-
quiorem sacris altaribus prospicis, tanto et*ᶜ *potiorem in locis congruentibus honorem impendere memineris, quatinus*ᵈ *mediator Dei et
hominum, te mediatorem cleri et plebis in hoc regni solio confirmet, et
in regno eterno secum regnare faciat, Ihesus Christus dominus noster,
rex regum et dominus dominantium. Qui cum Deo Patre et Spiritu
sancto vivit et regnat per omnia saecula saeculorum. Amen.*

136. ᵃquem *Ordo XXIII,77;* statum quam] quem *corr. to* locum quem C. —
ᵇsanctorum B. —ᶜei C *corr. from* et. —ᵈquatenus C.

137. Et en fin de ce, dictᵃ le verset qui s'ensuit.
Firmetur manus tua et exaltetur dextera tua.
Et le cueur respondit.
*Iusticia et iudicium praeparatio sedis tuae*ᵇ.
[fol. 83r] *Domine, exaudi orationem meam.*
Et clamor meus ad te veniat.
Dominus vobiscum.
Et cum spiritu tuo.

---

³⁹ A marginal note in *C* reads, "Le roy mené en son throsne royal."
⁴⁰ A marginal note in *C* reads, "Le royaume de France hereditaire."

Oremus.

137. ᵃ Et en fin se dist C. —ᵇ sedis eius C.

138. Oratio.

Deus, qui victrices Moisi manus in oracione firmasti, qui, quamvis aetate [lacesceret⁴¹], infatigabili sanctitate pugnabat, ut dum Amalech iniquusᵃ vincitur, dum prophanus nacionum populus subiugatur, exterminatis alienigenisᵇ haereditati tuae possessio copiosa serv[ir]etᶜ, opus manuum nostrarum piaᵈ nostre orationis exaudicioneᵉ confirma. Habemus et nos apud te, sancte Pater, dominum salvatorem, qui pro nobis manus suas tetendit in cruce, per quem etiam precamur, Altissime, ut eius potentia suffragante, universorumᶠ hostium frangatur impietas, populusque tuus, cessante formidine, teᵍ solum timere condiscat. Per dominum nostrum Ihesum Christum etc.

138. ᵃ iniqus B. —ᵇ alie inigenis B. —ᶜ servet B; serviet C, *but* serviret *Ordo XXIII,80.* —ᵈ piae B. —ᵉ exaudicionem B. —ᶠ diversorium B. —ᵍ et B.

139. Apres que ladicte oraison fut dicte, le roy estant assis en son siege au trosneᵃ, comme dict est, ledict archevesque dessubla et misᵇ jus sa mittre, et en grand amour, honneur et reverence baisa le roy en la bouche etᶜ print a crier a haulte voix : « Vivat rex in aeternum ! »

Et quand il eut ce dict, le peuple cria : « Vive le roy », et les trompettes et claronsᵈ prindrent a sonner melodieusement.

139. ᵃ siege ou throsne C. —ᵇ mist C. —ᶜ se *add. a.* —ᵈ clairons C; se *add. a.*

140. [fol. 83v] Semblablement apres luy le baiserent tous les autres pers, tant seculiers, comme ecclesiasticques, disant chacun en son ordre comme avoit faict ledict archevesque : « Vivat rex in aeternum ! » Et le peuple⁴² respondit comme dessus, en criant : « Vive le roy », les trompettes et clarons sonnansᵃ. Et quant tous les pers eurent ainsy faict, ledict archevesque commença a chanter a haulte voix : « Te Deum laudamus »,⁴³ qui fut achevé partyeᵇ par les orgues, partyeᵇ a choseᶜ faicte par les chantres du roy, et partie a plein chant communᵈ, pour avoir plustost faict, a cause du service qui estoit fort long. Et quand il fut achevé, ledit archevesque retourna en bas, avec les diacre et soubdiacreᵉ, pour aller dire la messe.

---

⁴¹ *lacesceret* is supplied from Ordo XXIII,80, var. *d.* The source must have been illegible here because *C* incorrectly reads *cassus* and because *B* inserts five dots in a blank space about the length of *infatigabili*, the following word.

⁴² A marginal note in *C* reads, "Vive le roy."

⁴³ A marginal note in *C* reads, "Te Deum laudamus."

140. ^a clairons sonnants C. —^b partie C. —^c à musique *a*. —^dcomme B. —
^e soubsdiacre C.

141. Ainsy que ledict archevesque descendoit pour retourner a l'autel dire la messe, comme dict est, le duc d'Orleans print son espee, en donna l'acolée^a au roy et le fit^b chevalier en armes.[44] Et ce faict, le roy print l'espée, et avant que monsieur^c de Reims commença^d sa messe a l'autel, fit IIII^{XX} XVII ^e chevaliers de diverses nacions et pais, dont les rois d'armes, heraulx^f et trompettes prindrent depuis, et receurent leurs noms et armes par escript.

141. ^a l'accolee C. —^b fist C. —^c monseigneur C. —^d commençast C. —^e fist
quatre vingt dix sept C. —^f heraults C.

142. Ce faict, les chantre et soubchantre^a dessus nommez commencerent l'introite de la messe, qui fut de la domimé commencerent^b « Exaudi », etc. Laquelle [fol. 84r] fut chantee par les chantres de la chappelle du roy le plus legerement que faire ce peult^c, et durant laquelle furent dictes^d audict pulpitre les messes ordinaires du roy sur ung autel pour ce illec preparé.

142. ^a chantres et soubschantre C. —^b qui fut de la dominee commançant C,
qui fut celle commençant *a*. —^c que faire se peut C. —^d dis B.

143. Monsieur l'archevesque de Sez fit^a a ladicte messe l'Epistre et office de soubzdiacre, et monsieur^b l'evesque de Sainct Pons office de diacre et dict l'Evangile, au commencement^c de laquelle le roy mit jus sa couronne de sa teste, se leva tout droict et se tint en cet^d estat jusques a ce qu'elle fut achevee[45] ; et en la fin d'icelle se r'asseit et remit sadite^e couronne sur son chief^f.

143. ^a Monseigneur l'evesque de Says leut C. —^b et fit office de soubsdiacre et
monseigneur C. —^c l'office de diacre et dist l'Evangile, au commancement C. —
^d cest C. —^e se r'assist, et remist sadicte C. —^f chef C.

144. Et apres que ledict evesque de Sainct Pons, faisant office de diacre, eut dict et prononcé ladicte Evangile, il print le livre aux Evangiles et le porta baisier au roy, et puis apres le porta baisier^a audict archevesque.

144. ^a baiser C.

145. Quand les chantres de la chappelle du roy, tenans^a la messe,

---

[44] A marginal note in *C* reads, "Le roy faict chevalier a son sacre par le duc d'Orleans."

[45] A marginal note in *C* reads, "le roy oste sa couronne de la teste, lors que l'Evangile se dict, et se leve debout."

eurent chanté l'offertoire, les unze pairs de France soustenans[b] la
couronne du roy, le amenerent[c] a l'offrande au grant autel,[46] et y offrit
ung pot d'argent doré plain de vin, ung gros pain de froment doré et treze
escus d'or pour besons[d], selon les anciens livres ; puis le remenerent en
sondit[e] siege, comme ils[f] l'avoient admené[g]. Et[47] en allant a ladite[h]
offrande, comme dict est, et en retournant audict pulpitre[i] en son siege
royal, monsieur[j] le mareschal de Gié, par luy a ce faire ordonné, [fol. 84v]
porta tousjours l'espee[48] toute nue devant luy, pour et ou lieu de monsieur[k] le connestable ; et durant l'aller et revenir[l], jouoyent les trompettes
et clarons[m].

145. [a] tenants C. — [b] soustenants C. — [c] l'amenerent C, *corr. from* l'amel-
nerent. — [d] besans C, *corr. from* besaons. — [e] sondict C. — [f] il B. — [g] amené C. —
[h] ladicte C. — [i] et *add.* C. — [j] monseigneur C. — [k] au lieu de monseigneur C. —
[l] l'allee et revenue C. — [m] clairons C.

146.　Tantost apres que le roy eut faict son offrande, et tandis qu'il s'en
retournoit, les prelatz et chanoines officians[a] a l'autel, firent l'offrande
accoustumee de pain et de vin pour celebrer, et offrirent deux hosties et
du vin, comme a double de ce qu'on a accoustumé[b], que ledict evesque[c]
consacra.

146. [a] officiants C. — [b] acoustumé C. — [c] archevesque C.

147.　En apres l'oroison dominicale par luy dicte, avant qu'il dict[a] :
« Pax Domini sit semper vobiscum », il se retourna vers[b] le roy et le peuple, la mittre sur sa teste, sa crosse en sa main senestre, et fit[c] sur le roy
et le peuple la benediction qui s'ensuit.[49]

147. [a] dist C. — [b] devers C. — [c] fist C.

148. Benedictio.
Benedicat tibi Dominus custodiensque [te[a]], *sicut voluit* [te[b]] *super
populum suum constituere regem, ita et in presenti seculo felicem et
aeternae felicitatis tribuat esse consortem. Amen.*

148. [a] te *om.* B, *here add. from* C. — [b] te *om.* B C, *here add. from Ordo
XXIII,103.*

149.　*Clerum ac populum, quem sua voluit opitulacione, tua sanctione*

---

[46] A marginal note in *C* reads, "Offrande du roy."
[47] A marginal note in *C* reads, "L'espee nue portee devant le roy allant à l'offrande."
[48] A marginal note in *C* reads, "L'espee nue portee devant le roy pour et au lieu du
connestable."
[49] A marginal note in *C* reads, "Benediction."

congregari, sua dispensatione et [fol. 85r] *tua administracione per diuturna tempora faciat feliciter gubernari. Amen.*

150. *Quatinus[a] divinis monitis parentes, adversitatibus omnibus carentes, bonis omnibus exuberantes, tuo ministerio[b] fideli amore obsequentes, et in presenti seculo pacis transquilitate[c] fruantur, et tecum aeternorum civium consorcio potiri mereantur. Amen.*

[*Quod ipse praestare dignetur, cuius regnum et imperium permanet in saecula saeculorum. Amen[d].*]

150. [a] Quatenus C. —[b] misterio B. —[c] tranquillitate C. —[d] Quod ipse ... Amen *om.* B, *here add. from* C.

151. *Et benedictio* ✠ *Dei omnipotentis* ✠, *Patris* ✠[a] *et Fili et Spiritus sancti super vos descendat et maneat semper.* [*Amen[b].*]

151. [a] ✠ *om.* C. —[b] Amen *om.* B, *here add. from* C.

152. Item, est a noter que l'archevesque, avant ladicte Epistre, [dist l'oraison[a]] et collecte[b] qui s'ensuit.

Quaesumus, omnipotens Deus, ut famulus tuus rex noster Carolus[c], qui tua miseracione regni suscepit gubernacula, virtutum omnium eciam[d] percipiat incrementa, quibus decenter ornatus et vitiorum monstra devitare, et ad te qui 'via, veritas et vita' [*es[e]*], *graciosus valeat pervenire. Per dominum nostrum Ihesum Christum etc.*

152. [a] dist l'oraison *om.* B, *here add. from* C. —[b] colecte B. —[c] Charolus C. — [d] etiam omnium C, *corr. from* etiam. —[e] es *om.* B, *here add. from Ordo XXIII,82;* est C.

153. Et pour la secrette, il print celle qui s'ensuit.

Munera, quaesumus Domine, oblata sanctifica, ut et nobis unigeniti tui corpus et sanguis fiant, et Carolo[a] regi nostro ad obtinendam anime, [fol. 85v] *corporisque salutem, et ad peragendum iniunctum officium, te[b] largiente, usquequaque proficiant. Per dominum nostrum etc.*

153. [a] Charolo C. —[b] et B.

154. Secunda post communionem[a] [50] fut celle qui s'ensuit.

Haec, Domine, oratio salutaris famulum tuum Carolum[b] regem nostrum ab omnibus tueatur adversis, quatinus[c] et ecclesiastice pacis obtineat tranquilitatem[d], et post istius temporis decursum ad aeternam perveniat hereditatem. Per dominum nostrum Ihesum Christum filium etc.

---

[50] *B's* reading is probably that of the source; its retention of the three Latin words shows that the author was working from a Latin text.

154. [a] Secunda post communionem] Sa communion C. —[b] Charolum C. —
[c] quatenus C. —[d] tranquillitatem C.

155. Quand ledict archevesque eut dict[a] : « Pax Domini sit semper
vobiscum », alors qu'on a acoustumé de donner baisier[b] la paix, ledict
evesque de Saint[c] Pons, diacre, print la paix dudict archevesque pour le
baisier[d] ; et ce faict, l'alla porter au roy en le baisant ; et apres qu'il l'eut
baisiée[e], tous les autres evesques estans[f] entour luy le baisierent[g] semblablement, ou il estoit assis en son siege roial.

155. [a] dit C. —[b] baisier] a baiser C. —[c] Sainct C. —[d] la baiser C. —[e] baisee C. —
[f] estants C. —[g] baiserent C.

156. Et quant ledict archevesque eut prins[a] et usé une ostie[b] sacree
et du precieux sang qu'il avoit consacré, avant que dire la postcommu-
nion, ne prendre perception de vin, il attendit acoudé sur l'autel, jusques
a ce que les pers ecclesiastiques et seculiers eurent amené[c] le roy de son
siege d'enhault empres le grand autel, soustenans [fol. 86r] tousjours sa
couronne comme devant ; lequel venu illec, entra en l'oratoire qu'on luy
avoit preparé empres ledict[d] grand autel, et la se reconcilia a son con-
fesseur. Puis s'en vinte[e] mettre a deux genoux[f] devant ledict autel, ou il
dit[g] son Confiteor, et apres eut l'absolution et benediction dudit[h] archevesque, et puis receut en grande devotion le precieux corps et le sang de
Nostre Sauveur[i] Iesus Christ. Et pour ce qu'il[j] ne peut tout user le sang
qui estoit ou[k] calice, ledict archevesque usa le surplus. Et print du vin
apres, mais il n'en bailla poinct au roy. [Puis il[l]] lava ses mains et
escheva[m] la messe.

156. [a] pris C. —[b] hostie C. —[c] ameiné C. —[d] le C. —[e] s'en vint] se vint C. —
[f] genoulx *corr. from* genouls C. —[g] dist C. —[h] dudict C. —[i] Saulveur C. —[j] qui
B. —[k] au C. —[l] Puis il *om.* B C, *here add. from* a. —[m] acheva C.

157. La messe finie, ledict archevesque osta la couronne de dessus la
teste du roy, et sy fut le roy despouillé des habitz royaulx apportez de
Saint[a] Denis en France, qui furent tous rendus[b] a l'abbé dudict Saint[a]
Denis.

Et le roy revestu d'autres habitz[c] de drap d'or, ledict archevesque luy
mit[d] sur sa teste une autre couronne plus petite et plus legere. Et en cet[e]
estat, tenant le sceptre en la main destre[f] et la verge en la main senestre,
fut conduit et mené au palais archiepiscopal pour disner et reposer,
l'espee nue tousjours precedant, que portoit ledict mareschal de Gié au
lieu du connestable, qui la tint durant le disner en tel estat devant le roy
estant a [fol. 86v] table.

157. [a] Sainct C. —[b] renduz C. —[c] d'aultres habits C. —[d] mist C. —[e] cest C. —
[f] dextre C.

158. En la fin de ladicte messe, ledict archevesque rendit et restitua ladicte saincte ampolle audit[a] abbé de Sainct Remy, qui ne la porta[b] pas si tost apres, par ce que les quatre barons qui la devoyent reconduire estoient allé[c] avecq le roy audict palais, auquel Domp[d] Guillaume Grossadier[e], grand prieur de l'abbaie de Sainct Remy les fut requerir. Et quant ils furent venus[f], ledict abbé, vestu d'un surplis et une chappe de drap d'or dessus, ayant ladicte saincte ampolle pendue a son col, monta sur la hacquenee que le roy luy avoit envoyé estant empres[g] du grand portail, et soubs le palium donné par le roy, la reporta processionnelle-ment en ladicte abbaye, ou, en la presence desdicts barons, elle fut remise en son lieu empres le corps de monsieur[h] sainct Remy.

158. [a] la saincte ampoulle au dict C. —[b] reporta C. —[c] allez C. —[d] Dom C. — [e] Grossaire C. —[f] venuz C. —[g] empres] au pas C. —[h] monseigneur C.

159. En souvenance et recordation de la conduitte et reconduitte[a] de ladicte saincte ampole, faicte par lesdicts quatre barons, iceulx ont faict mettre les bannieres[b] de leurs armes en ladicte eglize[c] Sainct Remy sur des lances mises sur les allees des vossures[d] d'entour le grant autel.

159. [a] conduicte et reconduicte C. —[b] banieres C. —[c] eglise de C. —[d] buos-sinnes C, *perhaps a misreading of* vuossines *or* vuossures; voûtes *a.*

160. Tantost que le roy fut retourné audit[a] palais, il alla a sa chambre et illec fut despouillé de la chemise qu'il avoit vestu, laquelle [fol. 87r] fut pour reverence et sainctet锓[b] de la tres saincte unction par luy receue, a laquelle elle avoit touché, portee[c] en l'eglise de Reims, et illec arse[e][d] et bruslee.

Et luy en fut vestu un autre[e]; et luy reabillé[f] et mis en poinct, alla en estat et habit royal seoir a sa[g] table pour disner a la grand table, a laquelle luy et[h] les pers disnerent, et y furent assis en l'ordre qui s'ensuit.

160. [a] audict C. —[b] sainctité C. —[c] porté B. —[d] arsé B C. —[e] aultre C. —[f] reha-billé C. —[g] sa *om.* C. —[h] tous *add.* C.

161. Premierement, le roy fut et estoit assis droict au milieu[a] du banc, ayant dessus[b] son palion de drap de velours parsemé[c] [51] de fleurs de lis[d] de fin or, couvrant a son endroit toute la table de largeur, et descendant par derriere bien bas contre la tapisserye qui [y[e]] estoit tendue. Et estoit ledict roy vestu d'une robbe de drap d'or, doublee de soye changent[f], ayant une couronne d'or sur sa teste.

---

[51] Each manuscript's reading makes sense: "cloth of velvet spangled with fleurs-de-lis" in *B*, and "cloth of blue velvet, sewn with fleurs-de-lis" in *C* ("son pallion de drap de veloux pers, semé de fleurs de Lys de fin or" in ed. *a*, p. 206). *C*'s reading is likely to be the correct one because it accords with the reading in no. 63 above (at var. *b*), where both manuscripts read "velours per (pers *C*), semé de...."

161. ᵃmillieu C. —ᵇluy *add.* C. —ᶜpers semé C. —ᵈlys C. —ᵉy *om.* B, *here add. from* C. —ᶠchangeant C.

162. Et devant luy, [surᵃ] la table du costé destreᵇ, y en avoit une plus grande sur ung coussin de drap d'or, et sur ladicte table a senestre y avoit une grande nef d'argent doré, en laquelle estoit le linge de bouche pour sa personne.

162. ᵃsur *om.* B, *here add. from* C. —ᵇdextre C.

163. A sa dextre estoit assis le plus prochain de luy l'archevesque duc de Reims. Apres luy, l'evesque duc [fol. 87v] de Laon. Apres, l'evesque duc de Langres. Apres, l'evesque comte de Chaalons. Et apres, l'evesque conte de Noyon. Et combien que l'evesque d'Amiens fitᵃ office pour celuy de Beauvais audict sacre, neantmoins il ne fut point assis a la table du roy.

163. ᵃfist C.

164. A saᵃ senestre estoit assis aupres le roy le duc d'Orleans. Apres, le duc d'Alençon. Apres, le comte de Clermont. Apres, le comte Daulphin. Apres, le conte de Bresse. Et au bout de la table le comte de Vendosmeᵇ, qui estoit mal disposé.

164. ᵃla C. —ᵇVandosme C.

165. Au devant de la table du roy, au travers de laditeᵃ salle, y avoit trois tables. En l'une desquelles, et la prochaine de celle du roy disnerent, et furent assis les huissiers d'armes de l'Hostel du roy. En celle de milieuᵇ, les rois d'armes et heraulxᶜ. Et en la tierce et derniere les trompettes et claronsᵈ.

Entour ladicte salle de tous costez estoient dressezᵉ autres tables, ausquelles furent assis et disnerent gens de divers estatz.

165. ᵃladicte C. —ᵇmillieu C. —ᶜheraults C. —ᵈclairons C. —ᵉdressees C.

166. A ce disner messire Gasion de Lionᵃ, seneschal de Toulouse, fitᵇ office d'escuier, tranchant devant le roy ; et les metzᶜ et services se faisoient et portoient par ceulxᵈ et en la maniere qui s'ensuit.

Premierement, au partir de la cuisine de bouche, [fol. 88r] les trompettes et claronsᵉ alloient toutᶠ devant sonnansᵍ melodieusement. Apres eulx, les roys d'armes et heraulsʰ. Apres euxⁱ, six maistres d'hostelʲ ordinaires, qui alloient deux a deuxᵏ. Et apres eulx, François de Lavalˡ, comte de Montfort, habitué comme ung pair luy faisant office de grand maistre d'Hostel, et derriere luy l'escuierᵐ qui portoit la viande.

166. ᵃGaston de Lyon C. —ᵇThoulouze fist C. —ᶜmets C. —ᵈceulx C. —

167. Sur la fin du disner, madame de Beaujeu, soeur du roy, entra en ladicte salle par l'huis[a] d'empres la chapelle, vestue d'une robbe de drap d'or. Et assez tost apres qu'elle y fut entree on leva la table. Et au lever de la table, le roy fit deux chevaliers, puis s'en alla en sa chambre pour reposer.

167. [a] l'huys C.

168. Ce jour le roy fut ouir vespres en l'eglise de Reims, qui furent tenues solennelles[a] par ledict archevesque.

Et en y allant, ouit et receut[b] les supplications et requestes des habitans seculiers dudict Reims, demandans affranchissementz[c] des tailles et de[s][d] menues impositions.

Et de ceulx de ladicte eglise demandans[e] ayde pour reparer icelle eglize.[52]

Apres lesdictes vespres s'en alla souper[f] et coucher audit[g] palais.

168. [a] solemnelles C, corr. to solemneles. —[b] receut et ouit C. —[c] demandants affranchissement C. —[d] de B C, but des a. —[e] esglise demandants C. — [f] soupper C. —[g] audict C.

169. Le lundy dernier jour de may, et le lendemain du [fol. 88v] jour dudict sacre, le roy et madame de Beaujeu allerent ouir messe a Sainct Remy, et saluer et visiter le corps de mondit[a] sieur[b] Sainct Remy. Et la messe ouye et leur devocion faicte[c], s'en allerent apres en l'eglize[d] de monsieur[e] Sainct Nicaise audit[f] Reims, puis s'en retournerent disner audict palais archiepiscopal.

169. [a] mondict C. —[b] seigneur C. —[c] fete B. —[d] l'eglise C. —[e] monseigneur C. — [f] audict C.

170. Apres que le roy eut disné et reposé de ce jour, il[a] s'en alla esbattre[b] hors de la ville, et saillit par la porte de Portemars[c],[53] et tira par selon les fossés[d] pardevant Portechaire[e], Portene[u]fve[f] et Dieulimire jusques sur la riviere a l'endroict de la tour de Chanterainne[g], en visitant l'ensaincte[h] et la fortiffication de la ville et les ouvrages qu'on y a fait[i] puis n'agueres.

Et quand il vint au devant de ladite[j] tour[k], s'arresta[l] et la regarda fort,

---

[52] In July 1481 a fire had badly damaged the cathedral, which was just nearing completion. Some features of the late-medieval cathedral were never restored.

[53] The Porte Mars is the longest surviving Roman triumphal arch, although only its lower part still exists. See also n. 15 above.

et comme il pouvoit sembler, prenoit grand plaisir a la regarder et aussi a regarder le tour et enseinte[m] et la longueur de ladicte ville.

Puis s'en retourna selonc lesdictz fossés[d], et rentra en ladicte ville par la porte de Portechaere[n], et s'en retira souper et coucher audict palais.

170. [a] il *om.* C. —[b] esbatre C. —[c] la porte de Portemars] la Porte Mars C. — [d] fossez C. —[e] Porte Chaire C. —[f] Portenefve B, Porte Neufve C. —[g] Chanteraine C. —[h] l'enceinte C. —[i] faict C. —[j] ladicte C. —[k] il *add. a.* —[l] s'arresta] arresta C. —[m] enceinte C. —[n] du *or* dit Portechaere B, de Portechaire C.

171. [fol. 89r] Le mardy premier jour de juing ensuivant, entre sept et huict heures de matin, le roy alla ouir messe en l'eglize de Reims, et au saillir de sa messe, au devant de ladicte eglise, monta sur son mulet, et se partit de ladicte ville de Reims par Portemars[a], et s'en alla disner a Cormissi[b],[54] petite ville fermee appartenant a l'archevesque de Reims.

Et d'illec tira au giste a Corbe[n]y[c], faire son pellerinage a monsieur[d] Sainct Marcoul, dont le precieux corps gist et repose illec, qui guerit[e] des escroelles, comme le roy.

171. [a] Porte Mars C. —[b] Cornussy C. —[c] Corbeni C. —[d] pelerinage a monseigneur C. —[e] guerist C.

172. Auquel lieu de Corb[e]ny, le lendemain[a] luy furent presentez six mallades[b] desdictes escroelles,[55] sur lesquelz il fit[c] les prieres et benedictions accoustumees, au moien desquelles ont esté, et sont, gueriz[d].

172. [a] Corbeni le landemain C. —[b] malades C. —[c] fist C. —[d] guariz C.

173. Dieu, par sa grace et a l'intercession de sa tresglorieux Vierge Mere[a] et de tous les sainctz, luy doinct[b] tellement[c] vivre en ce monde, qu'il ait enfin, et ses subjectz par son moyen, la gloire qui [fol. 89v] dure a toursjours[d]. Amen. Amen. Amen.

173. [a] de tres glorieuse Vierge Mere C, de la tres glorieuse Vierge Marie *a.* — [b] saincts luy doint C. —[c] faire *add. a.* —[d] tousjours.

---

[54] Cormicy (Marne) is about seventeen kilometers northwest of Reims, Corbeny (Aisne) about the same distance further on the road to Laon.

[55] A marginal note in *C* reads, "Le roy Charles VIII. guairit six malades des escroüelles."

Appendix I

Spelling Variants Not Retained in Ordo XX B

For possible philological purposes this appendix contains the many variant spellings that are not retained in Ordo XX B (as well as the spellings of manuscripts A and B). Those who copied the manuscripts of this ordo more often than not applied their own spelling, which is unlikely to have been that of their source; furthermore, their spellings are often inconsistent within a single manuscript. Only words that appear five or more times are included in this list.

1) *archevêque* and its article appear in so many forms in each manuscript that it is necessary to list them by manuscript. (There are fewer variants for *évêque*; it is not necessary to list them separately.)

A —l'arcevesque, li arcevesque, li arcevesques, les arcevesques

B —l'arcevesque, li arcevesque, li arcevesques, les arcevesques

C —li arcevesques, li arcevesquez, les arcevesquez

D —l'arcevesque, l'arcevesquez, l'archevesque, li arcevesques, li arcevesquez, li archevesques, li archevesquez, les archevesquez, lez archevesques

E —l'arcevesque, l'archevesque, le arcevesquez, li arcevesque, li arcevesquez, li archevesque, les arcevesques, les arcevequez

F —l'arcevesque, lui arcevesques, ly arcevesques, ly arcevesques, les arcevesques

H —l'archevesque, li arcevesques, li archevesque, li archevesques, les archevesques

K —l'archevesque, li archevesque, li archevesque, ly archevesque, ly archevesques, les archevesques

L —l'archevesque, li arcevesques, li archevesque, li archevesques, les archevesques

M —l'archevesque, li archevesque, li archevesques, ly archevesque, les archevesques

N —l'archevesque, li archevesque, ly archevesque, les archevesques

O_1—l'arcevesque, l'arcevesques, li arcevesque, li arcevesques, li archevesque, les arcevesques

O_2—l'arcevesque, li arcevesque, lui arcevesques, ly arcevêque, ly arcevesque, ly arcevesque, ly arcevesques, ly archeveque, les arcevêques, les arcevesques

b —l'archevesque, li archevesque, li archevesques, les archevesques

In the following list a superscript plus sign after a siglum indicates that that manuscript or edition contains more than one spelling.

2) *a donc* (H^+ K^+ M^+ N), *adomques* (E^+), *adomquez* (C^+), *adonc* (A^+ B^+ F^+ H^+ K^+ M^+ O_1 O_2^+ b^+), *adoncq* (N), *adoncques* (F^+ E^+ O_2^+), *adoncquez* (C^+ E^+), *adonques* (A^+ B^+ D^+ H^+ L b^+), *adonquez* (D^+), *adont* (C^+ D^+ E^+)

3) *ampole* (B^+ C D E L O_1 b^+), *ampolle* (B^+), *ampoule* (A F H^+ L^+ O_2^+ b^+), *ampoulle* (K H^+ L^+ M N O_2^+)

4) *aultre* (C^+ E^+ M), *autre* (A B C^+ D E^+ F H K L N O_1 O_2 *b*)

5) *a* (F^+), *avec* (A^+ F^+ H^+ K^+ L^+ M^+ N^+ O_1^+ O_2^+ b^+), *avecq* (D^+), *avecque* (D^+ L^+), *avecques* (A^+ B^+ C^+ D^+ E^+ F^+ H^+ O_1^+ O_2^+ b^+), *avecquez* (C^+ D^+ E^+), *avesques* (C^+ E^+), *avesquez* (C^+ D^+), *evesques* (C^+), *o* (A^+ B^+ C^+ E^+ F^+ H^+ K^+ L^+ M^+ N^+ O_1^+ O_2^+ b^+), *ovecques* (A^+)

6) *cest* (D F^+ O_2), *ceste* (A B C E F^+ N O_1^+), *cette* (H K L M O_1^+ *b*)

7) *choeur* (K M), *coeur* (K M N^+ O_1^+ O_2^+), *cuer* (A B C D F L O_1^+ O_2^+ *b*), *cueur* (E H N^+)

8) noun: *coronne* (A^+ B D F L O_2^+), *courone* (C^+ N^+), *couronne* (A^+ C^+ E^+ H K L M N^+ O_1 O_2 *b*), *couroune* (C^+ E^+)
verb: *coronner* (B D E), *couronner* (A C F H K L M N O_1 O_2 *b*)
past participle: *coroné* (E^+ O_2), *coronné* (A B D F L^+), *couroné* (K), *couronné* (C^+ D E^+ H K M N O_1 *b*), *courounee* (C^+ E^+), *courounés* (C^+ L^+)

9) *dit* (A^+ D^+ E^+ F^+ H K L M^+ O_1^+ O_2^+ b^+), *dict* (A^+ B C D^+ E^+ F^+ M^+ N), *dist* (D^+), *ditte* (O_1^+ O_2^+ b^+). This includes the forms *dit, dite, dites, dittes, la dit, ladit, dictes, la dicte, ladite*.

10) singular: *eschafault* (K^+ M^+), *eschafaut* (C K^+), *eschaffau* (F^+ M^+ N^+ O_1^+ b^+), *eschaffaut* (D^+ K^+ O_1^+), *eschaffeau* (O_1^+), *eschaufau* (A H L M^+ N^+), *eschaufault* (K^+), *eschaufaut* (B E K^+), *eschauffau* (F^+ N^+ O_2 b^+), *eschauffaut* (D^+ M^+)
plural: *echaufaux* (H), *eschafaus* (C), *eschaffaus* (O_1), *eschaffaux* (D), *eschaufaulx* (M), *eschaufaus* (B F^+ L), *eschaufaux* (E N), *eschaufauz* (A), *eschauffaus* (F^+ *b*), *eschauffaux* (F O_2)

11) *ester* (L O_2), *estre* (A B C D E F H K M N O_1^+ O_2^+ *b*), *etre* (O_1^+ O_2^+), *être* (O_1^+)

12) *faict* (C E^+ F K L M N O_1^+ b^+), *fait* (A B D E^+ H O_1^+ O_2 b^+), *faitte* (D *b*)

13) *grand* (H^+ K^+ L M^+ N^+ O_2), *grande* (H^+ K^+ M^+ N^+), *grant* (A B C D E F O_1 *b*)

14) *mectra* (A F^+ O_1^+), *mectre* (A E^+ F O_1^+), *mettra* (B C D E F^+ H K L M N O_1^+ O_2 *b*), *mettre* (B C D E^+ H K L M N O_1^+ O_2 *b*), *promecte*

(A E F O_1), *promette* (B C D H K L M N O_2 *b*), *promectre* (A O_1), *promettre* (B C D E H K L M N O_2 *b*)

15) *li per* (A B D O_1), *li pers* (A B C *b*), *ly per* (F O_2), *ly pers* (F O_2), *les pairs* (H K L M N), *les peres* (L O_1^+), *les pers* (A B C D E F O_1^+ O_2 *b*)

16) *quand* (H K L^+ M N^+ O_2), *quant* (A B C D E F L^+ N^+ O_1 *b*)

17) *sainc* (E), *sainct* (C H K N *b*), *saincte* (C E F K L N O_2 *b*), *sains* (C E), *saint* (A B D E F), *sainte* (A B D), *sainctes* (F L N *b*), *saintes* (A B D). These words are often abbreviated and are never spelled out in some manuscripts.

18) *ceptre* (A^+ B C D E^+ F O_1^+ O_2^+ *b*), *sceptre* (A^+ E^+ H^+ K L M N^+ O_2^+), *septre* (H^+ N^+ O_1^+)

19) *seur* (B^+), *sur* (A^+ C^+ D^+ E^+ F^+ H K M N O_1 O_2 *b*), *sus* (A^+ B^+ C^+ D^+ E^+ F^+ L *b*$^+$)

20) *tel* (F^+ L^+), *tele* (A B F^+), *telle* (C D^+ E F^+ H K L^+ M N O_1 O_2 *b*), *tiel* (D^+)

21) *un* (A B C D^+ H K L M N O_1^+ O_2^+), *ung* (D^+ E F O_1^+ O_2^+ *b*)

Appendix II

Synoptic Table of Ordines XXII–XXV

This synoptic table of the last medieval ordines provides a quick survey of the late medieval development, and it also illuminates the sources of the Ordines of Louis XI and Charles VIII (Ordines XXIV–XXV). The *livre rouge* version of Charles V's ordo is treated separately from its parent in order to show that it was not a source of the Ordo of Louis XI, but that it was the primary source of the Ordo of Charles VIII. Only the liturgical formulas are listed here; one must look at the rubrics in order to see the extensive changes between ca. 1250 and 1484.

The third column presents the order of the texts as they appear in Ordo XXIII, MS *A*, because that ordo contains nearly all texts that are in all the other ordines; the exceptions are nos. 14–15 in the *livre rouge* (= nos. 56–57 in the Ordo of Charles VIII). Where two texts, originally separated, were later treated as one text, that continuation is shown by means of an en dash (–) connecting the two parts in separate lines. If the order of formulas differs from the order in the Ordo XXIII, its number in Ordo XXIII is shown in square brackets in the third column; that does not mean that those formulas appear at those locations in Ordo XXIII, but is meant only as an aid in identifying different ordines' formulas with each other. Nos. 103 and 104 appear twice in the *livre rouge*.

The King's Ordo

Formula	Last Capetian Ordo	Charles V	Louis XI	*Livre rouge*	Charles VIII
O.s. Deus, qui famulum tuum		5	12	5	45
Ecce, mitto angelum meum		6	13	6	47
Israel, si me audieris		7	14	7	47
Deus, qui scis humanum		8	15	8	49
Domine, in virtute tua		9	16	9	50
O. Deus, celestium moderator		10	17	10	51
Deus, humilium visitator		11			
O preciosum munus				14	56
O.s. Deus, qui pietatis tue dono				15	57
A vobis perdonari petimus	6	17	21	17	65
Promitto vobis et perdono	7	18	22	18	66
Hec populo christiano	8	19	23	19	67

Formula	Last Capetian Ordo	Charles V	Louis XI	*Livre rouge*	Charles VIII
Deus inenarrabilis auctor		21		21	69
Exaudi, Domine, quesumus		23	28	23	72
Accipe hunc gladium	10	25	30	25–	74–
Accipe inquam hunc gladium		26		26	74
Confortare et esto vir	11	27	31	27	75
Deus, qui providentia tua	12	28	32	28	76
Prospice, omnipotens Deus		30		30	78
Benedic, Domine, quesumus		31		31	79
Deus, Pater eterne glorie		32		32	80
Gentem Francorum inclitam		33	34	33	83
Deus, qui populo tuo		34		34	84
Litany	16–20	[109–15]		109–15	87–93
Pater noster		[116]		116	94
Pretende, quesumus Domine		[117]		117	95
Actiones nostras, quesumus		[118]		118	96
Te invocamus, Domine sancte	22	36	37	36	97
Deus, qui populis tuis	23	37	38	37	98
In diebus eius oriatur	24	38	39	38	99
O.s. Deus, creator ac gubernator	25	39	40	39	100
Ungo te in regem	27	40	41	40	102
Unxerunt Salomonem Sadoch	28	41	42	41	103
Christe, perunge hunc regem	29	42	43	42	104
Deus, electorum fortitudo	30	43	44	43	105
Deus, Dei filius	31	44	45	44	106
Deus, rex regum et dominus		45			
Ungantur manus iste		47		47	109
Deus, qui es iustorum gloria		48		48	110
Omnipotens Creator		50		50	111
Circunda, Domine, manus		51		51	112
Deus, tocius creature		53		53	113
Deus, celestium terrestriumque		54			
Benedic, Domine, et sanctifica		55			
Accipe anulum	33	56	47	56	114
Deus, cuius es omnis potestas	34	57	48	57	115
Accipe sceptrum regie	35	58	49	58	116
Omnium, Domine, fons bonorum	36	59	50	59	117
Accipe virgam virtutis	37	60	51	60	118

Formula	Last Capetian Ordo	Charles V	Louis XI	*Livre rouge*	Charles VIII
Deus tuorum corona fidelium		61			
Benedicat te Dominus		[103]		103	
Clerum et populum		[104]		104	
Coronet te Deus corona	39	63	53	63	123
Accipe coronam regni		64		64–	124–
Accipe inquam coronam		65		65	124
Deus perpetuitatis	40	66	54	66	125
Extendat omnipotens Deus	41	67	55	67	126
Indulgeat tibi Dominus	42	68	56	68	127
Angelos suos bonos	43	69	57	69	128
Inimicos tuos ad pacis	44	70	58	70	129
Victoriosum te atque	45	71	59	71	130
Et qui te voluit	46	72	60	72	131
Benedic, Domine, hunc regem	47	73	61	73	132
Sta et retine a modo statum	48	[77]	62		
Omnipotens Deus det tibi	49	74	63	74	133
Benedic, Domine, fortitudinem	50	75	64	75	134
Sta et retine a modo statum		77		77	136
Firmetur manus tua		79		79	137
Deus, qui victrices Moysi		80		80	138
Benedicat tibi Dominus		[103]			148
Clerum ac populum		[104]			149
Quatinus divinis monitis		[105]			150
Et benedictio Dei		[106]			151
Quesumus, omnipotens Deus	52	82		82	152
Munera, quesumus Domine	53	83		83	153
Benedicat tibi Dominus		[103]		103	
Clerum ac populum		[104]		104	
Quatinus divinis monitis		[105]		105	
Et benedictio Dei		[106]		106	
Inclina, Domine, aurem tuam		[107]		107	
Hec, Domine, oratio salutaris	54	84		84	154

The Queen's Ordo

Adesto, Domine, supplicationibus	60	88	69	88	
O. eterne Deus, fons et origo		89		89	
Deus, qui solus habes		90		90	

Formula	Last Capetian Ordo	Charles V	Louis XI	*Livre rouge*	Charles VIII
O.s. Deus, hanc famulam tuam		91		91	
In nomine Patris et Filii	61	92	70	92	
Spiritus sancti, gracia		93		93	
Deus, Pater eterne glorie		94		94	
O.s. Deus, affluentem spiritum	62	[98]	71		
Accipe anulum fidei	64	95	72	95	
Deus, cuius est omnis potestas	65	96	73	96	
Accipe virgam virtutis		97		97	
O.s. Deus, affluentem spiritum		98		98	
Accipe coronam glorie	66	99	74	99	
Omnium, Domine, fons bonorum	67	100	75	100	
Quesumus, omnipotens Deus		[82]	77		
Munera, quesumus, Domine		[83]	80		
Domine sancte Pater		101		101	
Inclina, Domine aurem tuam	69	[108]			
Benedicat tibi Dominus	71	103	81		
Clerum ac populum	72	104	82		
Quatinus divinis monitis	73	105	83		
Et benedictio Dei		106			
Haec, Domine, oratio salutaris		[84]	85		
Inclina, Domine aurem tuam		108			
Litany		109–15			
Pater noster		116			
Pretende, quesumus Domine		117			
Actiones nostras, quesumus		118			

Appendix III

Addenda and Corrigenda to Volume I

I decided, after publishing Vol. I, that references to the French translations of Ordines XX and XXII would be clearer if I assigned each translation a separate letter, and unanticipated discoveries forced me to
renumber some parts of some of the ordines in Vol. II. I also recognized a
few errors that had escaped my attention (some errors are nearly
inevitable in a work as complex as this edition).

p. xiii, line 2: *for* pp. 271–85 *read* pp. 269–83
   line 9: Since the publication of Vol. I, the name of the Bibliothèque
   nationale in Paris has been changed to Bibliothèque nationale de
   France.
p. 5: The adoption of separate identifying letters for the French translations of Ordines XX A and XXII A makes it necessary to modify
   the Synoptic Table slightly. In the column of ordo numbers: *for*
   XX B *read* XX B-C; *for* XXII B *read* XXII B-C. Schramm did not
   know Ordines XX C and XXII B, so he provided no equivalent
   numbers for those texts.
p. 14, last paragraph, lines 9–10: *for* Ordo XXII A, MS *B*; Ordo XXIII, MSS
   A and *F read* Ordo XXII A, MSS *B* and *I*; Ordo XXIII, MSS *A* and *G*
p. 15, line 9: *for* Ordo XVII A) *read* Ordo XVII A, MSS *C* and *E*)
p. 21, line 8 of the full paragraph: *for* (Ordo XX B) *read* (Ordo XX C)
p. 28, line 7 from bottom: *for* MSS *A* and *E*) *read* MSS *A* and *F*)
p. 31, first full paragraph, last line: *for* 1270 *read* 1271.
p. 56, n. 1, line 3: *for* 1: 119–19 *read* 1: 118–19
p. 58, no. 1, lines 5–6: *place single quotation marks around* 'de rore caeli
   ... frumenti, vini' *and add note*: Gen. 27: 28
p. 66, last line of Introduction: *for* Ordo XXV,142, *read* Ordo XXV,138
p. 72, no. 5, line 2: *delete the period after* nostrum
p. 83, n. 8, line 1: *for* Charles the Bold *read* Charles the Bald
p. 84, n. 13: *for* Pet. *read* Petr.
p. 87, n. 1, line 6: *for* Charles the Bold *read* Charles the Bald
p. 89, n. 10, line 1: *for* Bibl. cap. *read* Archivio capitolare
p. 92, lines 1–2: *for* Vercelli, Bibl. cap. *read* Vercelli, Archivio capitolare
   ed. *A*, line 1: *for* reg. lat. 291 *read* Reg. lat. 291
p. 100, n. 33, line 1: *for* 1623 (a_1) *read* 1623 (b_{1b})
p. 134, n. 5, last line: *for* Ordo XXIII,117 and Ordo XXV,97 *read* Ordo
   XXIII,118 and Ordo XXV,96

p. 135, Ordo XI, MS D, line 3: *for* générale *read* général

p. 138, var. 6b: *for* malo d_1 *read* malo D d_1

p. 143, lines 5–6: *add a period after* West Frankish Ordo

p. 146, MS D, penultimate line: *for* générale *read* général
last line: *for* 3: 36, 356 *read* 3: 336, 356

p. 156, n. 6: Lanoë, "Un ordo de couronnement carolingien inconnu," was published as "L'ordo de couronnement de Charles le Chauve à Sainte-Croix d'Orléans (6 juin 848)," in *Kings and Kingship in Medieval Europe*, edited by Anne J. Duggan (London: King's College London Centre for Late Antique and Medieval Studies, 1993), 41–68.

p. 157, Ordo XIV, MS *C*, last line: *for* 161–62 *read* 177–78
n. 7, first line: *for* (p. 162, n. 16) *read* (p. 178, n. 16)
MS *D*: *add footnote at end*: Bibl. Apos. Vat., MS Barb. lat. 631 has been identified as possibly the personal pontifical of abbot Desiderius of Monte Cassino (Pope Victor III); see Richard L. Gyug, "The Pontificals of Monte Cassino," in *L'età dell'Abate Desiderio*, Vol. 3:1: *Storia, arte et cultura: Atti del iv Convegno di studi sul medioevo meridionale, Montecassino e Cassino 4–8 ottobre 1987*, Miscellanea cassinese 67 (Montecassino: Pubblicazioni cassinese, 1992), 413–39.

p. 166, var. 13e: *delete* ", *where the words* Officio ... benedictam *are part of the rubric* (*these words are omitted in Ordo XXIII,99*)"

p. 174, Ordo XV, MS O, line 4: *for* générale *read* général
MS Q, lines 3–4: *for* uniwersyteckie *read* uniwersyteckiej

pp. 190–91, no. 35: *add note at end*: "det tibi de rore celi ... benedictionibus repleatur" is mostly quoted from Gen. 27: 28–29 and "Omnipotens benedicat ... benedictionibus uberum" mostly from Gen. 49: 25.

p. 215, no. 55, line 2: *for* Sancti spiritus *read* Sancti Spiritus

p. 222, Ordo XVII A, MS G, line 2: *for* générale *read* général

p. 223, Ordo XVII A, MS I, line 2: *for* générale *read* général

p. 234, Ordo XVII B, MS F, line 4: *for* générale *read* général

p. 235, edd. a_1 and a_2: *for* recherches *read* recerches
n. 2, line 3 from end: *for* Lyons *read* Leiden
add to note 2 at end: "Lotarius Philoponus," 102–103 (see Ordo XXII A, n. 25) printed a translation back into Latin of Du Tillet's French translation.

p. 239, line 2: *for* nostre dame *read* Nostre Dame

p. 251, no. 7: Gloria patri *should be on a separate line*

p. 255, no. 16, line 8: *add footnote at* subdita sit,': Rom. 13: 1

p. 259, line 3: *for* ẹcclesiam *read* Ẹcclesiam

p. 262, no. 38, line 3 from end: *delete the comma after* vassis

p. 271, line 4 from bottom: *for* Receuils *read* Recueils

p. 272, line 1: *for* générale *read* général

p. 274, s.v. Du Tillet, line 3: *for* Receuil *read* Recueil

p. 275, s.v. Elze, "Ordines für die Königskrönung in Mailand": *add* vol. 1, *before* edited, *and for* 1992 *read* 1994

p. 276, s.v. Guillot: *delete the space after* Olivier

p. 280, s.v. Paris, Bibliothèque de l'Arsenal, line 2: *for* générale *read* général

p. 281, s.v. *Respublica*: *for* Lyons *read* Leiden

p. 282, s.v. Schreuer, "Über altfranzösische Kröungsordungen": *for* Kröungsordnungen *read* Krönungsordnungen

I neglected to list four texts in the Collection Godefroy of the Institut de France. They are all in volumes from which the printed edition of Godefroy, *Le cérémonial françois*, was published in 1649. None is of any real significance, and I list them here simply for the sake of completeness.

Paris, Bibl. de l'Institut de France, MS Godefroy 380, pp. 27–42: Ordo VII (Ordo of Charles the Bald), nos. 2, 4–7, 9, 11–15, 17–43. Mid-seventeenth century. Copied from edd. b_1 and *d*.

Paris, Bibl. de l'Institut de France, MS Godefroy 380, pp. 47–54: Ordo VII (Ordo of Charles the Bald), nos. 10–29. Mid-seventeenth century. Copied from ed. l_1.

Paris, Bibl. de l'Institut de France, MS Godefroy 382, pp. 51–55: Ordo XVII A (Philip I). Mid-seventeenth century. Copied from ed. *e*.

Paris, Bibl. de l'Institut de France, MS Godefroy 382, pp. 57–61: Ordo XVII A (Philip I). Mid-seventeenth century. Copied from ed. *b*.

Works Cited

This list is a bibliography of all printed works cited in Volumes I and II, as well as an index to citations of those works. Catalogs of manuscripts are alphabetized by city and institution.

Agustín, Antonio. [*Aeterne memoriae viri Ant. Augustini Archiepiscopi Tarraconen bibliothecae Graeca MS. Latina MS. mixta ex libris editis varior. linguarum.*] Tarragona: P. Mey, 1586 [i.e., 1587]. (Ordo VII, n. 14)

Amiet, Robert, ed. *The Benedictionals of Freising (Munich, Bayerische Staatsbibliothek, Cod. lat. 6430)*. Alternate title: *Bénédictionnaires de Freising*. Henry Bradshaw Society, vol. 88. Maidstone: British Legion Press, 1974. (Ordo IV, MS *A*, ed. *c*)

———, ed. *Pontificale Augustanum: Le pontifical du XIe siècle de la Bibliothèque capitulaire d'Aoste (Cod. 15)*. Monumenta liturgica ecclesiae Augustanae, vol. 3. Aosta: Typo-offset Musumeci, 1975. (Ordo VI, n. 23)

Andrieu, Michel. *Les Ordines Romani du haut moyen âge*. Vol. 1: *Les manuscrits*. Etudes et documents, fasc. 11. Louvain: Spicilegium Sacrum Lovaniense, 1931. Vols 2–4: *Les textes*. Etudes et documents, fasc. 23–24, 28. Louvain: Spicilegium Sacrum Lovaniense, 1948, 1949, 1956. (I: 38, n. 74; Ordo III, MS *A*; Ordo XVI, n. 2, MSS *A*, *B*)

———, ed. *Le pontifical romain au moyen-âge*. 4 vols. Studi e Testi, vols. 86–88, 99. Vatican City: Biblioteca Apostolica Vaticana, 1938–41. (I: 41, n. 77; Ordo XIV, MS *D*)

Annales Bertiniani. In Muratori, *Scriptores rerum Italicarum*, 2,1: 491–576. (Ordo VII, ed. *k*)

Annales Bertiniani. In Bouquet, *Recueil des historiens*. Nouv. éd. Vol. 6 (1870): 192–204. Vol. 7 (1870): 57–124. Vol. 8 (1871): 26–37. (Ordo VII, ed. *l*; Ordo VIII, ed. *e*)

Annales Bertiniani. Edited by Georg Heinrich Pertz. MGH Scriptores in folio, vol. 1. Hanover: Hahn, 1826. Reprinted in PL, 125. (Ordo VII, ed. *m*; Ordo VIII, ed. *f*)

Annales Bertiniani. Edited by Georg Waitz. MGH Scriptores separatim editi. Hanover: Hahn, 1883. (Ordo VII, ed. *o*; VIII ed. *h*)

Annales Bertiniani. Edited by Reinhold Rau. In *Quellen zur karolingischen Reichsgeschichte*, vol. 2. Darmstadt: Wissenschaftliche Buchgesellschaft, 1958. (Ordo VII, ed. *p*; Ordo VIII, ed. *j*)

Annales de Saint-Bertin. Edited by Félix Grat et al. Paris: Société de l'histoire de France, 1964. (I: 25, n. 47; Ordo V, n. 1; Ordo VI, n. 1;

Ordo VII, n. 1, lost MSS *6*, *7*, MSS *D*, *E*, *F*, *G*, ed. *q*; Ordo VIII, nn. 1, 7, lost MS *1*, ed. *k*; Ordo IX, n. 2)

Les annales de Saint-Bertin et de Saint-Vaast. Edited by Crétien Dehaisnes. Paris: Société de l'histoire de France, 1871. (Ordo VII, ed. *n*; Ordo VIII, ed. *g*)

The Annals of Fulda. Translated by Timothy Reuter. Ninth-Century Histories, vol. 2. Manchester: Manchester University Press, 1992. (I: 18, n. 26)

The Annals of St-Bertin. Translated and annotated by Janet L. Nelson. Ninth-Century Histories, vol. 1. Manchester: Manchester University Press, 1991. (I: 25, n. 47; Ordo VII, n. 16)

Annales Vedastini. Edited by Georg Heinrich Pertz. MGH Scriptores in folio, vol. 1. Hanover: Hahn, 1826. (Ordo X, n. 1)

Anselme de Sainte-Marie (or Anselme de la Vierge Marie [Pierre Guibours]). *Histoire généalogique et chronologique de la maison royale de France.* 3d ed. 9 vols. Paris: La Compagnie des Libraires, 1726–33. (Ordo XXV, nn. 8, 22, 27)

Auvray, Lucien, and René Poupardin. *Catalogue des manuscrits de la collection Baluze.* See Paris, Bibliothèque nationale de France.

Avignon, Museum Calvet. Labande, L. H. *Manuscrits de la Bibliothèque d'Avignon.* 3 vols. Catalogue général des manuscrits des bibliothèques publiques de France: Départements, vols. 27–29. Paris: E. Plon, Nourrit et Cie., 1894–1901. (I: 9, n. 13)

Baix, F. "Les sources liturgiques de la Vita Remigii d'Hincmar." In *Miscellanea Historica in honorem Alberti de Meyer*, 1: 211–27. 2 vols. Louvain: Bibliothèque de l'Université; Brussels: «Le Pennon», 1946. (Ordo VII, n. 42)

Baluze, Etienne, ed. *Beati Servati Lupi presbyteri et abbatis Ferrariensis, ordinis S. Benedicti, Opera.* Paris: F. Muguet, 1664. 2d ed. Antwerp: L. F. Gleditsch et filius, 1710. (Ordo X, ed. *a*; Ordo XI, ed. *d*)

——, ed. *Capitularia regum Francorum.* 2 vols. Paris: Franciscus Muguet, 1677. (Ordo V, ed. *e*; Ordo VI, ed. *e*; Ordo VII, ed. *g*; Ordo VIII, n. 5, lost MS *3*, edd. *c*, *p*; Ordo X, ed. *c*; Ordo XI, ed. *f*)

2d ed. 2 vols. Venice: A. Zatta, 1772–73. (Ordo V, ed. *e*; Ordo VI, ed. *e*; Ordo VII, ed. *g*; Ordo VIII, n. 5, edd. *c*, *p*; Ordo X, ed. *c*; Ordo XI, ed. *f*)

3d ed. Edited by Pierre de Chiniac. 2 vols. Paris: Benedictus Morin, 1780. Anastatic reprint of 3d ed. In Mansi, 17 bis and 18 bis. Paris: Hubertus Welter, 1902. (I: 40, n. 76; Ordo V, ed. *e*; Ordo VI, ed. *e*; Ordo VII, n. 7, lost MS *2*, ed. *g*; Ordo VIII, n. 5, edd. *c*, *p*; Ordo X, ed. *c*; Ordo XI, ed. *f*)

Bamberg, Königliche Bibliothek. Leitschuh, Friedrich. *Katalog der Handschriften der Königlichen Bibliothek zu Bamberg*. Vol. 1, pt. 1: *Liturgische Handschriften*. Bamberg: C. C. Buchner, 1898. (Ordo XVI, MS *B*)

Barbiche, Bernard. "Conseils pour l'édition des documents français de l'époque moderne." *Gazette des Beaux-Arts* (July 1980): 25–28. (I: 41, n. 77; I: 47, n. 83)

Baronius, Caesar. *Annales Ecclesiastici*. 12 vols. Antwerp: Ex officina Plantiniana, 1611–77. 13 vols. Venice: Stephanus Monti, 1738–42. 19 vols. Lucca: Leonardo Venturini, 1738–46. (Ordo VII, ed. *a*)

Bautier, Robert-Henri. "Sacres et couronnements sous les Carolingiens et les premiers Capétiens: Recherches sur la genèse du sacre royal français." *Annuaire-Bulletin de la Société de l'histoire de France, Année 1987* (1989): 7–56. (I: 22, n. 38; I: 23, n. 42; I: 24, n. 45; I: 25, n. 48; I: 37, n. 72; Ordo V, n. 6; Ordo VII, n. 1; Ordo IX, n. 2; Ordo XIII, n. 2)

——, ed. *Recueil des actes d'Eudes, roi de France (888–898)*. Chartes et diplômes relatifs à l'histoire de France. Paris: Imprimerie nationale, Librairie C. Klincksieck, 1967. (Ordo XI, nn. 3, 10, ed. *l*)

Bethmann, Ludwig. "Nachrichten über die von ihm für die *Monumenta Germaniae historica* benutzten Sammlungen von Handschriften und Urkunden Italiens, aus dem Jahre 1854." *Archiv der Gesellschaft für ältere deutsche Geschichtskunde* 12 (1874): 201–426, 474–758. (Ordo VII, n. 10, MS *C*; Ordo XVII A, MS *A*)

Bevy, Charles Joseph de. *Histoire des inaugurations des rois, empereurs, et autres souverains de l'univers, depuis leur origine jusqu'à présent*. Paris: Moutard, 1776. (Ordo XVII B, n. 2; Ordo XXII B-C, n. 7)

Biblia Vulgata iuxta Vulgatam Clementinam. 4th ed. Biblioteca de Autores Cristianos, vol. 14. Madrid: Biblioteca de Autores Cristianos, 1959. (I: 45, n. 81)

Binius, Severinus, ed. *Concilia generalia et provincialia*. 4 vols. in 5. Cologne: I. Gymnicus et A. Hierat, 1606. 4 vols. in 9. Cologne: Ioannes Gymnicus, 1618. 9 vols. Paris: C. Morelli, 1636. (Ordo XVII A, n. 11)

Bodin, Jean. *De republica libri sex*. Paris: Hattmannus Palthenius, 1586. (Ordo XVII A, ed. *a*)

——. *Les six livres de la République*. Paris: Jacques du Puys, 1576. Paris: Jacques du Puys, 1577. Geneva: pirated edition — no publisher, 1577. Paris: Jacques du Puys, 1578. Geneva, 1579. Paris: Jacques du Puys, 1580. Paris: Jacques du Puys, 1583. (Ordo XVII A, ed. *a*)

Bonne, Jean-Claude. "The Manuscript of the Ordo of 1250 and its Illuminations." In *Coronations: Medieval and Early Modern Monarchic Ritual*, 58–71. (I: 37, n. 67; Ordo XXI, nn. 4, 10, 54, MS *A*)

Bouchel, Laurent, ed. *Decretorum ecclesiae Gallicanae ... libri VIII.* Paris: Barthelemy Macé, 1609. (I: 20, n. 30; Ordo XXIII, ed. *c*)

Bouman, Cornelius A. *Sacring and Crowning: The Development of the Latin Ritual for the Anointing of Kings and the Coronation of an Emperor before the Eleventh Century.* Bijdragen van het Instituut voor Middeleeuwse Geschiedenis der Rijks-Universiteit te Utrecht, vol. 30. Groningen: J. B. Wolters, 1957. (I: 6, n. 10; I: 13, n. 22; I: 23, n. 43; I: 37, n. 71; Ordo I, n. 2, ed. *a*; Ordo II, ed. *c*; Ordo III, ed. *b*; Ordo IV, nn. 1, 2, ed. *d*; Ordo VII, n. 4; Ordo IX, n. 5, ed. *e*; Ordo XII, n. 1, ed. *a*; Ordo XIII, n. 2; Ordo XIV, ed. *b*; Ordo XVI, nn. 3, 5; Ordo XVII A, n. 4)

Bouquet, Dom Martin et al., eds. See *Recueil des historiens des Gaules et de la France.*

Branner, Robert. *Manuscript Painting in Paris during the Reign of Saint Louis: A Study of Styles.* Berkeley and Los Angeles: University of California Press, 1977. (Ordo XIX, MS *B*; Ordo XXI, MS *A*)

B[rial, Michel-Jean-Jacques]. "Auteur du formulaire pour le sacre de Philippe-Auguste." *Histoire littéraire de la France* 14 (1817): 22–26. (Ordo XXII B-C, n. 1)

Brown, Elizabeth A. R. *"Franks, Burgundians, and Aquitanians" and the Royal Coronation Ceremony in France.* Transactions of the American Philosophical Society, vol. 82, pt. 7. Philadelphia: American Philosophical Society, 1992. (Ordo XV, nn. 20, 41, MS *C*, ed. *g*; Ordo XVII A, n. 6; Ordo XVII B, nn. 1, 2; Ordo XX A, n. 7; Ordo XX B-C, n. 13; Ordo XXII A, nn. 1, 10, 25; Ordo XXII B-C, nn. 3–5, 8–10, 21, 23, 25, 27, MS *A*, ed. *c*)

———. *Jean du Tillet and His* Recueils *for the Kings of France.* Forthcoming. (Ordo XVII A, n. 6; Ordo XXII B-C, n. 6)

Brown, Elizabeth A. R., and Myra Orth. "Jean du Tillet et les illustrations du grand *Recueil des Roys.*" *Revue de l'Art* 115 (1997): 8–24. (Ordo XXII B-C, n. 6)

Brown, Michelle P. *A Guide to Western Historical Scripts from Antiquity to 1600.* Toronto and Buffalo: University of Toronto Press, 1990. (Ordo XXII A, n. 31)

Brugge, Stedelijke Openbare Bibliotheek. Poorter, A. de. *Catalogue des manuscrits de la Bibliothèque publique de la ville de Bruges.* Catalogue général des manuscrits des bibliothèques de Belgique. Gembloux: J. Duculot; Paris: Société d'éditions Les Belles lettres, 1934. (Ordo XV, MS *O*)

Brussels, Bibliothèque royale Albert Iᵉʳ. Gheyn, J. van den. *Catalogue des manuscrits de la Bibliothèque royale de Belgique.* Vol. 1: *Ecriture sainte et liturgie.* Brussels: H. Lamertin, 1901. (Ordo XIV, MS *E*; Ordo XV, MS *N*)

Buchner, Maximilian. "Nochmals die Krönungsordnung Ludwigs VII. von Frankreich: Eine Erwiderung." *Zeitschrift der Savigny-Stiftung für Rechtsgeschichte, germ. Abteilung* 33 (1912): 328–89. (I: 4, n. 7)

——. "Zur Datierung und Charakteristik altfranzösischer Krönungsordnungen mit besonderer Berücksichtigung des 'angeblichen' ordo Ludwigs VII." *Zeitschrift der Savigny-Stiftung für Rechtsgeschichte, germ. Abteilung* 31 (1910): 360–423. (I: 4, n. 7; Ordo XXII B-C, n. 12)

Bzowski (= Bzovius), Abraham. Continuation of Caesar Baronius, *Annales ecclesiastici* 14. Cologne: Apud Antonii Boëtzeri haeredes, 1625. (Ordo XXII A, n. 25)

Cabrol, Fernand, and Henri Leclercq. *Dictionnaire d'archéologie chrétienne et de liturgie*. 15 vols. in 30. Paris: Letouzey et Ané, 1924–53. Cited as DACL. (I: 11, n. 19; Ordo I, MS *B*; Ordo IX, MS *A*, ed. *d*; Ordo XI, MS *A*; Ordo XIII, MS *B*)

Cagin, Dom Paul. "Note sur le sacramentaire de Gellone." In *Mélanges de littérature et d'histoire religieuses publiés à l'occasion du jubilé épiscopal de Mgr de Cabrières, évêque de Montpellier, 1874–1899*. 2 vols., 1: 231–90. Paris: A. Picard, 1899. (Ordo I, MS *A*)

——, ed. *Le sacramentaire gélasien d'Angoulême*. Angoulême: Société historique et archéologique de la Charente, [1920]. (Ordo II, ed. *b*)

Cambridge, Fitzwilliam Museum. James, Montague Rhodes. *A Descriptive Catalogue of Manuscripts in the Fitzwilliam Museum*. Cambridge: Cambridge University Press, 1895. (Ordo IV, n. 3)

Capitularia regum Francorum. Edited by Alfred Boretius, Victor Krause, et al. Monumenta Germaniae Historica: Legum sectio 2, pts. 1–2. 2 vols. Hanover: Hahn, 1883–97. See also Baluze, Etienne, *Capitularia*, and Sirmond, Jacques, *Karoli Calvi*. (Ordo V, ed. *h*; Ordo VI, nn. 6, 16, ed. *h*; Ordo VII, nn. 12, 35, ed. *j*; Ordo VIII, nn. 5–6, 10, 12, edd. *i, s*; Ordo X, ed. *g*; Ordo XI, ed. *j*)

Carey, Frederick M. "The Scriptorium of Reims during the Archbishopric of Hincmar (845–882 A.D.)." In *Classical and Mediaeval Studies in Honor of Edward Kennard Rand*, edited by Leslie Webber Jones, 41–60. New York: Published by the Editor, 1938. (Ordo VII, n. 49)

Catalogus codicum manuscriptorum bibliothecae regiae. See Paris, Bibliothèque nationale de France.

Chantilly, Musée Condé. Henri, duc d'Aumale; Léopold Delisle; and Gustave Macon. *Chantilly: Le Cabinet des livres: Manuscrits*. 3 vols. Paris: Plon, Nourrit et Cie., 1900–11. (Ordo XV, MS *S*; Ordo XX A, MS *I*)

Chartier, M. "Cambrai (Diocèse)." In *Dictionnaire d'histoire et de géographie ecclésiastiques*, 11: 549–51. (Ordo XVI, n. 7)

Chevalier, Cyr Ulysse. *Sacramentaire et martyrologe de l'abbaye de*

Saint-Remy. Bibliothèque liturgique 7. Paris: Alphonse Picard, 1900. (Ordo XX A, MSS *A, B, C,* ed. *a*)

Chifflet, Pierre François. *Histoire de l'abbaye royale et de la ville de Tournus.* Dijon: P. Chavance, 1664. (Ordo XVII A, ed. *g*)

Codaghengo, A. "Un pontificale ad uso della chiesa milanese nel sec. XI." *Memorie storiche d. diocesi di Milano* 6 (1954): 240–51. (Ordo XIV, n. 7)

Comité International des Sciences Historiques: Commission Internationale de Diplomatique. "Colloque technique sur la normalisation internationale des methodes de publication des documents latins du moyen âge." Barcelona, 2–5 October 1974. Pp. 45. Typescript. (I: 41, n. 77; I: 47, n. 83)

Conciliorum omnium generalium et provincialium collectio regia. 37 vols. Paris: e Typographia regia, 1644. (Ordo XVII A, n. 11)

Consecratio et coronatio regis Francie. Paris: Guillaume Eustache, 1510 [o.s.]. (Ordo XXIII, ed. *a*)

Coronations: Medieval and Early Modern Monarchic Ritual. Edited by János M. Bak. Berkeley and Los Angeles: University of California Press, 1990. (I: 35, n. 63; I: 37, n. 67; Ordo VII, n. 1)

Couderc, C. "Note sur le manuscrit latin 12814 de la Bibliothèque nationale." *Bibl. de l'Ecole des Chartes* 49 (1888): 645–53. (Ordo XX B-C, n. 24)

Crosnier, Augustin-Joseph, et al., eds. *Sacramentarium ad usum aecclesiae Nivernensis.* Publications de la Société nivernaise, 8. Nevers: Paulin Fay, 1873. (Ordo XIII, ed. *b*)

David, Marcel. "Le serment du sacre du IXe au XVe siècle: Contribution à l'étude des limites juridiques de la souveraineté." *Revue du moyen âge latin* 6 (1950): 5–272. Reprinted as separate book. Strasbourg: Palais de l'Université, 1951. (Ordo XVI, n. 5)

Delachenal, Roland. *Histoire de Charles V.* 5 vols. Paris: A. Picard et fils, 1909–31. (Ordo XXIII, n. 27)

Delalande, Pierre, ed. *Conciliorum antiquorum galliae a Iac. Sirmondo S. I. editorum supplementa.* Paris: Societas Typographica Librorum Officii Ecclesiastici, 1666. (Ordo VIII, ed. *b*; Ordo X, ed. *b*; Ordo XI, ed. *e*; Ordo XIII, n. 1, ed. *a*; Ordo XVII A, ed. *h*)

Delisle, Léopold. *Le cabinet des manuscrits de la Bibliothèque impériale.* Histoire générale de Paris 10. 3 vols. Paris: Imprimerie impériale/nationale, 1868–81. (Ordo XX B-C, n. 10)

———. *Catalogue des manuscrits des fonds Libri et Barrois.* See Paris, Bibliothèque nationale de France.

———. "Mémoire sur d'anciens sacramentaires." *Mémoires de l'Institut National de France: Académie des Inscriptions et Belles-Lettres* 32

(1886): 57–423. (Ordo I, MS *A*; Ordo II, MS *C*, edd. *a*, *b*; Ordo IX, n. 3, MS *A*, ed. *b*; Ordo XI, MS *A*; Ordo XIII, MS *B*; Ordo XV, MS *A*)

———. "Notice sur les manuscrits du 'Liber floridus', composé en 1120 par Lambert, chanoine de Saint-Omer." Paris: C. Klincksieck, 1906; reprinted from *Notices et extraits des manuscrits de la Bibliothèque nationale* 38 (1906): 577–791. (Ordo XX A, MSS *D*, *E*, *F*, *G*; Ordo XX B-C, MS *Q*)

———. *Recherches sur la librairie de Charles V.* 2 vols. Paris: H. Champion, 1907. (Ordo XX B, lost MSS *6*, *7*, *8*)

Depreux, Philippe. "*Imbuendis ad fidem prefulgidum surrexit lumen gentibus*: La dévotion à saint Remi de Reims aux IXe et Xe siècles." *Cahiers de civilization médiévale* 35 (1992): 111–29. (Ordo V, n. 1)

Dereine, Charles. "Chantoine." In *Dictionnaire d'histoire et de géographie ecclésiastiques*, 12: 406. (Ordo XVII A, n. 8)

Derolez, Albert, ed. *Liber Floridus Colloquium: Papers Read at the International Meeting Held in the University Library, Ghent on 3–5 December 1967*. Ghent: E. Story-Scientia 1973. (Ordo XX A, n. 9)

Deshusses, Dom Jean. *Liber sacramentorum Gellonensis: Introductio, tabulae et indices*. Corpus Christianorum Series Latina, vol. 159 A. Turnhout: Brepols, 1981. (Ordo I, MS *B*, ed. *b*; Ordo II, n. 1)

Desportes, Pierre, et al. *Diocèse de Reims*. Fasti ecclesiae Gallicanae, 1200–1500, vol. 3. Turnhout: Brepols, 1998. (Ordo XXV, n. 27)

Devisse, Jean. *Hincmar, archevêque de Reims, 845–882*. Travaux d'histoire ethico-politique, 29. 3 vols. Geneva: Librairie E. Droz, 1975–76. (Ordo VII, n. 42)

Dewick, E. S., ed. *The Coronation Book of Charles V of France (1338–1380)*. Henry Bradshaw Society, vol. 16. London: Harrison and Sons, 1899. (Ordo XV, n. 4; Ordo XIX, n. 2; Ordo XX B-C, ed. *f*; Ordo XXI, n. 5; Ordo XXIII, MS *A*, ed. *g*, nn. 37, 40, 47, 57, 91, 97, 107, 153, 161)

Dictionnaire d'histoire et de géographie ecclésiastiques. Edited by Alfred Baudrillart et al. 23 vols. completed to date. Paris: Lelouzey et Ané, 1912–. (Ordo XVI, n. 7; Ordo XVII A, nn. 2, 8)

Dorez, Léon. *Catalogue de la collection Dupuy*. See Paris, Bibliothèque nationale de France.

Du Cange, Charles du Fresne, sieur. *Glossarium mediae et infimae latinatitis*. Edited by Léopold Favre. 10 vols. Niort: L. Favre, 1883–87. (Ordo VII, n. 19)

Duchesne, André, and François Duchesne, eds. *Historiae Francorum scriptores*. 5 vols. Paris: Sebastien Cramoisy; Gabriel Cramoisy, 1636–49. (Ordo V, ed. *b*; Ordo VI, ed. *b*; Ordo VII, edd. *d*, *k*; Ordo VIII, edd. *a*, *m*; Ordo XVII A, ed. *e*)

Duchhardt, Heinz, Richard A. Jackson, and David Sturdy, eds. *European Monarchy: Its Evolution and Practice from Roman Antiquity to Modern Times*. Stuttgart: Franz Steiner Verlag, 1992. (I: 37, n. 70)

Dumas, Dom Antoine, ed. *Liber sacramentorum Gellonensis*. Corpus Christianorum Series Latina, vol. 159. Turnhout: Brepols, 1981. (I: 46, n. 82; Ordo I, ed. *b*; Ordo II, ed. *e*; Ordo IX, n. 7)

Dümmler, Ernst. *Geschichte des Ostfränkischen Reiches*. 2d ed. 3 vols. Berlin: Verlag von Duncker und Humblot, 1887–88. (Ordo VI, nn. 3, 8, 9; Ordo VII, nn. 1, 37; Ordo VIII, nn. 3, 6; Ordo X, n. 1)

Dupuy, Pierre [often attributed to Pierre Pithou]. *Preuves des libertez de l'église gallicane*. [Paris: Pierre Chevalier], 1639. 2d ed. Paris: Sebastien Cramoisy et Gabriel Cramoisy, 1651. 3d ed. 2 vols. Paris: Sebastien Cramoisy et Gabriel Cramoisy, 1731. (Ordo XVII A, ed. *d*)

———. *Traité de la majorité de nos rois et des régences du royaume*. Paris: Chez la Veuve Mathurin du Puis et Edme Martin, 1655. (Ordo XXIV, n. 21)

Dürig, Walter. "Das Benedictionale Frisingense Vetus (Clm 6430 fol. 1–14)." *Archiv für Liturgiewissenschaft* 4 (1955): 223–44. (Ordo IV, n. 4)

Du Tillet, Jean. *Les mémoires et recerches*. Rouen: Philippe de Tours, 1578. (Ordo XVII B, ed. a_1; Ordo XXII B-C, ed. a_1)

———. *Les mémoires et recerches*. Troyes: Philippe des Chams, 1578. (Ordo XVII B, ed. a_2; Ordo XXII B-C, ed. a_2)

———. *Recueil des honneurs et rangs des grands*. Bound with Du Tillet, *Recueil des roys de France* (Paris: Jacques du Puys, 1580), and continuously paginated. Retitled *Recueil des rangs des grands de France* and, separately paginated, dated [N.p.] 1606, and bound with Du Tillet, *Recueil des roys de France* (Paris: Pierre Metayer, 1618). (Ordo XVII B, ed. *a*)

———. *Recueil des roys de France, leurs couronne et maison*. Paris: Jacques du Puys, 1580. Reprints. Paris: Jacques du Puys, 1586, 1587, and 1588. Paris: Houzé; Jamet and Pierre Metayer; Barthelemy Macé, 1602. Paris: Abel l'Angelier; Barthelemy Macé; Pierre Metayer, 1607. Reprint. Paris: Pierre Metayer, 1618. (Ordo XVII A, n. 26; Ordo XXII B-C, II: 420, MSS *B*, *C*, *D*, edd. a_3, a_4, a_5, nn. 25, 27)

———. *Joan. Tilii actuarii in suprema Curia Parisiensi celeberrimi Commentariorum et disquisitionum de rebus Gallicis libri duo, nunc primùm Latinè redditi*. Frankfurt am Main: Apud Andream Wechelum, 1579. (Ordo XXII A, n. 25)

Dykmans, Marc. *Le cérémonial papal de la fin du moyen âge à la Renaissance*. Bibliothèque de l'Institut historique Belge de Rome, vol. 24. Brussels and Rome: Institut historique belge de Rome, 1977. (Ordo XXII A, MS *E*)

Eichmann, Eduard. "Die sogenannte Römische Königskrönungsformel." *Historisches Jahrbuch* 45 (1925): 516–55. (Ordo IV, n. 1, ed. *b*; Ordo XIV, n. 2)

Elze, Reinhard. "Le consacrazioni regie." In *Segni e riti nella Chiesa altomedievale occidentale: Spoleto, 11–17 aprile 1985*, Settimane di studio del Centro italiano di studi sull'alto medioevo, vol. 33 (Spoleto, 1987): 43–61. (I: 33, n. 60)

——. "Ein karolingischer Ordo für die Krönung eines Herrscherpaares." In *Bullettino dell' Istituto Storico Italiano per il Medio Evo e Archivio Muratoriano* 98 (Rome, 1992): 417–23. (Ordo VI, n. 4)

——. "Königskrönung und Ritterweihe: Der burgundische Ordo für die Weihe und Krönung des Königs und der Königin." In *Institutionen, Kultur und Gesellschaft im Mittelalter: Festschrift für Josef Fleckenstein*, edited by Lutz Fenske, Werner Rösener, and Thomas Zotz, 327–42. Sigmaringen: Jan Thorbecke, 1984. (Ordo XIV, n. 3)

——. "Ein Krönungsordo aus Portugal." In *Memoriam Sanctorum Venerantes: Miscellanea in onore di Mons. Victor Saxer*. Studi di Antichità Cristiana, vol. 48, 323–34. Vatican City: Pontificio Istituto di Archeologia Cristiana, 1992. (I: 21, n. 35; I: 28, n. 54; Ordo XIV, ed. *e*)

——. "Ordines für die Königskrönung in Mailand." In *Cristianità ed Europa: Miscellanea di studi in onore di Luigi Prosdocimi*, vol. 1, edited by Cesare Alzati, 175–89. Rome, Freiburg and Vienna: Herder, 1994. (Ordo XIV, MS *C*)

——. "Ein vergessener Ordo für die Trauung und Krönung eines karolingischen Herrscherpaares." In *Ex ipsis rerum documentis: Festschrift für Harald Zimmermann zu seinem 65. Geburtstag*, edited by Klaus Herbers, Hans H. Kortüm, and Carlo Servatius, 69–72. Sigmaringen: Jan Thorbecke, 1991. (Ordo VI, n. 4)

——, ed. *Ordines coronationis imperialis: Die Ordines für die Weihe und Krönung des Kaisers und der Kaiserin*. MGH Fontes iuris Germanici antiqui, vol. 9. Hanover: Hahnsche Buchhandlung, 1960. (I: 2, n. 3; I: 7, n. 12; I: 28, n. 53; I: 34, n. 61; I: 35, n. 63; I: 36, n. 65; I: 38, n. 74; Ordo VII, n. 2; Ordo IX, n. 2; Ordo XIV, n. 7; Ordo XV, n. 3; Ordo XVI, nn. 4, 18, 19; Ordo XVII A, n. 4; Ordo XIX, n. 11)

Enright, Michael J. *Iona, Tara and Soissons: The Origin of the Royal Anointing Ritual*. Arbeiten zur Frühmittelalterforschung: Schriftenreihe des Instituts für Frühmittelalterforschung der Universität Münster, vol. 17. Berlin and New York: Walter de Gruyter, 1985. (I: 22, nn. 37, 39)

Erdmann, Carl. *Forschungen zur politischen Ideenwelt des Frühmittelalters*. Edited by Friedrich Baethgen. Berlin: Akademie-Verlag, 1951. (I: 6, n. 9; I: 21, n. 34; Ordo XIV, ed. *a*)

——. "Der Heidenkrieg in der Liturgie." *Mitteilungen des Instituts für österreichische Geschichtsforschung* 46 (1932): 129–42. (Ordo XIII, n. 3)

Eustache, Guillaume. See *Consecratio et coronatio regis Francie*.

Ewald, Paul. "Reise nach Italien im Winter von 1876 auf 1877." *Neues Archiv der Gesellschaft für ältere deutsche Geschichtskunde* 3 (1878): 139–81. (Ordo VII, MS *C*)

Fleckenstein, Josef. "Rex Canonicus: Über Entstehung und Bedeutung des mittelalterlichen Königskanonikates." In *Ordnungen und formende Kräfte des Mittelalters: Ausgewählte Beiträge*, 193–210. Göttingen: Vandenhoeck und Ruprecht, 1989. (I: 1, n. 1)

Fliche, Augustin. *Le règne de Philippe Ier, roi de France (1060–1108)*. Paris: Société française d'imprimerie et de librairie, 1912. (Ordo XVII B, n. 2)

Fransen, Gerard, and Stephan Kuttner, eds. *Summa 'Elegantius in iure diuino' seu Coloniensis*, vol. 1. Monumenta Iuris Canonici: Series A: Corpus Glossatorum, vol. 1. New York: Fordham University Press, 1969. (I: 41, n. 77)

Gallia christiana in provincias ecclesiasticas distributa. 16 vols. Paris: ex Typographia regia, 1739–1877. (Ordo XVII A, ed. *m*)

Gatticus, Joannes Baptista, ed. *Acta selecta caeremonialia sanctae Romanae ecclesiae*. 2 vols. in 1. Rome: Haeredes J. L. Barbiellini, 1753. (I: 20, n. 29; Ordo XXII A, ed. *b*)

Genoa, Biblioteca Durazzo-Giustiniani. Puncuh, Dino. *I manoscritti della raccolta Durazzo*. Genoa: Sagep, 1979. (Ordo XX A, MS *G*)

Gheyn, J. van den. See Brussels, Bibliothèque royale Albert Ier.

Godefroy, Frédéric. *Dictionnaire de l'ancienne langue française et de tous ses dialectes du IXe au XVe siècle*. 10 vols. Paris: Vieweg (1–4), and Bouillon (5–10), 1880–1902; reprints Vadus, Liechtenstein: Scientific Periodicals Establishment, and New York: Kraus Reprint Corporation, 1962; and Geneva and Paris: Slatkine, 1982. (Ordo XX B-C, nn. 61, 64, 66; Ordo XXIV, n. 22)

Godefroy, Théodore, ed. *Le cérémonial de France*. Paris: Abraham Pacard, 1619. (Ordo XXV, n. 5)

Godefroy, Théodore, and Denis Godefroy, eds. *Le cérémonial françois*. 2 vols. Paris: Sebastien Cramoisy et Gabriel Cramoisy, 1649. (I: 32, n. 59; Ordo V, ed. *d*; Ordo VI, ed. *d*; Ordo VII, ed. *f*; Ordo VIII, ed. *o*; Ordo XV, n. 4; Ordo XVII A, ed. *f*; Ordo XVII B, ed. *b*; Ordo XX A, n. 7; Ordo

XX B-C, ed. *a*, n. 56; Ordo XXI, ed. *a*; Ordo XXII B-C, ed. *b*; Ordo XXIII, ed. *e*; Ordo XXIV, n. 2; Ordo XXV, ed. *a*)

Goethe, Johann Wolfgang von. "Sprichwörtlich." In *Sämtliche Werke nach Epochen seines Schaffens: Münchner Ausgabe*, edited by Karl Richter et al. Vol. 9, *Epoche der Wahlverwandschaften: 1807-1814*, edited by Christoph Siegrist et al., 121-47. Munich: Carl Hanser Verlag, 1987. (I: 38)

Grevisse, Maurice. *Le bon usage*. 11th ed. Paris: Duculot, 1980. (II: 287, n. 2)

Guillot, Olivier. "Les étapes de l'accession d'Eudes au pouvoir royal." In *Media in Francia ...: Recueil de mélanges offert à Karl Ferdinand Werner*, 199-223. Maulévrier: Hérault-Editions, 1989. (Ordo XI, nn. 1, 3)

Guizot, François, ed. *Collection des mémoires relatifs à l'histoire de France*. 31 vols. Paris: J.-L.-J. Brière, 1823-35. (Ordo XVII B, ed. *c*)

Gumbert, J. P. "Recherches sur le stemma des copies du Liber Floridus." In *Liber Floridus Colloquium: Papers Read at the International Meeting Held in the University Library, Ghent on 3-5 December 1967*, ed. Albert Derolez, 37-50. Ghent: E. Story-Scientia, 1973. (Ordo XX A, n. 9)

Gyug, Richard L. "The Pontificals of Monte Cassino." In *L'età dell'Abate Desiderio*. Vol. 3, 1: *Storia, arte et cultura: Atti del iv Convegno di studi sul medioevo meridionale, Montecassino e Cassino 4-8 ottobre 1987*. Miscellanea cassinese, vol. 67, 413-39. Montecassino: Pubblicazioni cassinese, 1992. (Appendix III, II: 626)

Hardouin, Jean, ed. *Acta conciliorum et epistolae decretales, ac constitutiones summorum pontificum*. 11 vols. Paris: ex Typographia regia, 1714-15. (Ordo XVII A, ed. *k*)

Haueter, Anton. *Die Krönungen der französischen Könige im Zeitalter des Absolutismus und in der Restauration*. Zurich: Juris Druck Verlag, 1975. (Ordo VII, n. 6)

Hedeman, Anne D. "The Commemoration of Jeanne d'Evreux's Coronation in the *Ordo ad Consecrandum* at the University of Illinois." In *Essays in Medieval Studies: Proceedings of the Illinois Medieval Association* 7 (1990): 13-28. (Ordo XXII A, MS *B*, n. 42)

Heiming, Odilo, ed. *Liber sacramentorum Augustodunensis*. Corpus Christianorum Series Latina, vol. 159 B. Turnhout: Brepols, 1987. (Ordo II, MS *D*, ed. *f*; Ordo IX, n. 7)

Hennig, John. "Zur Stellung Davids in der Liturgie." *Archiv für Liturgiewissenschaft* 10 (1967): 157-64. (Ordo I, n. 7)

Hoffmann, Hartmut. *Buchkunst und Königtum im ottonischen und frühsalischen Reich*. 2 vols. Schriften der Monumenta Germaniae

Historica, vol. 30, pts. 1–2. Stuttgart: Anton Hiersemann, 1986. (Ordo IV, n. 3)

Hohler, C. E. "Some Service-Books of the Later Saxon Church." In *Tenth-Century Studies*, edited by David Parsons, 60–83, 217–27. London and Chichester: Phillimore, 1975. (I: 29, n. 56; I: 37, n. 68; Ordo XV, nn. 1, 2)

Huguet, Edmond. *Dictionnaire de la langue française du XVIᵉ siècle.* 7 vols. Paris: E. Champion, then Paris: Didier, 1925–73. (Ordo XX B-C, n. 63)

Huyghebaert, N. "Gervais de Château-du-Loir." In *Dictionnaire d'histoire et de géographie ecclésiastiques*, 20: 1078–83. (Ordo XVII A, n. 2)

Imbert, Jean, Gérard Sautel, and Marguerite Boulet-Sautel. *Histoire des institutions et des faits sociaux (Xᵉ–XIXᵉ siècle).* «Themis»: Textes et documents (Paris: Hachette, 1956). (Ordo XX B-C, n. 17)

Isambert, François André. See *Recueil général des anciennes lois françises.*

Isidore of Seville. *Isidori Hispalensis episcopi Etymologiarum sive originum libri XX.* Edited by W. M. Lindsay. Scriptorum Classicorum Bibliotheca Oxoniensis. 2 vols. Oxford: Clarendon Press, 1911. (Ordo VII, n. 49)

Jackson, Richard A. "The *livres bleu* and *rouge*, Two Coronation Manuscripts in the Cathedral of Reims." In ...*The Man of Many Devices, Who Wandered Full Many Ways...: Festschrift in Honor of János M. Bak*, ed. Balázs Nagy and Marcell Sebők (Budapest: Central European University Press, 1999), 176–86. (II: 286, n. 1; Ordo XXII A, lost MS 2, nn. 36, 37; Ordo XXIII, nn. 5, 12; Ordo XXIV, n. 5)

——. "Manuscripts, Texts, and Enigmas of Medieval French Coronation Ordines." *Viator* 23 (1992): 35–70. (I: 7, n. 11; I: 35, n. 62; I: 38, n. 75; Ordo III, n. 1; Ordo XIII, n. 5; Ordo XV, nn. 2, 6, 8, 14; Ordo XVI, n. 6; Ordo XVII A, n. 3; Ordo XIX, n. 1; Ordo XX A, n. 5; Ordo XXI nn. 2, 54; Ordo XXII A, nn. 2, 4)

——. "Les manuscrits des *ordines* de couronnement de la bibliothèque de Charles V, roi de France." *Le Moyen Age* (1976): 67–88. (Ordo Ordo XX B, lost MSS 6, 7, 8; Ordo XXII A, lost MS 3, nn. 6, 9; Ordo XXIII, nn. 1, 2, 13–15, 18–19, 21)

——. "Le pouvoir monarchique dans la cérémonie du sacre et couronnement des rois de France." In *Représentation, pouvoir et royauté à la fin du Moyen Age*, edited by Joël Blanchard, 237–51. Paris: Picard, 1995. (Ordo XX B-C, n. 2; Ordo XXV, n. 20)

——. *Vivat Rex: Une histoire des sacres et couronnements en France, 1364–1825.* Strasbourg: Association des Publications près les Universités de Strasbourg, 1984. French edition of *Vive le roi*. (I: 7, nn. 11–12; I: 31, nn. 57–58; I: 32, n. 59; Ordo VII, n. 6; Ordo XVII B, n. 12; Ordo XXII A, nn. 4, 21; Ordo XXIII, nn. 2, 5, 15; Ordo XXIV, n. 21; Ordo XXV, n. 16)

——. *Vive le Roi! A History of the French Coronation Ceremony from Charles V to Charles X*. Chapel Hill: University of North Carolina Press, 1984. (I: 7, nn. 11–12; I: 31, nn. 57–58; I: 32, n. 59; Ordo VII, n. 6; Ordo XVII B, n. 12; Ordo XXII A, nn. 4, 21; Ordo XXIII, nn. 2, 5, 15; Ordo XXIV, n. 21; Ordo XXV, n. 16)

——. "Who Wrote Hincmar's Ordines?" *Viator* 25 (1994): 31–52. (I: 25, nn. 48, 49; Ordo V, nn. 2, 5; Ordo VI, n. 2; Ordo VII, nn. 2, 3, 5, 54)

——, ed. "The *Traité du sacre* of Jean Golein." *Proceedings of the American Philosophical Society* 113 (1969): 305–24. (I: 11, n. 18; I: 21, n. 36)

James, Montague Rhodes. See Cambridge, Fitzwilliam Museum.

Kelley, Donald R. *Foundations of Modern Historical Scholarship: Language, Law, and History in the French Renaissance*. New York and London: Columbia University Press, 1970. (Ordo XVII B, n. 1)

Kings and Kingship in Medieval Europe. Edited by Anne J. Duggan. London: King's College London Centre for Late Antique and Medieval Studies, 1993. (Appendix III, II: 626)

Kuttner, Stephan. "Notes on the Presentation of Text and Apparatus in Editing Works of the Decretists and Decretalists." *Traditio* 15 (1959): 452–64; and 26 (1970): 432. (I: 41, n. 77)

Labande, L. H. "Le cérémonial romain de Jacques Cajétan: Les données historiques qu'il renferme." *Bibliothèque de l'Ecole des Chartes* 54 (1893): 45–74. (I: 9, n. 13)

Labbe, Philippe. *L'abrègé royal de l'alliance chronologique de l'histoire sacrée et profane*. Paris: Gaspar Meturas, 1651; reprinted 1664. (Ordo XX B-C, ed. *b*, n. 16)

——. *Nova bibliotheca manuscriptorum librorum*. Paris: Joannes Henavit, 1653. (Ordo VII, n. 13)

Labbe, Philippe, and Gabriel Cossart, eds. *Sacrosancta concilia*. 16 vols. Paris: Societas typographica librorum ecclesiasticorum, 1671–72. 21 vols. in 23. Venice: Sebastianus Coleti et Jo. Baptista Albrizzi q. Hieron. fil., 1728–33. (Ordo XVII A, ed. *j*)

Lancelot, Antoine. *Mémoires concernant les pairs de France, avec les preuves*. Paris: A.-U. Coustelier, 1720. (Ordo XVII A, ed. *l*)

Langlois, Charles Victor. *Registres perdus des archives de la Chambre des comptes de Paris*. Paris: Imprimerie nationale, 1916. (Ordo XX B-C, n. 11)

Lanoë, Guy. "L'ordo de couronnement de Charles le Chauve à Sainte-Croix d'Orleáns (6 juin 848)." In *Kings and Kingship in Medieval Europe*, 41–68. (Appendix III, II: 626)

———. "Un *ordo* de couronnement carolingien inconnu." See Guy Lanoë, "L'ordo de couronnement de Charles le Chauve." (Ordo XIV, n. 6, MS *A*)

Latouche, Robert. *Textes d'histoire médiévale, Ve–XIe siècle*. Université de Grenoble: Publications de la Faculté des Lettres, 2. Paris: Presses Universitaires de France, 1951. (Ordo XVII A, ed. *r*; Ordo XVII B, ed. *d*)

Leclercq, Henri. "Gellone (Sacramentaire de)." In DACL, vol. 6, pt. 1 (1924): 777–94. (Ordo I, MS *B*)

———. "Nevers." In DACL, vol. 12, pt. 1 (1935): 1151–67. (Ordo XIII, MS *B*)

———. "Reims." In DACL, vol. 14, pt. 2 (1948): 2279–81. (Ordo IX, ed. *d*)

———. "Tours." In DACL, vol. 15, pt. 2 (1953): 2570–2677. (Ordo XI, MS *A*)

Le Goff, Jacques, "A Coronation Program for the Age of Saint Louis: The Ordo of 1250." In *Coronations: Medieval and Early Modern Monarchic Ritual*, 46–57. (I: 35, n. 63; Ordo XXI, nn. 3, 10)

Leiden, Rijksuniversiteit Bibliotheek. Meyier, Karel Adriaan de. *Codices Vossiani Latini: Pars II: Codices in quarto*. Codices Manuscripti, 14. Leiden: Universitaire Pers, 1975. (Ordo XIV, MS *A*)

Lelong, Jacques. *Bibliothèque historique de la France*. 2nd ed. 5 vols. Edited by Fevret de Fontette and Barbeau de la Bruyère. Paris: Herissant, 1768–78. (Ordo XXII A, lost MS *1*, n. 13; Ordo XXIII, n. 17)

Lemaître, Jean-Loup. "Les livres liturgiques des paroisses du Rouergue au milieu du XVe siècle." In *L'encadrement religieux des fidèles au Moyen Age et jusqu'au Concile de Trente*, Actes du 109e Congrès national des Sociétés savantes, Dijon 1984: Section d'histoire médiévale et de philologie, 1: 379–90. Paris: Ministère de l'éducation nationale, Comité des travaux historiques et scientifiques, 1985. (I: 33, n. 60)

Le Noble, Alexandre. *Histoire du sacre et du couronnement des rois et reines de France*. Paris: Gaultier-Laguionie, 1825. (Ordo XVII B, n. 2; Ordo XXV, n. 5)

Leroquais, Victor. *Les pontificaux manuscrits des bibliothèques publiques de France*. 3 vols. Paris: Protat frères, 1937. (I: 11, n. 19; Ordo XII, MS *A*; Ordo XIII, MS *B*; Ordo XV, MSS *B, D, E, F, G, H, I, K, L, M, P, T*; Ordo XVIII, MSS *A, B*; Ordo XIX, MSS *A, B*; Ordo XX B-C, MS *C*; Ordo XXI, n. 5; Ordo XXII A, MSS *A, I, K*; Ordo XXIII, MSS *C, G*)

———. *Les sacramentaires et les missels manuscrits des bibliothèques publiques de France*. 4 vols. Paris: Protat frères, 1924. (I: 11, n. 19; Ordo I, MS *A*; Ordo II, n. 1; Ordo IX, MS *A*; Ordo XI, MS *A*; Ordo XIII, MS *B*; Ordo XV, MS *A*; Ordo XX B-C, MS *C*; Ordo XXIII, MS *B*)

Leroy, G. "Le livre du sacre des rois, ayant fait partie de la librairie de Charles V, au Louvre, actuellement conservé au British Museum, à Londres," *Bulletin historique et philologique du Comité des travaux historiques et scientifiques* (1896): 616–21. (Ordo XX B-C, ed. *e*)

Lescuyer, Mathieu. See Paris, Bibliothèque nationale, *Catalogue général des manuscrits latins, nº 8823–8921.* (Ordo XX B-C, MS *C*)

Levillain, Léon. "Le sacre de Charles le Chauve à Orléans." *Bibliothèque de l'Ecole des Chartes* 64 (1903): 31–53. (Ordo VI, n. 6; Ordo VII, n. 1)

Lewis, Andrew W. "Anticipatory Association of the Heir in Early Capetian France." *American Historical Review* 83 (1978): 906–27. (I: 2, n. 2)

Lieftinck, Gerard I. *Manuscrits datés conservés dans les Pays-Bas.* Vol. 1: *Les manuscrits d'origine étrangère (816–C. 1550).* Amsterdam: North Holland Publishing Co., 1964. (Ordo XX A, MS *F*; Ordo XX B-C, MS *Q*)

London, British Library. *Catalogue of Additions to the Manuscripts in the British Museum in the Years MDCCCXLI–MDCCCXLV.* London: George Woodfall and Son, 1850. (Ordo XXII A, MS *D*)

——. *Catalogue of Additions to the Manuscripts in the British Museum in the Years MDCCCLXXXII–MDCCCLXXXVII.* London: British Museum, 1889. (Ordo XX B-C, MS *D*)

——. *Catalogue of Manuscripts in the British Museum.* New Series I, Part I: *The Arundel Manuscripts.* London: British Museum, 1834. (Ordo XXII A, MS *H*)

Loriquet, Henri. See Reims, Bibliothèque municipale.

Lot, Ferdinand. "Les derniers Carolingiens: Lothaire Louis V. — Charles de Lorraine (954–991)." *Bibliothèque de l'Ecole des Hautes Etudes* 87. Paris: Emile Bouillon, Libraire Editeur, 1891. (Ordo XVII A, n. 16)

Magistretti, Marcus, ed. *Pontificale in usum ecclesiae Mediolanensis necnon Ordines Ambrosiani ex codicibus saecc. IX–XV.* Monumenta veteris liturgicae Ambrosianae, vol. 1. Milan: Apud Ulricum Hoepli, 1897. (Ordo XIV, MS *B*)

Mansi, Giovan Domenico, ed. *Sacrorum conciliorum nova et amplissima collectio.* 54 vols. in 60. Florence etc. Reprint. Paris: H. Welter, 1901–27. (I: 40, n. 76; Ordo V, ed. *e*; Ordo VI, n. 5, ed. *e*; Ordo VII, ed. *g*; Ordo VIII, edd. *c, p₃*; Ordo X, ed. *c*; Ordo XI, ed. *f*; Ordo XVII A, ed. *o*)

Marlot, Guillaume. *Histoire de la ville, cité et université de Reims.* 4 vols. Reims: L. Jacquet, 1843–46. (Ordo XX B-C, ed. *d*)

——. *Metropolis Remensis historia.* Vol. 1, Lille: N. de Rache, 1666. Vol. 2, Reims: Protase Lelorain, 1679. (Ordo XVII A, ed. *i*)

Martène, Dom Edmond. *De antiquis ecclesiae ritibus.* 1st ed. 3 vols. Rouen: Guillelmus Behourt, 1700–1702. (I: 17, n. 25; Ordo XI, ed.

a; Ordo XV, ed. *b*; Ordo XVIII, ed. *a*; Ordo XXI, ed. *b₁*; Ordo XXII A, ed. *a₁*)

2d ed. 4 vols. Antwerp: J. B. de la Bry, 1736–38. (Ordo IX, ed. *a*; Ordo XI, ed. *a*; Ordo XIII, n. 7; Ordo XV, ed. *b*; Ordo XVIII, ed. *a*; Ordo XXI, ed. *b₂*; Ordo XXII A, ed. *a₂*)

3d ed. 4 vols. in 2. Venice: J. B. Novelli, 1763–65. Reprints of 3d ed. Venice: Jo. Bapt. Novelli, 1783; and Venice: Remondini, 1788. (Ordo IX, ed. *a*; Ordo XI, ed. *a*; Ordo XIII, n. 7; Ordo XV, ed. *b*; Ordo XVIII, ed. *a*; Ordo XXI, ed. *b₃*; Ordo XXII A, ed. *a₃*)

Martimort, Aimé-Georges. *La documentation liturgique de Dom Edmond Martène: Etude codicologique.* Studi e Testi, vol. 279. Vatican City: Biblioteca Apostolica Vaticana, 1978. (Ordo IX, MS *A*; Ordo XI, MS *A*; Ordo XIII, MS *A*; Ordo XV, MSS *A, D, G, M, P, T*; Ordo XVIII, MS *B*; Ordo XIX, MS *A*; Ordo XX A, MSS *A, B, C*; Ordo XXI, MS *A*; Ordo XXII A, MS *A*; Ordo XXIII, n. 25)

———. *Les "ordines", les ordinaires et les cérémoniaux.* Typologie des sources du moyen âge occidental, fasc. 56. Turnhout: Brepols, 1991. (I: 7, n. 12)

Masson, Jean Papire. *Annalium libri quatuor.* Paris: N. Chesenu, 1577. 2d ed. Paris: N. Chesenu, 1578. (Ordo XVII A, ed. *b*)

Mayer, Hans Eberhard. "Das Pontificale von Tyrus und die Krönung der lateinischen Könige von Jerusalem: Zugleich ein Beitrag zur Forschung über Herrschaftszeichen und Staatssymbolik." *Dumbarton Oaks Papers* 21 (1967): 140–232. (Ordo XV, MS *J*)

Menard, Hugues. *Notae et observationes in Librum sacramentorum S. Gregorii Magni papae I.* Paris: Apud Dionysium Moreau, 1641. (Ordo IX, ed. *g*)

———, ed. *Divi Gregorii papae huius nominis primi, cognomento magni liber sacramentorum.* Paris: Apud Dionysium Moreau, 1642. (Ordo XV, ed. *a*)

———, ed. *Sancti Gregorii papae I. cognomento Magna, Opera omnia.* 4 vols. Paris: C. Rigaud, 1705. (Ordo IX, ed. *g*; Ordo XV, ed. *a*)

Meurier, Hubert (= Hubertus Morus). *De sacris unctionibus libri tres.* Paris: Apud Guillielmum Bichonium, 1593. (Ordo XXII A, nn. 36, 37, 55; Ordo XXIII, nn. 7, 67, 81, 90, 99, 101, 105, 111, 113, 118, 129, 138, 140, 152, 155, 156)

Migne, Jacques Paul, ed. *Patrologiae cursus completus latinae.* 221 vols. Paris: Jacques-Paul Migne, 1844–64. Cited as PL. (Ordo V, n. 3, edd. *c*, *g*; Ordo VI, n. 16, edd. *c*, *g*; Ordo VII, ed. *e*; Ordo VII, edd. *i*, *m*; Ordo VIII, n. 10, edd. *f₃*, *f₄*, *n*, *r*; Ordo IX, ed. *g*; Ordo X, ed. *f*; Ordo XI, ed. *i*; Ordo XV, ed. *a*)

Miner, Dorothy. "Since De Ricci — Western Illuminated Manuscripts Acquired since 1934: A Report in Two Parts: Part II." *The Journal of the Walters Art Gallery* 31–32 (1968–69): 40–117. (Ordo XIII, n. 6)

Mohlberg, Leonhard Cunibert. *Norme per le pubblicazioni di opere scientifiche.* Rerum Ecclesiasticarum Documenta. Series minor: Subsidia studiorum, 2. Rome: Casa Editrice Herder, 1966. (I: 41, n. 77)

——, ed. *Liber sacramentorum Romanae aecclesiae ordinis anni circuli (Cod. Vat. Reg. lat. 316/Paris Bibl. Nat. 7193, 41/56) (Sacramentarium Gelasianum).* Rerum Ecclesiasticarum Documenta. Series maior: Fontes, 4. Rome: Casa Editrice Herder, 1960. (Ordo II, MS *A*, ed. *d*)

Moreau, Edouard de. *Histoire de l'église en Belgique.* 2d ed. 5 vols. Brussels: L'Edition universelle, 1945–52. (Ordo VII, n. 18)

Molin, J. B. "Un pontifical de Meaux du XIIIe siècle." *Bulletin de la Société d'histoire et d'art du diocèse de Meaux* 6 (1955): 257–59. (Ordo XXII A, MS *A*, n. 17)

Morin, D. G. "Un recueil gallican inédit de *Benedictiones episcopales* en usage à Freising au VIIe–IXe siècles." *Revue Benedictine* 29 (1912): 168–94. (Ordo IV, MS *A*, ed. *a*)

Muratori, Lodovico Antonio, ed. *Scriptores rerum Italicarum.* 25 vols. in 28. Milan: Ex typographia Societatis Palatinae in Regia Curia, 1723–51. (I: 19, n. 28; Ordo VII, ed. *k*; Ordo VIII, ed. *a*)

Nelson, Janet L. "The Earliest Surviving Royal *Ordo*: Some Liturgical and Historical Aspects." In Nelson, *Politics and Ritual,* 341–60. (I: 10, n. 16)

——. "Hincmar of Reims on King-making: The Evidence of the *Annals of St. Bertin,* 861–882." In *Coronations: Medieval and Early Modern Monarchic Ritual,* 16–34. (Ordo VII, n. 1)

——. *Politics and Ritual in Early Medieval Europe.* London and Ronceverte: The Hambledon Press, 1986. (I: 10, n. 16; I: 23, n. 41; I: 24, n. 46; I: 25, n. 48; I: 29, nn. 55–56; I: 35, n. 64; I: 36, n. 66; Ordo V, n. 4; Ordo VII, nn. 7, 11, MSS *A*, *C*; Ordo VIII, n. 2)

——. "Ritual and Reality in the Early Medieval Ordines." In Nelson, *Politics and Ritual,* 329–39." (I: 36, n. 66)

——. See also *The Annals of St-Bertin.*

Netzer, H. *L'introduction de la messe romaine en France sous les Carolingiens.* Paris: Librairie Alphonse Picard et Fils, 1910. (Ordo XV, MS *A*, ed. *c*)

Obertyński, X. Zdzisław. *Pontificale Arcybiskupa Lwowskiego Jana Rzeszowskiego w Bibliotece Kapitulnej w Gnieźnie.* Lvov: Wydawnictwo Zakładu Narodowego Imienia Ossolińskich, 1930. (Ordo XV, n. 3)

Omont, Henri. *Catalogue général des nouvelles acquisitions françaises.* See Paris, Bibliothèque nationale de France.

——. "Recherches sur la bibliothèque de l'Eglise cathédrale de Beauvais." *Mémoires de l'Académie des Inscriptions et Belles-Lettres* 40 (1914): 1–93. (Ordo VII, lost MS *2*)

L'ordre et les cérémonies du sacre et couronnement du tres-chrestien roy de France. Paris: Nicolas Chesneau, 1575. (Ordo XXIII, ed. *b*)

Oxford, Bodleian Library. Black, William Henry. *A Descriptive Catalogue of the Manuscripts Bequeathed unto the University of Oxford by Elias Ashmole.* Catalogi codicum manuscriptorum bibliothecae Bodleiana, pars 10. Oxford: The University Press, 1845. (Ordo XX A, MS *J*)

Pacaut, Marcel. *Les structures politiques de l'Occident médiéval.* Collection U: Série histoire médiévale. Paris: A. Colin, 1969. (Ordo XVII B, ed. *e*)

Paris, Archives nationales. *Catalogue des manuscrits conservés aux Archives nationales.* Paris: E. Plon, Nourrit et Cie., 1892. (Ordo XVII B, MS *I*)

Paris, Bibliothèque de l'Arsenal. Martin, Henry, et al. *Catalogue des manuscrits de la Bibliothèque de l'Arsenal.* 11 vols. Catalogue général des manuscrits des bibliothèques publiques de France. Paris: E. Plon, Nourrit et Cie., 1885–1915. (Ordo XVII B, MS *F*; Ordo XX B-C, MS *K*)

Paris, Bibliothèque de l'Assemblée nationale. Coyecque, Ernest, and Henry Debraye. *Paris: Chambre des Députés.* Catalogue général des manuscrits des bibliothèques publiques de France. Paris: Plon-Nourrit et Cie., 1907. (Ordo XVII B, MS *G*)

Paris, Bibliothèque nationale de France. Auvray, Lucien, and René Poupardin. *Catalogue des manuscrits de la collection Baluze.* Paris: E. Leroux, 1921. (Ordo X, MS *B*; Ordo XI, MS *C*; Ordo XIII, MS *C*)

——. Auvray, Lucien, and Henri Omont. *Catalogue des manuscrits français: Ancien Saint-Germain français.* 3 vols. Paris, 1898–1900. (Ordo XX B-C, MS *L*)

——. *Catalogue des manuscrits français: Ancien fonds.* 5 vols. Paris: Firmin Didot, 1868–1902. (Ordo XVII B, MSS *A*, *D*; Ordo XX B-C, MSS *F*, *G*; Ordo XXII B-C, MS *A*)

——. *Catalogue général des manuscrits latins, n⁰ 8823–8921.* Edited by Jacqeline Sclafer and Marie-Pierre Lafitte. Paris: Bibliothèque nationale de France, 1997. (Ordo XX B-C, MS *C*; Ordo XXIII, n. 19)

——. *Catalogus codicum manuscriptorum bibliothecae regiae.* Vol. 3. Paris: e Typographia regia, 1744. (Ordo XVII A, MS *B*)

———. Delisle, Léopold. *Catalogue des manuscrits des fonds Libri et Barrois.* Paris: H. Champion, 1888. (Ordo VIII, lost MS *3*)

———. Dorez, Léon. *Catalogue de la collection Dupuy.* 3 vols. Paris: E. Leroux, 1899–1928. (Ordo XVII A, MS *D*; Ordo XX B-C, MS *E*)

———. Omont, Henri. *Catalogue général des manuscrits français,* 3 vols. Paris: Ernest Leroux, 1898–1900. Vol. 2: Lucien Auvray, *Ancien Saint-Germain français.* Paris: Ernest Leroux, 1898. (Ordo XX B-C, MS *L*)

———. Omont, Henri. *Catalogue général des manuscrits français: Ancien supplément français,* 3 vols. Paris: Ernest Leroux, 1895–96. (Ordo XXII A, MS *G*; Ordo XXIV, MS *A*)

———. Omont, Henri. *Catalogue général des manuscrits français: Nouvelles acquisitions françaises.* 4 vols. Paris: E. Leroux, 1899–1918. (Ordo XI, MS *D*; Ordo XIII, MS *D*; Ordo XVII A, MSS *C, G, I*; Ordo XVII B, MS *E*; Ordo XX B-C, MSS *H, P*; Ordo XXV, MS *B*)

Paris, Bibliothèque Sainte-Geneviève. Kohler, Charles. *Catalogue des manuscrits de la Bibliothèque Sainte-Geneviève.* 2 vols. Paris: E. Plon, Nourrit et Cie., 1893–96. (Ordo XVIII, MS *B*)

Patetta, Federico. "Nuove osservazioni sui mss. della collezione di canoni *Anselmo dedicata* e del capitolare di Lamberto." *Rivista Italiana per le Scienze Giuridiche* 11 (1891): 375–84. (Ordo VII, n. 10, lost MSS *3, 4, 5*)

Pertz, Georg Heinrich, ed. *Monumenta Germaniae Historica Leges* (in folio). Vol. 1. Hanover: Hahn, 1835. (Ordo V, ed. *g*; Ordo VI, ed. *g*; Ordo VII, ed. *i*; Ordo VIII, n. 5, lost MS *3*, edd. *f, r*; Ordo X, ed. *f*; Ordo XI, ed. *i*; Ordo XVII A, ed. *p*)

Petit, Joseph, et al. *Essai de restitution des plus anciens mémoriaux de la Chambre des comptes de Paris (Pater, Noster¹, Noster², Qui es in Coelis, Croix, A¹).* Université de Paris: Bibliothèque de la Faculté des Lettres, vol. 7. Paris: Félix Alcan, 1899. (Ordo XX B-C, n. 4, MSS *A, O₁, O₂,* nn. 11, 12, 14)

Pirot, François. "La bibliothèque de l'abbaye Saint-Laurent de Liège." In *Saint-Laurent de Liège: Eglise, abbaye et hôpital militaire: Mille ans d'histoire,* edited by Rita Lejeune, 125–36. Liège: Soledi, 1968. (Ordo V, n. 3)

Pithou, Pierre. See Dupuy, Pierre.

Prou, Maurice. *Recueil des actes de Philippe Iᵉʳ, roi de France (1059–1108).* Chartes et diplômes relatifs à l'histoire de France. Paris: Académie des Inscriptions et Belles-Lettres, 1908. (Ordo XVII A, MS *E*, ed. *q*)

Puniet, Dom Pierre de. *Le sacramentaire romain de Gellone.* Ephemerides Liturgicae. Rome, [193–]. (Ordo XV, n. 5)

Prynne, William. *Signal Loyalty and Devotion of Gods True Saints and Pious Christians (as also of Idolatrous Pagans) towards their Kings.* London: [no publisher], 1660. (Ordo XXIII, ed. *f*)

Quentin, Henry. *Jean-Dominique Mansi et les grandes collections conciliaires.* Paris: Ernest Leroux, 1900. (I: 20, n. 32)

Recueil des historiens des Gaules et de la France. Edited by Dom Martin Bouquet et al. 24 vols. Paris: Victor Palmé, H. Welter, Imprimerie nationale, 1738–1904. New ed. unchanged. Vols. 1–19. Paris: Aux dépens des librairies associés, 1869–80. (I: 19, n. 27; Ordo V, ed. *f*; Ordo VI, ed. *f*; Ordo VII, edd. *h, l*; Ordo VIII, edd. *e, q*; Ordo X, ed. *e*; Ordo XI, ed. *h*; Ordo XVII A, n. 16, ed. *n*)

Recueil général des anciennes lois françaises. Edited by François André Isambert et al. 29 vols. Paris: Belin-le-Prieur, 1822–33. (Ordo XXIV, n. 21)

Reims, Bibliothèque municipale. Henri Loriquet. *Reims.* 2 vols. in 3. Catalogue général des bibliothèques publiques de la France: Départements. Vols. 38–39. Paris: Plon-Nourrit et Cie., 1904–1906. (Ordo XVII A, MSS *F, H*; Ordo XXIII, n. 16, MSS *J, L*; Ordo XXIV, MS *B*)

Reinhard, Marcel, ed. *Textes et documents d'histoire, Agrégation d'histoire, 1959.* Paris: Hachette, 1960. (Ordo XX B-C, n. 17)

Respublica, sive status regni Galliae diversorum autorum. Leiden: ex officina Elzeviriana, 1626. (Ordo XVII B, n. 2; Ordo XXII A, n. 25)

Richardson, H. G. "The Coronation in Medieval England: The Evolution of the Office and the Oath." *Traditio* 16 (1960): 111–202. (I: 7, n. 12, Ordo XX A, n. 4)

Rouse, Richard A., and Mary A. Rouse. Review of Jenny Stratford, *The Bedford Inventories*, in *Speculum* 72 (1997): 226–28. (Ordo XXIII, n. 4)

Le sacre et couronnement du roy de France. Reims: Jean de Foigny, 1575. (Ordo XXIII, n. 27)

Saffroy, Gaston. *Bibliographie généalogique, héraldique et nobiliaire de la France.* 5 vols. Paris: Librairie Gaston Saffroy, 1968–88. (I: 4, n. 5)

Saint-Roch, Patrick, ed. *Liber sacramentorum Engolismensis: Manuscrit B.N. 816: Le sacramentaire Gélasien d'Angoulême.* Corpus Christianorum Series Latina, vol. 159 C. Turnhout: Brepols, 1987. (Ordo II, MS *C*, ed. *g*; Ordo XI, n. 5)

Saint Petersburg, National Library of Russia at Saint Petersburg. Staerk, Antonio. *Les manuscrits latins du Ve au XIIIe siècle conservés à la Bibliothèque impériale de Saint-Pétersbourg.* 2 vols. Saint Petersburg: F. Krois, 1910. Reprint. Hildesheim and New York: G. Olms, 1976. (Ordo XIII, ed. *c*)

Salmon, Pierre. See Vatican City, Biblioteca Apostolica Vaticana.

Schenk, Wacław. "Rękopisy liturgiczne od XIII do XV wieku w bibliotece uniwersyteckiej we Wrocławiu." *Archiwa, Biblioteki i Muzea Kościelne* 2 (Lublin, 1961): 185–206. (Ordo XV, MS *Q*)

Schramm, Percy Ernst. *Kaiser, Könige und Päpste.* 4 vols. in 5 parts. Stuttgart: Anton Hiersemann, 1968–71. (I: 25, n. 48; Ordo IX, nn. 4, 5, 8; Ordo IX, ed. *f*; Ordo X, n. 2, ed. *i*; Ordo XI, nn. 1, 3, 4, edd. *c, m*; Ordo XIII, nn. 2, 4, 6, ed. *e*; Ordo XIV, ed. *d*; Ordo XV, ed. *f*; Ordo XVII A, nn. 4, 16)

———. *Der König von Frankreich.* 2d ed. 2 vols. Weimar: Hermann Böhlaus Nachfolger, 1960. (I: 25, nn. 48–49; Ordo XV, n. 7)

———. "Die Krönung bei den Westfranken und Angelsachsen von 878 bis um 1000." *Zeitschrift für Rechtsgeschichte, kan. Abteilung* 23 (1934): 117–242. (I: 6, n. 8; Ordo IX, ed. *c*; Ordo X, ed. *h*; Ordo XI, edd. *b, k*; Ordo XIII, ed. *d*; Ordo XV, ed. *d*)

———. "Ordines-Studien II: Die Krönung bei den Westfranken und den Franzosen." *Archiv für Urkundenforschung* 15 (1938): 3–55, with "Nachträge zu den Ordines-Studien II–III," ibid. 16 (1939): 279–86. (I: 5; I: 6, n. 8; I: 25, n. 49; Ordo VI, n. 2; Ordo VII, n. 4; Ordo XIII, nn. 2, 4, 6; Ordo XVI, n. 3; Ordo XVII A, n. 3; Ordo XVIII, nn. 1, 4, 6; Ordo XIX, n. 1; Ordo XX A, n. 3; Ordo XXIII, nn. 3, 24; Ordo XXIV, n. 14)

Schreuer, Hans. "Noch einmal über altfranzösische Krönungsordnungen." *Zeitschrift der Savigny-Stiftung für Rechtsgeschichte, germ. Abteilung* 32 (1911): 1–40, with "Nachtrag," 312–15. (I: 4, n. 7)

———. *Die rechtlichen Grundgedanken der französischen Königskrönung: Mit besonderer Rücksicht auf die deutschen Verhältnisse.* Weimar: Hermann Böhlaus Nachfolger, 1911. (I: 4, n. 7; Ordo XX A, ed. *b*)

———. "Über altfranzösische Krönungsordnungen." *Zeitschrift der Savigny-Stiftung für Rechtsgeschichte, germ. Abteilung* 30 (1909): 142–92. (I: 4, n. 7; Ordo XX A, n. 2; Ordo XX B-C, n. 16, ed. *g*)

Schrörs, Heinrich. *Hinkmar, Erzbischof von Reims: Sein Leben und seine Schriften.* Freiburg i. B.: Herder'sche Verlagshandlung, 1884. (Ordo VII, nn. 11, 42)

Selden, John. *Titles of Honor.* 2nd ed. London: R. Whitakers, 1631. (Ordo XXIII, ed. d_1, nn. 57, 74)

3rd ed. London: T. Dring, 1672. (Ordo XXIII, ed. d_2)

———. *Tituli honorum ... juxta editionem Londinensem anni 1672.* Translated by Simon Johannes Arnold. Frankfurt: impressis Jeremiae Schrey, et Henrici Johannes Meyeri haered., literis Goderitschianis, 1696. (Ordo XXIII, ed. d_3)

Sherman, Claire Richter. "The Queen in Charles V's 'Coronation Book': Jeanne de Bourbon and the 'Ordo ad reginam benedicendam'." *Viator*, 8 (1977): 255–98. (Ordo XXIII, MS *A*)

Simson, Bernhard. *Jahrbücher des Fränkischen Reichs unter Ludwig dem Frommen*. Jahrbücher der deutschen Geschichte. 2 vols. Leipzig: Duncker und Humblot, 1874–76. (Ordo VII, nn. 46, 47, 48, 50)

Sirmond, Jacques. *Opera varia*. 5 vols. Paris: e Typographia regia, 1696. 2d ed. Venice: Bartolomaeus Javarina, 1728. (Ordo V, ed. *a*; Ordo VI, ed. *a*; Ordo VII, ed. *b*; Ordo VIII, n. 5, edd. *d, l*; Ordo X, ed. *d*; Ordo XI, ed. *g*)

———, ed. *Concilia antiqua Galliae*. 3 vols. Paris: Sebastien Cramoisy, 1629. (Ordo VI, n. 5; Ordo VII, ed. *c*)

———, ed. *Hincmari archiepiscopi Remensis opera*. 2 vols. Paris: Sebastien Cramoisy et Gabriel Cramoisy, 1645. (Ordo V, ed. *c*; Ordo VI, ed. *c*; Ordo VII, ed. *e*; Ordo VIII, n. 10, ed. *n*)

———, ed. *Karoli Calvi et successorum aliquot Franciae regum capitula*. Paris: Sebastien Cramoisy, 1623. (Ordo V, ed. *a*; Ordo VI, ed. *a*; Ordo VII, nn. 9, 12, 55, ed. *b*; Ordo VIII, nn. 5, 15, edd. *d, l*; Ordo XI, ed. *g*)

Sprengler, Anneliese. "Die Gebete der Krönungsordines Hinkmars von Reims für Karl den Kahlen als König von Lothringen und für Ludwig den Stammler." *Zeitschrift für Kirchengeschichte* 63 (= 4th series, vol. 1) (1950–51): 245–67. (I: 37, n. 71; Ordo VII, n. 1; Ordo VIII, n. 2)

Staerk, Antonio. See Saint Petersburg, National Library of Russia at Saint Petersburg.

Stratford, Jenny. *The Bedford Inventories: The Worldly Goods of John, Duke of Bedford, Regent of France (1389–1435)*. Reports of the Research Committee of the Society of Antiquaries of London, vol. 49. London: Society of Antiquaries of London, 1993. (Ordo XXIII, n. 4)

Symcox, Geoffrey, ed. "Repertorium Columbianum: Instructions for Contributors." Los Angeles, [1991?]. Pp. 9. Typescript. (I: 41, n. 77)

Tellenbach, Gerd. *Römischer und christlicher Reichsgedanke in der Liturgie des frühen Mittelalters*. Heidelberg: Carl Winters Universitätsbuchhandlung, 1934. In *Sitzungsberichte der Heidelberger Akademie der Wissenschaften: Philosophisch-historische Klasse*, vol. 25, Jahrg. 1934/35, erste Abhandlung. Heidelberg: Carl Winters Universitätsbuchhandlung, 1935. (Ordo II, n. 3)

Thieme, Ulrich, ed. *Allgemeines Lexikon der bildenden Künstler*. 37 vols. Leipzig: Verlag vom Wilhelm Engelmann/Verlag von E. A. Seemann, 1907–50. (Ordo XX B-C, n. 10)

Tobler, Adolf, and Erhard Lommatsch. *Altfranzösisches Wörterbuch*. 10 vols. to date. Berlin: Weidmannsche Buchhandlung, and Wiesbaden: Franz Steiner Verlag, 1925–74. (Ordo XX B-C, n. 59)

Vaesen, Joseph, and Etienne Charvay. *Lettres de Louis XI publiée pour la Société de l'Histoire de France.* 11 vols. Paris: Librairie Renouard, 1883–1909. (Ordo XXIV, n. 21)

Varin, Pierre, ed. *Archives administratives de la ville de Reims.* Collection de documents inédits sur l'histoire de France. Première série: Histoire politique. 3 vols. Paris: Imprimerie de Crapelet, 1839–48. (I: 20, n. 31; Ordo XX B-C, ed. *c*, n. 45; Ordo XXIV, ed. *a*, nn. 1, 8, 9, 11, 14, 16, 19, 36, 39, 41)

Vatican City, Biblioteca Apostolica Vaticana. *Les manuscrits de la reine de Suède: Réédition du catalogue de Montfaucon et cotes actuelles.* Studi e Testi, vol. 238. Vatican City: Biblioteca Apostolica Vaticana, 1964. (Ordo XVII A, MS *A*)

——. Pellegrin, Elisabeth, et al. *Les manuscrits classiques latins de la bibliothèque vaticane.* Documents, études et répertoires publiés par l'Institut de Recherche et d'Histoire des Textes, 2 vols. in 3. Paris: Editions du Centre national de la Recherche Scientifique, 1975–82. (Ordo XVII A, MS *A*)

——. Salmon, Pierre. *Les manuscrits liturgiques latins de la Bibliothèque Vaticane.* 5 vols. Studi e Testi, vols. 251, 253, 260, 267, 270. Vatican City: Biblioteca Apostolica Vaticana, 1968–72. (Ordo XIV, MSS *C*, *D*; Ordo XXII A, MSS *C*, *E*)

——. Wilmart, Andreas. *Codices reginenses latini.* Bibliothecae Apostolicae Vaticanae codices manuscripti recensiti. 2 vols. Vatican City: Biblioteca Apostolica Vaticana, 1937–45. (Ordo VII, MS *A*)

Vignier, Nicolas. *La bibliothèque historiale.* 3 vols. Paris: Abel l'Angelier, 1587. (Ordo XVII A, ed. *c*)

Vogel, Cyrille. *Introduction aux sources de l'histoire du culte chrétien au moyen âge.* Reprint with additional notes and bibliography. Biblioteca degli «Studi Medievali», 1. Spoleto: Centro Studi Alto Medioevo, 1981. (I: 2, n. 4; I: 11, n. 19; I: 12, n. 20)

Vogel, Cyrille, and Reinhard Elze, eds. *Le pontifical romano-germanique du dixième siècle.* 3 vols. Studi e Testi, vols. 226–27, 269. Vatican City: Biblioteca Apostolica Vaticana, 1963–72. (I: 28, n. 52; I: 38, n. 74; Ordo II, n. 2; Ordo XIV, nn. 1, 5, ed. *c*; Ordo XVI, nn. 5, 22; Ordo XVIII, n. 3; Ordo XIX, n. 11; Ordo XXII B-C, n. 25)

Waitz, Georg. "Die Formeln der Deutschen Königs- und der Römischen Kaiser-Krönung vom zehnten bis zum zwölften Jahrhundert." *Abhandlungen der historisch-philologischen Classe der Königlichen Gesellschaft der Wissenschaften zu Göttingen* 18 (1873): 3–92. (I: 4, n. 6; I: 21, n. 33; Ordo III, ed. *a*; Ordo XVI, ed. *a*)

Ward, Paul L. "An Early Version of the Anglo-Saxon Coronation Ceremony." *English Historical Review* 57 (1942): 350–61. (Ordo XV, ed. *e*)

Warren, F. E., ed. *The Leofric Missal as Used in the Cathedral of Exeter during the Episcopate of Its First Bishop A.D. 1050–1072.* Oxford: Clarendon Press, 1883. (I: 10, n. 17; Ordo II, nn. 3, 4, 5, 9, 11; Ordo V, nn. 6, 12, 14, 16, 17; Ordo VII, n. 4)

Weil, Lucien. "Le concile de Troyes de 878 et le sacre de Louis le Bègue." *Mémoires de la Société académique du département de l'Aube* 109 (1978): 63–71. (Ordo IX, n. 2)

Wolfenbüttel, Herzog August Bibliothek. Heinemann, Otto von, et al. *Die Handschriften der herzoglichen Bibliothek zu Wolfenbüttel.* Vierte Abteilung: *Die Gudischen handschriften.* Wolfenbüttel: J. Zwissler, 1913. (Ordo XX A, MS *D*)

Woolley, Reginald Maxwell. *Coronation Rites.* Cambridge Handbooks of Liturgical Study. Cambridge: Cambridge University Press, 1915. (Ordo XVIII, n. 4)

Index of Formulas

One must use this index with some caution for several reasons. 1) Two different formulas might have the same incipit; I distinguish these by listing them separately, which is why some formulas seem to appear twice in the index. 2) There are many minor variations in the incipits of several formulas; I list essentially similar formulas together by means of cross-references, or by listing some of the variations within parentheses. 3) Formulas often suffered internal change with the passage of time; this is particularly true of a few of the earlier formulas, so it is necessary to compare a given formula with its counterparts in other ordines. 4) Formulas originally distinct were sometimes later combined; I index most such formulas with cross-references in order to prevent the second element from apparently disappearing from the rite. 5) A single formula in some ordines might be treated as several formulas in others; this is especially true of benedictions, and in the edition I assigned a single number to a set of formulas that were originally a single formula; where I do so, I do not index any but the first of such formulas. The formulas that begin *Benedic, Domine, hunc* (or *hos*) are related, but are particularly subject to variations. Only the Latin formulas are indexed, not the French formulas or translations. Sets of short suffrages (as in Ordo XXI,19) are not indexed.

Benedic, Domine, hos presules principes (hunc presulem principem) qui regna regum omnium: II,9; II, n. 11.

Benedic, Domine, hunc praesulem principem, qui regna: V, n. 16.

Benedic, Domine, hunc praesulem (preelectum) principem, qui regna: XV,33; XXII A,47; XXIV,61.

Benedic, Domine, hunc principem nostrum ill. (hunc regem nostrum ill., hunc principem nostrum), quem ad salutem: III,1β; IV,5; XXIII,31; XXV,79; see also *Deus, qui congregatis in tuo nomine.*

Benedic, Domine, hunc principem (regem nostrum, regem nostrum N.) qui regna: IX,4; XVI,38; XVIII,11; XIX,17; XXI,22; XXIII,73; XXV,132.

Benedicat tibi Dominus custodiat et te: see *Benedicat tibi Dominus et custodiat te.*

Benedicat te Dominus custodiatque te: see *Benedicat tibi Dominus et custodiat te.*

Benedicat tibi Dominus custodiensque te: see *Benedicat tibi Dominus et custodiat te.*

Benedicat tibi Dominus et custodiat te: IX,9; XVI,44; XVIII,21; XIX,32; XXI,44; XXII A,71; XXIII,103; XXIV,81; XXV,148.

Benedictionem tuam, Domine, hic famulus tuus accipiat: VII,22.

Christe, Deus oriens ex alto: I,4.

Christe perunge hunc regem in regimen. Unde unxisti: XV,10; XV,13; XVI,20; XXI,29–30; XXII A,29; XXIII,42; XXIV,43; XXV,104.

Christus, Rex regum ex aevo qui regnat: XV,66.

Circunda, Domine, manus huius famuli tui: XXIII,51; XXV,112.

Clerum ac populum, quem sua voluit: VII,32; VIII,29; IX,10; XIII,19; XVI,45; XVIII,22; XIX,33; XXI,45; XXII A,72; XXIII,104; XXIV,82; XXV,149.

Concede nos famulos tuos: XXV,28.

Concede, quesumus omnipotens Deus, his sacrificiis: XVI,43; XVIII,27; XIX,41; XXI,52.

Confortare et esto vir, et observa: XV,19; XXII A,11; XXIII,27; XXIV,31; XXV,75.

Conserva quaesumus, Domine, hunc famulum tuum: VII,23.

Convertat vultum suum ad te: VIII,19.

Coronet te Dominus corona glorię atque iusticię: XIII, n.6.

Coronet te Dominus (Deus) corona gloriae atque iustitiae: VII,34; VIII,15; XIII,11; XV,22; XXII A,39; XXIII,63; XXIV,53; XXV,123.

Coronet te Dominus gloria et honore: VI,5.

Coronet te Dominus corona gloriae in misericordia: VII,29.

Da ei a tuo spiramine cum mansuetudine: see *Benedic, Domine, hos (hunc)....*

Da ei, Domine Iesu, in tuo spiramine cum mansuetudine: see *Benedic, Domine, hos (or hunc)....*

Deus, qui populis tuis indulgentia consulis: VII,18; VIII,13; XIII,6; XV,7; XVI,16; XXII A,23; XXIII,37; XXIV,38; XXV,98.

Deus, qui populis tuis virtute consulis: see *Deus, qui populis tuis indulgentia consulis*.

Deus, qui populo tuo eterne salutis: XXIII,34; XXV,84.

Deus, qui praedicando aeterni regis: II,7; II, n. 9; XV,62.

Deus, qui providentia tua caelestia: XV,21; XVI,26; XVIII,18; XXII A,12; XXIII,28; XXIV,32; XXV,76.

Deus, qui regnorum omnium et Romani Francorumque: see *Deus regnorum omnium et christiani maxime*.

Deus, qui scis genus humanum nulla virtute: XVI,7; XVIII,4; XIX,6; XXI,5; XXIII,8; XXIV,15; XXV,49.

Deus qui solus habes immortalitatem: XIV,11; XVI,53; XIX,49; XXI,62; XXIII,90.

Deus, qui trinos gradus hominum: XIV, n. 16.

Deus, qui victrices Moysi: III,2; XXIII,80; XXV,138.

Deus regnorum omnium et christiani maxime: II,3; II, n. 3; XV,57.

Deus, rex regum et dominus dominancium: XXIII,45.

Deus, tocius creature principium et finis: XXIII,53; XXV,113.

Deus tuorum corona fidelium, qui in capitibus: XXIII,61.

Deus tuorum corona fidelium, qui quos ad regnum: XIX,57; XXI,70.

Domine Deus, Pater omnipotens, hunc famulum tuum: XI,2.

Domine in virtute tua letabitur rex: XXIII,9; XXIV,16; XXV,50.

Domine memorabor: XIX,57; XXI,69.

Domine, salvum fac regem et exaudi nos: XVIII,5; XIX,7; XXI,6; XXV,29.

Domine, salvum fac regem in virtute tua: XVI,8.

Domine sancte Pater omnipotens, eterne Deus, honoris cunctorum auctor: XXIII,101.

Domine sancte Pater omnipotens, eterne Deus, creator ac gubernator celi et terre: see *Omnipotens sempiterne Deus, creator ac gubernator caeli et terrae*.

Domine sancte, Pater omnipotens, aeterne Deus, electorum fortitudo: V,9.

Domine sancte Pater omnipotens, eterne Deus, creator omnium, imperator angelorum, rex regnantium: see *Omnipotens sempiterne Deus, creator ac gubernator caeli et terrae*.

Domine sancte, Pater omnipotens, aeterne Deus, qui potestate virtutis: VI,4.

Domine, sancte Pater, omnipotens aeterne Deus, rex regum: V, n. 14.

Dominus Deus omnipotens, qui dixit ad Moysem: VIII,17.

Dona eis profutura consilia: VI, n. 4.

Ecce ego mitto angelum meum: see *Ecce mitto angelum meum, qui precedet te*.

Impono tibi coronam regalem, qua ornatus ita vivas: XIII,36.

Illuminet faciem suam super te: VIII,18.

Inclina, Domine, aurem tuam ad preces nostre humilitatis: see *Inclina, Domine Iesu, salvator omnium*.

Inclina, Domine Iesu, salvator omnium: XV,68; XXII A,69; XXIII,108.

In diebus eius oriatur omnibus aequitas: XV,8; XVI,17; XXII A,24; XXIII,38; XXIV,39; XXV,99.

In hoc regni solio te confirmet: XIX,37; XXI,48; XXII A,77; see also *Sta et retine amodo locum*.

In nomine Patris et Filii et Spiritus sancti, prosit tibi haec unctio olei: XIII,26; XV,49; XVI,54; XXII A,61; XXIII,92; XXIV,70.

In te speravi, Domine: XIX,56; XXI,68.

Indulgeat tibi Dominus omnia peccata: see *Indulgeat tibi mala omnia*.

Indulgeat tibi mala omnia (omia mala, omnia peccata): VII,25; VIII,21; XV,28; XVI,33; XXII A,42; XXIII,68; XXIV,56; XXV,127.

Inimicos tuos ad pacis caritatisque: VII,27; VIII,26; XV,30; XVI,35; XXII A,44; XXIII,70; XXIV,58; XXV,129.

Israhel, si me audieris, non erit in te: XVI,6; XIX,5; XXI,4; XXIII,7; XXIV,14; XXV,25; XXV,47.

Kyrieleyson (i.e., the beginning of the litany): XIX,10; XXI,14; XXII A,16; XXIII,109; XXV,87.

Me ac ęcclesiam mihi commissam: VIII,6.

Multiplicet in te copiam suae benedictionis: VIII,22.

Munera quaesumus, Domine, oblata: VII,41; XIII,16; XV,42; XV,64; XXII A,53; XXIII,83; XXIV,80; XXV,153.

Nos tibi semper et ubique gratias agere: XIX,25; XXI,36.

Nostris quaesumus, Domine, in regimine: VII,20.

Nubas in Christo obnupta nube caelesti: V,2.

Officio indignitatis nostre seu congregationis: XIV,13; XVI,59; XIX,51; XXI,64.

Omnipotens benedicat tibi benedictionibus celi desuper in montibus: see *Omnipotens Deus det tibi de rore caeli*.

Omnipotens Creator, qui homini ad ymaginem: XXIII,50; XXV,111.

Omnipotens Deus, celestium (celestium terrestriumque) moderator: see *Omnipotens sempiterne Deus, caelestium terrestriumque moderator*.

O. D. det tibi de rore caeli: XV,35; XXII A,49; XXIII,74; XXIV,63; XXV,133.

O. D. dignetur te semper et ubique: XII,2.

O. D., qui te populi sui voluit: XIX,42; XXI,53.

O. D. regali culmine tibi: XIII,21.

O. D. victoriosum te atque triumphatorem: see *Victoriosum te atque triumphatorem*.

Promitto vobis, sanctissimi patres, et perdono: see *Promitto vobis et perdono, quia unicuique de vobis.*

Prospice, omnipotens Deus, hunc gloriosissimum regem: see *Prospice, omnipotens Deus, serenis obtutibus.*

Prospice, omnipotens Deus, serenis obtutibus: II,1; IV,3; IX,12; XII,1; XIX,21; XXI,33; XXIII,30; XXV,78.

Quesumus, omnipotens Deus, rex noster N.: see *Quaesumus, omnipotens Deus, ut famulus tuus.*

Quaesumus, omnipotens Deus, ut famulus tuus: VII,39; XIII,15; XV,39; XV,41; XV,63; XXII A,52; XXIII,82; XXIV,77; XXV,30; XXV,152.

Quatinus divinis monitis parentes: IX,11; XVI,46; XVIII,23; XIX,34; XXI,46; XXII A,73; XXIII,105; XXIV,83; XXV,150; see also *Clerum ac populum, quem sua voluit opitulatione tuae.*

Quoniam prevenisti eum in benedictionibus: XIX,35.

Rectitudo regis est noviter ordinati et in solium sublimati. Haec tria praecepta populo christiano: XV,37; XVI,40.

Respice, Domine, munera populi tui: VII,40.

Sacramentorum tuorum, Domine, communio sumpta: VII,42.

Sacrificiis, Domine, placatus oblatis: XIX,45; XXI,56.

Sancta divinitas, usque in extremos fines: VI, n. 4.

Sancti Spiritus gratia humilitatis nostrae officio: see *Spiritus sancti gratia, humilitatis nostre officio.*

Sicut oculi servorum: XIX,52; XXI,65.

Sit in iudiciis equitatis singularis: see *Benedic, Domine, hos* (or *hunc*)....

Spiritus sancti (sancti Spiritus) gratia, humilitatis nostre officio: XIV,12; XVI,55; XIX,22; XIX,50; XXI,63; XXIII,93.

Spiritum sanctificationis, quaesumus Domine, Hludowico regi: IX,7.

Sta et retine amodo locum: XIV,8; XV,34; XVI,39; XVIII,25; XIX,36; XXI,48; XXII A,48; XXIII,77; XXIV,62; XXV,136; see also *In hoc regni solio te confirmet.*

Sub hoc anulo hortamur te: XIII,34.

Sub hoc baculo commendamus tibi gubernaculum regni: XIII,38.

Suscipe, Domine, preces et hostias: II,5; II, n. 4; XV,58.

Talique intentione repleri valeas: VIII,24.

Te invocamus, Domine sancte, Pater omnipotens: V,7; V, n. 12; XV,6; XVI,15; XXII A,22; XXIII,36; XXIV,37; XXV,97.

Tibi (Tibi semper) cum timore sit subditus: see *Benedic, Domine, hos* (or *hunc*)....

Tu summe retributor atque miserator: VI, n. 4.

Unde unxisti sacerdotes, reges et prophetas: see *Christe perunge hunc regem in regimen. Unde unxisti.*

Index of Bible Quotations and References

This index of Bible quotations and references lists the first appearance of a quotation or reference in a liturgical formula, along with the formula's incipit (see Vol. I: 45). For further instances of the quotation or reference, one must use the Index of Liturgical Formulas. If the reference is not to a liturgical formula, only the reference is given. The abbreviated names of the Bible's books are those of the modern Vulgate.

122: 1 — Ordo V,2, *Nubas in Christo obnupta nube caelesti.*
  Ordo XIX,52; Ordo XXI,65.
 144: 19 — Ordo VII,5, n. 30.
 149: 2 — Ordo XXV,4.
Prov. 8: 14 — Ordo VII,4, n. 25.
 21: 1 — Ordo VII,4, n. 28.
Sap. 4: 11 — Ordo VI,2, n. 7.
Is. 42: 7 — Ordo XIV,5, *Accipe virgam virtutis atque equitatis.*
Dan. 4: 14 — Ordo VII,4, n. 27.
1 Mach. 11: 13 — Ordo VII,15, n. 52.
Mt. 5: 28 — Ordo V,1, *Nubas in Christo obnupta nube caelesti.*
 9: 37–38 — Ordo VII,13, n. 40.
 19: 3–11 — Ordo XIX,55; Ordo XXI,67.
 21: 9 — Ordo XXV,4.
 28: 20 — Ordo VI,3, n. 15.
Mc. 10: 8–9 — Ordo VI,6, *Deus omnipotens, qui benedixit Adam.*
 10: 9 — Ordo V,4, *Accipe anulum, fidei et dilectionis signum.*
  Ordo VI,4, *Domine sancte, Pater omnipotens, eterne*
   Deus, qui potestate virtutis.
Io. 10: 9 — Ordo XIV,5, *Accipe virgam virtutis atque equitatis.*
 14: 6 — Ordo VII,39, *Quaesumus, omnipotens Deus, ut famulus.*
Act. 12: 5 — Ordo VI,3, n. 18.
Rom. 13: 1 — Ordo XVIII,10, n. 5.
  Ordo XIX,16; Ordo XXI,21.
 16: 27 — Ordo V,10, *Gloria et honore coronet te Dominus.*
Eph. 2: 14 — Ordo VII,4, n. 29.
 5: 22–33 — Ordo XIX,53; Ordo XXI,66.
 5: 31 — Ordo VI,6, *Deus omnipotens, qui benedixit Adam.*
1 Thess. 5: 8 — Ordo VI,4, *Domine sancte, Pater omnipotens, qui*
 potestate virtutis.
2 Tim. 4: 8 — Ordo VI,4, *Domine sancte, Pater omnipotens, qui potes-*
 tate virtutis.
Hebr. 1: 8–9 — Ordo XIV,5, *Accipe virgam virtutis atque equitatis.*
1 Petr. 2: 17 — Ordo XXV,4.
 3: 6 — Ordo VI,2, n. 13.
Apoc. 3: 7 — Ordo XIV,5, *Accipe virgam virtutis atque equitatis.*

Index of Manuscripts

This is both a complete list of all manuscripts edited, discussed, or cited and an index to those manuscripts. There are three sections: 1) identifiable lost manuscripts; 2) manuscripts that contain coronation texts, some of which were collated by other scholars (the apparatus always notes such instances); and 3) other miscellaneous manuscripts. References are first to edited manuscripts, then to volume and page or to ordo and siglum or note. Where a manuscript contains an ordo in this edition, I give a shortened form of the ordo's name in parentheses, and I refer only to that manuscript's siglum because the manuscript often appears repeatedly in the ordo's apparatus. On the other hand, if a description of an ordo's manuscript contains a reference to another manuscript, I refer to the ordo and siglum without the abbreviated form of the ordo's name. If former shelfmarks appear in the literature, they are cross-referenced to the current shelfmarks. I did not index references in the variants. Manuscripts that I have examined are marked with an asterisk (*), and those that I have collated only from microfilm, photographs, or photocopies are marked with a plus sign (+).

Lost Manuscripts

Arras, abbey of Saint-Vaast. Putative manuscript that was the source of Saint-Omer, Bibl. mun., MS 706. Ordo VII (Charles the Bald), lost MS *6*; Ordo VIII (Louis the Stammerer), lost MS *1*.

Beauvais, cathedral church. Manuscript containing Ordo VII (Charles the Bald), lost MS *2*; I: 111, 233; Ordo XVII B, ed. a_1.

— cathedral church. Manuscript containing Ordo XVII A (Philip I), lost MS *2*.

Clermont, abbey of Saint-Pierre of Chantoine. Manuscript containing Ordo XVII A (Philip I), lost MS *5*.

Liège, abbey of Saint-Laurent. Manuscript containing Ordo V (Judith), lost MS *1*; Ordo VI (Ermentrude), lost MS *1*; Ordo VII (Charles the Bald), lost MS *1*; and Ordo VIII (Louis the Stammerer), lost MS *2*.

Modena, Bibl. capitolare, MS II,2. Supposedly a copy of Vercelli, Archivio capitolare, MS 175. Ordo VII (Charles the Bald), lost MS *3*.

Paris, Bibl. nat., MS lat. 4761, formerly in the possession of Philibert de la Mare (or Marre). Ordo VIII (Louis the Stammerer), lost MS *2*.

— Chambre des comptes, register (*Mémorial*) *Croix.*
Fols. 25 and 27–29v or 30r: Ordo XX B (Translations of Ordo of Reims), lost MS *1*; Ordo XX B, n. 4, 14, 24, 52.

Fols. 199ff.: Ordo XXII A (Last Capetian Ordo), lost MS *4*; Ordo XXII B-C, II: 420; Ordo XXII B-C, n. 3.

— Chambre des comptes, register *Pater*. Fols. 163 and 164: Ordo XX B (Translations of Ordo of Reims), lost MS *2*.

— Chambre des comptes, register *Qui es in celis*. Fols. 27 and 29v: Ordo XX B (Translations of Ordo of Reims), lost MS *3*.

— Chambre des comptes, register *Noster²*. Fols. 250 and 252: Ordo XX B (Translations of Ordo of Reims), lost MS *4*.

— Chambre des comptes, register *Nouveau Croix* (or *Saint-Just* or *Saint-Just²*).

Fols. 30ff.: Ordo XX B (Translations of Ordo of Reims), lost MS *5*; Ordo XX B, n. 3.

Fols. 213ff.: Ordo XXII A (Last Capetian Ordo), lost MS *5*.

— Manuscripts from the royal library of Charles V and Charles VI. Ordo XX B (Translations of Ordo of Reims), lost MS *6*, n. 9; Ordo XXII A (Last Capetian Ordo), lost MS *3*; Ordo XXIII (Charles V), lost MSS *1*, *2*, and *3*.

— abbey of Saint-Germain-des Près. Putative manuscript from Fleury. Ordo VII (Charles the Bald), lost MS *7*.

Paris (?): Manuscript in the possession of Jacques Sirmond. Ordo XVII A (Philip I), lost MS *4*.

Reims, library of the abbey of Saint-Remi, MS 59, L. 8. Ordo XXII A (Last Capetian Ordo), lost MS *1*; Ordo XXIII, n. 131.

— library of the abbey of Saint-Remi. Manuscript dating from 1478. Ordo XXIII (Ordo of Charles V), lost MS *5*.

— library of the cathedral church. Manuscript of Julian of Toledo's *De comprobatione sextae aetatis*, and containing Ordo XVII A (Philip I), lost MS *1*.

— treasury of the cathedral church. Manuscript known as the *livre bleu*. Ordo XXII A (Last Capetian Ordo), lost MS *2*; II: 285; Ordo XXIII, nn. 16, 131; Ordo XXIV, II: 524–25, and n. 7.

— treasury of the cathedral church. Manuscript known as the *livre rouge*. Ordo XXIII (Charles V), lost MS *4*; II: 285–86; Ordo XXII A, n. 1; Ordo XXIV, II: 524, and nn. 5, 18; Ordo XXV, II: 555–56.

Reims (?), cathedral church (?). Manuscript entitled *Cy apres s'ensuit la venue du roy Charles VIIIᵉ de ce nom, a Reyms, pour recepvoir son sacre et couronnement*. Ordo XXV (Charles VIII), lost MS *1*.

Reims (?), municipal archives (?). Jehan Foulquart's treatise on the obligations of the *échevins* of Reims at a coronation. Ordo XXIV (Louis XI), lost MS *1*.

Saint-Denis. Manuscript deposited by Charles V in the abbey of Saint-

Denis on 7 May 1380. Ordo XXIII (Charles V), lost MS *3*; XX B, n. 9; Ordo XXIV, II: 524.

Saint-Thierry (monastery in Champagne). Manuscript of unknown content. Ordo XVII A, MS *G*, nn. 12 and 14, ed. *f₁*.

Tarragona (?). Manuscript belonging to Antonio Augustino. A copy of a manuscript belonging to Marc-Antoine Muret, which was copied from Modena, Bibl. cap., MS II,2. Ordo VII (Charles the Bald), lost MS *5*.

Toul. Manuscript belonging to André du Saussay, bishop of Toul. Ordo XVII A (Philip I), lost MS *3*.

Tours, archives of the abbey of Saint-Martin. Forged coronation oath of Hugh Capet. Ordo XVII A (Philip I), n. 16.

Unknown location. Manuscript belonging to Marc-Antoine Muret. Ordo VII (Charles the Bald), lost MS *4*.

Manuscripts of Coronation Texts

+   Angers, Bibl. mun., MS 80. Fols. 158v–159r: Ordo XII (Second Sacramentary of Tours), MS *A*.

      Aosta, Bibl. del Capitolo, MS 15. Eleventh-century queen's ordo: Ordo VI, n. 23.

+   Avignon, Museum Calvet, MS 1706. Fols. 15v, 17r–18r. Royal ordo in Jacques Cajetan's Roman ceremonial: I: 9–10.

+   Bamberg, Staatsbibl., MS Msc. Lit. 56. Fols. 146r–155v, 158r–160r: Ordo XVI (Cologne Dombibliothek 141), MS *B*.

+   Barcelona, Archivo de la Corona de Aragón, MS Ripoll 40.

      Fol. 4v: Ordo XI (Eudes), MS *B*.

      Fol. 29r: Ordo X (Carloman), MS *A*.

      Berlin, Deutsche Staatsbibl., MS Phillips 1667. Fols. 145v–146v. Ordo II (Sacramentary of Angoulême), MS *D*.

*   Besançon, Bibl. mun., MS 138. Fols. 190v–214v: Ordo XIX (Ordo of 1200), MS *B*; Ordo XXI, n. 36.

+   Brugge, Stedelijke Openbare Bibl., MS 318. Fols. 111v–121r: Ordo XV (Ratold Ordo), MS *O*.

      Brussels, Bibl. royale Albert Iᵉʳ, MS 389 = MS II 1013.

*   — Bibl. royale Albert Iᵉʳ, MS 2067–73. Fols. 109v–110v: Ordo XIV (Ordo of Eleven Forms), MS *E*; Ordo XXI, n. 49.

      — Bibl. royale Albert Iᵉʳ, MS 6439–6451. Ordo VII (Charles the Bald), MS *E*; Ordo VIII (Louis the Stammerer), MS *B*.

*   — Bibl. royale Albert Iᵉʳ, MS II 1013. Fols. 131r–142v: Ordo XV (Ratold Ordo), MS *N*.

+   Cambridge, Fitzwilliam Museum, MS J27. Fols. 77r–78v: Ordo I, n. 6;

*   — British Library, MS Egerton 931. Fols. 183v–203r: Ordo XXII A (Last Capetian Ordo), MS *D*; I: ix.

+   Milan, Bibl. del Capitolo Metropolitano, MS D 1–11. Fols. 103r–127v. Ordo XIV (Ordo of Eleven Forms), MS *B*; I: 40.

    — Bibl. del Capitolo Metropolitano, MS D 2–34. Lombard Ordo: Ordo XIV (Ordo of Eleven Forms), edd. *a* and *c*; I: 159.

*   Munich, Bayrische Staatsbibl., MS Clm. 6430. Fols. 50v–51v: Ordo IV (Benedictional of Freising), MS *A*.

*   — Bayrische Staatsbibl., MS Clm. 14510. Fols. 72v–74r: Ordo III (Sankt Emmeram), MS *A*.

+   Orléans, Bibl. mun., MS 144. Fols. 160r–168r: Ordo XV (Ratold Ordo), MS *L*.

*   Oxford, Bodleian Library, MS Ashmolean 842. Fols. 75r–76v: Ordo XX A (Ordo of Reims), MS *J*.

*   Paris, Arch. nat., KK 1442.

> Fols. 3r–8r, 9r–10v: Ordo XX B (Translations of Ordo of Reims), MS *N*; Ordo XXII A, II: 377–78.
>
> Fols. 11v–29r: Ordo XXII A (Last Capetian Ordo), MS *N*.
>
> Fols. 31r–32r: Ordo XVII B (Du Tillet's Translation of Philip I), MS *I*.
>
> Fol. 55r–v: (Louis XI's coronation oath), Ordo XXIV, n. 21.
>
> Fols. 56r–114r: Ordo XXV (Charles VIII), MS *F*.

*   — Arch. nat., P 2288.

> Pp. 706–12, 714–15: Ordo XX B (Translations of Ordo of Reims), MS O_1; Ordo XXIIA, II: 377–78.
>
> Pp. 716–25: Ordo XX B (Translations of Ordo of Reims), MS O_2; II: 378
>
> Pp. 1290–1317: Ordo XXII A (Last Capetian Ordo), MS *O*; Ordo XXIV, n. 30.

*   — Archives de la Compagnie des prêtres de Saint-Sulpice, MS 1928. Fols. 57r–98r: Ordo XXIII (Charles V), MS *F*; I: 12, n. 21; Ordo XXV, n. 24.

*   — Bibl. de l'Arsenal, MS 4227.

> Fols. 2r–4r, 5r–6r: Ordo XX B (Translations of Ordo of Reims), MS *K*; XXIIA, II: 377–78.
>
> Fols. 6v–19r: Ordo XXII A (Last Capetian Ordo), MS *L*.
>
> Fols. 20v–21v: Ordo XVII B (Du Tillet's Translation of Philip I), MS *F*; Ordo XX B, n. 18.
>
> Fol. 38r: (Louis XI's coronation oath), Ordo XXIV, n. 21.
>
> Fols. 39r–84v: Ordo XXV (Charles VIII), MS *D*.

*   — Bibl. de l'Arsenal, 378 H.F. = MS 4227.

*   — Bibl. nat., MS fran. 994. No. 5, pp. 93–100: Ordo XXII B-C (Translations of Last Capetian Ordo), MS *A*.

*   — Bibl. nat., MS fran. 2833. Fols. 184r–185v: Ordo XX B (Translations of Ordo of Reims), MS *F*.

*   — Bibl. nat., MS fran. 2848.
      Fols. 164v–166v: Ordo XVII B (Du Tillet's Translation of Philip I), MS *A*; Ordo XVII A, n. 1.
      Fols. 168r–178r: Ordo XXII B-C (Du Tillet's Translation of the Last Capetian Ordo), MS *B*.

*   — Bibl. nat., MS fran. 4596. Fols. 124v–129v: Ordo XX B (Translations of Ordo of Reims), MS *G*.

*   — Bibl. nat., MS fran. 5784. Fols. 45r–47v: Ordo XVII B (Du Tillet's Translation of Philip I), MS *D*; Ordo XVII A, n. 1.

*   — Bibl. nat., MS fran. 7310^3 = MS fran. 994.

*   — Bibl. nat., MS fran. 8334. Fols. 47r–70v: Ordo XXIV (Louis XI), MS *A*.

   — Bibl. nat., MS fran. 9475 = MS fran. 4596.

*   — Bibl. nat., MS fran. 14371.
      Fols. 318r–324v: Ordo XXII A (Last Capetian Ordo), MS G_1.
      Fol. 356r (Last Capetian Ordo), MS G_2.

*   — Bibl. nat., MS fran. 16600. Fols. 316r–321r: Ordo XX B (Translations of Ordo of Reims), MS *L*.

*   — Bibl. nat., MS nouv. acq. fran. 681. Fols. 27r–29r. Ordo XVII A (Philip I), MS *I*.

*   — Bibl. nat., MS nouv. acq. fran. 7122. Fol. 174r–v: Ordo XVII A (Philip I), MS *C*.

*   — Bibl. nat., MS nouv. acq. fran. 7232.
      Fols. 1r–4v, 5v–6v: Ordo XX B (Translations of Ordo of Reims), MS *H*; Ordo XXII A, II: 377–78.
      Fols. 7v–21v: Ordo XXII A (Last Capetian Ordo), MS *J*.
      Fol. 23r–v: Ordo XVII A (Du Tillet's Translation of Philip I), MS *E*; Ordo XX B, n. 18.
      Fol. 45r: (Louis XI's coronation oath), Ordo XXIV, n. 21.
      Fols. 47r–89v: Ordo XXV (Charles VIII), MS *B*.

+   — Bibl. nat., MS nouv. acq. fran. 7336.
      Fols. 45r–47r: Ordo XVII A (Philip I), MS G_1.
      Fols. 47r–48r: Ordo XVII A (copy of an extract from the lost manuscript in the monastery of Saint-Thierry), n. 12.
      Fols. 48v–49r: Ordo XVII A (Philip I), MS G_2.

*   — Bibl. nat., MS nouv. acq. fran. 7938. Fols. 117r–127r: Ordo XX B (Translations of Ordo of Reims), MS *P*.

* — Bibl. nat., MS lat. 12711. Fols. 142r–143v: Ordo VII (Charles the Bald), MS *F*; Ordo VIII, nn. 4, 7.

+ — Bibl. nat., MS lat. 12765. Pp. 307–311: Ordo XVII A (Philip I), MS *E*.

* — Bibl. nat., MS lat. 12814. Fols. 27r–30v: Ordo XX B (Translations of Ordo of Reims), MS *A*.

* — Bibl. nat., MS lat. 13313. Fols. 188r–198v: Ordo XV (Ratold Ordo), MS *B*; Ordo XVI, n. 6.

* — Bibl. nat., MS lat. 13314. Fols. 3r–44r: Ordo XXIII (Charles V), MS *G*; I: 14; Ordo XXV, n. 24.

* — Bibl. nat., MS lat. 13315. Fols. 101r–110r: Ordo XV (Ratold Ordo), MS *D*.

* — Bibl. nat., MS lat. 14192. Fols. 73r–81r, 82r–83r: Ordo XV (Ratold Ordo), MS *C*; I: 14; Ordo XXII B-C, n. 21.

* — Bibl. nat., MS lat. 17333. Pp. 107–114: Ordo XIII (Erdmann Ordo), MS *B*.

* — Bibl. nat., MS lat. 17335. Fols. 64r–80r: Ordo XV (Ratold Ordo), MS *P*.

* — Bibl. nat., MS nouv. acq. lat. 1202. Fols. 121r–143v: Ordo XXII A (Last Capetian Ordo), MS *A*.

* — Bibl. nat., MS Reg. 4654.3 = MS lat. 4375.

* — Bibl. Sainte-Geneviève, MS 148. Fols. 84v–92r: Ordo XVIII (Ordo of Saint-Bertin), MS *B*.

* Reims, Bibl. mun., MS 214. Fols. 3v, 219r, 221v–222r: Ordo IX (Sacramentary of Saint-Thierry), MS *A*.

* — Bibl. mun., MS 328. Fols. 70v–73r: Ordo XX A (Ordo of Reims), MS *A*.

* — Bibl. mun., MS 329. Fols. 3v–5v: Ordo XX A (Ordo of Reims), MS *B*.

* — Bibl. mun., MS 330. Fols. 104v–106v: Ordo XX A (Ordo of Reims), MS *C*.

* — Bibl. mun., MS 342. Fols. 69v–80r: Ordo XV (Ratold Ordo), MS *G*; II: 285; Ordo XX A, n. 1; Ordo XXI, n. 47, II: 341, 343; Ordo XXIII, n. 3.

* — Bibl. mun., MS 343. Fols. 126r–149r: Ordo XIX (Ordo of 1200), MS *A*; II: 285; Ordo XXI, nn. 6, 33, 36, II: 341; Ordo XXII A, n. 91; Ordo XXIII, n. 3.

* — Bibl. mun., MS 1485 (nouv. fonds). No. 3, pp. 1–35: Ordo XXIII (Charles V), MS *L*; Ordo XXIIA, n. 57; Ordo XXIV, n. 7.

* — Bibl. mun., MS 1489 (nouv. fonds).
No. 1, pp. 1–4: Ordo XVII A (Philip I), MS *H*.

+   Vatican City, Bibl. Apos. Vat., MS Barb. lat. 631. Fols. 155v–166r.
      Ordo XIV (Ordo of Eleven Forms), MS *D*; I: 40; Ordo XXI, n. 49.

*   — Bibl. Apos. Vat., MS Chigi C VI 182. Fols. 72r–85v: Ordo XXII A
      (Last Capetian Ordo), MS *C*; Ordo XXIII, n. 17.

*   — Bibl. Apos. Vat., MS Chisianus 468 = MS Chigi C VI 182.

*   — Bibl. Apos. Vat., MS lat. 4733. Fols. 61r–67r: Ordo XXII A (Last
      Capetian Ordo), MS *E*.

+   — Bibl. Apos. Vat., MS lat. 4982. Fols. 144r–145v: Ordo VII,
      (Charles the Bald), MS *C*; I: 15, 111.

+   — Bibl. Apos. Vat., MS lat. 13151. Fols. 52r–59v. Ordo XIV (Ordo
      of Eleven Forms), MS *C*.

*   — Bibl. Apos. Vat., MS Ottoboniani 811. Fols. 113r–114r: Ordo
      XVII A (Philip I), MS *A*; I: 14, 233.

*   — Bibl. Apos. Vat., MS Reg. lat. 291. Fols. 120v–121v: Ordo VII
      (Charles the Bald), MS *A*; I: 15, 111.

      — Bibl. Apos. Vat., MS Reg. lat. 316. Fol. 214r–v: Ordo II (Sacra-
      mentary of Angoulême), MS *A*.

      — Bibl. Apos. Vat., MS Reg. lat. 421. Fol. 25v (Carolingian coro-
      nation ordo): Ordo VI, n. 4.

*   — Bibl. Apos. Vat., MS Reg. lat. 574. Fols. 17r–19r: Ordo XX A
      (Ordo of Reims), MS *H*; I: 14.

+   Wolfenbüttel, Herzog August Bibl., MS Guelf 1 Gud. lat. 20. Fols.
      72v–73r: Ordo XX A (Ordo of Reims), MS *D*.

+   Wrocław, Bibl. Uniwersytecka, MS I F 380. Fols. 118r–126v: Ordo
      XV (Ratold Ordo), MS *Q*.

Other Manuscripts

      Angers, Bibl. mun., MS 102. Fols. 158ff.: royal mass. Ordo II, n. 1.

+   Baltimore, Walters Art Gallery, MS W. 28. Fol. 2r (sacramentary
      from Reims): I: 10; Ordo XIII, n. 6.

      Brussels, Bibl. royale, MS 1814–16. Fol. 186r–v (royal mass): Ordo
      II, n. 1.

      Leiden, Bibl. Univ., MS Voss. Lat. Fol. 31 (Lambert of Saint-Omer's
      Liber floridus): XX A, n. 6.

      Metz, Bibl. mun., MS 343. Fols. 159ff. (ninth-century sacramen-
      tary): Ordo II, n. 1.

+   Paris, Arch. nat., X¹ᵃ 9318, nos. 152–53 (Louis XI's coronation
      oath): Ordo XXIV, n. 21.

*   — Bibl. de l'Arsenal, MS 2002. Fols. 19v–24v (Jean Golein's trans-
      lation of William Durandus): I: 11, n. 18.

      — Bibl. nat., MS Barrois 73. (Recovered portion of lost MS lat.
      4761): Ordo VIII (Louis the Stammerer), lost MS *3*.

Plates

The earliest surviving manuscript containing a coronation text is the Sacramentary of Gellone (Ordo I, MS *A*), but I decided against including it here because there are several photographs of the manuscript in the edition by Dom Antoine Dumas (Ordo I, ed. *a*). Unfortunately, I did not always measure the manuscripts when I examined them. If I did, I state both the size of the page and the size of the text on that page, but if I did not, I note my source for the measurements, if any. I place in parentheses after the measurements the size of the plate as an approximate percentage of the full size.

Plate 1: Paris, Bibl. nat., MS lat. 816, fol. 168v (Ordo II, MS *C*). Sacramentary of Angoulême, the earliest manuscript that specifically mentions a coronation. Fol. 168v illustrates damage to the manuscript (see Ordo II, n. 10). Photograph Bibliothèque nationale de France, reproduced by permission.

Plate 2: Munich, Bayerische Staatsbibl., MS Clm. 14510, fol. 73r (Ordo III, MS *A*). Collection of Sankt Emmeram. Fol. 73r contains the earliest surviving example of the prayer *Deus, qui victrices Moysi* (see the Introduction to Ordo III). Photograph Bayerische Staatsbibliothek, reproduced by permission.

Plate 3: Munich, Bayerische Staatsbibl., MS Clm. 6430, fol. 50v (Ordo IV, MS *C*). Benedictional of Freising. Fol. 50v contains the first surviving appearance of the unction of hands in the coronation ceremony. Photograph Bayerische Staatsbibliothek, reproduced by permission.

Plate 4: Reims, Bibl. mun., MS 214, fol. 3v (Ordo IX, MS *A*). 297 × 260 mm (measurement from Leroquais, *Sacramentaires*) (text ca. 186 × 180 mm) (44%). The formula of Louis the Stammerer in the Sacramentary of Saint-Thierry. Photograph Institut de Recherche et d'Histoire des Textes, reproduced by permission of the Bibliothèque municipale de Reims.

Plate 5: Barcelona, Archivo de la Corona de Aragón, MS Ripoll 40, fol. 29r (Ordo X, MS *A*). *Petitio* and *promissio* of Carloman in the left column. Photograph Archivo de la Corona de Aragón, reproduced by permission.

Plate 6: Barcelona, Archivo de la Corona de Aragón, MS Ripoll 40, fol. 4v (Ordo XI, MS *B*). The oath of Eudes, with the curious monogram (see Ordo XI, n. 10). Photograph Archivo de la Corona de Aragón, reproduced by permission.

Plate 7: Saint Petersburg, National Library of Russia at Saint Petersburg, MS lat. Q.v.I, No. 35, fol. 85r (Ordo XIII, MS *A*). Pontifical from Sens. Title page of the Erdmann Ordo. Photograph Institut de Recherche et d'Histoire des Textes, reproduced by permission of the National Library of Russia at Saint Petersburg.

Plate 8: Brussels, Bibl. roy. Albert Iᵉʳ, MS 2067–73, fol. 109v (Ordo XIV, MS *E*). Beginning of the only surviving manuscript of the complete Ordo of Eleven Forms. Photograph copyright Bibliothèque royale Albert Iᵉʳ, Brussels, reproduced by permission.

Plate 9: Reims, Bibl. mun., MS 342, fol. 70r (Ordo XV, MS *G*). 320 × 235 mm (measurement from Leroquais, *Pontificaux*) (text ca. 199 × 144 mm) (47%). Marginal addition in the Ratold Ordo, moving the *tria precepta* to the beginning of the French ceremony. Photograph Institut de Recherche et d'Histoire des Textes, reproduced by permission of the Bibliothèque municipale de Reims.

Plate 10: Paris, Bibl. nat., MS lat. 1223, fol. 186r (Ordo XV, MS *M*). 238 × 152 mm (measurement from Leroquais, *Pontificaux*) (text ca. 185 × 105 mm) (73%). A page showing the shaky hand of an old or cold scribe. The former is more likely because the script is what one would expect in a manuscript copied half a century earlier. Photograph Bibliothèque nationale de France, reproduced by permission.

Plate 11: Vatican City, Bibl. Apos. Vat., MS Ottob. 811, fol. 113v (Ordo XVII A, MS *A*). 211 × 147 mm (text 165 × 98 mm) (74%). Gervais of Reims's list of participants at the coronation of Philip I, with a blank space for the abbot of Landevennec's name (see Ordo XVII A, n. 21). Photograph © Biblioteca Apostolica Vaticana, reproduced by permission.

Plate 12: Saint-Omer, Bibl. mun., MS 98, fol. 67r (Ordo XVIII, MS *A*). 276 × 180 mm (measurement from Leroquais, *Pontificaux*) (text ca. 195 × 116 mm) (65% — part of the top margin is cut off in the photograph). Odd scribal error providing for anointing of the king's feet in the Ordo of Saint-Bertin, no. 13. Photograph reproduced by permission of the Bibliothèque municipale de Saint-Omer.

Plate 13: Reims, Bibl. mun., MS 343, fol. 132v (Ordo XIX, MS *A*). 202 × 146 mm (measurement from Leroquais, *Pontificaux*) (text ca. 152 × 95 mm) (79%). Anointing formulas in the Ordo of 1200. Fol. 132v is typical of this manuscript's appearance. Photograph Institut de Recherche et d'Histoire des Textes, reproduced by permission of the Bibliothèque municipale de Reims.

Plate 14: Besançon, Bibl. mun., MS 138, fol. 190v (Ordo XIX, MS *B*). 323 ×

225 mm (measurement from Leroquais, *Pontificaux*) (text ca. 222 ×
145 mm) (50%). Decorated initial in the Ordo of 1200 (see Ordo XIX,
n. 4). Photograph Institut de Recherche et d'Histoire des Textes,
reproduced by permission of the Bibliothèque municipale de Besançon.

Plate 15: Reims, Bibl. mun., MS 328, fol. 70v (Ordo , MS XXA, MS *A*). 175
× 127 mm (text 135 × 95 mm) (measurements from Chevalier, *Sacramentaire*) (68%). First page of the oldest surviving copy of the Ordo
of Reims. Photograph Institut de Recherche et d'Histoire des Textes,
reproduced by permission of the Bibliothèque municipale de Reims.

Plate 16: Paris, Bibl. nat., MS lat. 12814, fol. 27r (Ordo XXB, MS *A*). 256 ×
182 mm (text 180 × 124 mm) (58%). First page of the French translation of Ordo of Reims from the only surviving *liber memorialis* (with
the long marginal note and the reference to *Croix* at the top of the
page). Photograph Bibliothèque nationale de France, reproduced by
permission.

Plate 17: Paris, Bibl. nat., MS 8886, fol. 58r (Ordo XXB, MS *C*). 390 × 295
mm (text 260 × 185 mm) (measurements by Lescuyer in Sclafer and
Lafitte, *Catalogue général des manuscrits latins*) (42% — part of
the top, bottom, and right margins are cut off in the photograph).
Beginning of the official French translation of the Ordo of Reims,
with a miniature that depicts the enthroned king (see Ordo XXB, n.
24). This miniature is the source for the miniature in Plate 19. Photograph Bibliothèque nationale de France, reproduced by permission.

Plate 18: Paris, Bibl. nat., MS lat. 8886, fol. 61r (Ordo XXB, MS *C*). 390 ×
295 mm (text 260 × 185 mm) (measurements by Lescuyer in Sclafer
and Lafitte, *Catalogue général des manuscrits latins*) (42% — part
of the top, bottom, and right margins are cut off in the photograph).
Beginning of the queen's ordo, with a miniature that depicts the
bestowal of the scepter (see Ordo XXB, n. 47). This miniature is the
source of the miniature in Plate 20. Photograph Bibliothèque
nationale de France, reproduced by permission.

Plate 19: Paris, Bibl. nat., MS Dupuy 365, fol. 22r (Ordo XXB, MS *E*). 259
× 192 mm (text 154 × 115 mm) (58%). Beginning of the official French
translation of the Ordo of Reims, with a miniature that depicts the
enthroned king (see Ordo XXB, n. 24). Photograph Bibliothèque
nationale de France, reproduced by permission.

Plate 20: Paris, Bibl. nat., MS Dupuy 365, fol. 25v (Ordo XXB, MS *E*). 259
× 192 mm (text 154 × 115 mm) (58%). Beginning of the queen's ordo,
with a miniature that depicts the bestowal of the scepter (see Ordo

XX B, n. 47). Photograph Bibliothèque nationale de France, reproduced by permission.

Plate 21: Paris, Bibl. nat., MS lat. 1246, fol. 15v (Ordo XXI, MS *A*). 215 × 150 mm (measurements from Bonne, "The Manuscript of the Ordo of 1250") (text ca. 138 × 90 mm) (75%). Evidence (in no. 25) of interim manuscript (see Ordo XXI, n. 17). Photograph Bibliothèque nationale de France, reproduced by permission.

Plate 22: Paris, Bibl. nat., MS nouv. acq. lat. 1202, fol. 126r (Ordo XXII A, MS *A*). 283 × 180 mm (text 171 × 115 mm) (61%). Sample page from the oldest surviving manuscript of the Last Capetian Ordo with the scribe's marginal addition (see Ordo XXII A, n. 43). Photograph Bibliothèque nationale de France, reproduced by permission.

Plate 23: Urbana, Univ. of Illinois Library, MS "Ordo ad consecrandum et coronandum regem et reginam Franciae," fol. 2r (Ordo XXII A, MS *B*). 262 × 170 mm (text ca. 165 × 117 mm) (72% — part of the top, bottom, and right margins are cut off in the photograph). Historiated initial at beginning of the litany that depicts the king kneeling while the archbishop and the clergy chant the litany. Photograph University of Illinois Library, reproduced by permission.

Plate 24: Vatican City, Bibl. Apos. Vat., MS Chigi C VI 182, fol. 83v (Ordo XXII A, MS *C*). 229 × 213 mm (text ca. 202 × 134 mm) (54%). Beginning of the queen's ordo with illustration in the bottom margin (see Ordo XXII A, n. 87). Photograph © Biblioteca Apostolica Vaticana, reproduced by permission.

Plate 25: London, The British Library, MS Egerton 931, fol. 187r (Ordo XXII A, MS *D*). Musical notation for the antiphon, *Confortare et esto vir* (see Ordo XXII A, n. 39). This is fairly typical musical notation for manuscripts of coronation ordines. Photograph The British Library, reproduced by permission of The British Library.

Plate 26: Paris, Bibl. nat., MS fran. 14371, fol. 320r (Ordo XXII A, MS G_1). 168 x 119 mm (text 124 × 84 mm) (100%). Beginning of the prayer of consecration in the smallest of all manuscripts containing a coronation ordo (see the Introduction to Ordo XXII A, II: 369–70). It is the only surviving manuscript copied directly from the ordo in *Croix*. Photograph Bibliothèque nationale de France, reproduced by permission.

Plate 27: Paris, Bibl. nat., MS fran. 994, p. 100 (Ordo XXII B-C, MS *A*). 344 × 262 mm (text ca. 227 × 161 mm) (46%). Sample page (containing the complete ordo for the coronation of a queen) from the early French translation of the Last Capetian Ordo. Photograph Bibliothèque nationale de France, reproduced by permission.

Plate 28: London, The British Library, MS Tiberius B.viii, fol. 46v (Ordo XXIII, MS *A*). 278 × 192 mm (text ca. 176 × 116 mm) (56%). Correction to the coronation oath of Charles V (see Ordo XXIII, n. 47). The miniature depicts the king taking the oath. Photograph The British Library, reproduced by permission of The British Library.

Plate 29: Paris, Arch. de la Compagnie des prêtres de Saint-Sulpice, MS 1928, fol. 60r (Ordo XXIII, MS *F*). Late medieval marginal additions to a copy of the *livre rouge* (see Ordo XXIII, nn. 38–39, 41). Photograph Institut de Recherche et d'Histoire des Textes, reproduced by permission of the Archives de la Compagnie des prêtres de Saint-Sulpice.

Plate 30: Paris, Arch. de la Compagnie des prêtres de Saint-Sulpice, MS 1928, fol. 89r (Ordo XXIII, MS *F*). The name "Ludovico" added above the line in *Munera quesumus* (see Ordo XXIII, n. 137). Photograph Institut de Recherche et d'Histoire des Textes, reproduced by permission of the Archives de la Compagnie des prêtres de Saint-Sulpice.

Plate 31: Paris, Bibl. nat., MS fran. 8334, fol. 47v (Ordo XXIV, MS *A*). 295 × 225 mm (text 226 × 140 mm) (52%). Typical page from the only complete copy of Foulquart's treatise. Photograph Bibliothèque nationale de France, reproduced by permission.

Plate 32: Paris, Bibl. nat., MS nouv. acq. fran. 7232, fol. 47r. 345 × 214 mm (text 245 × 145 mm) (50%). Sample page from a manuscript that preserves the contents of several lost manuscripts (here the first page of Ordo XXV, MS *B*). Photograph Bibliothèque nationale de France, reproduced by permission.

Plate 33: Paris, Bibl. nat., Rés. Li^{25}.1, fol. 2r (Ordo XXIII, ed. *a*). First page of the first printed edition of any French coronation ordo. Photograph Bibliothèque nationale de France, reproduced by permission.

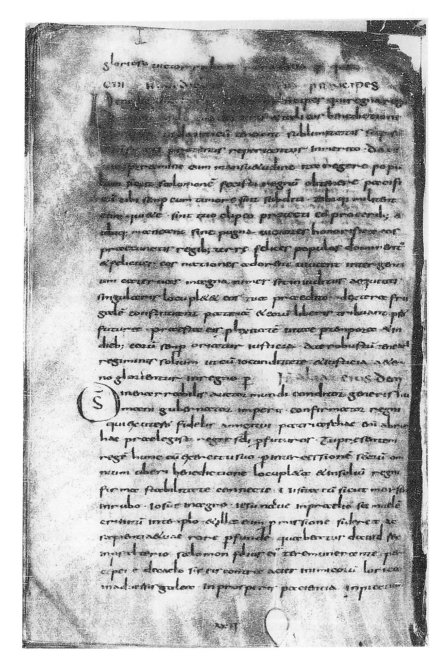

Plate 1: Paris, Bibl. nat., MS lat. 816, fol. 168v

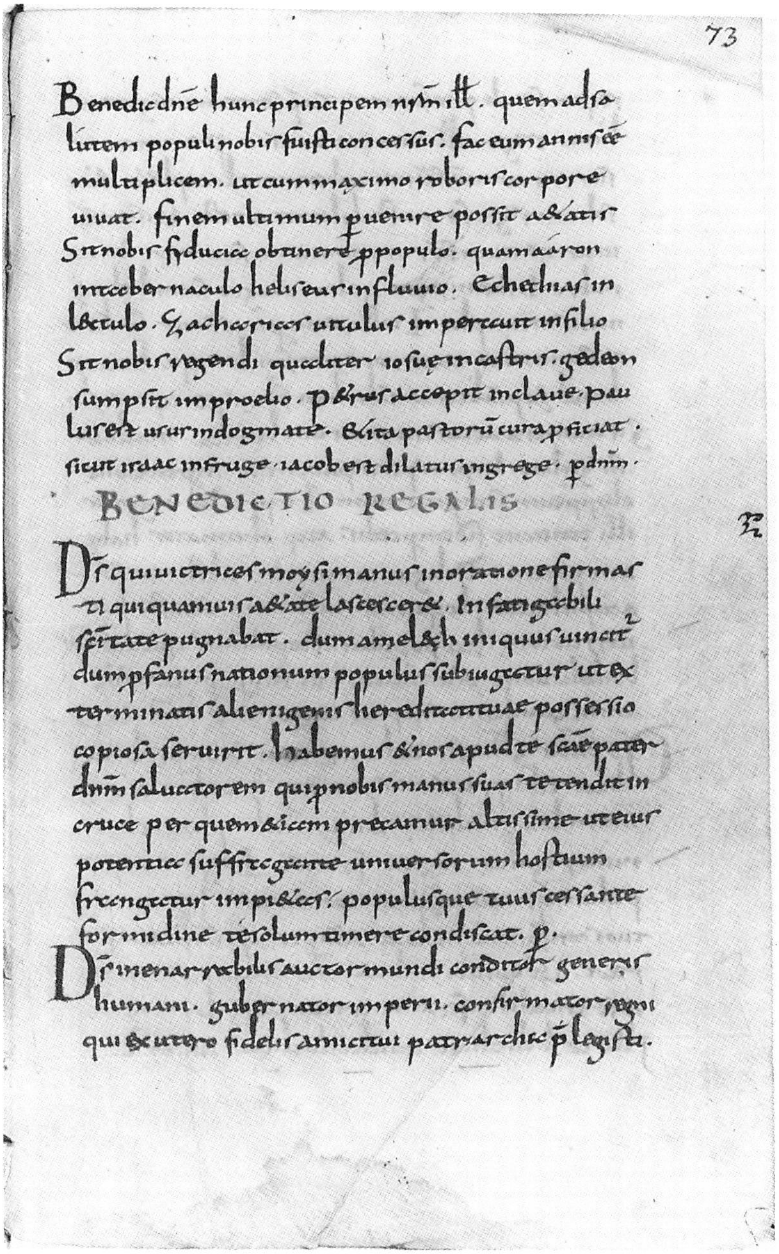

73

Benedic dñe hunc principem nr̄m ill. quem ad sa
lutem populi nobis fui sti concessus. fac eum animis ē
multiplicem. ut cum maximo roboris corpore
uiuat. finem ultimum puenire possit adᵃꞇꞃ
Sr̄ nobis fiduciae obtinere ꝑ populo. quam aaron
in tabernaculo helise us in fluuio. Echelias in
lectulo. zacharias uitulus impetrauit in filio
Sr̄ nobis regendi qualiter iosue in castris. gedeon
sumpsit in proelio. petrus accepit in claue. pau
lus ē usus in dogmate. & ita pastorū cura pficiat.
sicut isaac in fruge iacob est dilatus in grege. p dñm.

BENEDICTIO REGALIS

Dr̄ qui uictrices moysi manus in oratione firmas
ti qui quamuis aetate lassesceret. infatigabili
feritate pugnabat. dum amalech iniquus uinceretur
dum pfanus nationum populus subiugetur ut ex
terminatis alienigenis hereditatiuae possessio
copiosa seruiret. habemus & nos apud te sc̄e pater
dñm saluatorem qui p nobis manus suas tetendit in
cruce per quem &i cem precamur altissime ut eius
potentiae suffragante uniuersorum hostium
frangetur impietas. populusque tuus cessante
formidine te solum timere condiscat. p.

Dr̄ inenarrabilis auctor mundi conditor generis
humani. gubernator imperii. confirmator regni
qui & utero fidelis amici tui patriarchae p legisti.

Plate 2: Munich, Bayerische Staatsbibl., MS Clm. 14510, fol. 73r

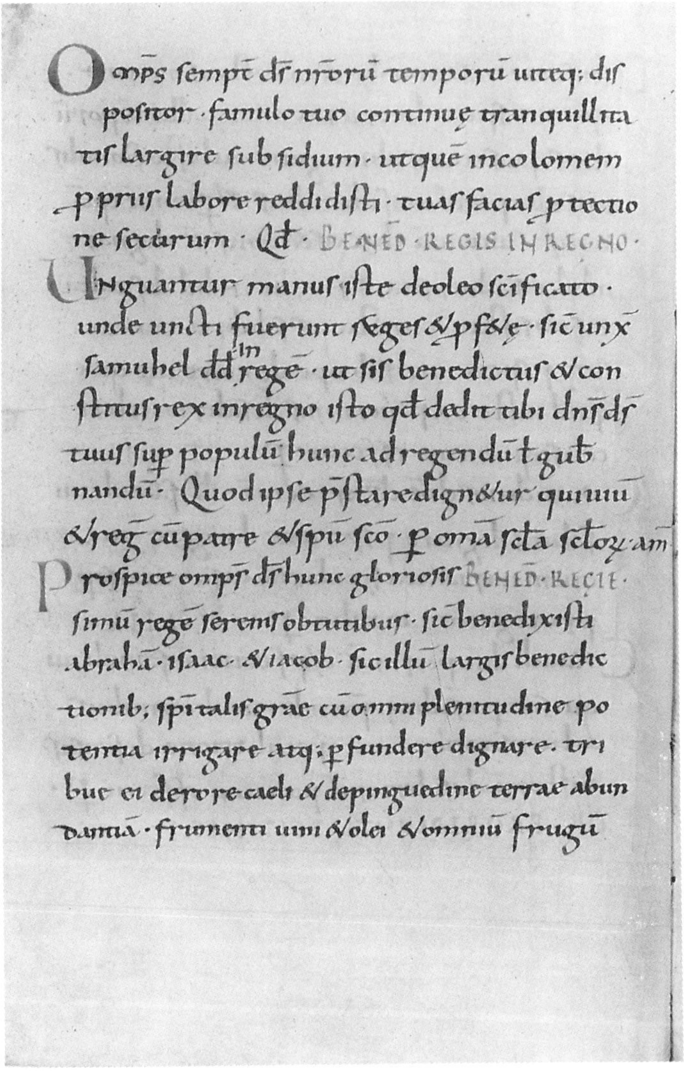

Omps sempt dr nroru temporu uteq; dis
positor · famulo tuo continue tranquillita
tis largire sub sidium · utque incolomem
pprns labore reddidisti · tuas facias ptectio
ne secarum · Qd · BENED · REGIS IN REGNO ·
Unguantur manus iste deoleo scificato ·
unde uncti fuerunt reges & pfete · sic unx
samuhel dd rege in · ut sis benedictus & con
stitus rex inregno isto qd dedit tibi dns ds
tuus sup populu hunc ad regendu t gub
nandu · Quod ipse pstare dignetur qui uiu
& reg cu patre & spu sco · p oma scla scloz am
Prospice omps ds hunc gloriosis BENED · REGIE ·
simu rege serens obtantibus · sic benedixisti
abraha · isaac · & iacob · sic illu largiris benedic
tionib; spritalis grae cu omm plenitudine po
tentia irrigare atq; pfundere dignare · tri
bue ei derore caeli & depinguedine terrae abun
dantia · frumenti uini & olei & omniu frugu

Plate 3: Munich, Bayerische Staatsbibl., MS Clm. 6430, fol. 50v

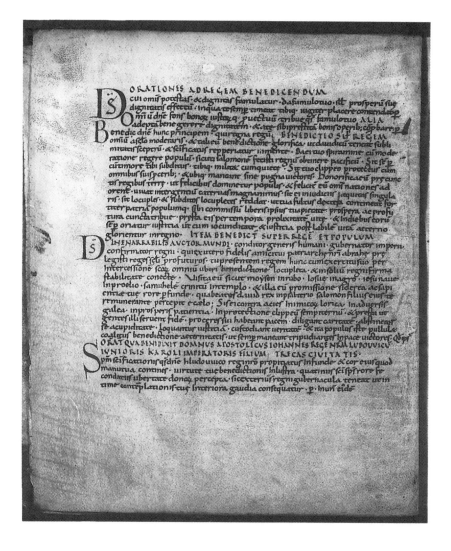

Plate 4: Reims, Bibl. mun., MS 214, fol. 3v

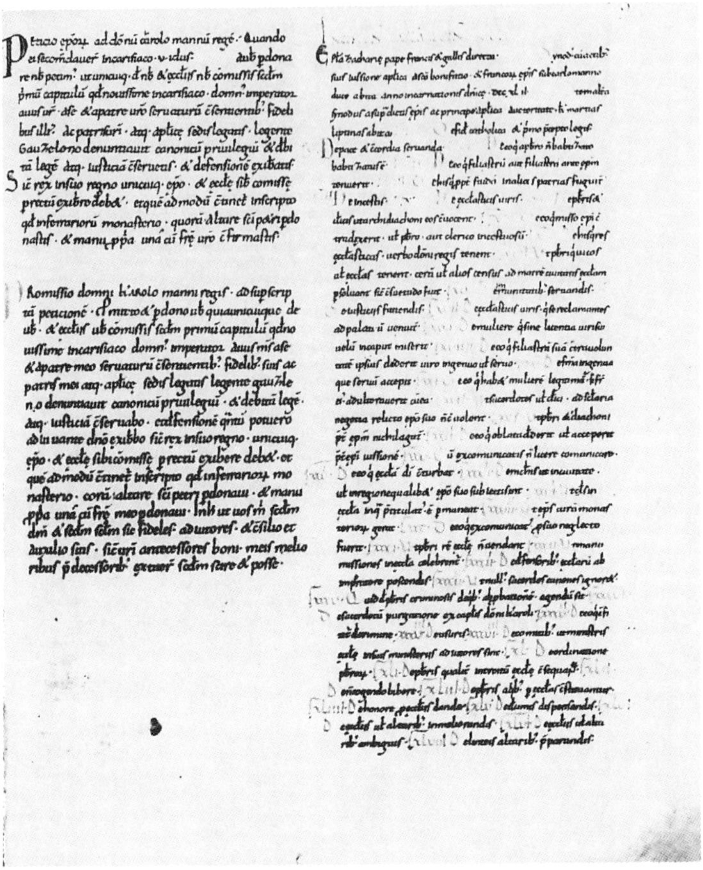

Plate 5: Barcelona, Arch. de la Corona de Aragón, MS Ripoll 40, fol. 29r

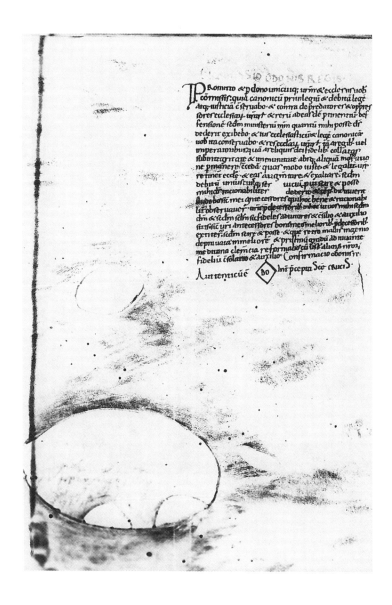

Plate 6: Barcelona, Arch. de la Corona de Aragón, MS Ripoll 40, fol. 4v

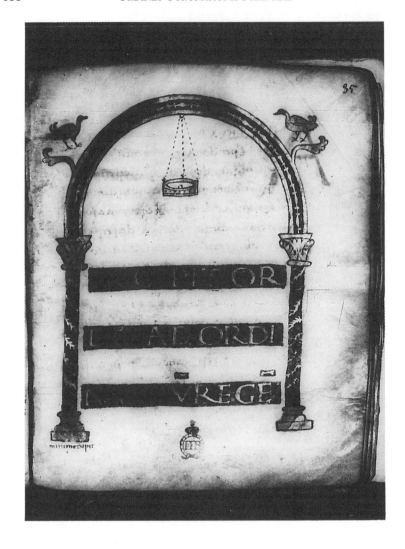

Plate 7: St. Petersburg, Nat. Lib. of Russia, MS lat. Q.v.I, No. 35, fol. 85r

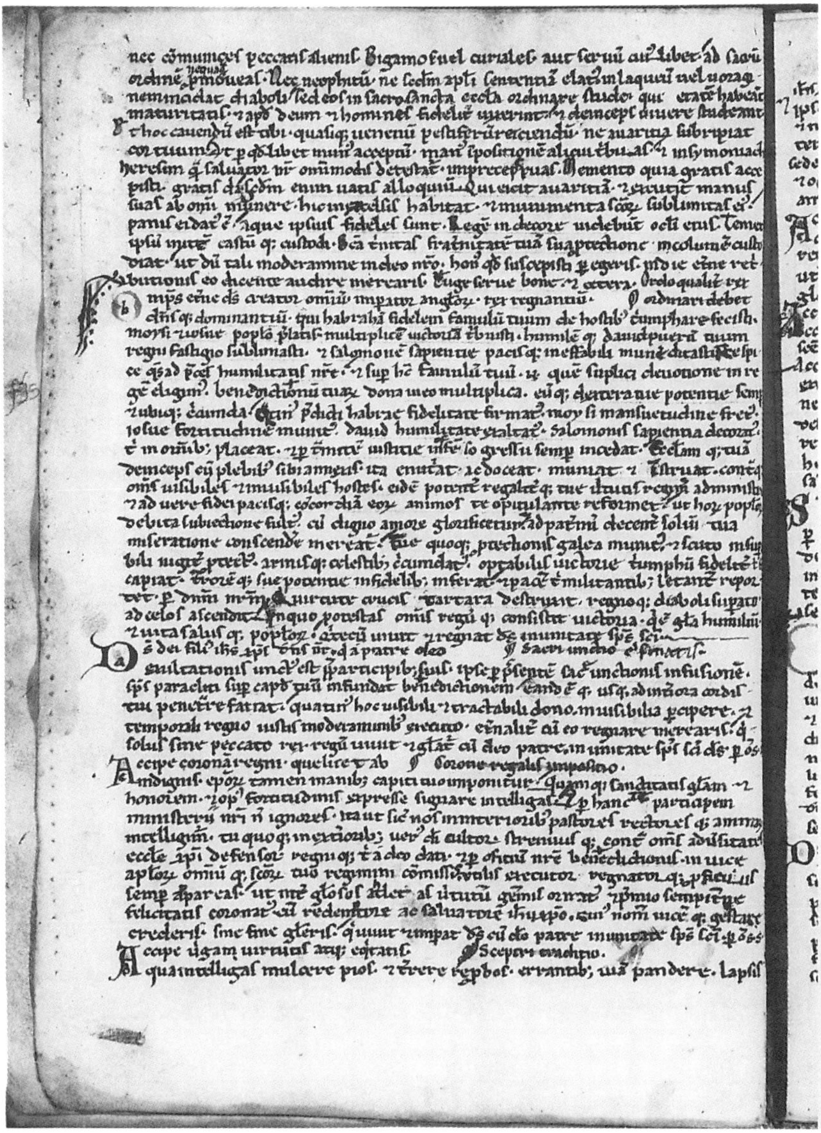

Plate 8: Brussels, Bibl. roy. Albert Ier, MS 2067–73, fol. 109v

70.

potuero adiuuante dño exhibebo. ficut rex
infuo regno unicuiq; epo æ ecctie fibi com
miffe prectum exibere debet. Deinde allo
quantur duo epi poptm inecctia. inqrentef
eorum uoluntate. æ fi concordef fuerint a
gant deo grãf dicentef. Te dm laudam. et
duo epi accipiant eu pman. æ deducant
ante altare. æ pfternet fe ufq; infine te dm
laud. Inuocatio fup R e ʒ e ɳ.

Te inuocamuf dñe fce pat ompf eterne
deuf. ut hunc famulum tuu. ɲ. que
tuæ diuinæ difpenfationif. prudentia inp
mordio plafmatu. ufq; inhc pfente diem
iuuenili flore letante crefcere conceffifti.
eum tuæ pietatif dono ditatu plenuq; grã
uertatif de die indie corã dõ æ hominib;
ad meliora femp pficere faciaf. ut fummi

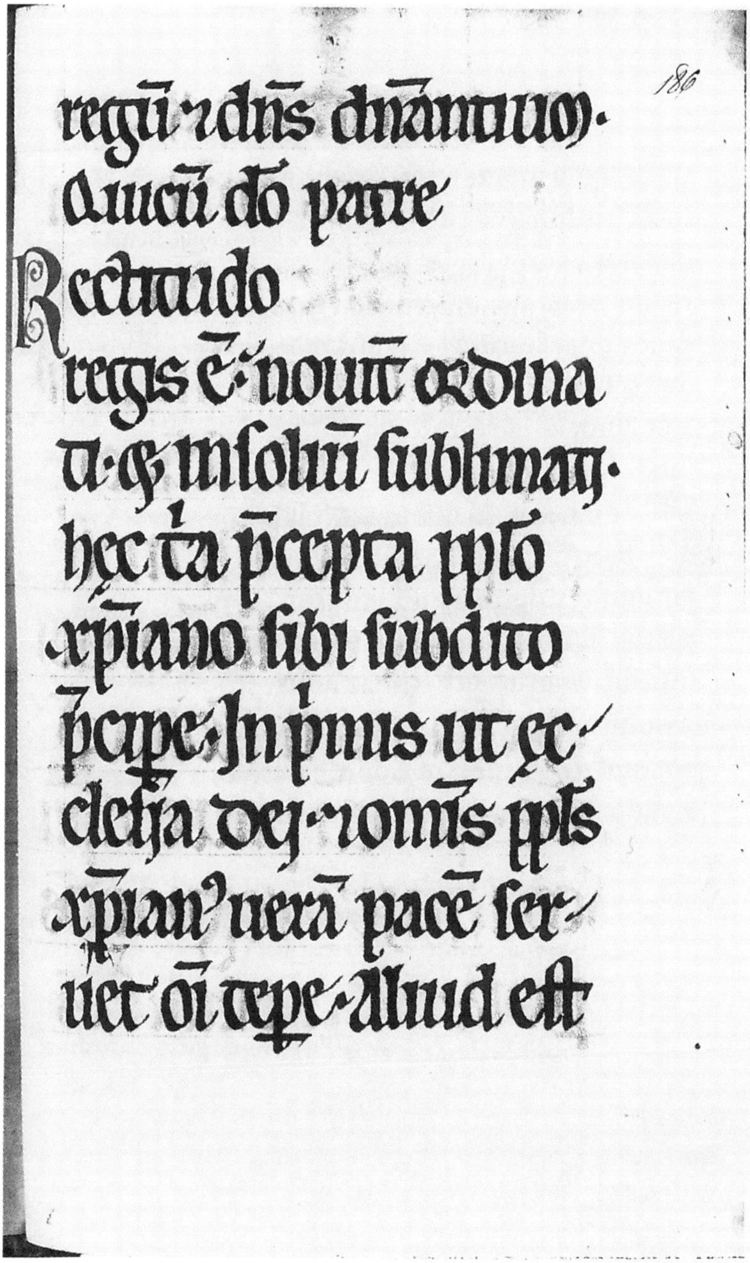

186

regū ꝛdn̄s chm̄ātuo).
Aucū do patre
Rectitudo
regis ē·nouū oꝛdina
ti·q̄ tn̄folū fublimat).
hęc ꝵa p̄cepta ꝑpl̄o
xp̄iano fibi fubdito
p̄cēpe·Jn p̄mis ut ęc
clefia dej·ꝛomn̄s ꝑpls
xp̄iau̅ ueꝛā pacē fer
uet oī tēpe·Aliud eft

Plate 10: Paris, Bibl. nat., MS lat 1223, fol. 186r

Guiddone ābuanēfi. Aganone ecluenfi. harduino linguonenfi.
Achardo cabillonenfi. Ifenbardo aurelianenfi. Imbro parifiacēfi.
Galtero meldēfi. hugone neūnenfi. Gaufrido aurafiodo
renfi. hugone trecaffino. Itero lemouicēfi. Guillelmo ecole
finēfi. Arnulfo ſcōnenfi. Vuereco nannetēfi. Et de abba
tib; herimaro ſcī remigu. Rainero ſcī benedicti. hugone
ſcī dionifii. Adroldo ſcī germani. Geruino ſcī Richari. Gua
thone ſcī ualeria.   ſcī Vuingaloei. Varino ſcī
uictori. Fulchone de forefta monaſtrō. Gerardo ſcī madarchi.
heinrico humolarienfi. Ooytzzone flouuenfi. Fulchone ſcī
michael laudunenfi. Archenueo laudunenfi. Guiddone mar
cianenfi. Rodulfo mofoniſi. Albro ſcī theoderici. Varino
albro ulatenfi. Vuenrico ſcī bafoli. hugone orbacēfi. Odi
lardo cathalaunēfi. Vandelgero clervenfi. Vualeranno
urdunēfi. Adalberone diuonenfi. Arnoldo putzarienfi.
Guillelmo trenozcēfi. hugone carrocēfi. Auefgaudo et
nomannēfi. hugone crifpmenfi. Accipiens baculū ſcī re
migu. differuit dtea et pacifice quīm adeo pineat maci
me electio regis. et ctecratio regis. coq ſcī remigi"
bludouicu rege baptizau. et ctecīutrO iffertuerenā
quīm pillu baculū hanc ctecranch poteſtate et tū gali
lie pmatu ormiſda papa ſcō declit remigio. et quīm
papa uictor ſibi et ecctie fue. Tunc annuente pinte
ei heinrico elegit eū mtegē. Loft eū: legatu romane
fedif. cū id fine pape nutu fieri licerai ee difērai ibi
tum   fit. honorif tū et amorif grā: tū ei ibi affuer le
gati. Loft hof archiepi et epi. abbatef et clerici. Loft
Vuiddo dux agtame: Loft: hugo fili' et legat'duef

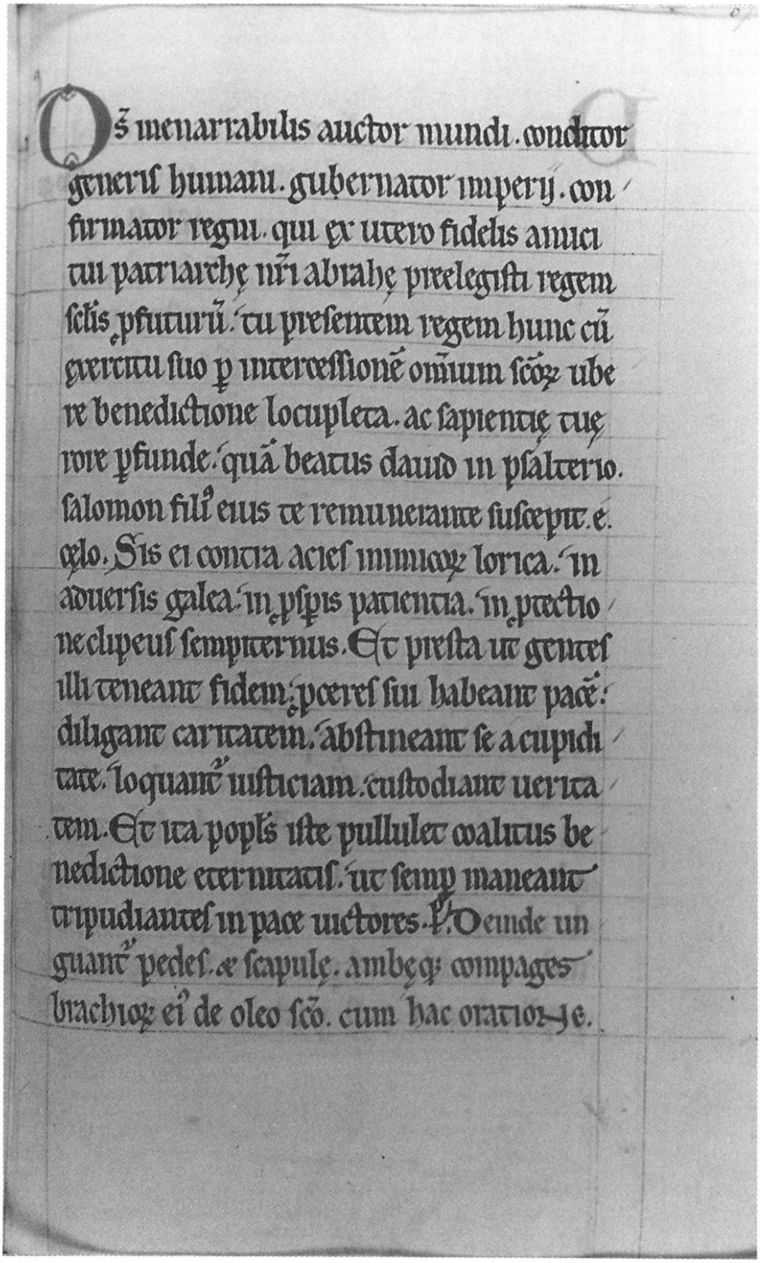

Os inenarrabilis auctor mundi. conditor
generis humani. gubernator impery. con
firmator regni. qui ex utero fidelis amici
tui patriarche nri abrahe preelegisti regem
scḷis pfuturū. tu presentem regem hunc cū
exercitu suo p intercessione oīum scōⱬ ube
re benedictione locupleta. ac sapientie tue
rore pfunde. quā beatus dauid in psalterio.
salomon filı eius te remunerante suscepit. e.
celo. Sis ei contra acies inimicoⱬ lorica. in
aduersis galea. in pspis patientia. in prelio
ne clipeus sempiternus. Et presta ut gentes
illi teneant fidem; poeres sui habeant pace:
diligant caritatem. abstineant se a cupidi
tate. loquant iusticiam. custodiant uerita
tem. Et ita popls iste pullulet coalitus be
nedictione eternitatis. ut semp maneant
tripudiantes in pace uictores. P. Deinde un
guant pedes. ⁊ scapule. ambeⱬ compages
brachioⱬ eı de oleo scō. cum hac oratioₑ ꝗe.

Plate 12: Saint-Omer, Bibl. mun., MS 98, fol. 67r

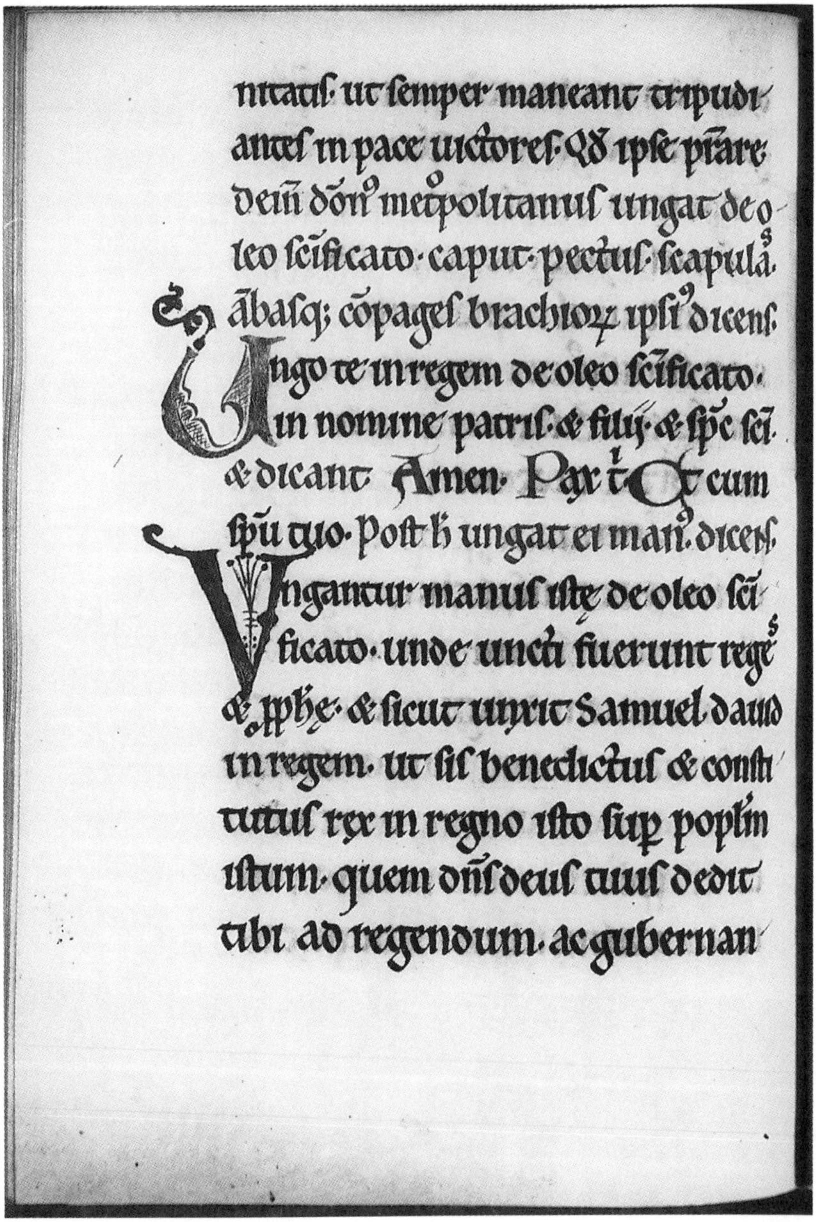

nitatis· ut semper maneant tripudi
antes in pace uictores· Q̅ ipse p̅stare·
deū dn̅o metpolitanus ungat de oleo
sc̅ificato· caput· pectus· scapulas·
Et ābasq; copages brachior̅ ipsi dicens·

Ungo te in regem de oleo sc̅ificato·
in nomine patris· & filij· & sp̅c sc̅i·
& dicant· Amen· Pax t̅ & cum
sp̅u tuo· post h ungat ei man̅· dicens·

Ungantur manus iste de oleo sc̅i
ficato· unde uncti fuerunt reges
& p̅phe̅· & sicut unxit Samuel dauid
in regem· ut sis benedictus & consti
tutus rex in regno isto sup̅ pop̅lm
istum· quem dn̅s deus tuus dedit
tibi ad regendum· ac gubernan

Plate 13: Reims, Bibl. mun., MS 343, fol. 132v

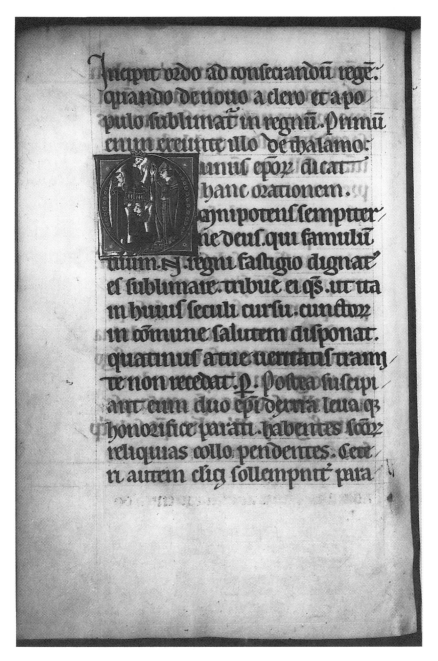

Plate 14: Besançon, Bibl. mun., MS 138, fol. 190v

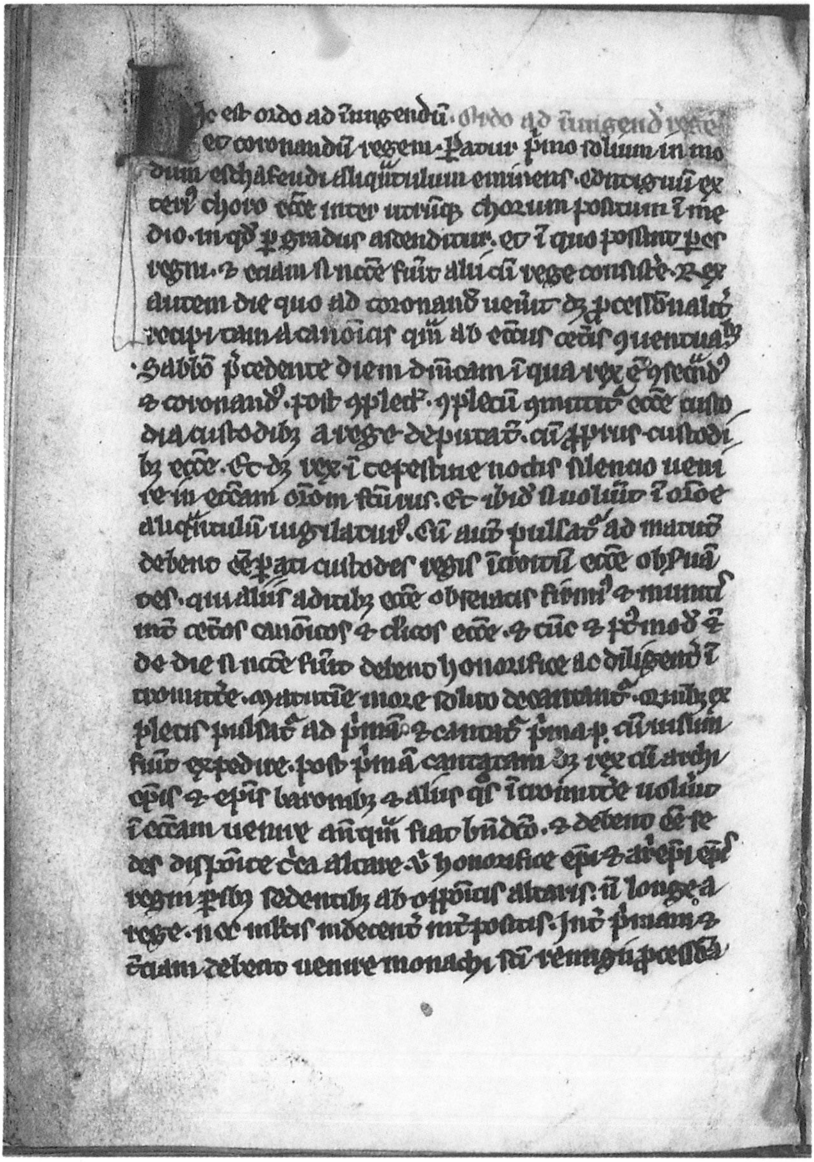

Plate 15: Reims, Bibl. mun., MS 328, fol. 70v

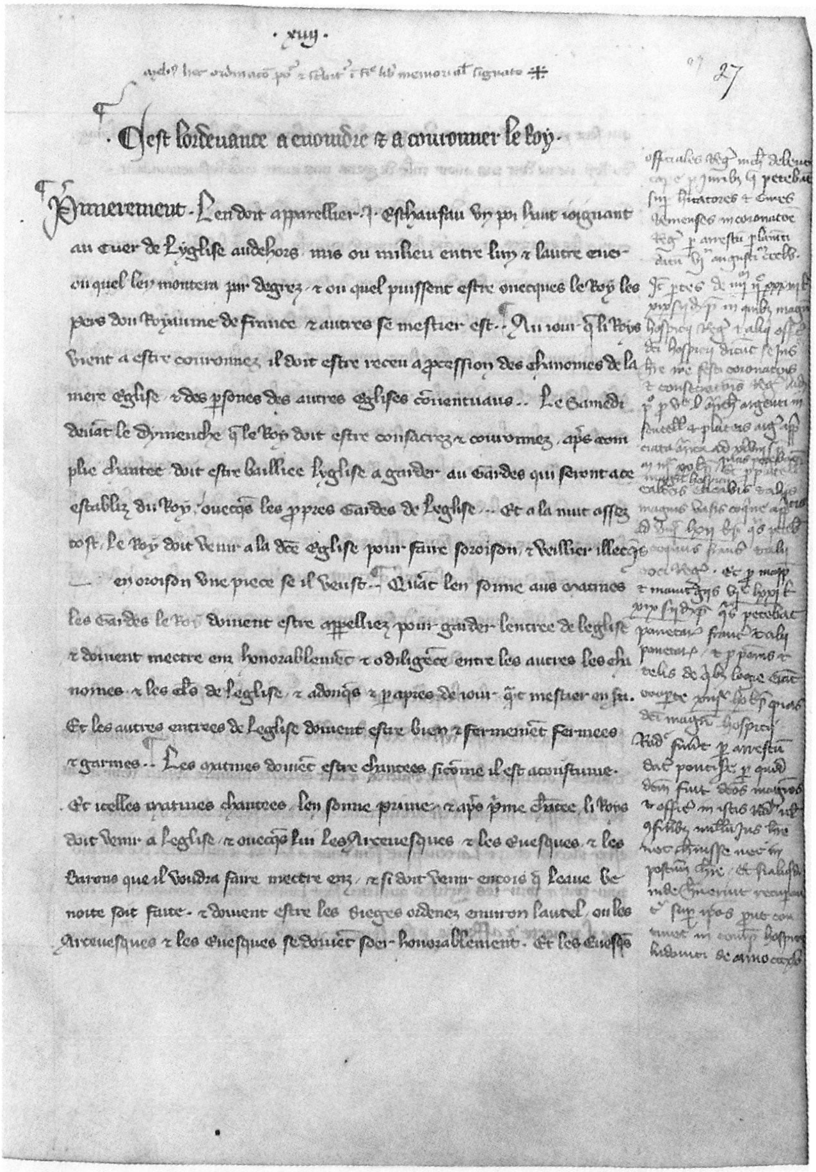

· xiiij ·

27

Cest lordenance a enoindre et a couronner le roy.

Plate 16: Paris, Bibl. nat., MS lat. 12814, fol. 27r

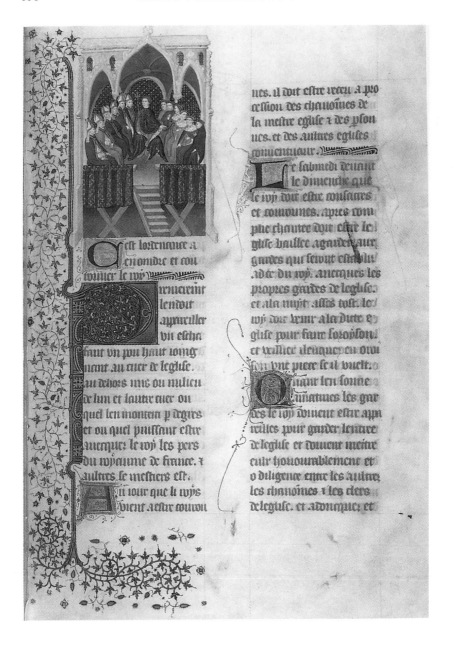

Plate 17: Paris, Bibl. nat., MS lat. 8886, fol. 58r

irstue de sope. et seir enonste
en duef tant seulement. et
ou pas non pas de linicion
le top ennoyec des eucils
mais duple simple sanre
fie Et apres linicion li ar
euesques la baille du preu
ceptie Dautie lilaineur que
le cepue to̅al. Et li la baille
vne veige semblont a la
veige to̅al [E]t apres
lan̅euesque tour seul li a
mer la couronne, en son
duef. la quelle couronne
nuse douent soustenir lei
baron de ca et de la. et en
telle maniere il les douent
mener a son eschafaut.
ou est assur en son liege
qu li est apparille. Et li
barons i les plus nobles
Dames douent estre enui
ron Ces choses acomplies
len doit chanter la messe
sollempnement. Et le
chanir et le soubechanir
douent garder le que. Et
lennauigle lejo le grigneur

r se il am
cut que
la wpne
Dope estre
enonste et couronnee auec
ques le roi. len li apparille
vn eschafaut Deuers la se
nestre partie du cuer. Et
lois doit estre mis lescha
faut du roi Deuers la dextre
partie du cuer vn pou plus
haulte que cellui a la wpne
Et puis que li wys sera
assis en son eschafaut en
la maniere deuant Dicte.
Et que li arcuesques seir
retourne alautel. il enom
dra la wpne qui doit estre

Plate 18: Paris, Bibl. nat., MS lat. 8886, fol. 61r

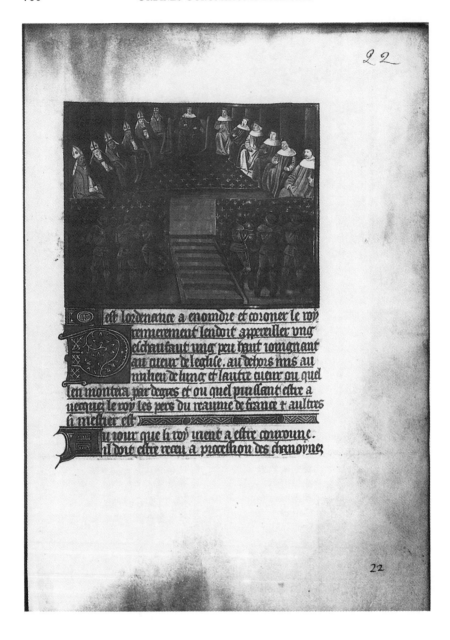

Plate 19: Paris, Bibl. nat., MS Dupuy 365, fol. 22r

il faillet en fa chere il dit les oioyfons qui en leurs
lieu font efcriptes en loidmaire. en celle maniere le
roy aflis en fa chiere et les pers du royaume aueques
luy qui foubtiennent la couronne. lareuegue reto
urne a lautier.

enfant comment la royne doit eftre enointe et couronnee.

Plate 20: Paris, Bibl. nat., MS Dupuy 365, fol. 25v

Plate 21: Paris, Bibl. nat., MS lat. 1246, fol. 15v

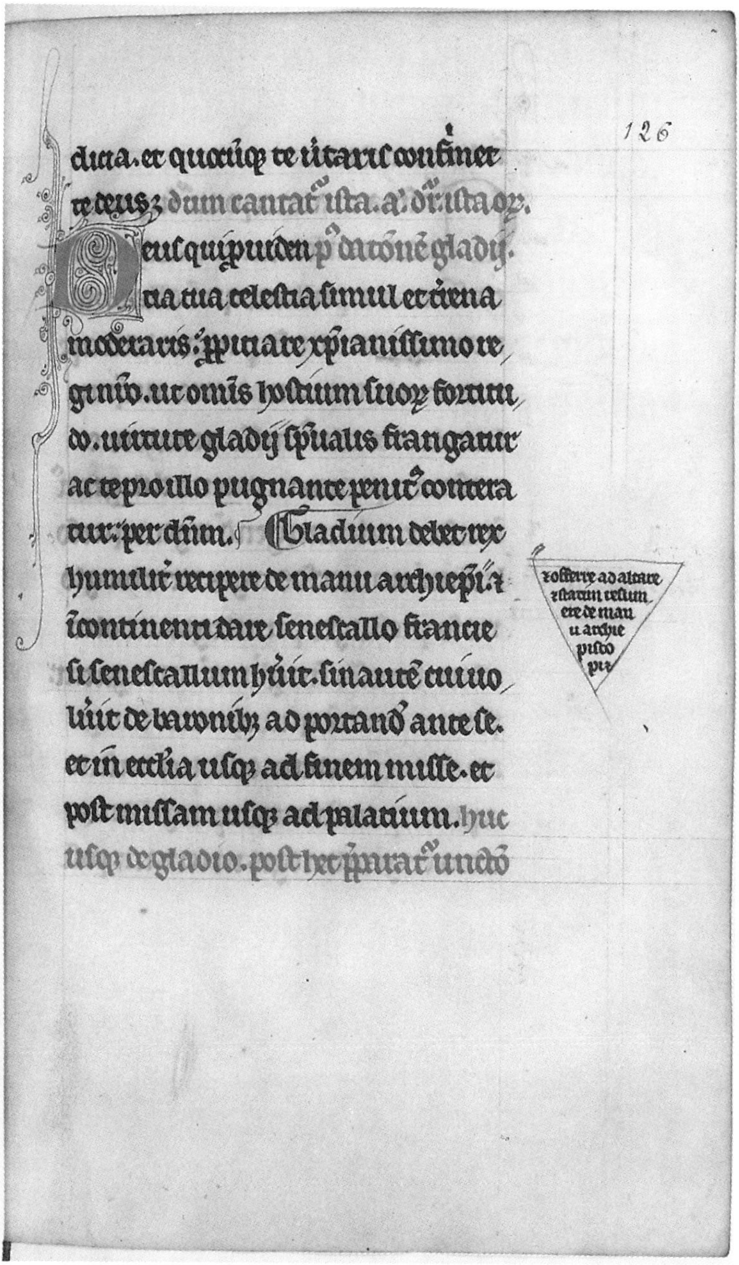

126

dicta. et quacunqʒ te utaris continet
te teusʒ dum cantat ista. al dr ista or.
Deus quipruden p racone gladij
na tua celestia simul et terrena
moderaris: propiciare xpianissimo re
ginio. ut omis hostium suoꝝ fortitu
do. uirtute gladij spualis frangatur
ac te pro illo pugnante penit continea
tur: per dnm. ¶ Gladium debet rex
humilit recipere de manu archiepi ꞇ
continuit dare senescallo francie
si senescallum habuit. si n aut cui uo
luit de baronibʒ ad portand ante se.
et in ecclia usqʒ ad finem misse. et
post missam usqʒ ad palacium. huc
usqʒ de gladio. post hec preparat undo

rostrare ad altare
et tam in restitu
ere de man
u archie
pisco
pi

Plate 22: Paris, Bibl. nat., MS nouv. acq. lat. 1202, fol. 126r

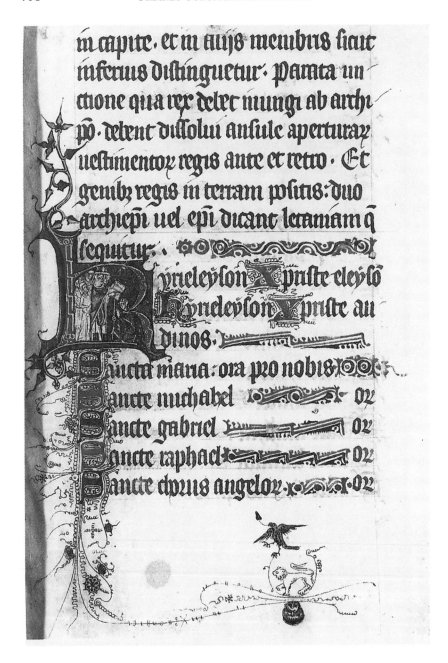

Plate 23: Urbana, Univ. of Ill. Lib., MS "Ordo ad consecrandum," fol. 2r

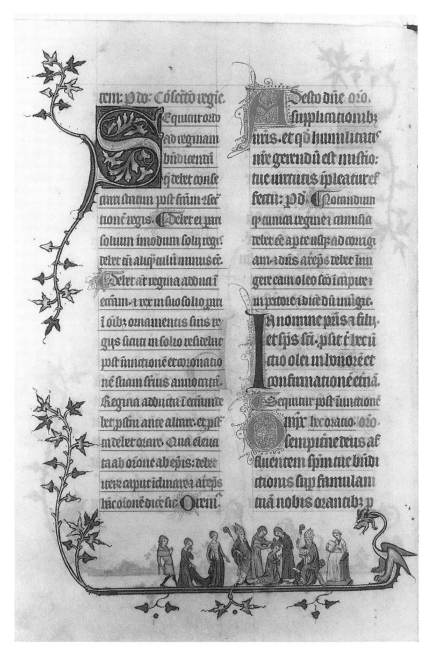

Plate 24: Vatican City, Bibl. Apos. Vat., MS Chigi C VI 182, fol. 83v

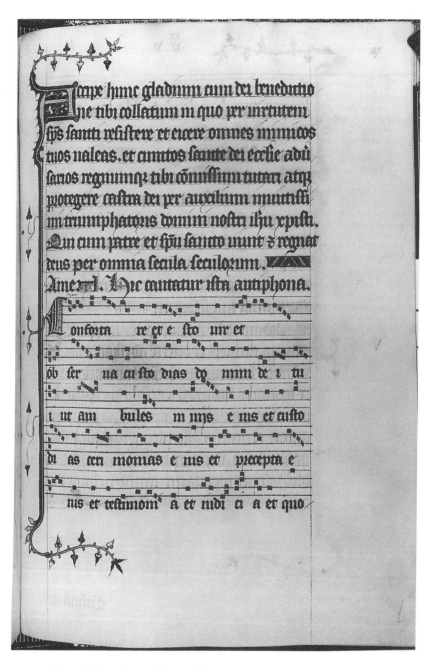

Plate 25: London, British Library, MS Egerton 931, fol. 187r

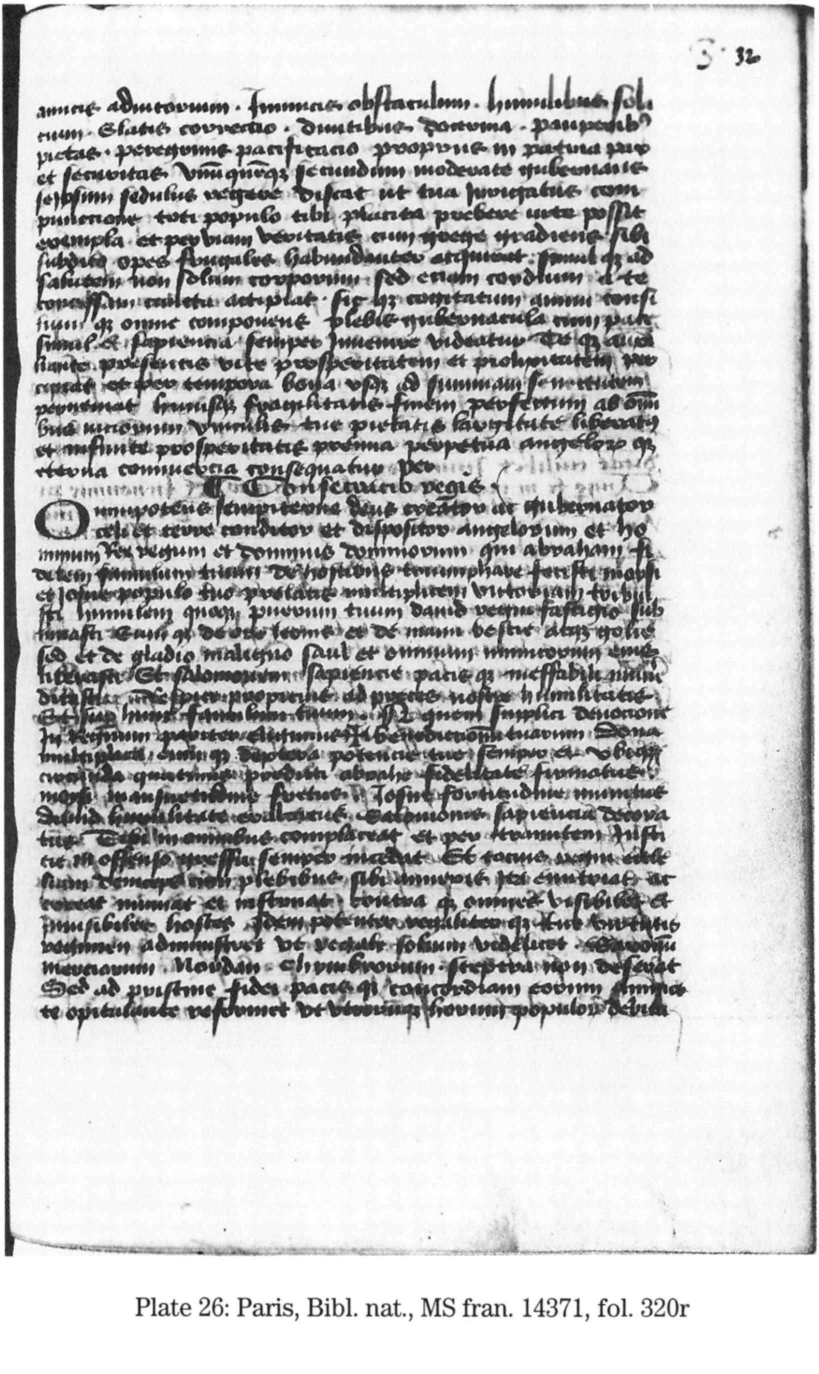

32

Plate 26: Paris, Bibl. nat., MS fran. 14371, fol. 320r

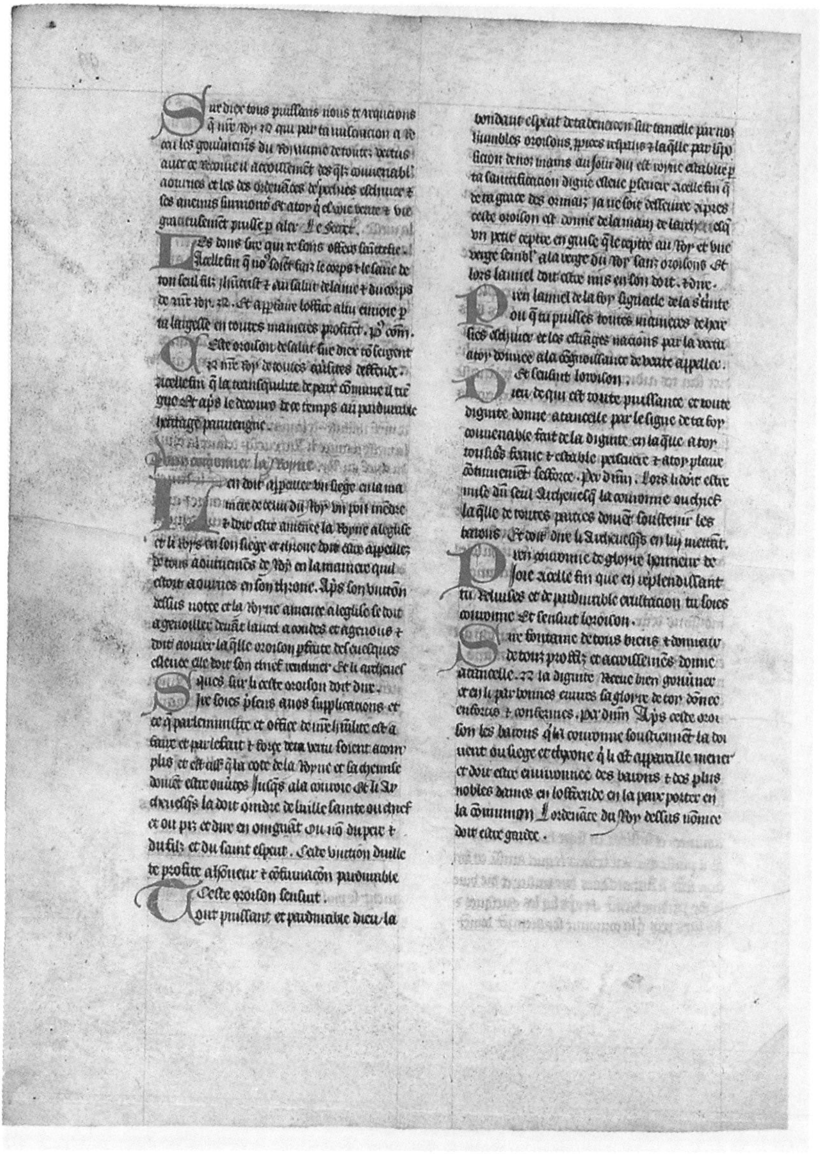

Plate 27: Paris, Bibl. nat., MS fran. 994, p. 100

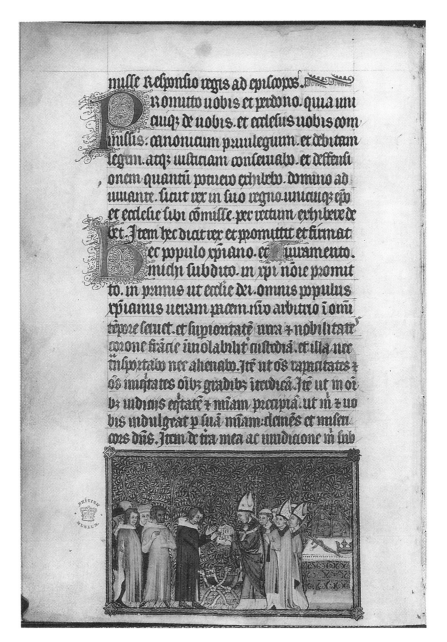

mulle Responsio regis ad epilcopos.
Romitto uobis et perdono. quia uni
pauq; de nobis. et ecclesus uobis com
millis: canonicum puuilegium. et debitam
legim. atq; iusticiam conseruabo. et deffensi
onem quantu potuero exhibebo. domino ad
iuuante. licut rex in luo regno uniicuiq; epo
et ecclelie libi comille. per rectum exhibere de
bet. Item hec diat rex et promittit et firmat
hec populo xpiano. et Iuuamento.
michi lubdito. in xpi noie promit
to. in pmus ut ecclie dei omnis populus
xpianus ueram pacem liio arbitrio i omi
tepore leruet. et luptontate nra + nobilitate
corone frade iuuolabilit custodia. et illa nec
tnlpoztabo nec ahenabo. Ite ut os rapacitates +
os iniquitates oib; gradib; iterdica. Ite ut in oi
b; iudiciis eqtate + miam precipia. ut m + uo
bis indulgeat p lua miam: clemés et miseri
cors dns. Item de tra mea ac iuurisdictione in lub

Plate 28: London, British Library, MS Tiberius B.viii, fol. 46v

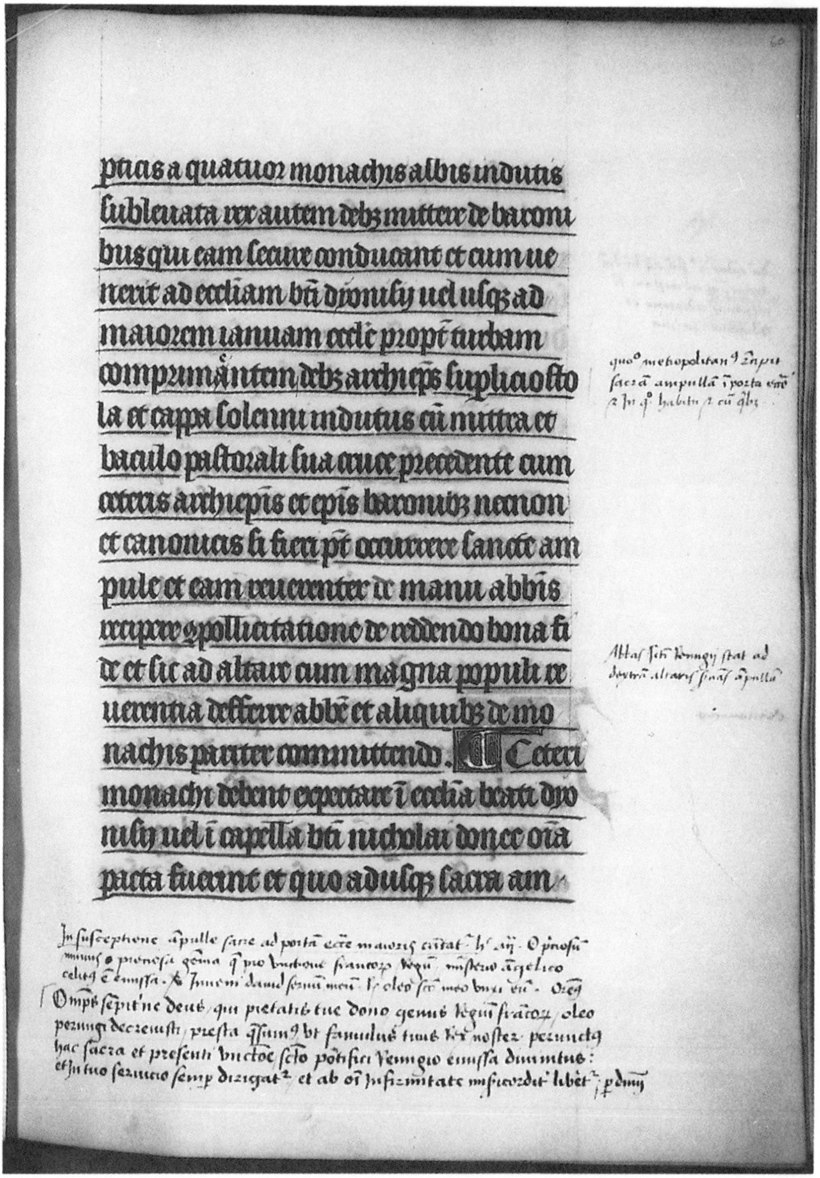

Plate 29: Paris, Arch. des prêtres de Saint-Sulpice, MS 1928, fol. 60r

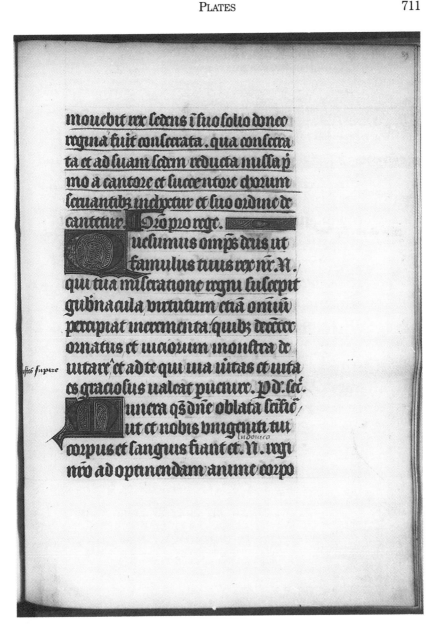

Plate 30: Paris, Arch. des prêtres de Saint-Sulpice, MS 1928, fol. 89r

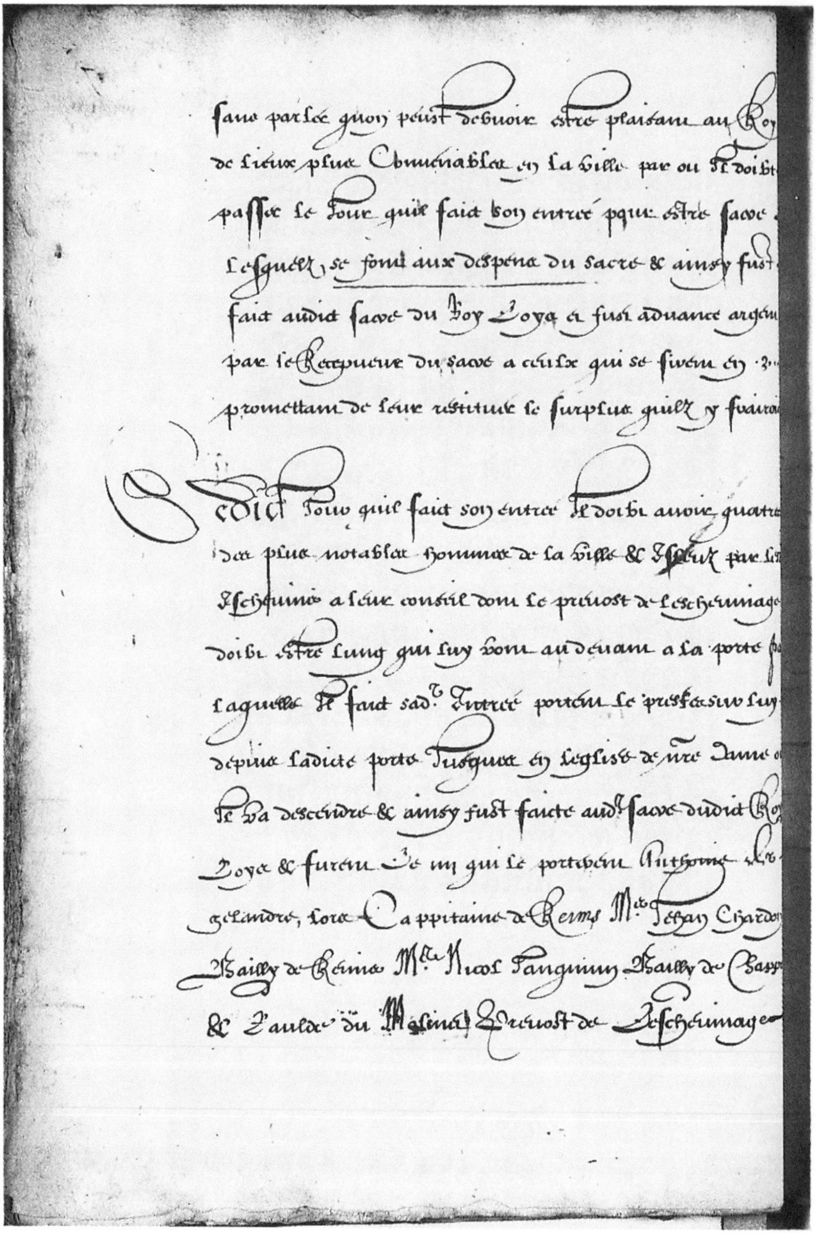

sans parler quon peust debuoir estre plaisant au Roy
de lieux plus Conuenables en la ville par ou il doibt
passer le Jour quil faict son entrée pour estre sacré
Lesquelz se font aux despens du sacre & ainsi fust
faict audict sacre du Roy Loys et fust aduancé argent
par le Receueur du sacre a ceulx qui se fiuent en ...
promettant de leur restituer le surplus quilz y feuront

¶ Et Jour quil faict son entrée il doibt auoir quatre
des plus notables hommes de la ville & esleuz par les
Eschquins a leur conseil dont le preuost de leschevinage
doibt estre lung qui luy vont au deuant a la porte par
laquelle il faict sad. Entrée portent le preste sur luy
depuis ladicte porte Jusques en leglise de nre Dame ...
Et la descendre & ainsy fust faicte audict sacre dudict Roy
Loys & furent de iiii qui le portèrent Anthoine ...
gelandres, lors Cappitaine de Reims Me Jehan Chardon
Bailly de Reims Me Nicol Sanguiny Bailly de Bass...
& Paulce du Meslnal Preuost de leschevinage

Plate 31: Paris, Bibl. nat., MS fran. 8334, fol. 47v

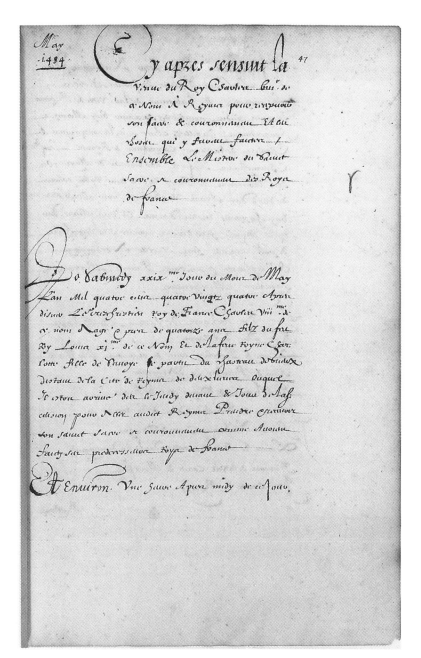

Plate 32: Paris, Bibl. nat., MS nouv. acq. fran. 7232, fol. 47r

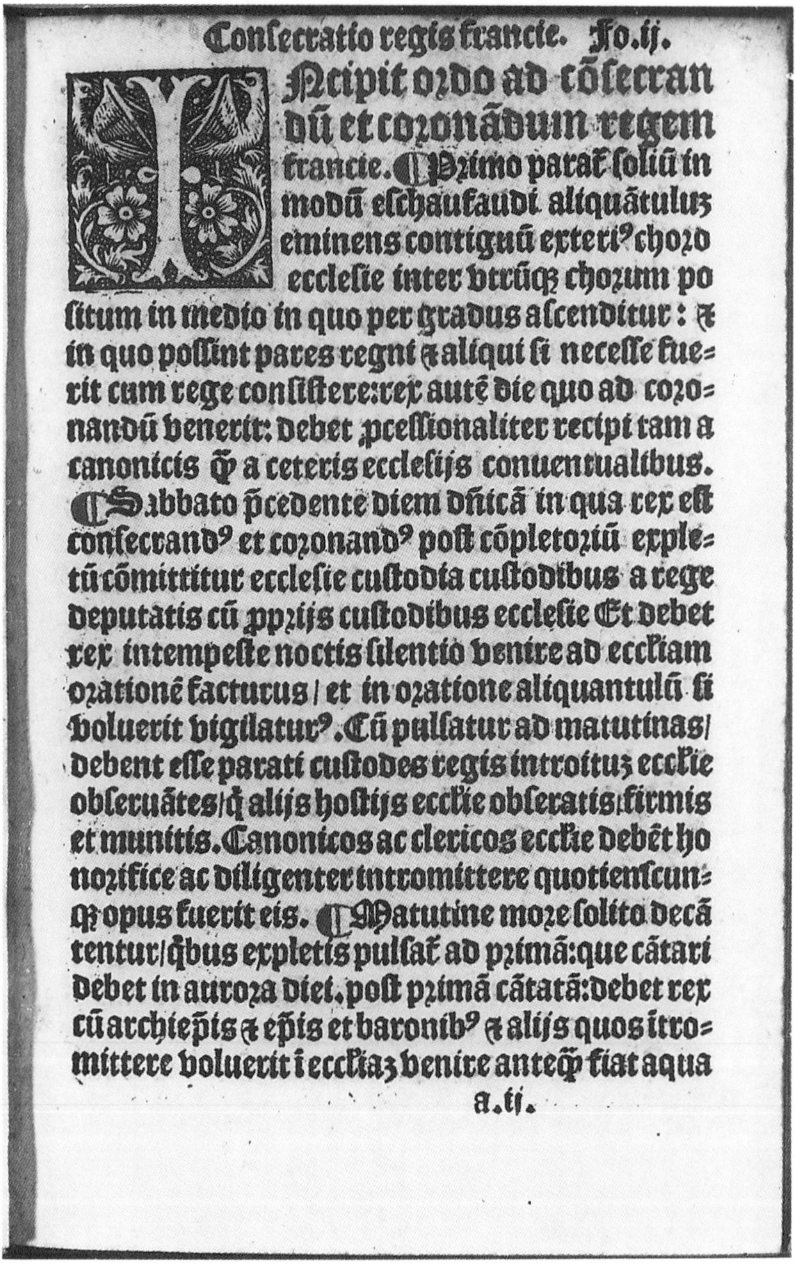

Consecratio regis francie. Fo.ij.

Ncipit ordo ad cõsecran
dũ et coronãdum regem
francie. ¶Primo paraf soliũ in
modũ eschaufaudi aliquãtuluz
eminens contiguũ exteri? choro
ecclesie inter vtrũcz chorum po
situm in medio in quo per gradus ascenditur: ꝗ
in quo possint pares regni ꝗ aliqui si necesse fue=
rit cum rege consistere:rex autẽ die quo ad coro=
nandũ benerit: debet ꝓcessionaliter recipi tam a
canonicis ꝗ a ceteris ecclesijs conuentualibus.
¶Sabbato ꝓcedente diem dñicã in qua rex est
consecrand⁹ et coronand⁹ post cõpletoriũ exple=
tũ cõmittitur ecclesie custodia custodibus a rege
deputatis cũ ꝓprijs custodibus ecclesie Et debet
rex intempeste noctis silentio benire ad eccłiam
orationẽ facturus / et in oratione aliquantulũ si
boluerit bigilatur⁹. Cũ pulsatur ad matutinas /
debent esse parati custodes regis introituz eccłie
obseruãtes / ꝗ alijs hostijs eccłie obseratis:firmis
et munitis. Canonicos ac clericos eccłie debẽt ho
norifice ac diligenter intromittere quottenscun=
cz opus fuerit eis. ¶Matutine more solito deca
tentur / ꝗbus expletis pulsaf ad primã:que cãtari
debet in aurora diei. post primã cãtatã:debet rex
cũ archiepis ꝗ epis et baronib⁹ ꝗ alijs quos ĩtro=
mittere boluerit i eccłiaz benire antecꝗ fiat aqua

a.ij.

Plate 33: Paris, Bibl. nat., Rés. Li²⁵.1, fol. 2r

General Index

References are to pages, not to elements of the ordines or their apparatus. If an ordo bears the name of a king, there is a single reference to that king in that ordo. Few of the many personal names in Ordines XVII and XXV are indexed; neither are the names of most of the buildings mentioned in Ordo XXV. I did not index the very many references to Biblical figures in the liturgical formulas. The names of scholars are indexed if their work is discussed, but not if their work is only cited or their aid acknowledged. Looking at all the references to a particular act, e.g., anointing of the king, will enable one to observe how that aspect of the ceremony did or did not change over time.